# Mac OS X Server Essentials v10.5

## Student Workbook

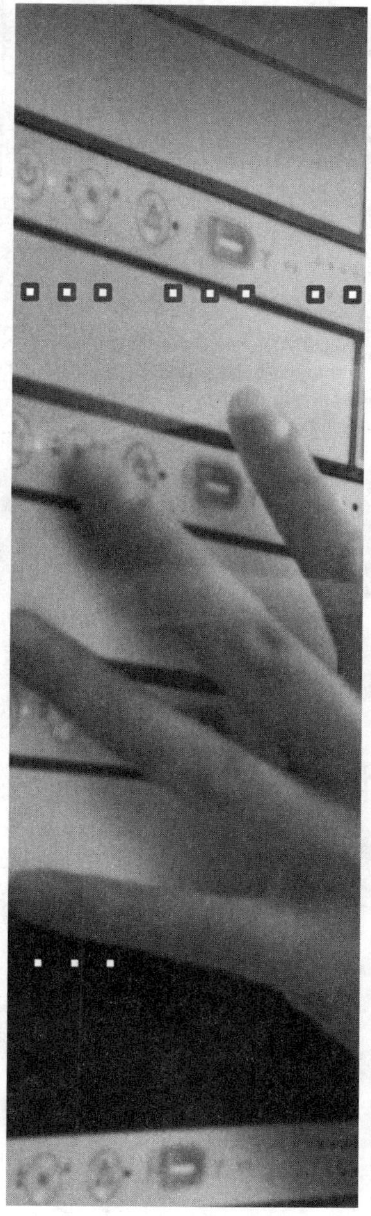

Apple Certified

**Mac OS X Server Essentials v10.5 Student Workbook**
Courseware Version 10.5.0
January 15, 2008

Published by Peachpit Press

Peachpit is a division of Pearson Education.



Project Editor: Rebecca Freed
Contributors: Andre LaBranche, David Long, Simon Wheatley
Development Editor: Schoun Regan
Production Editor: Danielle Foster
Copyeditor: Robyn G. Thomas
Tech Editor: John Signa
Proofreader: Valerie Witte
Compositor: Danielle Foster
Cover design: Mimi Heft
Interior design: Danielle Foster



ISBN-13: 978-0-321-55535-9
ISBN-10: 0-321-55535-X
9 8 7 6 5 4 3 2 1
Printed and bound in the United States of America

# Contents


## 1 Installation and Configuration 1

1.1–1.4 Installation and Configuration . . . . . . . . . . . 2

Exercise 1.1.1 Configure Mac OS X on the Client Computer. . . . 12

Exercise 1.2.1 Install Server Administration Software on the Mac OS X Computer. . . . . . . . . . . . . . . . . . . . 20

Exercise 1.3.1 Install Mac OS X Server Remotely (optional). . . . . 22

Exercise 1.4.1 Install Mac OS X Server Locally (optional). . . . . . . 27

1.5 Mac OS X Server Configuration. . . . . . . . . . 29

Exercise 1.5.1 Remote Configuration of Mac OS X Server. . . . . . 41

1.6–1.9 Mac OS X Server Administration Tools . . . 51

Exercise 1.6.1 Enable Service Configuration. . . . . . . . . . . . . . . . 61

Exercise 1.7.1 Export Service Configurations to Disk . . . . . . . . . 64

Exercise 1.8.1 View and Search Server Logs Using Server Admin (optional) . . . . . . . . . . . . . . . . . . . . 67

Exercise 1.9.1 Use Screen Sharing to Control Mac OS X Server . . . . . . . . . . . . . . . . . . . . . . . . . . . . . . . . . 69

Bonus Link Aggregate Networking . . . . . . . . . . . . 72

| | | |
|---|---|---|
| **2** | **Providing DNS Service** | 75 |
| **2.1** | **DNS Basics** | 76 |
| **Exercise 2.1.1** | View the Mac OS X Server Default DNS Information | 84 |
| **2.2–2.3** | **DNS Configuration** | 86 |
| **Exercise 2.2.1** | Configure a Basic DNS Zone | 97 |
| **Exercise 2.3.1** | Add Records to a Zone | 102 |
| **2.4–2.6** | **DNS Troubleshooting** | 107 |
| **Exercise 2.4.1** | Test and Troubleshoot DNS | 113 |
| **Exercise 2.5.1** | Log the DNS Service (optional) | 119 |
| **Exercise 2.6.1** | Use Recursion and Forwarders (optional) | 120 |
| **3** | **Authentication, Authorization, and Access Control** | 125 |
| **3.1** | **Authentication** | 126 |
| **Exercise 3.1.1** | Create Local User Accounts | 138 |
| **Exercise 3.1.2** | Add Comments and Keywords | 142 |
| **Exercise 3.1.3** | Import Local User Accounts | 145 |
| **Exercise 3.1.4** | Create Local Groups | 153 |
| **Exercise 3.1.5** | Associate Users and Groups | 157 |
| **3.2** | **Authorization** | 163 |
| **Exercise 3.2.1** | Use POSIX and File-System Access Control Management | 175 |
| **3.3** | **Service Access Controls** | 189 |
| **Exercise 3.3.1** | Configure Service Access Controls | 193 |

| | | |
|---|---|---|
| **4** | **Open Directory** | 199 |
| **4.1** | **Concepts** | 200 |
| **Exercise 4.1.1** | Examine the Local Data Store | 206 |
| **4.2** | **Configuration** | 208 |
| **Exercise 4.2.1** | Export Local Users and Groups | 225 |
| **Exercise 4.2.2** | Create an Open Directory Master | 227 |
| **Exercise 4.2.3** | Import Users and Groups into the Shared Directory | 234 |
| **4.3** | **Authentication** | 240 |
| **Exercise 4.3.1** | Configure Password Policies | 247 |
| **4.4** | **Archiving** | 252 |
| **Exercise 4.4.1** | Archive and Restore Open Directory Data | 255 |
| **5** | **File Services** | 259 |
| **5.1** | **Planning** | 260 |
| **Exercise 5.1.1** | View Preset Share Points and Permissions | 270 |
| **5.2** | **Protocols** | 274 |
| **Exercise 5.2.1** | Configure AFP File Sharing Service | 280 |
| **Exercise 5.2.2** | Manage AFP Service Settings | 288 |
| **Exercise 5.2.3** | Test AFP Service Settings | 293 |
| **Exercise 5.2.4** | Configure Samba File Sharing Service | 302 |
| **Exercise 5.2.5** | View Samba Log Files (optional) | 310 |
| **Exercise 5.2.6** | Configure the File Transfer Protocol Sharing Service (optional) | 316 |
| **Exercise 5.2.7** | Configure the Network File System Sharing Service | 324 |

| | | |
|---|---|---|
| **5.3** | **Configuration** | 328 |
| **Exercise 5.3.1** | Configure Automount Options and Quotas on Share Points | 331 |
| **Exercise 5.3.2** | Set a Time Machine Share Point (optional) | 336 |
| **6** | **Using the Mail Service** | 343 |
| **6.1** | **Configuration** | 344 |
| **Exercise 6.1.1** | Configure Basic Mail Service | 358 |
| **Exercise 6.1.2** | Enable a Group Mailing List | 367 |
| **6.2** | **Security** | 371 |
| **Exercise 6.2.1** | Secure the Mail Service | 382 |
| **Exercise 6.2.2** | Use SSL Certificates with the Mail Service | 387 |
| **6.3** | **Maintenance** | 391 |
| **Exercise 6.3.1** | Configure Mail Service Quotas (optional) | 398 |
| **Exercise 6.3.2** | Reconstruct and Rebuild Mail (optional) | 402 |
| **Exercise 6.3.3** | View Mail Log Files (optional) | 404 |
| **7** | **Using Web Services** | 407 |
| **7.1** | **Configuration** | 408 |
| **Exercise 7.1.1** | Configure Basic Web Services | 421 |
| **Exercise 7.1.2** | Create a Secondary Website | 430 |
| **7.2** | **Sharing** | 434 |
| **Exercise 7.2.1** | Use Realms to Restrict Access | 440 |
| **7.3** | **Security** | 447 |
| **Exercise 7.3.1** | Secure a Website Using SSL | 453 |

| | | |
|---|---|---|
| **8** | **Collaboration Services** | 457 |
| **8.1** | **Wiki Services** | 458 |
| Exercise 8.1.1 | Configure and Enable Wiki and Blog Services for Groups | 472 |
| Exercise 8.1.2 | Modify a User Blog | 478 |
| Exercise 8.1.3 | Tag and Search Blog Entries | 481 |
| Exercise 8.1.4 | Create and Edit a Group Wiki | 484 |
| Exercise 8.1.5 | Set Blog and Wiki Access Control | 488 |
| **8.2** | **Calendaring Services** | 493 |
| Exercise 8.2.1 | Configure and Use iCal Service | 505 |
| Exercise 8.2.2 | Create Resource and Location Records Using Directory | 508 |
| Exercise 8.2.3 | Configure iCal Accounts | 511 |
| Exercise 8.2.4 | Create and Respond to Events | 516 |
| Exercise 8.2.5 | Edit Web Group Calendars (optional) | 524 |
| **8.3** | **Messaging Services** | 527 |
| Exercise 8.3.1 | Configure the iChat Service and Application | 538 |
| Exercise 8.3.2 | Add Jabber Buddies and Communicate | 545 |
| Exercise 8.3.3 | View Chat Logs | 553 |
| **9** | **Deployment Solutions** | 557 |
| **9.1** | **Configuration** | 558 |
| Exercise 9.1.1 | Configure NetBoot Services | 566 |
| **9.2** | **Imaging** | 575 |
| Exercise 9.2.1 | Create a NetBoot Image | 579 |
| **9.3** | **Deployment** | 583 |
| Exercise 9.3.1 | NetBoot a Mac OS X Computer | 590 |

**10** **Managing Accounts** 595

**10.1** **Managed Preferences** . . . 596

**Exercise 10.1.1** Create Group Folders . . . 614

**Exercise 10.1.2** Set Managed Preferences for Users and Groups. . . . 618

**Exercise 10.1.3** Manage Computer Groups. . . . 624

**10.2** **Software Update Server** . . . 631

**Exercise 10.2.1** Configure and Enable Software Update Service . . . 637

**10.3** **Mobile User Accounts** . . . 640

**Exercise 10.3.1** Configure Mobile Accounts . . . 651

**11** **Optional Challenges** 657

Take the Challenge . . . 658

Plan the Implementation . . . 660

Server 1: Configure the Directory and Collaborative Services . . . 662

Server 2: Configure the File Server . . . 666

Server 3: Configure NetBoot Services (optional) . . . 669

Test Your Solution . . . 672

Reassess the Situation . . . 674

**Answer Key** . . . 677

## Notes

## Notes

## Notes

## Notes

# 1

# Installation and Configuration

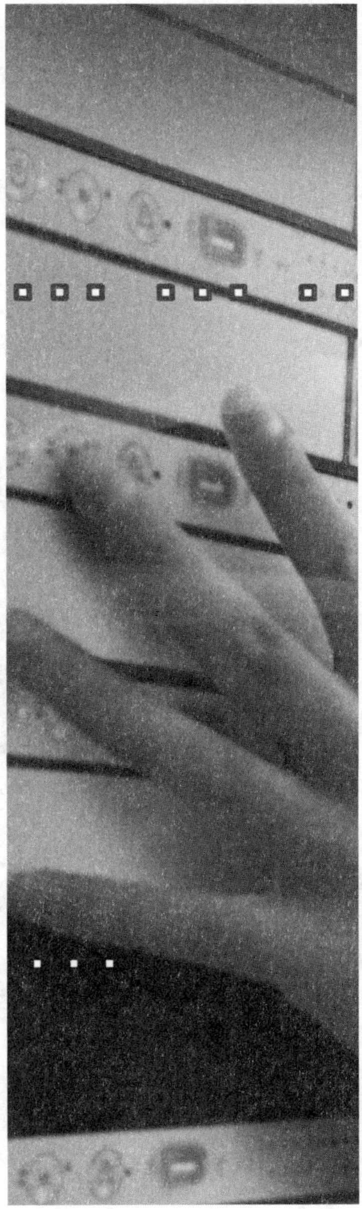


## 1.1–1.4 Installation and Configuration

**Exercise 1.1.1** Configure Mac OS X on the Client Computer

**Exercise 1.2.1** Install Server Administration Software on the Mac OS X Computer

**Exercise 1.3.1** Install Mac OS X Server Remotely (optional)

**Exercise 1.4.1** Install Mac OS X Server Locally (optional)

## 1.5 Mac OS X Server Configuration

**Exercise 1.5.1** Remote Configuration of Mac OS X Server

## 1.6–1.9 Mac OS X Server Administration Tools

**Exercise 1.6.1** Enable Service Configuration

**Exercise 1.7.1** Export Service Configurations to Disk

**Exercise 1.8.1** View and Search Server Logs Using Server Admin (optional)

**Exercise 1.9.1** Use Screen Sharing to Control Mac OS X Server

## Bonus Link Aggregate Networking

# 1.1–1.4 Installation and Configuration

Mac OS X Server is an extremely powerful and robust server operating system. Proper installation and configuration is critical to the life of the server. While there are more advanced methods of deploying a server image, such as NetBoot or NetInstall (something you will learn about in later lessons), at some point an initial installation and configuration must take place. Understanding all the initial options and properly recording those options makes subsequent installations much easier. Finally, even before an installation takes place, a planning meeting or list of objectives should be set to ensure exactly what is being expected of the server.

This lesson deals with the installation and configuration of Mac OS X Server, as well as the tools to maintain and manage it.

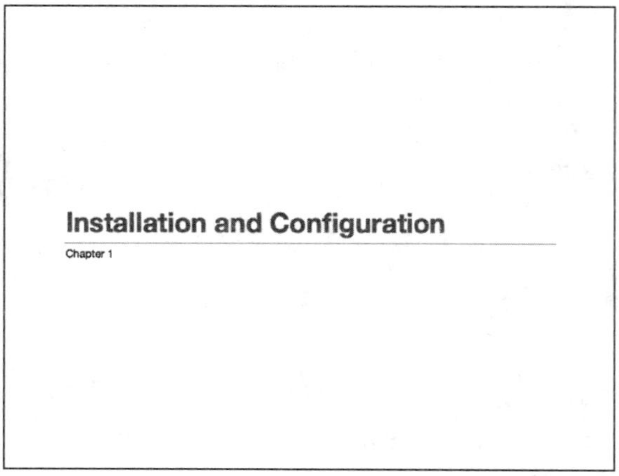

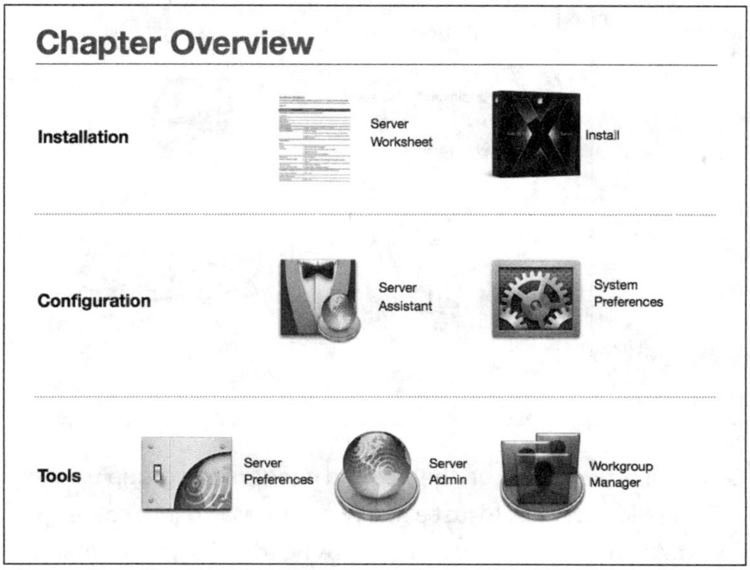


You can divide working with Mac OS X Server into three phases:

1. Planning and installation: Plan how the server will be set up, verify and configure the hardware, and install the server software.
2. Initial configuration: Use Server Assistant to perform the initial Mac OS X Server configuration. You can also use the Network preferences pane to update the interface configurations, including increasing performance by combining multiple Ethernet interfaces to act as one.
3. Tools/Maintenance: After the server is running, use utilities such as Server Admin and Workgroup Manager for ongoing server and account maintenance.

**Lessons 1.1-1.4**

Planning and Installation

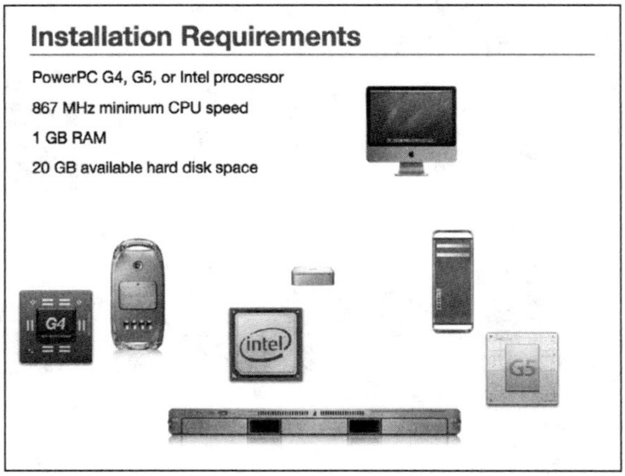


Choose a server based on the size and needs of the group using it. To provide services to just a few people, a Mac mini or older PowerMac G5 may suffice. Workgroups need a Mac Pro. Demanding server environments often require an Xserve, which is Apple's 1U rack-mount server.

> **Note** Xserve, Power Mac G5, and any Macintosh Server G4 or Power Mac G4 released later than February 2000 includes special hardware to detect an unexpected system shutdown and automatically restart the server machine. This feature works with Mac OS X Server's ability to detect and restart after an error in server service.

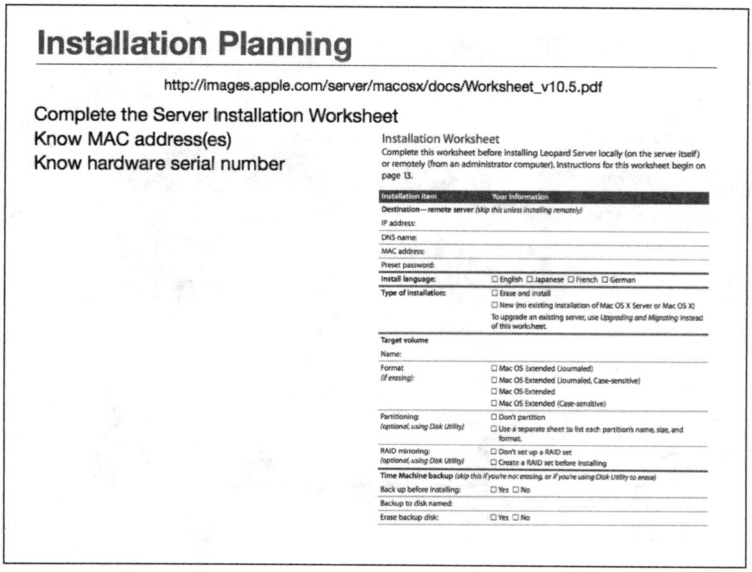


A server administrator should follow certain steps when setting up Mac OS X Server. The first step is to review your organization's server needs. Will the server be used mainly for web services, QuickTime streaming, calendaring and Wiki services, file and print services, or something else? Will it be a dedicated server or will it have multiple uses? When deciding how to use your Mac OS X Server, you might want to use the extensive planning document, included with the Mac OS X Server documentation.

## Partition Choices

Single partition

Separate partition

Multiple drives

Soft RAID

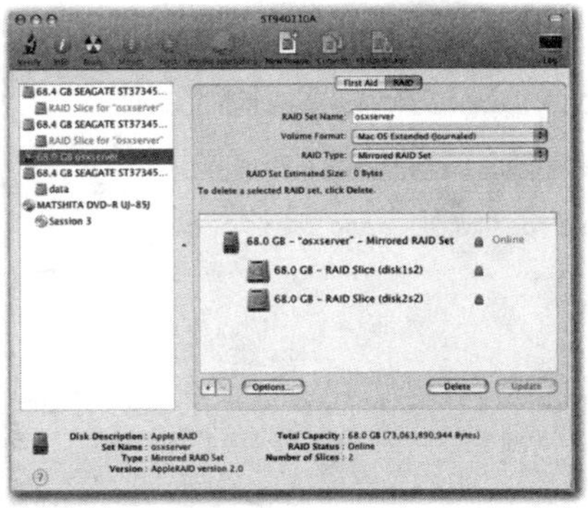

## Soft RAID Choices

RAID 0 - Striping

- Data is written across all drives
- When a drive in the group is lost, all data is lost.

RAID 0 - Concatenation

- Data fills first drive, then fills second, then third, and so on.
- When a drive is lost, all data on that drive is lost.

RAID 1 - Mirroring

- Data is written simultaneously to two drives.
- When one drive is lost, data is remains accessible.

## Supported Boot Disk Formats

Mac OS X Extended (Journaled)

- Appropriate for most installations
- Preferred for Wiki

Mac OS X Extended (Case-sensitive Journaled)

- Static websites with many files
- More specific URLs and links

Mac OS X Server can be installed on a single disk, partitioned drive or volume, supported RAID array, or removable device, as long as that device is bootable. You have options for how you partition your device, even if it's only one partition. Those are:

- GUID Partition Table—used to start up Intel-based Macs
- Apple Partition Map—used to start up a PowerPC-based Mac
- Master Boot Record—used to start up DOS and Windows-based computers

Once properly prepared, you have certain formatting options prior to installing Mac OS X Server, such as Mac OS Extended (Journaled) and Mac OS X Extended (Case-sensitive Journaled).

## Server Installation—Local

Boot from Mac OS X Server Install DVD.

Select device or partition.

Requires no other information or interaction.

Run Server Assistant locally.

## Server Installation—Remote

Boot from Mac OS X Server Install DVD.

Access server using server's MAC address(es) and first 8 digits of hardware serial number.

Install Server Admin Tools on Mac OS X.

Server searches local subnet for Macs booted from Mac OS X Server Install DVD.

Run Server Assistant remotely.

- Remote servers not on local subnet can be accessed if a public IP address has been assigned to the server via DHCP.

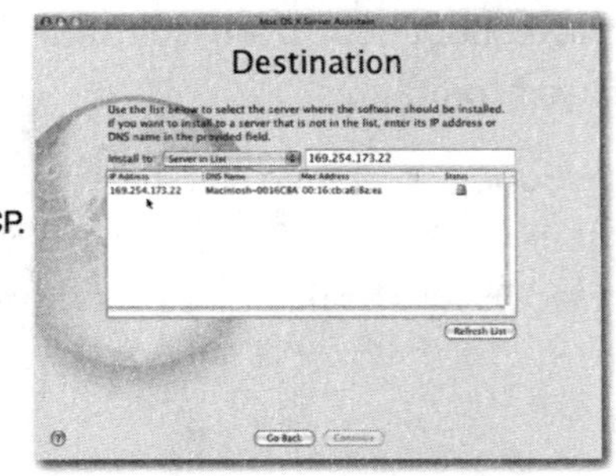

## Server Installation—Remote

Use Apple Remote Desktop or any VNC software to control the screen of a Mac booted from the Mac OS X Server Install DVD.

- No username is required.
- Password is first 8 digits of hardware serial number.
- The Local Subnet or known public IP is required.

You can choose to install Mac OS X Server either locally, sitting at the computer on which you are installing the software, or you can install it remotely. If you install remotely, you must have network access to the computer.

It is important to note that to install from any other computer you'll need both the hardware serial number and the Ethernet (or MAC) address(es) of the computer that will host your server software. Repeat the method of launching System Profiler—similar to when you confirmed your hardware requirements—and click Network contents to obtain the Ethernet (MAC) address(es). Write the address on your Server Worksheet along with the hardware serial number and other pertinent information. You can also find this information on the box label of every Mac and Xserve sold.

## Installation Without Internal DVD Drive

Boot server into FireWire Target Disk Mode.

- Connect to a Mac with the same CPU type.
- Boot from the Mac OS X Server Install DVD.

Connect removable optical drive using FireWire or USB cable.

- Insert Mac OS X Server Install DVD.

Boot another server running NetBoot service.

- NetInstall Mac OS X Server onto the computer.
- Image Restore

Mac OS X Server v10.5 also includes the ability to have the installation DVD in the remote machine and not at the server. In this scenario, you do not need physical access to the server, nor is the server required to have an optical drive. You can use other methods for remote installation.

## Installation Log

You can monitor progress of local installations via the install log.

You access the log using the Window menu.

Installation logs show errors, progress, or both.

You can save the log to a file.

Logs are excellent for obtaining baseline information when installing on a variety of Macs.

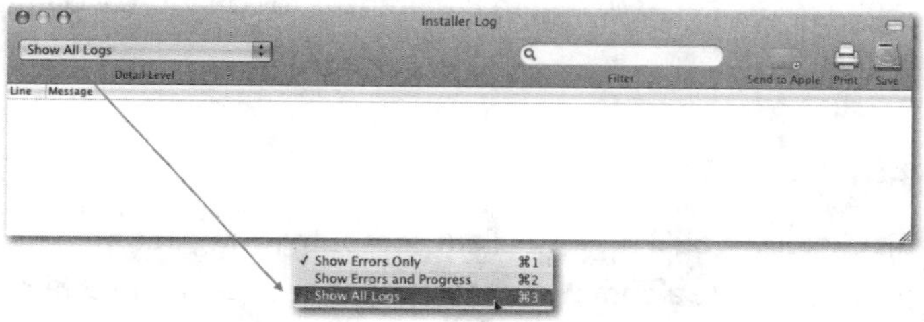


You can view the Installer log file during the installation process by selecting Installer Log from the Window menu. When you do so, a separate window appears at the bottom of the screen allowing you to view three types of events within the log file.

### Exercises

1.1.1 Configure Mac OS X on the Client Computer

1.2.1 Install Server Administration Software on the Mac OS X Computer

1.3.1 Install Mac OS X Server Remotely (optional)

or

1.4.1 Install Mac OS X Server Locally (optional)

## Exercise 1.1.1

# Configure Mac OS X on the Client Computer

## Objective

Use Setup Assistant and System Preferences to configure a client computer.

## Summary

In this exercise, you'll set up a client computer using Setup Assistant to create a administrator account and configure other basic settings. You'll use System Preferences to configure network, sharing, account, and energy saver settings. You'll also download student materials from the instructor server that you'll use throughout this class. Lastly, you'll apply any necessary system software updates.

Before you begin this exercise, ensure you have Mac OS X version 10.5 installed on your client computer. If it is not already installed, install it now using the Mac OS X Install DVD.

For this exercise your instructor will provide you a student number, which will be used to provide unique names for your classroom computers.

## Configure Basic Settings and Create Initial Administrator Account with Setup Assistant

In this section, you'll step through the Mac OS X Setup Assistant for initial system configuration.

1. At the Welcome screen, choose the appropriate country, and click Continue.
2. Choose the appropriate keyboard layout, then click Continue.
3. When asked about transferring information from another Mac, click Continue to proceed without transferring anything.

4 If prompted to choose a wireless connection, click Different Network Setup, choose "Local network (Ethernet)", and then click Continue.

5 Verify "Using DHCP" is the TCP/IP Connection Type, and click Continue.

6 When prompted for an Apple ID, leave both fields empty and click Continue.

7 In the Registration Information screen, press Command-Q to skip the registration process.

8 Click the Skip button.

9 In the Create Your Account screen, enter the following information:

- Name: `Client Administrator`
- Short Name: `cadmin`
- Password: `cadmin`
- Verify: `cadmin`
- Password Hint: None

If your Macintosh includes a built-in iSight camera, you will be prompted with the Select a Picture For this Account screen. Either take a snapshot or choose a picture from the picture library and click Continue.

10 Click Continue to create the administrator account.

11 In the Select Time Zone screen, click your time zone in the map, and then click Continue.

If you are not sure about your time zone, ask your instructor.

12 In the Set the Time and Date screen, verify the current time and date. If the time or date is incorrect, set it correctly, and then click Save. Click Continue.

13 In the Don't Forget to Register screen, click Done.

The Setup Assistant will quit, and the Finder will open.

14 If prompted to install software updates, click Not Now.

## Set the Computer Name and Turn On Remote Management

Because every student has entered the same account name information, all student computers have the same computer name. To distinguish your computer on the network, you need to set a unique computer name. Additionally, Mac OS X will not allow duplicate local host names, so you may see an error message indicating your local host name has been incremented from Client-Administrators-*machine name*.local to Client-Administrators-*machine name-n*.local, where *n* is a unique number based on when you configured your computer relative to other students. You'll also need to set a local host name associated with your student number.

1 Open System Preferences by clicking the icon in the Dock.

2 Click the Sharing icon in System Preferences.

3 Set the computer name to `clientn`, replacing *n* with your student number.

For example if your student number is 17, the computer name should be client17, all lowercase and no spaces, as shown in the following figure.

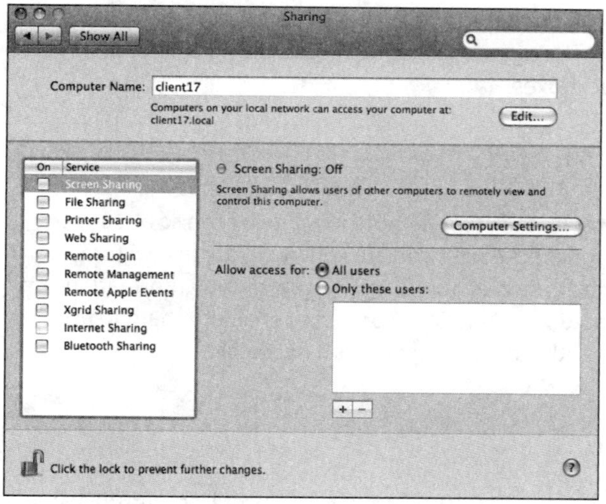


4 Press the Return key.

Notice that your local host name listed under your computer name updates to match your new computer name.

5 Make sure the Remote Login checkbox is selected.

If a warning about the sleep schedule appears, click OK.

6 Select the Remote Management checkbox. In the subsequent dialog that appears, hold down the Option key while selecting the Observe checkbox, as shown in the following figure. Click OK.

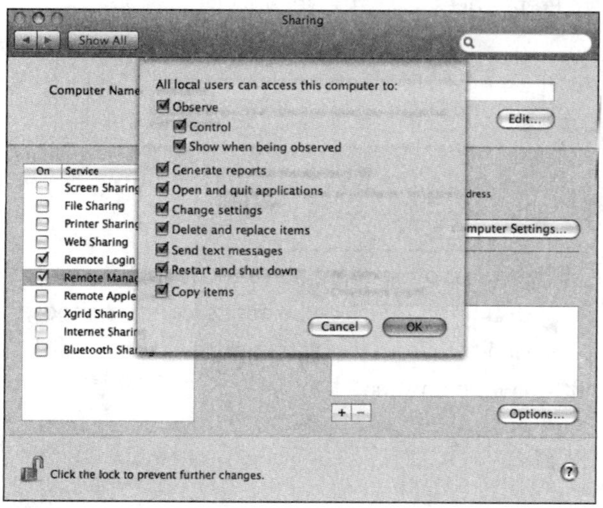

> **Note** Using the Option key in this dialog selects all checkboxes.

> **Note** By selecting Remote Management and all subsequent checkboxes, you are allowing your instructor to control your keyboard and mouse, gather information, and update your Mac OS X computer, enabling them to assist you with steps and exercises if necessary.

7 Click OK.

8 Click Show All to return to the main System Preferences pane.

## Turn Off All Interfaces Except Built-in Ethernet and Set Energy Saver Preferences

To prevent accidentally accessing another network, you will disable all active interfaces (such as a wireless connection with the Airport interface) other than the connected Ethernet interface. Active network interfaces are indicated in the list by a red, yellow, or green bullet. Inactive interfaces are labeled as such, and are faded out.

1 In System Preferences, click the Network icon.

2 Disable all interfaces other than the connected Ethernet interface. To disable an interface, select its icon and choose Make Service Inactive from the Action pop-up menu. Click the Apply button when finished.

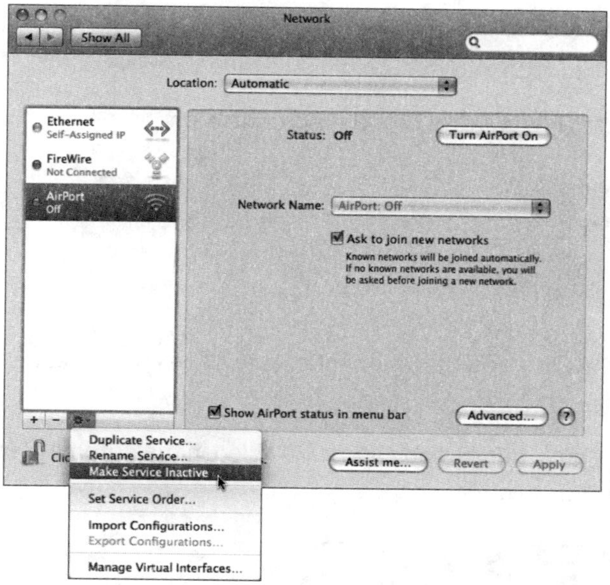


3 Return to the main System Preferences pane, then click the Energy Saver icon.

4 Click Show Details if necessary, then set the computer to never sleep.

This will prevent the computer from going to sleep while installing Mac OS X Server.

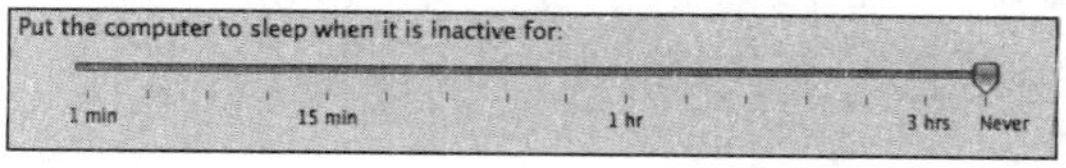


5 Click Show All to return to the main System Preferences pane.

## Turn Off Automatic Login

Next, you'll turn off automatic login for future exercises.

1 In System Preferences, click the Accounts icon.

2 Click the Lock, and then authenticate to allow configuration changes.

3 Click Login Options, and choose Disabled in the Automatic Login pop-up menu.

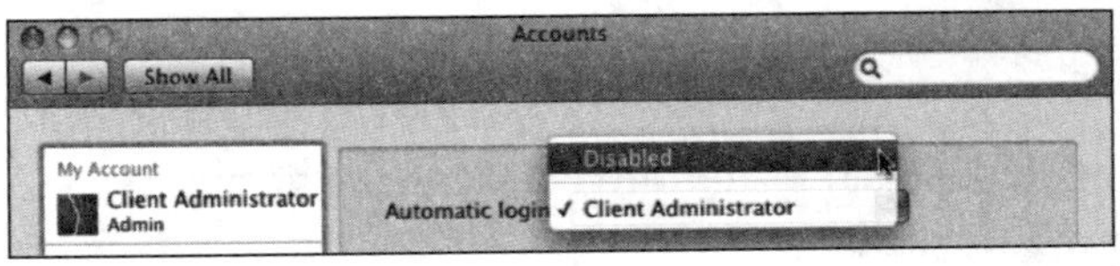


4 Quit System Preferences.

## Download Student Materials and Apply Software Updates

In this section you'll connect to the instructor server and download the student materials used for the course.

1 In Finder, choose New Finder Window from the File menu.

2 Select mainserver under the list of Shared computers.

Because mainserver allows guest access via Apple Filing Protocol (AFP), the Mac OS X computer logs in automatically and displays the available share points.

3 Open the `Public` folder.

4 Open a new Finder window and navigate to `/Users/Shared` on the Mac OS X computer.

5 Drag the `StudentMaterials` folder from the Public share point on the server to the Shared folder on the Mac OS X computer.

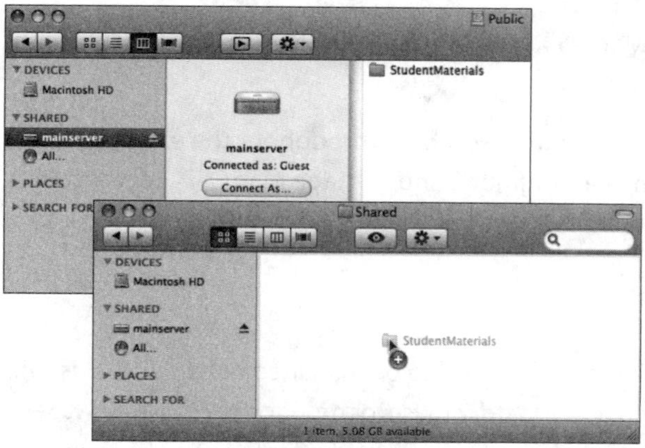


6 Once the copy is complete, disconnect from mainserver by clicking the Eject button.

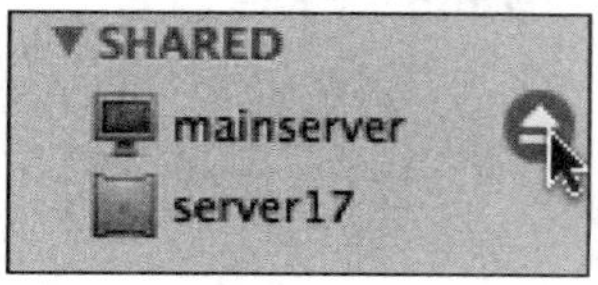


7 If there is an `Updates` folder inside the `StudentMaterials` folder, open it. Install any Mac OS X updates it contains. Restart if necessary.

To install a system update, double-click the disk image file to open it, and then run the installer that appears on the screen.

## Exercise 1.2.1

# Install Server Administration Software on the Mac OS X Computer

### Objectives

Install the Mac OS X Server administration software on the Mac OS X computer.

Use the administration software throughout the exercises to remotely install, configure, and manage Mac OS X Server over the network.

### Summary

Mac OS X Server is designed to be managed headless, that is, without access to a keyboard, mouse, or monitor. Each Mac OS X Server Install DVD contains a separate installer for the server administration software, which can also be freely downloaded from Apple's website. It is this software that you will be installing in this exercise.

1 Insert the Mac OS X Server Install DVD into your Mac OS X computer's DVD-ROM drive.

2 Open the `Other Installs` folder.

3 Double-click the `ServerAdministrationSoftware.mpkg` installer metapackage and follow the onscreen instructions to install the server administration software.

> **Note** A more recent version of installer metapackage may be in your Student Materials folder.

The administration software is installed in /Applications/Server. You will be accessing these tools frequently throughout this course.

4 For easy access, drag the `Server` folder onto the right side of the Dock.

***Question 1*** *What tools are installed inside the* `Server` *folder by the* `ServerAdministrationSoftware.mpkg` *metapackage?*

Exercise 1.3.1

# Install Mac OS X Server Remotely (optional)

## Objective

Perform a remote installation of Mac OS X Server using Server Assistant.

## Summary

Remote installation of Mac OS X Server requires knowledge of the server computer's hardware serial number and MAC address. In addition, the server must be restarted from the Mac OS X Server Install DVD. In this exercise, you'll install Mac OS X Server remotely on the server computer.

Remote installation has a couple noteworthy limitations compared to a location installation. Disk Utility is not available to partition the server's disk prior to installation. Also, it is not possible to customize the installation packages (for example, to remove extra languages and printer drivers) in a remote installation.

> **Note** You can use third-party software, such as Apple Remote Desktop or any Virtual Network Client (VNC) control software to control the keyboard and mouse of the computer on which you are installing Mac OS X Server. The VNC software is active when started from the Mac OS X Server Install DVD. There is no username and the password to control the server is the first eight digits of the hardware serial number of the computer. You will not be doing that type of installation in this course, but you should know you have that capability.

1 Locate and record your server's MAC address and hardware serial number. Your instructor may have this information for you.

   a MAC Address Ethernet 1 ____________________

   b MAC Address Ethernet 2 ____________________
   (if necessary)

   c Hardware Serial Number ____________________

2 Be sure the server computer is turned off, then hold down the Option key on the keyboard as you press the Power button.

   This "option-start" technique displays a list of available boot volumes, and works on most Mac models.

3 If your server computer has a DVD-ROM drive tray, press the Eject button on the keyboard. If there is not an Eject button, press F12 on the keyboard to open the DVD-ROM drive tray.

4 Insert the Mac OS X Server Install DVD, then press Eject (or F12) again to close the tray.

5 While the server is starting, open Server Assistant on the Mac OS X computer, located in /Applications/Server.

6 When the Mac OS X Server Install DVD icon appears, select it as the startup volume and press Return.

   You may also have the Server folder icon on your Dock, and you can access the Server tools from there.

7 To avoid interfering with the remote installation, place the server's keyboard and mouse out of reach.

8 Select "Install Mac OS X Server option on a remote computer," then click Continue.

   Server Assistant will display a list of all Mac OS X Server computers that are awaiting installation. Note that your server appears with a self-assigned IP address. Server Assistant uses Bonjour to locate any Mac OS X Server computers on the local network that are awaiting installation, which works even if there is no DHCP server on the network.

9 Use your server's MAC address to identify your server in the list. If it does not appear, try clicking Refresh List.

10 Select your server, then click Continue.

11 Enter the first 8 characters of your server's hardware serial number (uppercase because it is case-sensitive) at the prompt to authenticate, and click OK.

On older machines, it may be necessary to use "12345678" as the password.

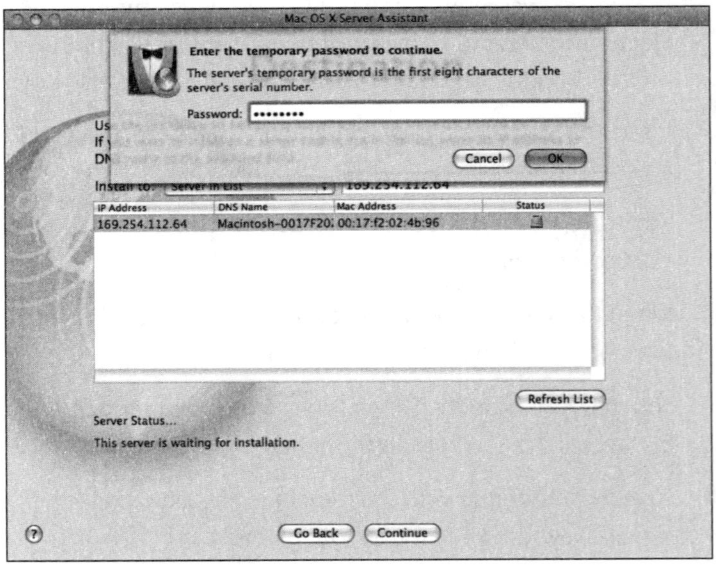


12 Choose the appropriate language, then click Continue.

13 Note the installation requirements.

The server's minimum CPU requirement is a G4 with a speed of 867 MHz or faster (any G5 or Intel processor is supported). 1 GB of system memory and 20 GB of available disk space are also required.

14 Click Continue to move past the Installation Requirements.

15 Agree to the software license by clicking the Continue and Agree buttons.

A list of volumes displays. As with Mac OS X, Mac OS X Server can be installed onto volumes that reside on external disks such as FireWire or USB drives. For best performance, install Mac OS X Server on an internal hard disk volume.

16 Select your server's primary internal hard disk drive as the install destination, then click Continue.

17 Notify your instructor when the installation begins.

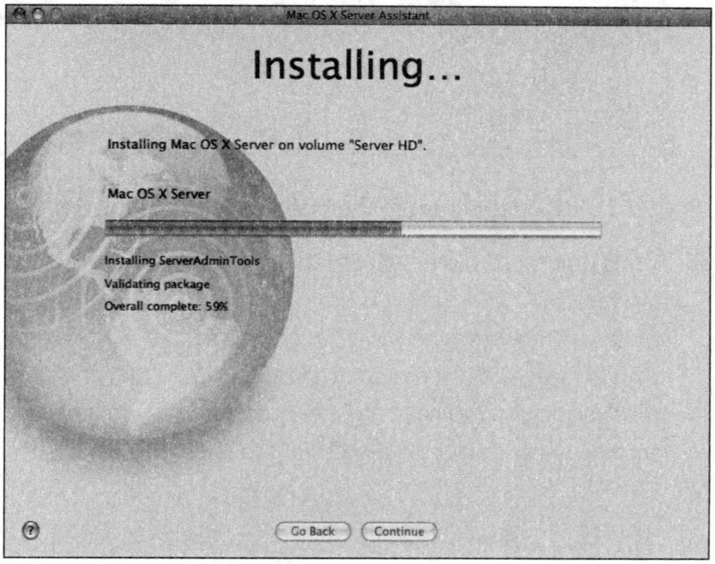

18 Once installation is complete, the server will restart.

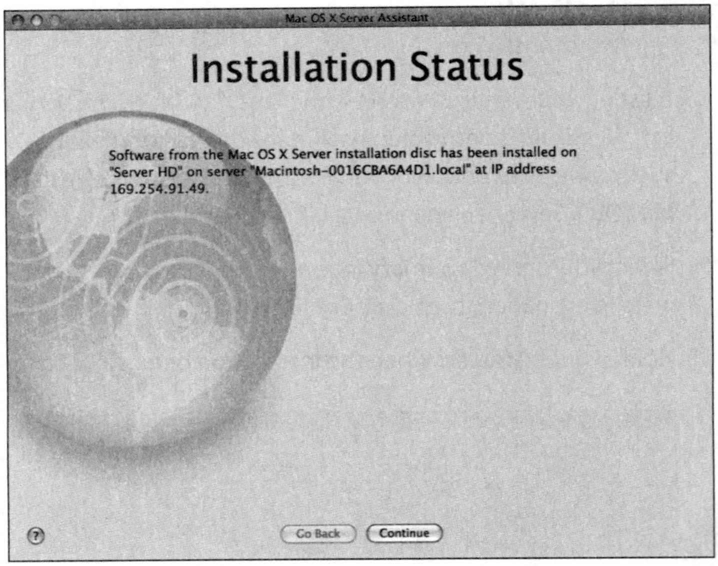


19 Click Continue to return to the main Server Assistant pane.

At this point, the server will use the newly installed server software. Mac OS X Server is now ready for configuration. Skip to Exercise 1.5, in which you will configure Mac OS X Server remotely using Setup Assistant. (Exercise 1.4 details the steps to install locally. You have already completed the installation remotely. Therefore, you should skip to Exercise 1.5)

## Exercise 1.4.1

# Install Mac OS X Server Locally (optional)

## Objective

Locally install Mac OS X Server.

## Summary

This exercise is an alternative to a remote installation, and should be skipped if a remote installation was performed.

Local installation of Mac OS X Server provides additional flexibility compared to a remote installation. When performing a location installation, it is possible to use Disk Utility to partition the server's disks. It is also possible to customize the list of components to install; for example, some servers may not need printer drivers and therefore should not be installed.

1 Be sure the server computer is turned off, then hold down the Option key on the keyboard as you press the Power button.

   This "option-start" technique displays a list of available boot volumes, and works on most Mac models.

2 If your server computer has a DVD-ROM drive tray, press the Eject button on the keyboard. If there is not an Eject button, press F12 on the keyboard to open the DVD-ROM tray.

3 Insert the Mac OS X Server Install DVD, then press Eject (or F12) again to close the tray.

4 When the Mac OS X Server Install DVD icon appears, select it as the startup volume.

5 Choose the appropriate language, then click the arrow to continue.

6 Before passing through the Welcome Screen, examine the Utilities menu at the top of the screen. Note the various tools available from the Mac OS X Server Install DVD.

7 Click Continue to pass the Welcome screen.

8 Agree to the software license by clicking the Continue and Agree buttons.

9 Select the Server HD partition as the install destination, then click Continue.

10 At the Install Summary screen, click Customize to view available customization options. For this class, leave all choices in their default states, then click Done.

11 Click Install to begin the installation.

12 A media check runs to validate the integrity of the media. If you know the media is in good shape, click Skip to halt this process and continue with the installation.

13 During installation, it is possible to view the installer log as it is being written. From the Window menu, select Installer Log.

> **Warning!** The server will not automatically restart when installation is complete if the installer log is open.

14 After installation finishes, click Restart.

# Mac OS X Server Configuration

1.5

**Lessons 1.5**

Mac OS X Server Configuration

## Server Configuration

Is performed with Server Assistant

Can be performed locally or remotely

Requires software serial number

Remote configuration also requires

- Server's MAC address(es)
- First 8 digits of hardware serial number

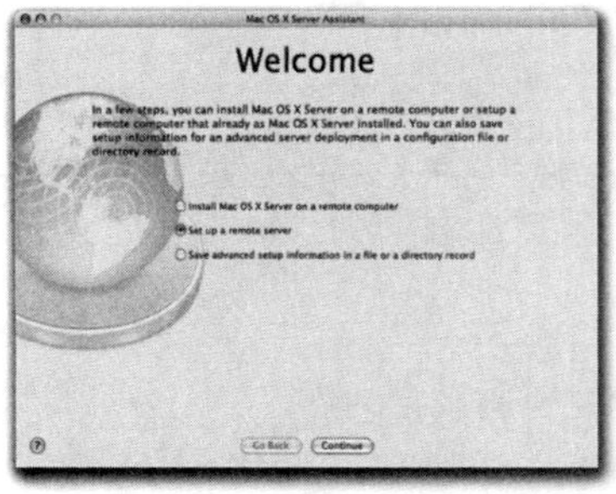

## Server Configuration Types

Standard

- Use for home office or small business

Workgroup

- Use for departments within an organization

Advanced

- Use for large organization using multiple services

Xsan Metadata Controller (hardware dependent)

- Use with Xsan
- Use when Fibre Channel cards are present

## Server Configuration Options

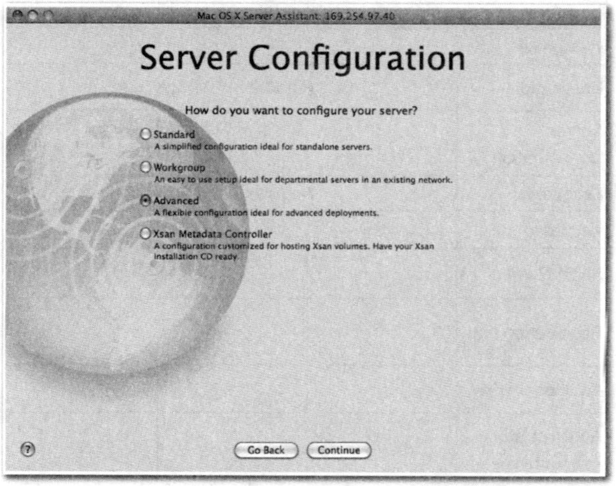


When using Server Assistant to set up a remote server, you are asked to select the destination computer and authenticate again using the first eight digits of the hardware serial number (or 12345678 if necessary for older computers). Local setup does not require these steps. At this point, both local and remote installations are similar, in that you now decide how you wish your server to be configured initially. You have three main configuration options:

- Standard
- Workgroup
- Advanced

## Configuration Matrix

| Screens | Standard | Workgroup | Advanced |
|---|---|---|---|
| Welcome | √ | √ | √ |
| Destination | Remote Install Only | | |
| Server Configuration | √ | √ | √ |
| Language | Remote Install Only | | |
| Keyboard | √ | √ | √ |
| Serial Number | √ | √ | √ |
| Registration Info | √ | √ | √ |
| Additional Info | √ | √ | √ |
| Administrator Account | √ | √ | √ |

## Configuration Matrix (cont'd)

| Screens | Standard | Workgroup | Advanced |
|---|---|---|---|
| Network Address Information | √ | √ | √ |
| TCP/IP Info | √ | √ | √ |
| Network Names | √ | √ | √ |
| Time Zone | √ | √ | √ |
| Date & Time | √ | √ | √ |
| Server Time Machine | √ | √ | |
| Initial Mail | √ | | |
| VPN Access | √ | | |

## Configuration Matrix (cont'd)

| Screens | Standard | Workgroup | Advanced |
|---|---|---|---|
| Enable Basic Services | | √ | |
| Directory Usage | | | √ |
| Client Time Machine | √ | √ | |
| Users and Authentication | | √ | |
| Add User Accounts | √ | √ | |
| Add New User Accounts | √ | √ | |
| Confirm Settings | | | √ |

When dealing with Standard or Workgroup configurations, you'll use Server Preferences.

## Standard and Workgroup Nuances

Use Server Preferences for configuration management.

Use Server Admin and Workgroup Manager when Standard or Workgroup configurations are upgraded to Advanced.

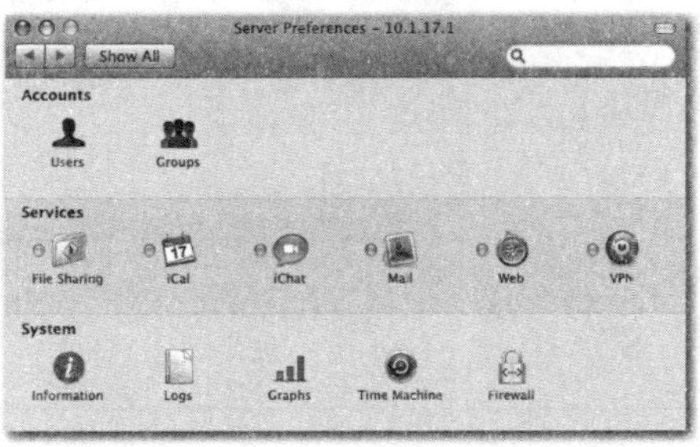

The screens that you walk through when configuring Mac OS X Server may differ depending on hardware, such as the Lights Out Management for Xserve.

## Local Administrator Account

Initial administrator account is the administrator of server services and of the local database.

- Password for local administrator is also password for local root account.
- Local root password should be changed after Mac OS X Server has been configured.

Edit Picture option only available in Standard and Workgroup configurations.

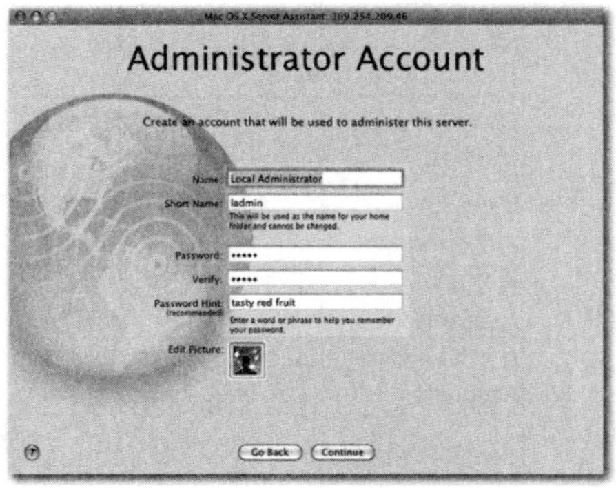


## Network Address Information

In Advanced configuration

- IPv6 can be turned off.

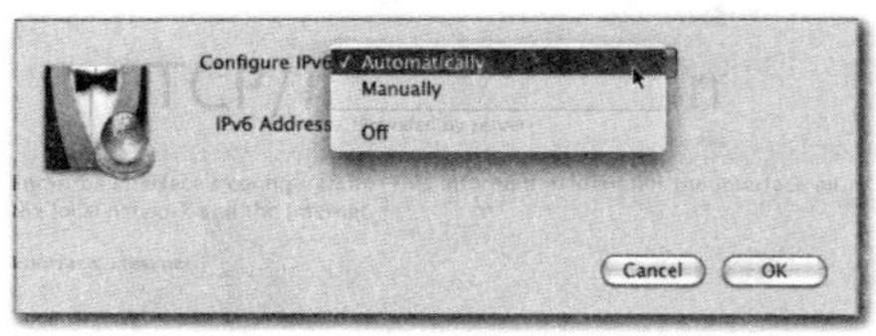


On Xserves

- Lights Out Management can be set up.

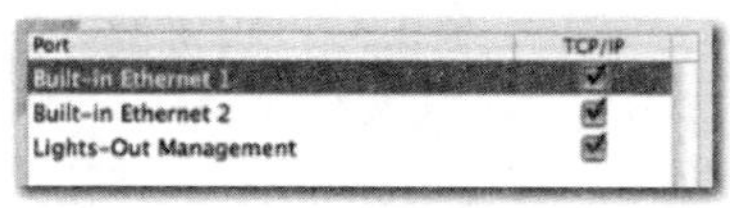

## Xserve Options

Lights Out Management

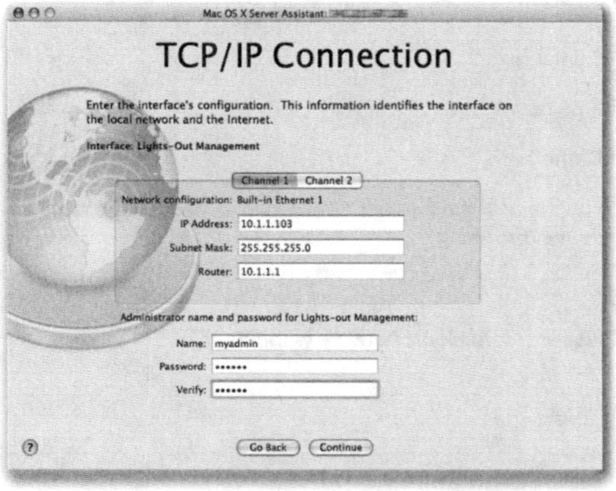


Network naming is important to Mac OS X Server as many services rely on the primary DNS name.

## Network Names

Mac OS X Server prefers to use DNS for name resolution.

- Any properly configured DNS server will suffice.
- Primary DNS name should match the IP address dedicated to the DNS server.
- Computer Name can contain spaces, Bonjour name cannot.
- Enable Remote Management checkbox is available only with Advanced configuration.

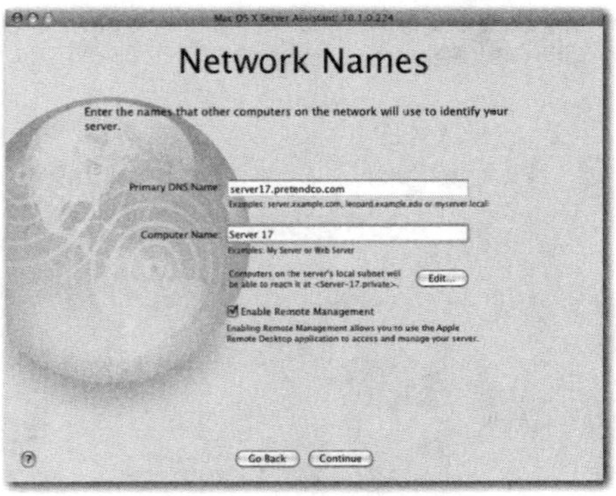

## Network Name Usage

Primary DNS Name

- Used to define
  - LDAP database
  - Kerberos realm

Computer Name

- Used to define how the name for the server appears over Mac OS X network when browsing

Local Name

- Used for users on the local network (subnet)

Should other volumes be present and mounted, a screen appears offering the opportunity to back up to an already configured server. Following that optional screen, a list of services is offered if you use the Workgroup configuration.

## Time Machine for Mac OS X Server

Standard and Workgroup configurations provide the ability to direct Mac OS X Server to backup data.

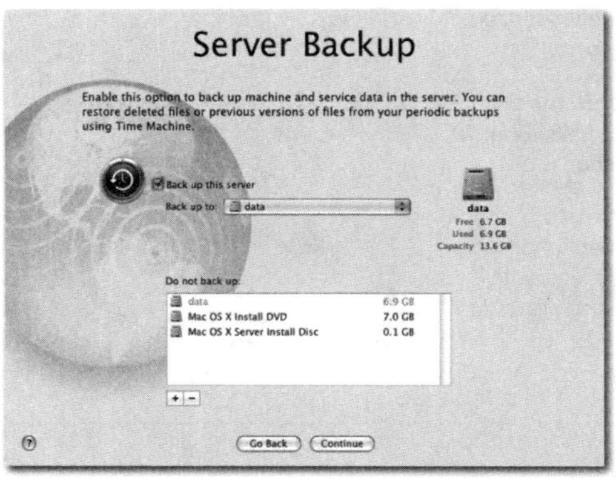

## Workgroup Configuration Setup Screen

Workgroup configurations provide the ability to enable certain services.

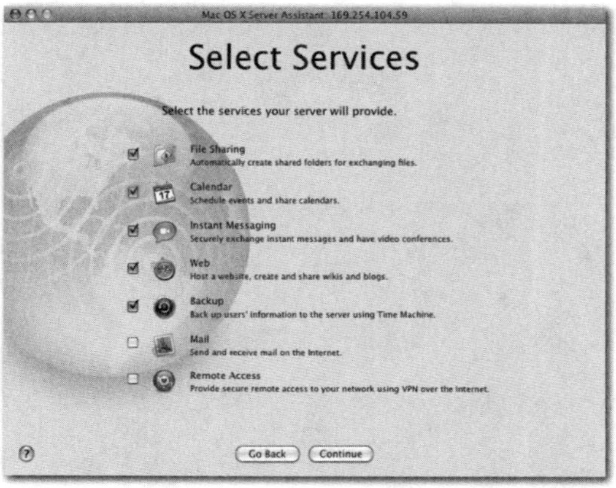


Directory usage is an important step, and unless the server is going to be connected to another directory server, it is best to leave it as a Standalone server, especially if using Advanced configuration. In Standard and Workgroup configuration, an Open Directory Master is created by default, unless you are connected to another directory system.

## Advanced Configuration Directory Usage

Advanced configurations provide the ability operate as a standalone or connect to a directory system.

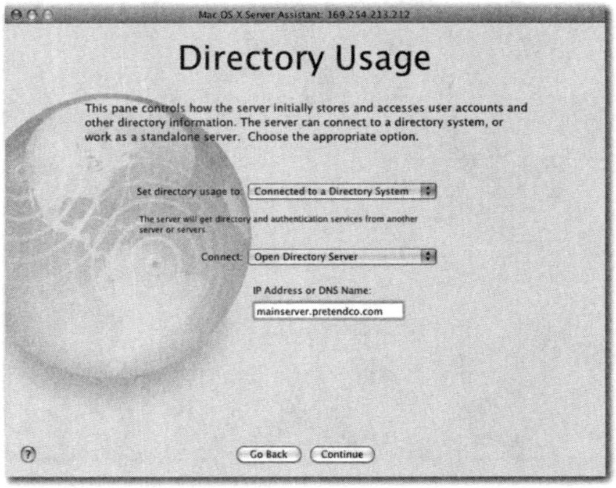


In Standard and Workgroup configurations, options appear to permit the Mac OS X Server to provide backup services via Time Machine and the ability to add user accounts prior to final configuration. This is useful when an administrator wishes to have another person enter user names but not have full access to the server.

## Client Time Machine Screen

Ability to direct Mac OS X computers to backup data to a Mac OS X Server. (Available only in Standalone and Workgroup setup configurations)

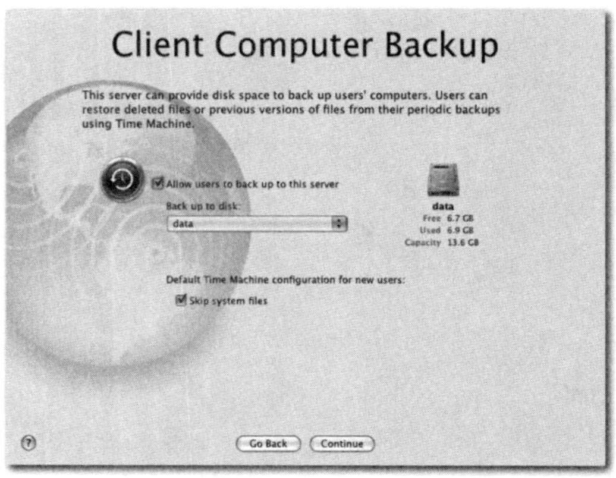

## Add User Accounts

Setup user accounts prior to initial server configuration.
(Available only in Standard and Workgroup setup configurations)

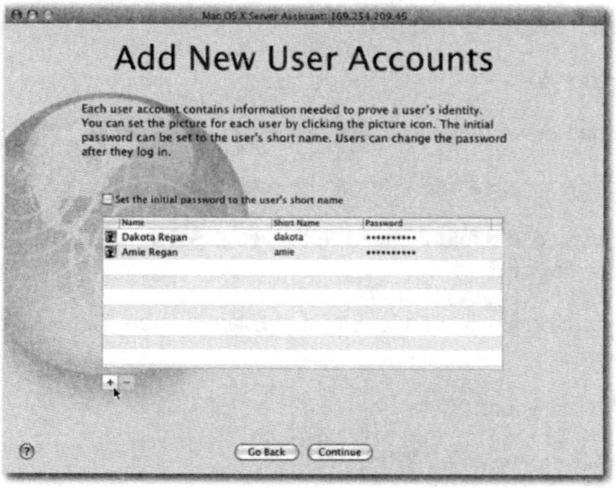


In Advanced mode, you have the chance to review all the settings and save configuration data in one of three methods.

## Confirm Settings

Review and save server configuration information.
(Available only in Advanced Configuration)

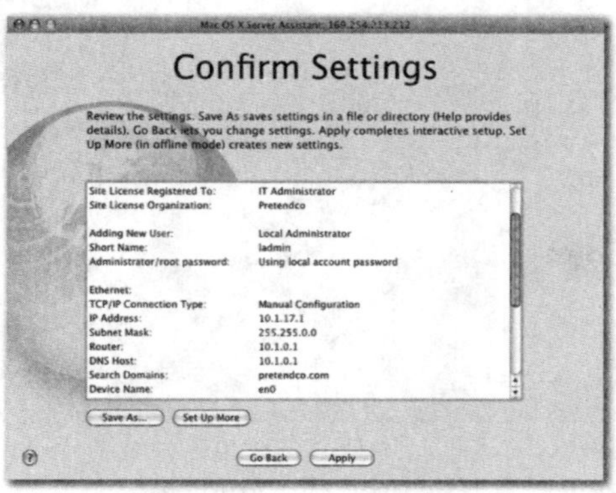

## Saving Server Configuration Data

Data can be saved three ways:

- Text file
  - Printable file of your information
- Configuration file
  - File is named with the MAC address(es)
    - Can be two files and files can be passphrase protected
  - File is placed in a folder called Auto Server Setup on USB or FireWire device
  - Configuration file is used to automatically configure a clean install of a server
- Configuration record
  - Record is stored on LDAP server

Exercise

1.5.1 Remote Configuration of Mac OS X Server

Server Preferences can be used to administer a Mac OS X Server setup in Standard or Advanced configuration. Server Admin can be used to administer certain additional services, but this must be approved by the administrator. Administrators also can upgrade their servers to Advanced configuration. After that, there is no way to use Server Preferences to manage the server again.

## Exercise 1.5.1

# Remote Configuration of Mac OS X Server

## Objective

Remotely set up Mac OS X Server in an Advanced configuration.

## Summary

Server configuration is performed directly after a local or remote installation of Mac OS X Server. During this initial configuration phase, several important aspects of your server will be configured, such as the primary administrator account name and password, network configuration, time and date, and the directory usage policy.

During configuration, you'll also set the administrative mode of the server. Mac OS X Server v10.5 features three distinct administrative modes: Standard, Workgroup, and Advanced. Standard and Workgroup modes are intended to ease the Mac OS X Server deployment process for standalone servers that host users and group accounts, or workgroup servers which use user and group accounts hosted on another directory server. The tradeoff between these two modes and the Advanced mode is reduced administrative complexity in exchange for a configuration focused on specific use cases. The Advanced configuration is the more similar to a Mac OS X Server v10.4 configuration, and provides access to all available services and maximum flexibility.

For this class, you'll use Server Assistant from the Mac OS X computer to set up the server in an Advanced configuration.

1 On Mac OS X, launch Server Assistant, if it is not already open.

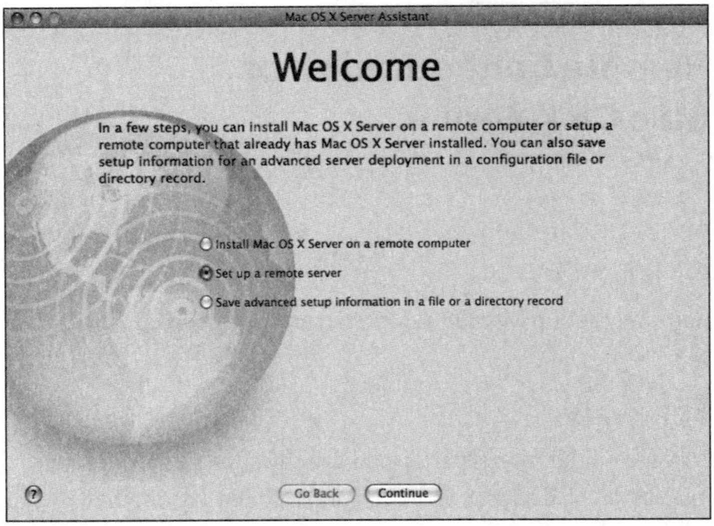


2 Select "Set up a remote server," then click Continue.

A list of servers awaiting configuration displays. Once again, Bonjour is used to locate your server on the local network, even though the server has a self-assigned IP address.

3 Locate your server in the list, using your server's MAC address. The MAC address is the 12-digit portion after the dash under the name.

If your server MAC address does not appear in the list but you see servers listed as "localhost," you can hover your cursor over the available IP addresses, and eventually a small yellow pop-up should appear showing the MAC address for the chosen IP in the list.

4 Select the Apply checkbox for your server.

5 Click once in the Password field to enable the field for text entry.

6 Type the first 8 characters of your server's serial number (all uppercase, the password is case-sensitive).

On older computers enter *12345678* as the password.

7 Click Continue.

You are presented with the Server Configuration screen. This is an important step in the Mac OS X Server setup. The configuration options listed allow Mac OS X Server to present an administrative interface that is most appropriate for how the server will be used.

> **Note** If you have fibre cards attached to an Xserve RAID, you will see a fourth option, Xsan Metadata Controller.

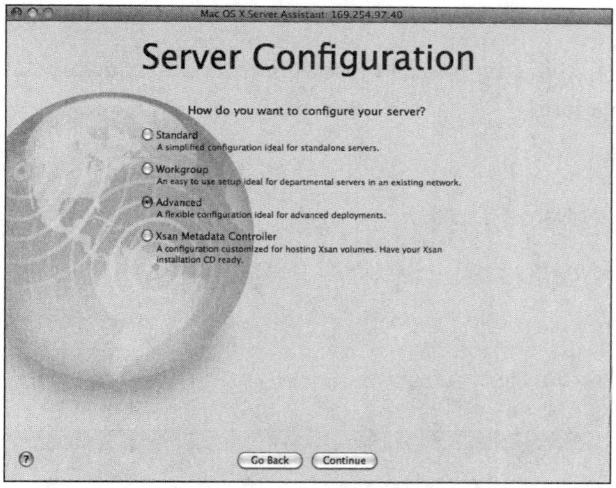


8 Select Advanced, then click Continue.

9 Choose the appropriate language, then click Continue.

10 Choose a keyboard layout, then click Continue.

11 Enter the Mac OS X Server serial number, registered user and organization, but do not click Continue yet.

Near the bottom right of the window is a 'tear-off' icon. This allows you to easily save the license information for later use.

12 Click and drag from the Tear-off icon to your desktop to save the serial number and license information to your disk.

13 To demonstrate loading the license information, clear a portion of the serial number that you just entered.

14 Drag the SerialNumber.SA icon from your desktop into the center of the Server Assistant window to load the configuration.

   The full serial number displays.

15 Click Continue to validate the serial number.

16 When prompted for Registration Information, click Continue.

17 Click Continue to bypass the questionnaire.

18 At the Administrator Account screen, enter the following information:

   - Name: `Local Administrator`
   - Short Name: `ladmin`
   - Password: `apple`
   - Verify: `apple`
   - Password Hint: `tasty red fruit`

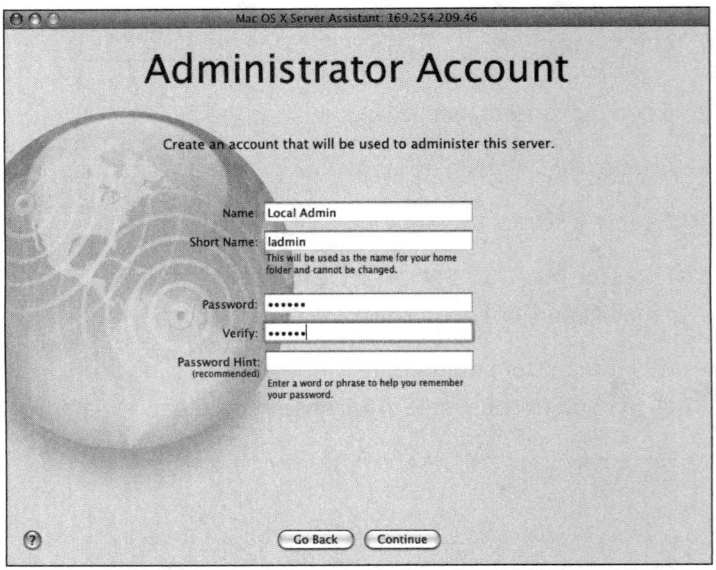

19 Click Continue.

20 In the Network Address panel, select "No, configure network settings manually," then click Continue.

21 Enter the following information to manually configure the Ethernet interface for the classroom environment:

- IP Address: `10.1.n.1` where *n* is your student number
- Subnet Mask: `255.255.0.0`
- Router: `10.1.0.1`
- DNS Servers: `10.1.0.1`
- Search Domain: `pretendco.com`

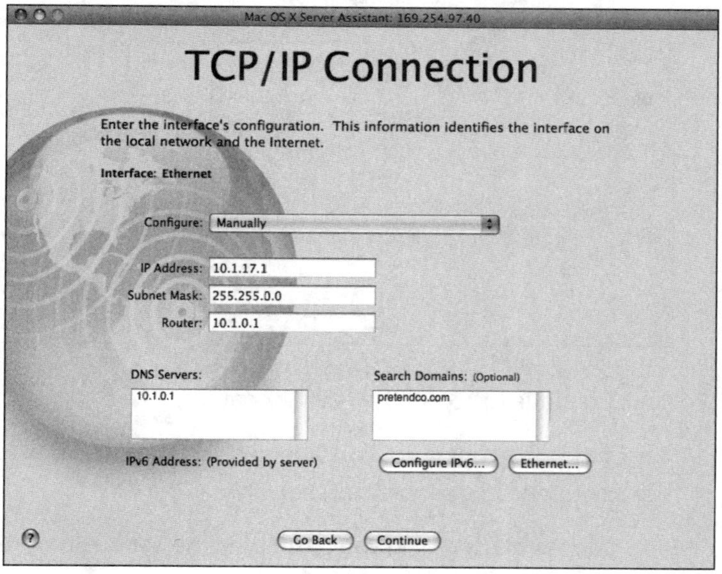


22 Click Continue to accept the network configuration.

**23** At the Network Names screen, enter the following information:

- Primary DNS Name: `server`*`n`*`.pretendco.com` where `n` is your student number, for example server17.pretendco.com
- Computer Name: *`servern`* where `n` is your student number, for example, *`server17`*
- Ensure Enable Remote Management is selected.

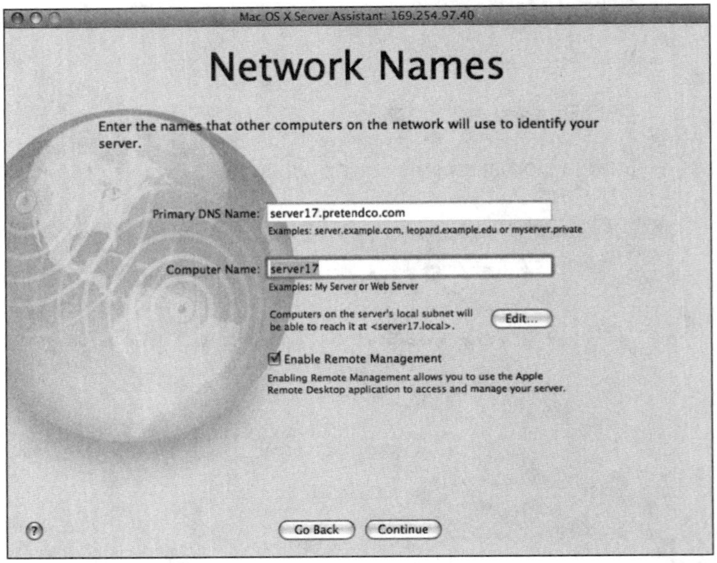


**24** Click Continue to accept the network names.

**25** Select the time zone. Click Edit, and deselect the checkbox to use a network time server, and click OK.

**26** If a screen appears asking you to set the time, set it appropriately for your location and click Continue.

You are prompted to configure Mac OS X Server's Open Directory role.

**27** Choose Standalone Server in the "Set directory usage to" pop-up menu.

In the Standalone role, the server uses a local, nonshared directory to store directory information (such as users and groups). When connected to another directory service, Mac OS X Server can use users and groups hosted on a remote server to provide authentication and authorization for services hosted by your server. You'll experiment with directory usage configurations later in the course, but for now, you'll use the Standalone Server configuration.

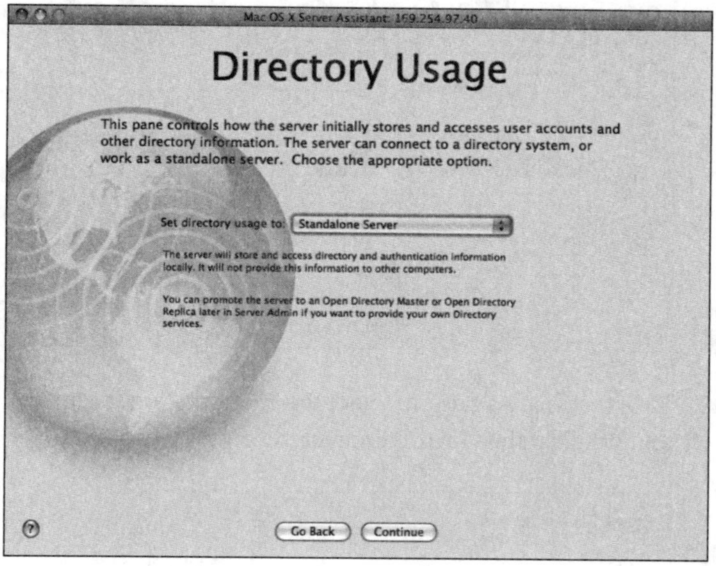


**28** Click Continue to proceed as a Standalone Server.

**29** Take a moment to confirm the server settings.

> **Note** At this point it is possible to save the server configuration to a file for later use. The configuration can be saved as a plain text file and also as a configuration file or record. The name of the file or record is the 12-digit MAC address of the server. There is also an option to use a passphrase for encryption. After an installation of Mac OS X Server but before configuration, Mac OS X Server automatically searches all available storage devices for a server configuration file located in a folder called `Auto Server Setup`. If found, those settings will be automatically applied. This feature helps facilitate fully automated initial Mac OS X Server configurations.

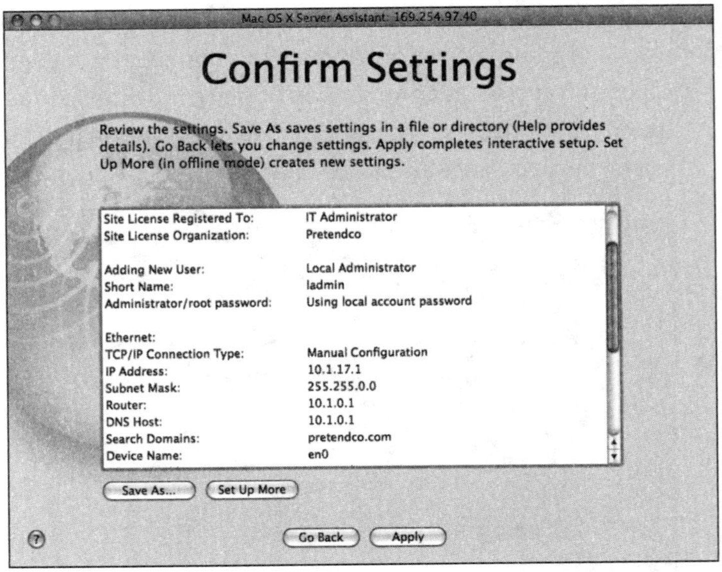


30 Click the Save As button, select the configuration file option, and deselect the "Save in Encrypted Format" checkbox.

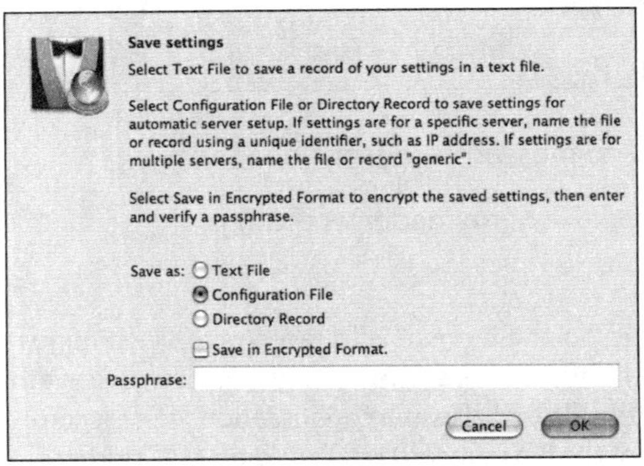


31 Click OK, select your Desktop from the list of locations to save this file, and save it to your Desktop without changing the name of the file.

If you see a dialog asking if you want to save more than one file, click No. Server Assistant recognizes a second Ethernet interface or the AirPort interface and wants to save a file for every interface.

32 Click Apply to apply the server settings.

33 Once server configuration is complete, a dialog appears asking what you want to do next. Minimize Server Assistant to your Dock for now.

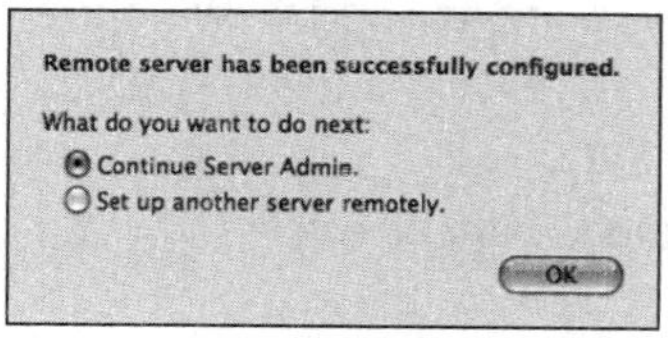


34 Open your `StudentMaterials` folder and in the `Ch01` folder, drag the Property List Editor to your `Applications` folder.

35 Double-click the server configuration file on your Desktop to view the initial configuration settings.

36 Click Open to agree to the dialog requesting permission to launch Property List Editor.

Property List Editor is an application available on the Xcode installer and was included in your student materials to allow easy viewing of files that are saved as property lists.

> **Note** The process of requesting user input when a new application is launched increases the security of Mac OS X by reducing the possibility a hidden application will launch and attempt to gain control of the system without the user's knowledge.

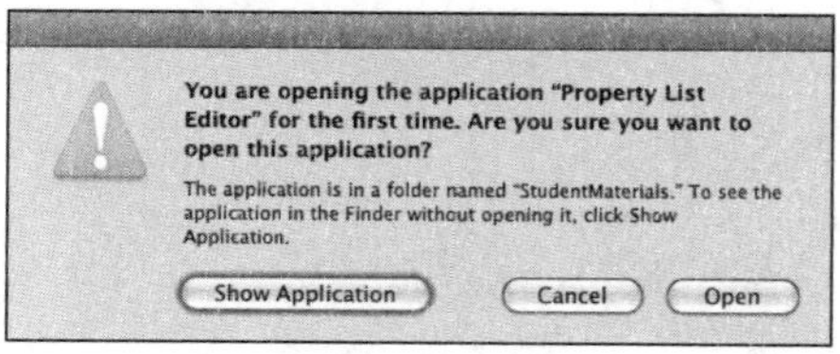

37 Click the disclosure triangle adjacent to the word Root to view the initial configuration settings for your server.

Note that all your initial configurations settings are stored in this file.

38 Quit Property List Editor when you are finished viewing the settings.

**Question 2** *What does Remote Management permit?*

# Mac OS X Server Administration Tools

1.6–1.9

## Lessons 1.6-1.9

Mac OS X Server Administration Tools

## Server Preferences

Is available only in Standard or Workgroup configurations

Provides limited service configurations

Allows Users and Groups data entry

Permits Time Machine setup

Permits Firewall setup

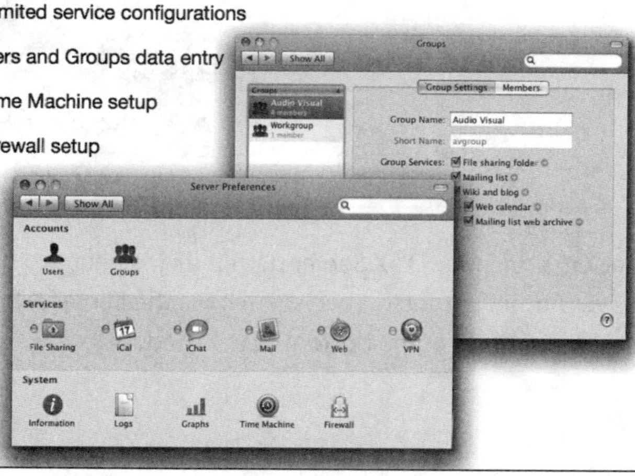

## Server Admin

Manages:

- All services
- Access Control
- Share Points
- Certificates

Facilitates the management of many servers at once

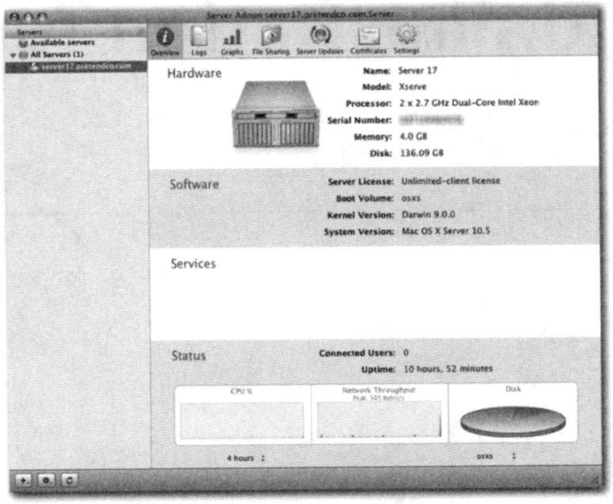

## Server Preferences to Server Admin

Standard or Workgroup modes display warnings when using Server Admin.

- A cannot revert message displays when upgrading to an Advanced configuration.

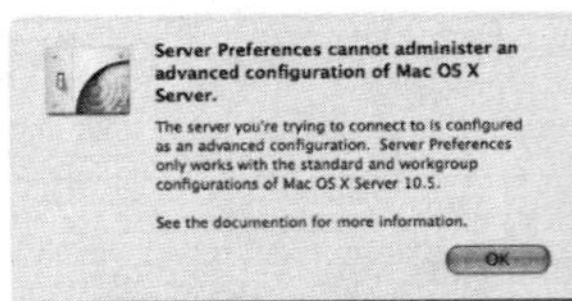


- Server Admin can be used for other services but may override automated settings applied during Standard or Workgroup configurations.

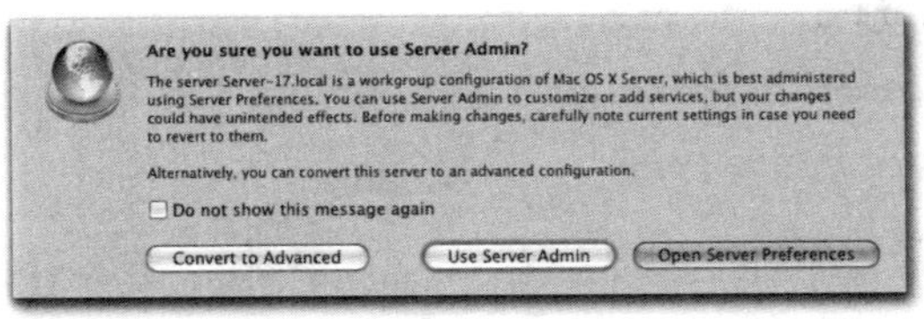


Mac OS X and Mac OS X Server permit their screens to be shared. Server Admin permits screen sharing via the Server Admin menu or Action button at the bottom of the window.

## Screen Sharing via Server Admin

Server Admin allows for remote control of a Mac OS X Server's keyboard and mouse.

User must authenticate as administrator.

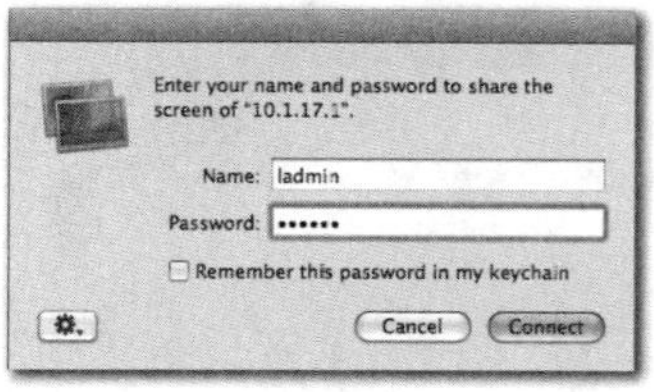


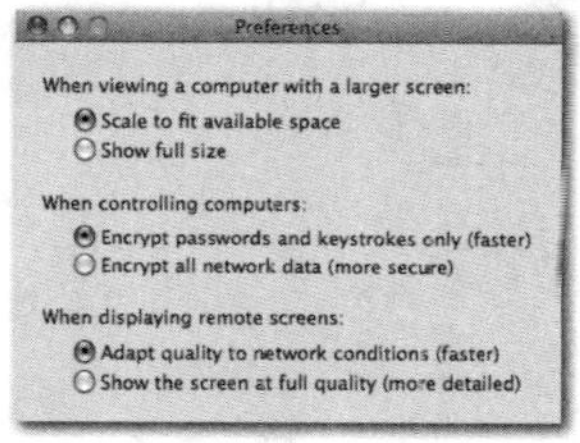

The Service Configuration Assistant allows a straightforward approach to configuring certain services.

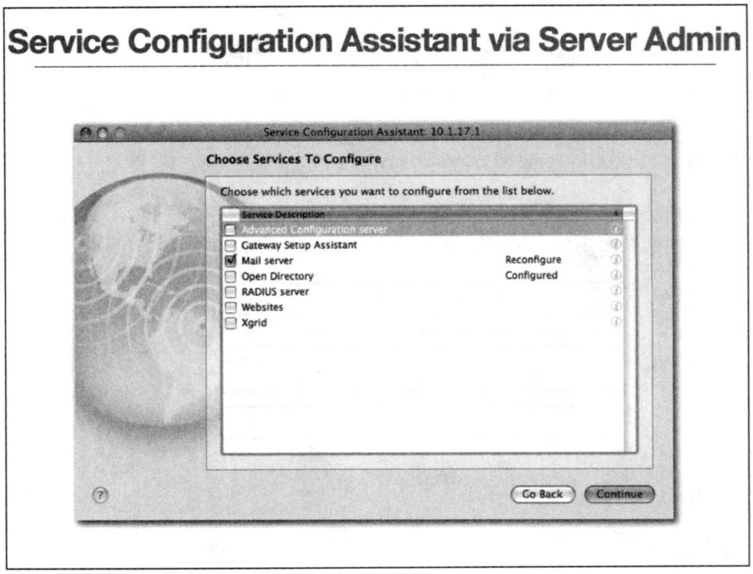


Several options exist when managing Mac OS X Server, separate from service management. Some of these options are: notification of certain system events, graphing various system parameters, updating the Mac OS X Server software remotely, and adjusting the date, time, name of the computer, and certificate management.

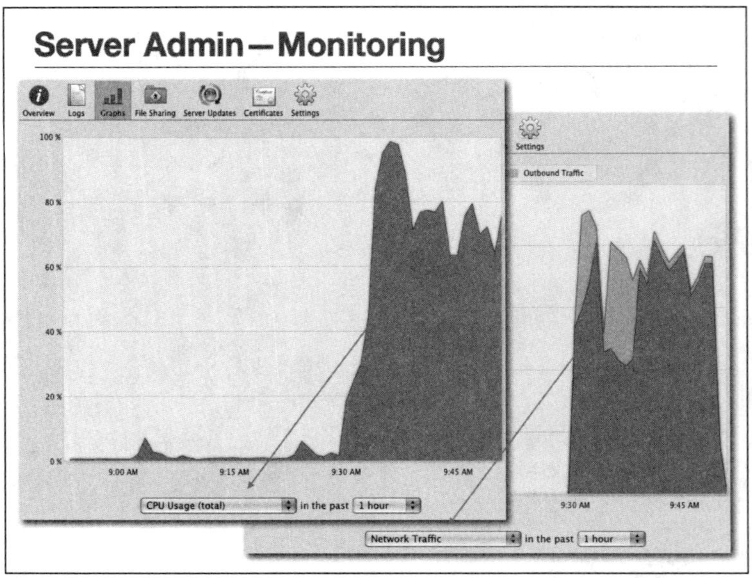

## Server Admin—Software Update

Server Admin or Software Update Preference Pane

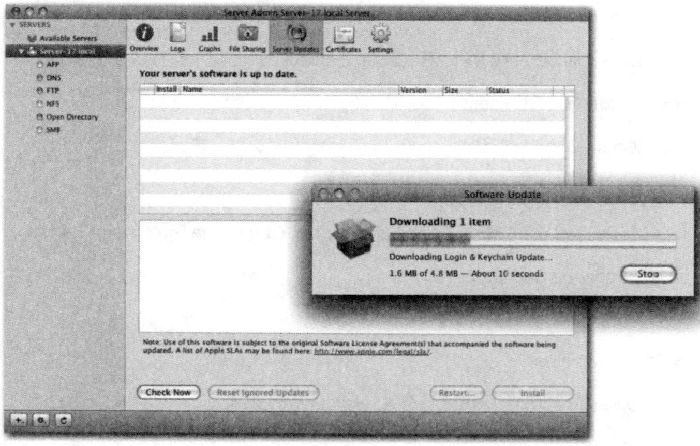


## Server Admin—Notifications

Permit email notifications when

- Disk space falls below a specified amount
- Software updates are available

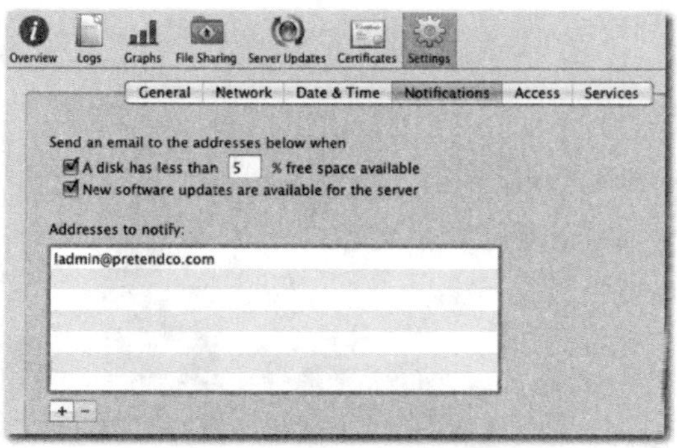


There are many services that can be configured and monitored on Mac OS X Server and each service has settings that can be saved as a file, to be used later or sent to another Mac OS X Server for identical service configuration.

## Server Admin—Adding Services

Server Admin enables or disables services:

- Network Services
  - DNS, DHCP, NAT, VPN, RADIUS, Firewall,
- Collaboration Services
  - iChat, iCal, Mail, Web,
- File Sharing and Media Services
  - AFP, SMB, FTP, NFS, Podcast Producer, QuickTime Streaming
- Maintenance Services
  - Software Update, NetBoot
- Other Services
  - Open Directory, Print, My SQL, Xgrid, WebObjects

## Server Admin—Service Monitoring

All services have log files.

Some services have graphs to monitor traffic.

Services that can be monitored using logs or graphs include:

- File Sharing
  - AFP, SMB, FTP
- Media
  - QuickTime Streaming
- Collaborative Services
  - Web

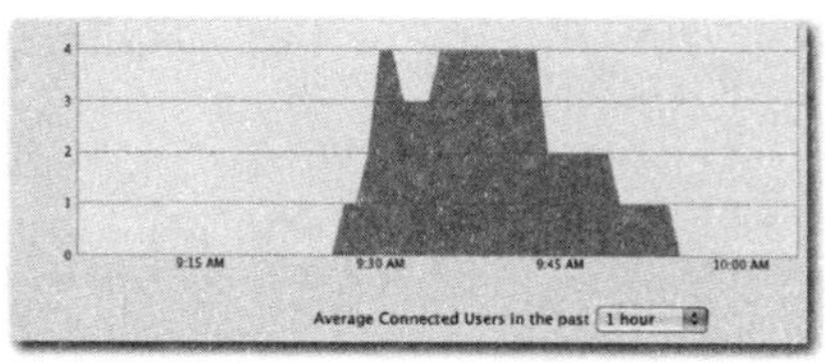

## Server Admin—Settings Files

Settings files save service configuration data including:

- Server Admin preferences
- File Sharing information
- Service configuration
- Server preferences

Settings files can be exported and imported.

- Service configuration files can be imported to other servers to replicate service for consistency or troubleshooting.

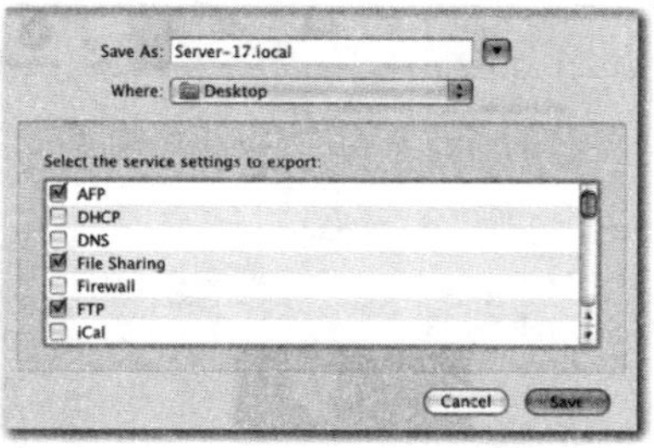


With Workgroup Manager you can perform client management and administer users, groups, computers, and computer groups. Account information can be entered individually or imported from a compatible file.

## Workgroup Manager

Manages

- Users
- Groups
- Computer groups
- Computers
- Managed preferences

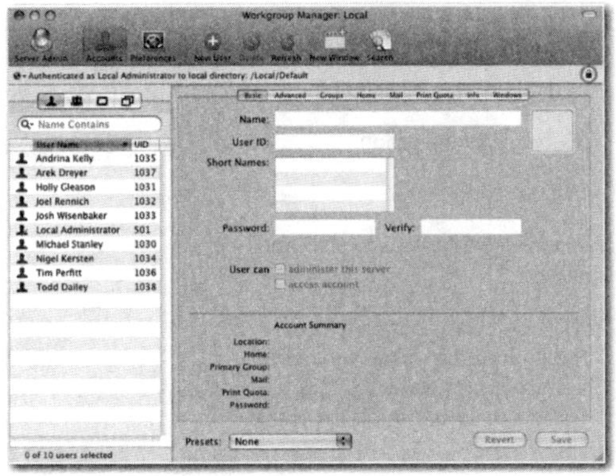

Server Monitor is used to view vital statistics for your Xserve. Server Widgets are also used to view certain system information, but can be used with any hardware that supports Mac OS X Server, not just the Xserve.

## Server Monitor

Functions as remote monitoring for Xserves

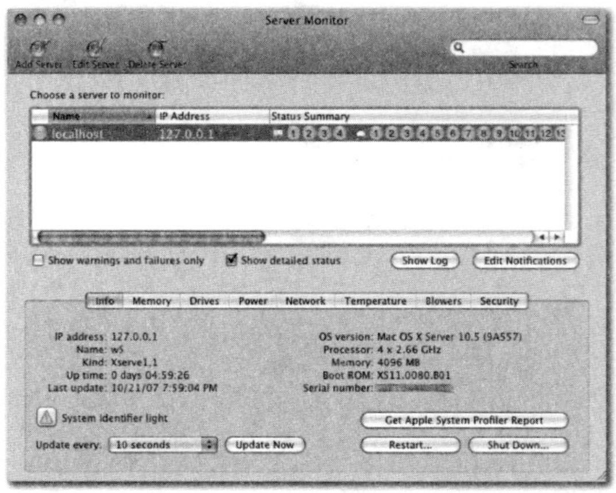

## Server Status Widget

Allows server status monitoring

- Several widgets can be launched at once for same server.
- Multiple views are available.

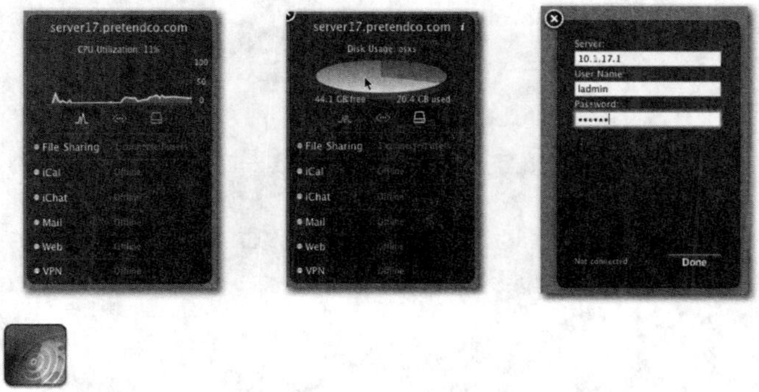


If Mac OS X Server does not install properly, there are methods of troubleshooting that process. Installation log files, media verification, and volume reformatting are possible ways to discover and potentially solve issues.

## Troubleshooting

Check logs

Check third-party hardware and software

Reformat hard drive

Evaluate potential hardware issues

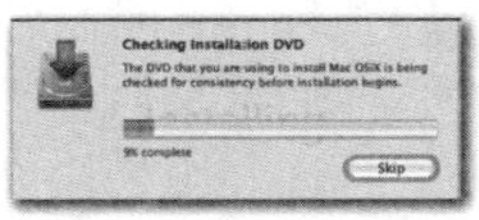

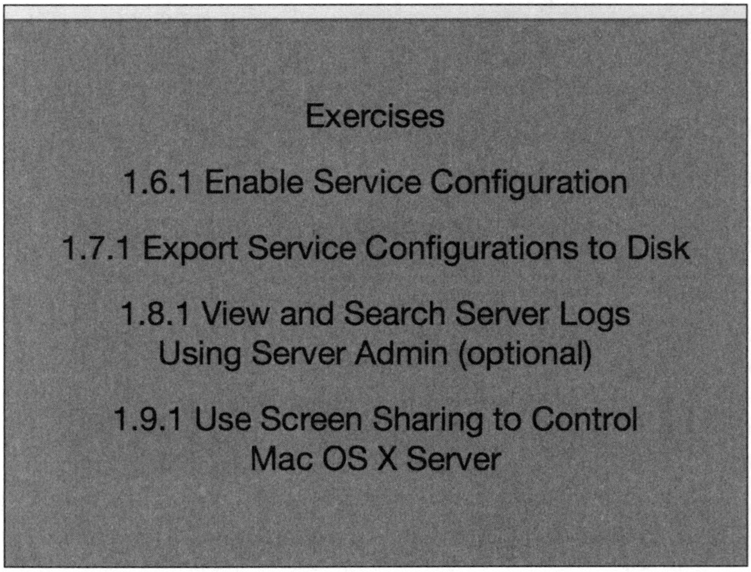
Exercises
1.6.1 Enable Service Configuration
1.7.1 Export Service Configurations to Disk
1.8.1 View and Search Server Logs Using Server Admin (optional)
1.9.1 Use Screen Sharing to Control Mac OS X Server

## Exercise 1.6.1

# Enable Service Configuration

## Objective

Enable service configuration for various Mac OS X Server services.

## Summary

The primary tool for managing services when Mac OS X Server is configured in Advanced mode is Server Admin. To simplify the user interface and prevent accidental configuration of services, Server Admin allows each service configuration to be enabled or disabled. A service that is enabled for configuration is shown in the list of services for your server, whereas a service that is not enabled for configuration is not shown. Service configuration may be enabled or disabled at any time regardless of whether the service has been actually configured. Disabling a service configuration does not affect the configuration or state of the service, merely its inclusion in the list of services shown by Server Admin.

1 Maximize Server Assistant in your Dock, select the option Continue Server Admin, and click OK.

2 Locate Server Assistant on your Dock, and quit Server Assistant.

3 When prompted, enter the following server address and login information:

- Address: `servern.local` Where *n* is your student number, for example server17.local.
- User Name: `ladmin`
- Password: `apple`

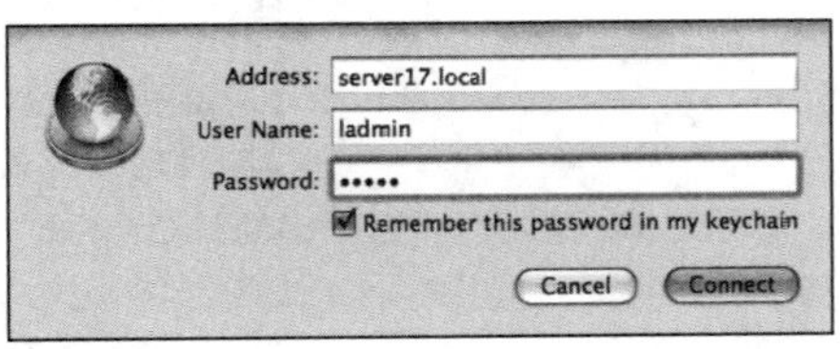

4 Click Connect.

Because this is a new installation, no services have been enabled for configuration yet. Server Admin offers to show the Service Configuration screen to allow you to enable services for configuration.

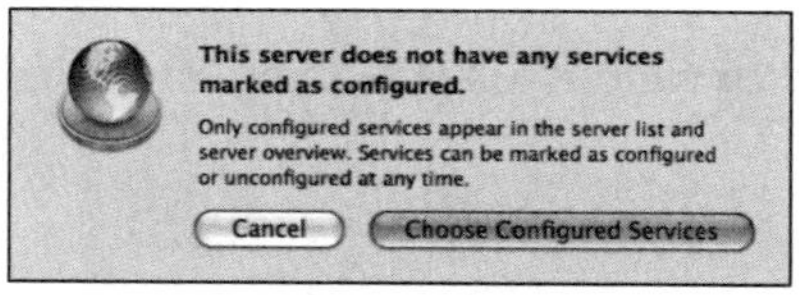


5 Click Choose Configured Services to turn on service configuration for selected services.

6 Select the following services for configuration: AFP, DNS, FTP, iCal, iChat, Mail, NetBoot, Open Directory, SMB, Software Update, and Web.

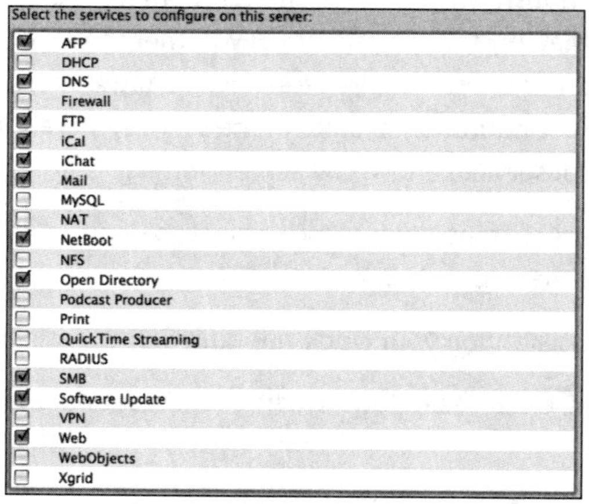


7 Click Save to turn on configuration for the selected services.

Click the disclosure triangle adjacent to your server's entry in the Servers list to display the list of services for which configuration is turned on.

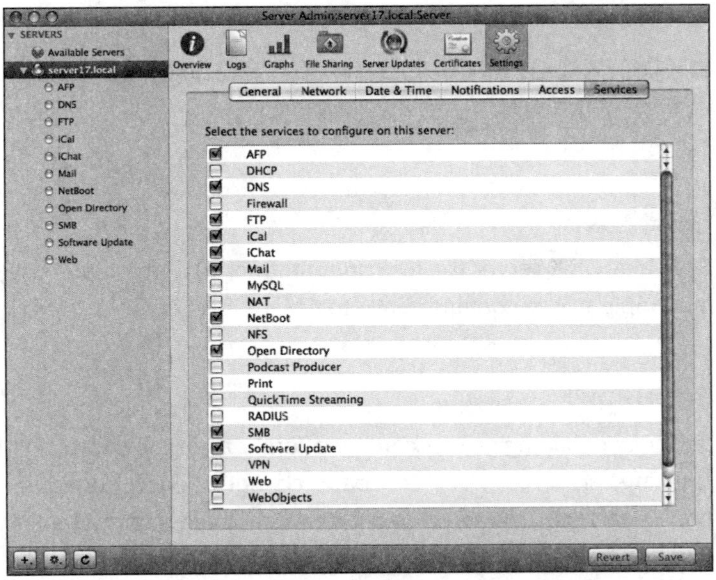
Server Admin:server17.local:Server
SERVERS
Available Servers
server17.local
AFP
DNS
FTP
iCal
iChat
Mail
NetBoot
Open Directory
SMB
Software Update
Web
Overview
Logs
Graphs
File Sharing
Server Updates
Certificates
Settings
General
Network
Date & Time
Notifications
Access
Services
Select the services to configure on this server:
AFP
DHCP
DNS
Firewall
FTP
iCal
iChat
Mail
MySQL
NAT
NetBoot
NFS
Open Directory
Podcast Producer
Print
QuickTime Streaming
RADIUS
SMB
Software Update
VPN
Web
WebObjects
Revert
Save

Exercise 1.7.1

# Export Service Configurations to Disk

## Objective

Save Mac OS X Server service configurations to disk for later use, and apply stored configurations to a Mac OS X Server.

## Summary

Saving and loading service configurations is an excellent way to help facilitate version control or "roll back" changes. Service configurations created on one server may be easily applied to other servers. In addition to saving time, this allows the administrator to ensure that a service is configured identically across multiple servers.

In this exercise, you'll add some simple settings to the SMB and AFP services, export the service configuration, revert the changes to the service configurations, and then import the configuration files.

> **Note** You don't need to start a service in order to configure it, or to export and import service configurations.

1. Open Server Admin, and view your server's list of services.
2. Select the SMB service from the service list on the left.
3. Click the Settings button in the toolbar.
4. Click the Access tab.
5. Select "Allow Guest Access" for the SMB service.

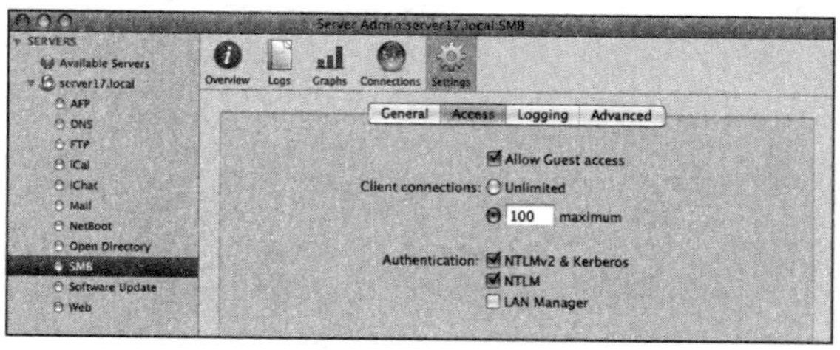

6 Click Save.

7 Select the AFP service, click the Settings button in the toolbar, click the Access tab, and select "Enable Guest Access." Click Save.

Now that you've added some basic configuration to the AFP and SMB services, export the configurations to a file.

8 From the Server menu, select Export > Service Settings.

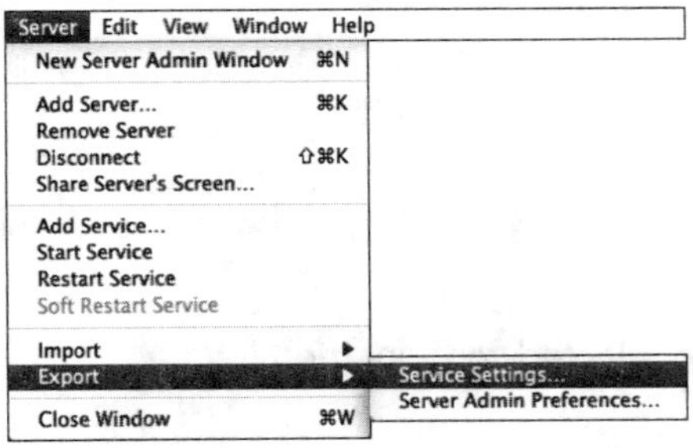


You are prompted to select which service configurations to include in the saved file.

9 Choose Desktop from the pop-up menu as the destination, then click Save.

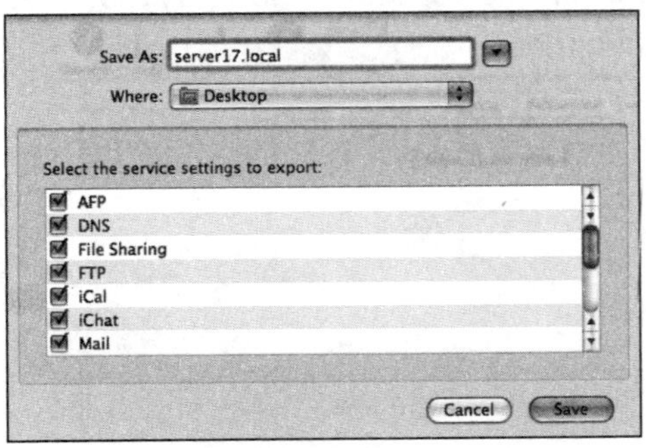


Now you'll make some changes to the AFP and SMB services, import the saved configuration, and verify the settings from the file are restored.

10 Turn off guest access for the AFP and SMB services, saving changes as you go.

11 From the Server menu, select Import > Service Settings.

12 Navigate to the Desktop, and select the configuration file you previously saved.

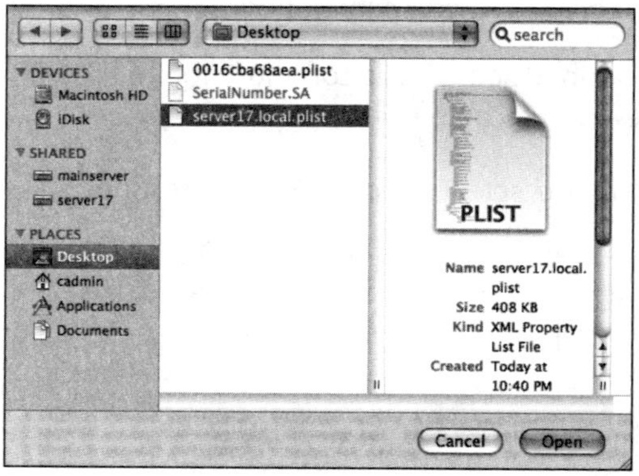


13 Click Open to load the selected configuration file.

You are given the option to select which of the saved service configurations in the file you wish to load. This helps prevent unwanted service configurations from being applied on your server.

14 Click OK to apply all saved configurations.

15 Examine the AFP and SMB access settings to verify that guest access is once again turned on.

Exercise 1.8.1

# View and Search Server Logs Using Server Admin (optional)

## Objective

Remotely view and search server logs using Server Admin.

## Summary

Log files are a critical tool for server administrators. Occasionally, some errors are only visible in a log file, and not via any graphical interface. Without looking at log files, the administrator may be unaware of an error condition. Additionally, it is of utmost importance to familiarize yourself with what various log files look like when the server is operating normally, so that if problems occur, you'll know which log messages are abnormal.

There are two kinds of logs you can view with Server Admin: logs specific to a service, which can be viewed by selecting a service name, and also server-wide logs that do not relate to a specific service, or which contain events that may affect all services. Server-wide logs are found by clicking the server name in the list, then clicking the Logs button in the toolbar.

1. Open Server Admin, authenticating if necessary, and select your server in the list.

2. Click the Logs button in the toolbar to display the primary system log.

   You can view other logs by selecting them from the pop-up menu at the bottom of the window. Notice that the file system path of the displayed log file is shown beneath the toolbar.

   Take a few moments to examine the various server logs by selecting them from the pop-up menu.

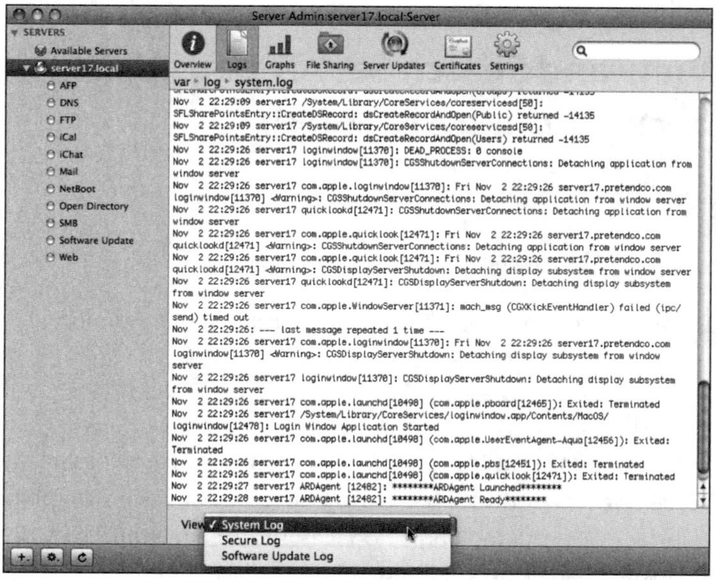

Try using the search field at the top right of the window to focus on specific log messages. To find a message that is logged each time the server starts, search for "regents."

3 In the search field at the top right of the window, enter the word *regents* and press Return.

## Exercise 1.9.1

# Use Screen Sharing to Control Mac OS X Server

## Objective

Use Server Admin and Screen Sharing to remotely observe and control the screen of a Mac OS X Server over the network.

## Summary

Server Admin includes a shortcut to Screen Sharing, which allows remote observation and control of the server's console. The administration software provides a complete set of tools for configuring and maintaining Mac OS X Server, but there are times when direct control of the console is desired, for example, to perform a series of file or folder copy operations using Finder. In this exercise, you'll use Screen Sharing to control your server computer, download the student materials from the instructor server, and optionally apply server updates.

1 In Server Admin, select your server in the server list.

2 From the Server menu, select Share Server's Screen.

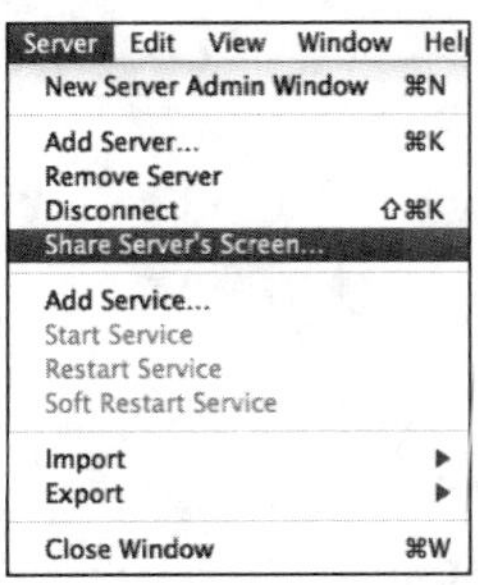

3 Enter the server administrator credentials at the login prompt.

4 Click Connect.

A Screen Sharing window appears, displaying your server's screen. The server should be at the login window.

5 Log in as `ladmin`.

6 As you did on the Mac OS X computer, connect to mainserver and copy the student materials to your server's `/Users/Shared` folder.

7 Apply any server software updates in the `StudentMaterials` folder.

Software updates can be selected and applied remotely using Server Admin, if the server has an Internet connection, but since some classrooms may not be connected to the Internet, server updates are distributed in the student materials.

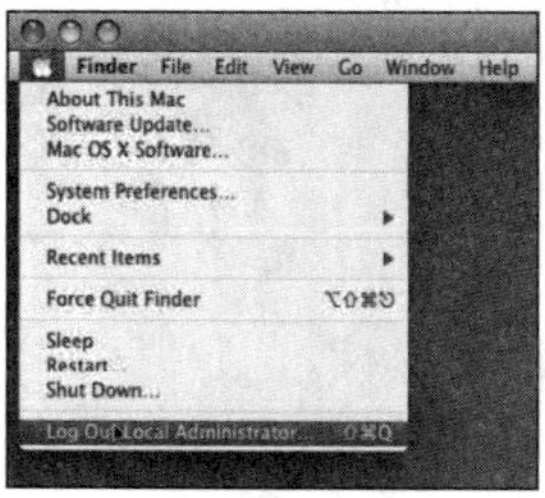


To install a system update, double-click the disk image file to open it, and then run the installer that appears.

8 When finished, restart the server if necessary.

9 If no restart is required, use Screen Sharing to log out of the admin account, then quit Screen Sharing.

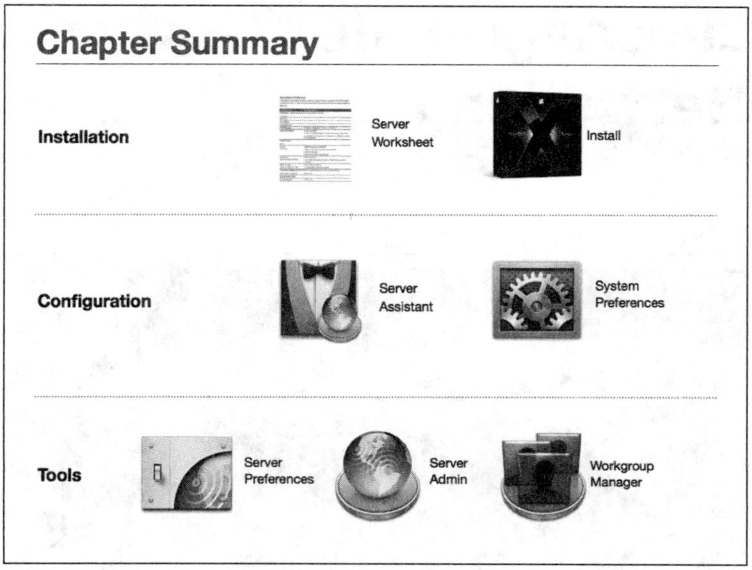


Summary: You now have all the information required to install and configure your Mac OS X Server. Keep in mind that Mac OS X Server is extremely powerful; however, as you will learn, certain services require more power than others. Therefore, you may want to plan for additional Mac OS X Servers to insure uninterrupted service if your organization's plans require that level of service.

# BONUS Link Aggregate Networking

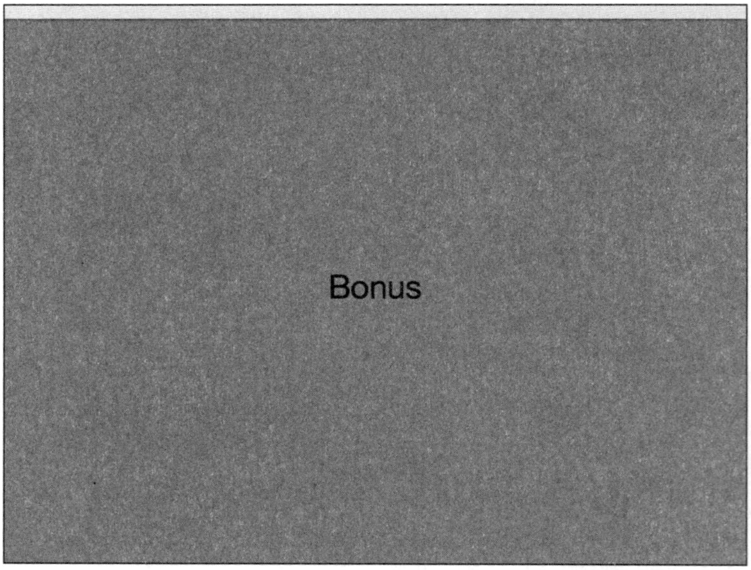


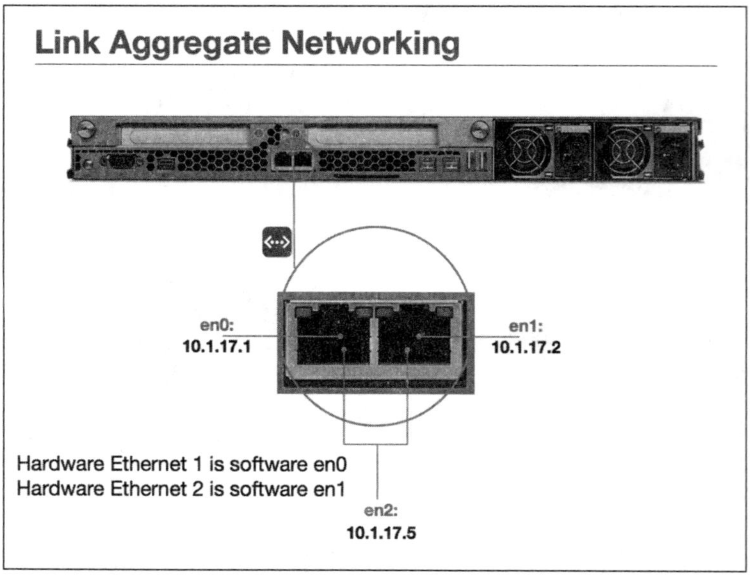

## Ethernet Link Aggregation

Provides ability to bind two Ethernet links together to act as single interface

- Two 1-GB interfaces become one 2-GB interface.
- Aggregation is setup with the Network Preference Pane.

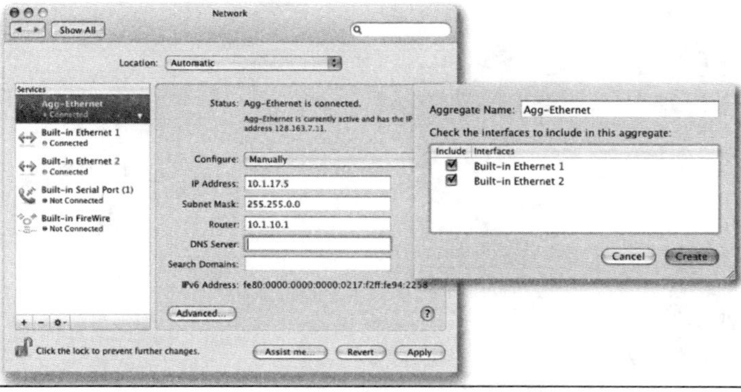


## Software Update

## Apple Remote Desktop

Allows remote control of the screen and mouse for tasks such as:

Sending

- Packages
- UNIX commands
- Events

Monitoring

- Events
- Volumes

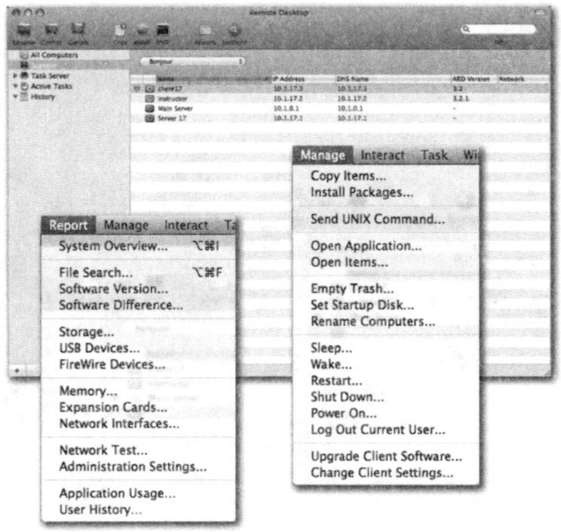

# 2

# Providing DNS Service

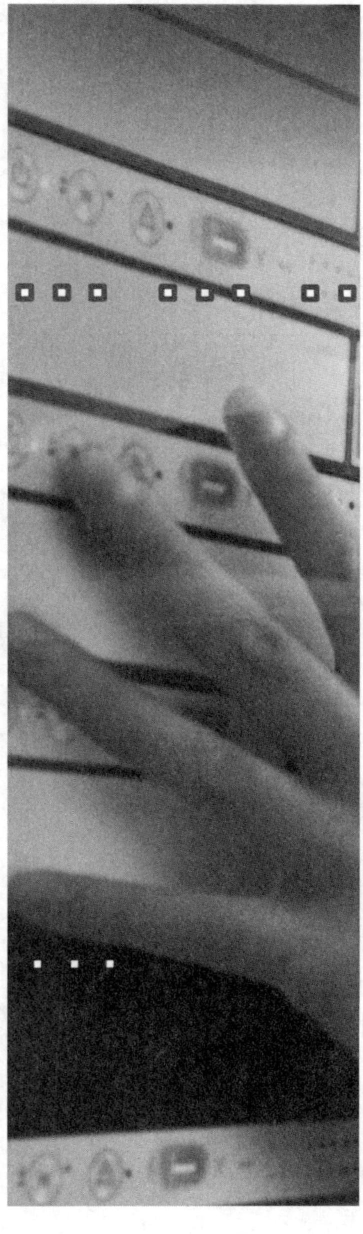


**2.1** DNS Basics

**Exercise 2.1.1** View the Mac OS X Server Default DNS Information

**2.2–2.3** DNS Configuration

**Exercise 2.2.1** Configure a Basic DNS Zone

**Exercise 2.3.1** Add Records to a Zone

**2.4–2.6** DNS Troubleshooting

**Exercise 2.4.1** Test and Troubleshoot DNS

**Exercise 2.5.1** Log the DNS Service (optional)

**Exercise 2.6.1** Use Recursion and Forwarders (optional)

# 2.1 DNS Basics

The Domain Name Service (DNS) is a critical part of the Internet. Mapping IP addresses to computer and domain names means maintaining a global structure of computers and routers to manage all the requests and directing them to the appropriate systems. A fundamental understanding of how DNS works and how to set up a basic domain name service on Mac OS X Server is important, because the lack of a properly functioning DNS server in the organization can lead to problems later down the road.

This lesson covers the basics of the domain name service and how to apply this knowledge directly to a Mac OS X Server by configuring the server to host a domain name service.

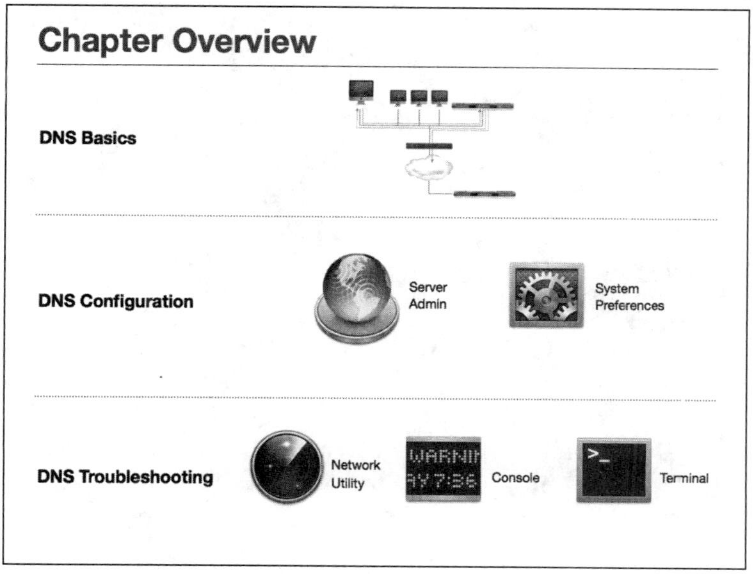


DNS on Mac OS X Server can be divided into three sections:

- DNS Basics: Understanding the fundamental architecture and skeleton of how DNS functions on the Internet.
- DNS Configuration: Using Server Admin to configure the Domain Name service on Mac OS X Server, and then using System Preferences to ensure the Mac OS X Server (and other computers) can see the new DNS server.
- DNS Troubleshooting: Using a variety of tools to ensure DNS is set up and working properly.

## Lesson 2.1

DNS Basics

## Domain Name System (DNS)

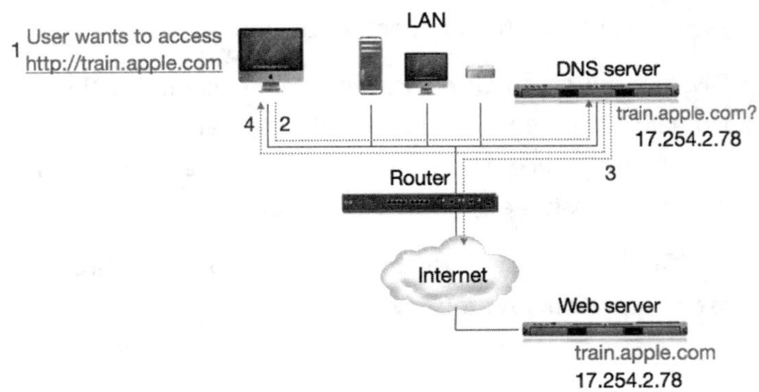


Here's a simple example for understanding DNS. Imagine a user who wants to access a website, such as Apple's training site. That user is connected to the correct server for Apple's training department by entering http://train.apple.com in a browser. The graphic depicts what is actually happening behind the scenes on the Internet to make this connection occur.

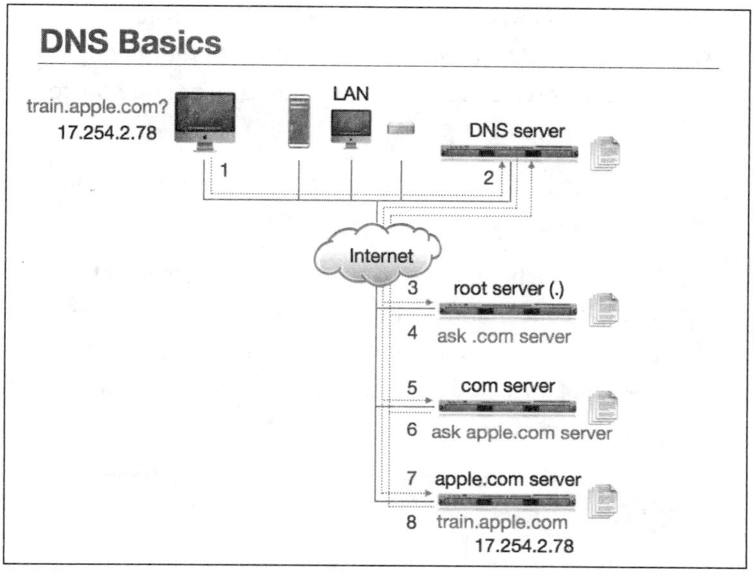


DNS combines a global search space with a local, relatively easy way to maintain the search space. It does this through a hierarchical structure in which each organization is responsible for maintaining its DNS information.

1 Again, we have a user who enters http://train.apple.com, perhaps from Japan.

2 The Japanese company maintains its DNS service running locally on a server. However, this server may not know how the DNS structure is handled across the Pacific and must contact one of 13 root servers across the globe.

3 These root servers subsequently return information concerning how to contact one of the `.com` DNS servers to the requestor—in this case the Japanese company's DNS server.

4 The Japanese DNS server subsequently contacts one of the `.com` servers asking for `apple.com`.

5 The `.com` server then locates the appropriate record (possibly by contacting other `.com` DNS servers or redirecting the request) and returns the information concerning how to contact `apple.com`.

6 The Japanese DNS server subsequently contacts apple.com asking for `train.apple.com`

7 The DNS service handling all the `apple.com` servers returns information concerning how to contact `train.apple.com` and the Japanese DNS server hands over that information—in the form of an IP address—to the client that originally made the request.

## Fully Qualified Domain Names

A top level domain generally starts with one of the following:

| | | |
|---|---|---|
| .com | .edu | .org |
| .gov | .net | .mil |

An organization registers their domain and anchors it to a top level domain through a registrar.

- pretendco.com

A computer has a name within that organized domain.

- server17.pretendco.com

The fully qualified domain name (FQDN) for that computer is:

- server17.pretendco.com.

The structure of DNS can be broken down into three main parts: the domain, the zone, and the computer name.

## Fully Qualified Domain Names-FQDN (cont'd)

A computer must have an IP address.

- 17.2.254.78

In order for other computers to reach it easily, the IP address should be associated with the FQDN.

- server17.pretendco.com. is 17.2.254.78

The name should also be associated with the IP.

- 17.2.254.78 is server17.pretendco.com.

A Domain Name Service server holds the files that map names to IP addresses and the IP addresses to names.

- When testing, this is called forward and reverse lookups.

A practical approach to structuring DNS is to plan out the names of the computers and other devices, and then map them to the appropriate IP addresses. This approach will help you to understand the overall structure of DNS and drive home the idea behind a Fully Qualified Domain Name.

## Reasons for Running DNS

If you have no other DNS server:

- You should be your own DNS.

If your DNS administrator cannot properly configure their DNS server to resolve BOTH forward and reverse lookups for your Mac OS X Server:

- You should be your own DNS.

If you are setting up a Master/Replica tiered environment and you are relying on a single DNS server, which, if it goes down, halts your entire structure:

- You should be your own DNS.

The reasons administrators rely on DNS is that it creates an easy way to locate and remember machines. LDAP also relies heavily on DNS to segregate information into logical parts, such as the top-level domain (`com`), the zone (`pretendco`), and the computer (`mainserver`). On the computer there are likely to be users (user accounts), groups (group accounts), computers (computer accounts), printers (printers), share points that can be mounted automatically (mounts), and so on. It is this division that LDAP uses when searching for a particular object on a particular computer in a particular zone in a particular domain. Apple's ACSA level courses go into great detail about the structuring of LDAP with respect to Mac OS X Server.

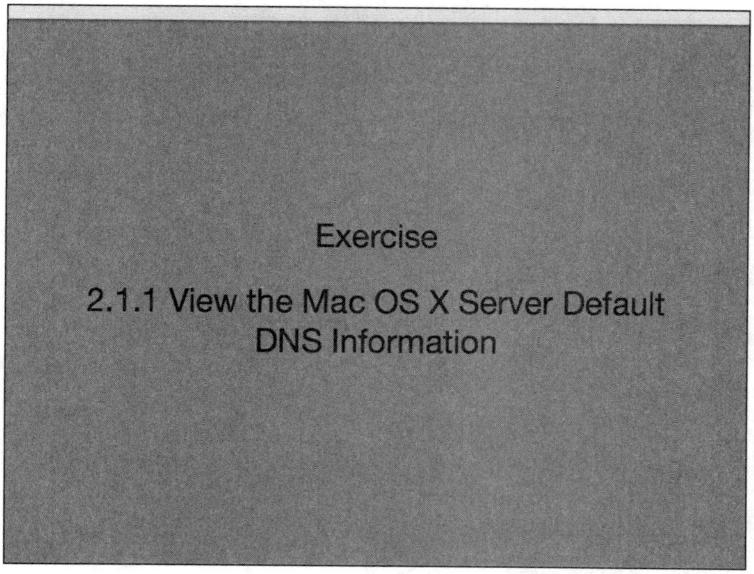
Exercise
2.1.1 View the Mac OS X Server Default
DNS Information

Exercise 2.1.1

# View the Mac OS X Server Default DNS Information

## Objective

Identify where DNS information is stored on Mac OS X Server.

## Summary

As a technical coordinator, you might be asked to explain DNS. Start by explaining where DNS files are stored. Your server computer maintains most of its DNS configuration files in the `/private/var/named/` folder.

## View Your Current DNS Information

Use the command line to view your main DNS files.

1 On your client computer, open Terminal.

**Warning!** It is import that you use proper case when typing in the Terminal. UNIX commands and paths are case-sensitive and errors can occur when not using the proper case.

2 Use `ssh` to connect to your server by typing `ssh ladmin@10.1.`*n*`.1` where *n* is your student number.

3 Press the Return key.

4 Enter `yes` when prompted, and press the Return key.

```
Terminal — ssh — 80×24
Last login: Wed Nov 14 01:42:49 on ttys000
client17:~ cadmin$ ssh ladmin@10.1.17.1
The authenticity of host '10.1.17.1 (10.1.17.1)' can't be established.
RSA key fingerprint is 4c:cd:c1:fc:e5:8f:37:b2:00:a6:2a:d2:f0:98:cb:54.
Are you sure you want to continue connecting (yes/no)? yes
```

5 Enter your `ladmin` password when prompted. You will not see any movement in the Terminal.

6 Press the Return key.

7 In the Terminal window, navigate to /private/var/named by typing the `cd /private/var/named/` command.

8 List the contents of this folder by typing the `ls -Al` command. The first and last characters in the command are the lowercase letter l.

9 Press Return. The default DNS configuration files display.

Mac OS X Server 10.5 has some additional configuration files located in `/private/etc/dns/`. You do not need to navigate to the folder to see the contents.

10 List the contents of the `/private/etc/dns/`folder by typing the `ls -Al /private/etc/dns/` command.

11 You can read the contents of any of the files using the `less` command:

```
less /private/etc/dns/publicView.conf.apple
```

Notice the file says "PLEASE DO NOT MANUALLY MODIFY THIS FILE!"

12 Press Q on your keyboard to quit viewing the file, and leave the Terminal window open.

# 2.2–2.3 DNS Configuration

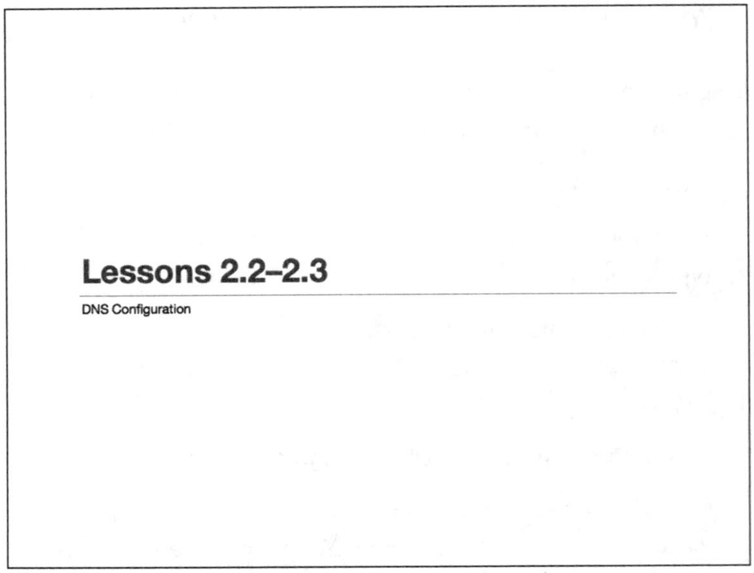

## DNS Service on Mac OS X Server

Mac OS X Server prefers to have a DNS entry, but does not need to be a DNS server if another one is available.

Standard and Workgroup configurations look back at themselves to ensure their names are correct.

- 127.0.0.1 is called loopback and is automatically entered in the Network Preference pane.
  - Machine looks back at itself.
- Advanced configuration requires setting up DNS manually.
  - Server Admin is used to configure DNS service.
- DNS lookups should be able to resolve the fully qualified domain name to the IP address and the IP address to the fully qualified domain name.

Mac OS X Server can be used as a DNS server, when no other DNS server is present on the network. It is possible and feasible to have more than one DNS server on a network and Mac OS X Server can be the DNS server for all Mac OS X clients. Also, when setting up a Mac OS X Server in a Standard or Workgroup configuration, Mac OS X Server automatically configures and starts DNS to resolve itself internally.

## Setting Up DNS on Mac OS X Server

1. Plan your DNS structure, including names and IP addresses.
2. Connect to Server Admin, and enable the DNS service.
3. Add your zone and edit your initial machine record.
4. Add additional machine records (optional).
5. Add aliases (optional).
6. Add Mail Exchange records (optional).
7. Start DNS.
8. Enter your DNS values in the Mac OS X Server Network Preference pane.
9. Test and troubleshoot.

The steps to setting up DNS on Mac OS X Server are straightforward. The first step is to plan the names and IP addresses for devices on your network.

## Zones

A zone is a name that has an IP address associated with it.

- apple
- pretendco

Zones are mapped to larger zones that keep track of IP to name matches.

- com
- edu

Zones control other devices (computers and printers) under their names.

- train
- mainserver

Examples:

- train.apple.com.
- mainserver.pretendco.com.

Zones are the basic organizational unit of DNS. Zones contain records and are defined by how they acquire those records and how they respond to DNS requests. There are three kinds of zones: master zone, slave zone, and forward zone (often called forwarders). For this course, you will deal only with a master zone.

## Add a Zone

Add your zone to the list.

Carefully check spelling because errors will cause DNS to fail.

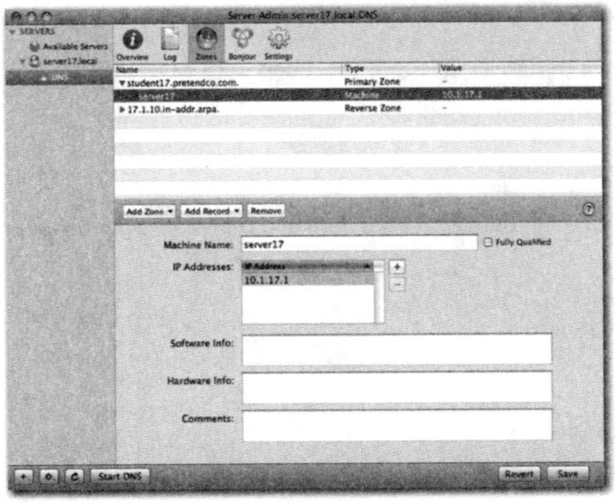


To add a zone:

1 Select the DNS service, and click the Zones icon in the toolbar.

2 Click the Add Zone button, and choose Add Primary Zone (Master).

3 Select the example zone from the list and edit the Primary Zone Name and Machine name to represent your domain and your computer name.

4 Save the changes.

## Machine Records

Zones control other devices (computers and printers) under their names.

- mainserver = 10.1.0.1
- server17 = 10.1.17.1
- client17 = 10.1.17.2
- printer17 = 10.1.17.3
- switch17 = 10.1.17.4
- router17 = 10.1.17.5
- iphone17 = 10.1.17.6

Each device must have a machine record within the zone.

Machine records, also called A records (for Address), are devices that require an IP address to name mapping that you want included in your zone. For example, a second server may need a name associated with its IP address.

## Add Machine Records

Add other machines to your zone.

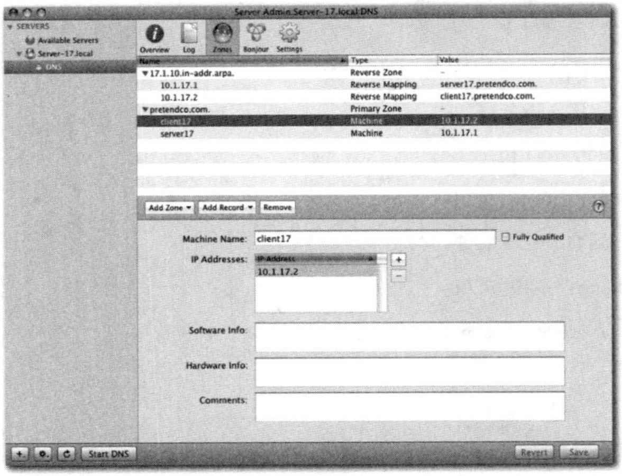


You add machine records by selecting the zone and choosing from the Add Record pop-up menu.

## Alias Records

Within, a zone a device can have more than one name

- mainserver.pretendco.com =10.1.0.1
    - www.pretendco.com = 10.1.0.1
    - afpserver.pretendco.com = 10.1.0.1
    - icalserver.pretendco.com = 10.1.0.1

Alias, or CNAME (canonical name), records are secondary names for the same IP address.

## Add Aliases

Aliases allow a machine to answer to more than one name.

- server17.pretendco.com is 17.2.254.78
- www2.pretendco.com is server17.pretendco.com

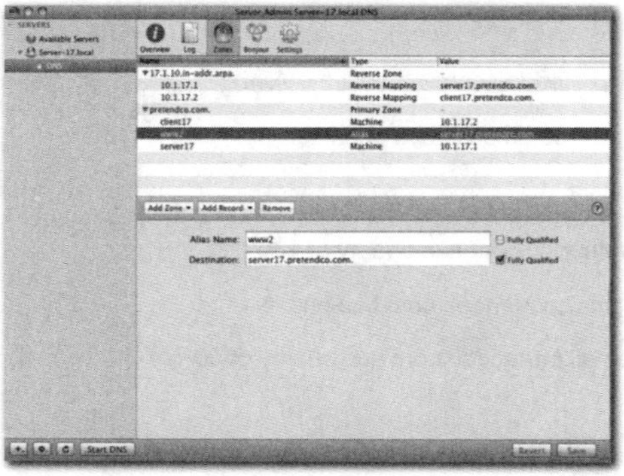


You add alias records in the same way as adding machine records, by selecting the zone and choosing from the Add Record pop-up menu.

## Mail Exchanger (MX Record)

Mail Exchange records are used by SMTP (mail protocol):

- Primary zone record
    - mainserver.pretendco.com
    - Mail Exchanger (MX Record)
        - mail.pretendco.com

Mail Exchange records can have priorities:

- More than one mail server can be used
    - mail.pretendco.com has priority of 10
    - canadamail.pretendco.com has priority of 20
    - europemail.pretendco.com has priority of 30

Mail Exchange (MX) records allow for mail services to talk to one another and transfer mail between them, generally using Simple Mail Transfer Protocol (SMTP). An MX record is useful when dealing with more than one mail server. Priorities are assigned to mail servers in case one server goes down; the next server in line will pick up the duties of the first.

## Add an MX Record

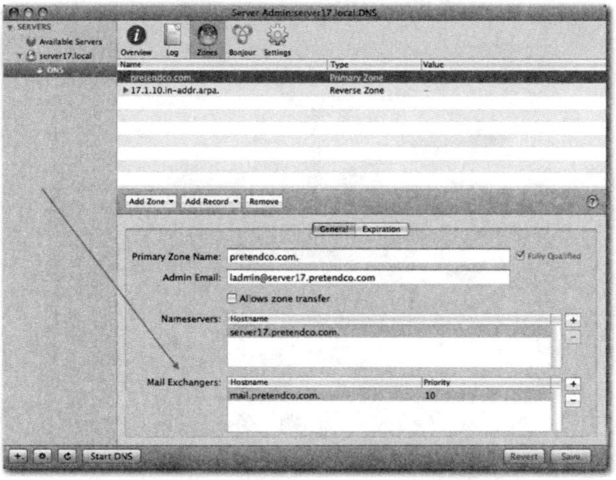


You add MX records by selecting the zone and adding them in the Mail Exchangers section at the bottom of the window.

## Start DNS

Almost all services in Server Admin are started/stopped by using the Start/Stop *service name* button.

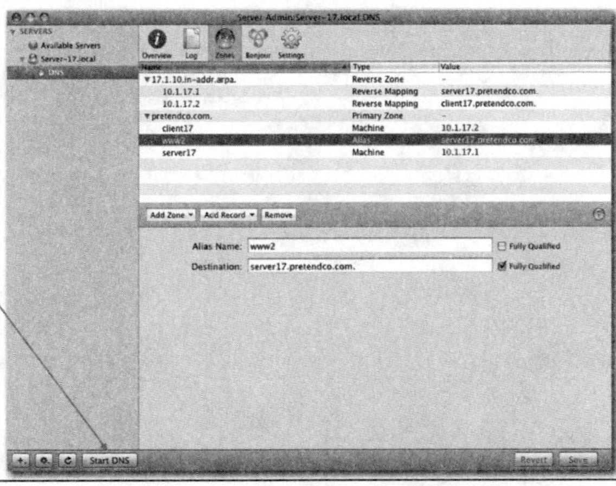


All services can be started and stopped using the Start DNS/Stop DNS button at the bottom of the window.

## Entering DNS Values

Your server must be able to see itself and resolve itself.

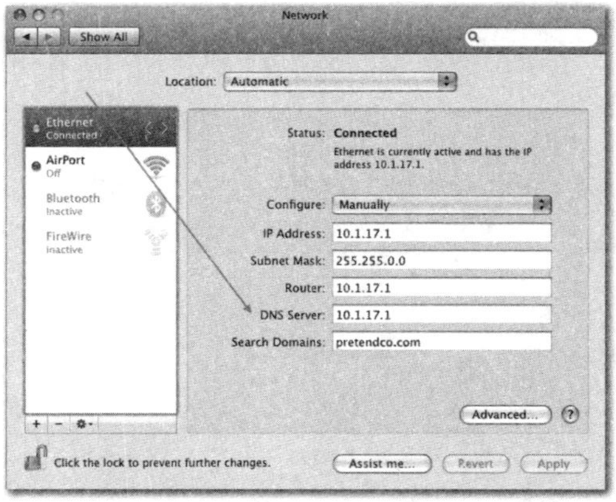


Once the DNS service is running, DNS information can be entered for Mac OS X Server Network settings. If a DNS entry already exists, a secondary entry can be added. The primary entry should be the DNS server containing the record for that Mac OS X Server. Client computers needing information from the DNS server should have this data entered into their networking information.

Exercises

2.2.1 Configure a Basic DNS Zone

2.3.1 Add Records to a Zone

## Exercise 2.2.1

# Configure a Basic DNS Zone

## Objective

Set up a basic zone on Mac OS X Server.

## Summary

You've already been instructed on how to activate services using Server Admin. You will use that knowledge to activate the DNS service so you can work with it. Even though your instructor is running the DNS service, you can also run your own DNS service by entering your own zone file information on your Mac OS X Server.

1 Open Server Admin, authenticate as your Mac OS X Server administrator if necessary, and connect to your Mac OS X Server.

2 Select your server from the list, click Settings in the toolbar, click Services in the toolbar, deselect all services except the DNS service, and click Save. Only the DNS service appears in the services list now.

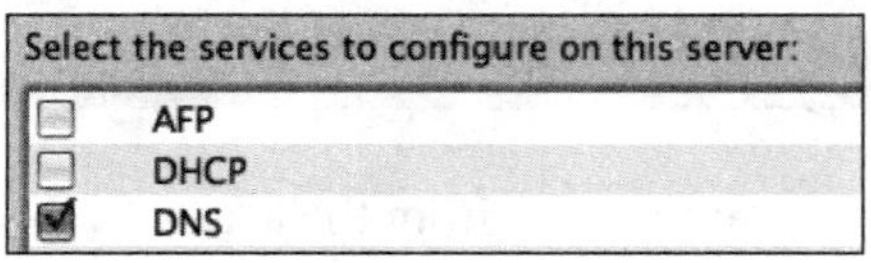


3 Select DNS on the left under server*n*.local, where *n* is your student number.

4 Click Zones in the toolbar.

5 Click the Add Zone button and choose Add Primary Zone (Master) from the list.

You'll see two entries created, a Primary Zone and a Reverse Zone.

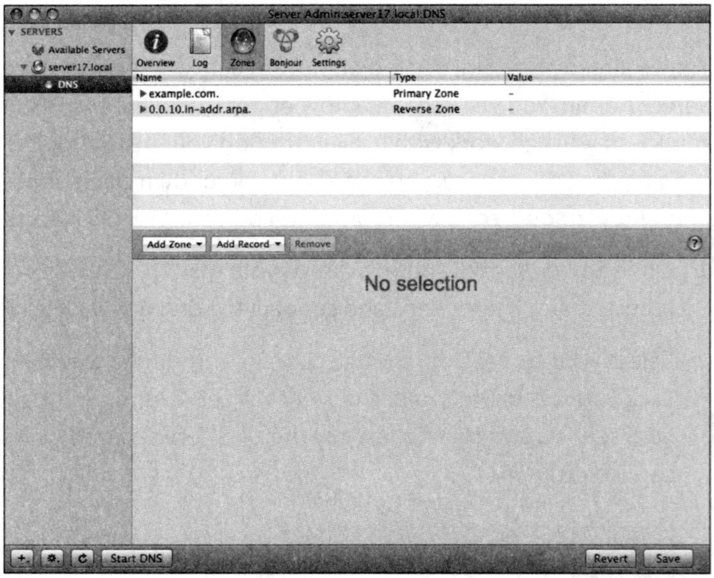


6 Select the Primary Zone example.com from the list.

This is the preset zone Mac OS X Server provides.

7 Enter the following information in their respective fields, using your student number wherever an *n* appears:

- Primary Zone Name: `student`*n*`.pretendco.com.`
- Admin Email: Leave blank
- Allows zone transfer: Select the checkbox
- Nameservers: `server` (There is no student number included in the value for this field.)
- Mail Exchangers: Leave blank

Later, when you save and start DNS, student*n*.pretendco.com will be your new domain.

8 Do not click Save yet.

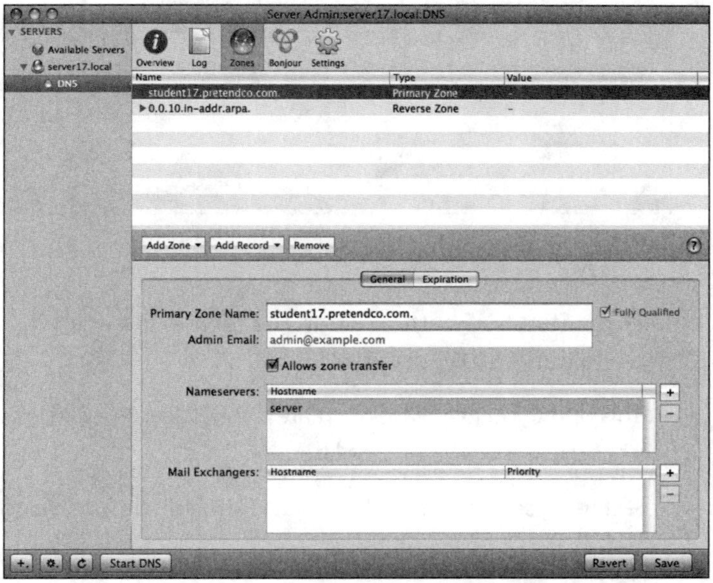


9 Click the disclosure triangle next to student*n*.pretendco.com and select *ns* from the list.

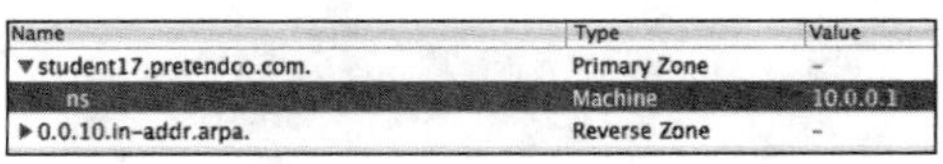

10 Change the Machine Name from `ns` to `server`. There is no student number included in the value for this field.

11 Double-click the default IP address, and change it to `10.1.`*`n`*`.1` where *n* is your student number.

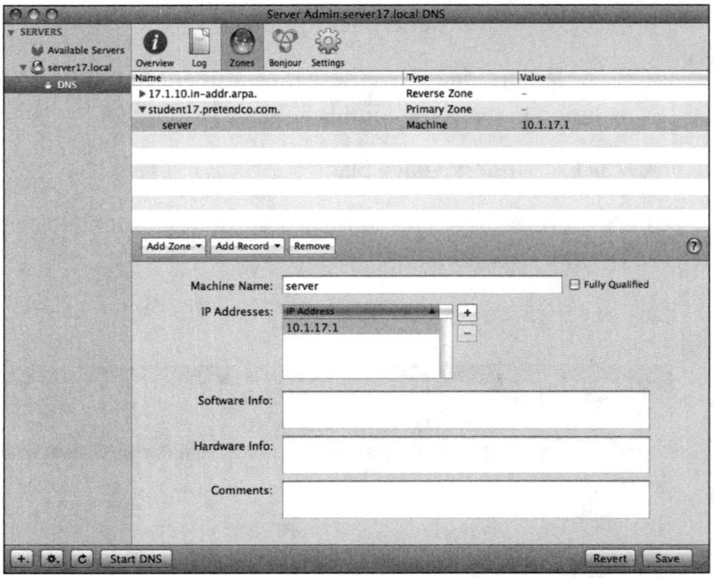


12 Click Save.

13 Click the Start DNS button to start the service, then click it again to turn the DNS service off.

At this point you just want to create the DNS service files. You'll start and use the DNS service later.

14 Select Reverse Zone in the list, and click the disclosure triangle.

15 Select Reverse Mapping from the list.

The IP address maps back to your server. What you see is your server's Fully Qualified Domain Name (FQDN).

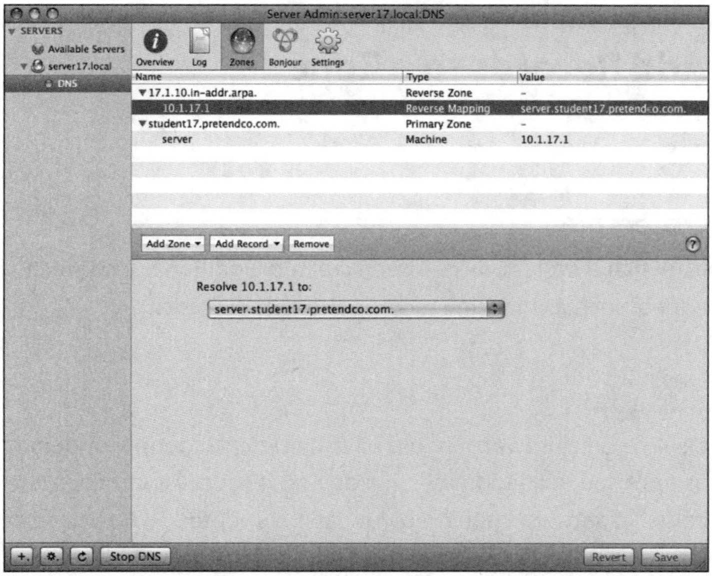


16 Display the Terminal window you opened in the previous exercise.

17 Run the `ls -Al` command on the `/private/var/named/`, and then run the `less` command on `/private/etc/dns/publicView.conf.apple`

If you forget how to run these commands, refer to the "View the Mac OS X Server Default DNS Information" exercise.

The list now includes additional settings files for the student*n*.pretendco.com zone you created. In this class, you'll use Server Admin to make several changes that create and configure files on your disk. It's useful to be familiar with those file locations when troubleshooting.

18 In the Terminal window, while still in `/private/var/named/`, enter `less db.studentn.pretendco.com.` and press Return.

This command displays the contents of your zone file. There is a new entry for the student*n*.pretendco.com file, but it just refers to another file. You can change directories to the location of this file and view its contents as well.

19 Press Q to quit viewing the file and minimize Terminal to the Dock.

Exercise 2.3.1

# Add Records to a Zone

## Objective

Now that a basic zone has been created, additional records can be added, such as machine records and alias records.

## Summary

Devices on a network should have names that people understand, as opposed to IP addresses. If a device's IP address changes, the zone file and associated records can be updated so the name can be mapped to the new IP address. Also, having more than one name for a server can help manage access to other services.

1 Return to Server Admin, select the DNS service if not already selected, and click Zones in the toolbar.

   You'll add machine records and aliases to your DNS entry and observe the result.

2 Select the student*n*.pretendco.com zone to edit it. If the disclosure triangle is closed, open it.

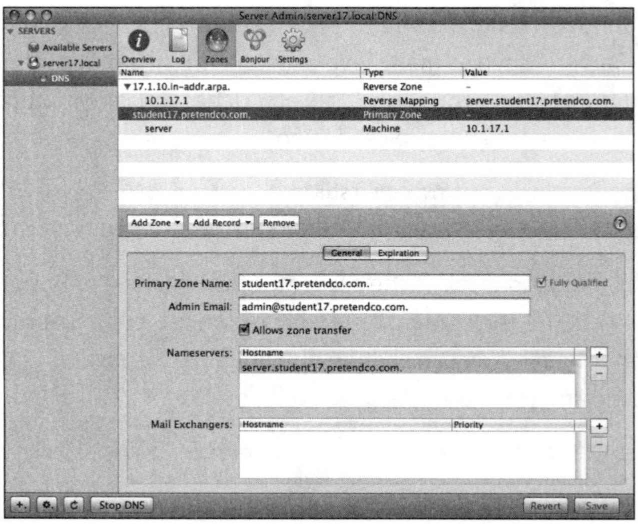

3 Click Add Record, and choose Add Machine (A) from the pop-up menu.

4 Select the new entry labeled *newMachine.*

5 Enter the following information (replacing *n* with your student number):

- Machine Name: `client`*n*
- IP Address: Replace the default value with `10.1.`*n*`.2`

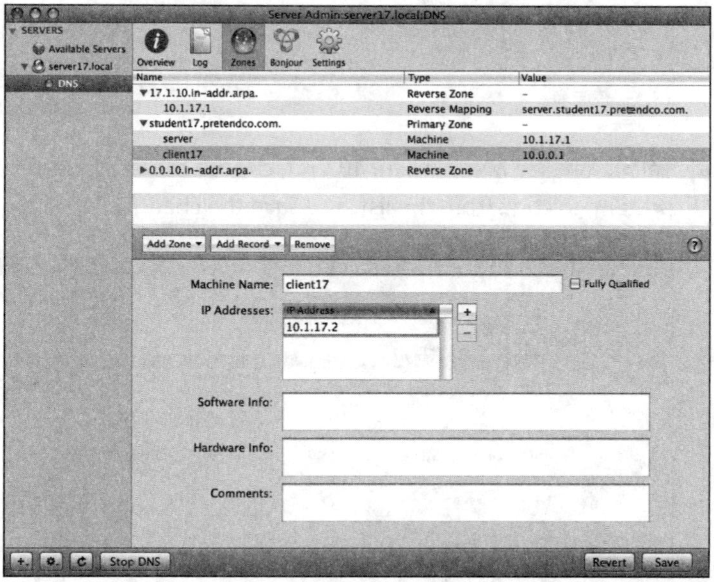

6 Repeat steps 3–5, creating new A records using the following information:

- Machine Name: `secure` IP Address: `10.1.`*n*`.1`
- Machine Name: `mail` IP Address: `10.1.`*n*`.1`

7 Click Save.

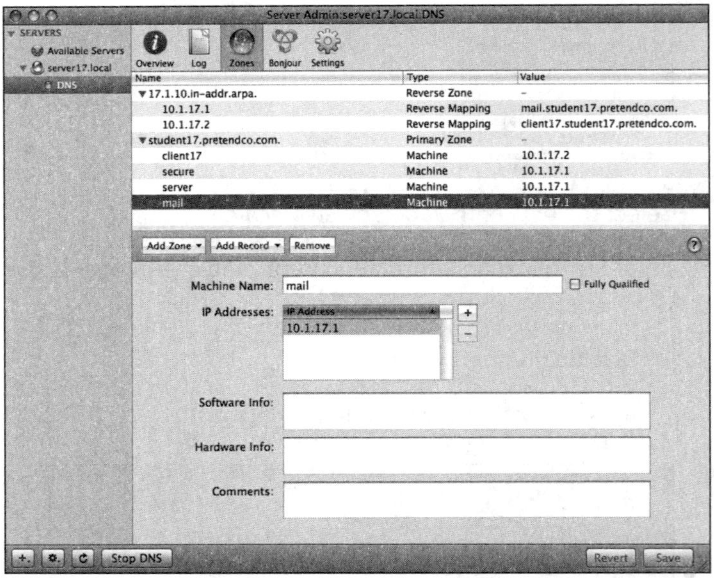

8 Select Reverse Mapping for 10.1.*n*.1, choose server.student*n*.pretendco.com. from the list, and save the changes.

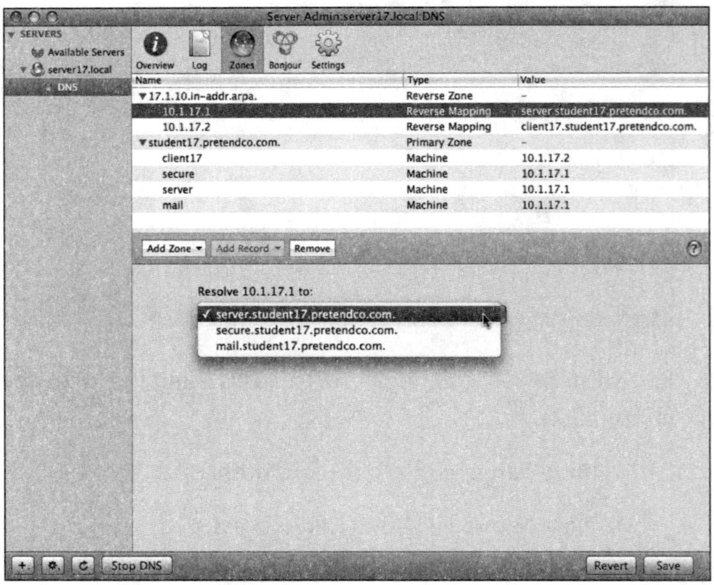

9 Click back on your student*n*.pretendco.com zone, click Add Record, and select Add Alias (CNAME).

10 Select the new entry labeled *newAlias* and enter the following:

- Alias Name: `stdn` (where *n* is your student number)
- Destination: `clientn` (where *n* is your student number)
- Make sure both Fully Qualified checkboxes are deselected.

11 Repeat steps 9–10 using the following aliases (CNAME):

- Alias Name: `www`
- Destination: `server`
- Ensure both Fully Qualified checkboxes are deselected.

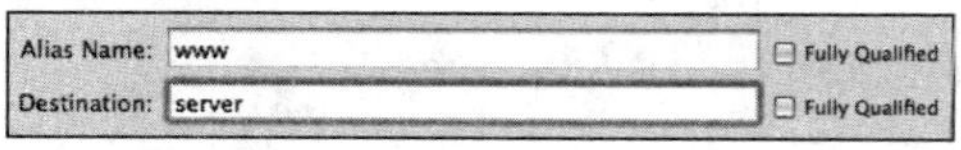


- Alias Name: `ical`
- Destination: `server`
- Ensure both Fully Qualified checkboxes are deselected.

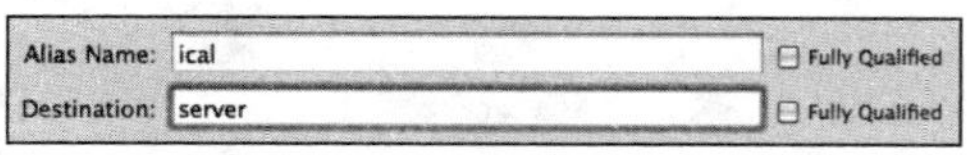


- Alias Name: `chat`
- Destination: `server`
- Ensure both Fully Qualified checkboxes are deselected.

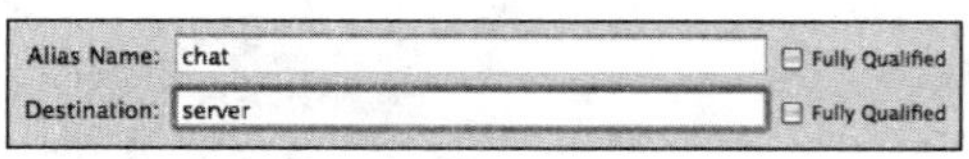

12 Click Save.

13 Click through all your new Aliases and Machine records. Notice the Fully Qualified checkbox is selected for the Destination and the FQDN. The period (.) is automatically inserted.

14 Maximize the Terminal from your Dock.

15 In the Terminal window, enter `less /private/var/named/zones/db.studentn.pretendco.com.zone.apple` and press Return.

This command will display your zone file. You'll see new entries. The entries will have your student number associated with the IP address and at least one alias that points to your server's IP address, among the changes.

16 Press q to return to the command prompt in the Terminal window and then enter `exit` to disconnect from the ssh connection to your Mac OS X Server.

17 Minimize your Terminal to the Dock.

18 Use Server Admin to start the DNS service.

# DNS Troubleshooting

2.4–2.6

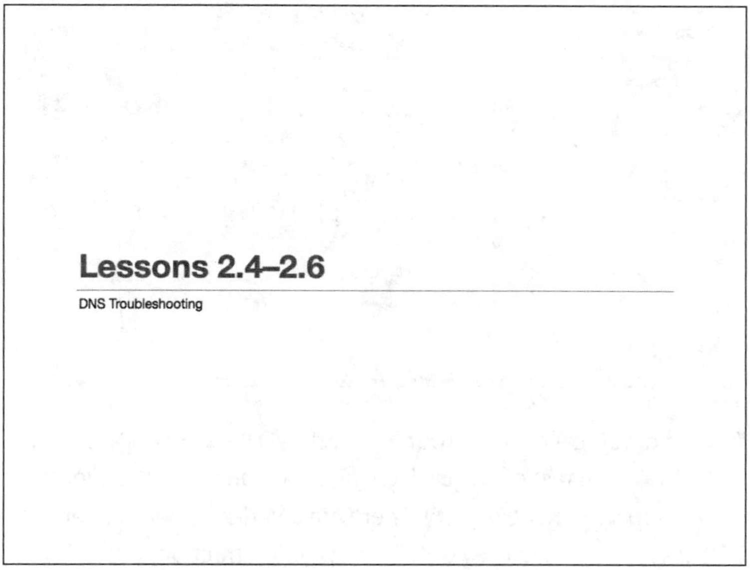

## Test DNS

Ensure forward and reverse lookups using the Lookup tab in Network Utility.

Also check aliases or other machine records.

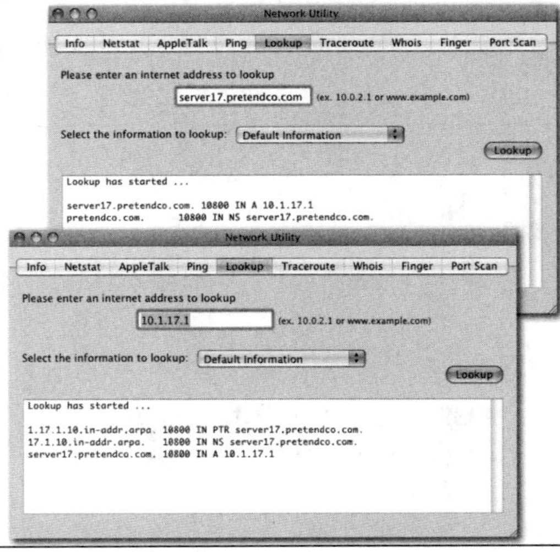


A great graphical tool for troubleshooting DNS issues is Network Utility. The real test of any DNS change is when your DNS clients are able to use the new entry. There are a variety of ways to ensure DNS is working. Because you've set up only a fraction of the DNS services available, you'll test to see if DNS is configured properly using both ping and lookup from your client computer. Using both the Ping and the Lookup panes of Network Utility will allow for testing of your DNS service on your server.

## DNS Logging

**Log files assist in diagnostics and troubleshooting.**

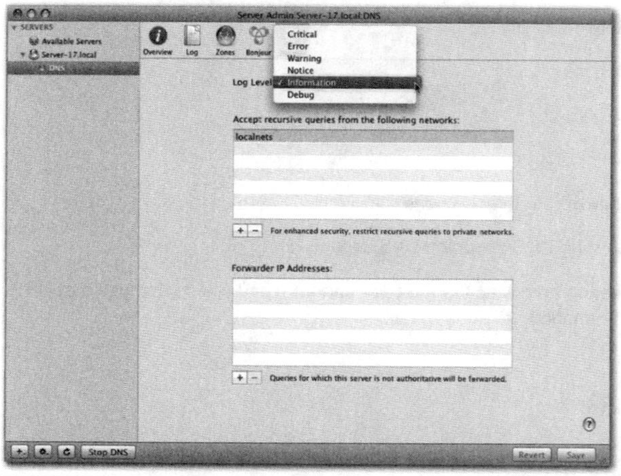


After setting up DNS, it is important to view and watch the log files for any errors, anomalies, or unusual requests—such as a barrage of requests from a single computer that may indicate that computer may have something awry.

## DNS Troubleshooting

Tools and techniques used to troubleshoot DNS:

- Network Utility
- Console
  - DNS Logs
- Terminal
- Network Preference pane
- Starting DNS/Stopping DNS service
- Testing from Mac OS X Server and from any clients that use that DNS information

You have several methods of troubleshooting DNS at your disposal, including rechecking the entry in the Network Preference pane, ensuring the network location has not changed, pinging the DNS server to ensure it is working properly, checking the DNS server for firewall rules that may block DNS, and cycling the DNS service.

## Getting DNS to Clients

Two methods for configuring DNS on client computers.

- DNS information can be pushed down dynamically with DHCP.
- DNS information can be entered on the client computer.

Both can be used by Mac OS X (Static and Dynamic assignment).

DNS information can be pushed out to clients via the DHCP service, along with the IP address subnet mask and router. A Mac OS X computer with manually entered DNS information can still use DNS information from a DHCP server.

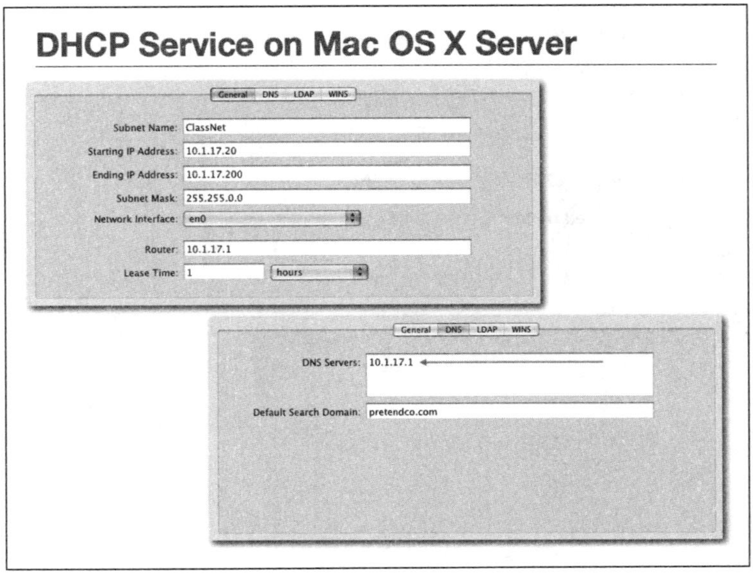


When entering information in the DHCP settings, you can send out information on more than one DNS server.

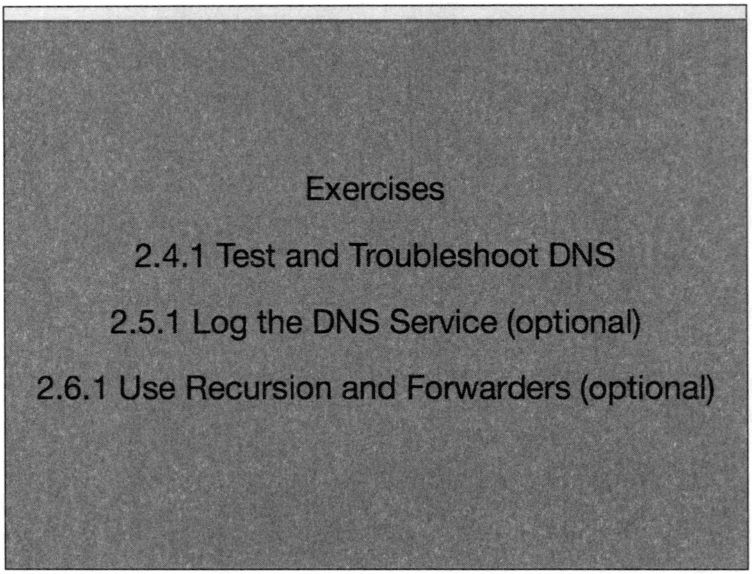

Exercise 2.4.1

# Test and Troubleshoot DNS

## Objective

Now that DNS has been set up on your server, you'll tell your Mac OS X Server to see itself. Next, you'll tell your Mac OS X Server computer to use its own DNS service. Finally, you'll use Network Utility to verify that DNS is working properly.

## Summary

Once DNS is running, checking the validity of the records is critical. If records do not map correctly, users may not be able to access resources and services by name and must resort to using IP addresses to locate and use them.

## Setting DNS Entries on your Mac OS X Server and Mac OS X Computer

You'll set DNS entries on both your Mac OS X Server and Mac OS X computer to use the DNS service you set up.

1 Return to Server Admin and select Share Server's Screen from the Server Admin menu. Authenticate if necessary.

   You are now controlling your Mac OS X Server.

2 Open System Preferences, select the Network Preference pane, and edit the following:

- DNS Server: `10.1.`*n*`.1`
- Search Domains: `student`*n*`.pretendco.com`

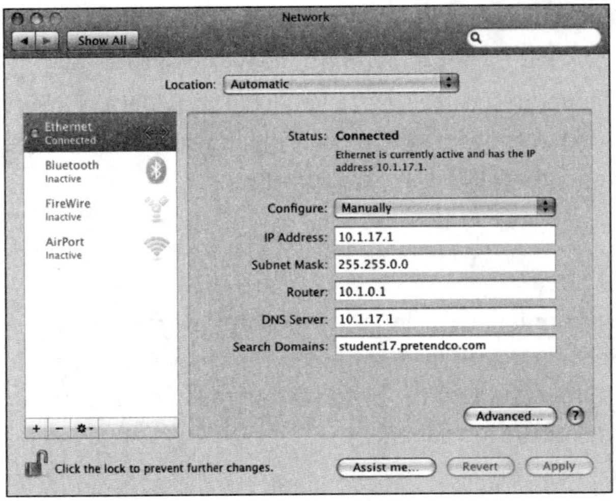


You just told your Mac OS X Server to see its own DNS service.

3 Click Apply, then close System Preferences on your Mac OS X Server, and close Screen Sharing.

4 On your Mac OS X computer, open System Preferences, select your Network Preference pane, and choose Edit Locations from the Locations pop-up menu.

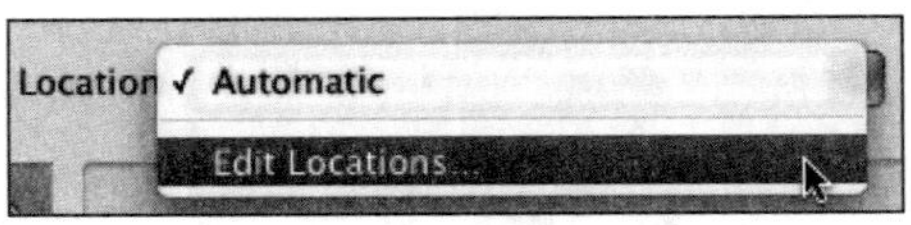

5 Add a new location called `Static`, click Done, and disable any other network interfaces except the Ethernet interface.

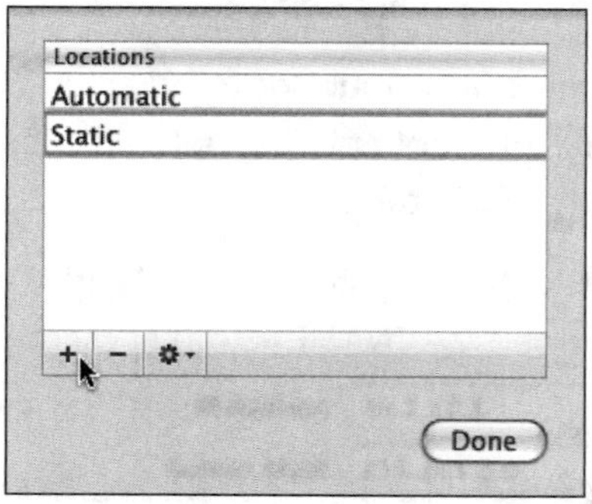


6 Enter the following information, and click Apply:

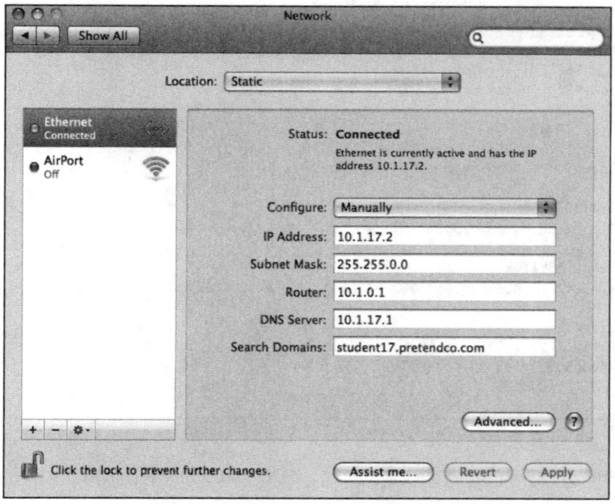


- IP Address: `10.1.`*`n`*`.2`
- Subnet Mask: `255.255.0.0`
- Router: `10.1.0.1`
- DNS Servers: `10.1.`*`n`*`.1`
- Search Domains: `student`*`n`*`.pretendco.com`

7 Click Apply and then close System Preferences.

You have now entered the DNS information on your Mac OS X computer. You will now test the DNS service.

## Testing and Troubleshooting DNS

Now, with DNS entries on both your Mac OS X Server and Mac OS X computer, you'll test to ensure DNS is functioning properly.

1. Select the Terminal application from your Dock, and enter `dig std`*`n`*`.student`*`n`*`.pretendco.com` (replacing both *n*'s with your student number), and press Return.

   You can see that the results of the `dig` are successful and that what you entered returned the CNAME record of client*n*.student*n*.pretendco.com.

```
client17:~ cadmin$ dig std17.student17.pretendco.com

; <<>> DiG 9.4.1-P1 <<>> std17.student17.pretendco.com
;; global options:  printcmd
;; Got answer:
;; ->>HEADER<<- opcode: QUERY, status: NOERROR, id: 6141
;; flags: qr aa rd ra; QUERY: 1, ANSWER: 2, AUTHORITY: 1, ADDITIONAL: 1

;; QUESTION SECTION:
;std17.student17.pretendco.com. IN      A

;; ANSWER SECTION:
std17.student17.pretendco.com. 10800 IN CNAME   client17.student17.pretendco.com.
client17.student17.pretendco.com. 10800 IN A    10.1.17.2

;; AUTHORITY SECTION:
student17.pretendco.com. 10800  IN      NS      server.student17.pretendco.com.

;; ADDITIONAL SECTION:
server.student17.pretendco.com. 10800 IN A      10.1.17.1

;; Query time: 3 msec
;; SERVER: 10.1.17.1#53(10.1.17.1)
;; WHEN: Wed Nov 14 03:45:44 2007
;; MSG SIZE  rcvd: 123
```

2. In Terminal enter `host 10.1.0.1` and press Return.

   Because your Mac OS X computer is using the DNS service on your Mac OS X Server, it does not know about the instructor's server. While it would still be able to connect over the IP address, it would not be able to connect using the fully qualified domain name.

3. You must now quit, not close, the Terminal application.

4 Open Network Utility in the Utilities folder, click the Ping tab, and perform a ping on the following:

- `10.1.0.1`
- `10.1.`*n*`.1`
- `server`*n*`.pretendco.com`
- `client`*n*`.pretendco.com`
- `server.student`*n*`.pretendco.com`
- `ical.student`*n*`.pretendco.com`
- `chat.student`*n*`.pretendco.com`
- `mainserver.pretendco.com`

5 Ping other students' IP addresses and Fully Qualified Domain Names.

**Question 1** *Why are you able to ping some fully qualified domain names but not others?*

---

6 With Network Utility open, click the Lookup tab, and perform a lookup on the following:

- `10.1.0.1`
- `10.1.`*n*`.1`
- `server`*n*`.pretendco.com`
- `client`*n*`.pretendco.com`
- `server.student`*n*`.pretendco.com`
- `ical.student`*n*`.pretendco.com`
- `chat.student`*n*`.pretendco.com`
- `mainserver.pretendco.com`

> **Note** The Lookup tab actually performs a process called `dig`, not lookup.

7 Look up other students' IP addresses and Fully Qualified Domain Names.

*Question 2 Why are you able or not able to look up other students' fully qualified domain names?*

---

8 Open Screen Sharing and repeat the ping and lookups using Network Utility on your Mac OS X Server. You should see identical results, which indicated DNS is working properly.

9 Use the Apple menu on your Mac OS X Server to log out, quit Screen Sharing and the Network Utility, and close any open windows.

## Exercise 2.5.1

# Log the DNS Service (optional)

## Objective

The default level for logging is great for a newly set up DNS server, but once the setup is working smoothly, you should lower the log level to give some performance and resources to other services.

## Summary

Logging any service is crucial to troubleshooting and optimizing that service by viewing the various transactions that happen and correlating the transactions to the network and CPU usage.

1. In Server Admin, select the DNS service, and click Settings in the toolbar.
2. From the Log Level pop-up menu, choose Debug.
3. Click Save.

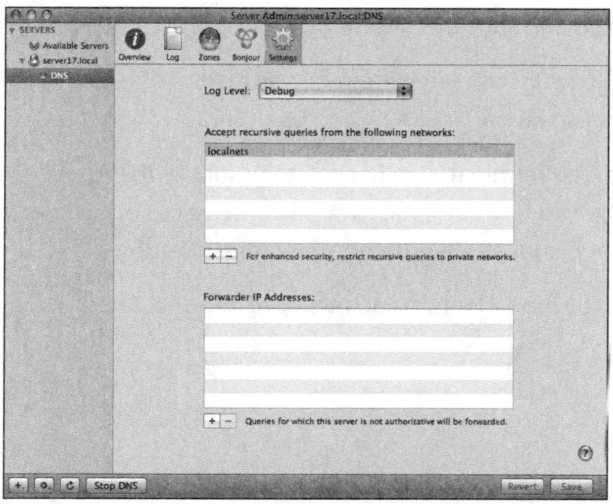


As you step through the next exercise, notice how much detail is added to the logs.

## Exercise 2.6.1

# Use Recursion and Forwarders (optional)

## Objective

You can control what information your DNS server hands out as well as who answers the requests being made.

## Summary

Recursion allows other users within your company, but not necessarily on the same subnet, to use your name server for queries.

1. In Server Admin, select the DNS service, and click Settings in the toolbar.
2. Select *localnets,* and click the Minus (-) button on your server to remove the recursive lookup.
3. Click Save
4. Fully stop and start the DNS service.

   This will restart the service, effectively reading the configuration files again.

5. Launch the Terminal from Recent Items (under the Apple menu), enter `dig server.studentn.pretendco.com`, where *n* is your student number, and press Return.

   Notice the lookup returns no recursive information.

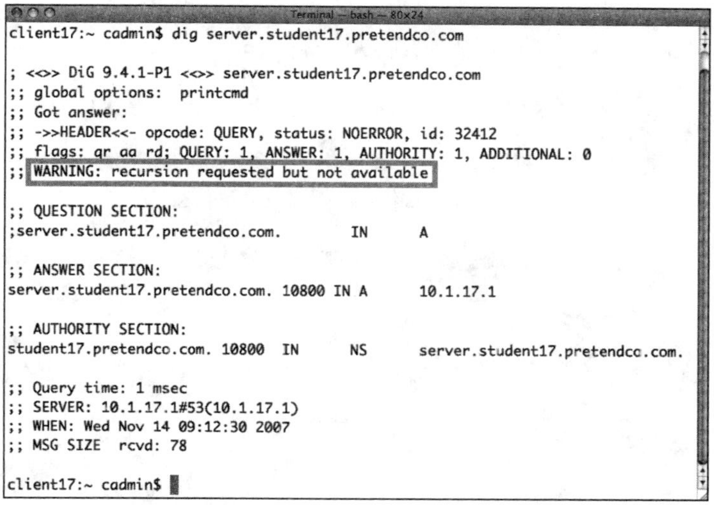


6 Check the log file for information related to the denial of the `dig` command.

7 Return to the DNS settings, and in the "Accept recursive queries" window, double-click the word *none* and enter `10.1/16` in the field.

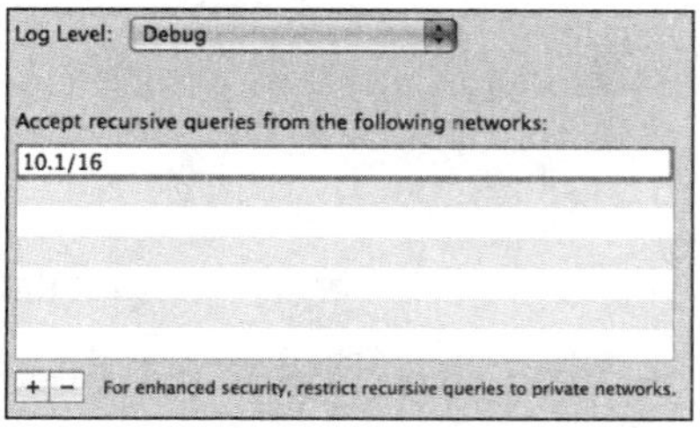


8 Click Save.

9 Fully stop and start the DNS service.

10 In the Terminal, press the Up arrow on your keyboard to reenter the previous command, and press Return.

Notice the lookup now returns recursive information. You'll now lower the log level and add a forwarder to take some load off your Mac OS X Server's DNS service.

11 In Server Admin under the DNS service, select Settings from the toolbar, and then set the Log Level to Error.

This reduces the level of logging and consumes less CPU usage.

12 Click the Add (+) button under Forwarder IP Addresses, and enter `10.1.0.1`, which is the instructor DNS server.

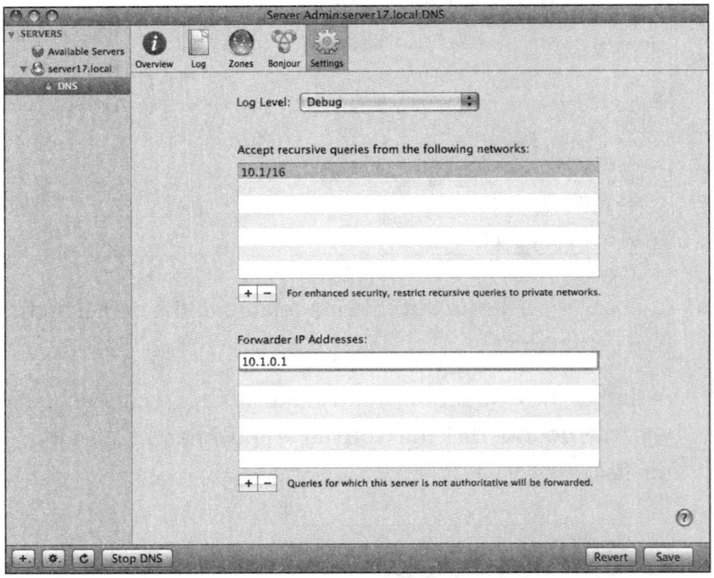


13 Save the changes, and stop and start the DNS service.

14 Using both `dig` and Network Utility, test the new forward settings.

The forwarder is used to take some of the load off the name server and use the more robust corporate name server to look up information outside of the zone.

15 Now, add a forwarder for a classmate's server and use `dig` to verify that you are able to forward a request to the classmate's server.

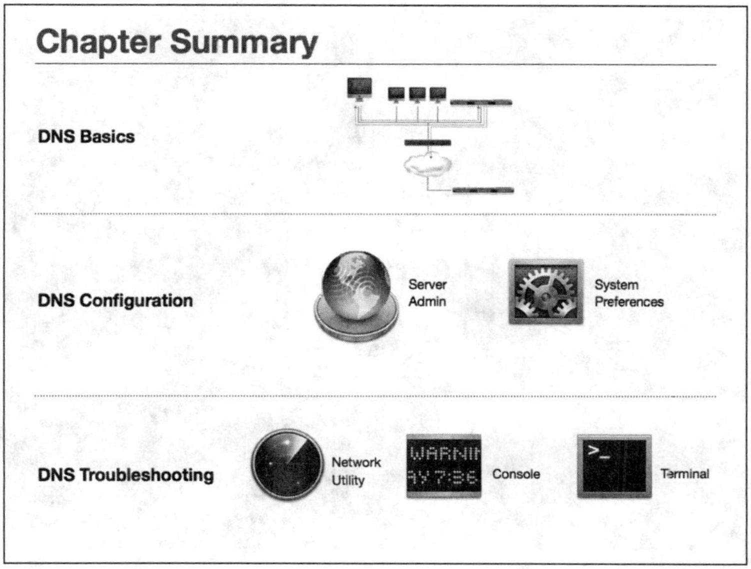


Understanding basic DNS can assist you in segregating, securing, and making your network devices (such as client computers, server, printers, and mobile devices) easier to locate by authorized users.

DNS is a complicated topic that covers a wide range of configuration options and settings. Now that you better understand the importance and essence of DNS, you can plan an efficient and exact DNS structure in which your Mac OS X Server will reside.

Apple
Certified

# 3

# Authentication, Authorization, and Access Control

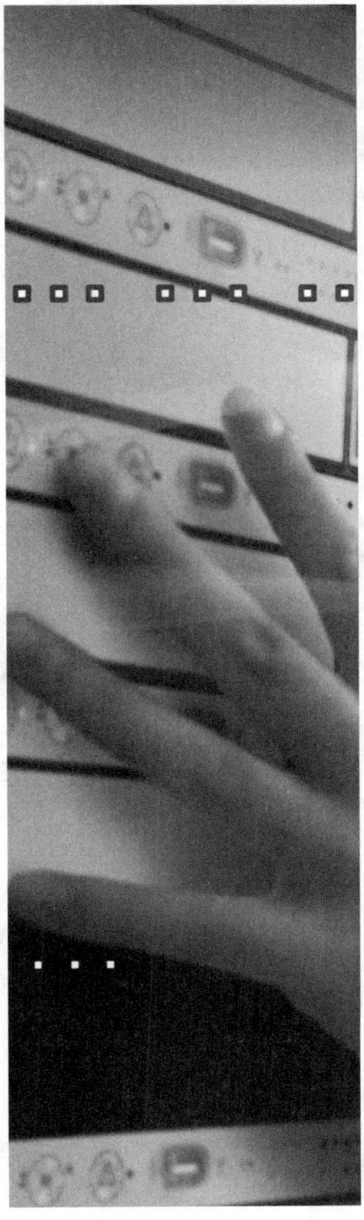


## 3.1 Authentication

**Exercise 3.1.1** Create Local User Accounts

**Exercise 3.1.2** Add Comments and Keywords

**Exercise 3.1.3** Import Local User Accounts

**Exercise 3.1.4** Create Local Groups

**Exercise 3.1.5** Associate Users and Groups

## 3.2 Authorization

**Exercise 3.2.1** Use POSIX and File-System Access Control Management

## 3.3 Service Access Controls

**Exercise 3.3.1** Configure Service Access Controls

# 3.1 Authentication

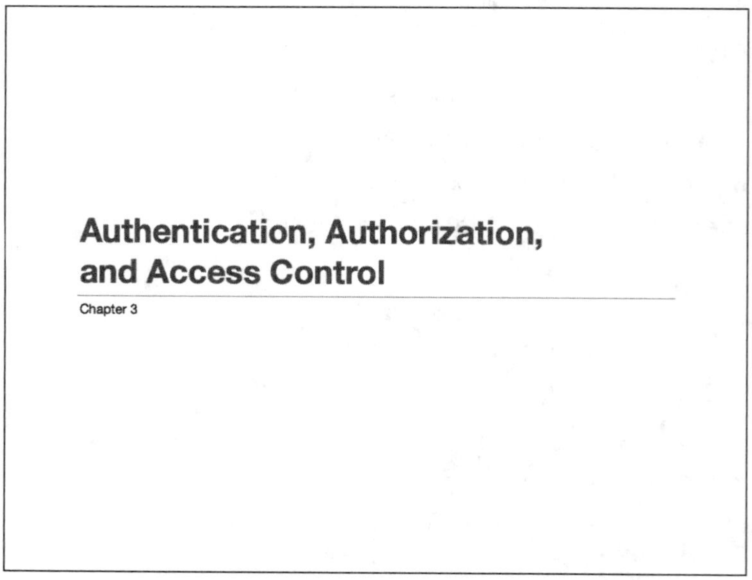

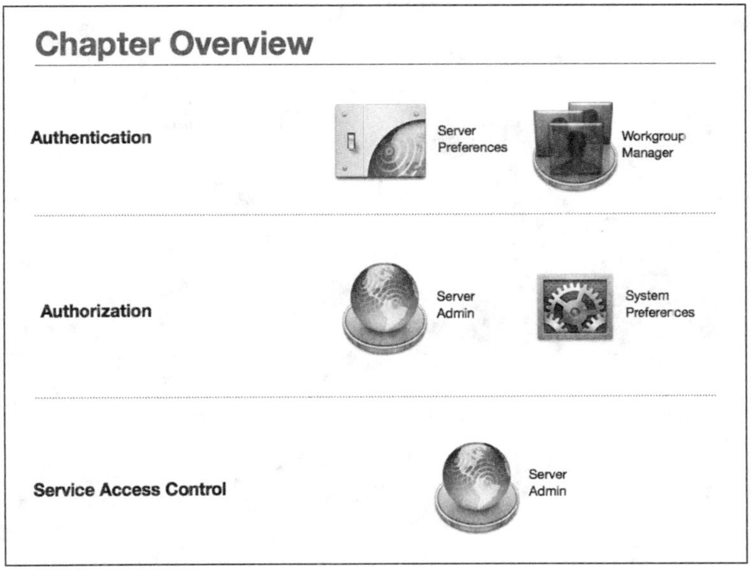


This lesson deals with authentication—the process of identifying a user and their credentials, authorization—where the user is permitted to go (which folders, volumes, and/or share points), and access control—granular permissions on folders, volumes, share points, and services.

When dealing with users and groups, it is important to understand how the users and groups can work with Mac OS X Server. There are three main topics in this chapter:

- Authentication
- Authorization
- Access Control

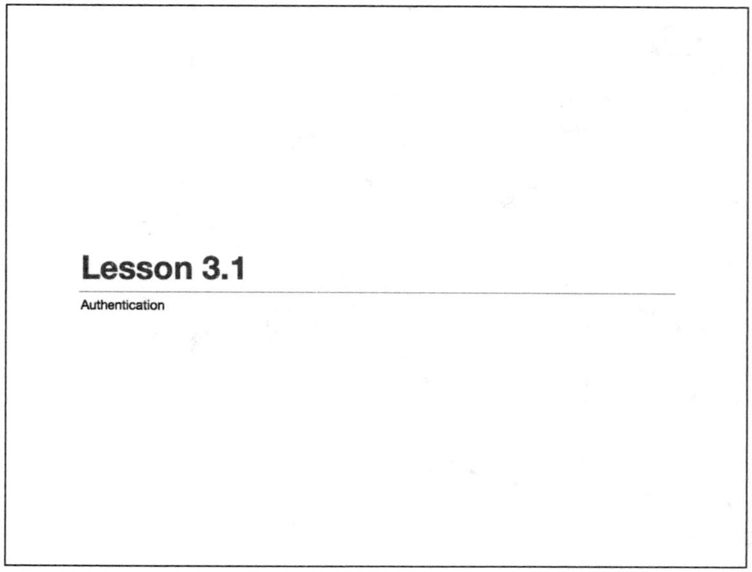
Lesson 3.1
Authentication

## Authentication Versus Authorization

Authentication

- Users of an account provide information to allow access to the account.
- Users provide user name and password for authentication.

Authorization

- The system checks permissions set for a file, folder, share point, or service.
- The system grants access granted based on the user's identity or group membership.

*Authentication* is the process by which a person identifies which user account he or she will use on the system. This is similar to, but slightly different from, saying that authentication is how a person proves his or her identity to a system. This distinction is useful because multiple people may share the same user name or password, or one person may have multiple user accounts on the same system. In each case, the name and password identify which user account the person wants to use. While there are other methods of authenticating a user account, such as smart cards or voice print, a name and password are the most common.

*Authorization* is the process that determines what a person with an authenticated user account is allowed to do on the system. Authorization is associated with user account file–access permissions that are set through Mac OS X or set through the Mac OS X Server administration tools.

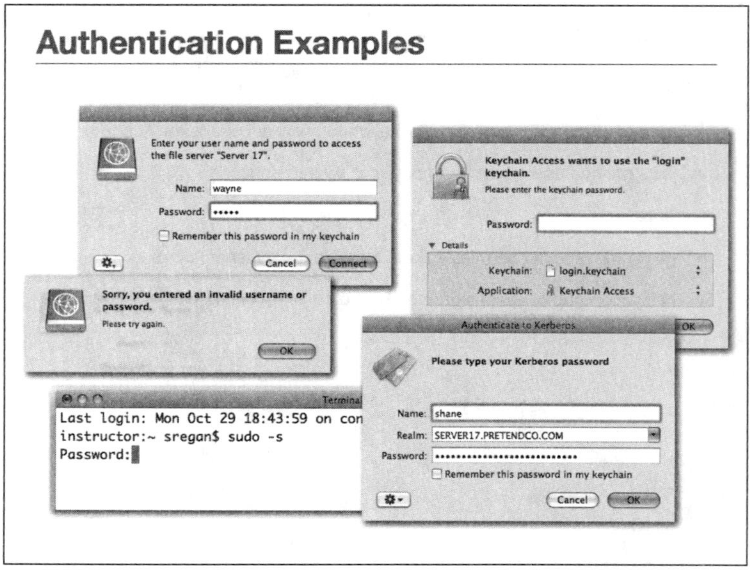


Here are some examples of authentication. While not shown, Login Window is also an excellent example of authentication.

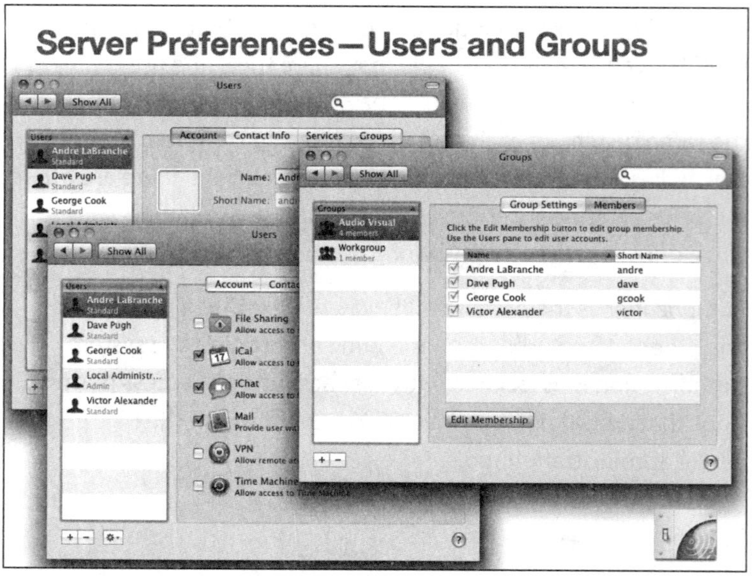


Server Preferences is used to manage users and groups when using Mac OS X Server in either the Standard or Workgroup configuration. In Advanced mode, Server Preferences cannot be used.

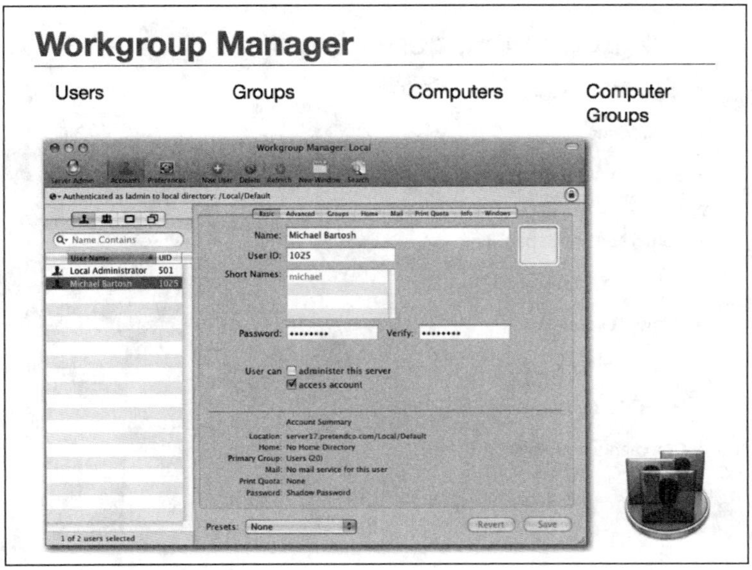


A practical approach to structuring DNS is to plan out the names of the computers and other devices, and then map them to the appropriate IP addresses. Doing so helps to understand the overall structure of DNS and drives home the idea behind a Fully Qualified Domain Name.

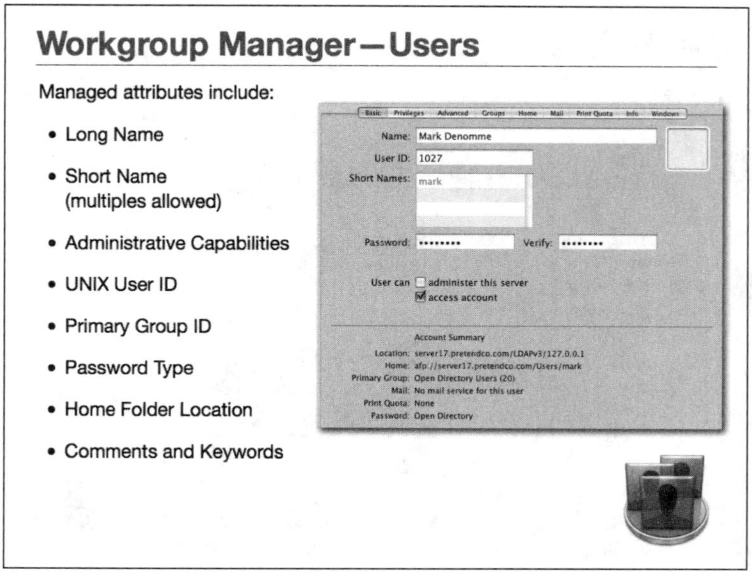


When adding users to Workgroup Manager, there are several items associated with that user, such as long name, short name, UNIX user ID, and so on. These are called attributes. The term *attributes* is used to describe items associated with an account. In some cases, an attribute can have more than one value. For example, a user John Signal has the attribute short name with a value of johnsignal.

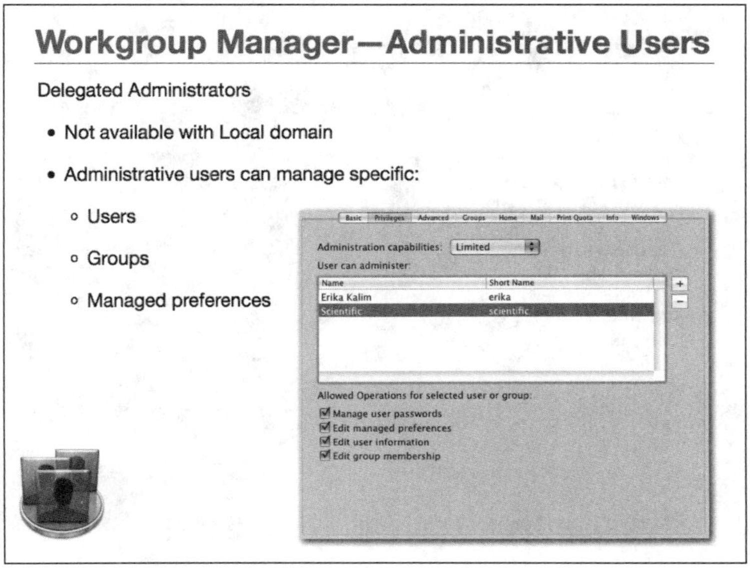


Often, Mac OS X Server administrators want other administrators be responsible for their department/grade/organization. Workgroup Manager permits administrators to have limited management of other users and/or groups. The Privileges tab appears only when a Mac OS X Server is configured in a certain way, which will be discussed in the next chapter.

## Workgroup Manager—Groups

Groups can contain other groups, nested groups, which allows for more granular management.

To ways to manage users and groups with identical results:

- Add users to groups (Groups tab)
- Add groups to users (Users tab)

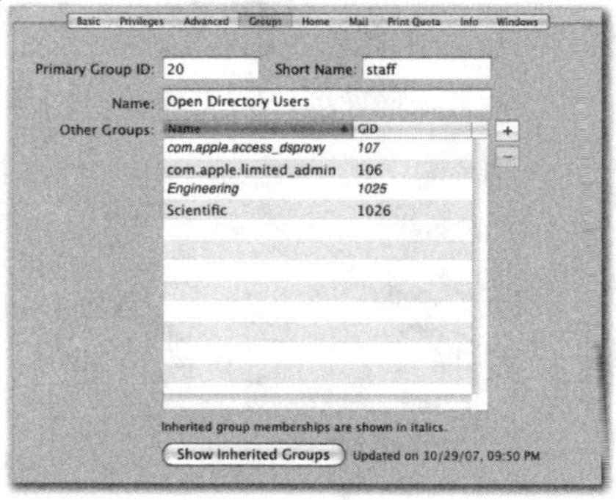


* Inherited groups are shown in *italics*

Groups are collections of users and can include other groups—called nested groups. There are two main methods to manage groups. The Groups account tab permits the administrator to add users to groups. The Groups pane under each User account (shown in the slide) shows the groups to which that user belongs, including any nested or inherited groups.

## Importing and Exporting Users and Groups

Workgroup Manager can import users and groups from files.

- Certain criteria must be specified:
    - Beginning UNIX user ID
    - Primary Group ID
    - Ignore top (first, header) record
    - Ability to use templates (presets) for records
    - Verbose logging to track input
- Passwords are not exported because of potential security risk.
- Third-party tools are available to assist in management (Passenger).

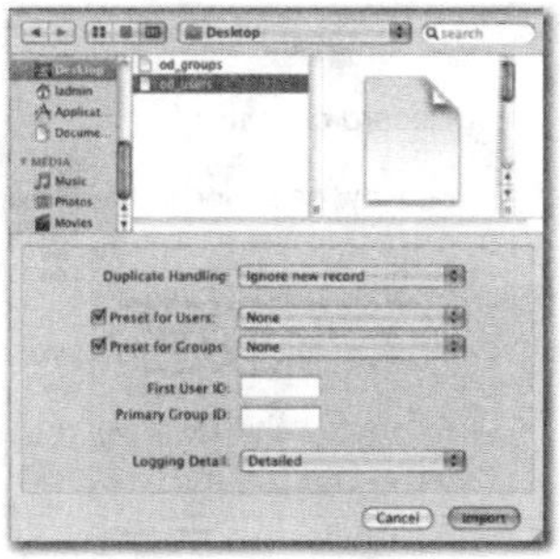

Often, an administrator may want to move accounts from one computer to another, perhaps they are moving away from another directory service and over to Mac OS X Server. Flat files that are configured properly can be used by Workgroup Manager to import users and groups. Using Workgroup Manager, passwords can be imported; they cannot be exported.

## Importing Users or Groups from a Text File

Flat files can be used to import users or groups.

- WGM requests certain information:
  - Record delimiter
    - How each line in the file ends
  - Attribute delimiter
    - How each attribute is separated on the line
  - Attribute value delimiter
    - How the attribute values are separated in the line
  - Escape character
    - Value for that character, if any

If you have ever used Microsoft Excel or FileMaker Pro, you understand the basics of a database. When creating or massaging a file to import, you need to know what the columns (in the case of Excel) or the fields (in the case of FileMaker Pro) need to contain and how those items are separated (tab, comma, return character, space, and so on).

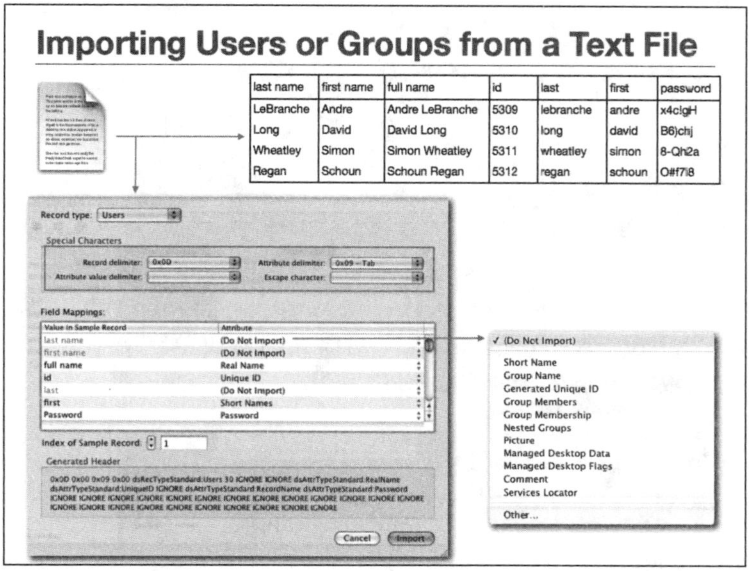


Returning to the discussion of attributes, if you know what attributes are required for a user or group to have a good experience, then you can enter those attributes for every user and then save the file. When you open Workgroup Manager and start to import the file, you simply map your field names to what Workgroup Manager wants.

## Exercises

3.1.1 Create Local User Accounts

3.1.2 Add Comments and Keywords

3.1.3 Import Local User Accounts

3.1.4 Create Local Groups

3.1.5 Associate Users and Groups

## Exercise 3.1.1

# Create Local User Accounts

### Objective

Mac OS X Server uses a list of local accounts for accessing resources such as files when running Apple file services. You'll use the Workgroup Manager to add two sample local users to your Mac OS X Server's local database.

### Summary

Because you have not configured your computer to share account information, you'll get a notification about your directory node not being visible on the network. You'll learn about directory services in Chapter 4, "Open Directory."

For any PretendCo users to access your server, they need to have an account on the server. Use Workgroup Manager, the primary tool for creating and managing user accounts, to add two users: Shane Onnue and John Signal.

1 On your Mac OS X computer, open Workgroup Manager, and connect to your server using the fully qualified domain name, server.student*n*.pretendco.com (where *n* is your student number), and the ladmin account.

2 Click OK when the local directory warning appears.

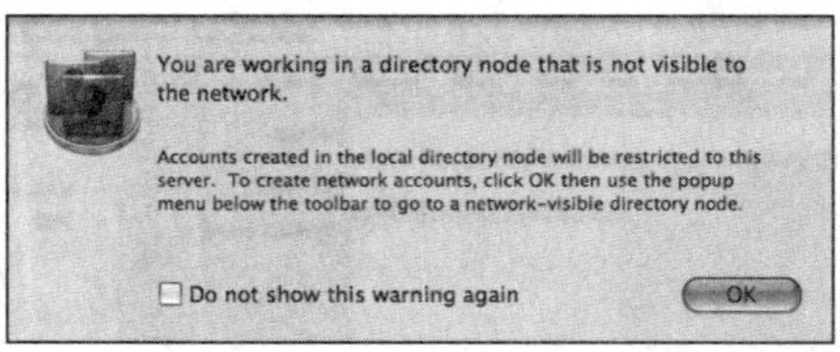


3 Click the Accounts icon in the toolbar.

This will display the list of users in the local directory.

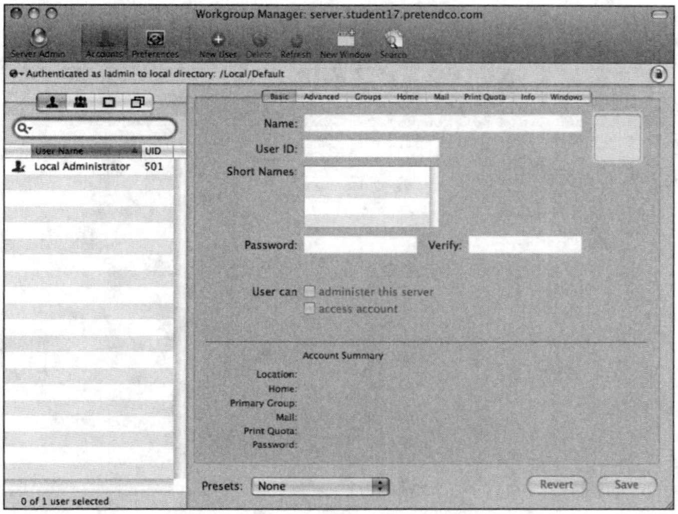


This is the local directory of your Mac OS X Server. The structure of this directory is identical to the local directory on Mac OS X. The user currently permitted to make changes to the directory is the user Local Administrator (The short name ladmin can also be used.).

4 Click New User in the toolbar.

If the button is dimmed, click in the list of users to activate the button.

5 Click the Basic tab, enter the following information for the first new user:

- Name: `LeRoy Venison`
- Short Names: `leroy`
- Password: `leroy`
- Verify: `leroy`

6 Leave the other settings at their default values and do not select "User can administer the server."

At the bottom of the window, leave Presets set to None.

7 Double-click the empty line below leroy in the Short Names field to add another short name.

8 Type `lvenison` in the Short Names field.

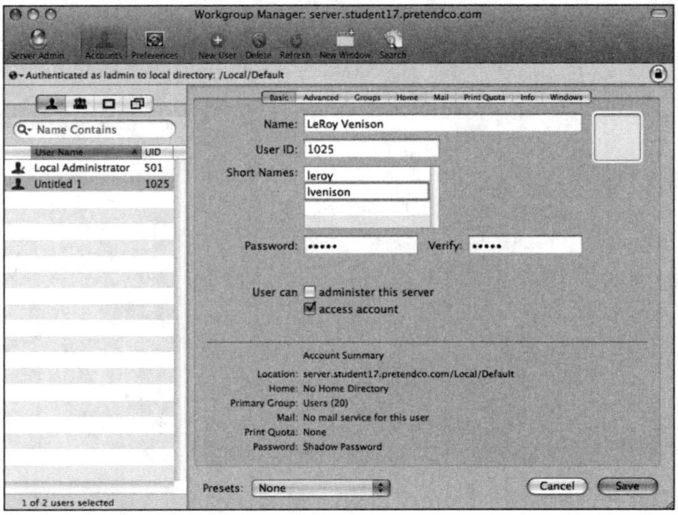


9 Click Save.

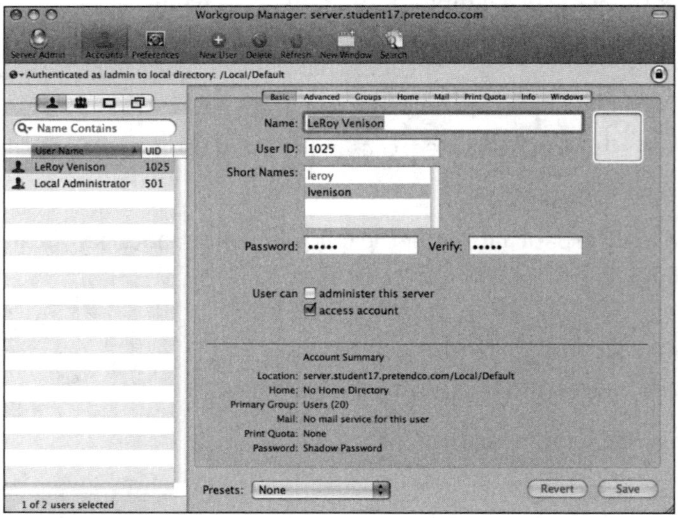


The new user name appears in the list of users on the left side of the Workgroup Manager window. You should also see that the first short name is now dimmed, indicating that it cannot be changed. Notice that the name and alternate short names can be edited after this point.

**10** Add a second user, John Signal, with the following values:

- Name: `John Signal`
- Short Names: `john`
- Password: `john`
- Verify: `john`

Leave the other settings at their default values.

**11** Click Save.

**12** Select the existing Local Administrator account from the list of current users.

Notice that the administrator account has the "User can administer the server" option selected.

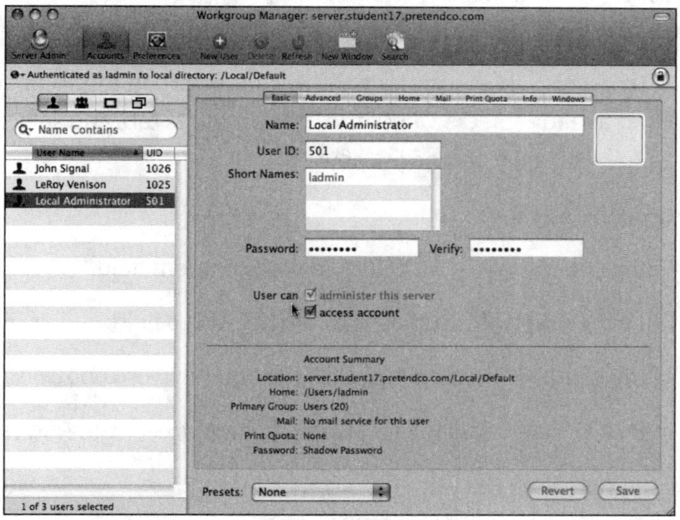


**13** Compare the two new accounts with the administrator account.

***Question 1*** *What are the differences between the accounts?*

## Exercise 3.1.2

# Add Comments and Keywords

### Objective

You can configure advanced features such as comments and keywords for accounts. These features are useful for organizing users or searching for particular users based on something other than name or UNIX user ID.

### Summary

You'll be adding comments and keywords to specific user accounts. You will then search the local database for users with those keywords.

1 In Workgroup Manager, click the Accounts icon in the Toolbar if not already selected, click the User accounts tab, and select LeRoy Venison from the list of users.

2 Click the Advanced tab.

3 Enter `Employee#: 8675309` in the Comment field.

4 Click the Add (+) button next to the Keywords field.

5 In the window that appears, click the Edit Keywords button.

6 In the "Manage available keywords" window, click the Add (+) button.

7 Enter `Manager` in the text field.

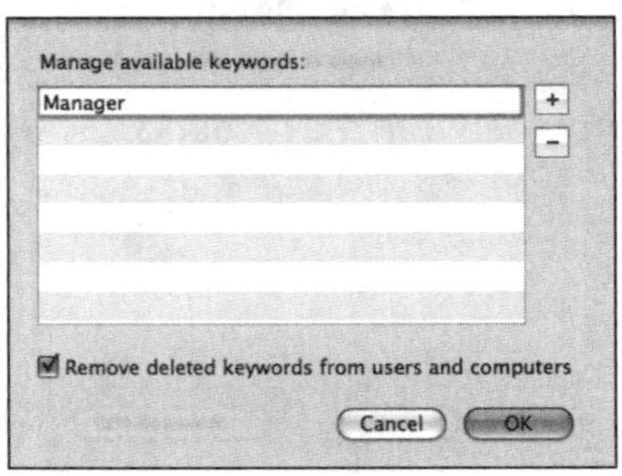

8 Click the Add (+) button again.

9 Type `Marketing`, in the same field.

10 Add a third keyword, `Engineering`.

11 Click OK to save the new keywords.

12 In the "Select the keywords" window, select Manager, and click OK to add the Manager keyword to LeRoy's user account.

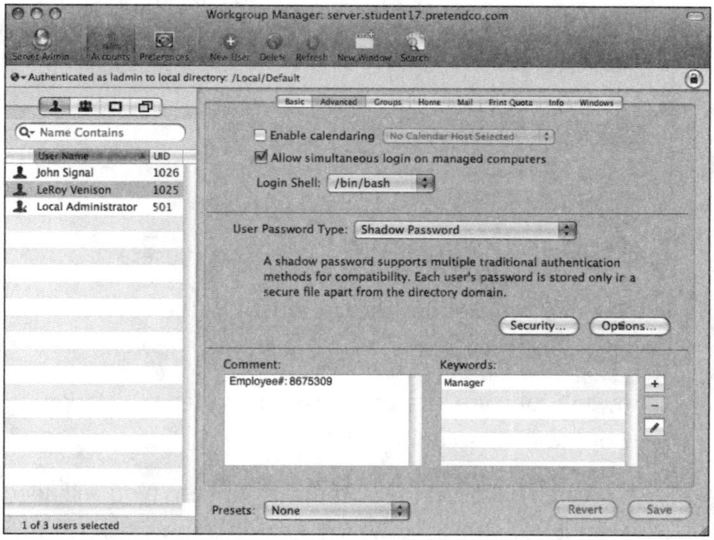


13 Click Save.

14 Add the Marketing keyword to LeRoy's account.

15 Add the Marketing and Engineering keywords to John's user account.

16 Add `Employee#: 2241955` to the Comment field for John's user account, and click Save.

17 In the Search field above the Users list, choose Keyword Contains from the small arrow, and type `Manager`.

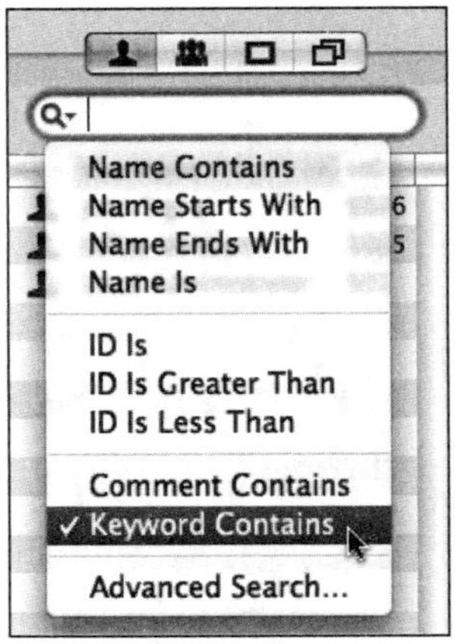


Only LeRoy's account should be listed in the user list.

18 In the Search field above the Users list, choose Keyword Contains, and type `Mar`.

LeRoy and John are listed because you added the Marketing keyword to their accounts.

19 In the search field, choose Comment Contains (you will need to select it from the list of search criteria using the small arrow), and type `224`.

Only John should be listed in the user list because his account's comment contains 224 in his employee number.

20 Remove 224 from the search field.

## Exercise 3.1.3

# Import Local User Accounts

### Objective

When you are setting up a new server and will be supporting more than just a few users, you'll probably import the users from a configured text file instead of adding each of them individually. In this exercise, another system administrator at PretendCo has provided you with a file containing formatted user records for you to use with your server.

### Summary

Workgroup Manager can import users from text files. If Workgroup Manager cannot easily detect the type of separation for attributes used in the text file, a dialog appears asking for some clarification on how the attributes are separated and what categories the attributes use.

1. In Workgroup Manager, click Accounts in the toolbar, and click the Users tab.
2. From the Server menu, select Import.
3. Navigate to and select `/Users/Shared/StudentMaterials/CH03/employee-dumpfile.txt`.

   If the student materials have not been downloaded to your Mac OS X computer you can get them from your instructor's server and save them in /Users/Shared/.
4. Accept all default values in the Import dialog, and click Import.

5 In the dialog that appears, select Users from the Record type pop-up menu.

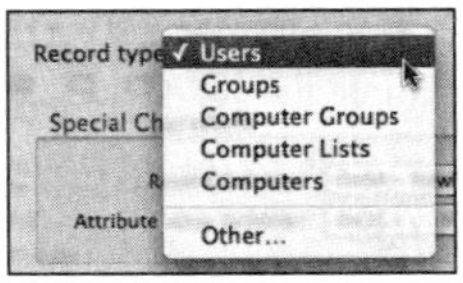


6 For the Special Characters select:

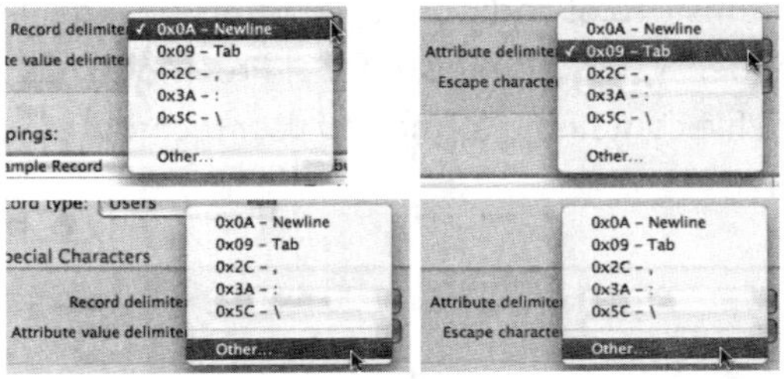


- Record delimiter: 0x0A—Newline
- Attribute delimiter: 0x09 - Tab
- Attribute value delimeter: 0x00 (nothing will show)
- Escape character: 0x00 (nothing will show)

The "nothing" character (0x00) can be selected from the "Other" selection as seen in the following figure.

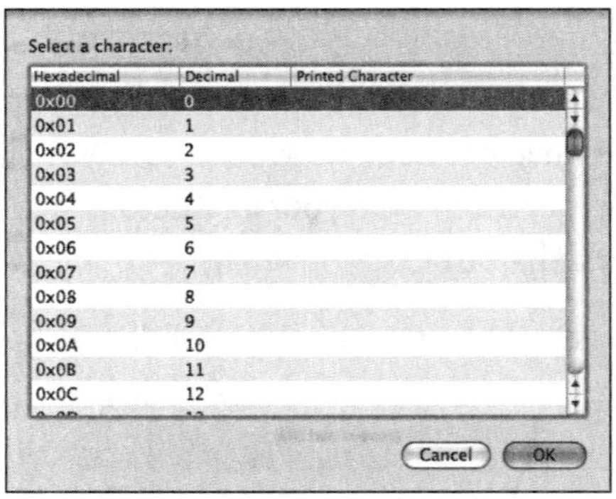

7 After you select all four character mappings, your dialog should appear as shown in the following figure:

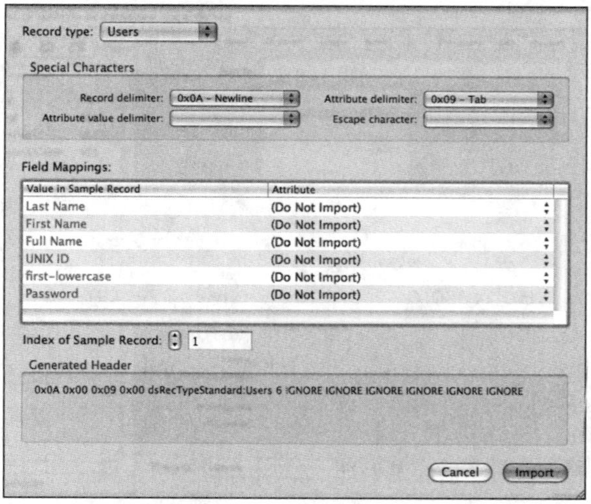


8 In the Index of Sample Record field, click the up arrow and scroll through all the user accounts that are going to be imported. Scroll back to record 1 before proceeding to the next step.

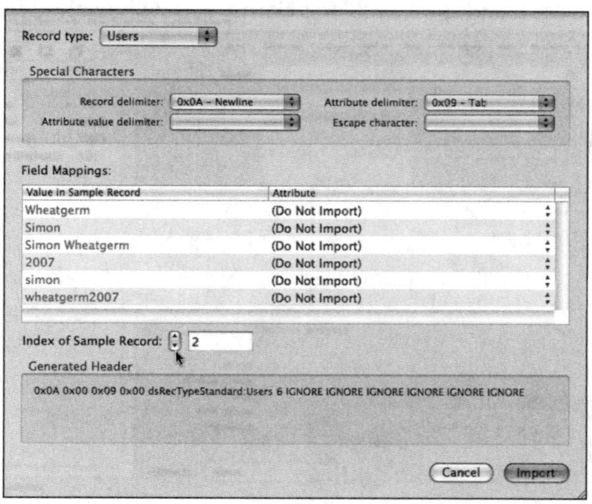


Notice that record 1 is actually the header of the file. Workgroup Manager allows you to scroll through the records before you map the attributes to ensure you are mapping them correctly.

*Question 2 What is the password for Simon Wheatgerm? What is the password for Schoun Vegan?*

9 Ensure you are on record 1. For the Field Mappings in the Attribute column, in any row, click the words, "Do Not Import." A pop-up menu appears. Map the following (Value column to Attribute column):

- Full Name (value) to Real Name (attribute)
- UNIX ID (value) to Unique ID (attribute)
- first-lowercase (value) to Short Names (attribute)
- Password (value) to Password (attribute)

10 For the values Last Name and First Name, you will be choosing "Other" from the list of attributes.

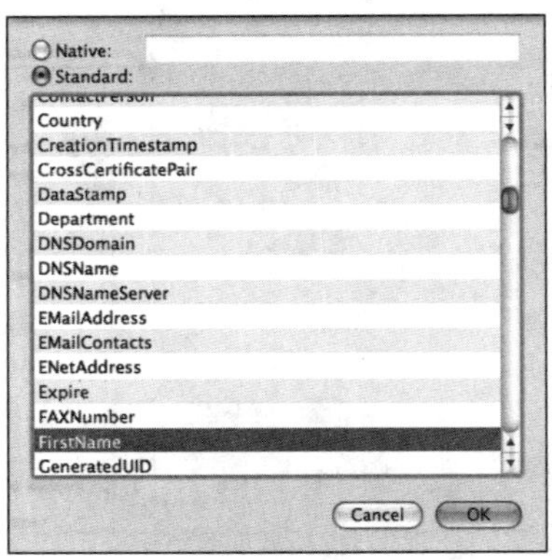

11 Map the last two values:

- Last Name (value) to LastName (attribute)
- First Name (value) to FirstName (attribute)

> **Note** There are over 170 various attributes that can be mapped, covering all types of values. All available attributes are under the "Other" option.

12 When you are finished mapping and before you click Import, your dialog should appear as shown in the following figure:

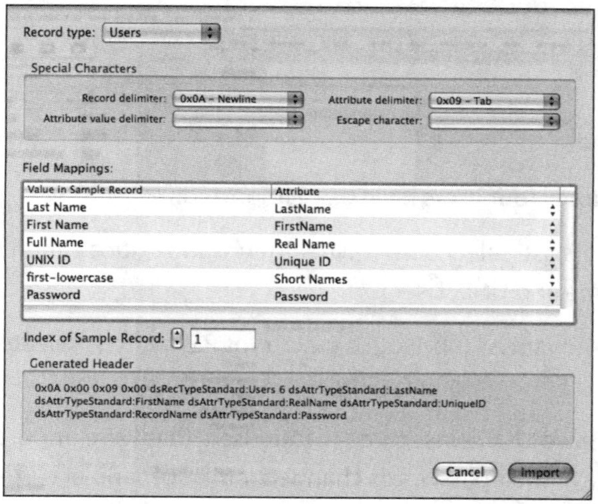


> **Warning!** If you scroll past record 5 in the next step, you will have to remap all your field mappings.

**13** Scroll through the records again to see how the maps appear.

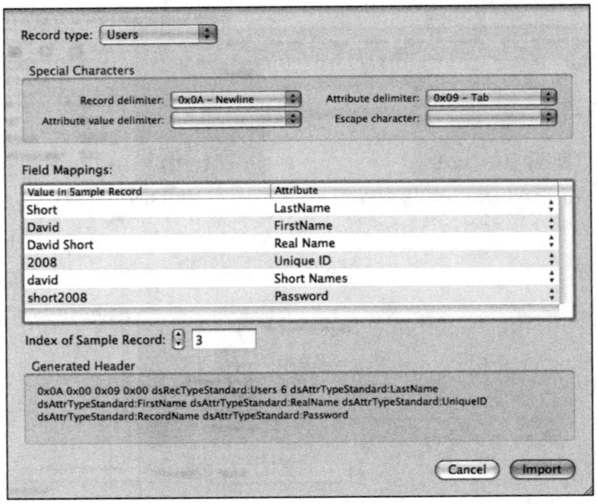


**14** Click Import.

An additional four users have been imported.

**15** In the Users list, select Simon Wheatgerm, and notice Simon's short name and UNIX User ID.

**16** Click the Advanced tab. Notice that Crypt Password is selected to indicate Simon has a crypt type password.

Crypt passwords are insecure. All four users that were imported should have their passwords changed if this scenario occurred on a Mac OS X Server in use.

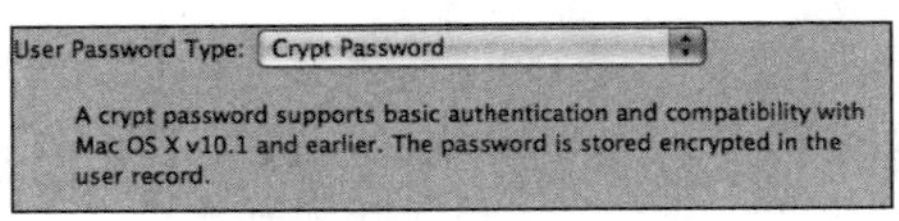

17 Click the Info tab. Note that Simon's first name and last name were correctly imported.

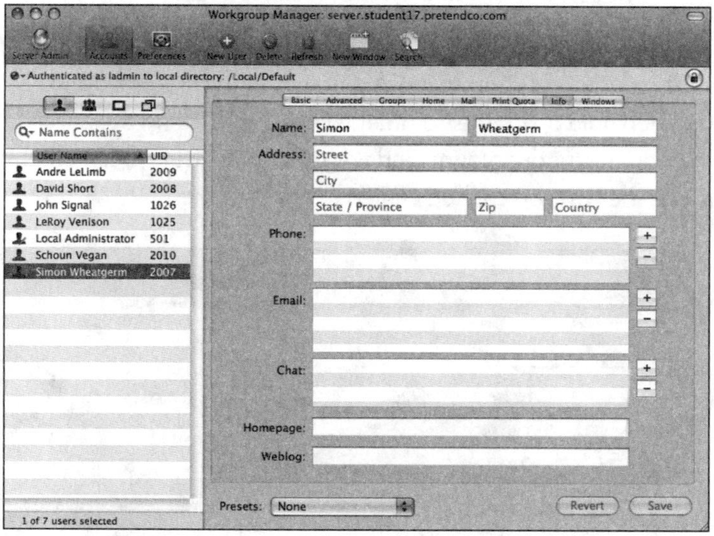

You'll import more users from a properly formatted file, such as one created by Workgroup Manager on another server.

18 From the Server menu select Import.

19 Navigate to and select the /Users/Shared/StudentMaterials/CH03/PretendCo-Employees file.

20 Leave all the other settings at their default values.

21 Click Import.

An additional eight users have been imported.

Because passwords are not included in the users import file, you need to set a password for each of the new accounts. For now, you will set all the accounts to use the same password, `changeme`.

22 In the Users list, click the UID column to sort by UNIX user ID, select all the newly imported accounts and the four accounts previously imported. Click the Advanced tab.

A simple way to select all the user accounts is to select one account, press Command-A to select all the accounts, and then hold down the Command key while clicking the Local Administrator account (and any other preexisting accounts such as the two you created earlier) to deselect them.

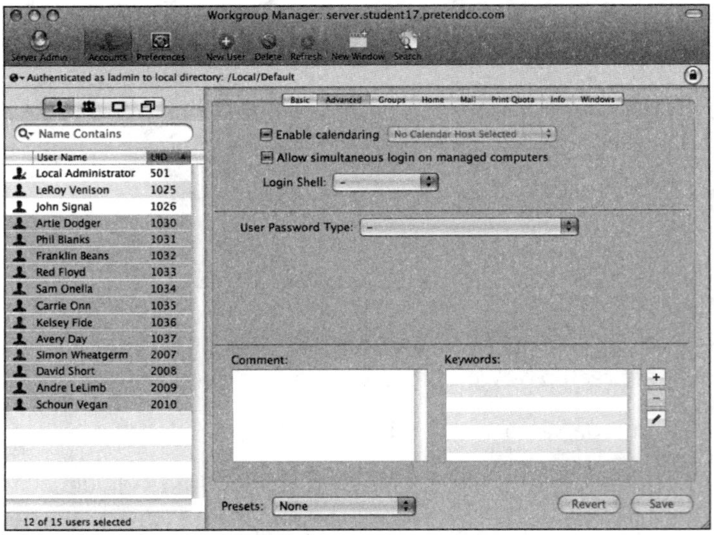

23 Select Shadow Password from the User Password Type pop-up menu.

24 Enter `changeme` in both the Password and Verify fields.

25 Click OK then click Save. You have imported users from two different types of files.

Exercise 3.1.4

# Create Local Groups

## Objective

The PretendCo users who are accessing your server can be broken down into four categories: Marketing, Engineering, Management, and Projects. In this exercise you will create four groups, one for each department. You'll also create three additional groups for Employees, Contractors, and Server Administrators. You 'll then assign the previously created users to their proper groups.

## Summary

Because you can search user accounts based on keywords, you could use the keywords to logically organize large numbers of user accounts and then group them into a group account.

1 In Workgroup Manager on your Mac OS X computer, click Accounts in the Toolbar.

2 In the left side of the window, click the Group tab.

> **Note** Workgroup Manager shows one local group, _guest. More local groups—initially hidden by Workgroup Manager—can be seen by choosing "Show System Users and Groups" from the View menu.

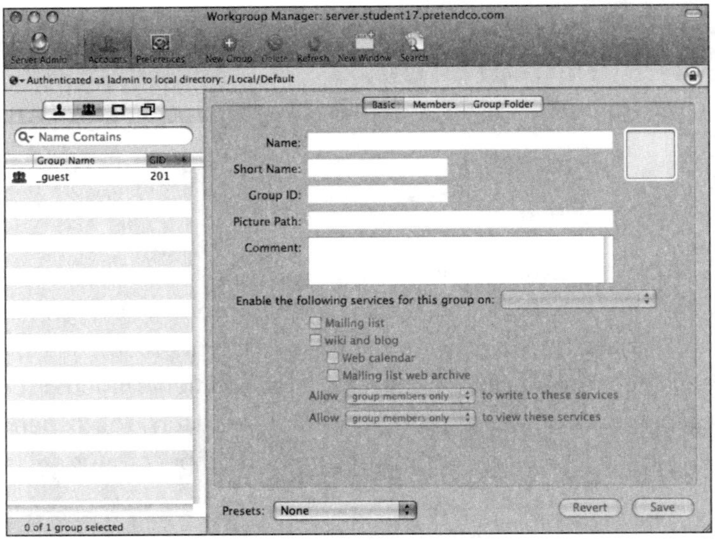


3 In the toolbar, click the New Group button to create a new group.

4 Enter the following information for the first new group:

- Name: `Engineering`
- Short Name: `engr`

Leave all other fields at their default values.

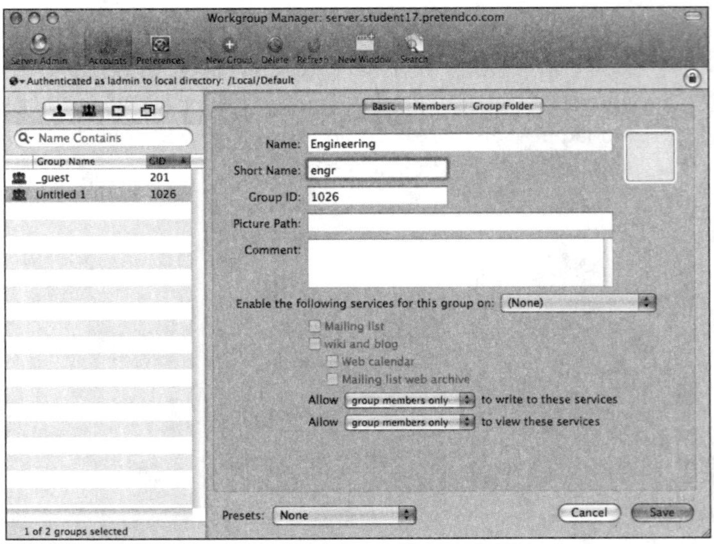

5 Click Save.

6 Create a second group:

- Name: `Marketing`
- Short Name: `mktg`

Leave all other fields at their default values.

7 Click Save.

8 Create the remaining groups with the following information:

| Name | Short Name |
|---|---|
| Employees | employees |
| Contractors | contractors |
| Projects | projects |
| Management | management |
| Technical Admins | tadmins |

Leave all other fields at their default values.

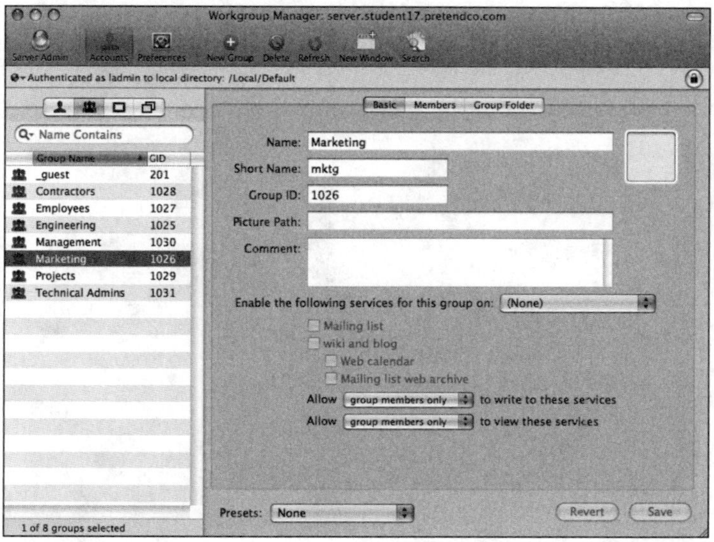


9 Click Save.

**Note** If you try to create a group called "admin" you will get a notice that a group with that name already exists.

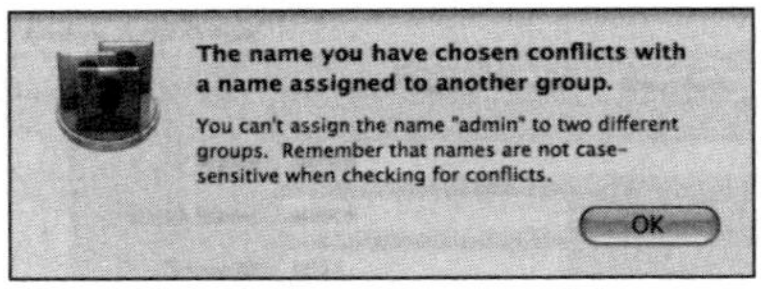

Exercise 3.1.5

# Associate Users and Groups

## Objective

Now that you have created your groups, you need to assign them the users that you created in the previous exercises. You'll do this using two different methods: adding users to a group, and adding group membership to a user account. The most common approach for populating groups with users is to select a group and then add one or more users to the group. On your server, you'll select a group and then add users to the group based on keywords. Finally, you'll add groups to groups to create nested groups.

## Summary

When finished, the PretendCo Employee group will consist of three groups: Marketing, Engineering, and Management. Although you could populate the Employees group with all the individual Marketing, Engineering and Management user accounts, the easiest approach is to simply add the three groups to the Employees group.

## Adding Users to Groups

You'll use Workgroup Manager to add users to groups.

1 Select the Marketing group from the Groups list.

2 Click the Members tab, click the Add (+) button to the right of the Members list.

The Users and Groups drawer appears. You can resize the drawer to see user names, UNIX User IDs, and Short Names.

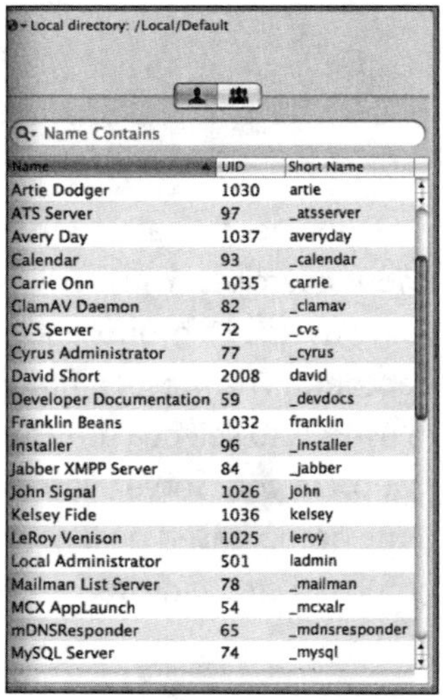


3 Click back on the User account tab. From the pop-up menu in the Search field, choose Keyword Contains and type `Mar`.

   This locates all the users with the Marketing keyword. The four user accounts listed should LeRoy, John, Artie, and Phil.

4 Now that you found the members of the Marketing group, click back on the Groups account button. Click the Marketing group, select the Members tab, and open the Users and Groups drawer.

5 Using the Command key, select the four users who are members of the Marketing group.

   Again, the four user accounts are LeRoy, John, Artie, and Phil.

   It might be helpful to click on the Name or UID column in the Users and Groups drawer to locate the users in each group.

6 Drag the selected users to the Members list.

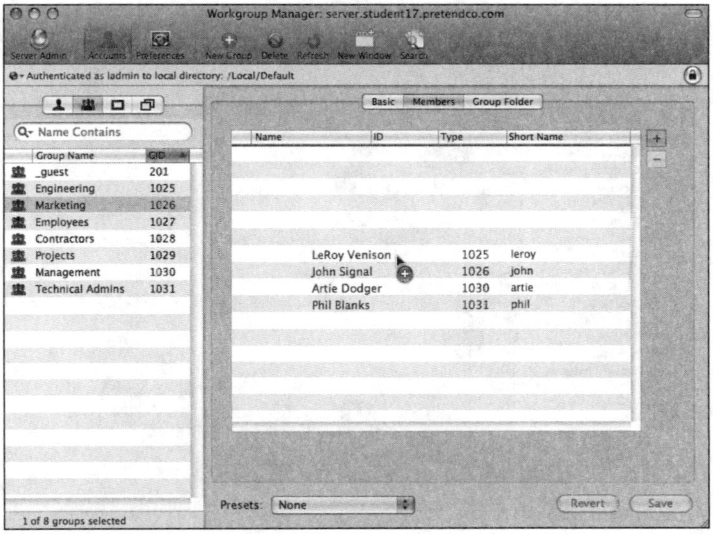

7 Click Save.

8 Repeat steps 1–7 to add the appropriate users to the Engineering and Management groups.

## Adding Group Membership to a User Account

While you could easily use the same process you used in the previous section to add users to our newly created groups—this time we'll try an alternate approach by adding the groups to a new user's account.

1 Click the Users button on the left side of the Workgroup Manager window.

2 Add a new user with the following information:

- Name: `Shane Onnue`
- Short Names: `shane`
- Password: `shane`
- Verify: `shane`

Leave the other settings at their default values.

3 Click Save.

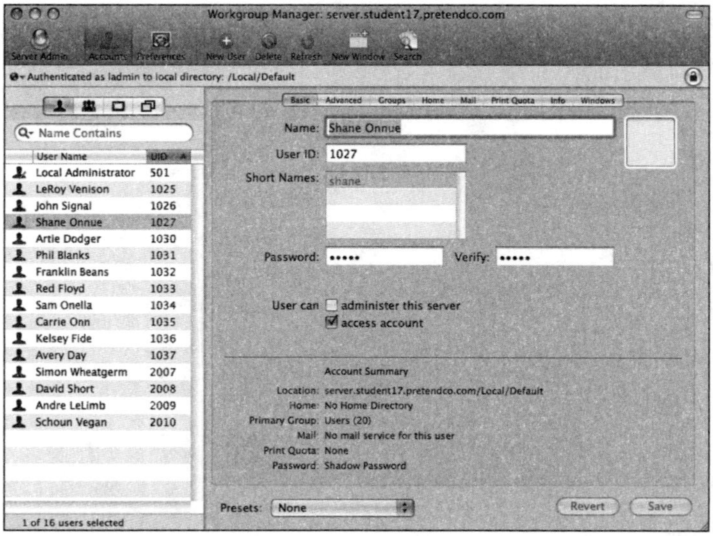


4 Click the Groups tab to the right of the Advanced tab.

5 Click the Add (+) button to add a group.

The Groups drawer appears, displaying the list of groups currently defined on the system.

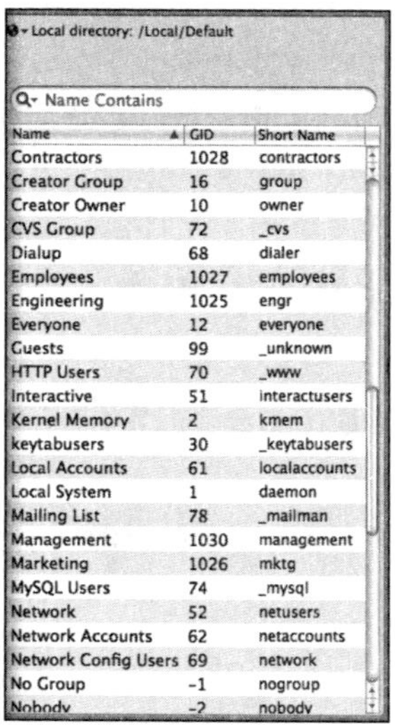

This list includes both groups that you created and system-defined groups that Mac OS X Server created during installation.

6 Select the Contractors group and drag it from the Groups drawer to the Other Groups text field.

Notice that as you drag the group, the pointer changes to a plus sign. This indicates that you are adding this group to the group list.

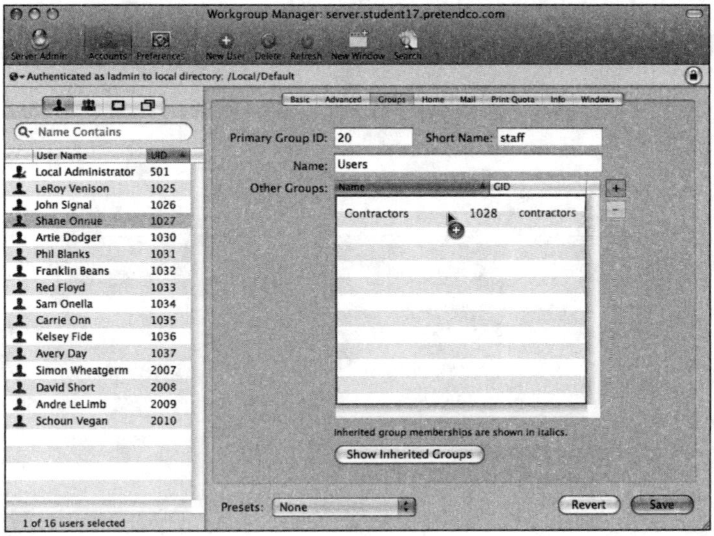

7 Repeat for the tadmins group.

8 Click Save.

You have successfully added multiple group memberships to Shane's account. You will now add groups to groups.

9 Click the Group Account button on the left side of the Workgroup Manager window.

10 Select the Employees group from the Groups list.

11 Click the Members tab, click the Add (+) button to the right of the Members list to open the Users and Groups drawer.

12 In the Users and Groups drawer, click the Groups button and then click the GID column to sort the list by their UNIX Group ID.

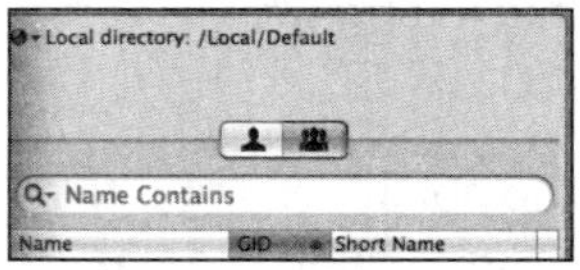


13 Select the Marketing, Engineering, and Management groups and drag them to the Members list.

All members of the Marketing, Engineering, and Management groups now have access to anything that the Employees group does.

14 Click Save.

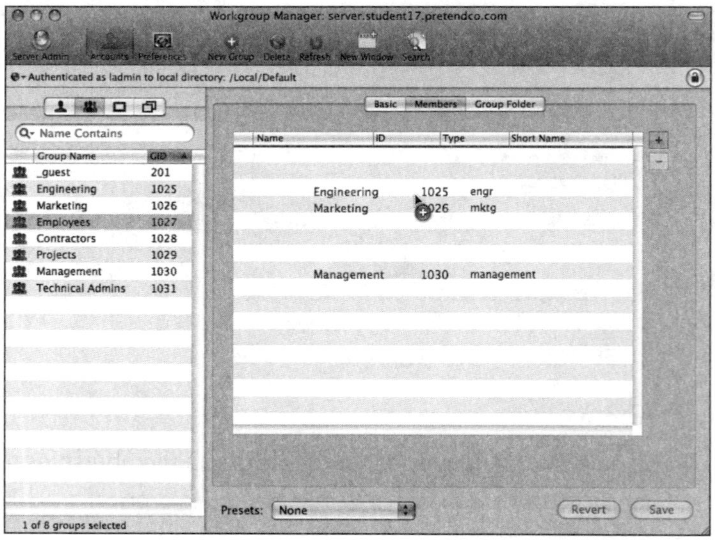


## Summary

You have created, imported, and managed local users and groups on Mac OS X Server.

# Authorization 3.2

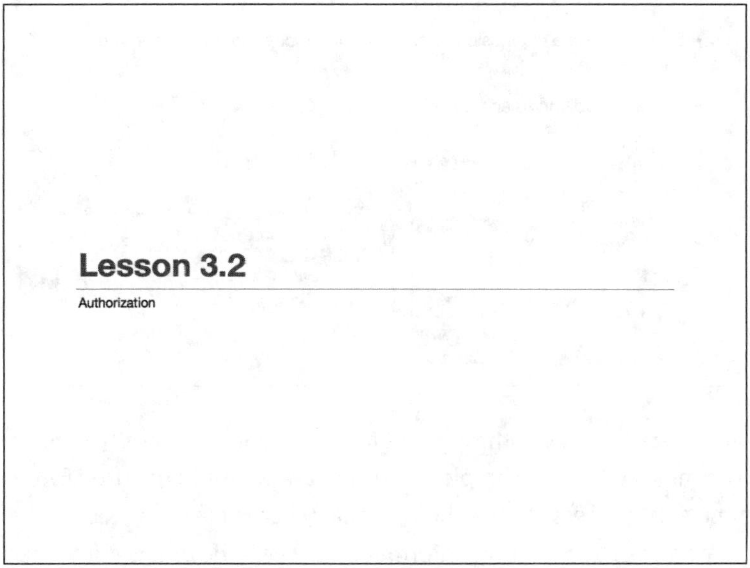


The lesson deals with the process of authorization, both POSIX style permissions and file system access control.

## Authorization

POSIX Permissions—Always set for every file and folder

File-system ACLs

- Optional for any folder or share point in Mac OS X Server
- Enables flexible expression of privileges for accessing folders and their enclosed files
- Works in addition to and can override POSIX permissions

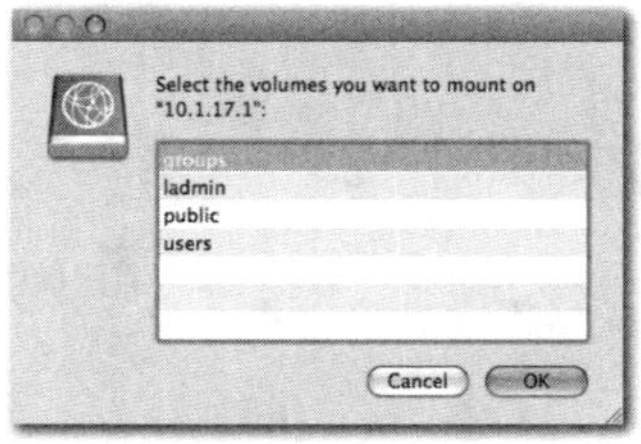


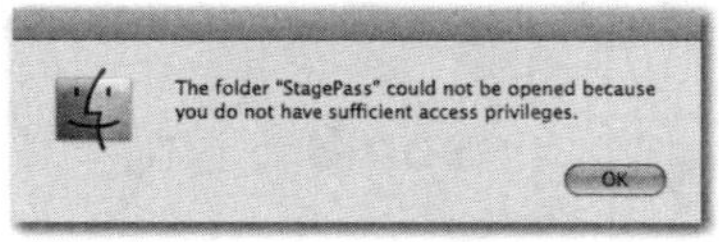


Authorization is used throughout Mac OS X and Mac OS X Server. The most common example is usually transparent to the user: Every time a user accesses a file, the computer checks file permissions against the user's account information to see if the user is authorized to use the file. In Mac OS X and Mac OS X Server, owner and group permissions are associated with every file, folder, and application.

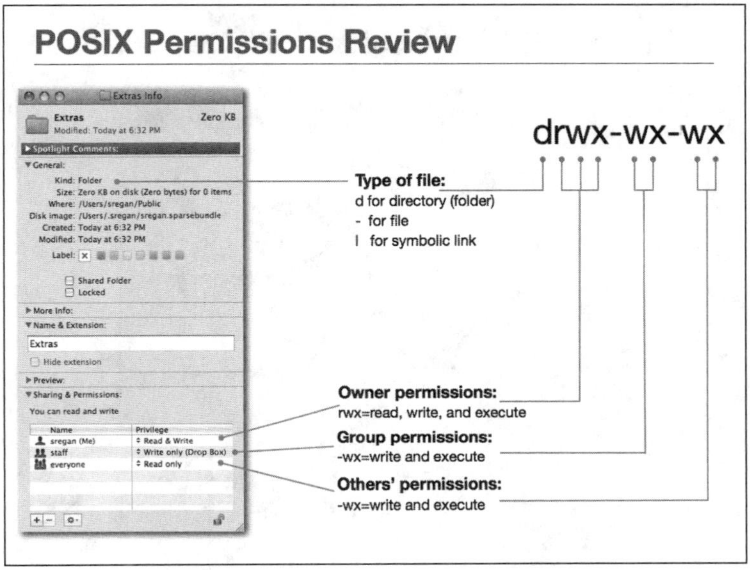


Portable Operating System Interface (POSIX) permissions are the permissions that have been used on Mac OS X and Mac OS X Server since day one. They are still used both on Mac OS X and Mac OS X Server, and they exist for every file system file or folder on the file system. POSIX permissions are the traditional UNIX-style permissions that enable you to apply read, write, and execute permission for three groups of users: the owner, the group, and all other users. The initial permissions that you see in the Get Info window of Mac OS X are POSIX permissions.

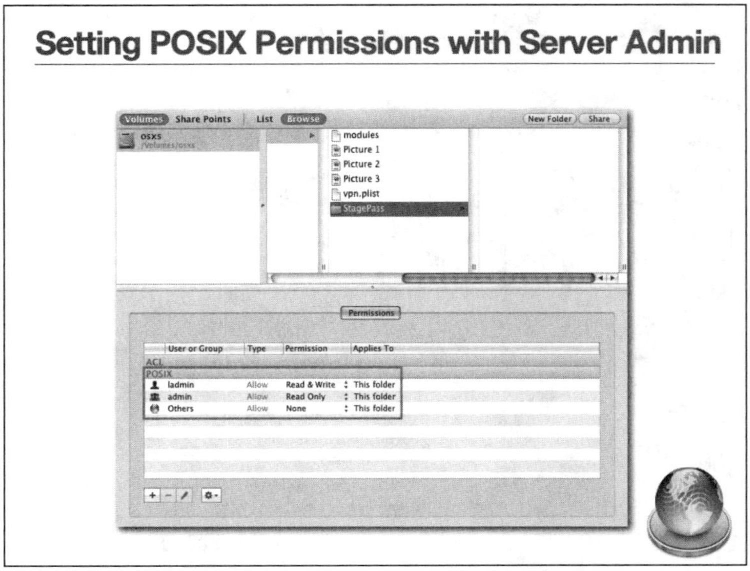


Server Admin is used to set POSIX permissions on Mac OS X Server. While you can use the Get Info window, it is advisable to only use Server Admin for setting ownership and permissions on Mac OS X Server.

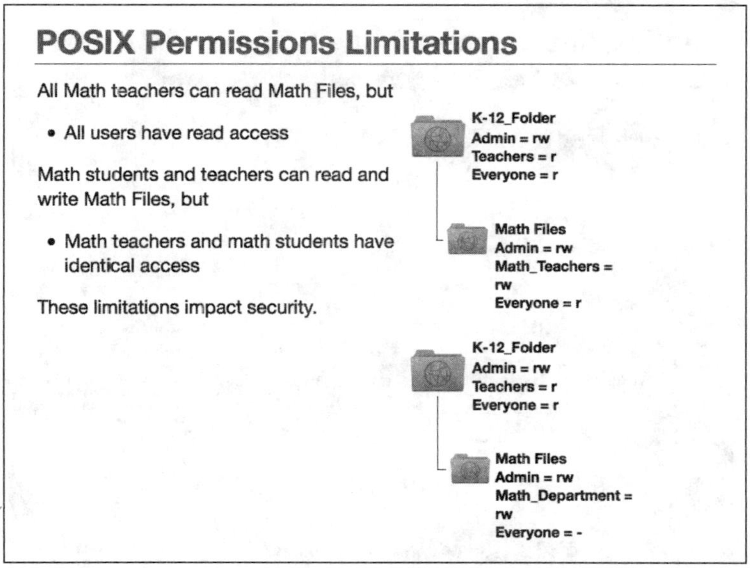


POSIX permissions have certain limitations, such as only allowing permissions for the owner of the folder (referred to as the user), the group associated with the file, and everyone else (called other). Also, permissions can be set only for Read Only, Read/Write, Write Only, and No Access.

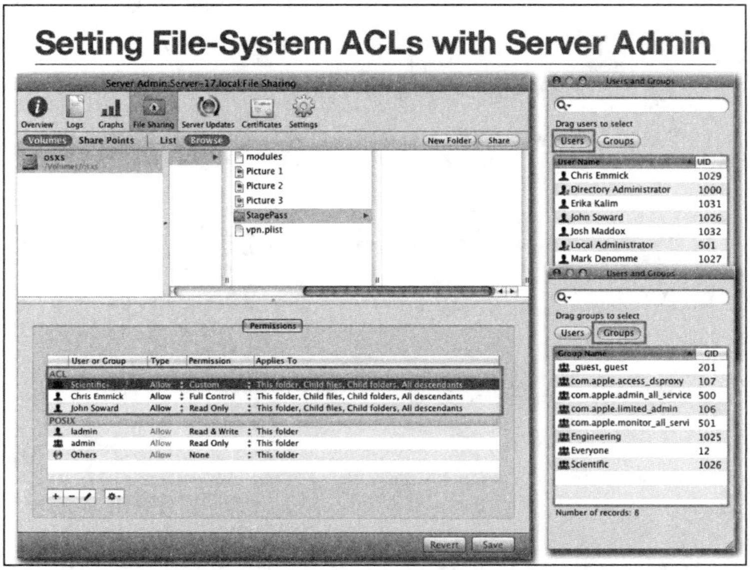


File system access controls permit a wide range of access similar to that of Windows systems. With file system access controls, administrators can expand the options for accessing share points well beyond POSIX permissions.

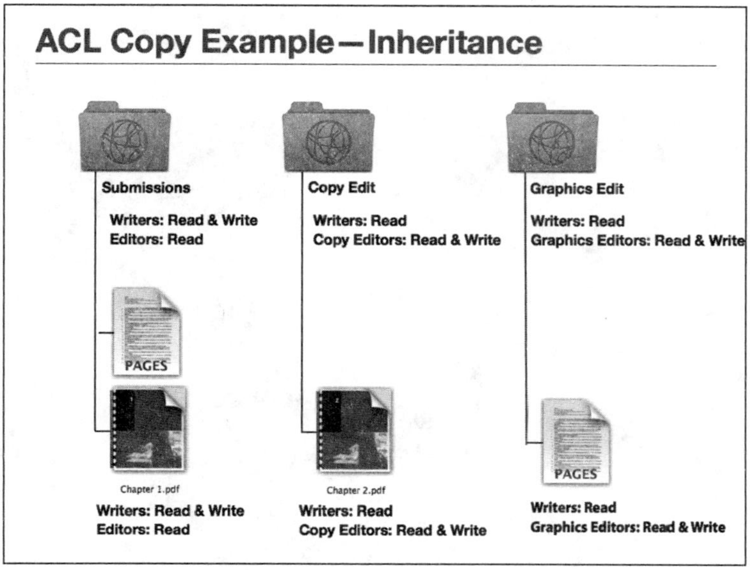


Inheritance with ACLs is fairly straightforward. A folder that has more than one group associated with that folder allows access on that folder to be inherited down through subfolders.

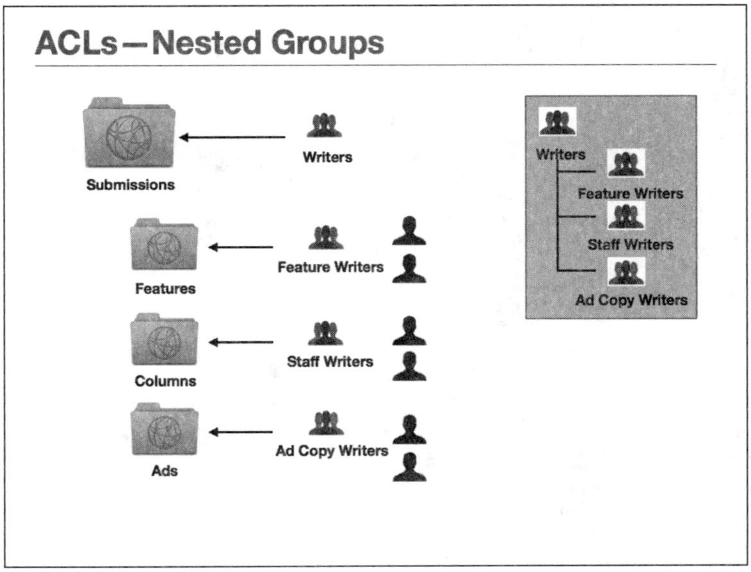


Nested groups allow administrators to set permissions at a higher level, thus reducing the complexity of the overall permissions. However, if a greater granularity is required, it can be obtained by restricting some of the nested groups.

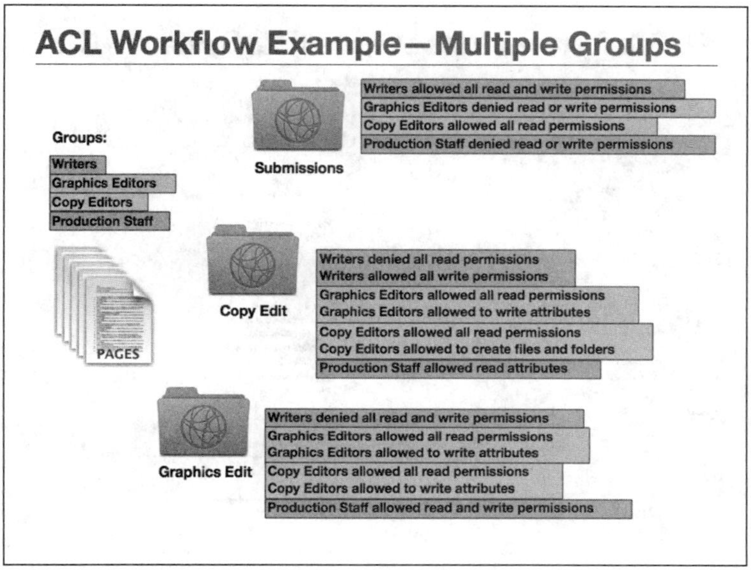


This slide illustrates possible complex scenarios when using file system access controls. Read each level of access carefully and examine how that access will affect the workflow.

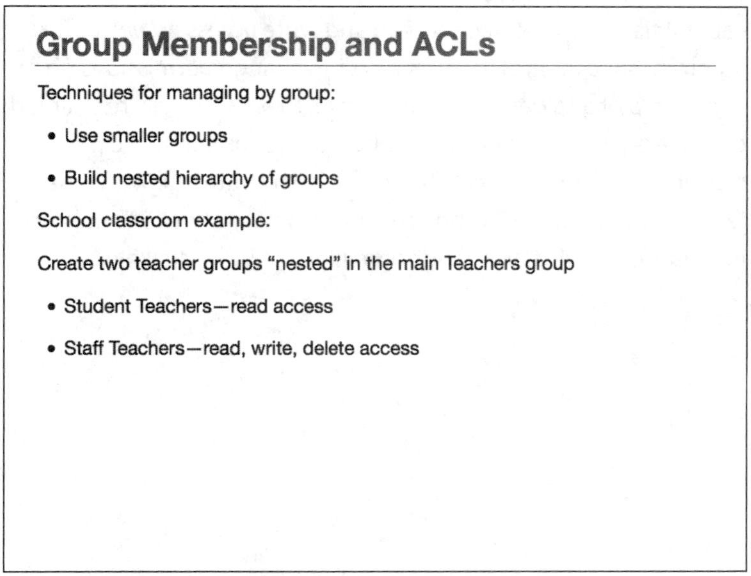


Management of groups, rather than users is usually more effective.

**POSIX Permissions Versus File-System ACLs**

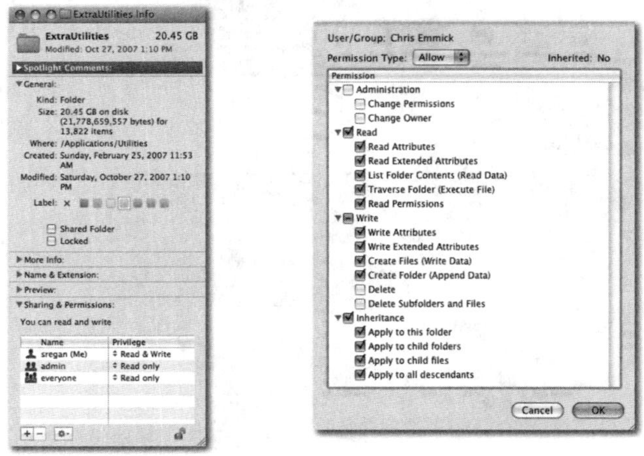


ACLs provide you the ability to set a finer grain of control over access settings that are compatible with the Windows environment. Seventeen additional settings can be made on a folder (or share point) from inside Server Admin. This allows a richer set of capabilities to be defined for read and write access as well as for administrative control (such as who can change permissions on or ownership of a folder). In Server Admin, these settings are enabled on folders, not individual files, although files obtain these permissions through inheritance. This folder-level control allows a finer level of management, without having to worry about administering permissions for thousands or millions of individual files.

## File-System ACLs—How They Work

Access Control Entry (ACE)—bound to a specific file-system location:

- Enabled for a group or users
- Based on UUIDs
- Allow or deny
  - Example—john allow delete
- Access Control List (ACL)—a group of ACEs (Access Control Entries)

Order of processing:

- First match in list determines access
- If match found, ACLs override POSIX permissions

When you use Server Admin to define ACLs, you are creating individual access control list entries (ACEs). These entries and lists are specific to a file-system location and are set on container objects—either share points or folders.

## Access Control—First Match Allow Example

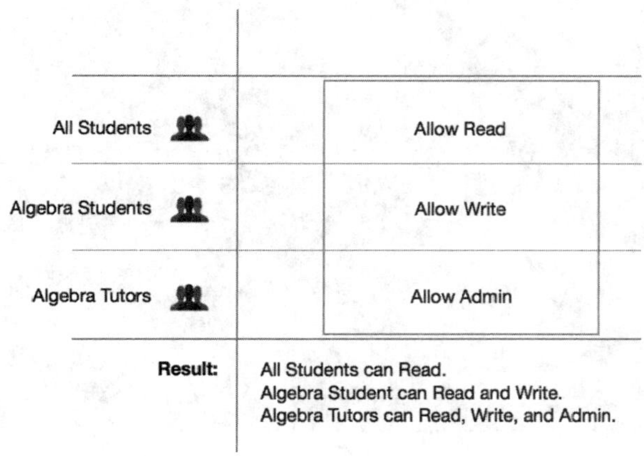


Allow matches are cumulative for all matches that apply to a user, whether from user or group matches.

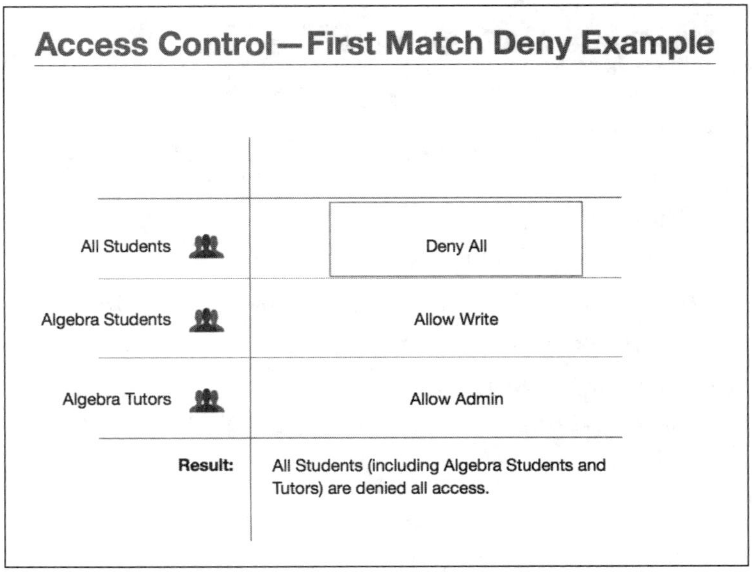


Deny matches apply on the first match and will override all other access controls below the deny match on the folder for the specified group.

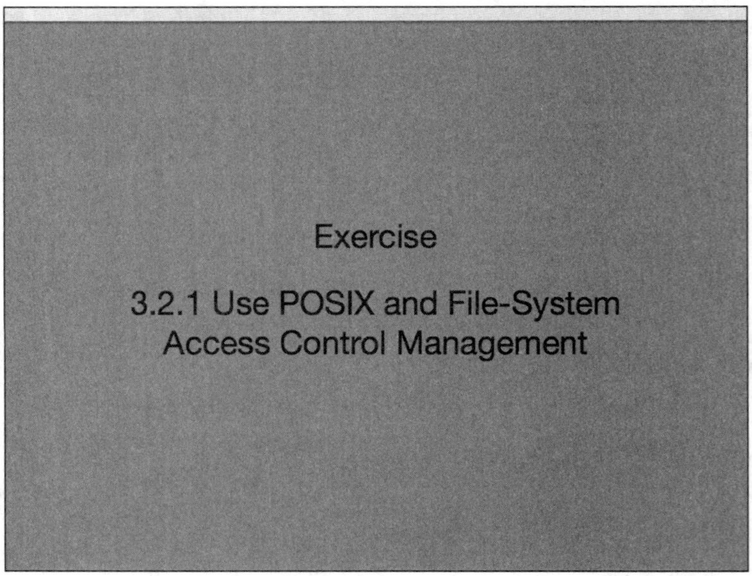

## Exercise 3.2.1

# Use POSIX and File-System Access Control Management

## Objective

In this exercise you'll be creating a folder hierarchy and a means of controlling user and group access to those folders. Using only file system access control lists (ACLs), you will follow the path of an example project from development to release. You'll discover that access to a file is determined by where the file is located in the system, rather than who created or "owns" the specific file.

> **Note** Changes in Workgroup Manager only take effect when you save them. It is good practice to frequently save changes.

## Summary

To properly configure your server, you'll need to know about the intended workflow of your users. PretendCo has four main groups: Engineering, Marketing, Projects, and Contractors. Each group needs different access to files at different times during the flow of a project.

## Creating the Folder Structure

In this exercise, the folder structure is project-based, not department-based. As a document meets a particular milestone, it will be moved from one location to another. You'll create project folders and assign ACLs for those folders to control workflow. This may be different from the way you managed documents with POSIX permissions.

The first step is to create a project folder hierarchy. You can create the folders in the Finder, but you can also use Server Admin to create the folders. Server Admin allows you to create folders on your server remotely.

1 On your Mac OS X computer, open Server Admin, and connect to your server.

2 Click the File Sharing icon in Server Admin's toolbar, and then click the Browse button.

This view allows you to navigate volumes and set permissions on folders not contained in a share point.

3 In the left column, select the Server HD volume.

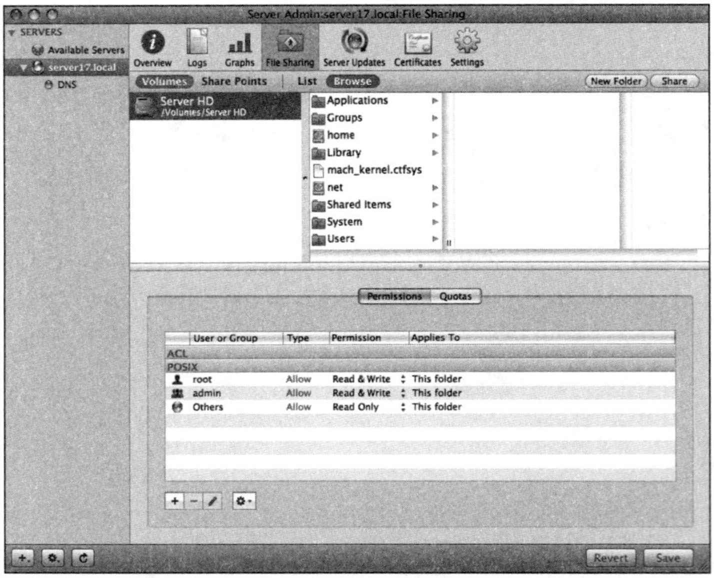


In this example, the name of the volume is Server HD.

The permissions panel shows that at the moment, only POSIX permissions have been set.

4 Select Shared Items in the second column.

5 Click the New Folder button in the top-right corner of the window.

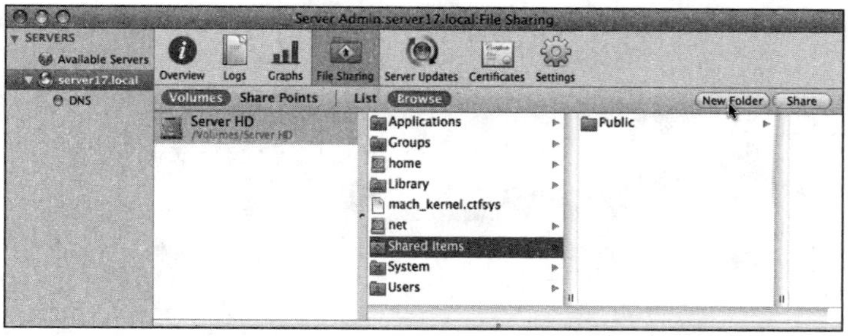


This command creates a new folder within the Shared Items folder.

If the New Folder button is grayed out, make sure you have at least one service configured under your server's entry in Server Admin. You should have DNS configured and running from Chapter 2.

6 Enter `Project Lion` in the Name field.

This folder will be used for the development projects.

7 Click Create then click Save.

8 Select the Project Lion folder in the list. Inside the new folder create three subfolders: (Note: You should click back on the Project Lion folder before creating each folder to ensure they are created inside the Project Lion folder, and not nested inside each other.)

- Development
- Pre-Release
- Release

9 Click the Share button to share the Project Lion folder and its contents. Click Save.

This option turns the Project Lion folder into a share point that can be mounted by your users.

10 Click the Share Points button to view all the share points, including your Project Lion folder.

11 Select the Project Lion folder in the share points list to confirm all the subfolders.

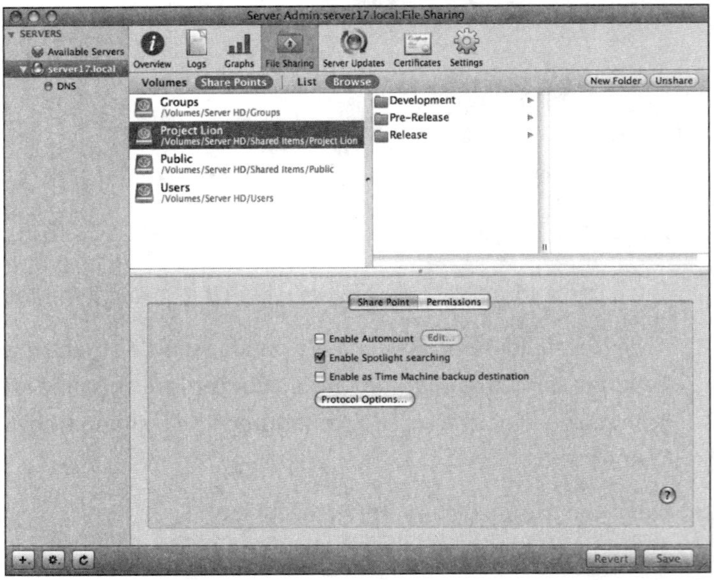


*Question 3* *What other folders are set up as shared folders on Mac OS X Server?*

## Setting Ownership and Permissions for the Development Folders

You've created the folder structure, and now you need to assign ownership and permissions. You'll assign the ownership of each folder to groups.

1 Ensure the File Sharing button is selected in the toolbar of Server Admin.

2 Click the Share Points button and the Browse button, if not already selected.

3 Select the Development folder from the list.

4 Verify the initial POSIX access settings:

- Owner—`ladmin`—Read & Write
- Group—`admin`—Read & Write
- Others—Others—Read Only.

The Development folder will be left with POSIX permissions for the first phase of the exercise to illustrate the power of using ACLs.

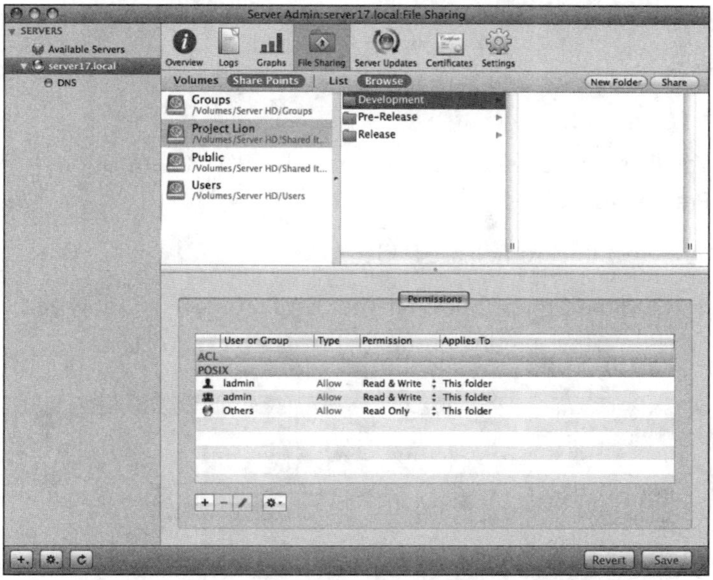


5 Click the Add (+) button near the bottom of the window to open the Users & Groups window.

You can drag users and groups to the Permissions pane to change permissions.

6 Set the Owner for the Development folder to `john`.

7 Set the Owner permissions for the Development folder to Read & Write.

8 Set the Group for the Development folder to Engineering (short name of the Engineering group is engr).

9 Set the Group permissions for the Development folder to Read & Write

10 Set the Others permissions for the Development folder to None.

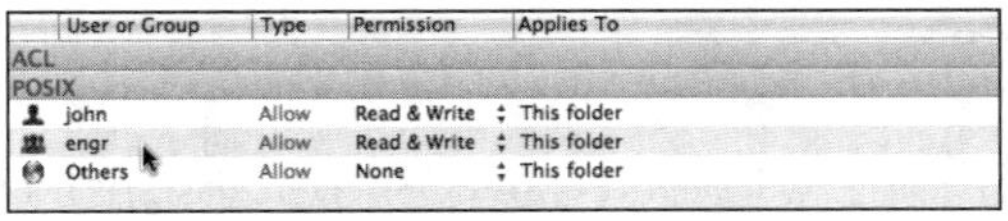


11 Click Save.

## Setting the Access Control for the Pre-Release Folder

You'll use an access control list instead of POSIX permissions for the Pre-Release folder.

1 Select the Pre-Release folder.

2 Click the Groups button in the Users & Groups window and drag the Marketing group to the Access Control List.

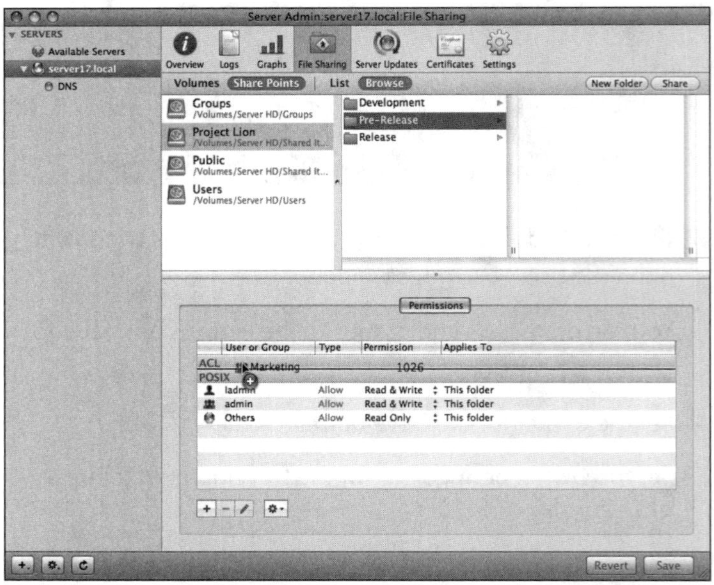


A new ACL entry is created.

3 Select the Marketing entry in the Access Control List.

4 Select Full Control from the Permission column.

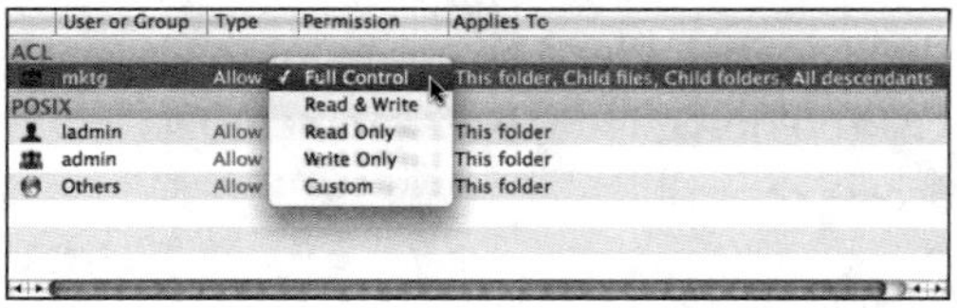


5 Drag the Engineering group to the Access Control List.

6 Select the Engineering group in the Access Control List and select Custom from the Permission column.

7 In the window that appears, configure permissions to allow read and write access for the Engineering group, but not allow the group to delete files or folders.

8 Do not change the configuration for inheritance.

You've allowed the Engineering group to edit items, but members of the group will not be able to remove them.

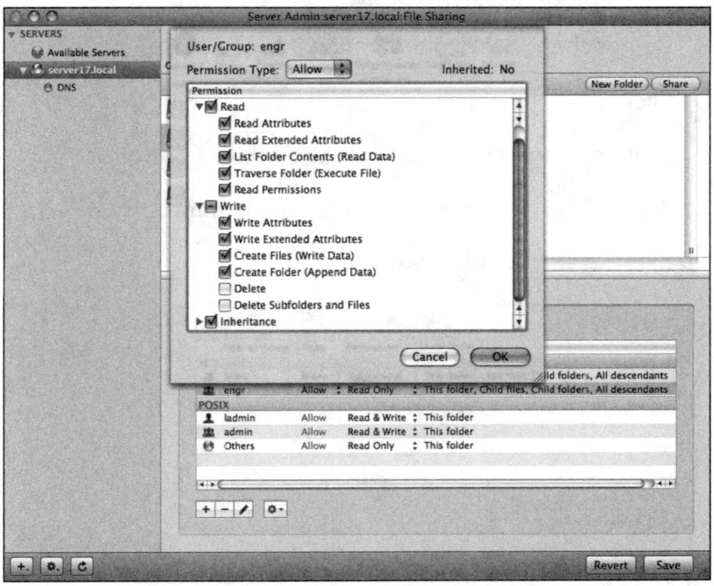


9 Click OK, and click Save.

## Setting the Access and Permissions for the Release Folder

Just as you did for the Pre-Release folder, you need to set the access controls for the Release folder. The group for the Release folder will be Projects. You don't need to assign members in that group to establish access control.

1. Select the Release folder.
2. Click the Groups button in the drawer, and drag the Projects group to the Access Control List.
3. Select the Projects entry in the Access Control List and give the Projects group Full Control.
4. Drag the Marketing group to the Access Control List.
5. Select the Marketing group in the Access Control List and select Custom from the Permission column.
6. In the window that appears, configure permissions to allow read and write access for the group, but not allow the group to delete files or folders.
7. Do not change the configuration for inheritance.
8. Click OK.
9. Drag the Engineering group to the Access Control List.
10. Select Read Only from the Permission column.
11. Click Save.

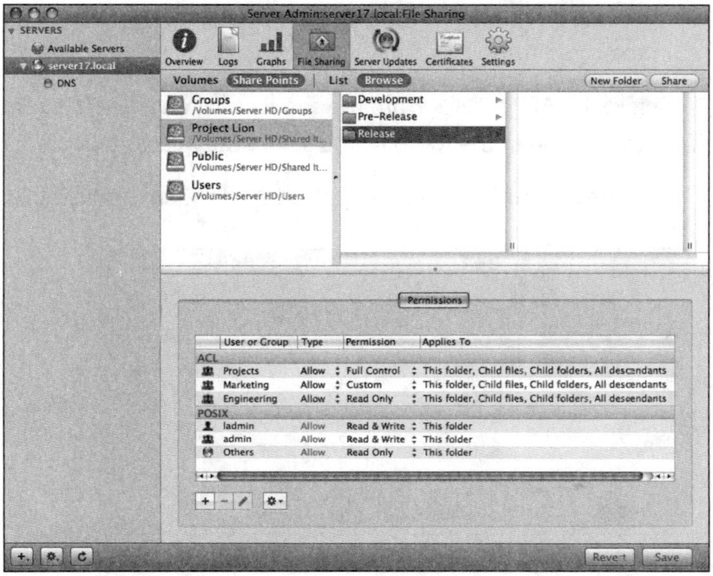


## Creating New Users

You've created the folder structure. Now, you'll create additional users for this workflow using Workgroup Manager.

- Name: `Sandy Shores`
- Short name: `sshores`
- Password: `sshores`
- Group: `Projects`
- Name: `Elizabeth Town`
- Short Name: `etown`
- Password: `etown`
- Group: `Contractors`

## Watching the Workflow

You've now configured the server with the proper project folders and appropriate users and groups. You'll create a document and watch the access during a normal workflow.

1 In Server Admin, enable the AFP service using the Settings icon in the toolbar.

2 Select the AFP service from the services list on the left, click the Settings icon in the toolbar, and select the Access tab.

3 Change the Authentication method to Standard and click Save.

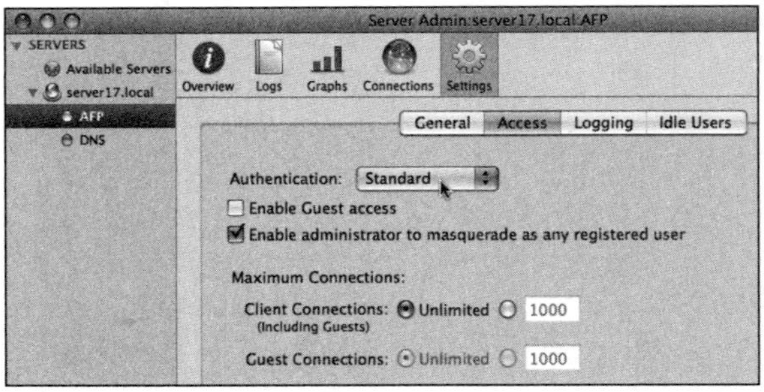


4 Start the AFP service.

5 In the Finder on the Mac OS X computer, select "Connect to Server" from the Go menu and enter `server`*n*`.local` in the dialog.

6 Authenticate as john with john's password.

7 Select the Project Lion share point.

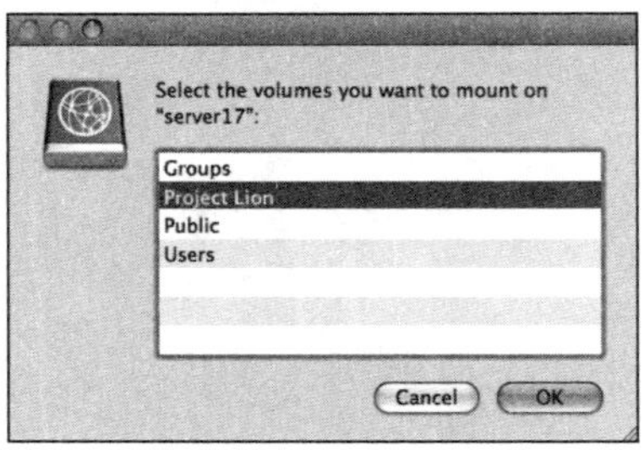


8 On your desktop, create two text files with the TextEdit application: One named Engineering Spec, and one named First Source. These files do not need to contain any text.

9 Copy the files into the Development folder.

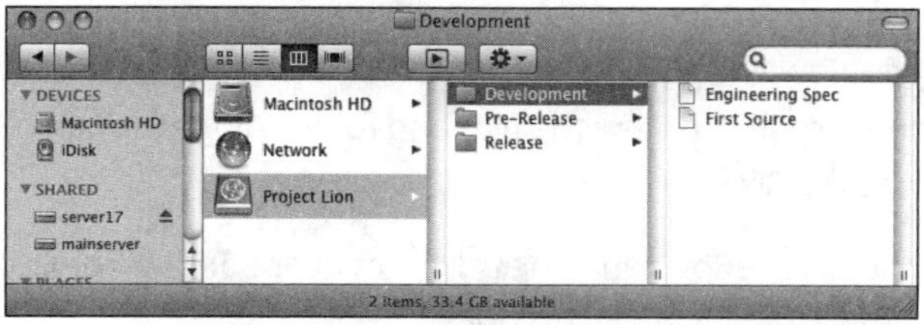


John Signal has Full Access to the Development folder.

10 Create a subfolder inside Development called Code, and move the First Source file into the new folder.

11 Option-drag the Code folder from Development to Pre-Release.

For our example, dragging the Code folder to the Pre-Release folder simulates the completion of a milestone, the end of a cycle, or specific time period.

12 Disconnect as John Signal and connect as LeRoy Venison. Mount the Project Lion share point.

13 Attempt to view the permissions on the files in the Development folder.

As a member of the Marketing group, LeRoy Venison does not currently have access to the Development folder. Because there are no ACLs for the Development folder and LeRoy Venison isn't a member of the Engineering group, he cannot see the files in the Development folder.

14 View the files in the Pre-Release folder.

15 Create a new folder in Pre-Release called Reviewed.

16 Edit the file First Source text file (located in the Code folder) by adding some text to the content of the file.

17 Use the Save As command to save the file in the Reviewed folder. Use the same name for the new version of the text file, First Source.

18 Move the Reviewed folder from the Pre-Release to the Release folder.

   This action indicates a project is ready for production. The LeRoy Venison account can view the files and folders once they are moved to the Release folder.

19 Disconnect as LeRoy Venison and connect as Sandy Shores. Mount the Project Lion share point.

20 Attempt to view the documents in the Development, Pre-Release, and Release folders.

21 Create a new folder inside the Release folder named Ready, and copy (option-drag) the file First Source (from the Reviewed folder) into it.

   The other groups should still have read access to the Ready folder.

22 Disconnect as Sandy.

## Adding Groups to the Access Path

You've configured access to the program folders, and viewed how the access changes when a document or folder is moved from one container to another. You'll now add groups to groups and see how that impacts the access.

1 Connect back to the Project Lion share point as the contractor Elizabeth Town.

2 Verify that you can read the data in the Pre-Release and Release folders.

3 Disconnect as Elizabeth Town.

4 Select the File Sharing icon from the toolbar in Server Admin.

5 Click the Browse button and navigate to the Development folder.

6 Click the Add (+) button in the Permissions pane to display the Users and Groups window.

7 Click the Groups button in the Users & Groups drawer.

8 Drag the Engineering group to the Access Control List and select Full Control from the Permission column.

You've added ACLs to the Development folder. You'll now give the Contractors group access to the Development folder.

9 Drag the Contractors group to the Access Control List.

10 Select the Contractors group in the Access Control List and select Custom from the Permission column.

11 In the window that appears, configure permissions to allow read and write access for the Contractors group, but not allow the group to delete files or folders.

12 Do not change the configuration for inheritance.

13 Click OK, and click Save.

You've given the Contractors group access to the Development folder. The Marketing and Projects groups still do not have access. You could have just added the Contractor group to the Engineering group but this would have given the Contractors group more access than you desired. You'll look at that scenario next.

## Adding Deny Type Access

You just configured access to the Development folder for the Contractors group. An easier way to do that would have been to add the Contractors group to the Engineering group once you set the Development ACLs. That action would have given additional access. With Deny you can still limit users and groups.

1. Open Workgroup Manager and connect to your server.
2. Click Accounts, and then click the Groups tab.
3. Add the Contractors group to the Engineering group.
4. Click Save.
5. In Server Admin, click File Sharing and Navigate to the Pre-Release folder.
6. If the Users and Groups window is not open, click the Add (+) button.
7. Click the Groups button in the Users & Groups drawer.
8. Drag the Contractors group into the ACL pane, positioning it above the Engineering ACL entry.
9. Select the Contractors group, and choose Deny from the Type column and Full Control from the Permissions column.
10. Click Save.

    The Deny access for the Contractors group is enforced before other access is granted as part of the Engineering group.

    For this exercise do not change the ACLs on the Release folder. Take some time to log in as various users and notice how your access changes. The Contractors group was denied access to the Pre-Release folder but picked up Engineering access to documents in the Release folder.

# Service Access Controls 3.3

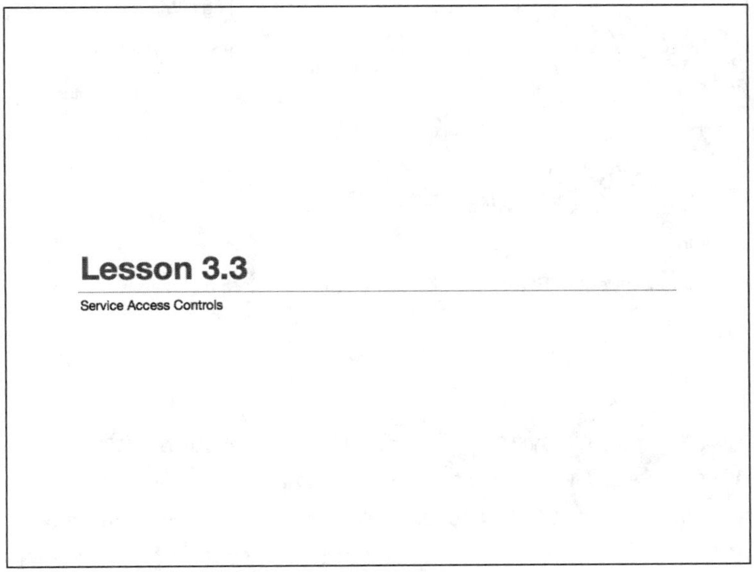


This lesson deals with service access control, which allows restricting the use of various services to specific users and/or groups.

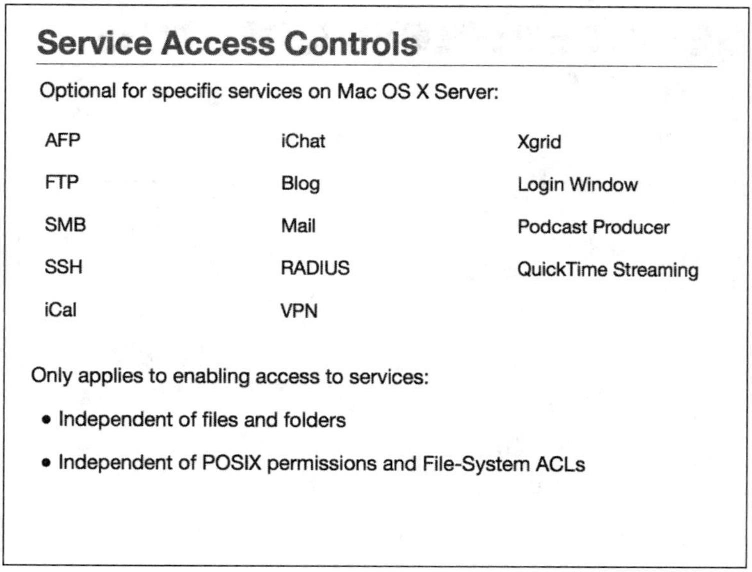


In addition to file-system ACLs, Mac OS X Server supports service ACLs, or SACLs, which are separate from file-system ACLs in implementation and purpose, despite the similar name. Service ACLs enable you to define who has access to specific services on Mac OS X Server. You could use SACLs to allow all users to log in via AFP, but restrict ssh (Secure Shell) connections to administrators.

## Enabling Service Access Controls

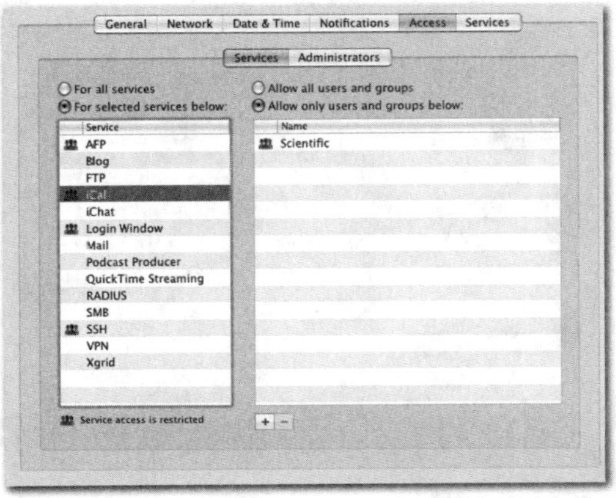


The interface for permitting SACLs is found in Server Admin under the Settings icon.

## Administrative Service Access Controls

Administrators can delegate service duties to others.

- Delegate full administration
- Delegate monitoring

| | | | |
|---|---|---|---|
| AFP | NAT | Print | Login Window |
| FTP | VPN | Web | Open Directory |
| SMB | RADIUS | WebObjects | Podcast Producer |
| NFS | iCal | Xgrid | QuickTime Streaming |
| SSH | iChat | Firewall | File Sharing |
| DNS | Blog | MySQL | Software Update |
| DHCP | Mail | NetBoot | |

You can use SACLs to control who has administrative access to services. For example, who can manage the service, and who can monitor the service.

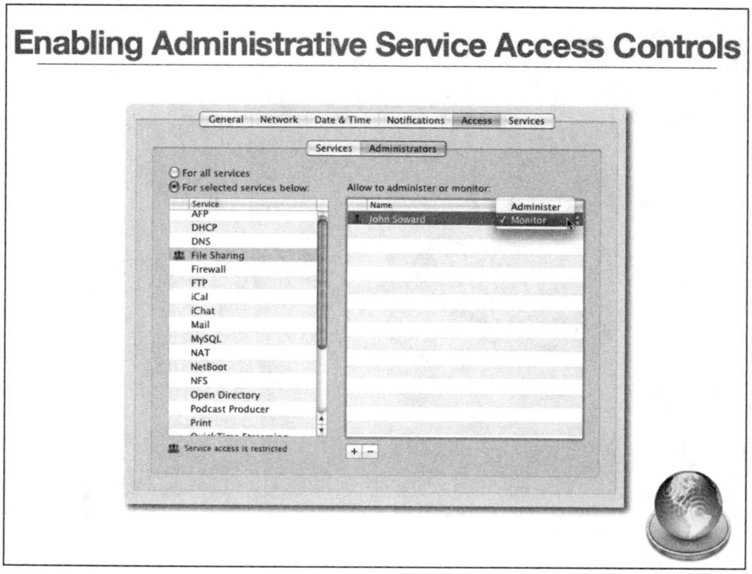


Take care when delegating access to manage services. Monitoring services can be done by a separate user.

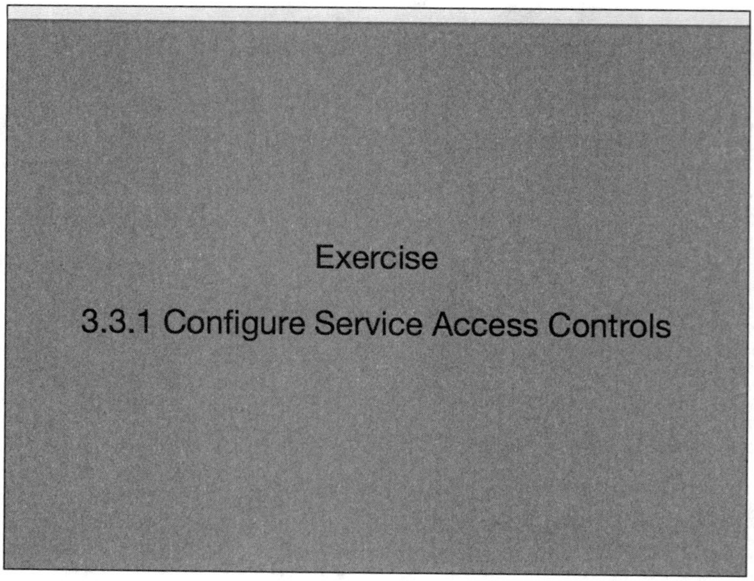

## Exercise 3.3.1

# Configure Service Access Controls

## Objective

To better secure a Mac OS X Server, access controls can be placed on services, just as they were placed on share points. For example, you may want just a certain group of users to have access to share points over SMB, and a small group of users to have access to the server via ssh.

## Summary

Administrators of Mac OS X Server may want to delegate control of services to other administrators and secure services to certain groups, helping to ensure share points and other access is limited to only those groups who have correct access.

1. If not open, launch Server Admin, authenticate as your local server administrator, and select your server from the list on the left.
2. Click the Settings icon, and then choose the Access tab.

   You'll be restricting AFP access to the Employees group, so anyone outside the Employees group will not be able to access the share points over AFP.
3. Click the Services tab, select the option "For selected services below," and select AFP from the list.
4. Select the "Allow only users and groups below."

> **Warning!** If you were to click save now, no one would be able to access your server via AFP because you have not defined any user or group yet.

5 Click the Add (+) button, select the Employees group from the list, and drag it into the field.

6 Click Save.

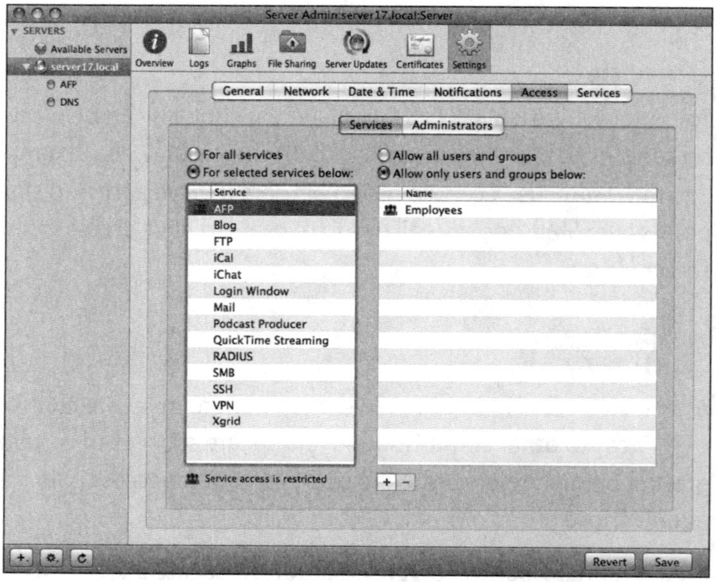

7 Repeat steps 3-6 for the Login Window service but only allow the user ladmin.

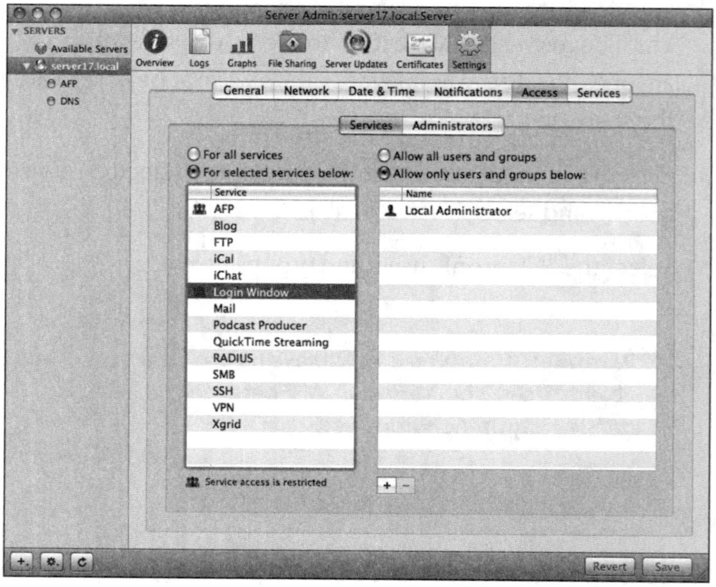

8 From your Mac OS X computer, attempt to use Connect to Server to connect to your server, using server*n*.local as the address as the following people:

- `leroy`
- `ladmin`
- `franklin`

***Question 4*** *Who can connect, and who cannot connect?*

_______________________________________________

_______________________________________________

_______________________________________________

_______________________________________________

9 Using Screen Sharing, connect to your server and log out if you were logged in. At the Login Window, attempt to log in as any user other than ladmin.

Your log in attempt will fail because ladmin is the only user permitted to use the Login Window.

10 Quit Screen Sharing, open Workgroup Manager, and connect to your server. Select LeRoy's account, and click the Groups tab.

11 Click the Show Inherited Groups button at the bottom of the window.

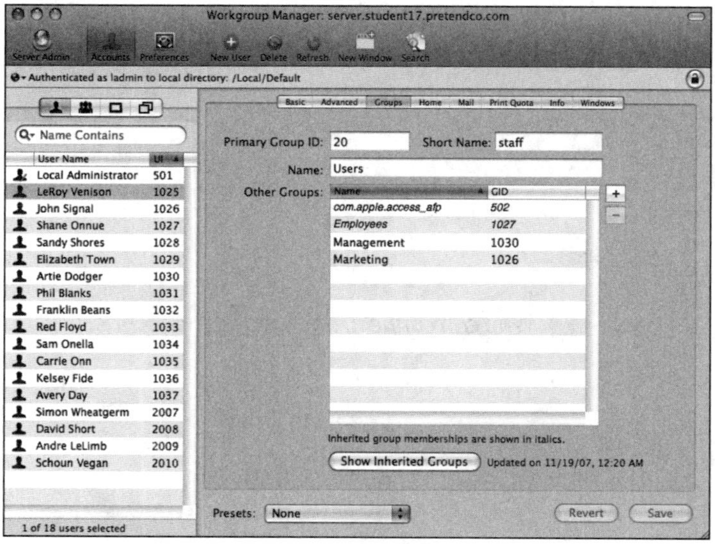


Notice that LeRoy has two inherited groups, the Employees group and another group, the com.apple.access_afp group, which dictates who has access to the server via AFP.

12 Select the ladmin account and review the inherited groups.

The ladmin account does not have any inherited groups, but you'll see the com.apple.access_loginwindow group, indicating that ladmin can access the Login Window.

13 Select the AFP service from the service access control list in Server Admin, and select the option "Allow all users and groups" to remove the restriction of the AFP service to just the Employees group.

14 Click Save.

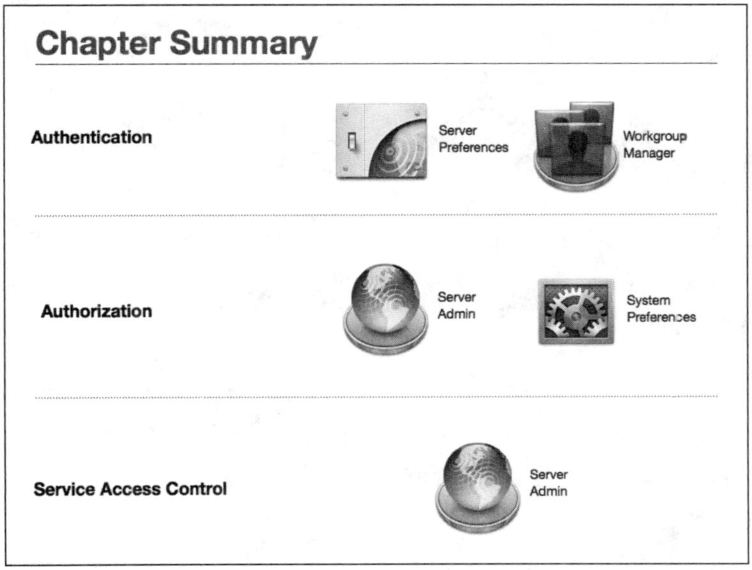
Chapter Summary
Authentication
Server Preferences
Workgroup Manager
Authorization
Server Admin
System Preferences
Service Access Control
Server Admin

Apple Certified

# 4

# Open Directory

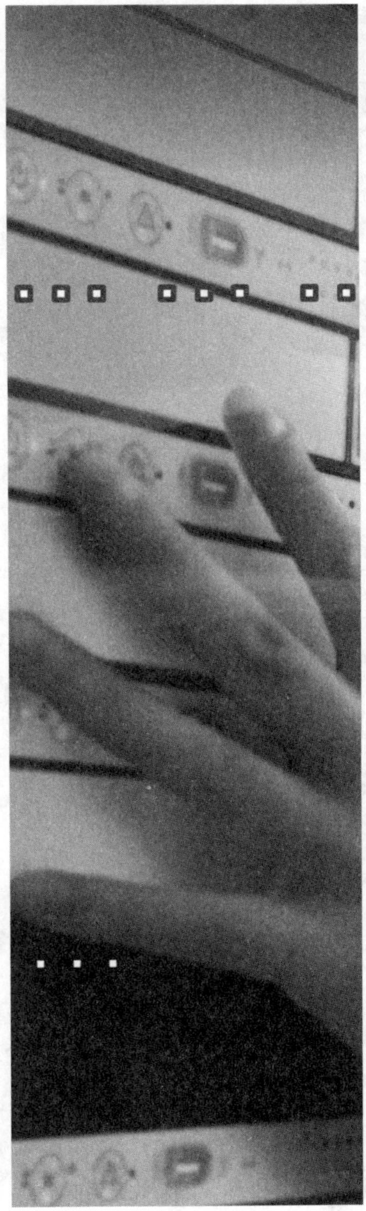


## 4.1 Concepts

**Exercise 4.1.1** Examine the Local Data Store

## 4.2 Configuration

**Exercise 4.2.1** Export Local Users and Groups

**Exercise 4.2.2** Create an Open Directory Master

**Exercise 4.2.3** Import Users and Groups into the Shared Directory

## 4.3 Authentication

**Exercise 4.3.1** Configure Password Policies

## 4.4 Archiving

**Exercise 4.4.1** Archive and Restore Open Directory Data

# 4.1 Concepts

This lesson deals with understanding how Directory Services can benefit an infrastructure of computers by providing features that are not available when local directory data is not shared.

Following are the slides for this chapter and any accompanying student and instructor notes. Following each lesson are its corresponding student exercises.

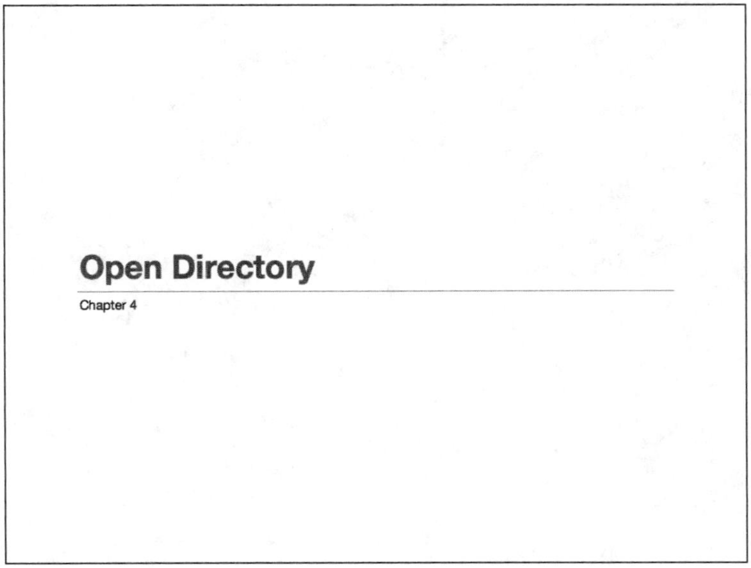


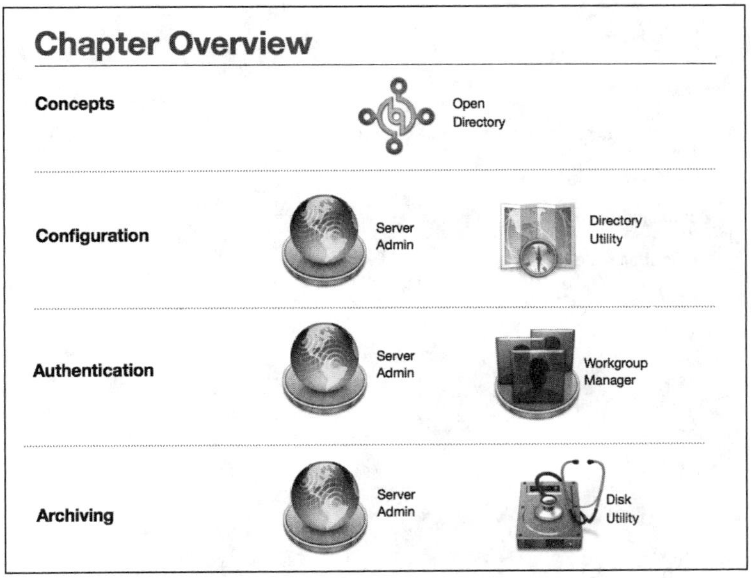


Open Directory on Mac OS X and Mac OS X Server can be divided into logical learning objectives: Concepts, Configuration, Authentication, and Archiving.

## Lesson 4.1

Concepts

## Directory Concepts

Issues:

- Multiple user accounts on multiple computers
- Lack of consistency

Solutions:

- Centralized data store
- Directory made available to all bound computers

Computers that are not connected to any centralized structure cannot be managed by any one source and are essentially owned by each system's local administrator on that particular computer.

## Advantages of Centralized Directories

User experience is standardized.

- Controlled experience based on user, group, or computer affiliation

Network resources can be managed effectively.

- Printers, servers, share points can be accessed easily and uniformly

User is not tied to a single system.

- User data stored remotely

Provides central authentication.

- Single sign-on for services such as Mail, iChat, iCal, File Sharing, VPN

When computers are connected to a central authentication source, several aspects of the computing experience can change. First, user authentication and authorization can be handled on a global level, not just on a computer-by-computer level. Second, management of all computers can take place at the discretion of the directory administrator. Third, resources can be managed more effectively.

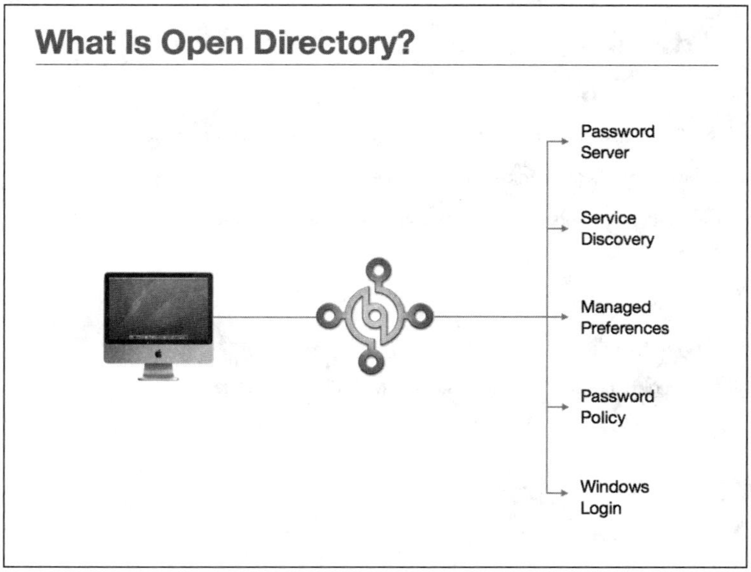


Open Directory is Apple's marketing name for several aspects of the user experience.

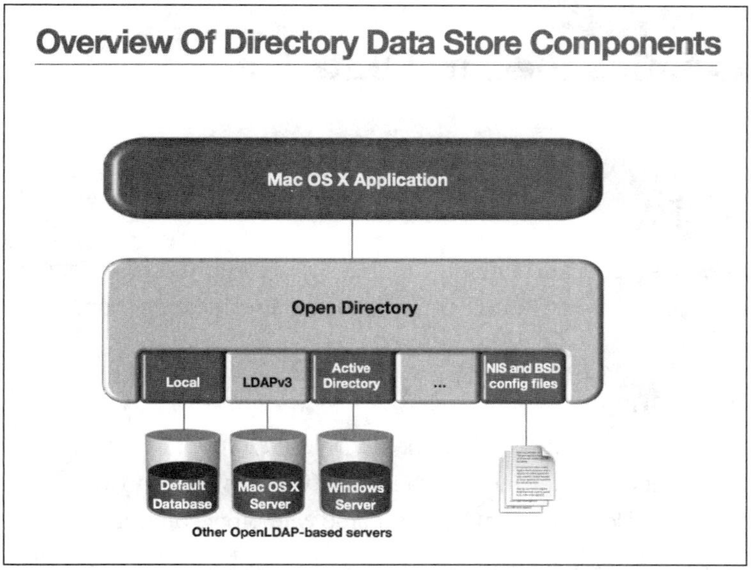


Basically, the structure of Open Directory allows it to look for information on other computers, which can be Mac OS X Servers or other types of directory servers. Once found, Open Directory attempts to correlate the appropriate information from that server to the Mac OS X computer. The information can be user-related, group-related, computer-related, or any combination.

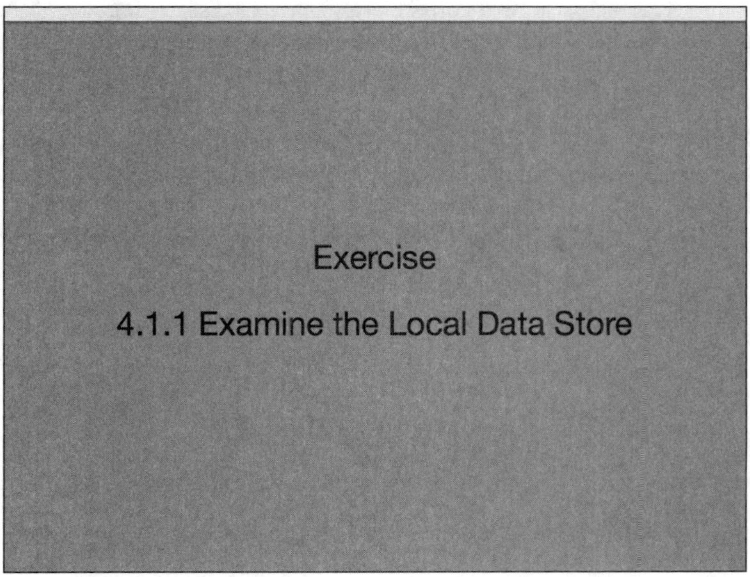

## Exercise 4.1.1

# Examine the Local Data Store

## Objective

View the local data store on your Mac OS X computer, and view the local data store on Mac OS X Server using an ssh connection.

## Summary

Local data stores contain information on users, groups, mount points, and other items that enhance the usability of Mac OS X and Mac OS X Server. This local data store is not shared with other computers.

1 On your Mac OS X computer, open the Terminal, and type `sudo -s` at the prompt.

   This command places you into a root shell. Notice the first time warning when using the `sudo` command.

   > **Warning!** Use of `sudo`, especially `sudo -s`, should be restricted and reserved for occasions when becoming root is a necessity. An incorrect letter can spell disaster for a volume, because UNIX does not have an undo function.

2 Enter your *cadmin* password, and press Return. Notice the shell changes to reflect you are now in effect the root user.

   You will now change directories so you can see your local data store.

3 Type the following on one line, and press Return:

   ```
   cd /private/var/db/dslocal/nodes/Default/
   ```

   You are now inside your local data store.

4 Type `ls -l` and press Return to view the directories inside your local data store.

***Question 1*** *What are the names of the local directories that have the potential to hold local directory data store information?*

5. Type `cd users/` and press Return to go to the users directory. Once inside that directory, type `ls -l` and press Return to view the contents.
6. You will see several user files.
7. Type `more cadmin.plist` and press Return to view the contents of the file. Use the Space bar to move down through the file one page at a time.
8. Notice that the cadmin user file contains parameters necessary for the user to work with Mac OS X.
9. Press Q when you reach the end of the file.
10. Type `exit` and press Return to escape out of your root shell.
11. Type `ssh ladmin@10.1.`*`n`*`.1` and press Return (where *n* is your student number).
12. Enter the password for ladmin when requested, and press Return.

    You are now connected to your Mac OS X Server.

13. Repeat steps 1-10 only changing step 7, where you will enter `ladmin` instead of `cadmin`, and look in the ladmin user file in step 8 instead of the cadmin file.

    You'll notice that you have more users in your Mac OS X Server's local data store. This is because you have added users throughout the Chapter 3, "Authentication, Authorization, and Access Control," exercises.

14. View the contents of the group directory if you like. If you are unsure as to how to navigate in the Terminal using the `cd` command, ask your instructor for guidance.
15. When finished, type `exit` and press Return to exit out of the root shell, then type `exit` and press Return again to exit the ssh connection to your Mac OS X Server.
16. Quit the Terminal application.

# 4.2 Configuration

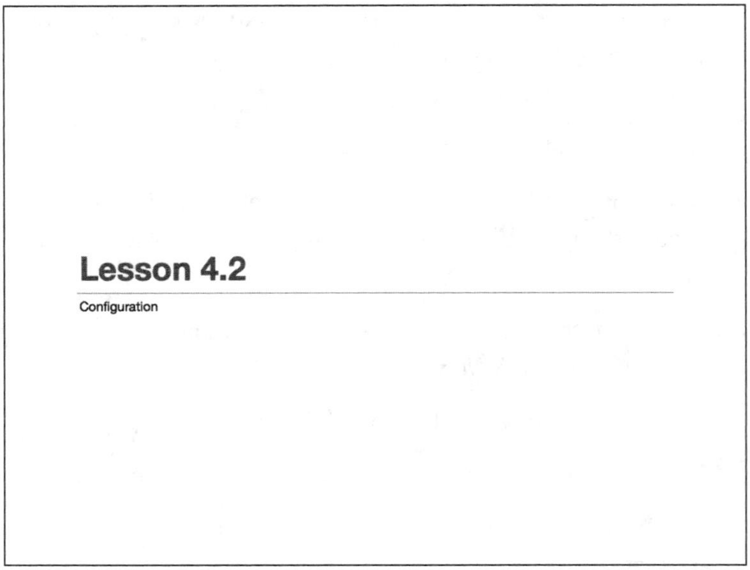


Explore the possible scenarios surrounding the Open Directory service on Mac OS X Server.

## Open Directory Roles

Standalone

Connected to directory system

Open Directory Master

Open Directory Replica

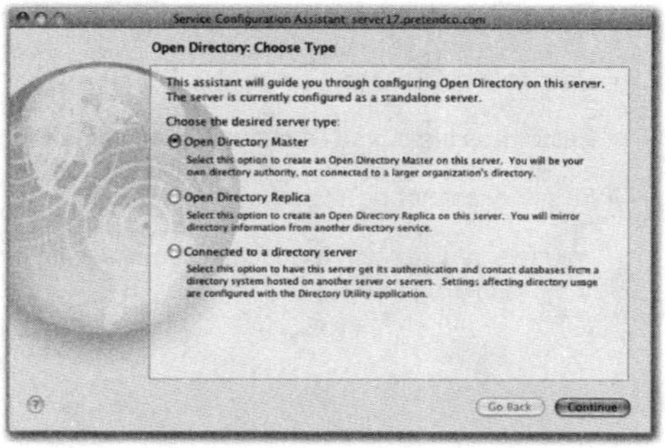


Server Admin launches Service Configuration Assistant to change roles.

There are four different roles that can be specified when using Mac OS X Server's Open Directory service. They are: Standalone server, Connected to another directory system, an Open Directory Master, or an Open Directory Replica.

## Standalone

Advanced configuration at setup:

- Option available to make standalone.

Local data store:

- User data store is identical to Mac OS X.
- Passwords are stored as shadow passwords with hashes.
- Directory cannot be shared.
    - Users can connect to the standalone server, but experience no single sign-on.

A Standalone server is just that, a Mac OS X Server that does not share its information with regard to users, groups, or other attributes. Users can connect to the Mac OS X Server and use most of its services, but the administrator lacks control over the local accounts on all the client computers. A standalone server keeps users and groups in the local database, similar to that of a Mac OS X computer. There is little difference with respect to directory services between a standalone Mac OS X Server and a Mac OS X computer.

## Standalone Window

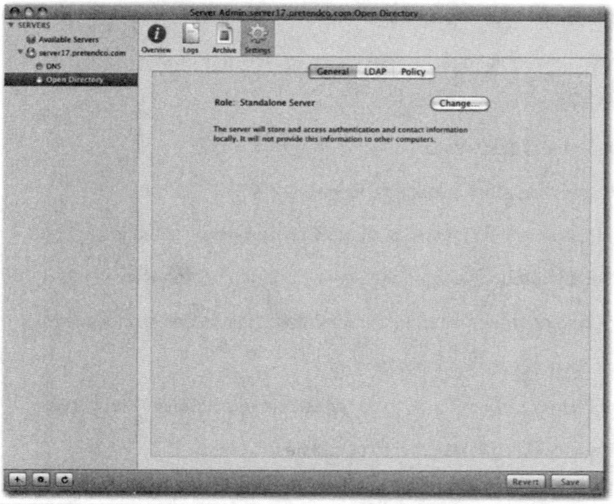


When Open Directory Services are enabled on a server set up with the Advanced configuration, the choice how the server was configured with regard to the directory structure in the Server Assistant is shown here. Recall the two choices were, Connected to a Directory System and Standalone.

## Connected to Directory System

Advanced configuration at setup:

- Option available to make Connected to Directory System.

Similar to Standalone:

- Single local data store:
  - User data store is identical to Mac OS X.
  - Passwords are stored as shadow passwords with hashes.
- User and group management stays on other directory server.
  - Directory trusts other server for authentication and authorization.
- The local directory cannot be shared.
- This role is an excellent choice for servers used primarily for services.
- Directory Utility is required to complete process.

When choosing Connected to a Directory System, administrators are not creating a secondary database to store user, group, and other information. Rather they are relying on another directory service to provide them with that information. Trust about authentication is given up to another directory service. This Mac OS X Server does not authenticate any users other than the local administrator and any other local users or groups.

## Connected to a Directory System

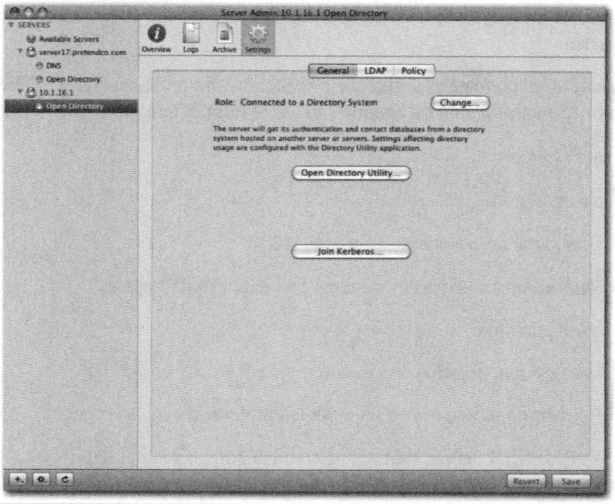


When choosing Connected to a Directory System, administrators must run the Directory Utility and "bind" their Mac OS X Server to another directory server, such as another Mac OS X Server, eDirectory, or Active Directory.

## Open Directory Master

Standard and Workgroup configurations create OD Master automatically during setup.

Advanced configuration at setup permits Standalone or Connected to Other Directory Server and can be changed to OD Master at later time.

Two data stores:

- Local data store
  - User data store is identical to Mac OS X.
  - Passwords are stored as shadow passwords with hashes.
- Shared data store
  - User data is stored in one location
  - Passwords stored in two different locations and synchronized.
    - Password Server, Kerberos database (for single sign on)

An Open Directory Master creates a secondary database that can be shared with other computers. This database can store more than just user, group, and computer information. The database is an LDAP version 3 database based on OpenLDAP. Along with the shared LDAP database, an Open Directory Master also provides two more authentication methods for the shared LDAP directory, Password Server and a Kerberos Key Distribution Center.

## Open Directory Master

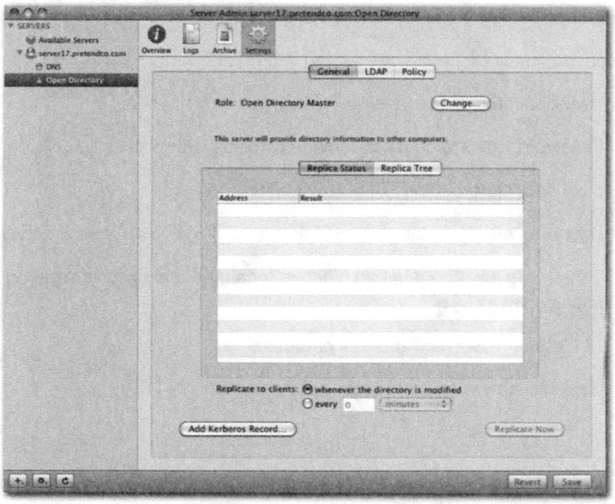


Once an Open Directory Master (OD Master or ODM) is created, the Open Directory Service window reflects the change and shows the status of the OD Master and any replicas of that OD Master.

## Open Directory Replica

Two data stores:

- Local data store:
  - User data store is identical to Mac OS X.
  - Passwords are stored as shadow passwords with hashes.
- Replica data store of Open Directory Master:
  - User data are now stored in two locations (Master and Replica servers).
  - Passwords are stored in two different locations and synchronized on each server.
    - Password Server, Kerberos database
  - Replicas can be nested—replicas of replicas.

Open Directory Replicas are essentially clones of the Open Directory Master. They clone the LDAP database, the Password Server database, and the Kerberos database. Client computers can be configured to authenticate against either the Open Directory Master or the Replicas, thus spreading the authentication load across several servers.

## Open Directory Replica

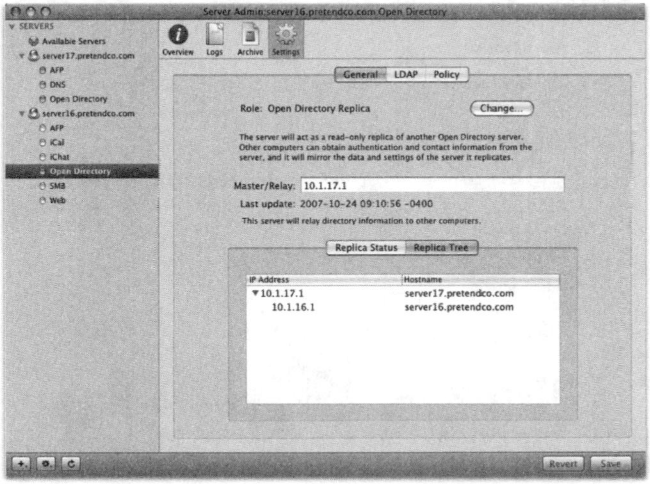


Open Directory Replicas are listed in the window of an Open Directory Master. Replicas of Replicas are listed there as well.

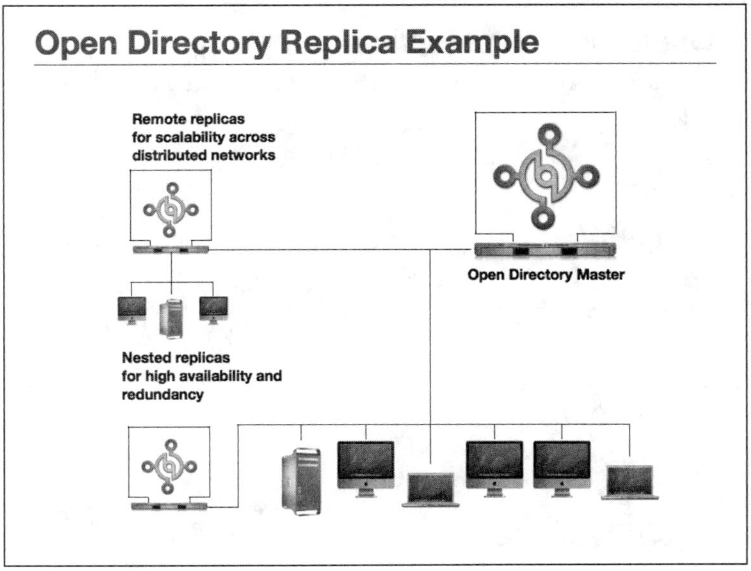


A possible scenario for deploying an Open Directory Master and Replica might include a school district that keeps an Open Directory Master at the school board office, with Replicas placed at each school. When students log in to their bound computers, their computers contact all replicas and the master and attempt to authenticate to the first responder. In this scenario, the local replicas in each school normally answer the requests of the clients in their respective school.

## Replica Limitations

Maximum number of replicas of an Open Directory Master

- 32

Maximum number of replicas of replicas

- 32

There are a certain number of replicas that can be used within a single Open Directory deployment, and the number of replicas include the replicas of replicas.

## Changing Open Directory Configuration

Server Admin launches Service Configuration Assistant to change roles.

- Step-by-step walkthrough process
- Server should resolve forward and reverse correctly prior to changing roles (DNS must be set up properly).

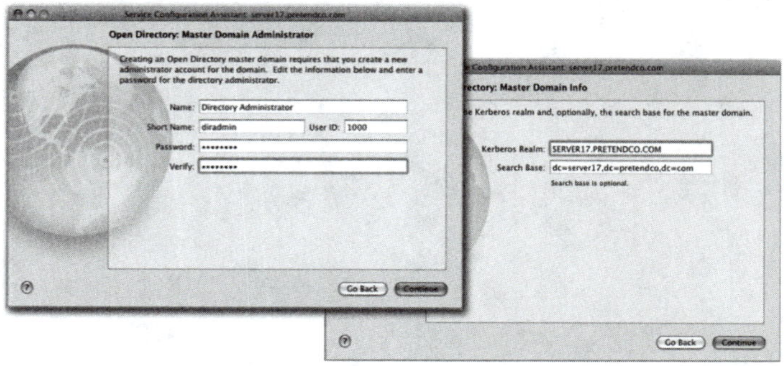


The Service Configuration Assistant is used to change the roles of the Open Directory Server. When creating an Open Directory Master, the important factor in most situations is that the Kerberos realm name and the LDAP search base match. In certain cases, administrators may wish to have these different, however, for basic Mac OS X Server Open Directory Master configuration, these should match. Anything else appear in these fields may cause a DNS error.

## Adding Shared Database Users

Similar to adding local users, except database is shared.

- Passwords are called Open Directory passwords, not Shadow Passwords.
- As with Local database, Workgroup Manager is used to manage users and groups.

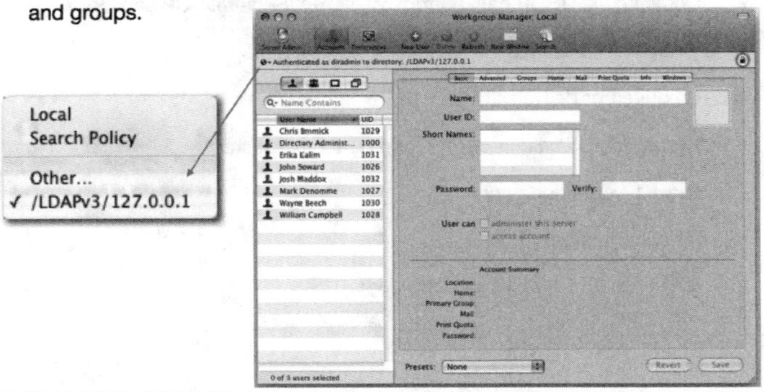


Workgroup Manager is used to add users to the newly created LDAP database in the same way users were added to the local database with one exception. LDAP users and LDAP administrators can be delegated to control various groups, thus restricting certain administrators to managing certain groups.

## Delivering Open Directory Location Data to Clients

Open Directory servers must be known by Mac OS X clients.

- Directory Utility
  - Manual setup
  - Obtained via DHCP packet from Mac OS X Server DHCP service
    - Option 95 in DHCP specification (RFC 2131)

Data is required or delivered.

- Fully qualified domain name of Open Directory Master
  - server17.pretendco.com
- LDAP search base
  - dc=server17,dc=pretendco,dc=com

Once an Open Directory Master has been created, clients must know about the server in order to use it for authentication. A few methods for telling the client about the ODM include manually entering the data into a Mac OS X computer or delivering the data along with the DHCP packet.

## DHCP Supplied LDAP Data Setup

Mac OS X Server DHCP Service

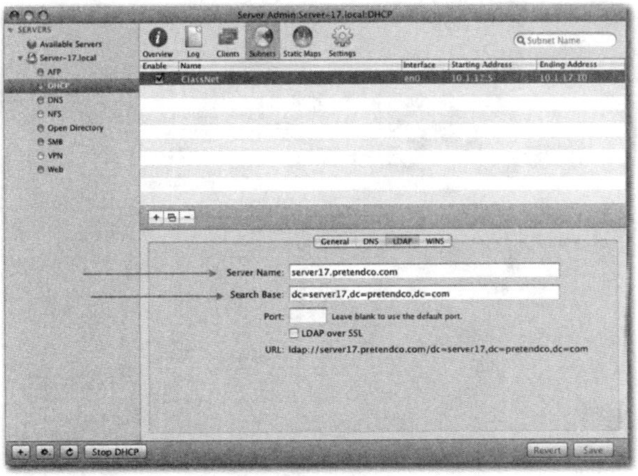


When setting up a DHCP server, the LDAP data that Mac OS X computers require can be entered into the appropriate fields within Server Admin.

## DHCP Supplied LDAP Data Delivery

Mac OS X Client

- Obtains IP information
- Obtains LDAP information
- Server displays in Directory Servers list

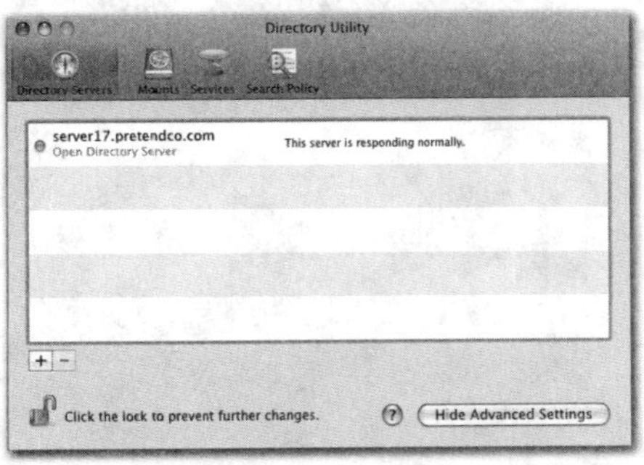


The Directory Utility is used to bind Mac OS X computers to servers providing directory services.

## Troubleshooting—Log Files

Server Admin Open Directory Service

- Several log files to view

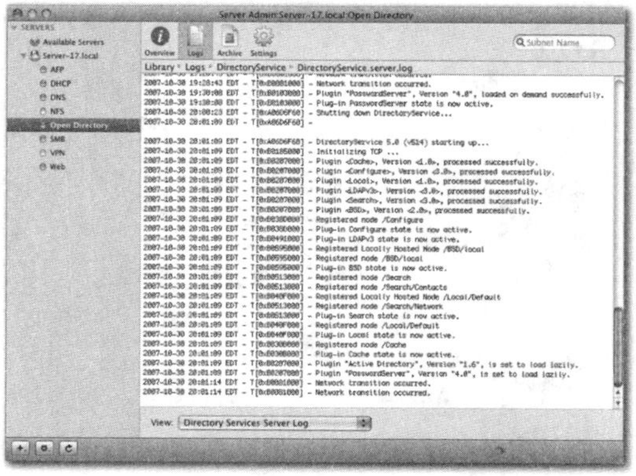

When using the Open Directory services to provide a variety of roles on Mac OS X Server, you can use the log files to examine events as they occur.

### Exercises

4.2.1 Export Local Users and Groups

4.2.2 Create an Open Directory Master

4.2.3 Import Users and Groups into the Shared Directory

## Exercise 4.2.1

# Export Local Users and Groups

## Objective

Learn to move users and groups from one server to another.

## Summary

You'll be selecting all the users except the local administrator and exporting them as a file. You'll do the same with the groups.

1 On your client computer, open Server Admin and use Screen Sharing to connect to your server.

2 Log in to your server as ladmin.

3 Open Workgroup Manager, and connect to your server.

4 Dismiss the dialog notifying you about working in a local directory.

5 Click the Accounts icon in the toolbar, and select the Users button.

6 Select all the users except the Local Administrator.

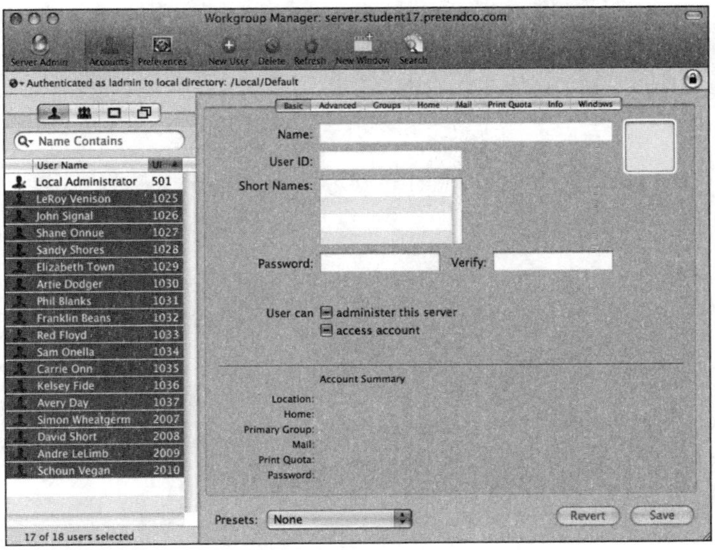

7 Choose Export from the Server menu, and save the file as `servern-users` to your Desktop (where *n* is your student number).

8 Click the Groups button, select all the groups except the _guest group, and export those to your Desktop in a file saved as `servern-groups` (where *n* is your student number).

You'll be importing these users and groups later into another directory.

9 With all the groups selected (except _guest), click the Delete icon in the toolbar. Confirm the deletion, and click OK to any error dialogs that appear.

10 Click the Users button, and repeat the process, deleting all users except the Local Administrator.

11 Quit Workgroup Manager by pressing Command-Q or choosing Quit under the Workgroup Manager menu. Do not click the red close button in the upper-left corner. Clicking the red close button will only close the window and leave Workgroup Manager running. Do not quit Screen Sharing.

## Exercise 4.2.2

# Create an Open Directory Master

### Objective

Demonstrate how to configure Mac OS X Server in the Open Directory Master role to provide shared directory data to other computers on the network.

### Summary

The first rule in creating an Open Directory Master is to ensure DNS is working properly and your server is responding as expected. You'll begin to create an Open Directory Master, discover that certain data does not appear the way you expect, fix the problem, and continue to create an Open Directory Master.

The Open Directory Master configuration uses several network services that are very sensitive to DNS and network configuration. Before you configure Mac OS X Server as Open Directory Master, it's important to verify network and DNS settings. Though Mac OS X Server can use several network interfaces and IP addresses at once, one IP address and DNS name must be designated as the primary address and name for your server. The primary IP address and DNS name should always be used when configuring Open Directory on your server, and when configuring other computers to connect to your Open Directory Master.

Many common real-world server issues can be traced to network or DNS configuration problems, so it's very important to verify proper network and DNS configuration before you begin configuring Open Directory.

Now you are ready to configure Open Directory to create a new shared directory and initialize authentication services for use by other computers on the network. In particular, three new network services will be running once Open Directory Master configuration is complete: an LDAP service to provide access to shared directory data, and two authentication services—Password Server and Kerberos. In the following steps, you'll configure your server as an Open Directory Master, and verify the success of the configuration.

1 On your Mac OS X computer, open Server Admin, and connect to your server.

2 Enable the Open Directory service so it appears in the services list.

  If you need to review how to enable the Open Directory service, refer to Chapter 1, "Installation and Configuration."

3 Select the Open Directory service, and click the Settings icon in the toolbar.

  You can see your server is a Standalone server, which is how you set it up in Server Assistant.

4 Click the Change button to launch the Service Configuration Assistant.

5 Select the Open Directory Master option from the list, and click Continue.

  You have two other options, to create an Open Directory Replica or to connect your server to another directory server.

6 On the Master Domain Administrator window, leave the defaults and enter a password of `diradmin` (the same as the Short Name), and click Continue.

This account will be the administrator of your secondary database. When finished, you'll have two administrators that do not know about each other, one administrator for each database.

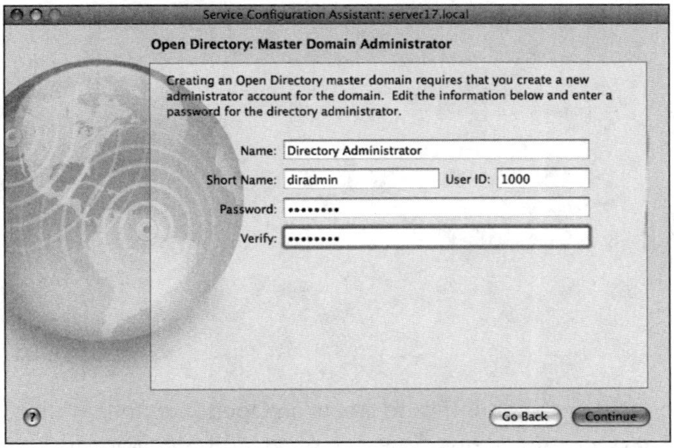


7 In the next dialog, do not click Continue. View your Kerberos Realm and your Search Base.

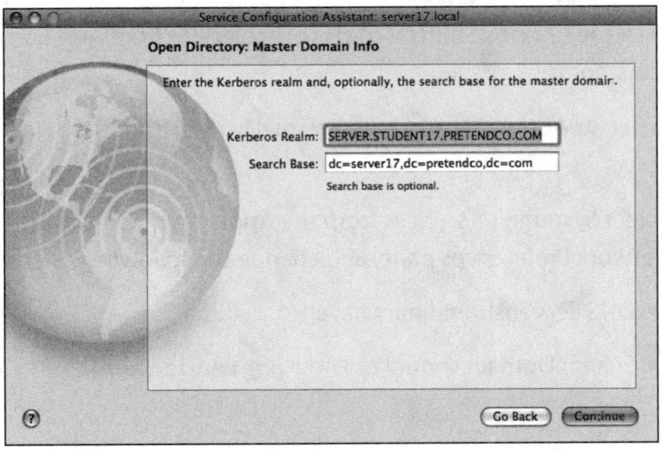


***Question 2*** *Do they match?*

***Question 3*** *Why or why not?*

If you were to continue and create an Open Directory Master, your server would not act as expected. Authentication and Authorization would break under most circumstances. You must go back and change your DNS to look at the instructor server to ensure the realm name and the search base are the same.

8 Click the red close button to close the Service Configuration Assistant.

9 In Server Admin, select Share Server's Screen from the Server menu.

10 Select System Preferences from the Apple menu, select the Network Preferences pane, and change the following:

- DNS Server should only have: `10.1.0.1`
- Search Domain should only be: `pretendco.com`

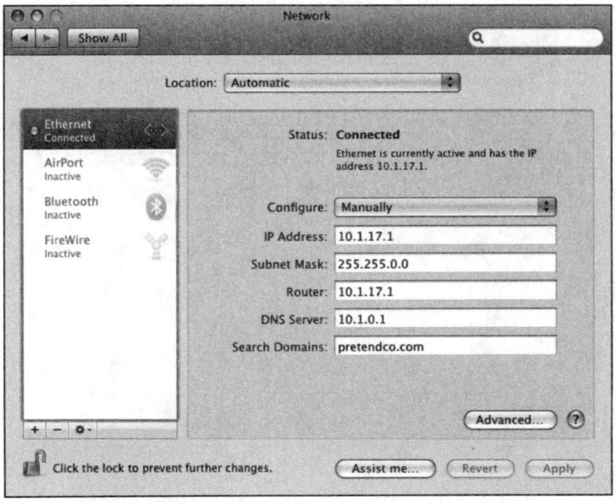


11 Apply the changes, close System Preferences, and close screen sharing.

12 Repeat the same changes to the Network preferences on your Mac OS X computer.

You have now told both your Mac OS X computer and your Mac OS X Server to look at the instructor's server for DNS resolution. Your DNS, although still running, is ignored.

13 In Server Admin, click the Change button under Open Directory to run the Service Configuration Assistant again.

14 Repeat steps 5–7, stopping to view your Kerberos Realm and Search Base again.

**Question 4** *Do they match?*

---

**Question 5** *Why or why not?*

---

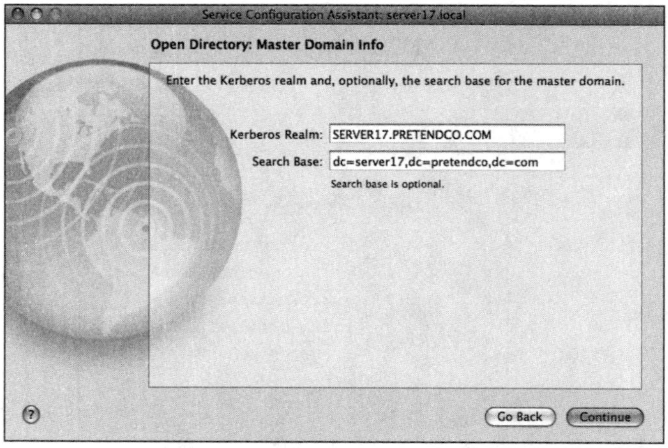


15 Click Continue, view the confirm settings screen, and click Continue again.

16 Click the Close button to close the Service Configuration Assistant. Your Mac OS X Server is now an Open Directory Master.

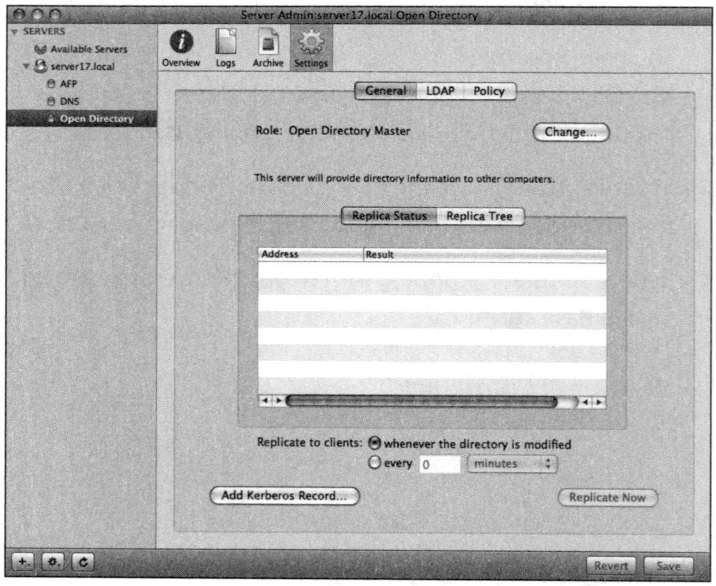


After configuring Mac OS X Server as Open Directory Master, verify that the configuration changes were successful. This verification can also be performed any time you suspect there may be problems with Open Directory services on your server.

17 In Server Admin, select the Overview icon of your server's Open Directory configuration in the toolbar.

18 Verify that LDAP Server, Password Server, and Kerberos are all running.

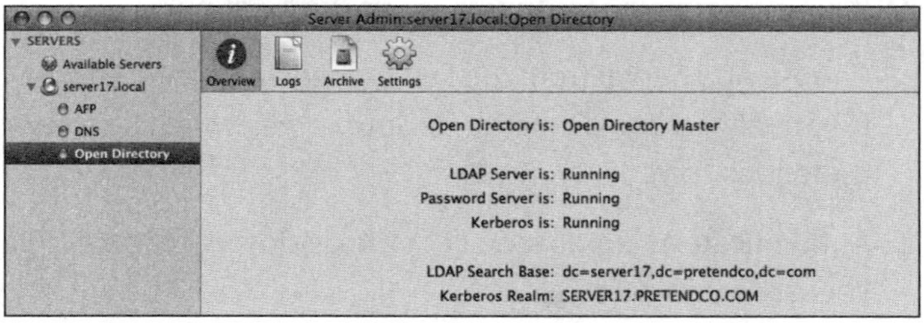


If one or more services are not running, use Server Admin to check the Open Directory logs for the inactive service(s) to look for possible reasons for the problem. If you are having an issue with a recently configured Open Directory Master, the Configuration Log (actually named the slapconfig.log) can be particularly useful.

19 To view the Open Directory configuration log, click the Logs button in the toolbar, and then choose Configuration Log from the View menu.

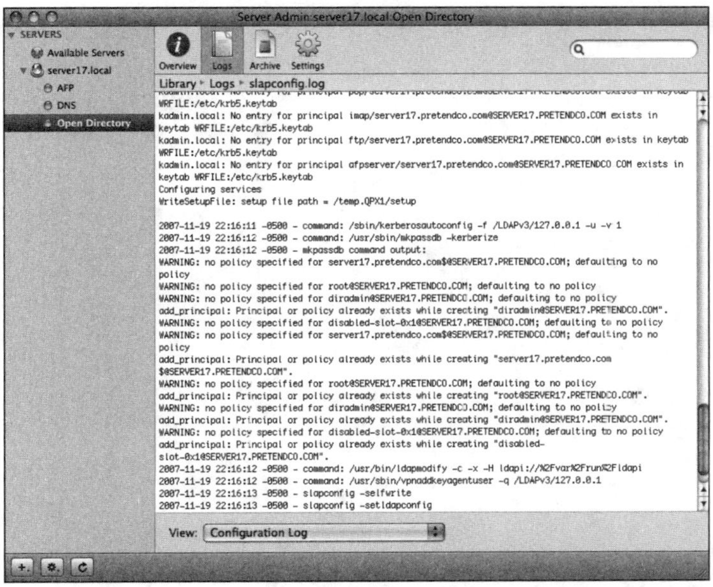

Your server is now running a second database that you will populate with users.

20 Select servern.local in the server list and choose Remove Server from the Server menu.

21 Click the Remove button to confirm the deletion.

22 Choose Add Server from the Server menu and enter the new fully qualified domain name for your server, which is server*n*.pretendco.com.

23 Authenticate as ladmin and click the disclosure triangle to view your services again.

## Exercise 4.2.3

# Import Users and Groups into the Shared Directory

## Objective

Import user and group records into the shared directory of a Mac OS X Server configured as an Open Directory Master.

## Summary

Importing users and groups into a shared directory is similar to importing into the local directory, which you did in Chapter 3 using Workgroup Manager. Now that we have two directories to manage with Workgroup Manager, it's important to verify that operations are performed in the correct directory—local or shared.

1. With Screen Sharing, open Workgroup Manager on your server.
2. Enter your server's DNS name in the Address field.
3. For User Name and Password, use the local administrator user name and password (ladmin). You can authenticate later to the shared directory as diradmin.

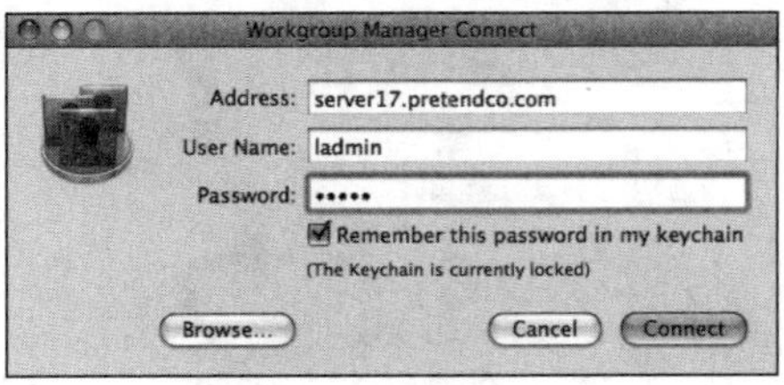


4. Click Connect, and notice you are not looking at the local directory anymore.
5. In the Workgroup Manager window, click the globe icon under the toolbar to display a pop-up menu containing the list of available directories.

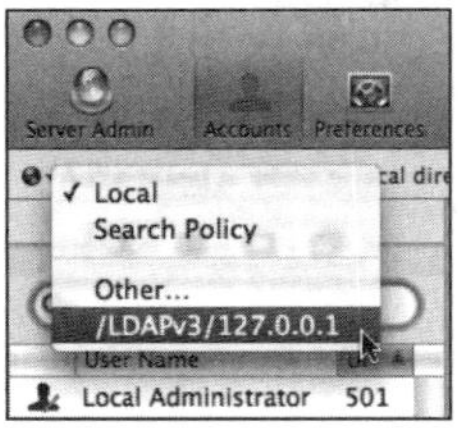


This menu is an important part of the Workgroup Manager user interface. The list of directories you can view is the same regardless of which administrator account you used in Workgroup Manager to connect to your server. However, you can only make changes in a directory when authenticated as an administrator of that directory. To make changes in a different directory, select it from the list, and then click the lock icon on the right to authenticate as an administrator in that directory.

Workgroup Manager remembers which directory you most recently used, and will display that directory the next time you connect with Workgroup Manager.

6 Verify that /LDAPv3/127.0.0.1 is the selected directory, and click the lock icon on the right, and enter the shared directory administrator's username and password (diradmin and diradmin).

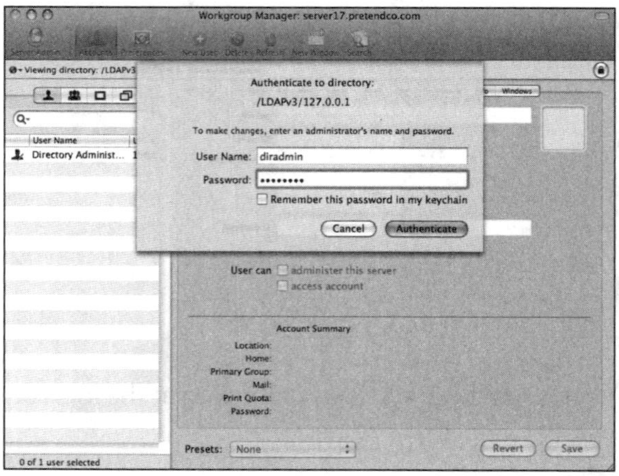


You are now authenticated to import users and groups.

7 To import user accounts from a file, choose Import from the Server menu.

A file selection dialog appears that allows you to choose a file containing user or group account records stored in a character-delimited format. Additionally, there are options for setting the first user ID used for the imported users — the first user gets the specified user ID, the next user ID is one greater than the previous, and so on. Specifying user ID during import only works if there is no user ID information stored in the user record file. A group ID may also be specified, but will only be used if absent in the user record file. If not specified in the file or when importing, group IDs for imported users will be set to 20, which corresponds to the group called Open Directory Users.

8 In the file selection dialog, navigate to your Desktop folder, and select server*n*-users, where *n* is your student number.

9 Click Import.

The users are imported and displayed, as shown in the following figure.

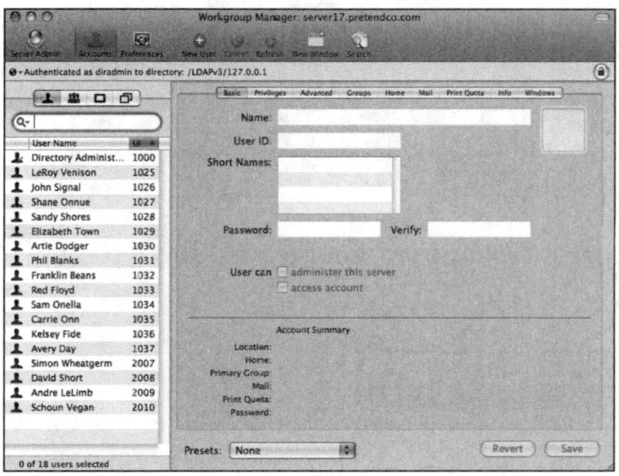

Because there is no password data in the users file you imported, you will need to assign passwords to the new users. To fully use the services available in the Open Directory Master, such as password policies and Kerberos, the user password type should be set to Open Directory.

10 In Workgroup Manager, select the users imported from the users file.

This process may be easier if you click the UID column header to sort the list of users by user ID. To select all of the imported users, select the first imported user, hold down the shift key, and then select the last imported user. Make sure you do not select the Directory Administrator.

11 Click the Advanced tab to view the Advanced configuration pane.

The checkboxes and menus display a dash to indicate an indeterminate state. This is a visual cue that you are able to change settings for multiple records at once.

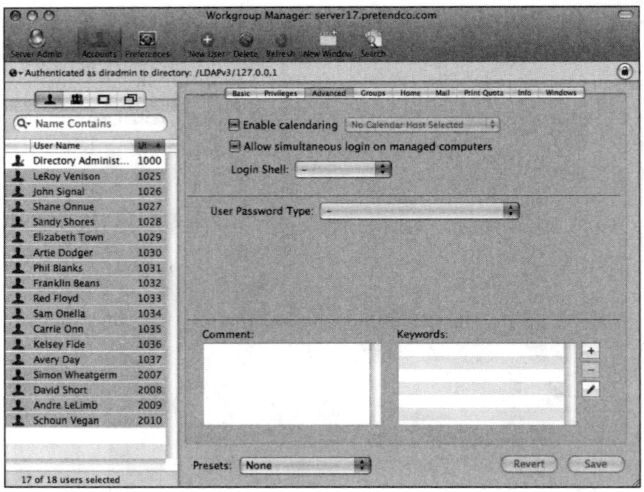


12 Choose Open Directory from the User Password Type pop-up menu.

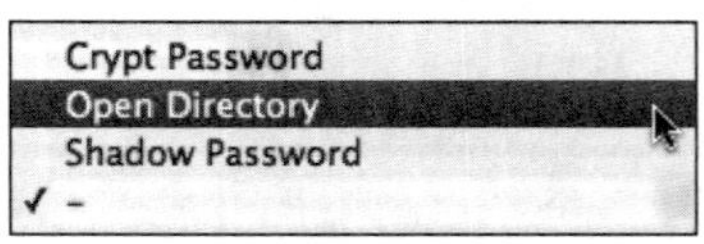

13 Enter `changeme` as the new password.

14 Click OK, click Save, and then click the Groups button on the left to import your groups.

15 Verify that you are working in the shared directory by making sure that /LDAPv3/127.0.0.1 is the selected in the directory pop-up menu under the toolbar.

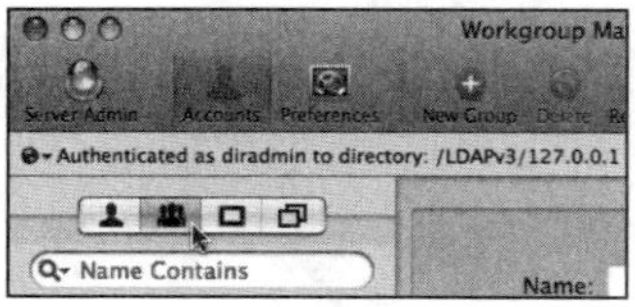


16 Choose Import from the Server menu and import the server*n*-groups file (where *n* is your student number) in your Desktop folder.

If your groups do not import, quit Workgroup Manager, reopen it, and remove any groups you see. Then import a file located inside /Users/Shared/StudentMaterials/CH04/ called groups.

17 The new groups are imported and displayed.

18 You will have to add the Engineering, Marketing, and management groups back to the Employee group and click Save.

Take a few moments to examine the memberships of these groups using the skills you learned in Chapter 3.

19 Quit Workgroup Manager and Screen Sharing.

# 4.3 Authentication

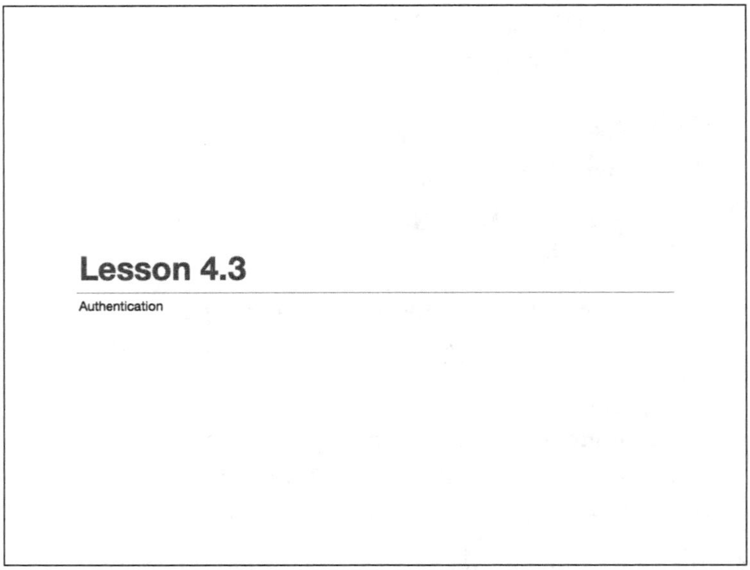


The way users authenticate to obtain access to services can be a potential point of attack in attempts to gather information about the user and the password. In a Mac OS X Server directory structure, there are two main methods for user authentication, Password Server and Kerberos. Each method has distinct qualities and features of which you should be aware. Directory structures such as Open Directory also allow administrators to set password policies. Password policies can help organizations standardize their passwords. This is a crucial part of managing a directory infrastructure and is often regulated.

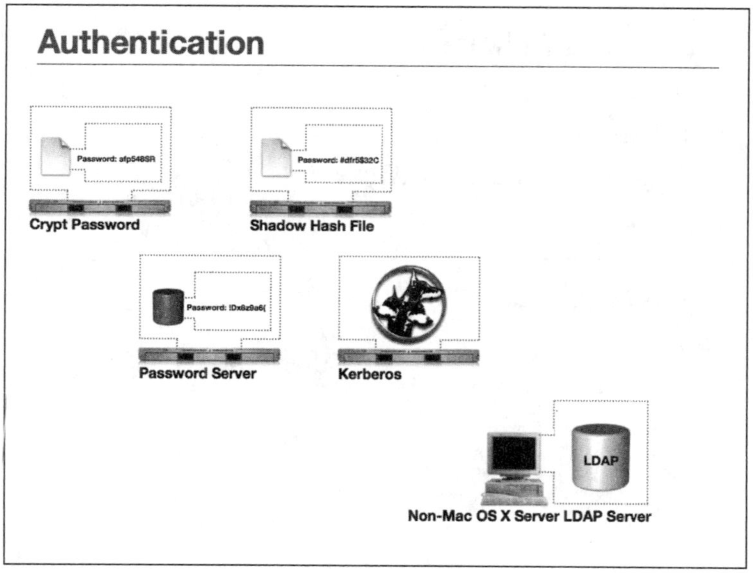


Authentication information can be stored in several different formats. Mac OS X and Mac OS X Server can use almost all of these formats.

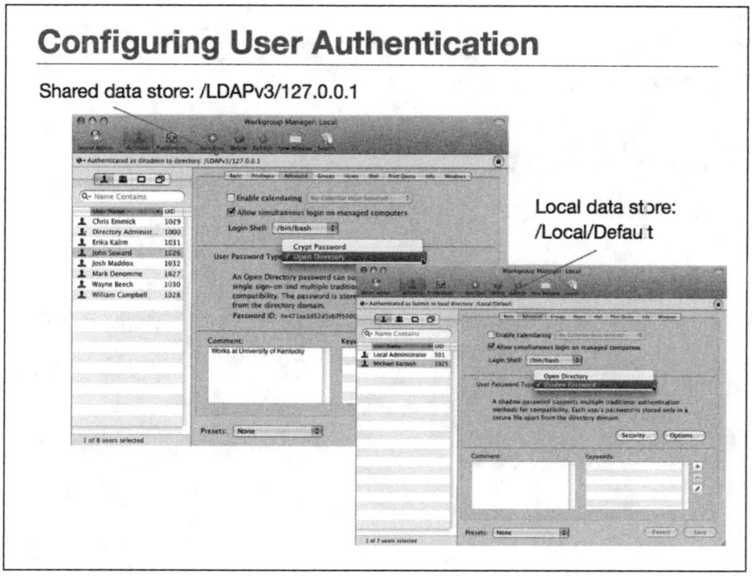


Depending on the directory data store, there are a variety of options when saving user passwords. When looking at the local data store, passwords can be saved slightly differently than those of the LDAP data store.

## Password Policies

Two methods:

- Per-User Policy
- Global Policy

Two types:

- Login restrictions
- Password rules

Two rules:

- Per-user policies *may* override global policies.
- Administrators are exempt.

There are two methods of password policies, per-user policies and global policies. The types of policies that can be set are login restrictions and password rules.

## Password Policies

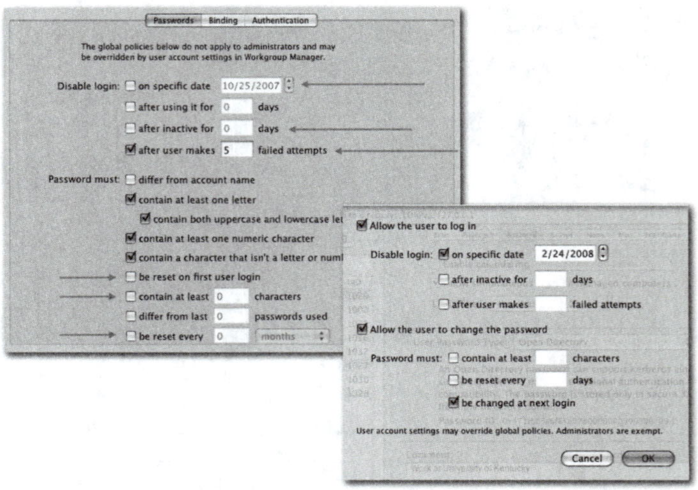


In some cases, global polices have the same options as per-user policies. In those cases, the per-user policies may override the global policies.

## Password Server

Permits the retention of older authentication methods:

- Recoverable methods
  - WebDAV
  - APOP
- Hash methods
  - CRAM-MD5
  - NTLMv1 and NTLMv2
  - NT LAN-Manager

Password Server can store passwords for use where Kerberos cannot be used. When storing the password, Password Server can retain the password differently, depending on how the password will be used. There are less secure methods of storing the password that can be disabled if not used.

## Kerberos

Terminology

- Key Distribution Center
  - Issues tickets based on requests
- Ticket Granting Ticket
  - First ticket received by requester
- Service Ticket
  - Subsequent tickets obtained for services

Kerberos is an authentication method involving three main components, the Kerberos Key Distribution Center which issues tickets, the services that can accept tickets, and the users that obtain tickets. These tickets are used in lieu of passwords.

## Kerberos KDC

Contains user "secrets."

Once authenticated against KDC:

- Tickets are granted for services.
- Additional password entry is not required.
- The effect is a single password at login, then access to services without password.
    - Called Single Sign-On.
- Services must leverage Kerberos.
- Mac OS X Server services integrate with Kerberos KDC.
- KDC and Password Server stay in sync.

The Kerberos KDC stores users and these users have secrets. The secret is the user's password, stored securely. Once a user sends their username to the KDC, a system of generated keys are used to confirm and authenticate the user. Once authenticated, the tickets can be granted, starting with the Ticket Granting Ticket, which allows the user to obtain more tickets for services they will use, such as Mail services, Calendaring services, Chat services, and file services.

## Troubleshooting—Directory Service

Problem:

- User cannot log in from Login Window.

Problem Resolution:

- LDAP misconfiguration
  - DHCP data incorrect
- Password incorrect
- Time skew—5 minutes or more
- No Home folder defined
- AFP or SMB service not active
- Firewall settings

As noted earlier, troubleshooting directory services can involve troubleshooting the LDAP database and also troubleshooting any authentication issues, which may involve Password Server and/or Kerberos.

Exercise

4.3.1 Configure Password Policies

Exercise 4.3.1

# Configure Password Policies

## Objective

This exercise demonstrates how to configure and verify password policies that apply to user accounts in a shared directory. You will learn how to apply password policies that target selected users, and also policies that apply globally for all users in the shared directory.

## Summary

Password policies are useful limitations and restrictions that affect how your server authenticates its users. They are typically used to help enforce good password security, and to help prevent other account security problems from occurring, for example by automatically disabling a temporary account at a specific date or after a period of inactivity. There are two types of password policies that can be configured in Mac OS X Server: per-user policies and global policies. Global policies are configured with Server Admin, and per-user policies are configured with Workgroup Manager.

## Configuring Global Password Policies

1 Open Server Admin, and select your server's Open Directory service from the list.

2 Click the Settings button in the toolbar.

3 Click Policy and then click the Passwords tab to display the global password policy configuration pane.

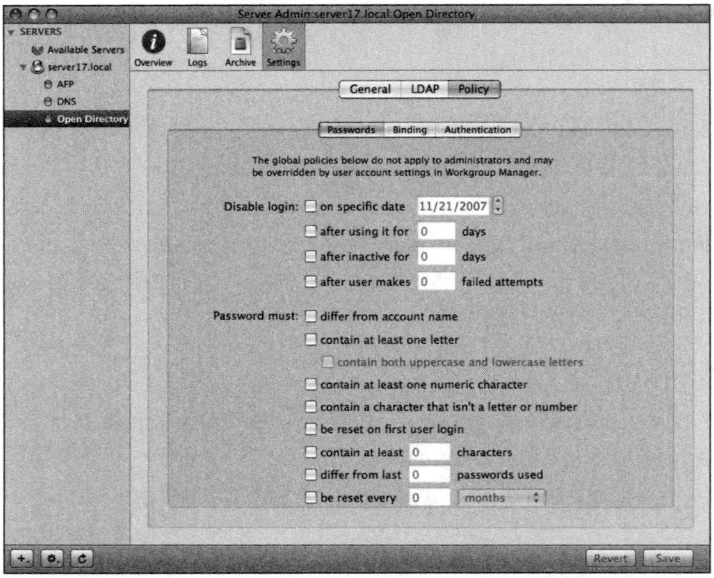


For this exercise, you'll create password policies that require passwords to:

- Differ from account name
- Contain at least one numeric character
- Contain at least 8 characters

4 Configure the password policies just described and then click Save.

5 Using Workgroup Manager, select Andre LeLimb in your server's shared directory.

6 Click the Advanced tab to view the password options (among other options) for this account.

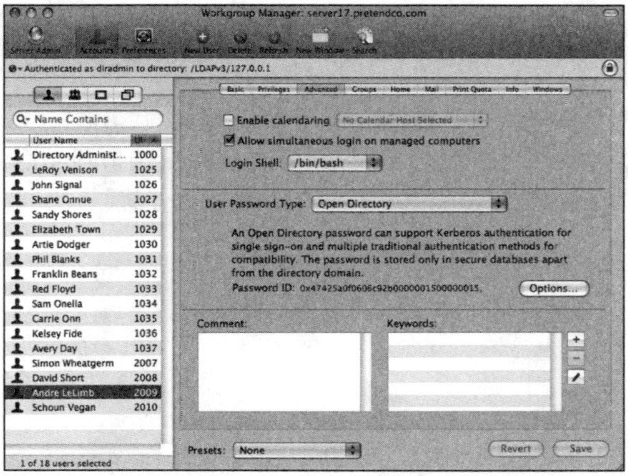


7 Click the Options button to display the password policy configuration for this account.

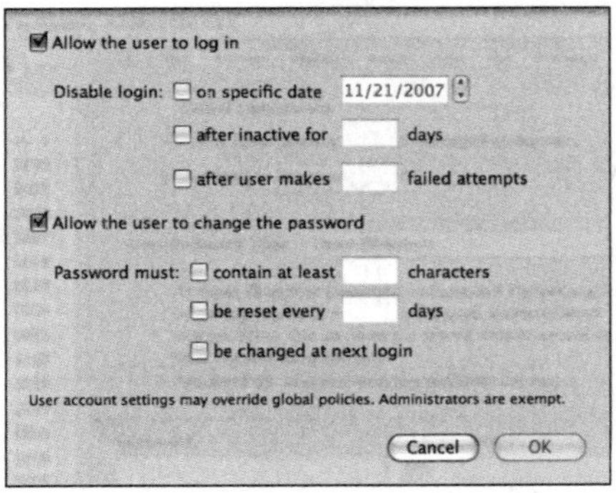


8 Configure this account to require a password change at the next login, click OK, and then click Save.

9 For the user named David Short, configure a password policy that does not allow the user to log in and save the changes.

Notice that David's account now has a red X by his account in the user list, indicating that he cannot currently use his account.

In order to validate that the password policies are in place, you'll connect to your server from your client computer. Though the password policies apply to most of the services that can be provided by your server, for this exercise you'll use the AFP service, because it requires no extra configuration, and provides an interface for users to change their password before they log in.

10 In Server Admin, verify that the AFP service indicator is green to ensure that AFP is running.

11 Stop the AFP service, and start the AFP service again. This reduces the chance that the service access controls that were implemented (and then removed) in Chapter 3 can cause an error.

12 In the Finder on your Mac OS X computer, choose Go > Connect to Server.

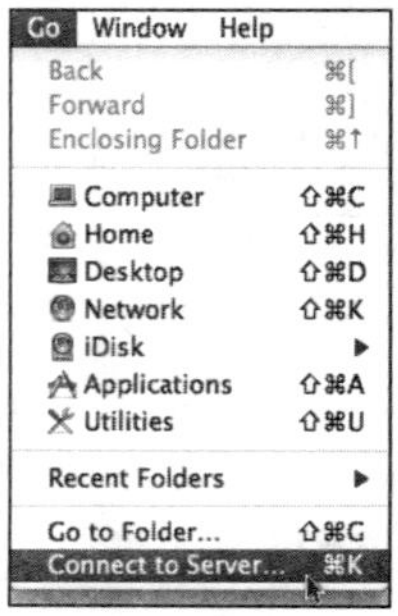


13 Enter your server's DNS name (server*n*.pretendco.com), and then click Connect.

14 Log in with the username, `andre`, and password, `changeme`.

Due to the user password policy set earlier with Workgroup Manager, Andre is now required to perform a password change.

15 Enter `changeme` as the old password and `abcd1234` as the new password.

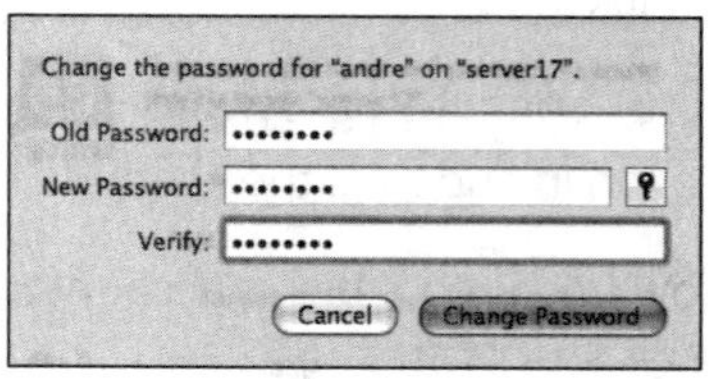


16 Click the Change Password button to change Andre's password, and continue to log in as Andre.

If the volume selection window appears, it means the login with the new password was successful.

17 Click Cancel to close the AFP connection.

Next you will perform a user-initiated password change using a different account to test the global password policies.

18 Log out of your client computer and attempt to log in as Simon.

You cannot log in as Simon because your client computer is not yet bound to your server. You will be doing this in the next chapter; when doing so, you will be required to change Simon's password.

19 Log back into your client as cadmin.

20 Choose Change Password from the gear menu.

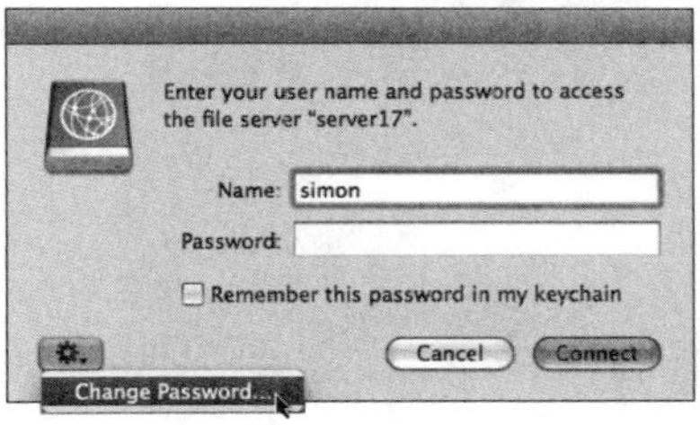


21 Enter `changeme` as the old password and `123abc` as the new password.

This fails because of the global password policy that requires passwords to contain at least 8 characters.

22 Change the password for `simon` to `abcd1234`.

> **Note** If you get an error, stop and start the AFP service, and change the password to the full 8 characters.

23 Attempt to connect to your server via AFP as David Short.

This login fails due to the user password policy that has disabled authentication for this user.

24 Experiment with other global and user password settings, using the steps in this exercise to configure and test the policies.

25 When you are finished, stop the AFP service using Server Admin.

# 4.4 Archiving

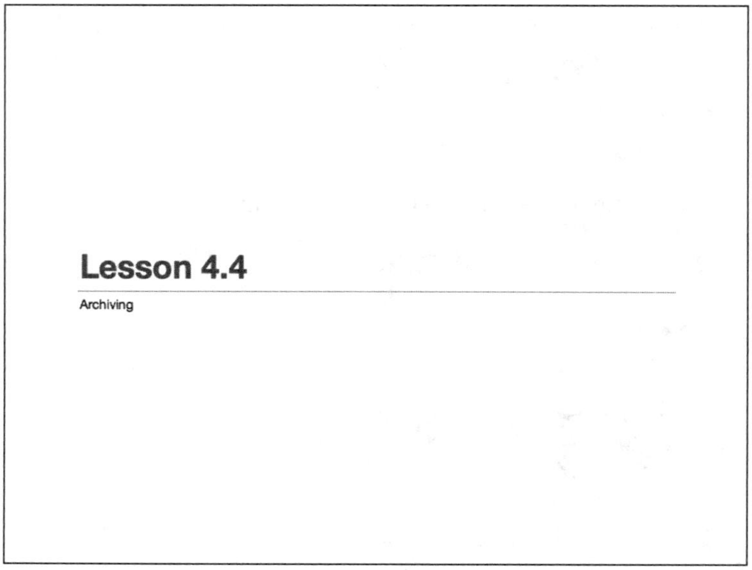


Archive and restore Open Directory components.

## Open Directory Archive

Archive several files and directories critical to Open Directory:

- Location for archive is chosen.
- Administrator enters password once.
- Encrypted disk image is created.
- Files and directories are duplicated.

Key files/folders:

- backup.ldif
- passwordserver_backup
- Kerberos files

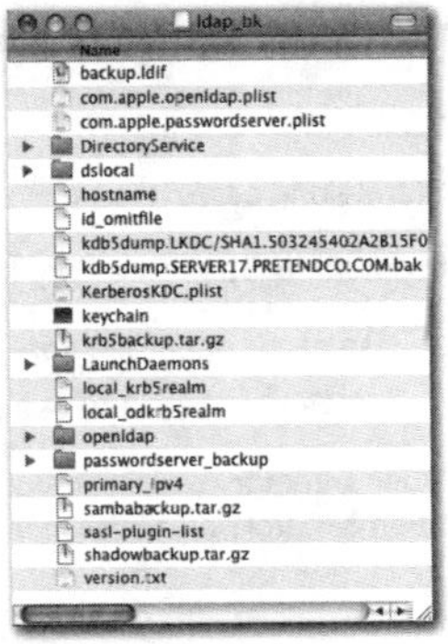


Archiving Open Directory information is a critical aspect of maintaining and managing a server. This information can be used to restore a server or recreate a server. When creating the archive, an encrypted disk image is created to store the archived files. There is only one password entry field so ensure you are entering the correct password, otherwise you may not be able to restore your archive when you need it most.

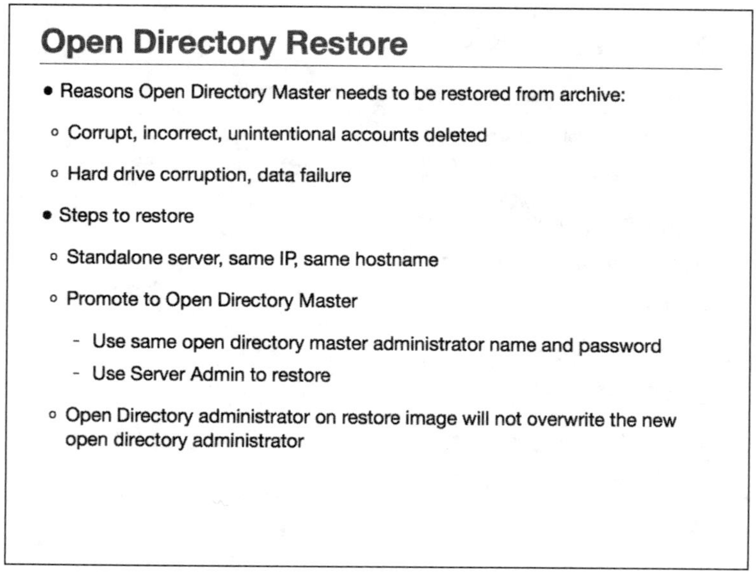


The critical archived data files include the Kerberos database files, the password server database, and the LDAP (shared) database. Other files critical to the operation of the server are also archived.

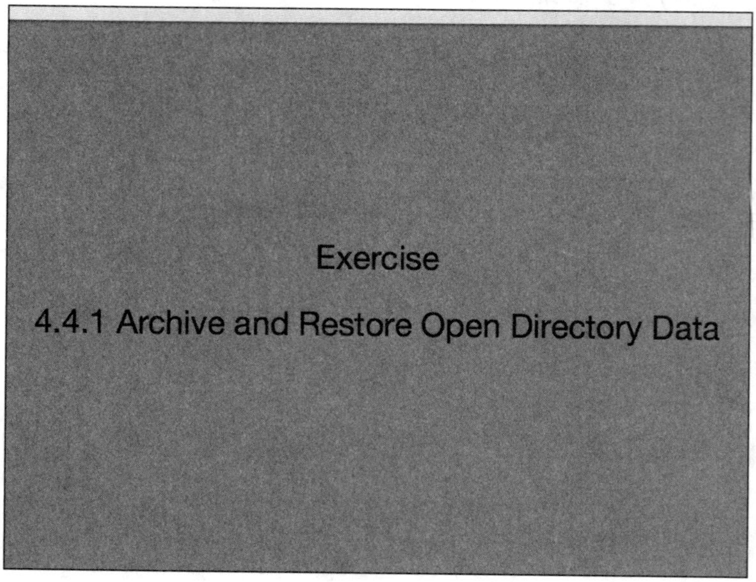

Exercise 4.4.1

# Archive and Restore Open Directory Data

## Objective

Illustrate how to archive and restore Open Directory data and related files critical to the functionality of your server.

## Summary

The archived file used to store the directory data and related files is an encrypted disk image. When using Server Admin to archive the data, a single password with no consistency check is used to encrypt the disk image. Take care to enter the password correctly the first time. Once archived, you will take your Mac OS X Server down to a standalone server, recreate an Open Directory Master, and restore the archived data to return your server to a known state.

1. Quit Workgroup Manager, if its open.
2. In Server Admin, select the Open Directory service, and choose the Archive icon in the toolbar.
3. Click the Choose button, select the /Users/Shared/ folder on your server, and click the dialog's Choose button to continue.
4. Click the Archive button, and enter the name for your archive as server*n*-archived-data-Month-Date (where n is your student number, Month is the current month, and Date is the current date).

   It is advisable to enter the date into the name of the archived file so you can quickly refer to the file should you have several archives to choose from.

5 Enter the word `apple` for the password, and click OK to create the archive.

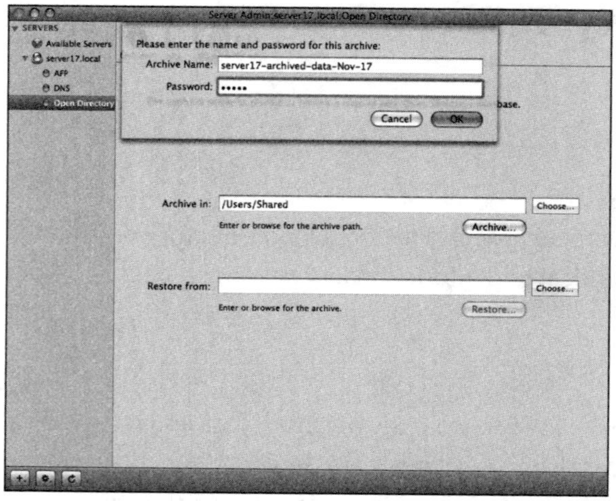


Your Open Directory archive is now on an encrypted disk image on your Mac OS X Server inside the /Users/Shared/ folder called server*n*-archived-data-*Month-Date*.

Now, you'll take your server back down to a Standalone server, thus deleting the LDAP database, Password Server, and the Kerberos KDC used for single sign-on for your shared LDAP directory.

6 Click the Settings icon in Open Directory, and click the General tab.

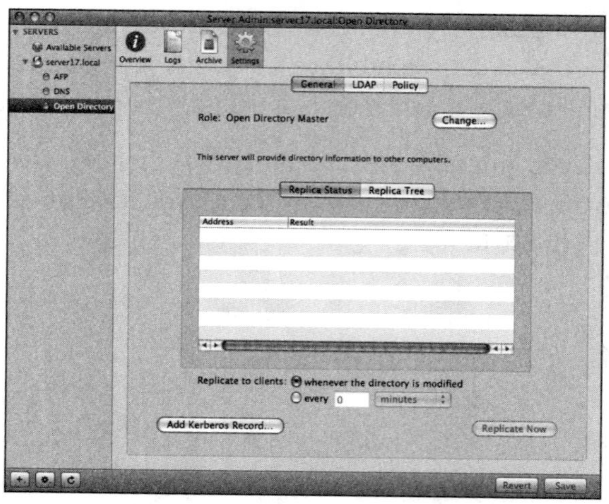

7 Click the Change button to launch the Service Configuration Assistant again.

8 Change your server to a Standalone server, and walk through the dialogs.

   Your server is now a Standalone server and does not have an LDAP database anymore.

   All the users and groups you had are now gone, as they were a part of the LDAP database.

9 Click the change button again and walk through the Service Configuration Assistant, creating an Open Directory Master again using the same password (diradmin) for the Directory Administrator account.

10 Once the Open Directory Master is created, click the Archive icon in the toolbar of Open Directory.

11 Click the Choose button next to Restore, navigate to the /Users/Shared/ folder, and select your disk image.

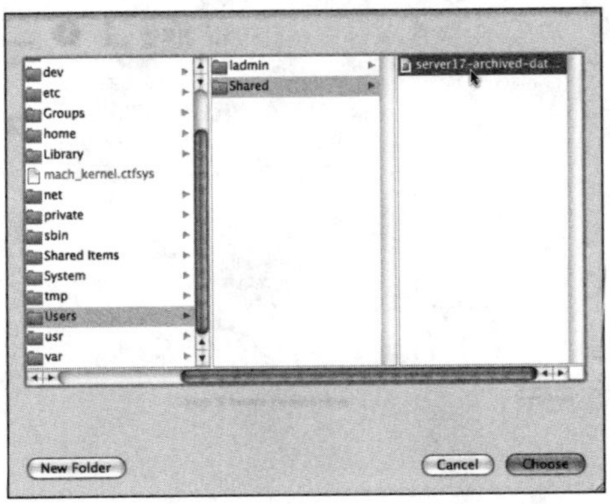


12 Click the Choose button to close the dialog, and return to Server Admin.

13 Click the Restore button and enter the password (`apple`) for the encrypted disk image.

14 You can now open Workgroup Manager and view all your LDAP accounts, restored properly after they were previously archived.

## Chapter Summary

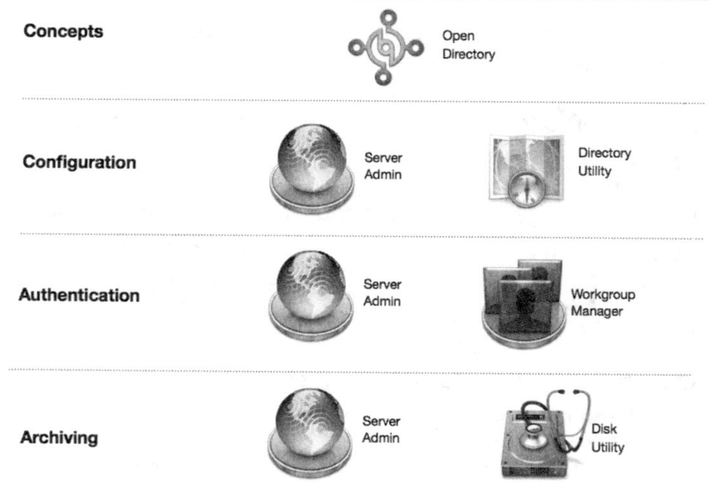


Apple Certified

# 5

# File Services

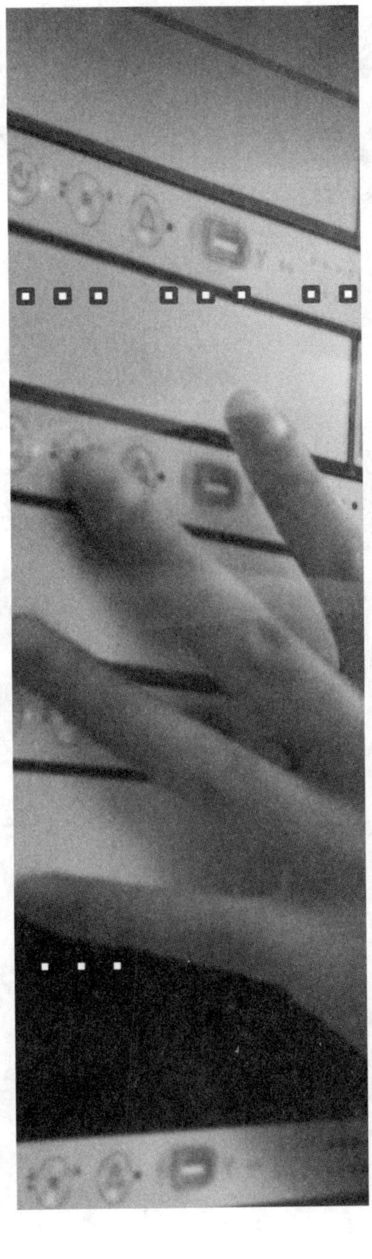

## 5.1 Planning

**Exercise 5.1.1** View Preset Share Points and Permissions

## 5.2 Protocols

**Exercise 5.2.1** Configure AFP File Sharing Service

**Exercise 5.2.2** Manage AFP Service Settings

**Exercise 5.2.3** Test AFP Service Settings

**Exercise 5.2.4** Configure Samba File Sharing Service

**Exercise 5.2.5** View Samba Log Files (optional)

**Exercise 5.2.6** Configure the File Transfer Protocol Sharing Service (optional)

**Exercise 5.2.7** Configure the Network File System Sharing Service

## 5.3 Configuration

**Exercise 5.3.1** Configure Automount Options and Quotas on Share Points

**Exercise 5.3.2** Set a Time Machine Share Point (optional)

# 5.1 Planning

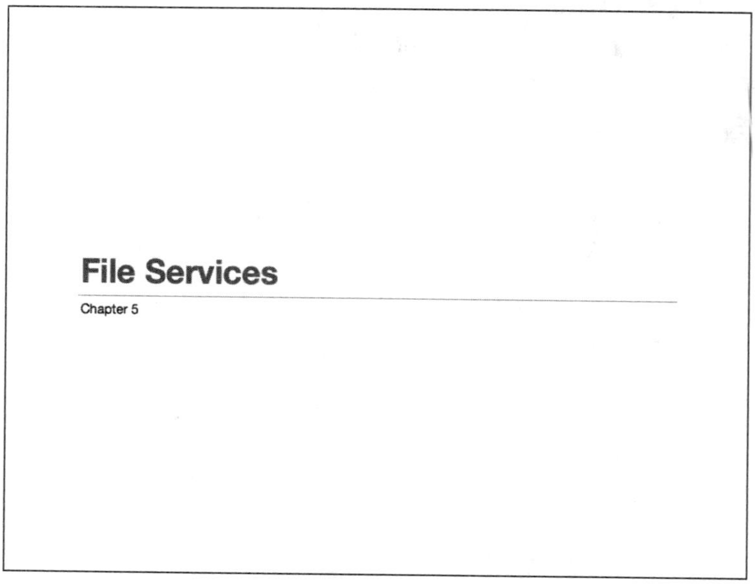

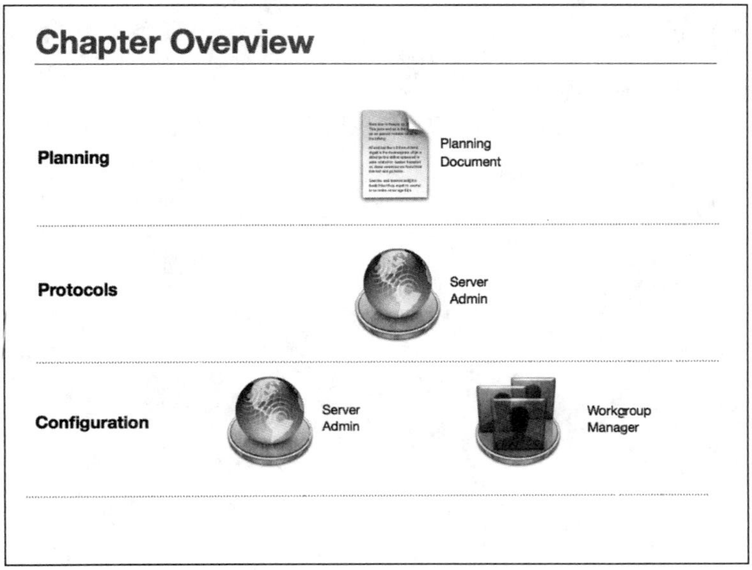


When sharing files, it is important to divide the task into smaller parts to ensure mistakes are not made and errors, if any, are located, analyzed, and corrected prior to a wider share point rollout within your organization.

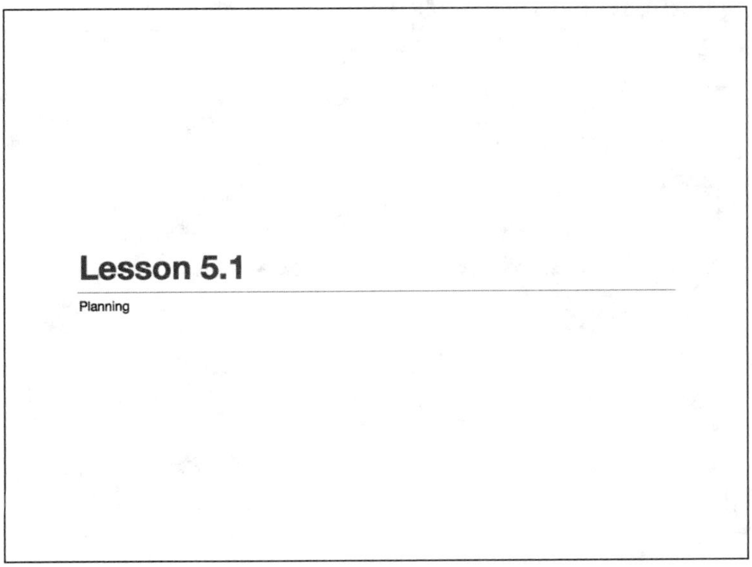


This lesson deals with the proper planning and the issues surrounding sharing files over various protocols using Mac OS X Server.

## File Sharing Challenges

- File Sharing Protocols
- Client Operating Systems
- Various Access Levels
- Case-Sensitive Files

Certain challenges come with sharing files. Levels of access, multiple protocols, and a variety of operating systems, can all affect how share points are used in your organization.

## File Sharing Protocols

AFP

- Apple Filing Protocol
- Primarily Apple Clients

SMB

- Server Message Blocks
- Windows, Apple, *NIX Clients

FTP

- File Transfer Protocol
- All Clients

NFS

- Network File System
- Apple, *NIX Clients

There are four main file sharing protocol options, AFP, SMB, FTP, and NFS. Each has options and parameters that you'll explore in this chapter.

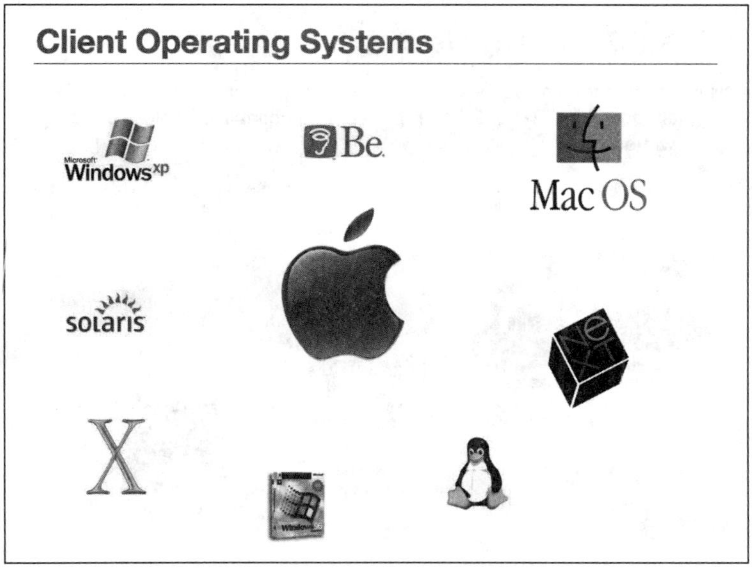


The wide variety of client operating systems, including legacy systems, can be a challenge when setting up share points.

### Various Access Levels

- Administrators
- Limited Administrators
- Groups
- Nested Groups
- Guests

Levels of access can be established for share points. These include administrators that have access only to manage or monitor various sharing protocols, nested group access, and whether or not to allow guest access.

## Case-Sensitivity Issues

Files copied from a case-sensitive file system to a non-case sensitive file system over AFP, FTP, or NFS will prompt for confirmation before being overwritten.

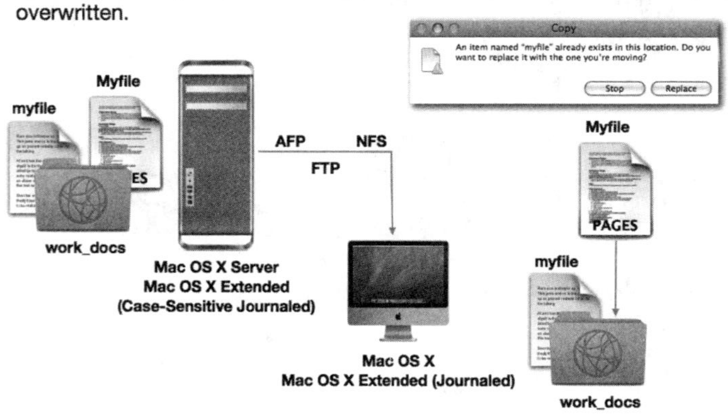


Case-sensitive file systems can cause issues when transferring files. AFP, FTP, and NFS are all case-sensitive, but SMB is not. When moving files from a case-sensitive file system to a non case-sensitive file system over AFP, an alert displays, prompting for confirmation before the file is overwritten, even though the case is different on the two files.

## Case-Sensitivity Issues

Files copied <u>from</u> a case-sensitive file system <u>to</u> a non-case sensitive file system over SMB may <u>NOT</u> be asked to be overwritten and may take a second copy attempt to succeed.

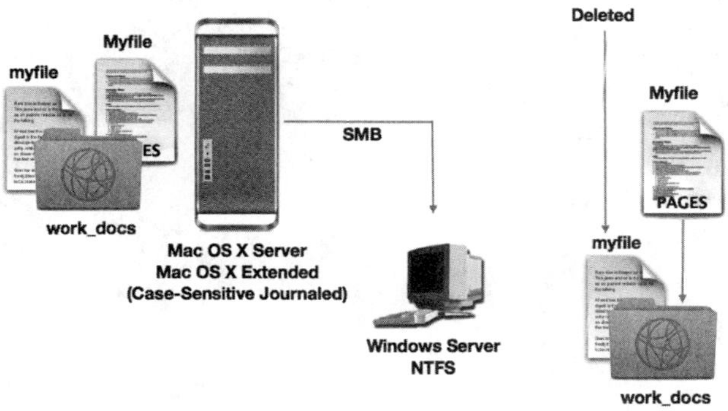


When using the SMB protocol, a transferred file may produce a dialog asking to overwrite the file. An error will likely occur when attempting to replace the file. The local copy is deleted but the file transfer does not occur. A second attempt will transfer the file without error.

## File Sharing Solutions

- Proper Planning
- Protocol Selection
- Access Control

There are three file sharing solution areas when attempting to resolve file sharing issues; proper planning, protocol selection, and access control.

## Planning File Service Layout

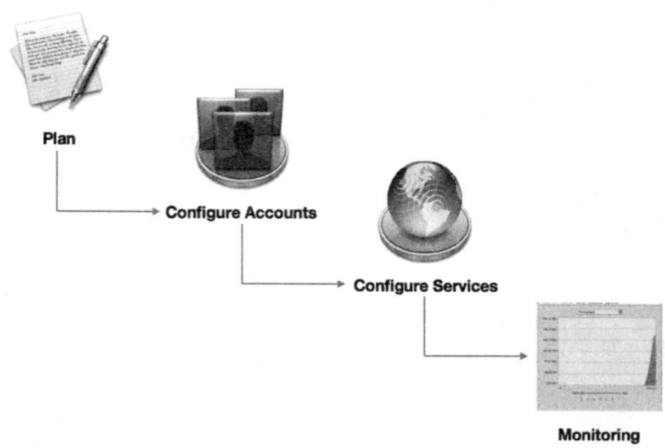


Planning is key to successful file sharing implementation, especially when trying to avoid duplicates file shares and complex access controls.

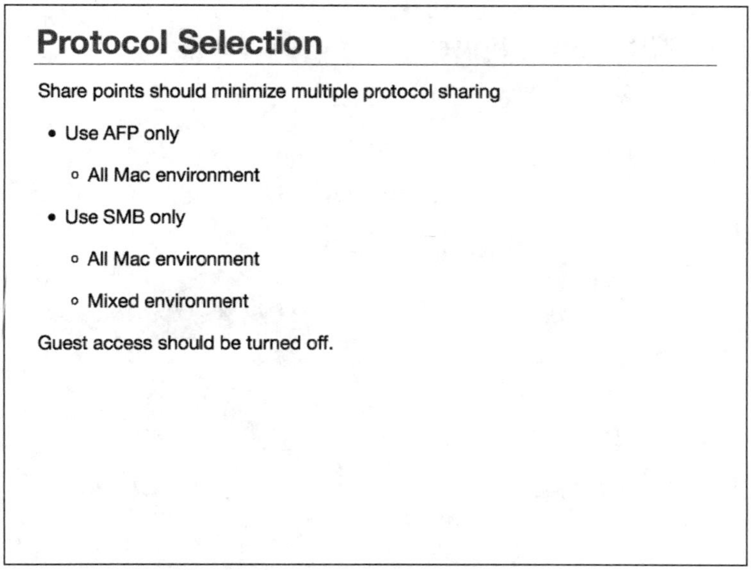


Making wise decisions on the protocols used for the share points helps reduce the chance of errors.

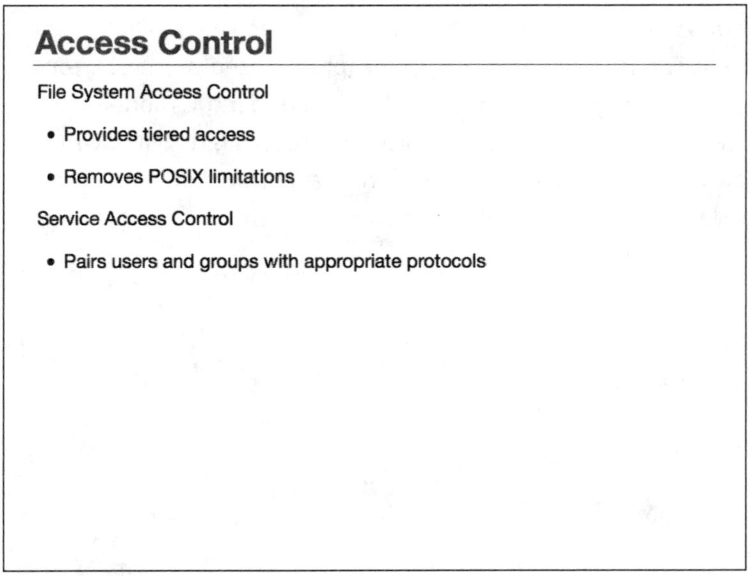


Access control is key to user and group management of share point access, as you saw in Chapter 3. Service access control helps with the management of the file sharing service.

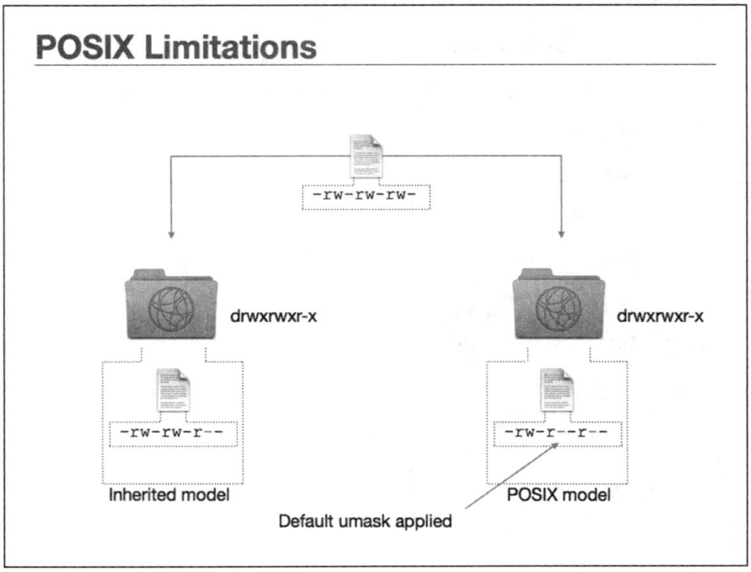


POSIX permissions can limit the overall use of a share point. Using standard POSIX permissions, when a folder is created, the owner or user of the folder has read and write access but the group and others have ready only. Permissions have been limited automatically. This is also known as a umask (pronounced yoomask). You cannot change these predefined values. Under this model, if you create an item in a folder in which the group has read and write permission, the item will not inherit that permission. If you want to let other group members edit the new item, you must change permissions manually.

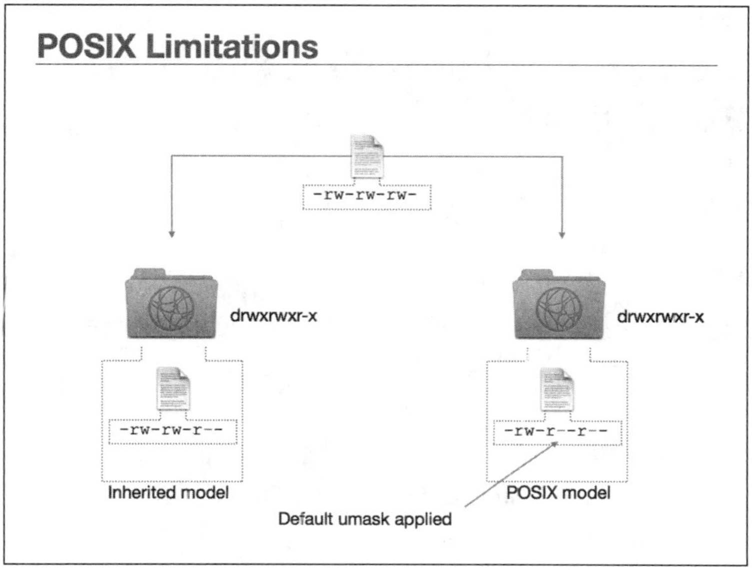


As you saw in Chapter 3, Server Admin is used to manage share points, permissions, and mounting options.

Exercise

5.1.1 View Preset Share Points and Permissions

## Exercise 5.1.1

# View Preset Share Points and Permissions

## Objective

Understand how the default Mac OS X Server share points are configured and shared.

## Summary

You'll open Server Admin and view the default share points and their respective protocol options.

1 Connect to your server using Server Admin, and click the File Sharing icon in the toolbar.

2 Click the Share Points button, and then click the List button to view all your preset share points.

3 Click the Share Point tab in the lower section of the screen.

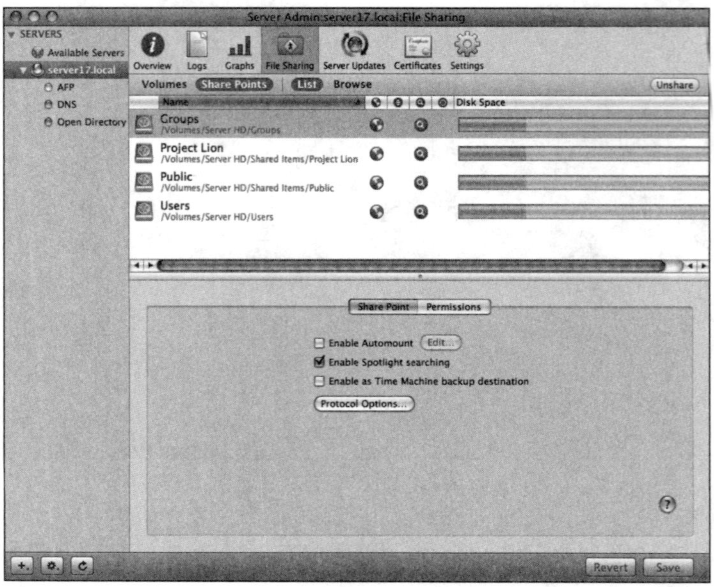

In the share point list, the columns contain icons that indicate the status of each share point. The columns are:

- Name: Displays the name of the Share Point
- Globe icon: Indicates whether Guest access is on or off for that share point.
- Arrowed icon: Indicates whether the share point is configured to automount.
- Spotlight icon: Indicates whether the share point is configured to be searched by Spotlight when mounted on a connected user's Mac OS X computer.
- Time Machine icon: Indicates whether the share point is configured as a Time Machine mount.
- Disk Space: Indicates the amount of space available on that share point (remember that some share points can be separate volumes).

4 Move your cursor over the share point icons to view the help tool tip indicating you do not have a share point that is an automount and that all share points are configured to be searched via Spotlight.

5 Select the Users share point in the list.

**Question 1** *Where is the Users share point located?*

---

6 Click the Share Point tab.

7 Click the Protocol Options button, and click through the various protocol tabs.

8 You will see all protocols except NFS are configured by default to share the Users share point. Also notice that guest access is turned on for all preset share points.

9 Close the Protocol Options dialog and click the Permissions tab to view the default POSIX permissions for the Users share point.

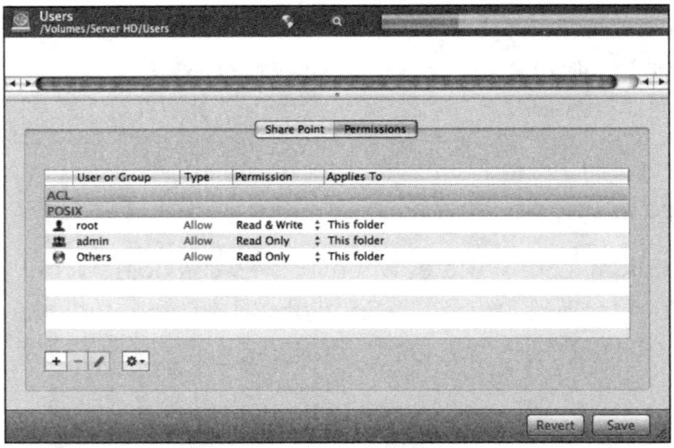


10 Select the Volumes button, select your Server HD volume, and click the Quotas tab.

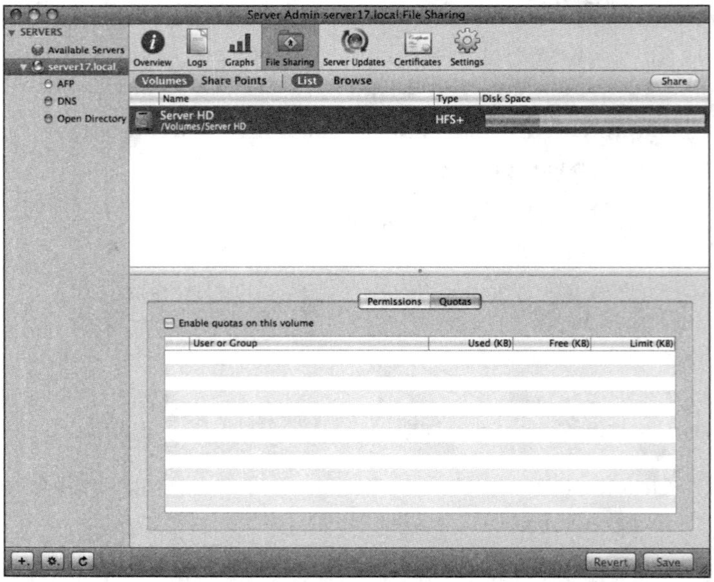

> **Note** Quotas, while based on users and/or groups, are also based on volumes, not folders. If a user has a quota, their quota is based on every folder where they are the owner of the items within that folder. For example, Shane has his home folder and has read and write access to five share points, where he is still the owner of any files he places in these share points. His quota is a combination of all files in all locations where he is the owner of files.

11 Select "Enable quotas on this volume" for your Server HD volume, and click Save.

You've turned on quotas, even if you choose not to enforce any.

12 Click the Share Points button to view all the preset share points.

13 Click the Share Point tab in the lower section of the screen.

You've viewed the default share points on Mac OS X Server and turned on quotas for the Server HD volume.

# 5.2 Protocols

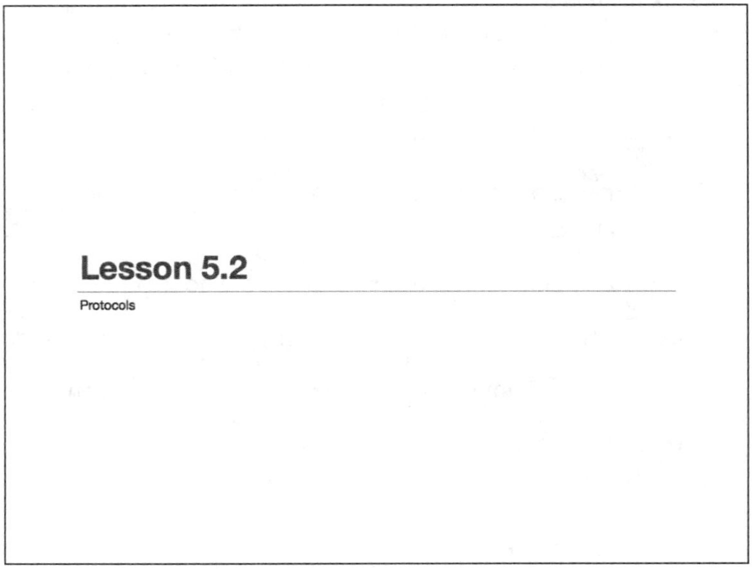


This lesson covers the four main protocols (AFP, SMB, FTP, and NFS) and their respective options.

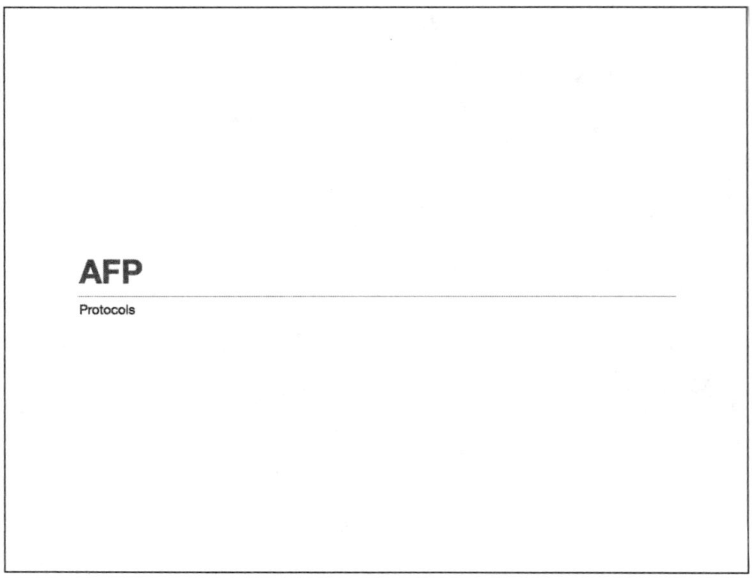

## Apple Filing Protocol—Service Configuration

Primary options

- Login and disconnect messages.
- Attempts both authentication methods.
  - Kerberos (attempted first)
  - Standard
- Administrator can masquerade as any user.
  - Enter user's name and administrator password to authorized user share points.
- Local network browsing permitted via Bonjour.

The AFP service has a variety of options, such as deciding how to authenticate users (Standard authentication or Kerberos), allowing guest access, error and access logging, greeting messages, Bonjour browsing, and more. With regard to guest access, you'll recall that guest access is on for every share point created. However, unless guest access is turned on for the AFP service, guests will not be able to connect to all the share points. This feature is similar in SMB and FTP.

## Apple Filing Protocol—Logs

Access Logging

Error Logging

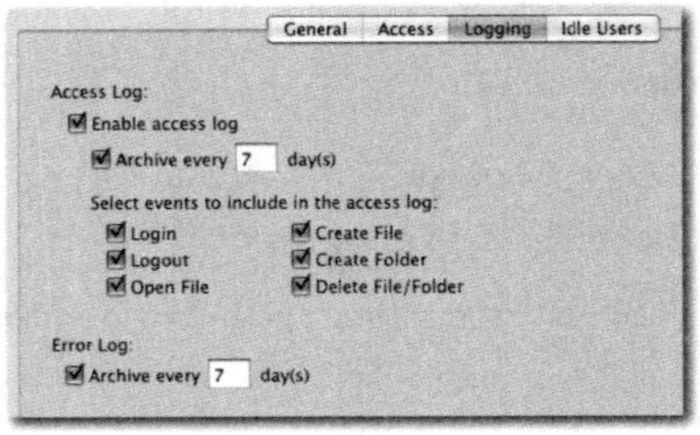


There are two main AFP log files, the access log and the error log. The access log can be configured to keep track of six different parameters, and the error log indicates service shutdowns and other anomalies associated with the AFP service.

## Apple Share Point Options

When choosing to share a volume or folder over AFP:

- Allow guest access (must be turned on for the AFP service as well).
- Change share point name.
- Use a permissions model for copied items.
    - POSIX
    - Inherit permissions

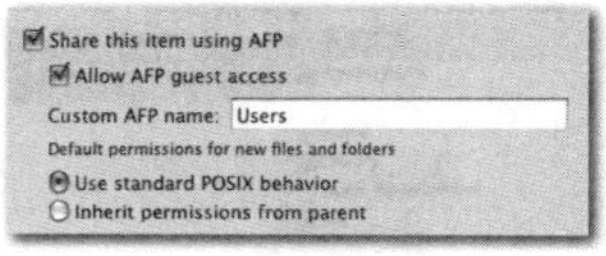


When selecting a share point to share over AFP, guest access can be turned off for the share point and a custom name used to mask the true name of the share point. You can decide how items copied into the share point will behave with respect to their permissions.

Demo

Walk-Through of Apple File Sharing and Share Point Options

The instructor will demo the AFP service and AFP share point options.

## Apple Filing Protocol—Service Access

Restrict AFP for certain users and groups

Dictate who can administer or monitor the AFP service

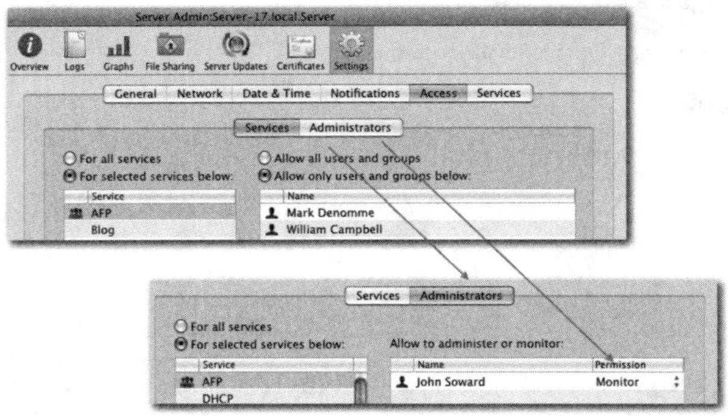


Setting controls on who can access, manage, and monitor the AFP service helps secure that service against users who have accounts on the Mac OS X Server, but are not authorized to access share points over AFP.

## File Sharing Protocol Comparison

| | AFP | SMB | FTP | NFS |
|---|---|---|---|---|
| Native Platform | Mac OS | Windows | Multi-platform | *NIX |
| Security | Encrypted - Standard or Kerberos | Encrypted - NTLMv2 or Kerberos | Clear text or Kerberos | Clear text, encrypted, or Kerberos |
| Browsable | Bonjour | NetBIOS | Bonjour | Bonjour |
| Example URL | afp://server17.pretendco.com/SharePoint | smb://server17.pretendco.com/SharePoint | ftp://server17.pretendco.com/ | nfs://server17.pretendco.comSharePoint |

This is the first slide in a series (one slide at the end of each protocol lesson) that compares and contrasts authentication information, if the share point can be browsed, and the full syntax of the share point URL.

Exercises

5.2.1 Configure Apple File Sharing Service

5.2.2 Manage AFP Service Settings

5.2.3 Test AFP Service Settings

## Exercise 5.2.1

# Configure AFP File Sharing Service

### Objective

Demonstrate some of the most useful features of Apple File Service on Mac OS X Server.

### Summary

You'll share a folder via AFP and set permissions and control connections with Server Admin.

### Share a Folder via Apple File Service

In this exercise, you'll use Server Admin to make a folder on your server computer, which is shared via Apple File Service. Before a folder can be shared via any protocol, you must set up the folder for sharing.

1. Open Server Admin, and select your server. Authenticate if necessary.
2. Click File Sharing in the toolbar.
3. Click the Volumes and Browse buttons.
4. Navigate to and select the /Shared Items folder.
5. Click the New Folder button in the top-right corner of the window.
6. Enter `Apple File Share Point` in the name field.

7 Click Create, and click Save. Then select the Apple File Share Point folder, and make sure it is highlighted.

8 Click the Share button, and then click Save.

The item is now shared. By default, Mac OS X Server shares items over AFP, SMB, and FTP. Because you want this item to be viewable only by AFP clients, you'll modify the default setting so that it is shared only via Apple File Service (AFP).

9 Click the Protocol Options button.

10 In the AFP window, make sure that "Share this item using AFP" is enabled (it should be turned on by default).

11 Select the radio button for "Inherit permissions from parent."

12 Click the SMB button to show the Windows File Settings.

13 Deselect the checkbox for "Share this item using SMB."

14 Click the FTP button to show the FTP Settings.

15 Deselect the checkbox for "Share this item using FTP."

16 Click OK, and then click Save.

Now, your shared folder is visible only to computers and authorized users connecting over the AFP service.

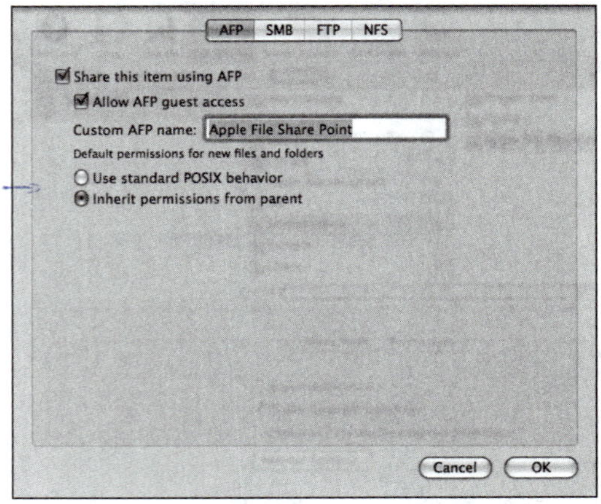


## Start Apple File Service

Because you want to share this folder using Apple File Service, you must configure AFP service with Server Admin and then start the AFP service.

If AFP services are already running, you'll only need to verify your AFP set up using the steps below.

1 Open Server Admin, and select your server.

2 Select the AFP service.

3 Click Settings, and then click the General tab.

4 Make sure that Enable Bonjour registration is selected.

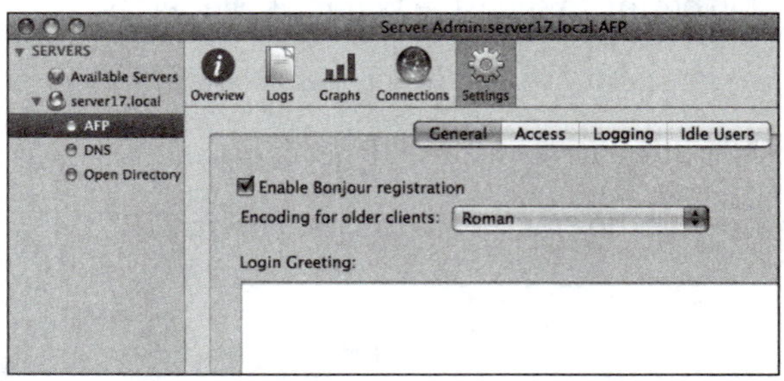

5 Click the Access tab, and choose Standard from the Authentication pop-up menu.

6 Select "Enable Guest access."

7 Click Save.

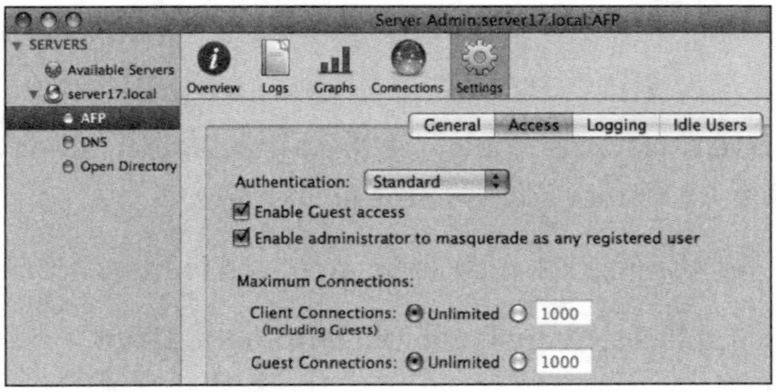


8 Apple File Service should be turned on. If it isn't, start it by clicking the Start AFP button.

If it was already on, stop and restart AFP services to ensure the changes have taken effect.

9 On your Mac OS X computer, use Connect to Server in the Finder to connect to your server at server*n*.local (where *n* is your student number).

10 Connect as a guest, and click Connect.

> **Note** Notice that you are connecting via AFP even though you did not type `afp://` prior to the address. This is because Connect to Server defaults to `afp://`, so there is no need to type in the prefix.

11 Select the Apple File Share Point volume.

12 Click OK.

13 Verify that the Apple File Share Point volume is mounted.

14 Unmount the Apple File Share Point volume.

## Configure Permissions on the Shared Folder

Now that you've shared the Apple File Share Point folder, modify the permissions to restrict access to the files.

1 Using Server Admin, click the File Sharing icon in the toolbar.

2 Select the Apple File Share Point folder from the Share Points list.

3 Create two new folders in your Apple File Share Point folder:

   Save the changes after each folder creation and click back on another share point, or you may end up creating nested folders.

   - Press Releases
   - Lion Development

4 Select the Lion Development folder.

5 In the Permissions pane, change the POSIX permissions as follows:

   - Owner: `leroy`, Read & Write
   - Group: `admin`, Read & Write
   - Others: None

6 Click Save.

7 Your Apple File Share Point should now appear as follows:

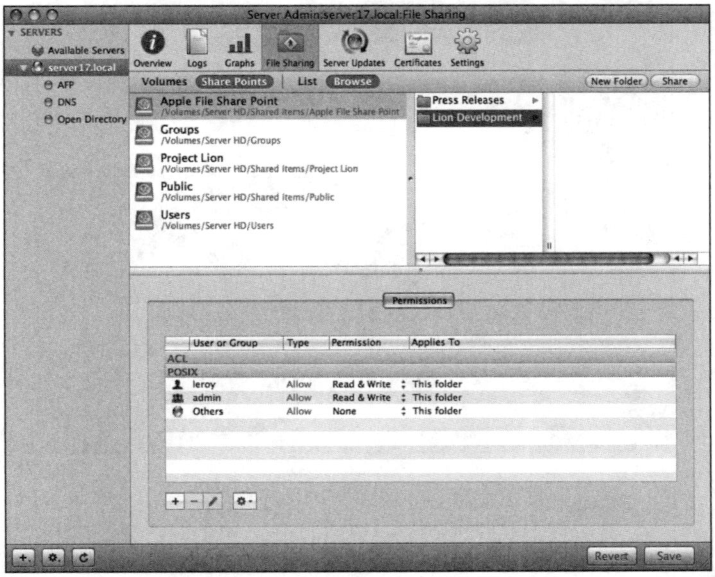


## Assigning Shared Groups to Share points

1 If not selected, click the File Sharing icon in the Server Admin toolbar.

2 Select the Lion Development folder.

3 Click the Add (+) button in the Permissions pane.

4 Click the Groups button in the Users and Groups window and drag the Engineering and Marketing groups to the Access Control List.

5 Click Save.

6 Select the Press Releases folder, and change the POSIX permissions to the following:

- Owner: `diradmin`, Read & Write
- Group: `mktg`, Read & Write
- Others: Read Only

7 Click Save.

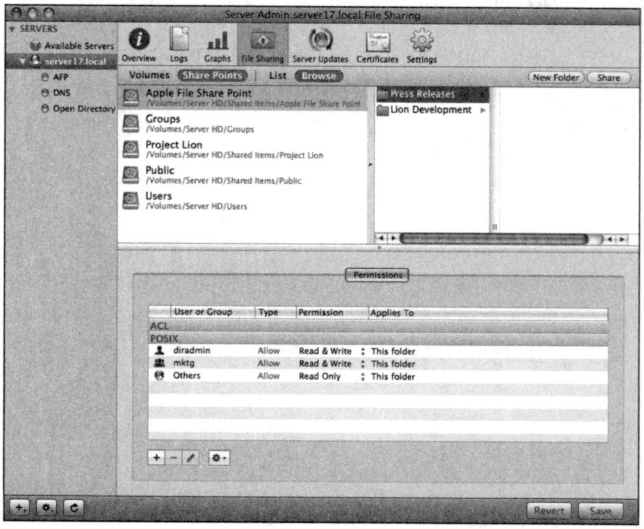

## Testing the Share Point

1 From your Mac OS X computer, connect to your AFP server as `leroy` (password: `changeme`).

2 Mount the Apple File Share Point folder.

3 Use TextEdit to save a file called New Features in the Lion Development folder.

4 Unmount the share point.

5 Connect to the same share point, this time as john.

   Because John is a member of Marketing, he has read only access to the Lion Development folder.

6 Use TextEdit to save a file called Public Announcement in the Press Releases folder.

7 Unmount the share point.

8 Connect again as Red Floyd (a member of Engineering).

   ***Question 2*** *What kind of access does Red have to the Press Releases folder?*

   ______________________________________________

9 Unmount the share point.

Exercise 5.2.2

# Manage AFP Service Settings

## Objective

Demonstrate some of the most useful features of Apple File Service on Mac OS X Server.

## Summary

You'll share a folder via AFP and set permissions and control connections with Server Admin.

## Restrict Connections to the Server by the Authentication Method

Now, you'll restrict who can connect through Apple File Protocol to your server to those users that use Kerberos.

1. In Server Admin, select the AFP service from the list under your server's entry.
2. In the toolbar, click the Settings icon, and then click the Access tab.
3. Choose Kerberos from the authentication method pop-up menu, and deselect Enable Guest Access.
4. Click Save.

## Set Up Home Folder Automounts

Now, you'll set up the home folder for other users of this server.

1. In Server Admin, click the File Sharing icon in the toolbar.
2. Click the Share Points button, and select the Users share point from the list.

3 Click the Share Point tab, and select Enable Automount.

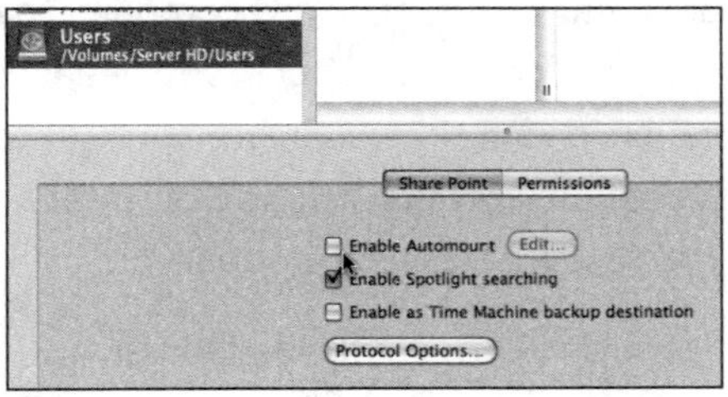


4 A dialog appears showing that you'll be adding this mount point to the shared directory.

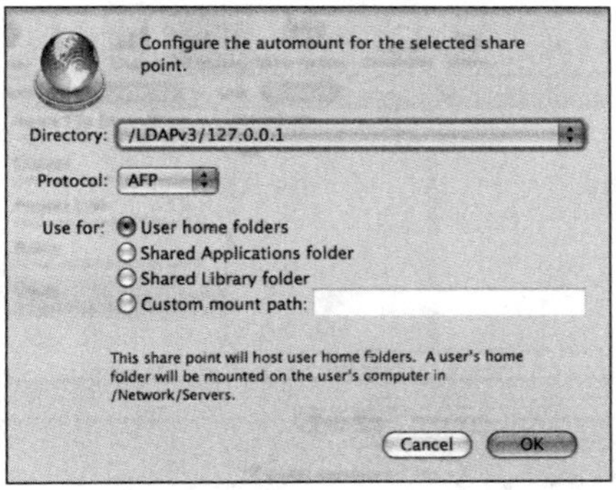


Verify that /LDAPv3/127.0.0.1 is the directory selected for automount and that AFP is the protocol for mounting.

5 Verify "User home folders" is selected, and click OK.

6 Authenticate as `diradmin`.

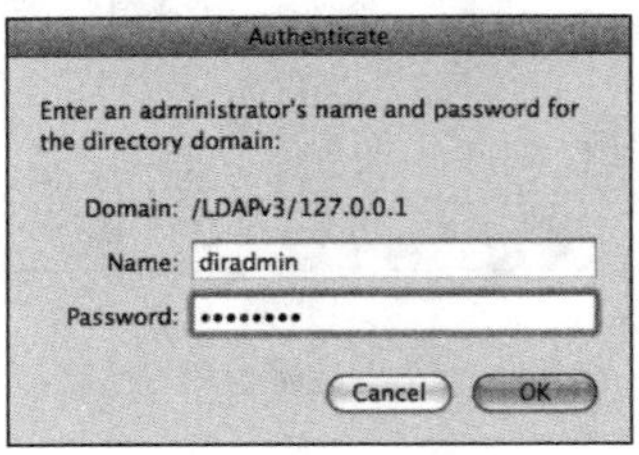

7 Click Save.

You've allowed this share point to mount on any computer that can see your shared directory. For this to happen, you needed to save this mount information in your shared directory. You already know that you've saved users and groups. You've just saved a mount point. It is a record, just like a user or group record.

8 Open Workgroup Manager, and connect to your server.

9 Ensure you are looking at the shared (LDAP) directory, and click the Lock icon in the upper right, if necessary authenticate as diradmin.

10 Click the Accounts icon in the toolbar

11 Click the Users tab, and select all user accounts except for diradmin.

12 Click the Home tab. The new AFP home folder share point is listed.

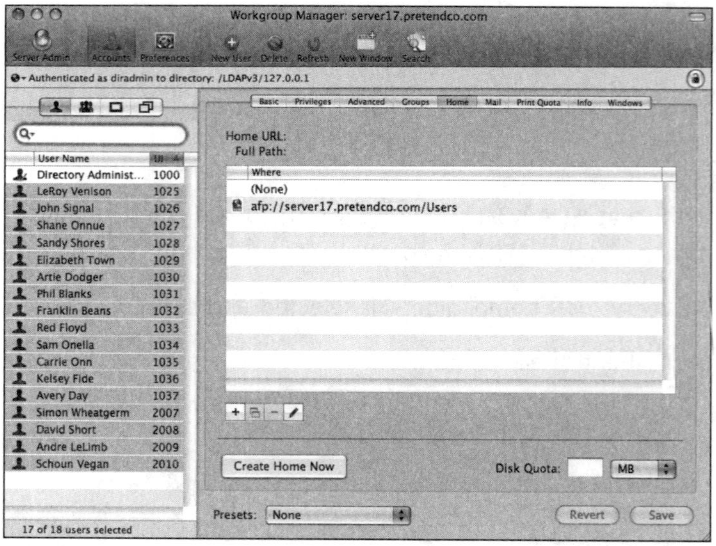


13 Select afp://server*n*.pretendco.com/Users (where n is your student number).

14 Click the Create Home Now button, and then click Save.

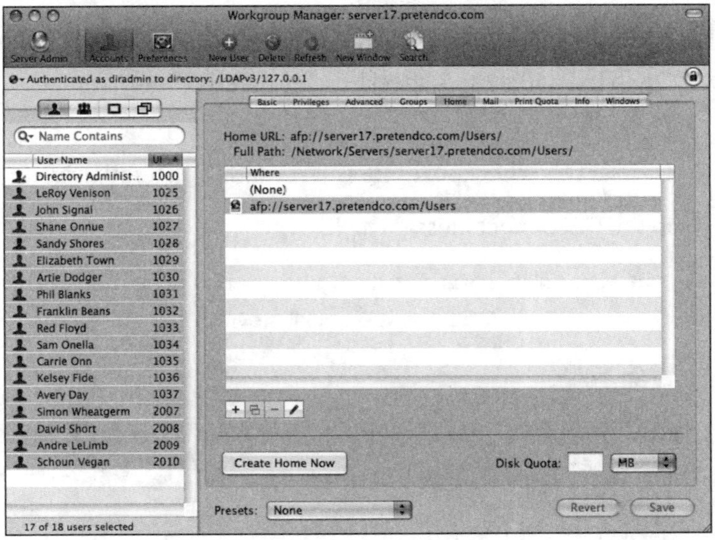

You've added two values to all the users' attributes; the Home URL and the Full Path. All the users have a long name, short name, and so on. They now have a location where they can locate their home folder. That location—in this case—is inside the Users folder on server*n*.pretendco.com. You can see the share point path is listed in the field and shown as the Home URL. The Full Path, which in this case is /Network/Servers/server*n*.pretendco.com/Users/, is actually where the share point will show on the computers that can read this shared (LDAP) directory.

15 Use Screen Sharing to control the screen of your Mac OS X Server and open the /Users folder to ensure home folders for all users have been created.

## Configure Idle User Settings

Now you'll set up Idle Users settings for AFP services on this server.

1 In Server Admin, select the AFP service from the list under your server's entry.

2 Click the Settings icon in the toolbar, and click the Idle Users button.

3 Deselect the Allow clients to sleep option, select the Disconnect idle users checkbox, and set the time limit to `10` minutes.

4 Deselect the checkboxes for Guests and Registered users.

5 In the Disconnect Message field, type

```
You are not using this share point and there-
fore will be disconnected now. Have a nice day.
```

6 Click Save.

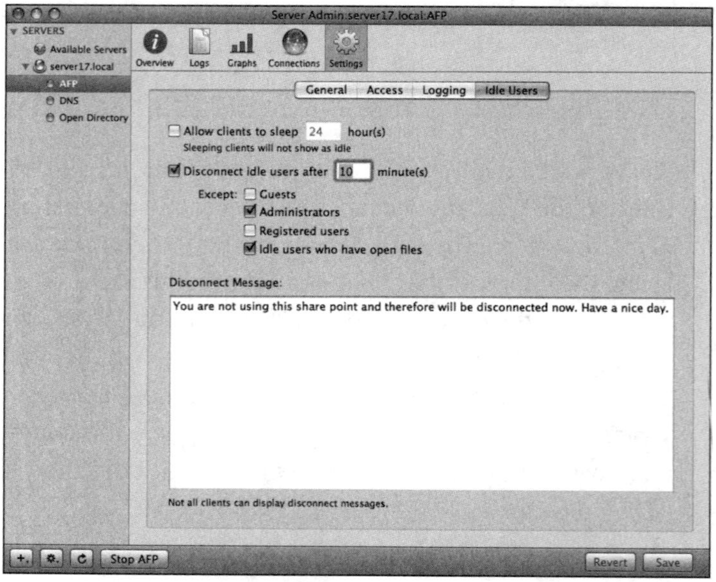


7 Stop and restart AFP services.

## Exercise 5.2.3

# Test AFP Service Settings

## Objective

Ensure file sharing and the home directories are set up correctly by properly testing them prior to rolling them out.

## Summary

You'll test your AFP connection, watch it fail, bind your Mac OS X computer to your Mac OS X Server's shared directory, and retest your AFP connection.

1 Using your Mac OS X computer, try to connect to your server as `schoun` (password: `changeme`).

***Question 3*** *What happens when you try to connect?*

Now, you must bind your Mac OS X computer to the Mac OS X Server.

2 Open your Directory Utility inside the /Applications/Utilities/ folder, click the Lock icon in the lower-left corner, and authenticate as your client administrator.

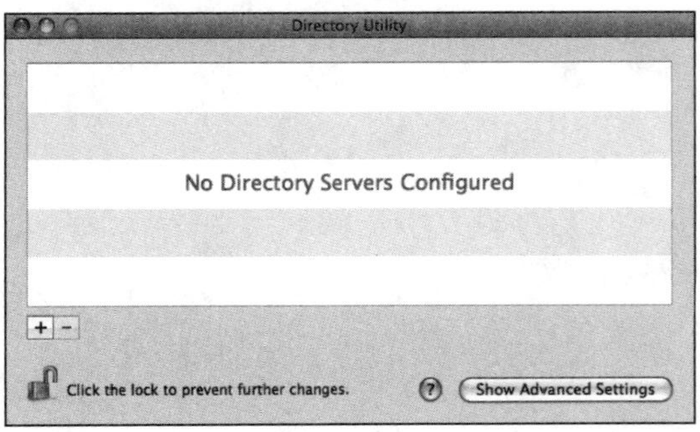

3 Click the Add(+) button, enter `servern.pretendco.com` (where *n* is your student number), and click OK.

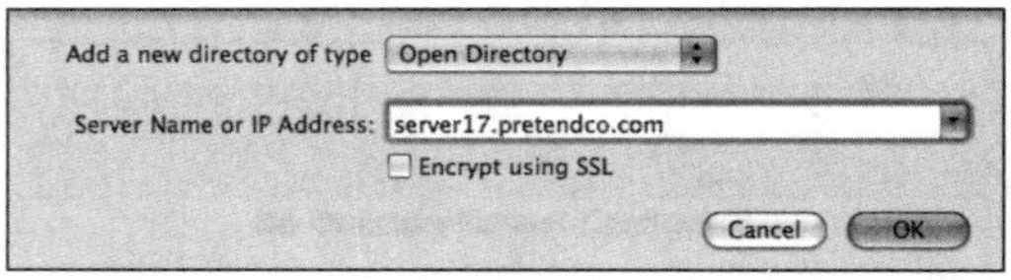


Your Mac OS X computer will contact your Mac OS X Server, locate the shared database, and bind to that server. Several files are being updated and created on your Mac OS X computer, allowing it to use the server for authentication. You'll see the server is responding normally.

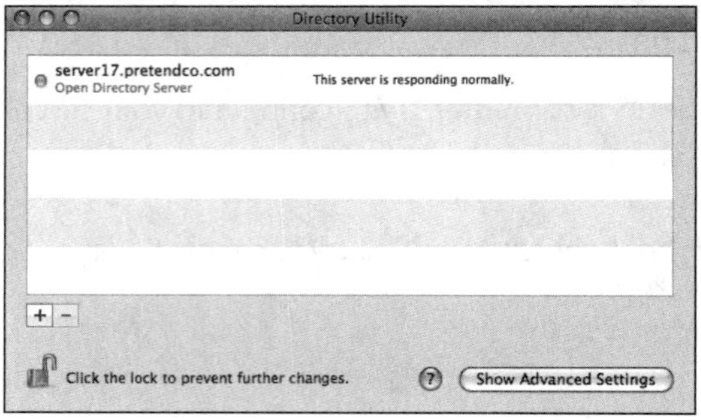


4 Quit Directory Utility.

5 Attempt to log in via AFP to the Mac OS X Server as schoun.

6 Authenticate and select the schoun share point.

7 Open /System/Library/CoreServices/Kerberos, and view your tickets.

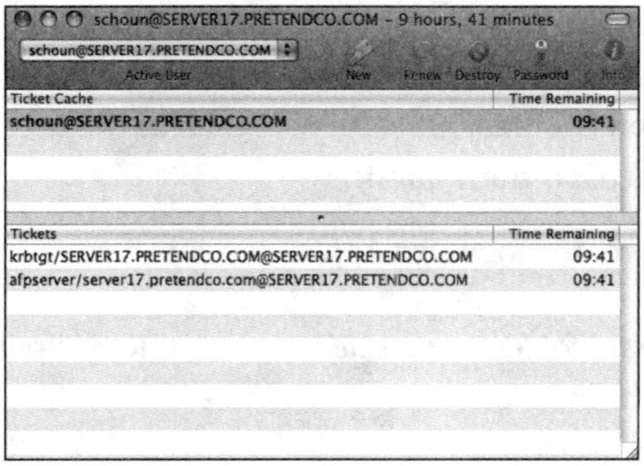


You have an afpserver ticket.

8 Quit the Kerberos application and unmount the schoun share point.

9 Choose Go > Connect to Server, and mount the Apple File Share Point.

Notice you did not have to provide a password this time.

10 Unmount the share points.

11 Connect to your AFP server again.

***Question 4*** *Were you prompted to authenticate?*

12 Unmount the share point, destroy all existing Kerberos tickets, and log out from your client.

13 Now, log out, and log back in as artie.

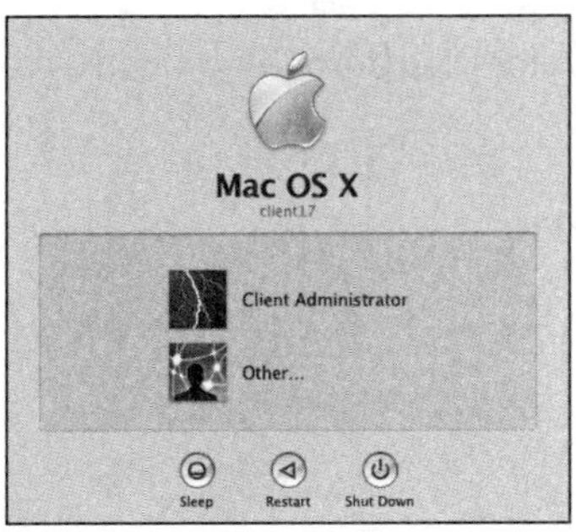

You've logged in to your Mac OS X computer as a user that does not exist on your Mac OS X computer. You have a home directory, located on your Mac OS X Server. As far as the user is concerned, the process is transparent.

14 Connect to your server to mount the Apple File Share Point folder.

*Question 5 Which subfolders does artie have access to without further authentication?*

---

15 Unmount the AFP volume from your Mac OS X computer, and log out as artie.

16 Log back in as cadmin and use Workgroup Manager to reenable David's account.

17 Destroy any existing Kerberos tickets, and then connect to the Apple File Share Point folder, and authenticate as david.

18 Close the Finder window for this share point (DO NOT EJECT IT).

19 Open Server Admin, authenticate, and select AFP from the list under your server's entry.

20 Click Connections in the toolbar and watch David's AFP connection gradually change from Normal to Disabled/Asleep.

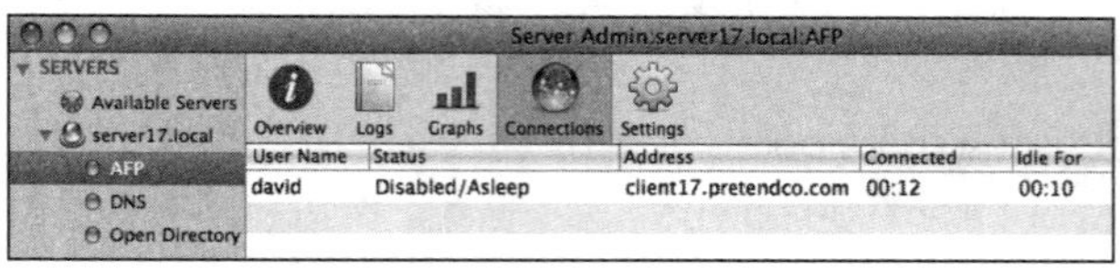


21 Unmount the share point.

22 Open /System/Library/CoreServices/Kerberos, and destroy any tickets that are active.

## SMB

Protocols

## Server Message Block—Service Configuration

Primary options

- Server Roles:
    - Standalone
    - Domain Member
    - Primary Domain Controller (PDC)
    - Backup Domain Controller (BDC)

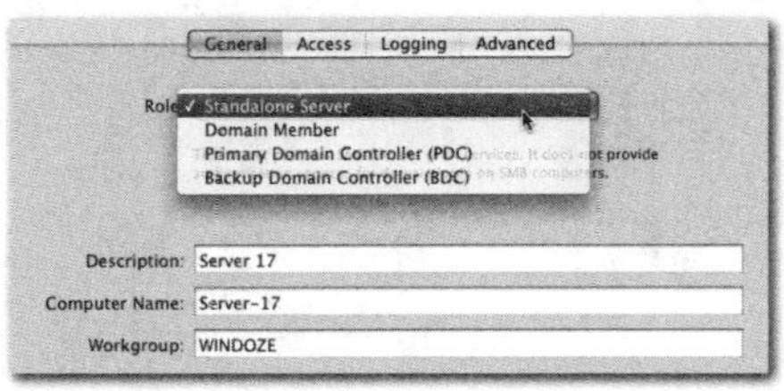


The SMB service has a variety of options, most notably the roles that the service can become. The SMB service can mimic a Primary Domain Controller or Backup Domain Controller to permit authentication from older Windows clients. It can also be a member of an existing Windows domain or stand on its own as a single SMB service running on a Mac OS X Server.

## Server Message Block—Service Configuration

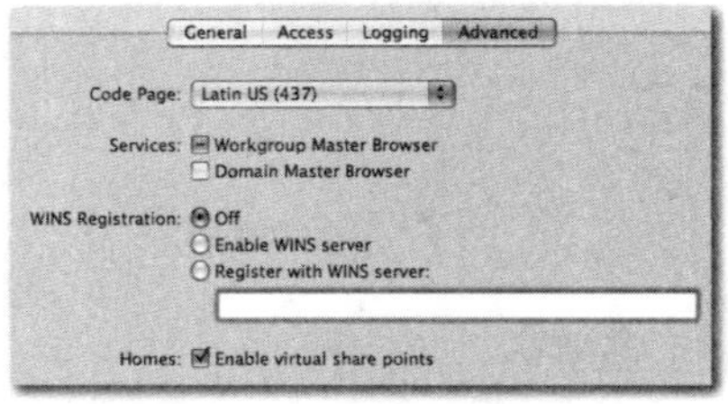


Primary options

- Authentication methods
  - Kerberos, NTLMv2
  - NTLMv1
  - LAN MANAGER
- Mac OS X Server SAMBA service participation in elections:
  - Workgroup Master Browser
  - Domain Master Browser
- Register with or become WINS server
- Verbose logging capabilities

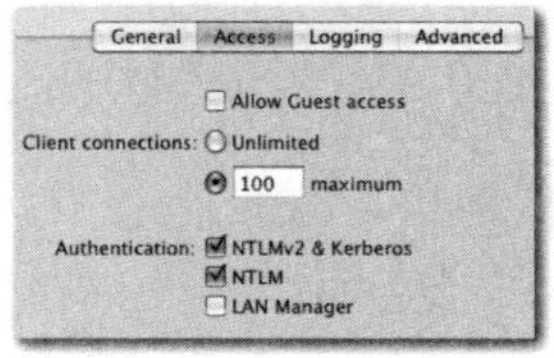


Among the options that SMB can provide are different authentication methods, including Kerberos and NTLMv2. Older Windows clients require less secure authentication methods. Virtual share points permit users to log into a Mac OS X Server and have the same home folder regardless of whether they are using Windows or Mac OS X to log in.

## SMB Share Point Options

When choosing to share a volume or folder over SMB:

- Guest access (must be enabled on the SMB service as well)
- Custom share point name
- Opportunistic locks/strict locking
- Permissions model for copied items
  - Inherit Permissions
  - Assign Permissions

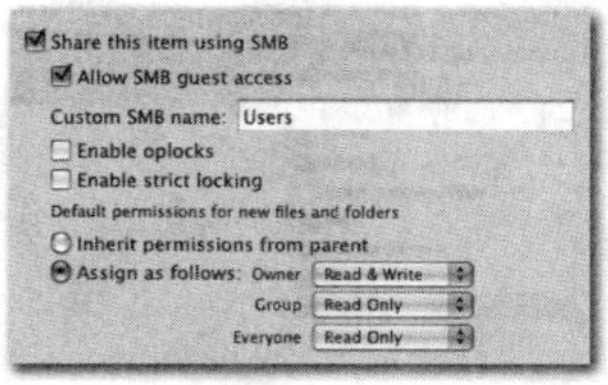


Share point options consist of changing the name and guest access, default permissions, and file locking. The use of oplocks (opportunistic locks) and strict locking permits files to be treated differently by users depending on who opened the file first. Strict locking opens files by a second user as read-only, while opportunistic locks cache file changes locally and should only be used when sharing over SMB only.

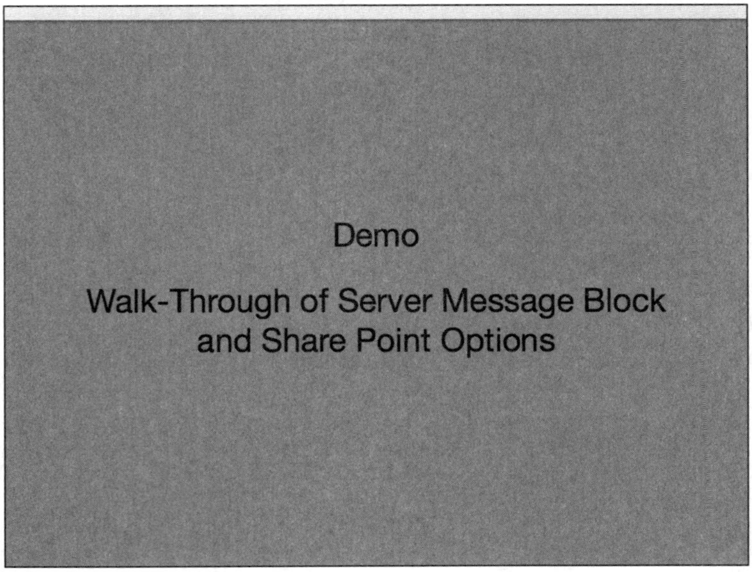


The instructor will demo the SMB service and SMB share point options.

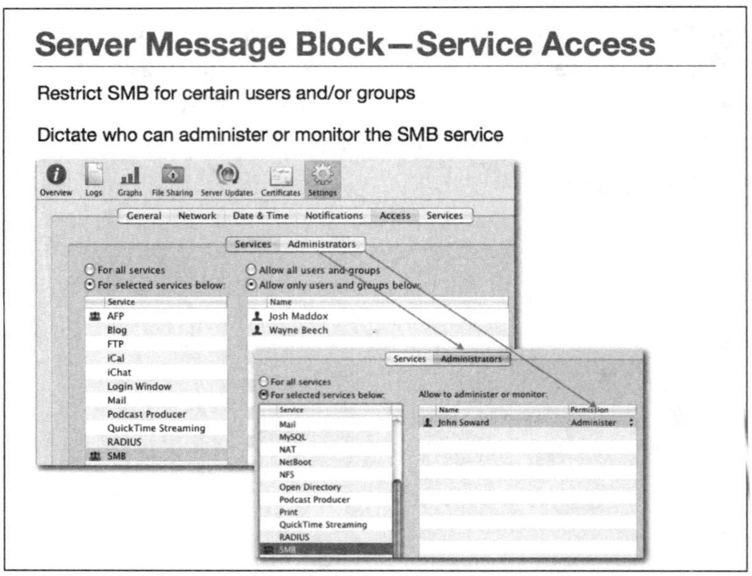


Setting controls on who can access, manage, and monitor the SMB service helps secure that service against users who have accounts on the Mac OS X Server but are not authorized to access share points over SMB.

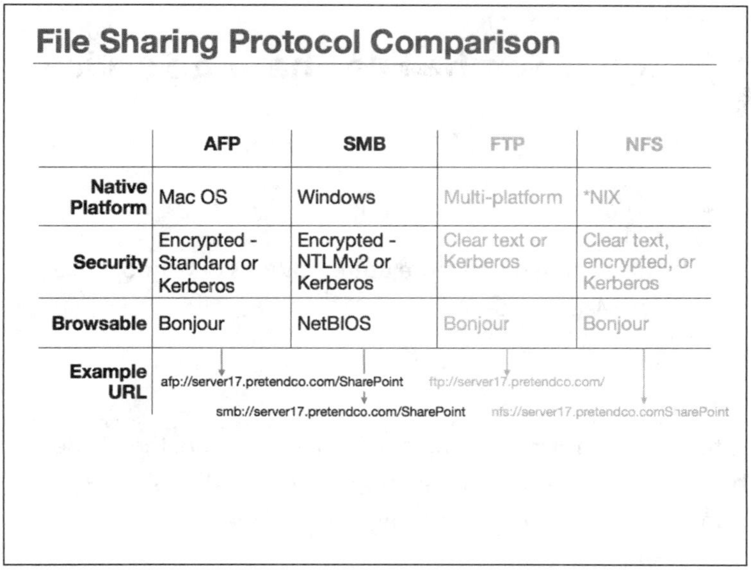

## File Sharing Protocol Comparison

| | AFP | SMB | FTP | NFS |
|---|---|---|---|---|
| Native Platform | Mac OS | Windows | Multi-platform | *NIX |
| Security | Encrypted - Standard or Kerberos | Encrypted - NTLMv2 or Kerberos | Clear text or Kerberos | Clear text, encrypted, or Kerberos |
| Browsable | Bonjour | NetBIOS | Bonjour | Bonjour |
| Example URL | afp://server17.pretendco.com/SharePoint | smb://server17.pretendco.com/SharePoint | ftp://server17.pretendco.com/ | nfs://server17.pretendco.comSharePoint |

This is the second slide in a series (one slide at the end of each protocol lesson) that compares and contrasts authentication information, if the share point can be browsed, and the full syntax of the share point URL.

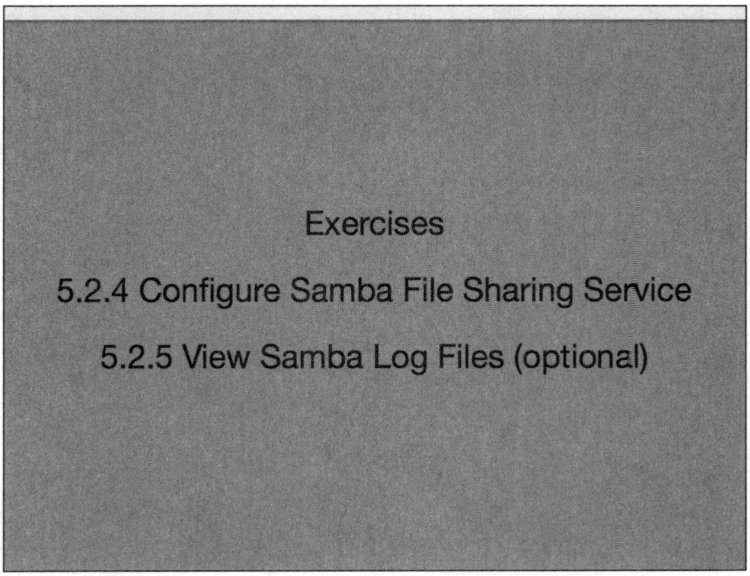

## Exercise 5.2.4

# Configure Samba File Sharing Service

### Objective

Demonstrate some of the more useful features of Windows file services on Mac OS X Server.

### Summary

After creating a Windows share point, you'll explore the Windows browsing features and browse to your Windows File Share Point using the Connect to Server command in Finder.

### Share a Folder for Windows Clients

In this exercise, you'll use Server Admin to share a folder over SMB.

1 In Server Admin, click the File Sharing icon in the toolbar.

2 Click the Volumes and Browse buttons to navigate the contents of the hard drive.

3 Navigate to and select /Shared Items.

4 Click the New Folder button in the upper-right corner of the window.

5 Enter `Windows File Share Point` in the name field.

6 Click Create, and click Save.

7 Select the Windows File Share Point folder, making sure it is highlighted.

**8** Click Share, and then click Save.

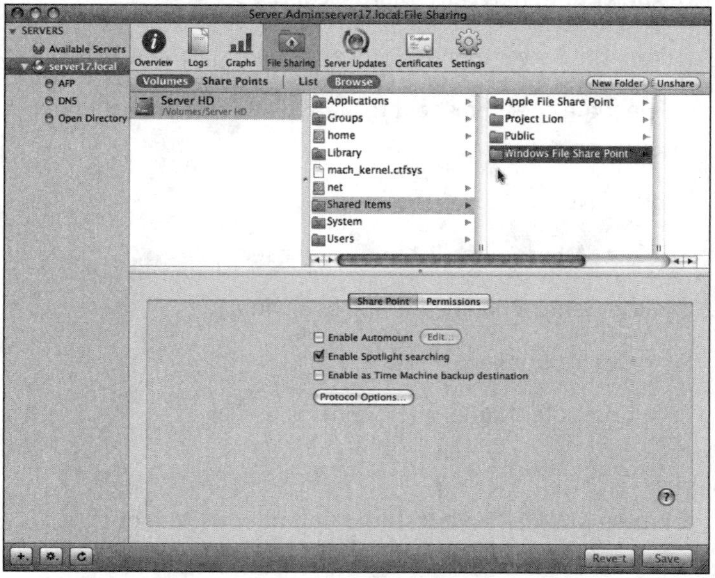


**9** Click the Protocol Options button, and deselect AFP and FTP services for this item.

Click the SMB button, and type `Windows` in the "Custom SMB name" field.

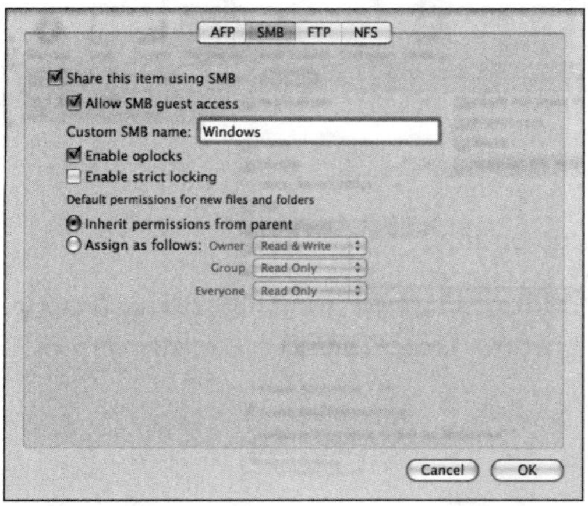


**10** Click OK, and then click Save.

Any Windows clients will see a share point called Windows instead of Windows File Share Point.

## Start Windows File Service

Use Server Admin to start Windows services.

1 From the Server menu in Server Admin, choose Add Service.

2 Select the checkbox next to SMB to add it to the list under your server on the left.

3 Click Save.

4 Select SMB from the list under your server.

5 In the General pane enter the following:

- Description: server*n*
- Computer Name: server*n*
- Workgroup: WG_*NUMBER*

Where *NUMBER* is your student number written out, for example SEVENTEEN.

Leave other settings as default.

6 Click Save.

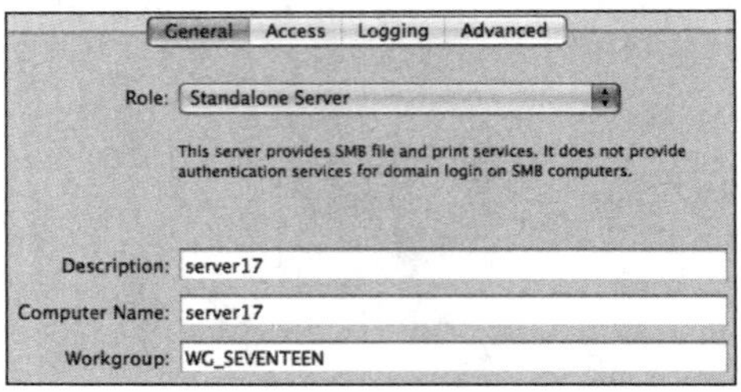


7 Click the Advanced button.

8 Select "Register with WINS server" from the WINS Registration options, and then enter 10.1.0.1 in the "Register with WINS server" text field.

9 Click Save.

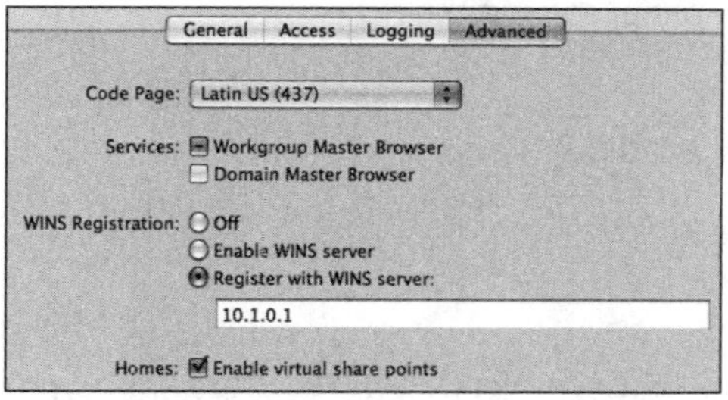


10 Click the Access tab.

11 Verify the "Allow Guest access" checkbox is selected.

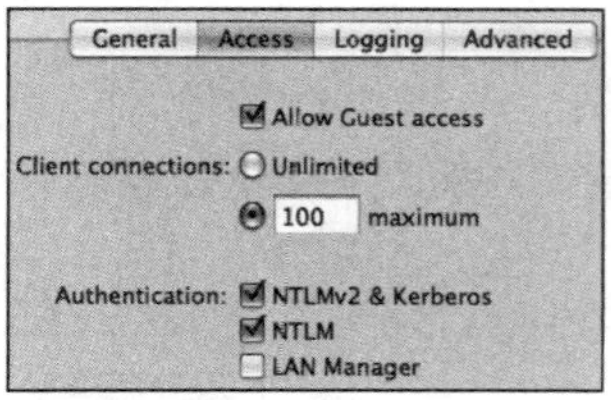


12 Click Save.

13 Click Start SMB (bottom left) to start the SMB service.

## Configure Permissions on the Shared Folder

Now that you've shared the Windows File Share Point folder, modify the permissions to restrict access to the files.

1 In Server Admin, click File Sharing in the toolbar.

2 Click the Share Points and Browse buttons.

3 Navigate to and select the Windows File Share Point folder.

4 Create two new folders in your Windows File Share Point folder:

Save the changes after each folder creation and select another share point, then select the Windows File Share Point again, or you might create nested folders.

- Public Items
- Longhorn Development

5 Select the Longhorn Development folder.

6 In the Permissions pane, change the POSIX permissions as follows:

- Owner: `leroy`, Read & Write
- Group: `admin`, Read & Write
- Others: None

7 Click the Add (+) button in the Permissions pane and drag the Engineering and Marketing groups to the Access Control List.

8 Click Save.

9 Your Longhorn Development folder permissions should appear as shown in the following figure:

10 Click Save.

11 Select the Public Items folder, and change the POSIX permissions as follows:

- Owner: ladmin, Read & Write
- Group: mktg, Read & Write
- Others: None

12 Click Save.

## Case-Sensitivity Issues with SMB Volumes

In this exercise, you'll use the client computer to connect to Windows file services on the server computer over SMB and try to copy some files.

1 Use the TextEdit application to create a text file. You can enter anything for content.

2 Save the text file as myfile.rtf (all lowercase letters, no spaces) on your Desktop.

3 Choose Connect to Server from the Go menu in the Finder.

4 Type the volume address `smb://servern.local` (where *n* is your student number).

5 Authenticate as leroy, and click OK.

6 When prompted to select a share point, select windows.

At this time, all SMB share point names appear in lower case.

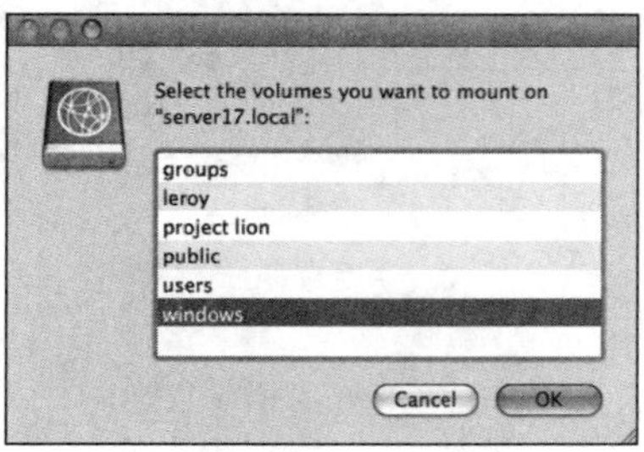


7 Click OK.

8 Copy the myfile.rtf file you created from Mac OS X to the mounted network volume windows into the Public Items folder.

9 Change the name of the myfile.txt file on the local computer to MyFILE.rtf (notice the case difference).

10 Try to copy the renamed file to the same location on the server.

11 When the server asks you to confirm, click Replace.

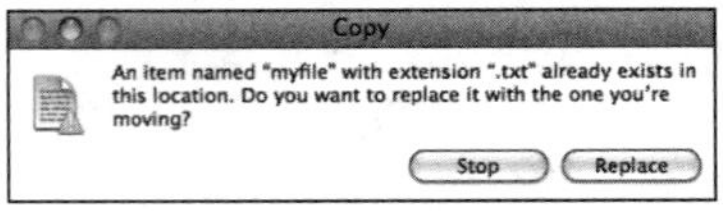


Your MyFILE.rtf overwrites the myfile.rtf file. If this were a case-sensitive file system, the file would still be erased.

12 Open the Kerberos application from your Recent Items list under the Apple menu.

Notice that LeRoy obtained a ticket granting ticket and a CIFS (Common Internet File System) ticket for connection via SMB.

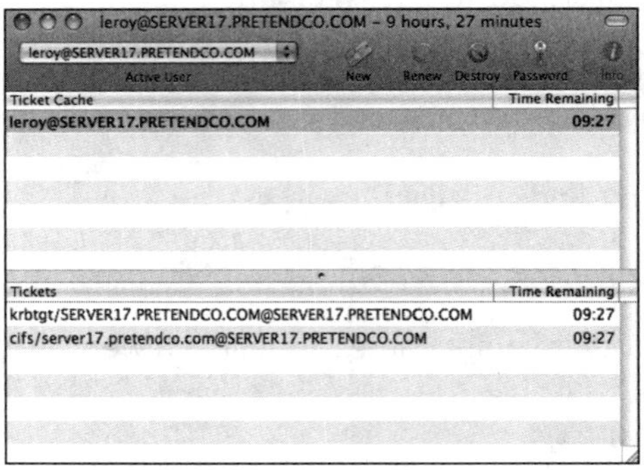

13 In the Finder, choose Go > Connect to Server, and enter `afp://servern.local`. Click Connect, and mount the Apple File Share Point.

14 Close the window that appears, but in the Kerberos application notice that you gained another ticket, an afpserver ticket. Because you were granted this ticket, you did not have to authenticate again to mount the Apple File Share Point.

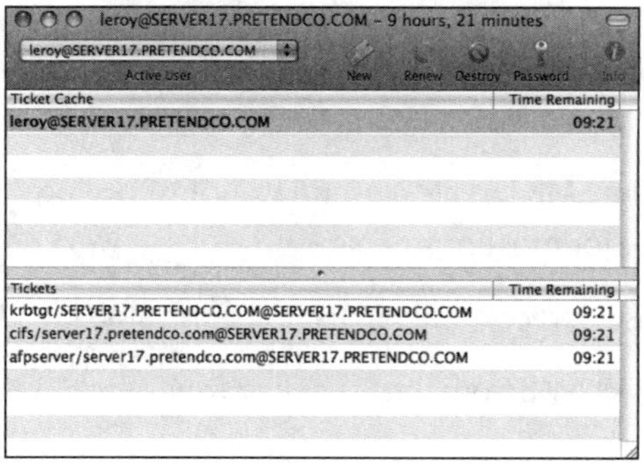


15 Click the Destroy icon in the toolbar of the Kerberos application to destroy all the tickets.

**Question 6** *Can you still copy files to both mount points even though you don't have any tickets? Why or why not?*

## Exercise 5.2.5

# View Samba Log Files (optional)

## Objective

Demonstrates some of the more useful features of the log files on Mac OS X Server.

## Summary

While you'll focus on the SMB log files, useful troubleshooting information is available for most protocols.

In this exercise, you'll use Server Admin to examine the SMB log file.

1. In Server Admin, select SMB from the list below your server's entry.
2. Click Settings in the toolbar.
3. Click the Logging button, set the Log Level to High, and click Save.
4. Unmount any share points using the Eject button in the Sidebar of your Finder.
5. Stop and restart the SMB service.
6. Connect to your server via SMB and mount the windows share point (authenticate as john).
7. Copy the MyFILE.rtf file to the Public Items folder again.
8. Unmount the share point.
9. In Server Admin, click Logs in the toolbar, and choose the SMB File Service Log from the bottom pop-up menu.
10. Scroll through the log file for the SMB service.

    You'll see messages for starting and stopping the SMB service and messages showing the mount request just made.

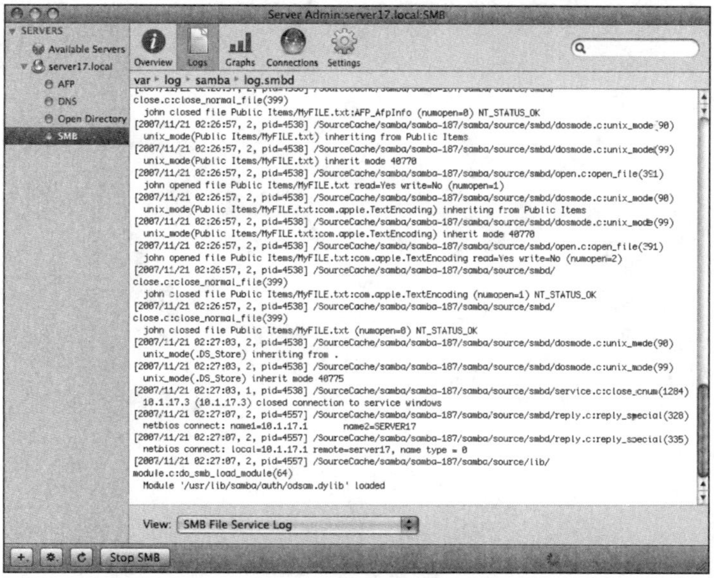


11 Select the SMB Name Service Log from the bottom pop-up menu.

You'll see messages pertaining to the browser elections for your workgroup.

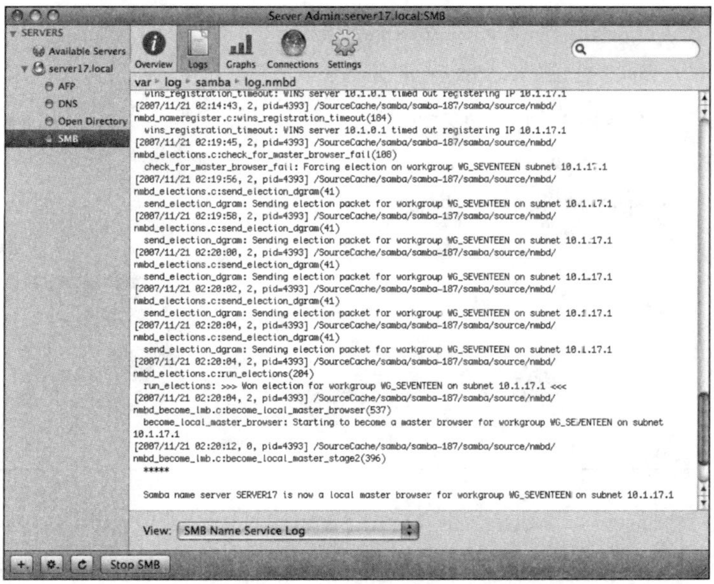

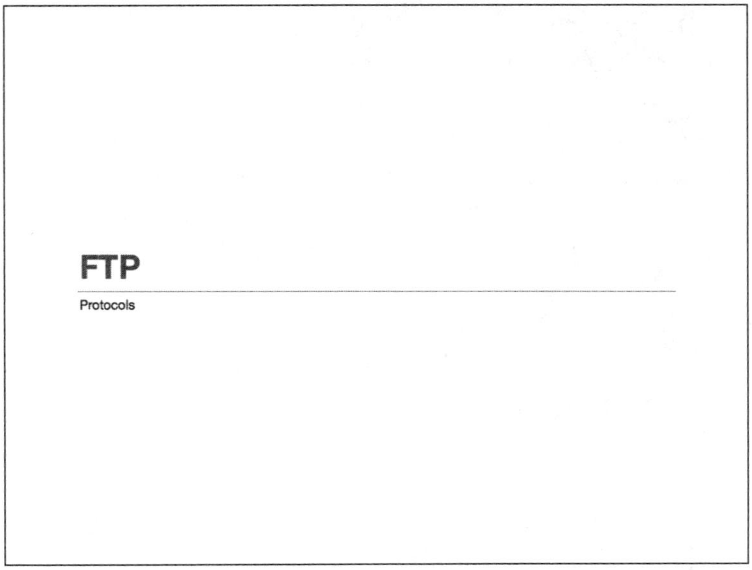


FTP is a ubiquitous file sharing service that has been around for a very long time. Mac OS X Server can offer FTP services.

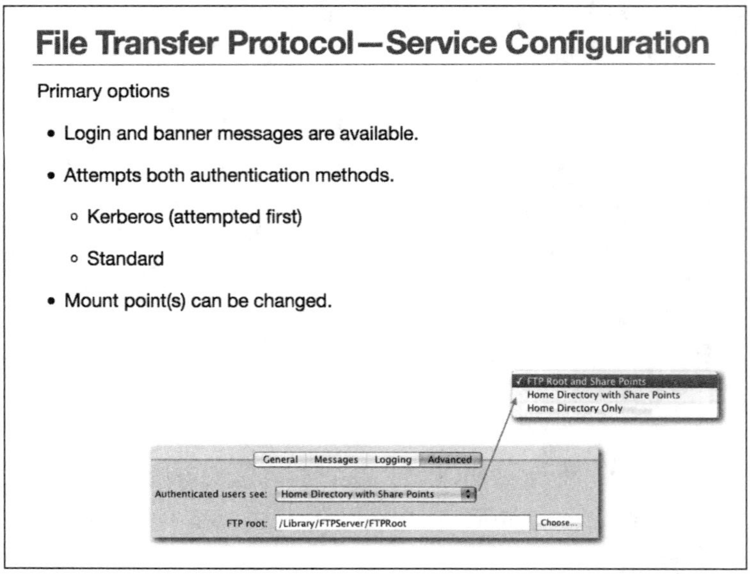


FTP has been around for several years and is a very common way to transfer files and folders back and forth from clients to servers. Mac OS X Server can use the FTP service and maintains a list of options for securing and customizing the FTP service.

## File Conversion

Uncompressed/compressed files and/or folders requested from FTP share points on the server can be delivered compressed/uncompressed*

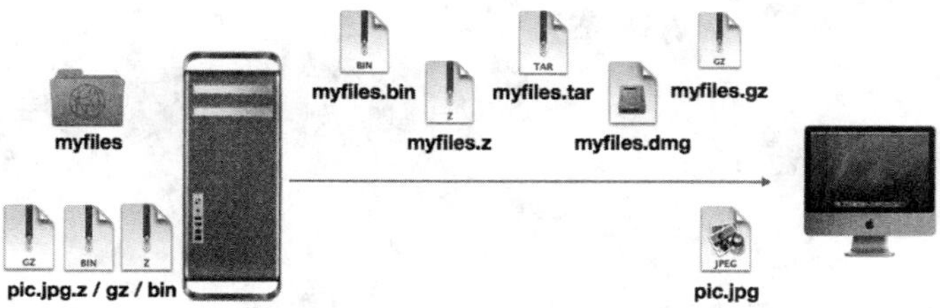


* Mac OS X Server, FTP Service Active, File Conversion On

Users can upload compressed files to an FTP server. When those same files are requested, they are delivered to the user requesting the files as uncompressed. The FTP service recognizes the name of the file and decompresses the file on the fly for the user.

## FTP Share Point Options

When choosing to share a volume or folder over FTP:

- Guest access
- Custom share point name

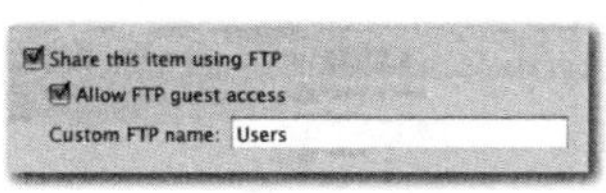


When setting up a share point for access over FTP, administrators can change the name of the share and permit or deny guest access.

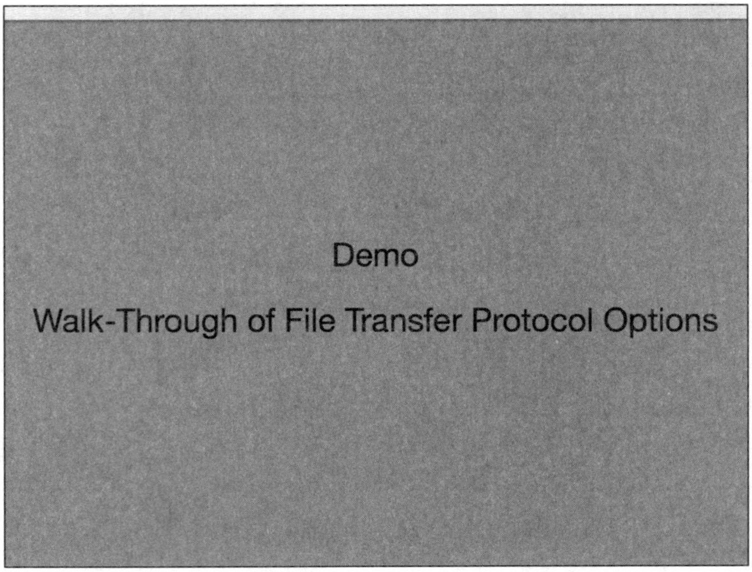


The instructor will demo the FTP service and FTP share point options.

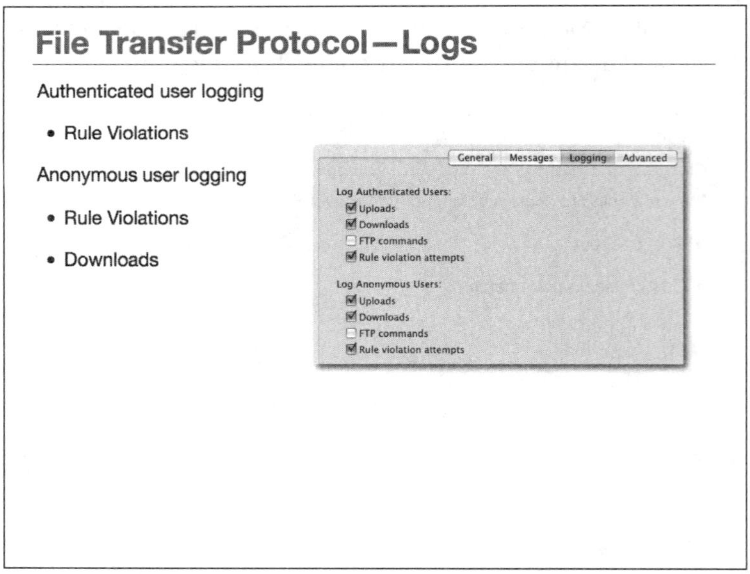


FTP logging can be very verbose and administrators may want to turn on all types of logging when first setting up FTP share points to obtain a baseline on how much network access is being used and who is using all the bandwidth.

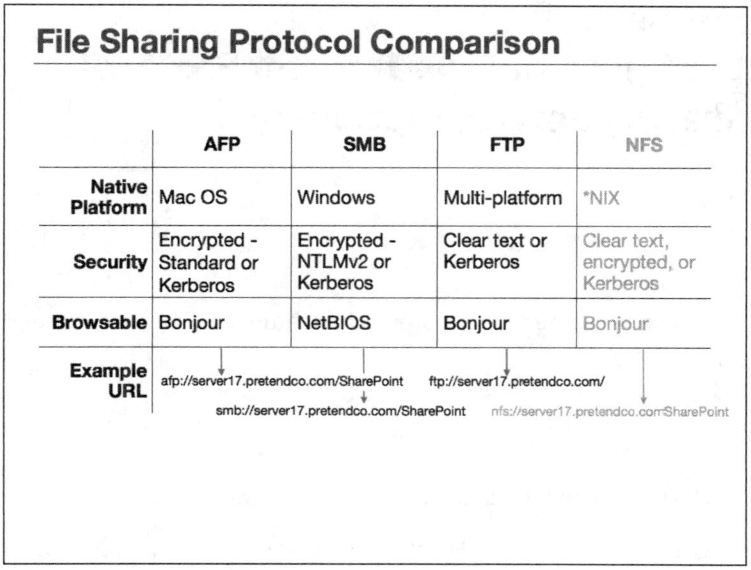

## File Sharing Protocol Comparison

| | AFP | SMB | FTP | NFS |
|---|---|---|---|---|
| **Native Platform** | Mac OS | Windows | Multi-platform | *NIX |
| **Security** | Encrypted - Standard or Kerberos | Encrypted - NTLMv2 or Kerberos | Clear text or Kerberos | Clear text, encrypted, or Kerberos |
| **Browsable** | Bonjour | NetBIOS | Bonjour | Bonjour |
| **Example URL** | afp://server17.pretendco.com/SharePoint | smb://server17.pretendco.com/SharePoint | ftp://server17.pretendco.com/ | nfs://server17.pretendco.com/SharePoint |

This is the third slide in a series (one slide at the end of each protocol lesson) that compares and contrasts authentication information, if the share point can be browsed for, and the full syntax of the share point URL.

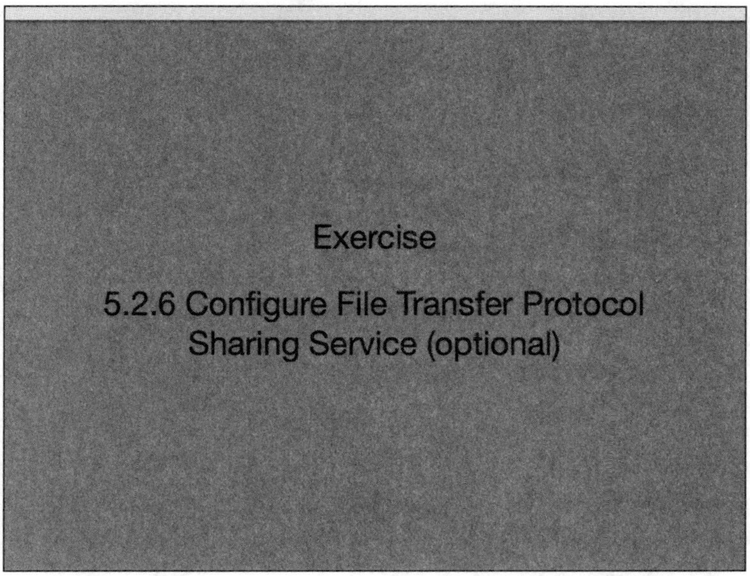

Exercise 5.2.6

# Configure the File Transfer Protocol Sharing Service (optional)

## Objective

Demonstrate some of the more useful features of FTP file service on Mac OS X Server.

## Summary

You'll view the default share point setup for the FTP service.

1. Using Server Admin, click the File Sharing icon in the toolbar.
2. Click the Volumes and Browse buttons to navigate the contents of the hard drive.
3. Navigate to and select /Shared Items.
4. Click the New Folder button in the upper-right corner of the window.
5. Enter `FTP File Share Point` in the name field.
6. Click Create, and click Save.
7. Select the FTP File Share Point folder, and make sure it is highlighted.

8 Click Share, and then click Save.

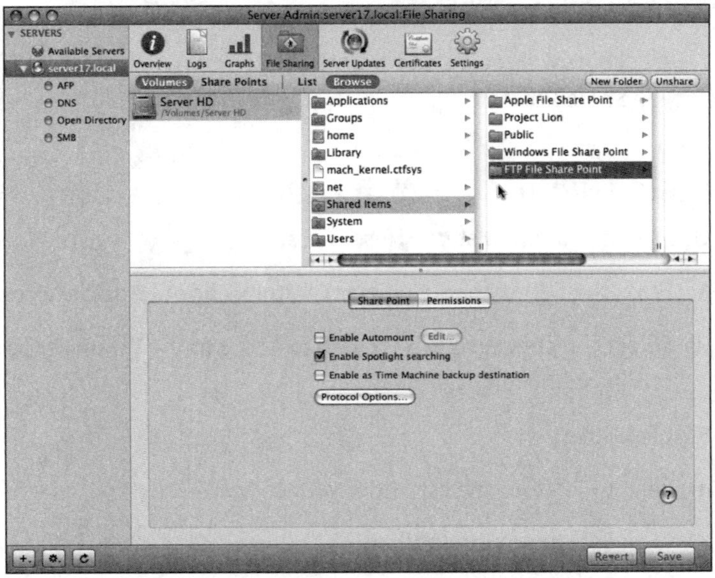


9 Click the Protocol Options button, and deselect AFP and SMB services for this item.

10 Click the FTP button and type `FTP Share` in the "Custom FTP name" field.

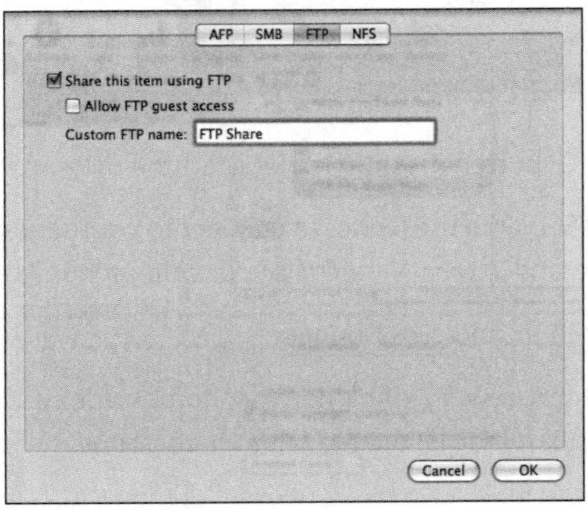

11 Deselect guest access.

12 Click OK, then click Save.

All clients will see a share point called FTP Share instead of FTP File Share Point.

## Start FTP File Service and Connect as a User

Use Server Admin to start FTP services.

1 From the Server menu in Server Admin, choose Add Service…

2 Select the checkbox next to FTP to add it to the list under your server on the left.

3 Click Save.

4 Select FTP from the list under your server.

5 Click Settings in the toolbar.

6 Click the Advanced tab, choose "Home Directory with Share Points" in the "Authenticated users see" pop-up menu, and click Save.

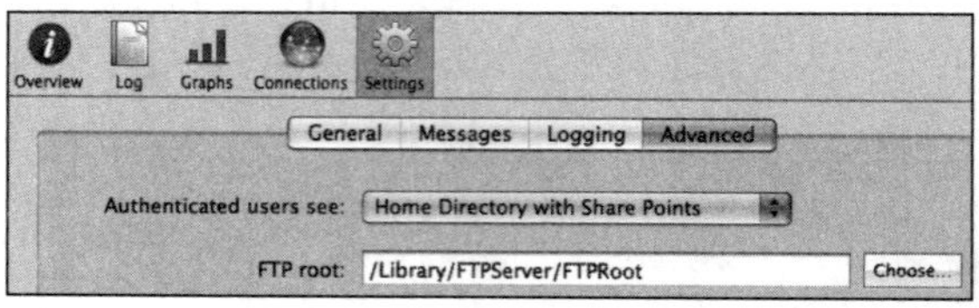


7 Click the Start FTP button (bottom left) to start the FTP service.

8 Use Connect to Server in the Finder to connect to your server at ftp://server*n*.pretendco.com (where *n* is your student number).

9 Authenticate as john, and click Connect.

10 A window appears showing john's network home folder, and inside the FTPRoot folder, all the available share points.

11 Close the window, and unmount the FTP share point.

The NFS service is different from other file sharing services in that it does not generally require user authentication. It trusts the client computer, not the person sitting in front of the computer.

## Network File System—Service Configuration

Primary options

- Number of threads can be set:
  - Default set to 8.
  - Set transmission protocol choice.

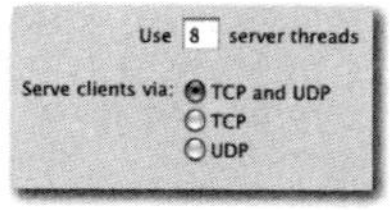


- NFS are exports:
  - Sharing begins once a directory is shared.
  - No service to turn on.
- NFS often used for automounts:
  - Share points that appear within the client file system are actually located on the server.

NFS is a protocol that is used to mount shares regardless of who is logged into a client computer. Uses include network Fonts folders, remote Applications folders, and other folders that are required for users to have access to but not necessarily to write to. The NFS service has only a few options because most of the NFS configuration comes from management of the share point.

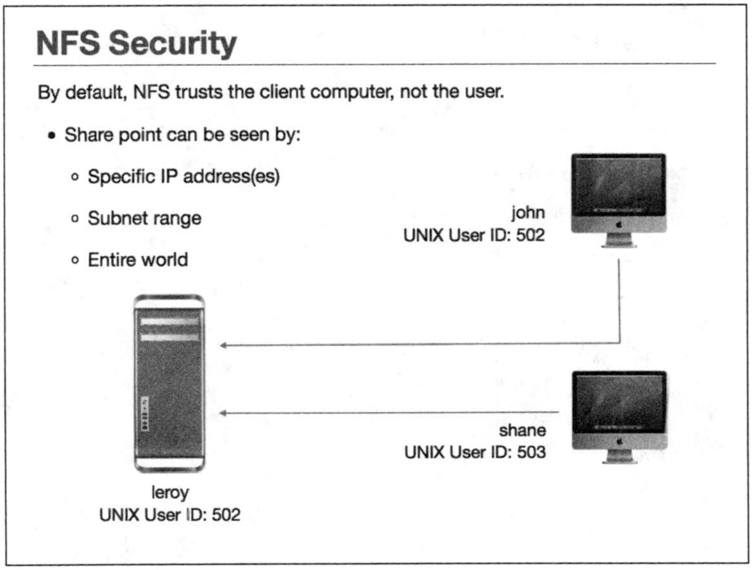


Unlike other protocols, NFS trusts the client computer, not the user who's logged in to that computer. This can potentially be an issue and can be restricted by reducing the number of computers that have access based on IP address or subnet. NFS mounts that are required for all computers use an option to share themselves with the world.

## NFS Share Point Options

Secure Mapping

- Map root to root (good)
- Map root to nobody (better)
- Map all to nobody (best)

Authentication

- Kerberos
  - With or without data integrity and privacy
    - Integrity = Checksum
    - Privacy = Encryption

Read Only and subdirectory redirection options

Users who connect to an NFS share can potentially have access that administrators do not want them to have. This is due to the fundamental nature of how NFS operates. To guard against this, administrators have the option of treating an incoming client as the UNIX user "nobody." The "nobody" user gets the permissions that are set for "everyone" (in the command line this shows up as "others"). The "Root to Root" option maps all users except root to "nobody." The "All to Nobody" option maps all users to "nobody." The "Root to Nobody" option maps only root to "nobody."

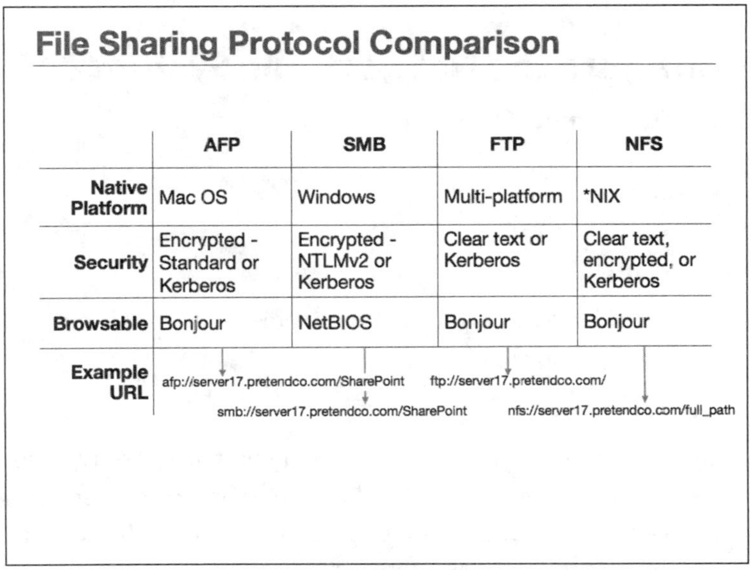

## File Sharing Protocol Comparison

| | AFP | SMB | FTP | NFS |
|---|---|---|---|---|
| **Native Platform** | Mac OS | Windows | Multi-platform | *NIX |
| **Security** | Encrypted - Standard or Kerberos | Encrypted - NTLMv2 or Kerberos | Clear text or Kerberos | Clear text, encrypted, or Kerberos |
| **Browsable** | Bonjour | NetBIOS | Bonjour | Bonjour |
| **Example URL** | afp://server17.pretendco.com/SharePoint | smb://server17.pretendco.com/SharePoint | ftp://server17.pretendco.com/ | nfs://server17.pretendco.com/full_path |

This is the fourth slide in a series (one slide at the end of each protocol lesson) that compares and contrasts authentication information, if the share point can be browsed, and the full syntax of the share point URL.

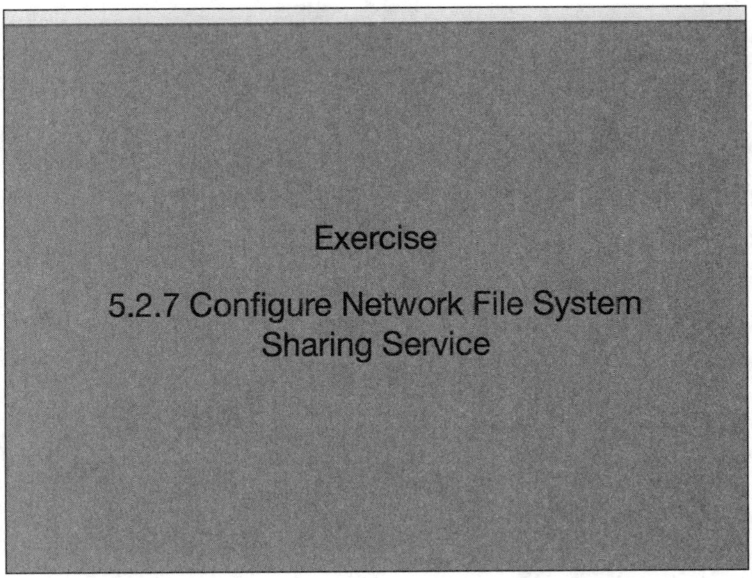

## Exercise 5.2.7

# Configure the Network File System Sharing Service

### Objective

Set up an NFS share point and mitigate some of the risks involved.

### Summary

Differing slightly from the other file sharing protocols discussed so far, NFS provides share points to others based on a computer's IP address and allows for user authentication. You'll view the default share point setup for the NFS service.

### Use Server Admin to Set Up an NFS Share Point

In this exercise, you'll use Server Admin to set up an NFS share point that is accessible from your Mac OS X computer.

1 Use Screen Sharing to control your server, and then use the Finder in the server to create a folder in /Shared Items called Templates.

2 Copy the template and text files from the Student_Materials/CH05/Templates/ folder to this new folder.

3 Quit Screen Sharing so you are not controlling your server in the GUI anymore.

4 On your Mac OS X computer, open Server Admin if it's not already open, and connect to your server.

5 From the Server menu choose Add Service.

6 Select the NFS checkbox, and click Save.

7 Select the newly added NFS service from the list on the left.

8 Click the Start NFS button at the bottom to start this service.

There is no need to make any changes to the settings for NFS.

9 Next, select your server's entry in the list on the left.

10 Click File Sharing in the toolbar.

11 Click the Volumes and Browse buttons, and navigate to the /Shared Items folder.

12 Select the Templates folder to highlight it.

13 Click Share, and click Save.

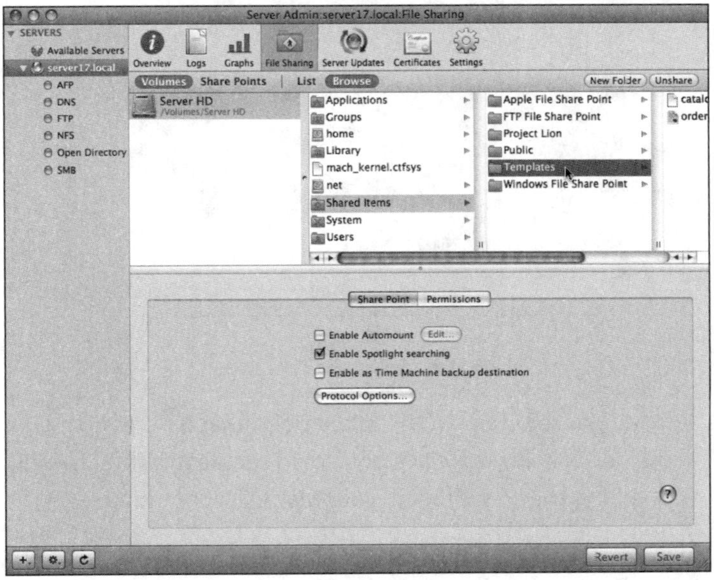

14 In the Share Points pane, click Protocol Options.

15 Turn off sharing for AFP, SMB, and FTP.

16 Click the NFS button, and select "Export this item and its contents."

17 Choose Subnet from the pop-up menu.

18 Enter the following information:

Subnet address ______________ 10.1.0.0 ____________________

Subnet mask ________________ 255.255.0.0 ________________

19 Verify the Mapping option is set to Root to Nobody.

This helps secure the NFS share against anyone logging in as root.

20 For Minimum Security, select "Kerberos v5 with data integrity and privacy."

21 Select the Read Only checkbox.

Your dialog should look like the following figure:

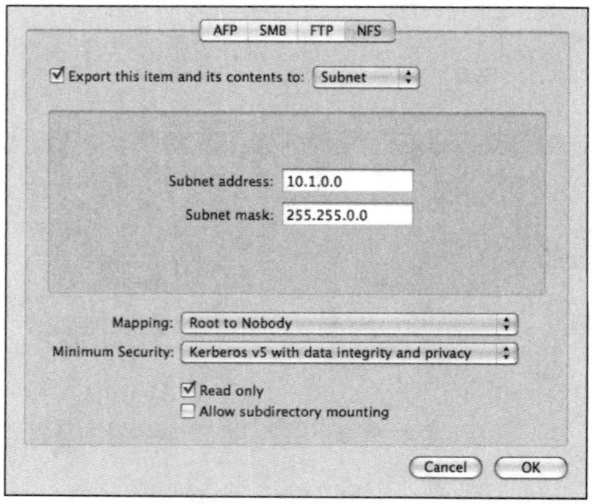


22 Click OK, and then click Save.

Now, you've set up an NFS share point that is accessible on the network in your class. You could secure it further by only selecting the IP address of your Mac OS X computer.

## Access the NFS Share Point

Now that the share point has been set up, we will access it in a secure manner.

1 Open /System/Library/CoreServices/Kerberos, and destroy any tickets you may currently have as any user.

2 Click New Ticket in the toolbar, and obtain a new TGTicket as sam.

Normally, once sam logs in to the Mac OS X computer, he would already have a TGT from the server. If you already have a TGT for sam you do not have to get a new ticket. We do this step manually here because we are logged in as cadmin—who may not have connected and obtained a TGT yet.

3 In Finder, connect to the NFS share point by entering `nfs://servern.pretendco.com/Shared Items/Templates` in the address.

4 The share point should mount, giving you access to the two Pretendco templates.

5 Check your Kerberos application, and you'll notice a new ticket for sam.

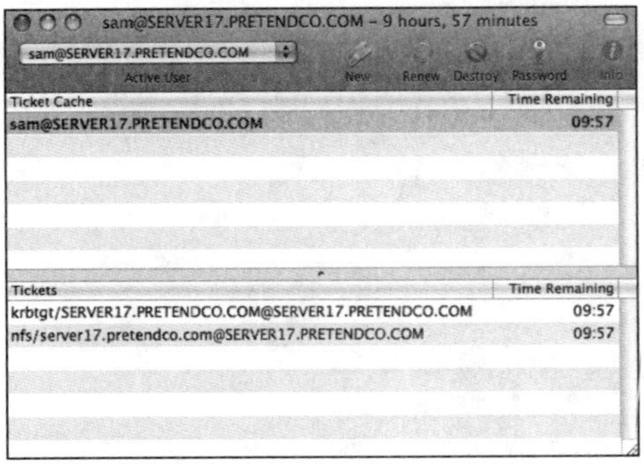


6 Eject the NFS volume.

# 5.3 Configuration

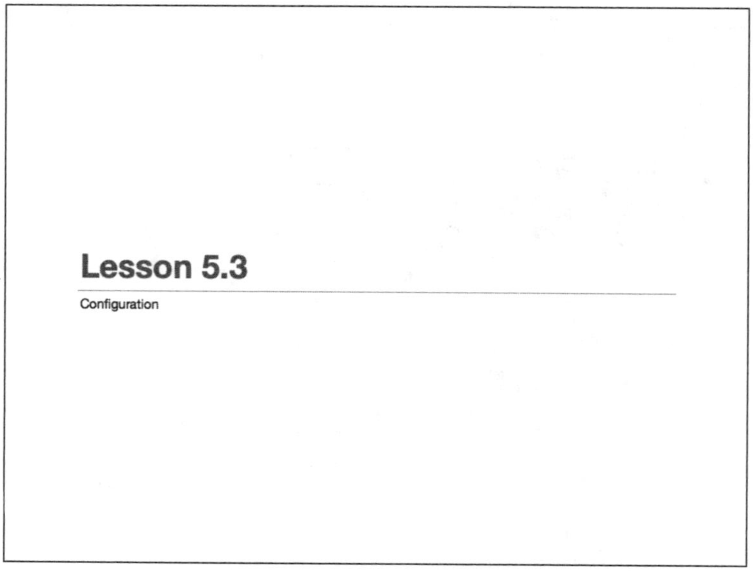


This lesson deals with automounting of shared folders, quotas, and using shared folders as Time Machine backup locations.

## Review—Share Point Options

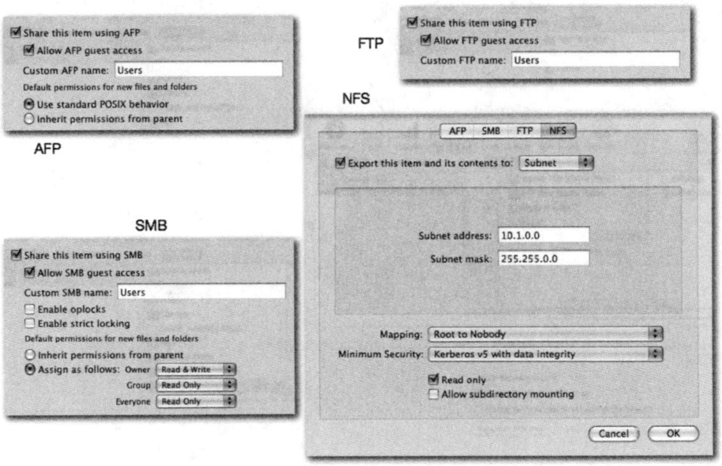


It's a good idea to review all the share point options for all four protocols so you'll have a better idea how to properly plan your shares.

## Advanced Share Point Features

Enable Spotlight Searching

- Enables mounted share point to be searched via Spotlight.
  - AFP and SMB only

Time Machine destination

- Permits mounted share point to become backup destination.

Quotas

- Quotas are based on volumes, not share points.
  - User quotas are set using Workgroup Manager.

Enhancements to share points can include Spotlight searching for AFP or SMB mounted share points, Time Machine backup share points for Mac OS X computers, and quotas for users and groups.

## Automounting Share Points

Share points can be configured to automatically mount when a computer is started.

- Shared over AFP or NFS.
- Server administrator dictates where the share point appears on the client file system.
  - /Network/Servers
  - /Network/Applications
  - /Network/Library
  - Custom path

Two folders commonly automounted are Users folder and Groups folder.

Automounting share points can greatly increase the usability of shares by not requiring the user or group to manually mount the share prior to using it.

Exercises

5.3.1 Configure Automount Options and Quotas on Share Points

5.3.2 Set a Time Machine Share Point (optional)

Exercise 5.3.1

# Configure Automount Options and Quotas on Share Points

## Objectives

Configure options for automount home folders.

Place limitations on home folders, preventing server share points from becoming full.

Use your Open Directory Master to provide access to a centralized share point containing applications. The share point will be mounted automatically when the Mac OS X computer starts up.

## Summary

Using enhancements like automounts and user-based quotas increases the functionality of the share points for users.

## Configure Network Home Folder Quotas

You've configured the network home folders but now you'll place limits on home folder capacity.

1 Restart your server.

**You enabled quotas in an earlier exercise, but for quotas to be enforced, you must restart your server.**

On your client computer, notice what happens to any share points you've mounted and your server tools, such as Server Admin and Workgroup Manager, when you restart your server without unmounting and disconnecting first.

2 Once your Mac OS X Server has rebooted, open Workgroup Manager, and connect to your server.

3 Click Accounts in the toolbar, and authenticate as diradmin for the shared LDAP Directory.

4 Click the Users button on the left, and select Elizabeth's account.

5 Click the Home button, and place a quota limit of 5 MB on her home folder.

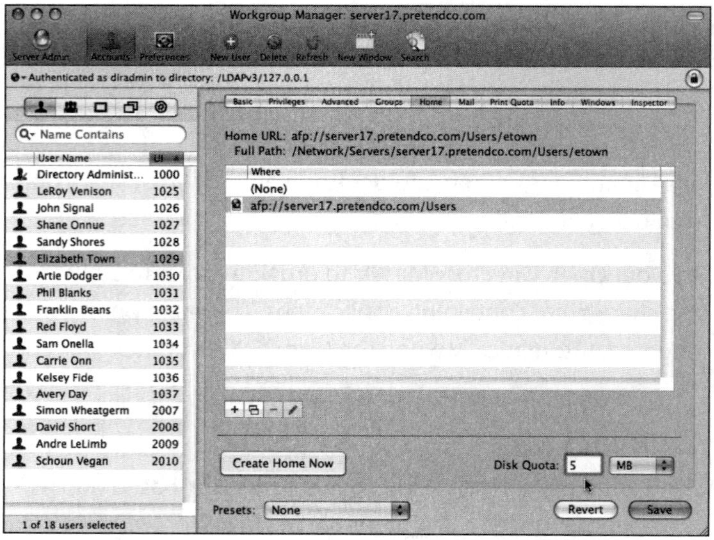


6 Click Save.

You'll see the effect of home folder quotas shortly.

## Set Up an Automatically Mounted Applications Folder

In this exercise, you'll create a new folder, copy some applications into it, and share its contents as a network mount.

1 Use Screen Sharing to control your server, and then use the Finder in the server to create a folder in /Shared Items called Applications.

2 Copy (option-drag) Directory and Podcast Capture from /Applications/Utilities/ to /Shared Items/Applications.

3 Quit Screen Sharing so you are not controlling your server in the GUI anymore.

4 On your Mac OS X computer, open Server Admin if it's not already open, connect to your server, and select the AFP service.

5 Click the Settings icon in the toolbar, click the Access tab, and confirm that "Enable Guest access" is selected. If it is not, select it.

6 Click Save if necessary.

7 Select your server in the list on the left.

8 Click File Sharing in the toolbar.

9 Click the Volumes and Browse buttons.

10 Navigate to and select the /Shared Items/Applications.

11 Click the Share button.

12 Click Save.

13 In the Share Point pane, select Enable Automount.

14 Choose /LDAPv3/127.0.0.1 from the Directory pop-up menu.

15 Verify that AFP is chosen as the protocol.

16 Select Shared Applications folder.

17 Before you click OK, your dialog should match the following figure:

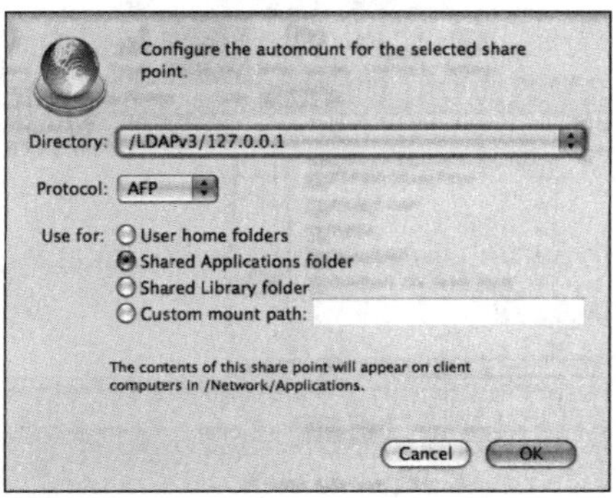

18 Click OK, and authenticate as diradmin.

19 Click Save, and quit Server Admin.

You've added another mount point record like the Users mount point record you added.

## Access Shared Applications from a Client

Shared volumes mount automatically only at startup. Simply logging in as a network user does not force the volume to mount.

1 Restart the Mac OS X computer.

It may take a few seconds for the Others button to appear in the login window.

2 Once the Other button appears in the login window, log in as Elizabeth (short name: etown, password: changeme).

3 In the Finder, click the All button under SHARED on the left.

4 Navigate to Applications and open the Directory application.

**If Directory launches, your Mac OS computer has successfully accessed a shared application.**

5 Quit Directory.

***Question 7*** *What happens if you drag the Podcast Capture application from the Shared applications folder to your desktop?*

6 Choose Go > Connect to Server, enter smb://server*n*.local and mount the windows share point.

7 Choose Go > Connect to Server again, and enter `nfs://servern.pretendco.com/Shared Items/Templates` and click Connect.

8 Open the Kerberos application, and view all the tickets.

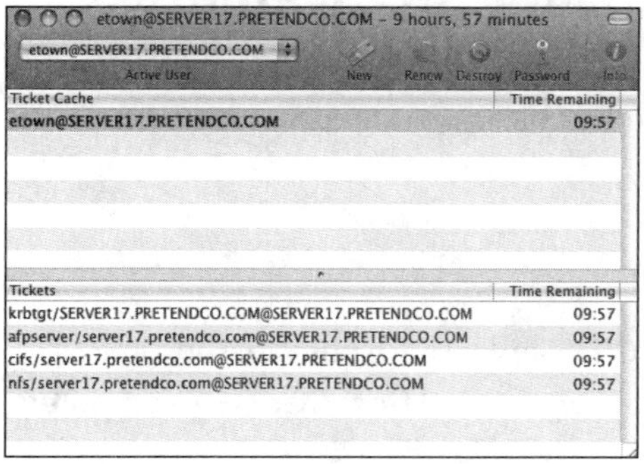


**Question 8** *How many tickets do you have and for what services?*

**Question 9** *How do you account for each ticket being in the list?*

9 Log out as Elizabeth.

10 Log in as cadmin, and launch Server Admin.

## Exercise 5.3.2

# Set a Time Machine Share Point (optional)

### Objective

Step through the Mac OS X Server share point-based Time Machine repository that can be used from Mac OS X computers.

### Summary

Create a second partition on your server and turn it into a share point that will be used as a Time Machine share point.

### Set Up Server Backup Share Point

As one of the first steps for this mechanism, you'll create a share point for Time Machine operations. Usually you would dedicate a separate storage. Here, you'll use Disk Utility to dynamically create an additional partition for backup purposes.

1. Use Screen Sharing to control your server, and open /Applications/Utilities/Disk Utility.
2. Select your server's hard drive from the source list.
3. Click the Partition button to show the partition settings and click the Add (+) button to add an additional partition.

4 Select the second partition, and name it Backups.

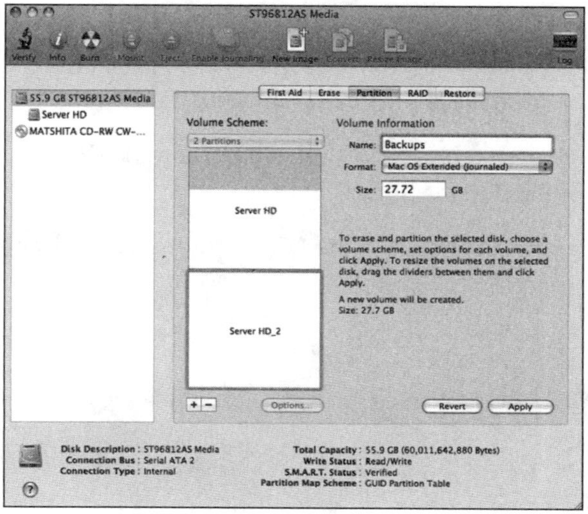


5 Click the Apply button.

6 At the Partition Disk dialog, click Partition.

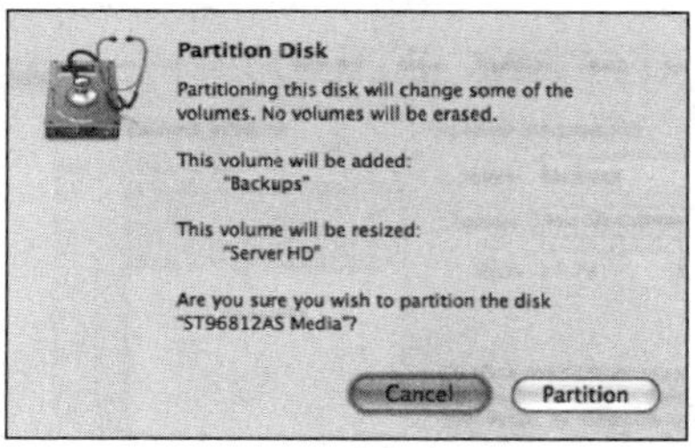


7 After a minute or so, a new partition is created. You'll use this for Time Machine backups.

> **Note** You've just partitioned a drive on-the-fly using built-in tools that are on any Mac OS X v10.5 computer.

8 Quit Screen Sharing so you are not controlling your server in the GUI anymore.

9 Open Server Admin, and select your server's entry in the list.

10 Click File Sharing in the toolbar and then click Volumes.

11 Select the Backups volume, and click Share.

12 Select the checkbox to Enable as Time Machine backup destination from the Share Points pane and click Save.

13 Click Permissions tab, and then open the Users and Groups window by clicking the Add (+) button.

14 Drag the Marketing group to the ACL list for this volume, and give that group Full Control.

15 Click Save.

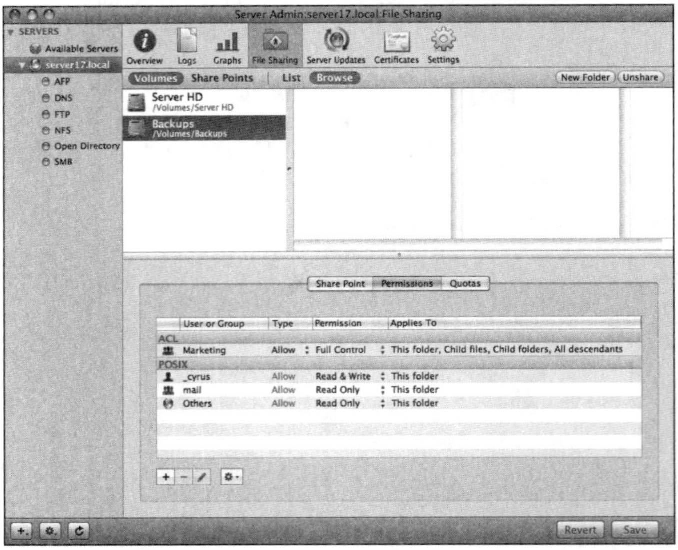


Use Server Admin to change AFP authentication from Kerberos to Standard, and stop and start the AFP service.

16 If the AFP service is not running, start it now.

17 Quit Server Admin, and then click the Time Machine icon in the dock.

The first time you run Time Machine, you'll see a dialog prompting you to set a location for backups.

18 Click Open Time Machine Prefs, and click the slider switch to ON.

19 Select your server's backup share point, and click Use for Backup.

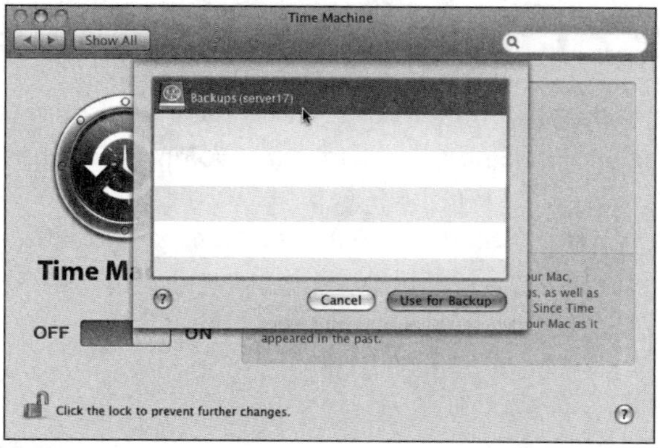

20 Authenticate as a member of the Marketing group who has access to this share point.

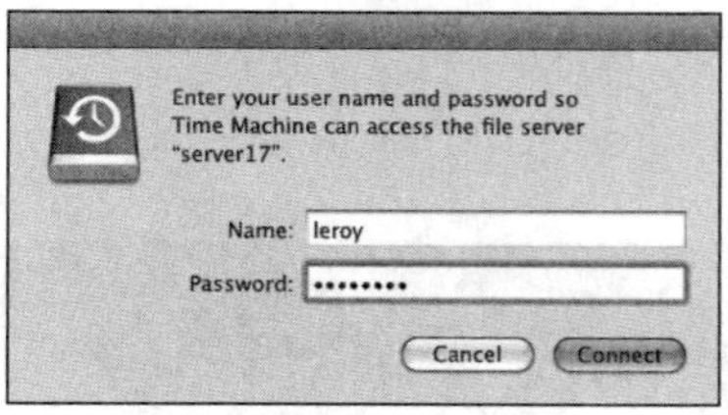

21 Click the Options button, and add the following folders to be excluded from backup:

- /System (Exclude all system files when asked)
- Applications
- Developer (if Xcode is installed)
- Library

You can use Command-Click to select multiple folders.

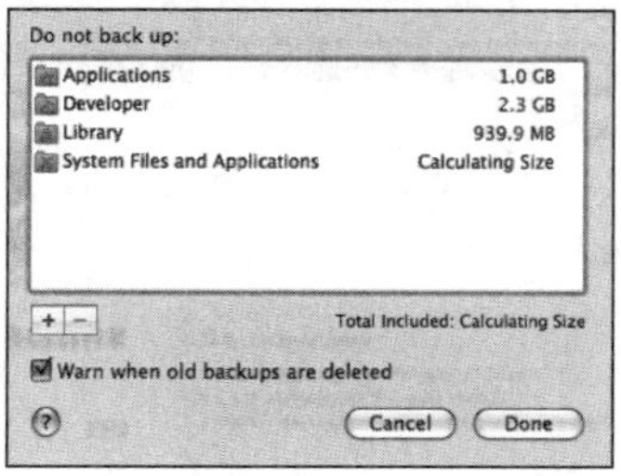

22 Click Done.

Notice that the Time Machine system preferences will note that next backup is just under two minutes away.

23 Once one backup is complete, use Screen Sharing to connect to your server, and use Finder to navigate to /Volumes/Backups.

*Question 10* *What file(s) do you see in the share points folder?*

The duration of the backup process varies depending on the contents of the /Users folder on the client.

24 Open the Address Book application and delete the card for cadmin.

25 Click the Time Machine icon in the dock.

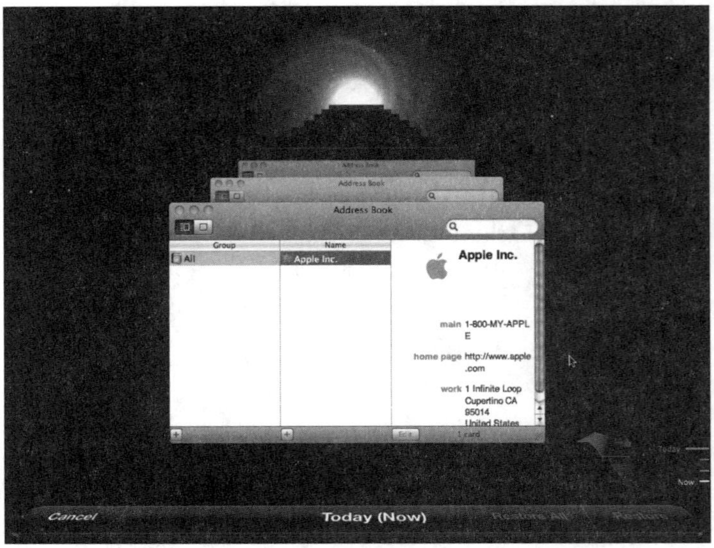


26 Since the last backup, the only change has been the removal of an Address Book card for cadmin.

27 Click the Back Arrow once to show the Address Book with the cadmin card present.

28 Click to select the cadmin address book card.

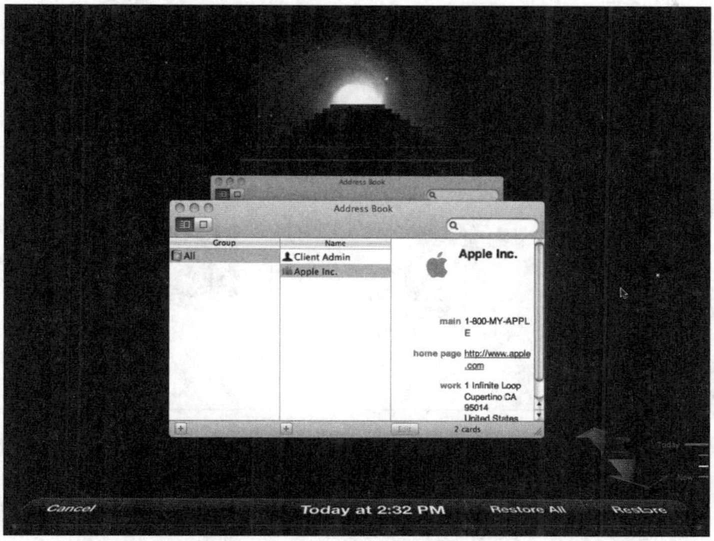


29 Click Restore.

30 The Time Machine window fades and your Address Book now has the cadmin card restored.

31 Quit any open applications, and unmount any network shares.

Now, you've used all four file sharing protocols in a variety of uses. You should be able to properly plan and execute file sharing services for your organization.

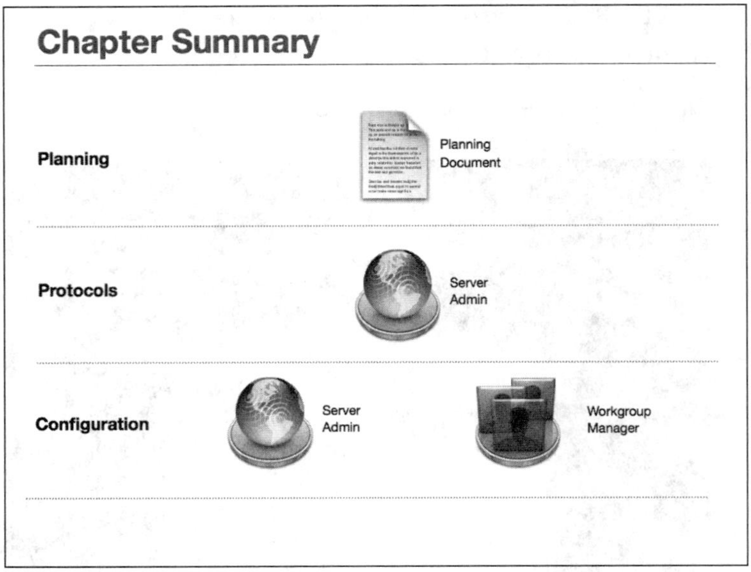
Chapter Summary
Planning
Planning
Document
Protocols
Server
Admin
Configuration
Server
Admin
Workgroup
Manager

Apple
Certified

# 6

# Using the Mail Service

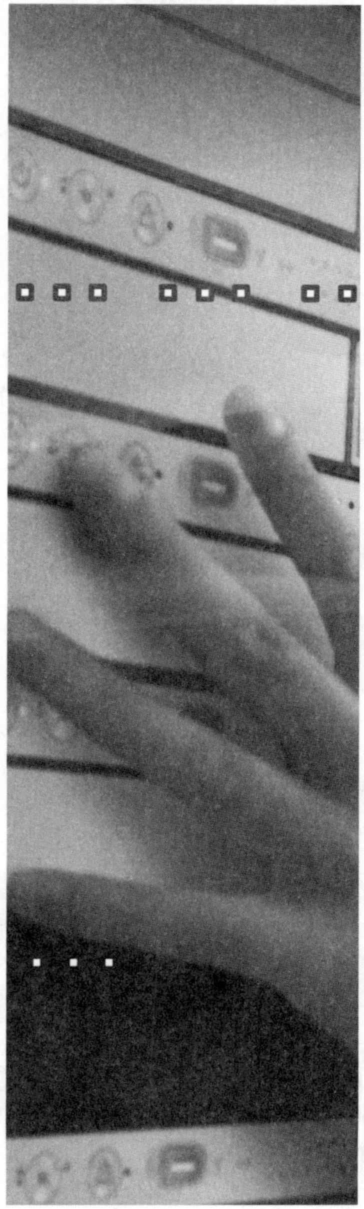


## 6.1 Configuration

**Exercise 6.1.1** Configure Basic Mail Service

**Exercise 6.1.2** Enable a Group Mailing List

## 6.2 Security

**Exercise 6.2.1** Secure the Mail Service

**Exercise 6.2.2** Use SSL Certificates with the Mail Service

## 6.3 Maintenance

**Exercise 6.3.1** Configure Mail Service Quotas (optional)

**Exercise 6.3.2** Reconstruct and Rebuild Mail (optional)

**Exercise 6.3.3** View Mail Log Files (optional)

# 6.1 Configuration

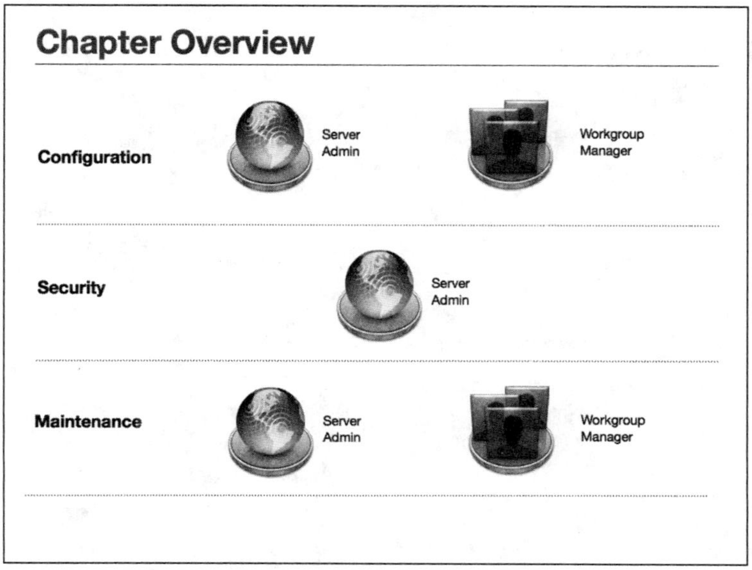


Mac OS X Server's mail service can be divided into three logical sections.

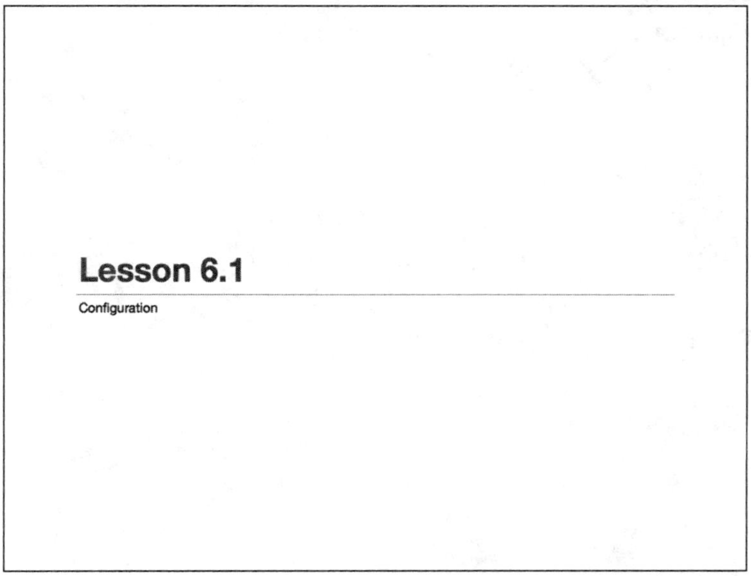


This lesson deals with the basics of Mail service terminology, reasons for running a mail service, and mail service configuration on Mac OS X Server.

## Mail Service

- Mail service advantages
- How mail servers function
- Mail protocols
- Mail service initial configuration
- Enable mail for users
- Mailing lists
- Mail service clustering
- Mail database hosting

There are several aspects to consider when running a mail service. Among them, what advantages are to be gained by taking a mail service in-house? Do you need to run mailing lists? How is the mail database stored?

## Mail Service Advantages

Control of mail service database

Increased security

Reduced traffic on the network

Running a mail service in-house has several advantages: increased security by hosting the mail database behind your walls, decreased outgoing traffic when mail is sent between staff members, and full control over the functionality of the mail service.

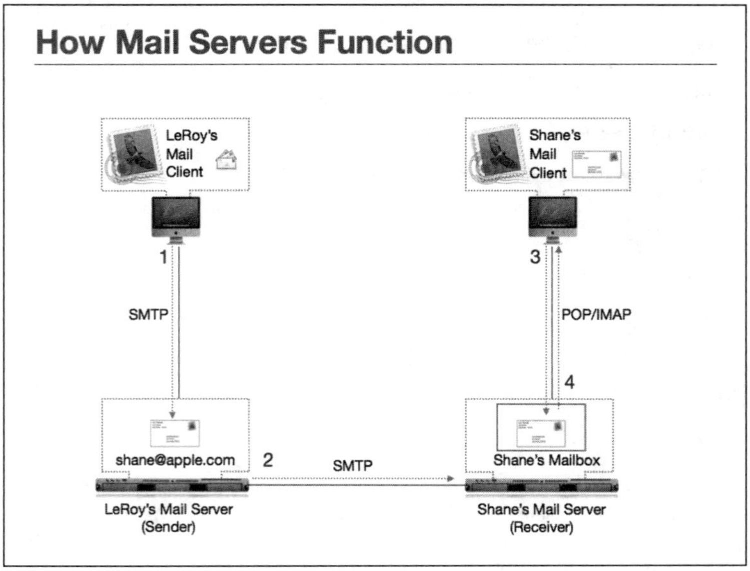


Basic mail delivery takes place on the mail services' server. The clients send mail, and the mail services' server passes that mail between them. The mail then sits on the recipient's mail service server, waiting to be requested.

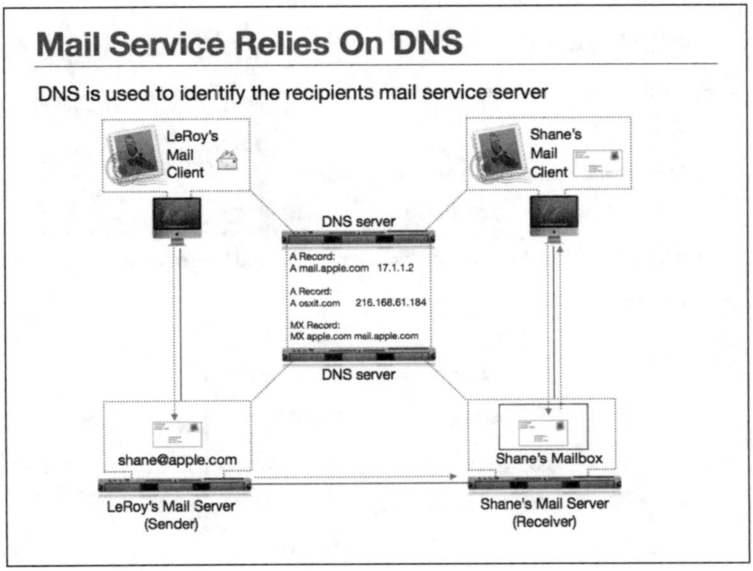


DNS plays a crucial role in how mail servers work. Without proper DNS, mail servers would fail to function on a name level. It may still be possible to send mail via IP address only.

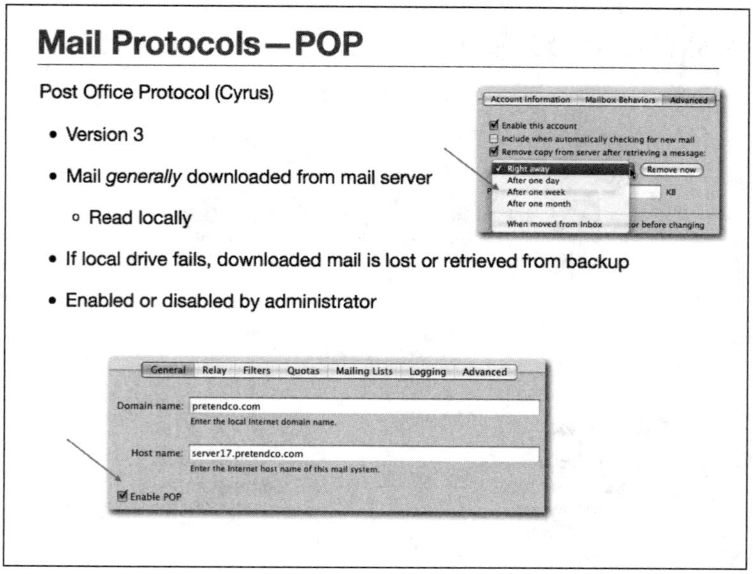


Post Office Protocol (POP) is a common mail retrieval protocol used on mail services where disk space and network connections are at a premium. POP is preferred in these environments because a mail client will connect to the server, download the mail, remove it from the server, and disconnect very quickly. Although good for the server, POP mail servers are typically less user-friendly because they don't support server-side folders and may cause difficulties for a user connecting from multiple computers.

## Mail Protocols—IMAP

Internet Message Access Protocol (Cyrus)

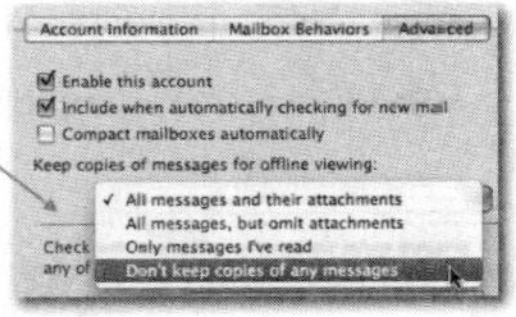


- Version 4
- Mail *generally* kept on mail server
  - Read when connected to mail server
- Mail can be read from any system connected to the mail server
- Enabled or disabled by administrator

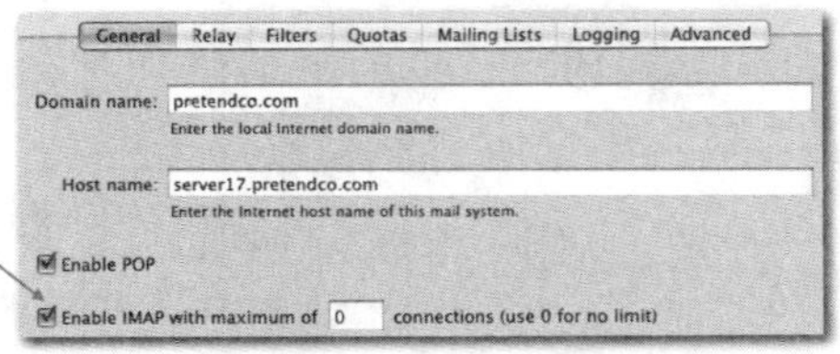


Internet Message Access Protocol (IMAP) is commonly used by mail services that want to provide more features to the user. IMAP allows storage of all mail and mail folders on the server, where they are usually backed up. A mail client will often remain connected to the mail service for the duration of the user session. This can result in quicker notification of new messages. The downside to using IMAP is that it puts a greater strain on the resources of the mail service.

## Mail Protocols—SMTP

Simple Mail Transfer Protocol (Postfix)

- Sends mail from client to mail server
- Relies on DNS
  - If names are used instead of IP addresses
- Sends mail between SMTP servers
- Enabled or disabled by administrator

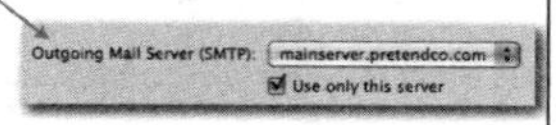


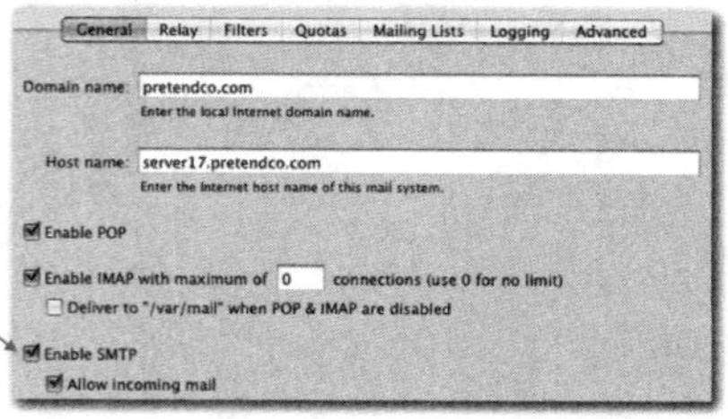


SMTP is used to send mail. When mail is sent to a server, it is stored until the server is ready to send it to the recipients' SMTP server.

## Mail Service Initial Setup

Server Admin launches Service Configuration Assistant.

- Mail services starts automatically after the Assistant completes.
- Server Admin is used to manage mail service.

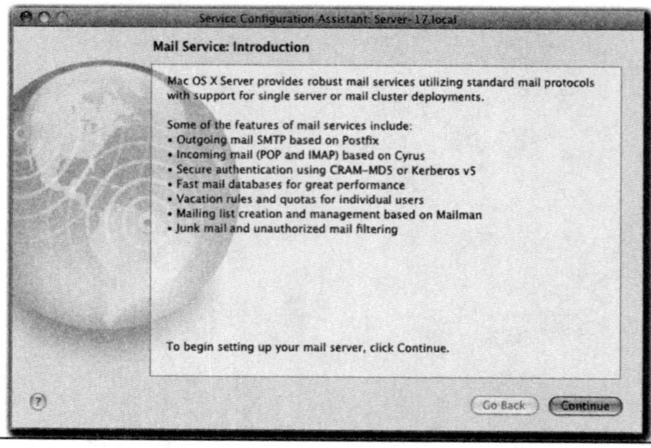


The initial setup of the mail service is handled in Server Admin. A Mail service plug-in to the Service Configuration Assistant handles the duties of basic mail service setup. From there, additional mail settings can be made using just Server Admin.

## Mail Service Manual Configuration

Options on the General tab are not available during automatic setup.

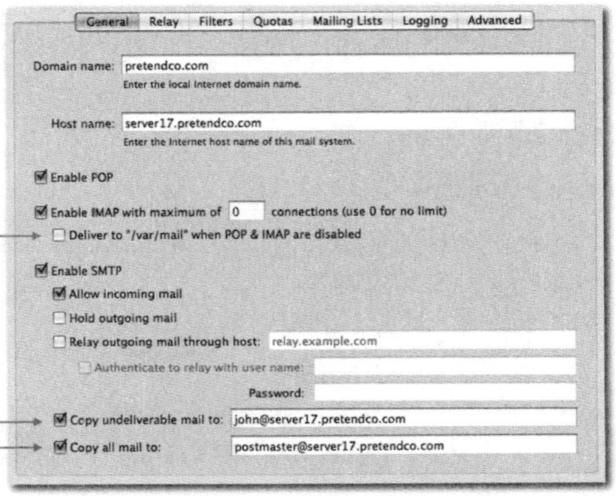


Manual configuration of the mail service allows for more granularity. You can redirect mail that has been addressed improperly or copy all mail to an account for archival and search purposes.

## Mail Enabled for Users

Workgroup Manager

- Select the user and the Mail tab to set quota and alternate mail store information

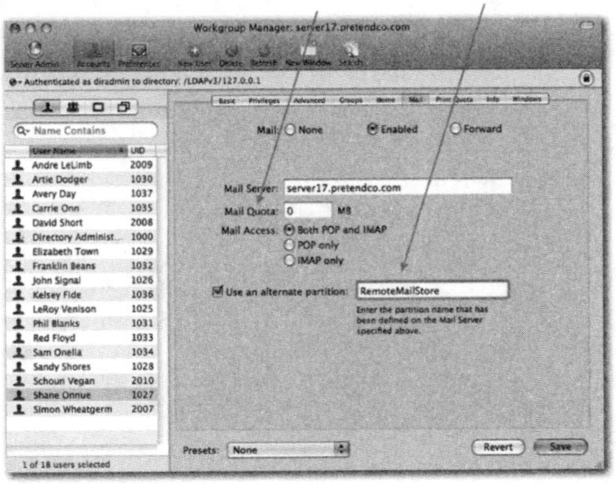


After the basic setup of the mail service, a user's mail information is set up using Workgroup Manager.

## Mailing Lists

Collection of users who receive identical messages

- Group mailing lists
  - Automatic configuration of Open Directory group-based mailing lists
- Mailman mailing lists
  - Users can self subscribe
  - User and group options
    - List administration
    - Post
    - Subscribe

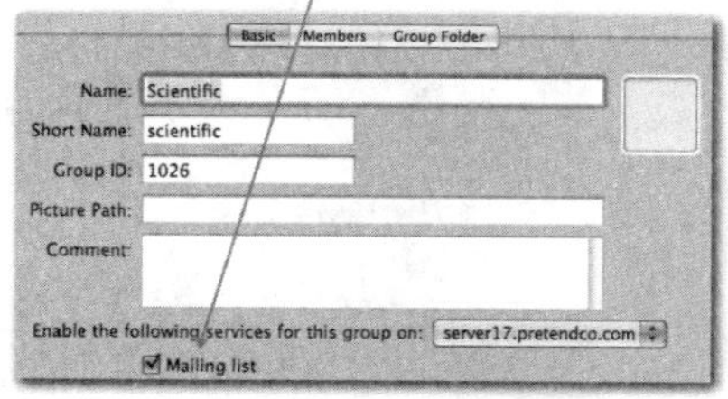


You can use Server Admin to set up mailing lists. This functionality is based on an open source project called Mailman and allows you to create a mail address on your server that will distribute a copy of every message it receives to all the members of that list.

## Mailing Lists

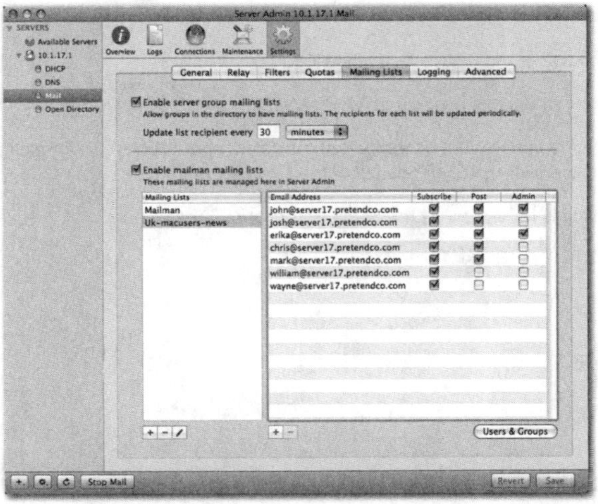


The GUI for managing Mac OS X Server's Mailman mailing lists is based on an open source initiative. A webpage can also be used to access the mailing list options.

## Mail Service Clustering

Several mail servers access a single database and mail storage.

- Each server must have Xsan installed.
- Each server uses their own SMTP service.
  - If one service fails or a server shuts down, another server automatically takes over the SMTP duties of the failed server.

Clustering is turned on via the Service Configuration Assistant.

A mail cluster is a group of servers that share a single mail store among them for the purposes of redundancy and load balancing. Each participating server shares a common file system using Xsan. The messages are kept in the shared file system and can be accessed from any of the servers once they've been configured to participate in the cluster.

## Mail Database Hosting

An entire database or portions of the database can be stored on other volumes, such as

- Extra partition
- Extra drive
- Xserve RAID

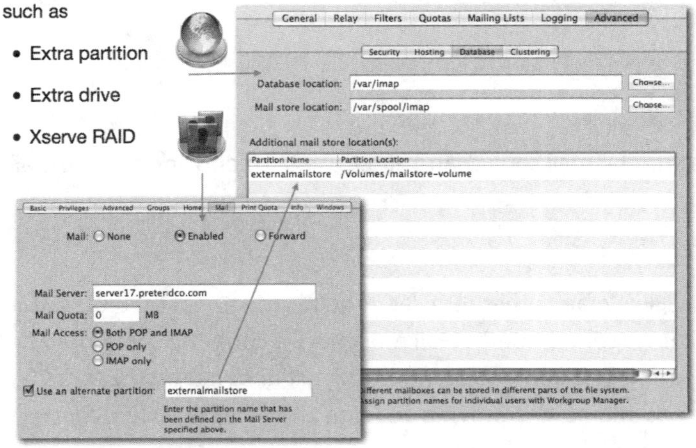


The mail service database can be hosted on any volume and should that volume fill up, secondary mail stores can be used.

### Exercises

6.1.1 Configure Basic Mail Service

6.1.2 Enable a Group Mailing List

## Exercise 6.1.1

# Configure Basic Mail Service

## Objective

Set up the mail service and allow users to send and receive mail.

## Summary

Mail, like many other services, requires the use of several services for it to work properly. Mail must have a correctly configured and running DNS server. Second, you must understand the users' needs and how to provide a secure and reliable system for them to communicate.

1. From the Server menu in Server Admin, choose Add Service.
2. Select the Mail checkbox to add it to your list of services.
3. Click Save.
4. Select Mail from the list under your server.
5. Click the Settings icon in the toolbar.
6. Click the General tab, and configure the settings as follows:
   - Domain name: `pretendco.com`
   - Host name: `server`*`n`*`.pretendco.com` (where *n* is your student number)
   - Select the checkboxes for the following:
     - POP
     - IMAP
     - SMTP
   - Allow incoming mail
   - Copy undeliverable mail to: `diradmin@server`*`n`*`.pretendco.com`

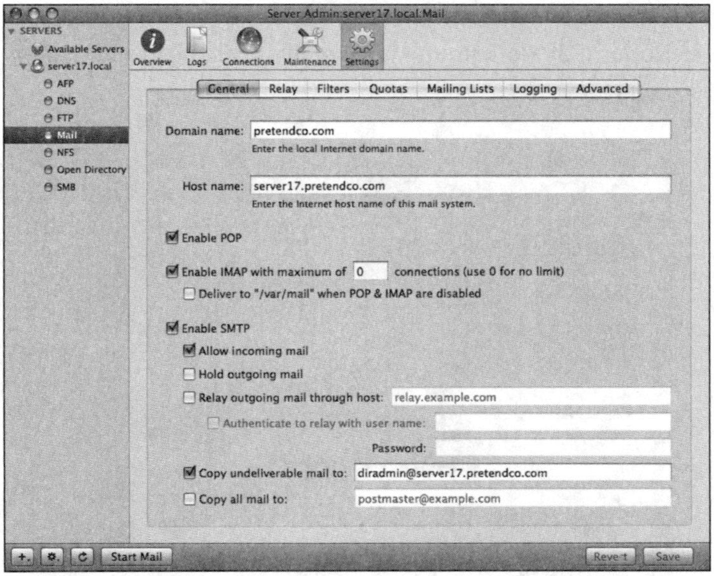


7 Click the Logging tab, and set the log levels for SMTP and IMAP/POP to Debug. Leave Junk Mail Virus log level set to Critical.

8 Click Save.

9 Click the Start Mail button to start the Mail service.

You've just completed the basic setup for Mac OS X Server's mail service. Now, you'll turn on mail for a user account and test the mail service.

10 Open Workgroup Manager, and ensure you are looking at your shared LDAP database.

11 Select all the users, including the Directory Administrator in the Users list.

12 Click the Mail tab, and select the Enabled option for Mail. Notice that Workgroup Manager fills in all the proper parameters for you.

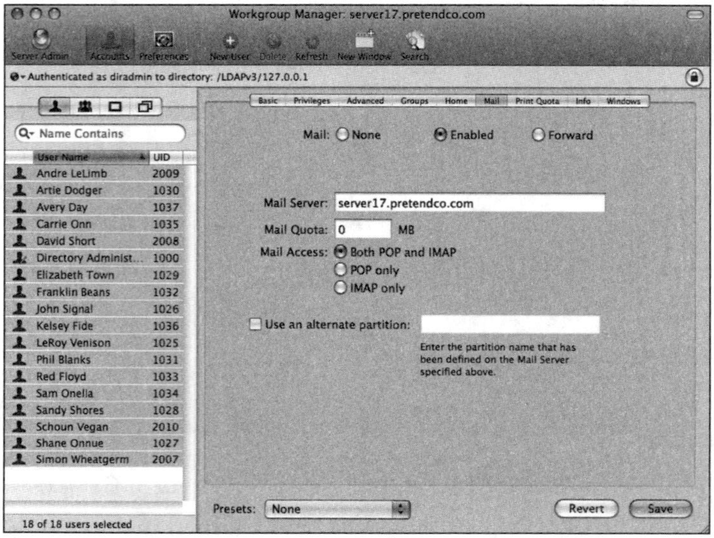


13 Click Save.

You've just turned on mail services for all your users. Now, you'll use Mac OS X's Mail application to test sending and receiving mail.

14 Click the Mail application icon in your Dock, or locate the Mail application inside the /Applications folder.

The Welcome to Mail window appears.

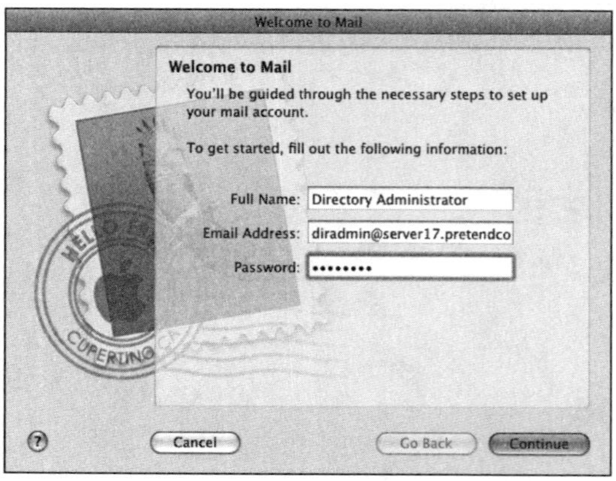

15 Enter the following information:

- Full Name: `Directory Administrator`
- Email Address: `diradmin@server`*`n`*`.pretendco.com`
- Password: `diradmin`

16 Click Continue.

17 In the Incoming Mail Server screen, choose IMAP from the Account Type pop-up menu, and enter the following information:

- Description: `Directory Administrator's Account`
- Incoming Mail Server: `server`*`n`*`.pretendco.com`
- User Name: `diradmin` (should already be entered for you)
- Password: `diradmin` (should already be entered for you)

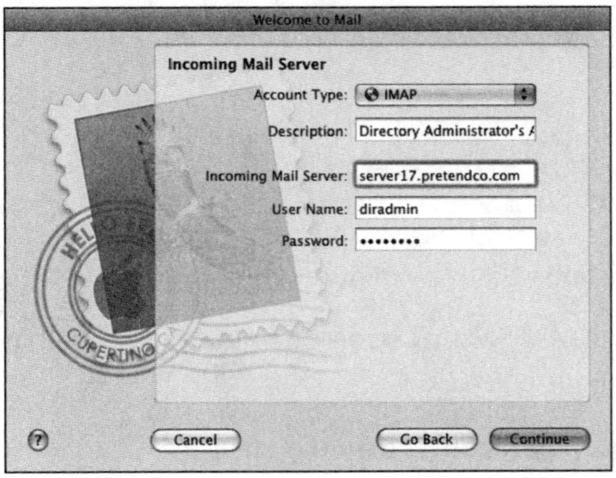


18 Click Continue.

19 Click Continue to cancel any certificate alerts that appear.

20 In the Outgoing Mail Server screen, enter the following information:

- Description: `Server n` (where *n* is your student number)
- Outgoing Mail Server: `servern.pretendco.com`
- Select "Use only this server."
- Do not select or enter any authentication at this time.

You're not requiring authentication to send mail. This can be a security risk and will be changed later in this chapter.

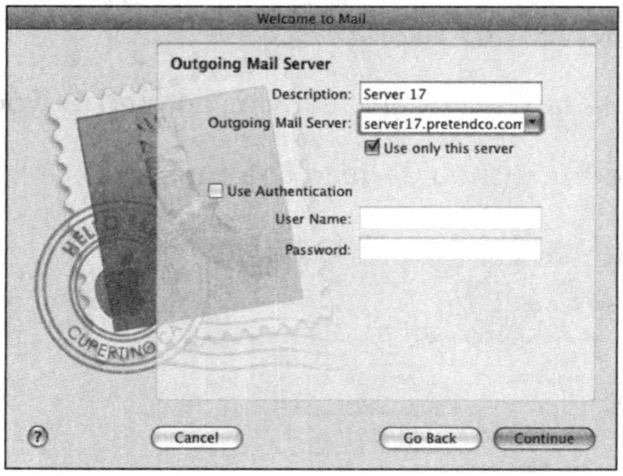


21 Click Continue and wait a few minutes.

22 In the Outgoing Mail Security screen, do not change anything, and click Continue.

You've just set up how you'll be sending mail.

23 View the Account Summary screen, and ensure the "Take account online" checkbox is selected.

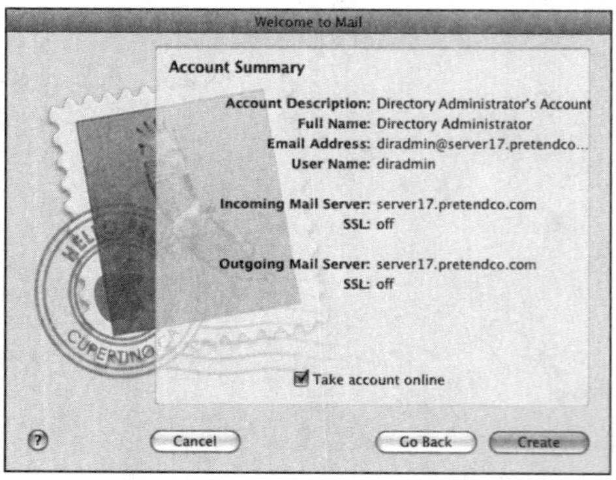

24 Click Create.

You've just created a mail account for your Directory Administrator. Now, you'll ensure you can send and receive mail for your account.

25 When the Mail application opens, click Don't Show to dismiss the What's New dialog.

26 Click the New Message icon in the toolbar, and address the mail to diradmin@server*n*.pretendco.com. Enter a subject line and some text in the body of the message.

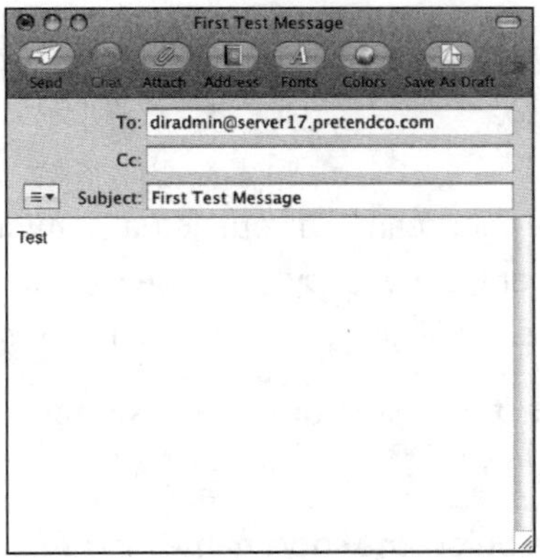


27 Click Send.

28 Click your Inbox if it's not already selected, and click the Get Mail icon in the upper left of your toolbar.

You should see the mail you just sent to yourself. This indicates the mail service is operating properly.

29 Click New Message, and send five separate mail messages to the following people with `TPS Reports` entered in the subject line.

- schoun@server*n*.pretendco.com
- simon@server*n*.pretendco.com
- david@server*n*.pretendco.com
- andre@server*n*.pretendco.com
- steve@server*n*.pretendco.com

***Question 1** Did your mail server balk at all when sending mail messages to people who do not have their Mail accounts set up yet?*

30 Click the Get Mail icon in the toolbar. You've got mail.

***Question 2** Steve is not a user in Workgroup Manager. What happens to the mail that is addressed improperly?*

You may not want to use the short name of your actual administrator for account management, or you may want users to have mail aliases. In the next steps, you'll give two users mail aliases.

31 In Workgroup Manager, select the Directory Administrator account and click the Basic tab.

32 Double-click the empty line below the short name diradmin, and enter `postmaster`. Press the Return key, and click Save.

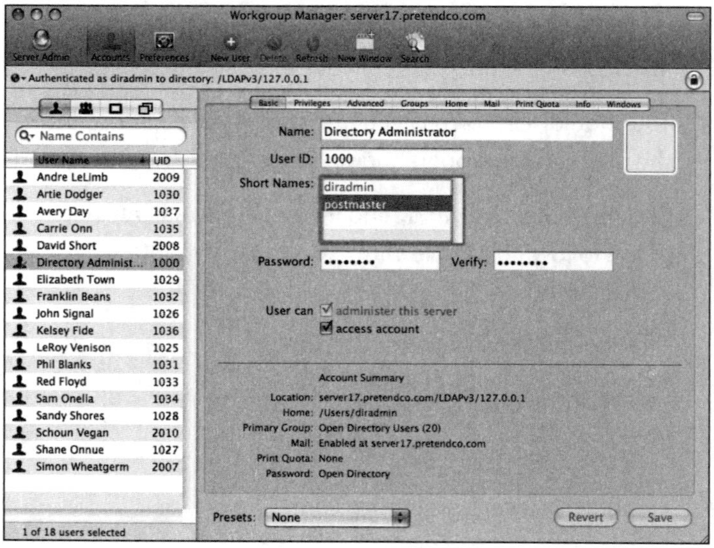

33 Repeat steps 32 and 34 for the user Simon, enter the additional short name `development`, and save the changes.

34 In Server Admin, select the Mail service from the list of services, select the Settings icon in the toolbar, and click the General tab.

35 Change the undeliverable mail address to `postmaster@servern.pretendco.com`, and click Save.

36 In your Mail application, send two mails, one to `development@servern.pretendco.com` and one to `doug@servern.pretendco.com`.

37 Check mail. You'll see mail addressed to doug but still delivered to diradmin. You do not have to edit your mail account in the Mail application to receive mails to aliases of your account name. You can test this by sending mail to postmaster@server*n*.pretendco.com and checking Mail to see you received it.

Later in this chapter, you'll set up Mail for Simon and see all the mail he has received.

38 Send one more mail to David, this time adding a large attachment.

39 Click the New Message icon, and address the mail to `david@servern.pretendco.com`, enter the subject line `My new application`, but do not send it yet.

40 Open your Applications folder in column view, and select Dictionary, but do not open it.

41 Control-click Dictionary, and choose Compress Dictionary from the list. When the archive finishes compressing, open another Finder window, and drag the archive to the /Users/Shared/ folder. Also drag it to your open mail window as an attachment for David. Click Send.

42 Control-click and compress the Chess application, and drag the compressed file to the /Users/Shared folder for a later exercise.

**43** Send one more mail, this time to the Instructor, (instruct@mainserver.pretendco.com). Enter `From Student n` in the subject line and the word `Hello` in the body of the message.

**44** Ask the instructor to verify receiving the mail and ask for a reply.

**Question 3** *How can you send mail to the instructor?*

## Exercise 6.1.2
# Enable a Group Mailing List

## Objective

Create a group, and set up a group mail list for the new group.

## Summary

Mac OS X Server allows two types of mail lists: group mail lists that are central to groups in the shared LDAP directory, and Mailman lists, which are lists that others outside the central group can join. Mail lists are useful for communicating with others about centralized topics. Mac OS X Server allows for the easy creation and management of mail lists.

1 In Server Admin, select Mail from the list under your server.

2 Click the Settings icon in the toolbar and click the Mailing Lists tab.

3 Select "Enable server group mailing lists," and click Save.

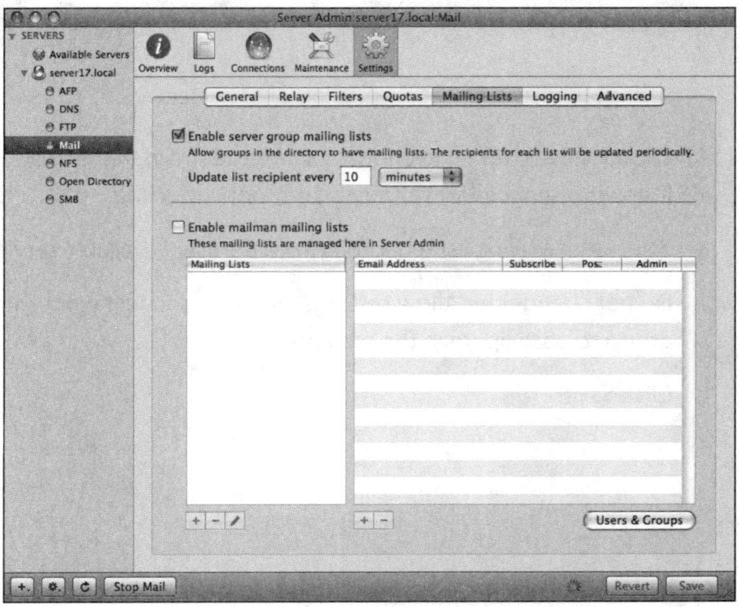

4 In Workgroup Manager, create a new group called Developers with developers as the short name. Add the following users:

- Simon
- David
- Andre
- Schoun
- Elizabeth

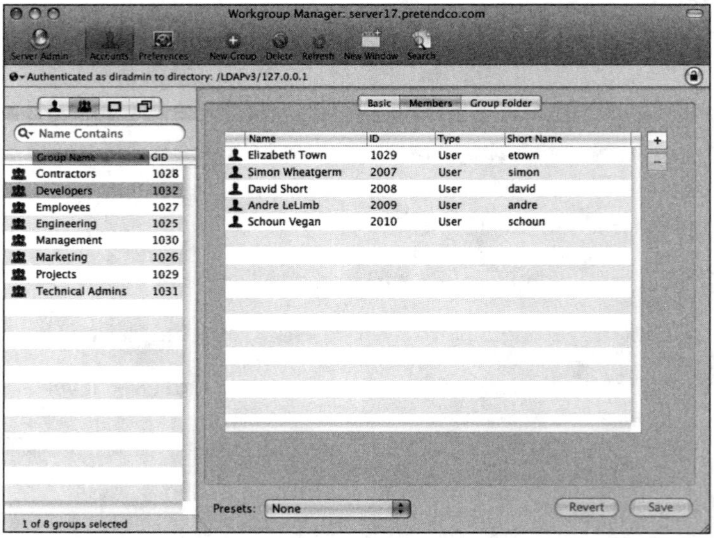

5 Click the Basic tab, and choose your server from the "Enable the following services for this group on" pop-up menu.

6 Select the "Mailing list" checkbox from the list of available services.

7 Do not change the Allow settings, because you just want this group to participate in the mailing list.

8 Click Save.

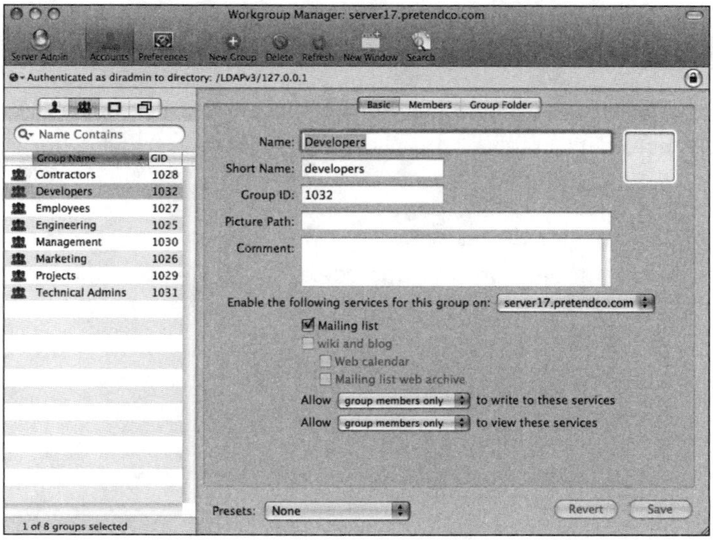


9 Log out as cadmin, and log in as Schoun (short name: schoun and password: changeme).

10 Setup mail for Schoun as you did for Directory Administrator.

You may be prompted about a certificate after Mail opens.

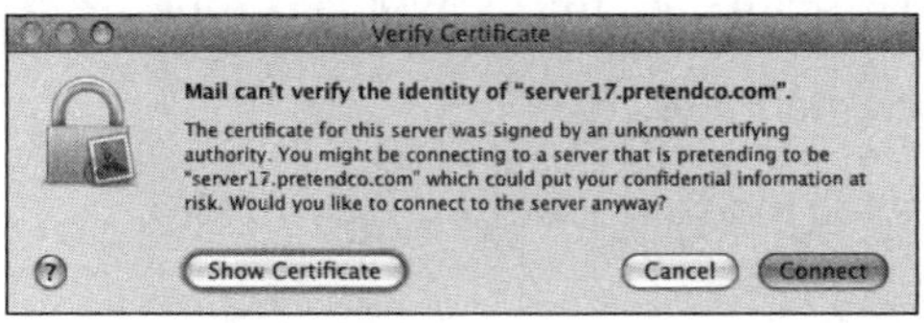


11 Click Show Certificate, and select the "Always trust 'Default' when connecting to 'server*n*.pretendco.com' " checkbox.

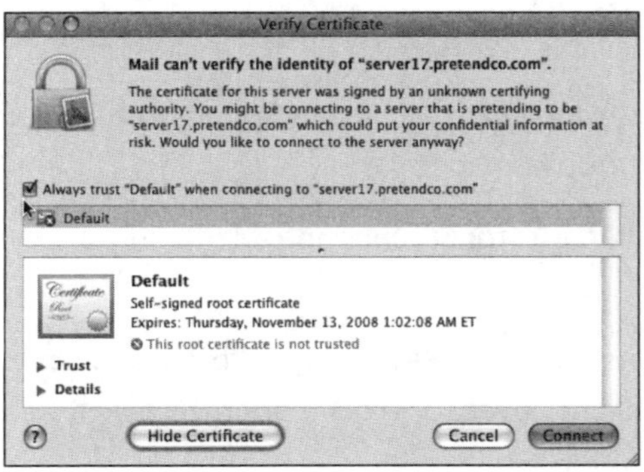

12 Click Connect. You'll have to authenticate as cadmin to always trust the certificate.

This occurs because Mac OS X Server creates a certificate, names it Default, and Mail will try to use this certificate for encryption.

13 Send mail to `developers@servern.pretendco.com`, and enter a subject line and some text.

14 Check your mail. Notice you received the message. This is because schoun is a member of the developers group.

You'll check Simon's mail later.

15 Log out as Schoun, log in as Elizabeth, and set up Mail.

*Question 4 Can Elizabeth set up mail? Why or why not?*

16 Log out as Elizabeth, log in as cadmin, and open both Server Admin and Workgroup Manager.

17 Enable group mailing lists for Engineering, Marketing, and Employees.

18 Add the Developers group to the Employees group, so when mail goes out to all employees, the developers receive it too.

19 Leave Server Admin and Workgroup Manager open.

# Security

# 6.2

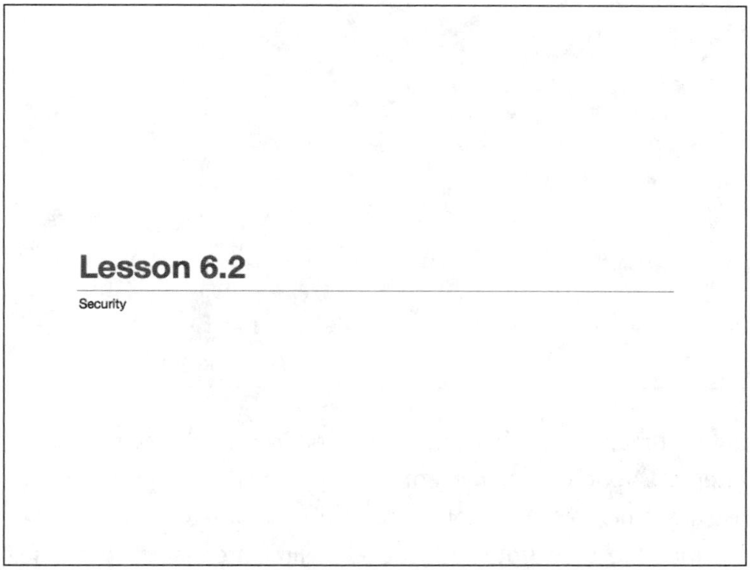


A mail service that is not properly protected can be attacked in several ways. These include snooping passwords, using your mail service to send junk mail, and getting viruses.

## Mail Security Issues

Authentication

Unencrypted Messages

Open Relays

Junk Mail

Viruses

Internet mail is one of the most used services available on the Internet. Along with significant use comes significant abuse. Mail, like any other Internet-enabled service, has numerous options that can increase its security and reduce or eliminate the risk for abuse. This lesson focuses on three primary areas of abuse and what can be done to reduce their impact on your users.

- Password security focuses on ensuring that your users' passwords are safe and that frequent checking of mail does not expose their passwords.
- Spam prevention actually has two components. First, you want to keep other users from using your server for delivering their spam to others, and second, you want to reduce the amount of spam your users receive.
- Virus detection protects the integrity of your users' computers by keeping known viruses out of their mail.

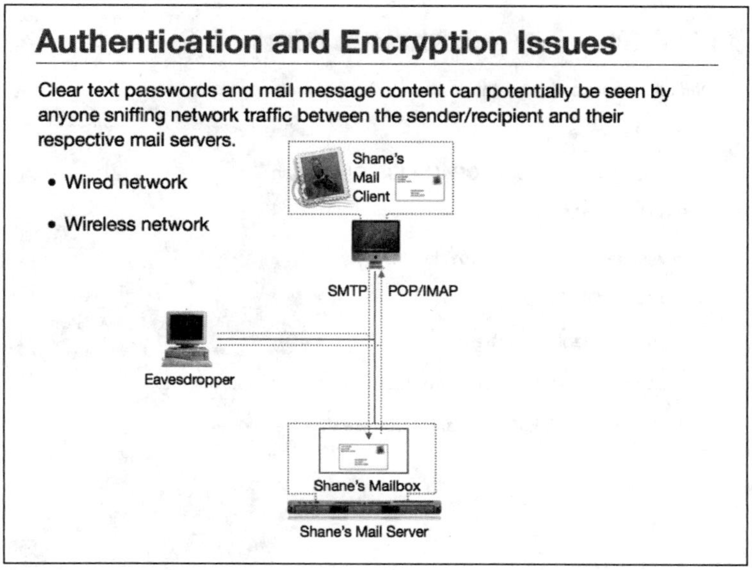


Any time a user must authenticate to a service over the Internet, particularly over insecure wireless networks, their password is at risk. You can reduce this risk by taking advantage of higher levels of password hashing and by enabling encryption.

## Mail Security—Authentication

Default authentication methods used by mail service protocols

- SMTP = None
  - Available = Kerberos, CRAM-MD5, Clear, Plain
- IMAP = CRAM-MD5 or Clear
  - Also available = Kerberos, Login, Plain
- POP = APOP, Clear
  - Also available = Kerberos

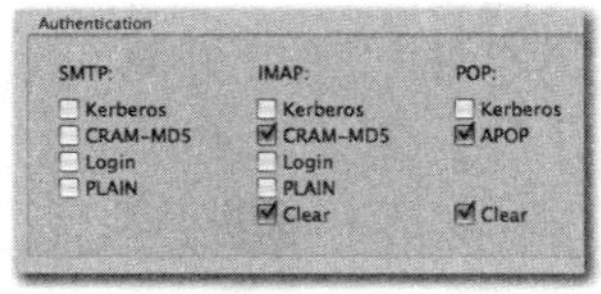


More secure methods obscure the password from eavesdroppers.

- Kerberos uses tickets, no passwords are ever transferred.

The mail service in Mac OS X Server offers a number of different authentication mechanisms. Each has varying levels of security, but more importantly, does not have support in every mail client used. When selecting authentication methods, it's important to determine which mail clients your users will be running and which authentication methods they support. Authentication methods range from Clear or PLAIN, which send passwords over the network unencrypted, to Kerberos, which is considered one of the most secure because passwords are never sent over the network. If none of your users will be using a particular authentication method, you should disable that method. Additionally, if you want to force your users to only use more secure methods, you should disable the less-secure mechanisms such as Clear and PLAIN or require the connection to use SSL.

## Unencrypted Messages

By default, mail messages sent through Mac OS X Server mail service are unencrypted.

- Secure Sockets Layer can encrypt mail.
  - Prevents others from seeing mail content.
  - Two options
    - Use but not required
    - Required

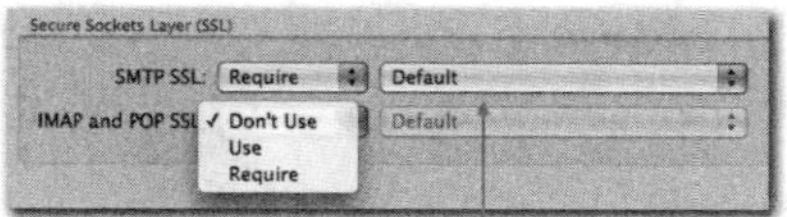


  - Mandates the use of a certificate.
    - Mac OS X Server creates a certificate named Default.

To further protect the user's password and protect the message content as well, you can use SSL encryption. This provides the same level of protection used by secure websites. Unless you have incompatible clients or don't want to manage SSL certificates for your server, you will want to set both of the SSL options to Require.

## Open Relay Issues

Open relays allow junk mail senders to use SMTP protocol of a mail server to send mail to thousands of users.

- Open relays often get blacklisted.
- Other SMTP mail servers refuse to accept messages from blacklisted mail server.

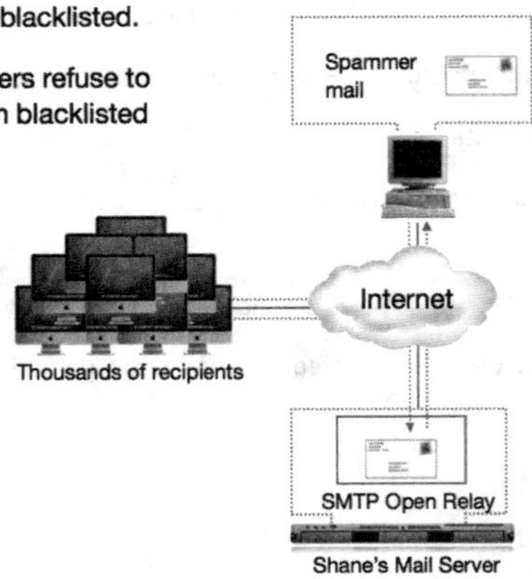


Servers that allow anyone to send messages through them are known as open relays. Such servers can quickly be blacklisted.

## Restricting SMTP Relay

By default, Mac OS X Server restricts mail service to an IP range of internal IP addresses.

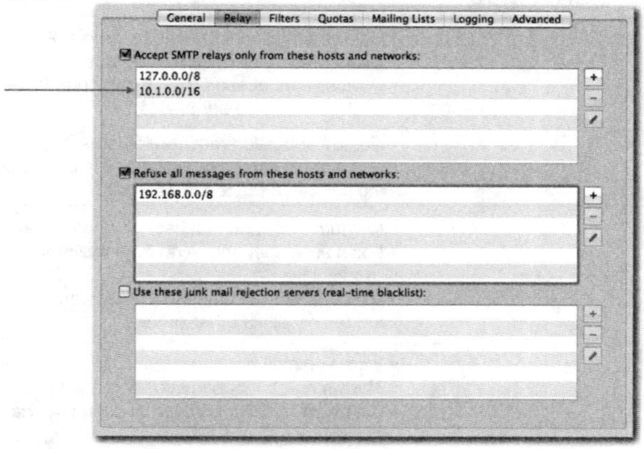


Preventing your mail service from becoming an open relay is fairly easy. Mac OS X Server places the IP range of your server (as defined by your subnet mask) in the field to restrict acceptance of other SMTP servers to just those on your local subnet. You can add or alter this behavior depending on your requirements.

## SMTP Relay Combinations

| SMTP Authentication | Restricted SMTP Relay | Result |
|---|---|---|
| On | Off | • No Authentication required for incoming mail<br>• Users must authenticate to send mail<br>• Devices cannot send mail (e.g., printer low-toner warning) to outside addresses |
| On | On | • No authentication required for incoming mail<br>• Local users must authenticate unless they are sending from a trusted IP address |
| Off | On | • No Authentication required for incoming mail<br>• Local users can only send from mail from trusted IP addresses<br>• Users on untrusted IPs (e.g. road warriors) must send their mail via other servers |
| Off | Off | • Incoming mail operates normally<br>• The server cannot be used for outgoing mail<br>• Clients must be configured to send mail via some other server (e.g. the ISP's) |

A very secure mail service is one that requires authorization before sending mail and restricts access to itself by not accepting connections from open relays.

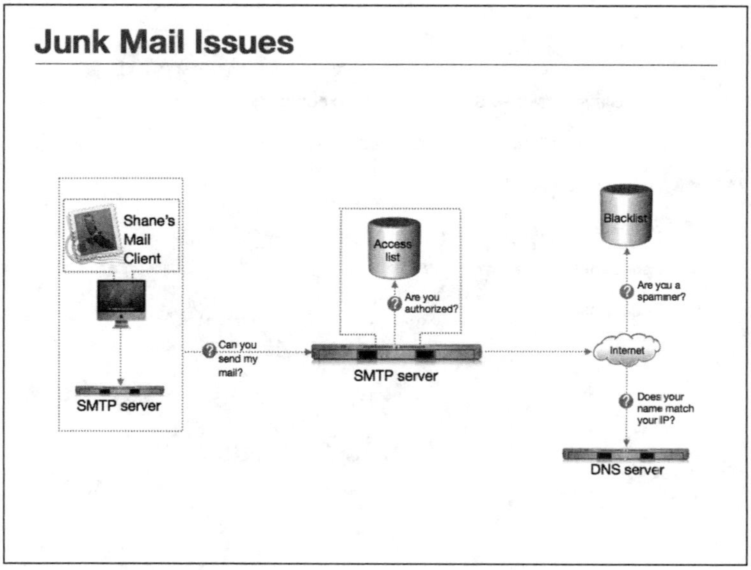


It is important to take an overall view of how junk mail can be handled. At each stage in this process, junk mail could be halted in one way or another. You've already seen how to authenticate prior to sending mail and restrict your mail service from acting as an open relay. You now need to take a look at how your mail service treats the mail it receives.

## Restricting Junk Mail

Mac OS X Server includes SPAM Assassin to combat junk mail.

- Advanced algorithms evaluate and score suspect mail.
- Adjustable parameters
  - Score level
  - Languages
  - Locations

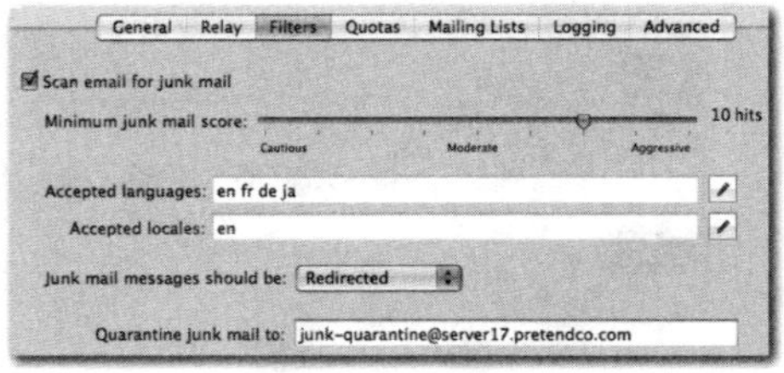


Administrators should try to reduce the amount of junk mail users receive. One method is to block known sources of junk mail. Although this will stop junk mail from known spam servers, you also risk blocking legitimate messages delivered through a server that was misidentified as a spam server.

## Handling Known Junk Mail

Defined junk mail can be dealt with in the following ways:

- Delivered with attached subject line
- Deleted
- Bounced
  - Not recommended
- Redirected
  - Deleted, bounced, and redirected junk mail can be handled with optional notification.

Once junk mail is located, you can decide how to handle it.

## Managing Virus Detection

Mac OS X Server includes ClamAV to combat mail viruses.

Defined mail with attached viruses can be dealt with in the following ways:

- Deleted
- Bounced
- Redirected
  - All methods offer optional notification to recipient and secondary account.

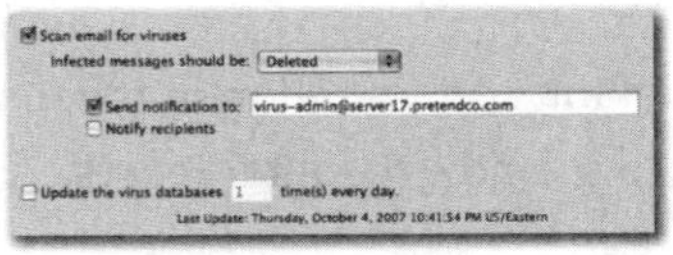


Virus definitions should be updated frequently.

Scanning for mail viruses can help maintain the health of your mail service and prevent being blacklisted because one of your users transmits a virus to another mail service.

Exercises

6.2.1 Secure the Mail Service

6.2.2 Use SSL Certificates with the Mail Service

## Exercise 6.2.1

# Secure the Mail Service

## Objective

Look at the default configuration of the mail service and make adjustments to see how the filter reacts.

## Summary

Once you have a mail server running, your users will begin to complain about SPAM and viruses in mail. Security surrounding your mail service is crucial since most people rely on healthy mail services to communicate.

1 Select the Mail service from your services list in Server Admin.

2 Click the Settings icon in the toolbar, and select the Relay tab.

3. Notice your subnet is listed, and you can add other mail servers to the refusal list or blacklist.

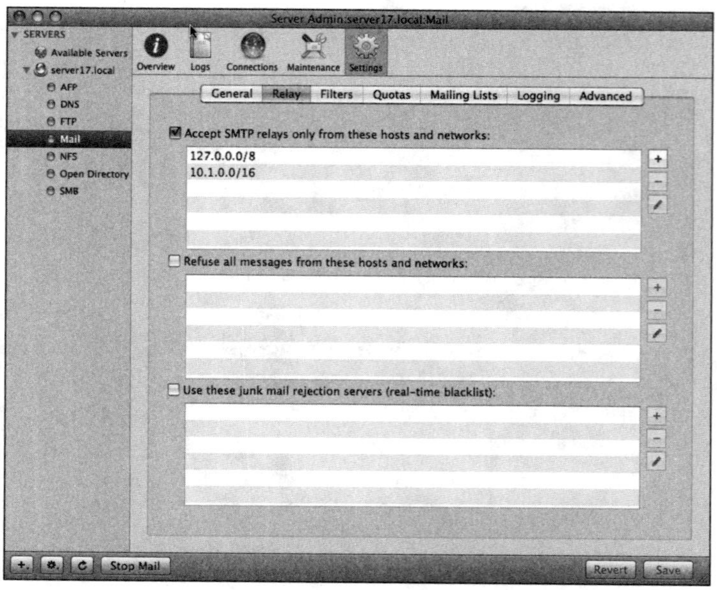

4 Click the Advanced tab and the Security tab. Notice the default authentication settings for SMTP, POP, and IMAP.

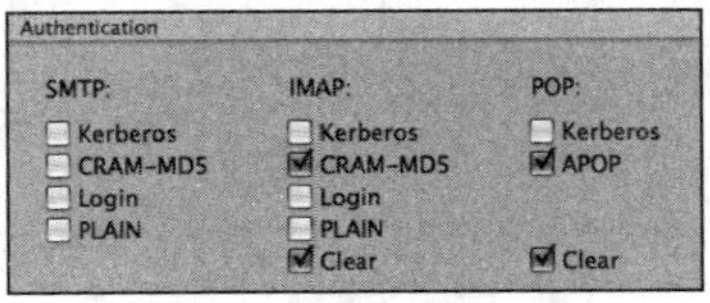


For IMAP, CRAM-MD5 is selected by default but so is Clear authentication. Because you are not using POP, the settings for POP do not matter at the moment, although you should restrict it anyway in case a user requires POP. SMTP is also not restricting who can send mail because there is no authentication required.

5 Select Kerberos for all three protocols, deselect everything else, and click Save.

You've restricted both sending and receiving mail. Users must be in the Kerberos database to obtain a ticket granting ticket, and then obtain a ticket for any other services they wish to use.

6 Click the Filters tab, and view the options for filtering junk mail and mail viruses.

7 Turn on scanning for junk mail and viruses. Ensure that Deleted is chosen from the "Infected messages should be" pop-up menu, and select the checkbox to enable "Notify recipients." Enter `postmaster@servern.pretendco.com` in the "Quarantine infected mail to" field.

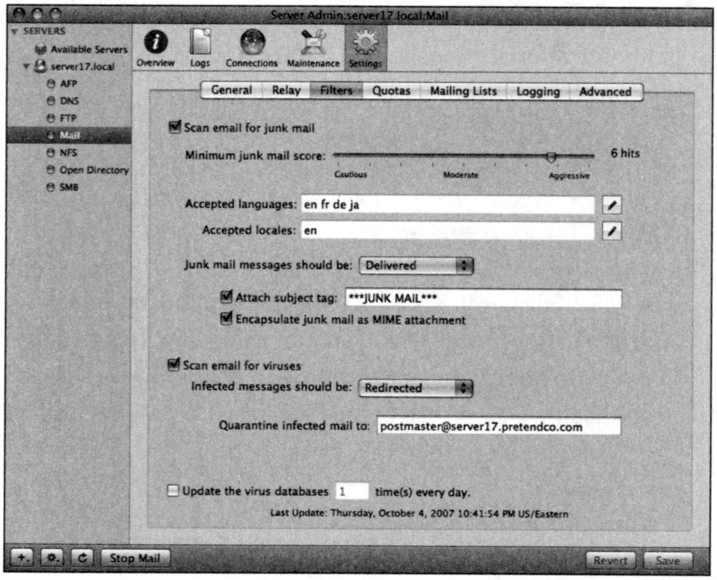


8 Click Save.

9 Log out as cadmin, and log in as david (password: changme).

10 Setup David's mail account, and do *not* enter any passwords in the password fields.

11 Set up David's mail account for IMAP. There will be three opportunities to enter a password, but make sure you never enter a password. In the Outgoing Mail Server dialog, enable Use Authentication, but only enter your user name (leave the password blank).

Note that this does not specify which type of authentication to use, but you will be using Kerberos authentication.

***Question 5*** *Why does setting up David's mail differ from that of Schoun's and the Directory Administrators?*

12 You should have new mail waiting for you. View the mail messages.

13 Attach the text file called gtube.txt, located in /Users/Shared/StudentMaterials/CH06/, to a new mail message to developers@server*n*.pretendco.com.

14 Give your message the subject line `SPAM mail` and send the message.

15 Create another new message to the developers group, this time attaching the file clam.exe, which contains a virus.

16 Give your message the subject line `Virus mail`, and click Send.

You want to ensure everyone in your group receives the junk mail and the virus.

17 Check for new mail if necessary. You'll see two new mail messages, one addressed to you because you are a member of the group Developers, the other a message about the mail containing a virus.

18 Leave the Mail application open, and choose Go > Connect to Server in your Finder. Enter `smb://servern.local`, and click Connect. Select the project lion share point. Notice you did not have to provide a password.

19 Open /System/Library/CoreServices/Kerberos, and view all the Kerberos tickets you have.

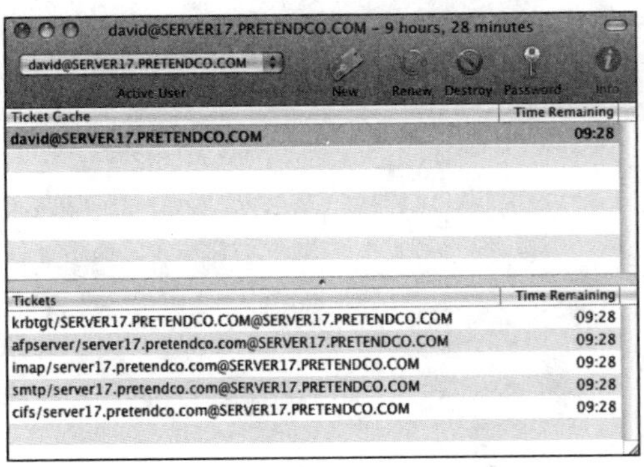


***Question 6*** *What is each ticket for and how did you obtain them?*

20 Quit the Kerberos application, minimize but do not close or quit the Mail application, and open Server Admin. Because you are logged in as David, you'll have to locate Server Admin in the /Applications/Server/ folder.

21 Connect to your server, and authenticate as ladmin (password: apple).

22 Select the Mail service, and click the Connections icon in the toolbar to view david's IMAP connections.

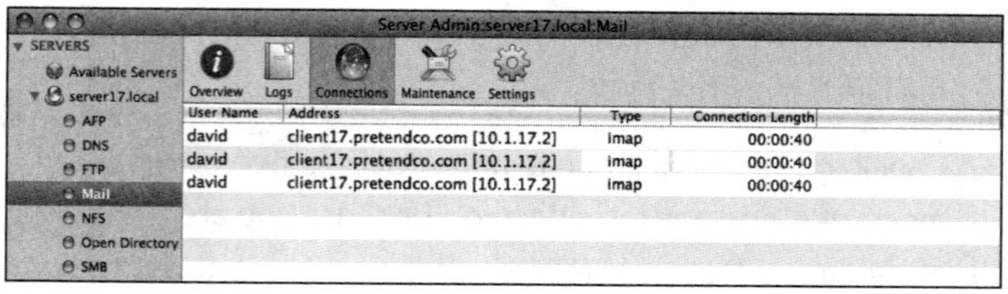


**Question 7** *Why does David have more than one IMAP connection?*

23 Do not close any running applications or log out as David.

## Exercise 6.2.2

# Use SSL Certificates with the Mail Service

## Objective

Use Secure Sockets Layer (SSL) certificates to better secure your users' mail.

## Summary

Recall that when you set up Schoun's email, you authenticated as cadmin to always trust the certificate named Default from the Mac OS X Server. This certificate is now inside your System keychain and is trusted by any user who logs into your Mac OS X computer. You'll change the Mail service to require and use this certificate and edit David's mail preferences to take advantage of it.

1 While still logged in as david, and connected to Server Admin as ladmin, ensure the Mail service is selected in the services list.

2 Click the Settings icon in the toolbar, and click the Advanced tab. Click the Security tab is selected.

3 Choose Require from the SMTP SSL pop-up menu.

4 Choose Use from the IMAP and POP SSL pop-up menu.

   These settings will require a certificate for sending mail, but will only use one for IMAP and POP if available.

5 Choose Default for the Certificate for both SMTP and IMAP/POP.

   This certificate was created when Mac OS X Server is first configured.

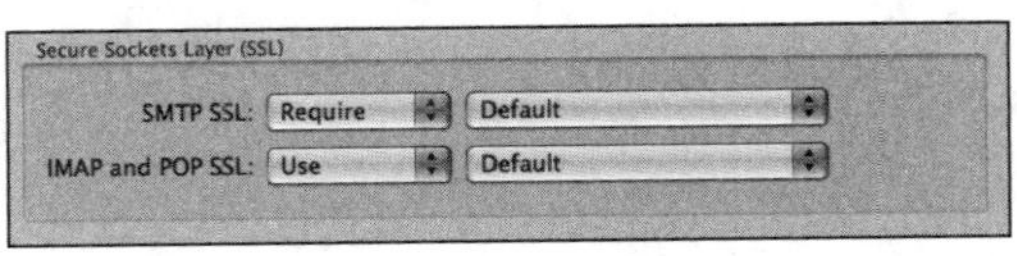

6 Click Save.

7 Click the Mail application in the Dock to maximize it, and send an email to Simon.

You get an error about the authentication.

8 Click Edit Message to return to the Message, and close the message without saving it.

9 Under the Mail menu, choose Preferences, and click on the Accounts icon in the toolbar.

10 Select David's account, and choose Edit Server List from the Outgoing Mail Server (SMTP) pop-up menu.

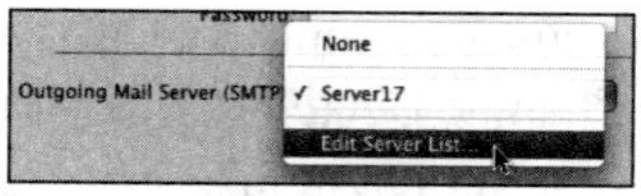


11 Click the Advanced tab, select "Use Secure Sockets Layer (SSL)," and click OK.

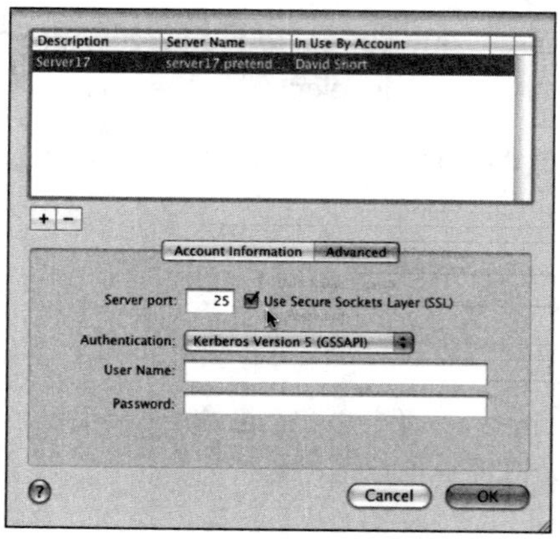


12 In David's account, click the upper Advanced tab, and select Use SSL, if not already selected.

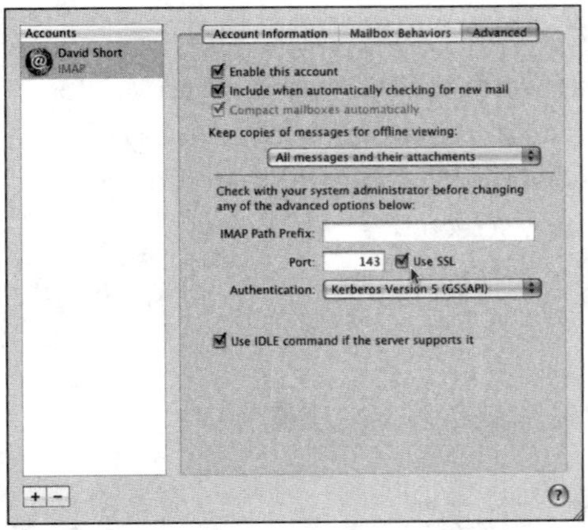


13 Close the Preferences window, and save the changes to David's account.

14 Send the email to Simon.

15 Create another email and send it to developers@server*n*.pretendco.com.

16 Check your mail. You should have successfully sent and received mail using SSL.

17 Quit Server Admin, and open System Preferences, and click the Accounts preferences pane.

Notice David is listed as a network account. This is because his home folder is located on server*n*.pretendco.com.

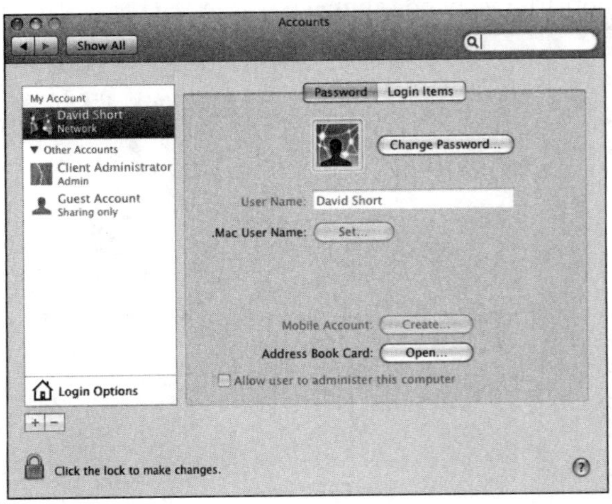

18 Quit any open applications, and log out as David.

19 Log in as simon (password: abcd1234), and set up Mail for simon, again, without any passwords entered in any of the password fields. Remember to choose Kerberos for the Outgoing Mail Security screen.

20 On the final screen, view the information to confirm SSL is turned on.

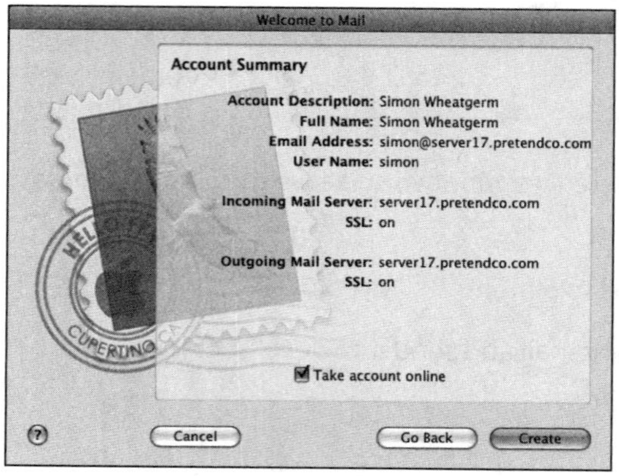


21 View all of simon's mail and reply to the developers group message about the meetings. Respond that you'll be delighted to attend all of them. Send it to confirm you can receive mail, and you can send mail as well.

22 Use the Kerberos application to view Simon's tickets, and log out as simon after viewing them.

# Maintenance

# 6.3

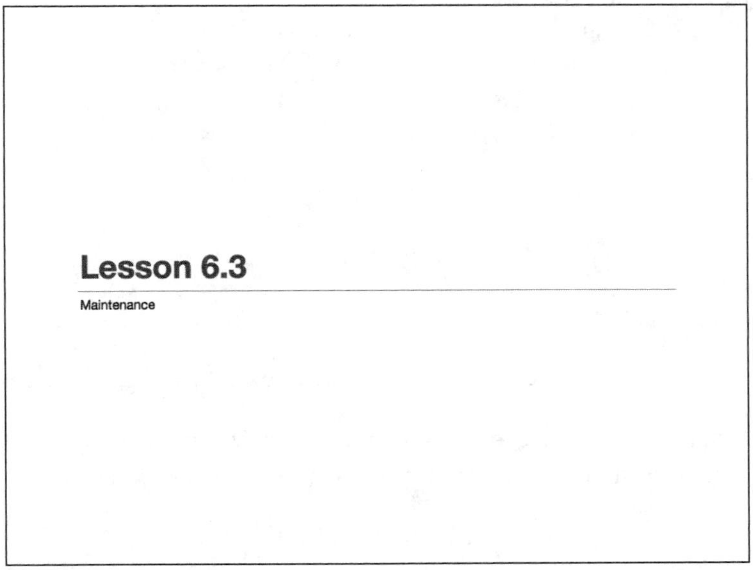


Running a mail service is generally critical to an organization, therefore, maintenance procedures, including setting mail quotas, and training users to use other methods of large file transfers should be implemented. Knowing how to attempt a repair on the mail database or reconstruct a user's mailbox can quickly satisfy upset users.

## Mail Server Maintenance

Setting Mail quotas

Logging Mail server details

Reconstructing user mailboxes

Repairing IMAP databases

Several maintenance features are built in to Mac OS X Server's mail service, including quota management and extremely detailed logging abilities.

## Setting Mail Quotas

Refusal of messages over a given size

- Limits overuse of mail server as transfer method for large files

Enable and enforce quotas

- If mailbox exceeds given size
  - Send customized warnings
  - Disable mail

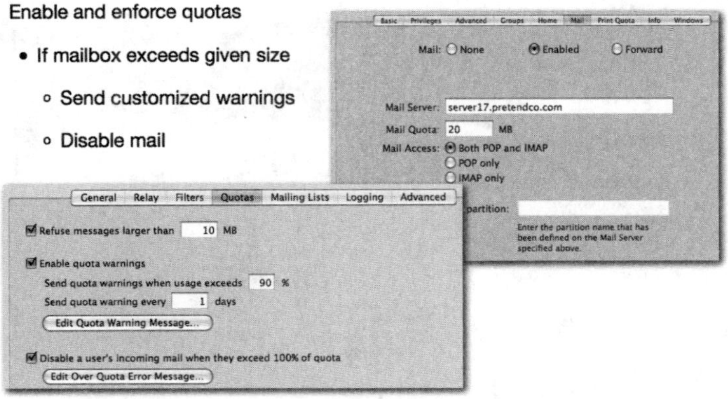


Setting a low overall quota for attachments is the best way to keep a mail server from bogging down while attempting to deliver extremely large files. Per-user quotas can also be set and warning messages about the size of quotas can be customized.

## Logging Mail Service Details

Several logs associated with mail services

- mailaccess.log logs information related to
  - IMAP
  - POP
  - SMTP
- Mailing list logs
- Virus and junk mail logs

Custom log archival

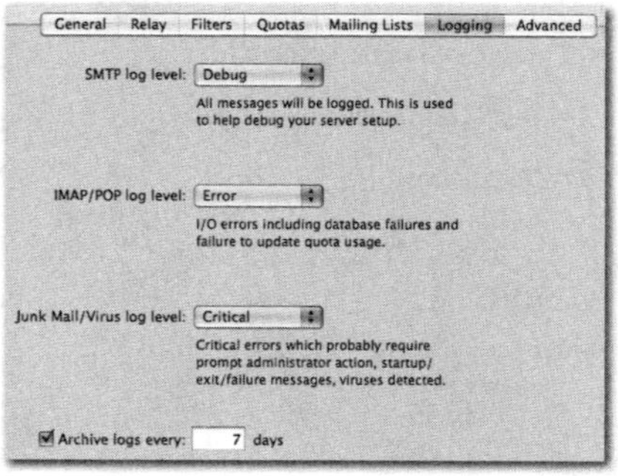


The three parameters that are open to a variety of logging levels are the SMTP service, the IMAP/POP services, and virus and junk mail. Mailing list logs are not open to changing the logging levels in Server Admin.

## Mail Access Log

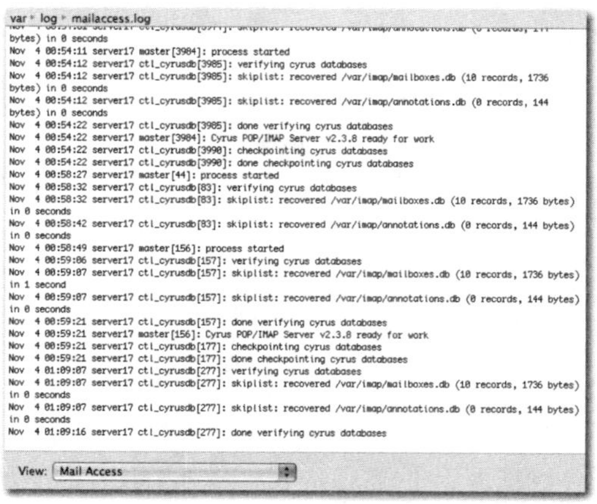


Using Server Admin, administrators can view and search several mail-related log files.

## Logging Levels

Debug

- Logs everything, can become extremely large

Critical

- Most events that require administrator notification, virus detection

Error

- Mail database errors, quota errors

Information

- Mailbox openings, delivery and authentication attempts

Warning

- Mail client inactivity, virus scanning output

Notice

- All authentication attempts, successful and unsuccessful

Six logging levels exist for the three main log files. Do not leave verbose logging on unless mail log files are archived frequently; searching very large log files can consume time when attempting to troubleshoot an issue.

## Reconstructing User Mailboxes

Mailboxes can become corrupt.

- Reconstruct mailboxes on a per user basis.

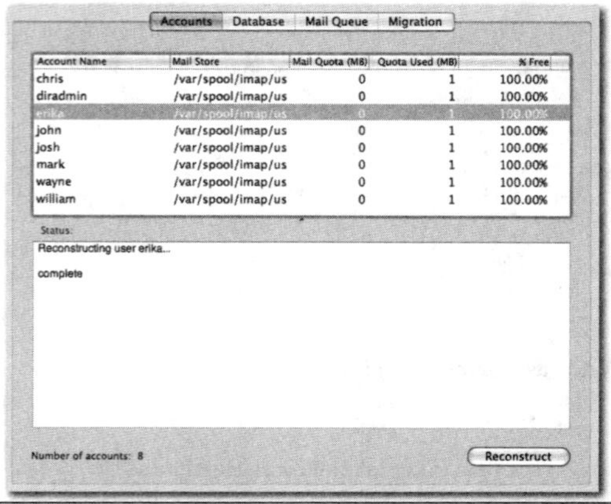


User mailboxes may need to be reconstructed at times. If possible, have the user quit their Mail application when attempting a reconstruction on their mailbox to avoid checking mail while the mailbox is being reconstructed.

## Repairing IMAP Databases

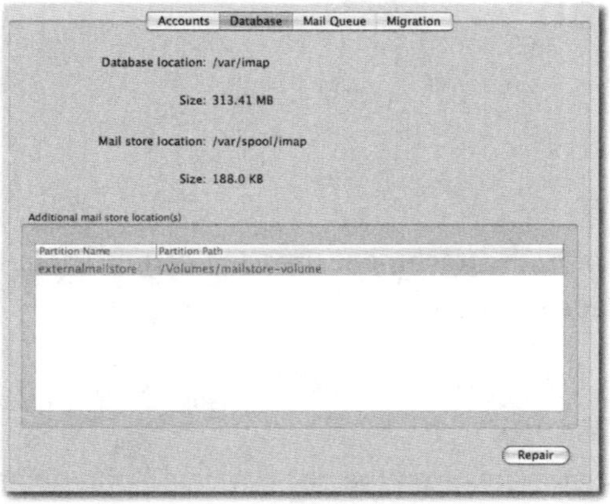


In some cases, the entire mail database can be corrupt and no users can get their mail. In this case, attempts to rebuild the entire mail database can be attempted. It is advisable to back up the mail database prior to an attempted rebuild, in case a hardware failure occurs during the rebuild which can exacerbate the problem. The location of the mail database can be viewed under the mail service settings of Server Admin.

Exercises

6.3.1 Configure Mail Service Quotas (optional)

6.3.2 Reconstruct and Rebuild Mail (optional)

6.3.3 View Mail Log Files (optional)

## Exercise 6.3.1

# Configure Mail Service Quotas (optional)

## Objective

Set quotas for both attachment sizes and certain users. Edit the quota message users see.

## Summary

Mail attachments are often the primary cause of problems in a mail service. In addition, users may not clean out their mailboxes regularly, leading to storage issues.

1 Log in as cadmin, open Server Admin, and select the Mail service from the list.

2 Click the Settings icon in the toolbar.

3 Click the Quotas tab, and select "Refuse messages larger than" if not already enabled, and set the size to 4MB.

4 Select "Enable quota warnings," if not already enabled, and send quota warnings when usage exceeds 70 percent.

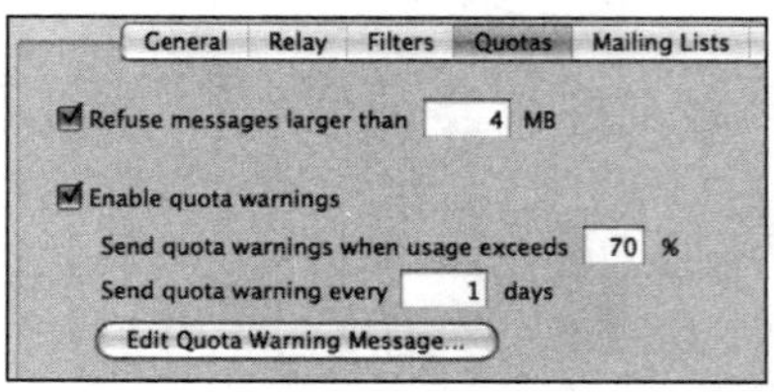

5 Edit the quota warning message so it originates from postmaster@server*n*.pretendco.com, and has an appropriate subject line and body text. Click OK.

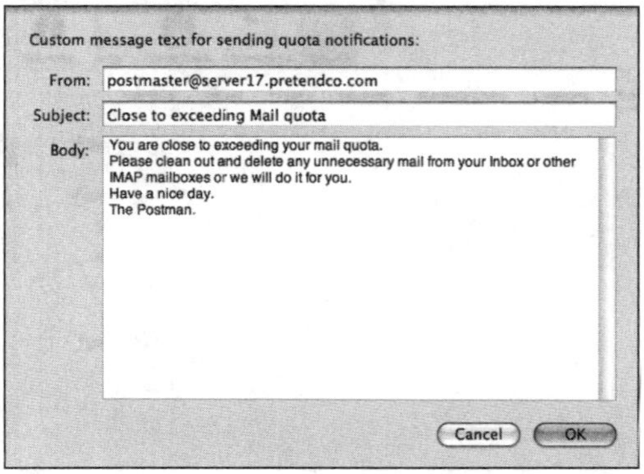


6 Click Save.

7 Open Workgroup Manager, and select Andre's account.

8 Click the Mail tab, and set Andre's Mail Quota to `4`MB, and click Save.

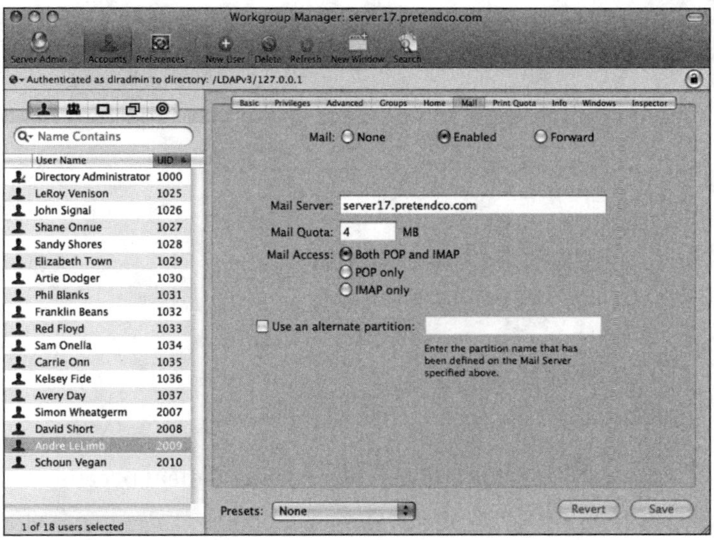


9 Open Mail, and open the Mail preferences for Directory Administrator.

10 Edit both your SMTP settings and your IMAP settings to use Kerberos and SSL.

*Question 8* *What happened when you attempted to change the settings?*

11 Test the new settings by sending david an email and copying yourself.

12 Check your mail to ensure you are receiving mail.

13 Create a new mail message to Andre, and attach the Dictionary.zip file from the /Users/Shared/ folder.

14 Send the message, and view the dialog that appears.

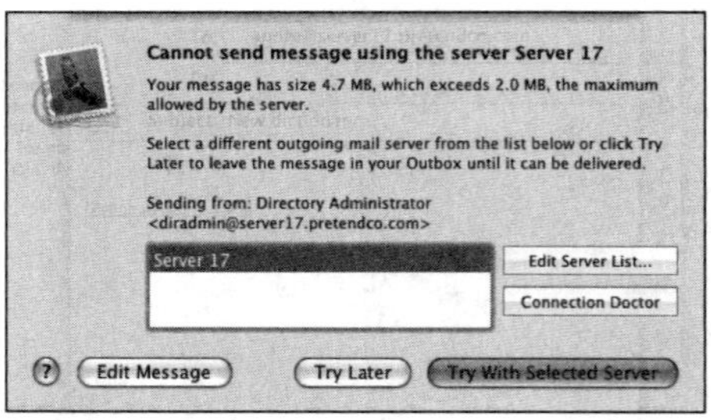


15 Click Edit Message and remove that attachment because it exceeds the message quota.

16 Attach the Chess.zip file inside /Users/Shared, and send the message.

**17** Create a new message to Andre, attach the same Chess.zip file, and send it.

You are sending two large files to Andre so his personal mail quota will be close to exceeding his limit.

**18** Log out as cadmin, and log in as andre (password: abcd1234).

**19** Configure Mail for Andre, remembering to not use any passwords and to use Kerberos for the Outgoing Mail Security screen.

**20** Click the small alert icon next your IMAP inbox, and view the message.

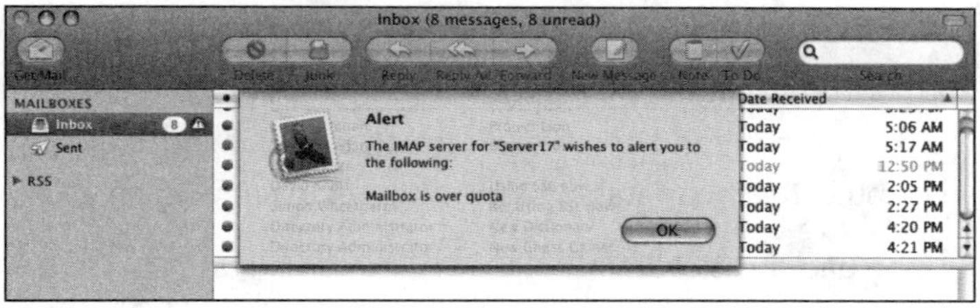


**21** Attempt to delete the two mail messages that put Andre over the quota.

***Question 9*** *What happens when you try to delete them and how can this be corrected?*

---

---

**22** Quit Mail and log out as Andre.

## Exercise 6.3.2

# Reconstruct and Rebuild Mail (optional)

## Objective

Reconstruct a user's mailbox because it may not be working properly. In some cases, the mail database itself is corrupt and requires rebuilding.

## Summary

You'll assume that the Directory Administrator's mailbox is not working properly and needs reconstruction. Assuming it failed, you will rebuild the mail database in an attempt to remedy the issue.

1 Log back in as cadmin.

2 Open Server Admin, click the Mail service, and click the Maintenance icon in the toolbar.

3 Click the Accounts tab and notice who is over quota on their account.

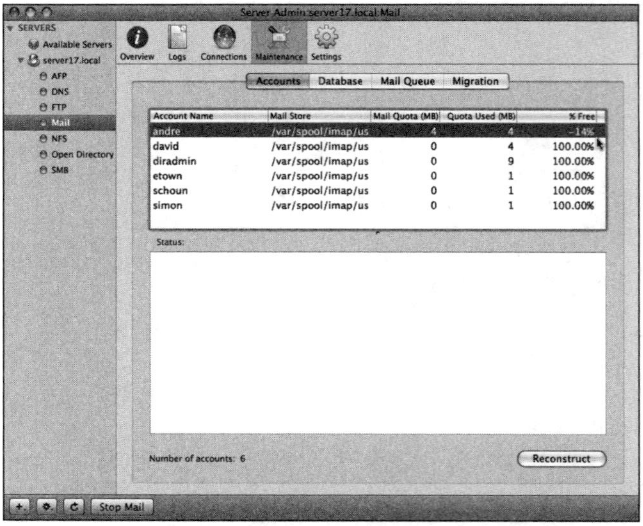

4 While Andre is over his quota, it is not his mailbox that needs reconstruction.

5 Select diradmin in the list, and click the Reconstruct button in the lower right.

6 Click on other users to reconstruct their mailboxes. Notice the status in the lower portion of the window.

7 Click the Database tab, and view the storage statistics on the mail database.

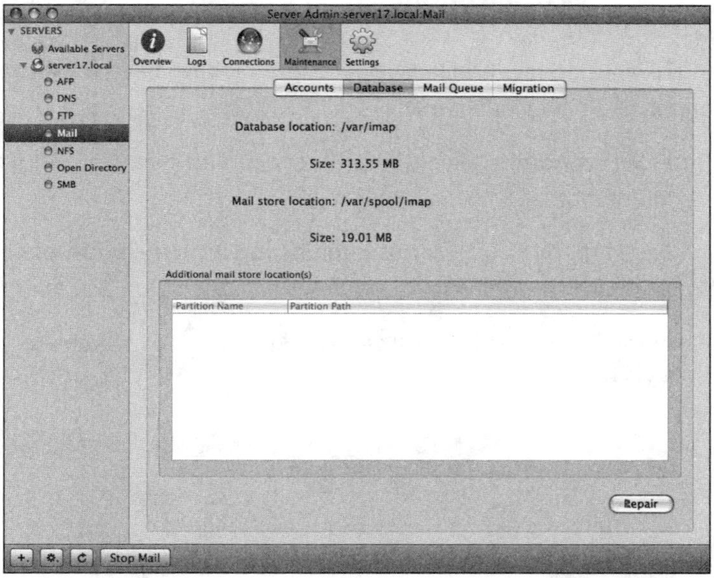


8 Click the Repair button in the lower right. Notice the progress indicator (looks like a spinning gear), indicating the mail database is being rebuilt.

## Exercise 6.3.3

# View Mail Log Files (optional)

## Objective

View and use log files to watch for anomalies or issues surrounding mail.

## Summary

You'll view log files and look for viruses that have been found and watch users check their mail.

1 In Server Admin, select the Mail service, and click the Logs icon in the toolbar.

2 Select the Junk Mail/Virus Scanning log from the pop-up menu and view the log file.

3 In the Search field, enter the word `infected` to search the log entries.

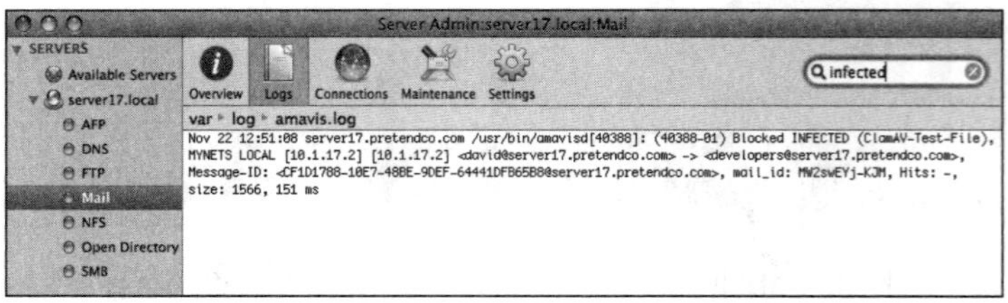


4 Notice there is an entry when David sent the virus attachment.

5 Remove the word infected from the Search field.

6 Select IMAP from the View pop-up menu, and scroll through the file, looking at the entries from when you were checking mail in this chapter.

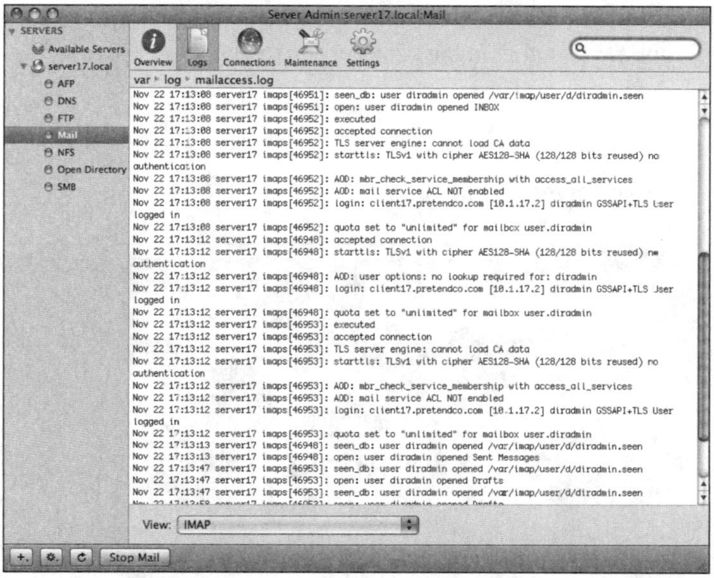


7 Select SMTP from the View pop-up menu, and scroll through the file, looking at the entries from when you were sending mail in this chapter.

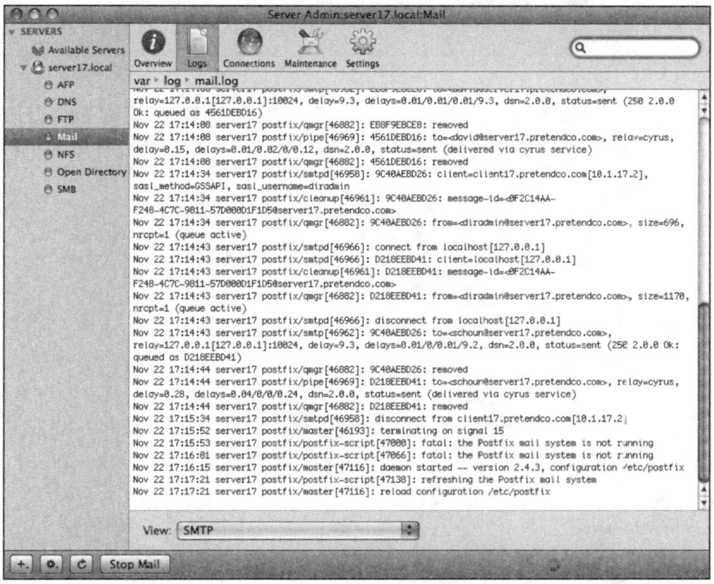

*Question 10 What log files are being searched by both the IMAP and SMTP entries in the View pop-up menu?*

8 Leave Server Admin open.

## Chapter Summary

| | | |
|---|---|---|
| **Configuration** | Server Admin | Workgroup Manager |
| **Security** | Server Admin | |
| **Maintenance** | Server Admin | Workgroup Manager |

# 7

# Using Web Services

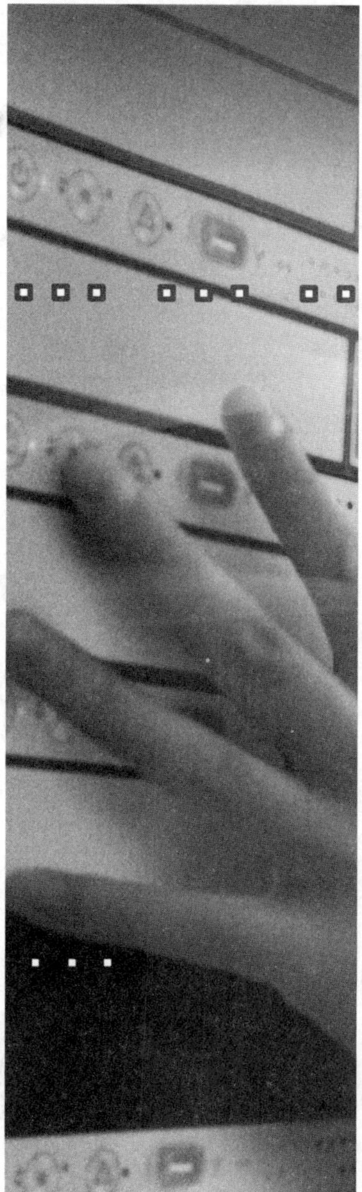


## 7.1 Configuration

**Exercise 7.1.1** Configure Basic Web Services

**Exercise 7.1.2** Create a Secondary Website

## 7.2 Sharing

**Exercise 7.2.1** Use Realms to Restrict Access

## 7.3 Security

**Exercise 7.3.1** Secure a Website Using SSL

# 7.1 Configuration

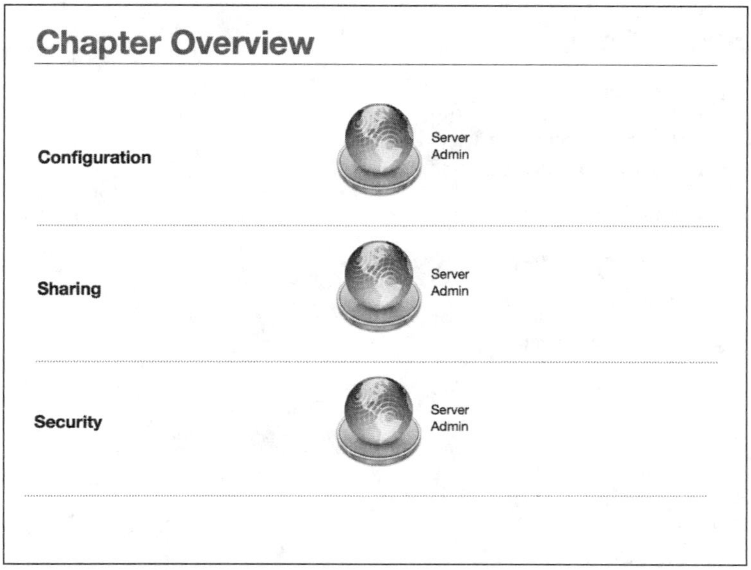


Mac OS X Server's Web Services can be divided into three logical sections, and all Web Services configuration is done with Server Admin.

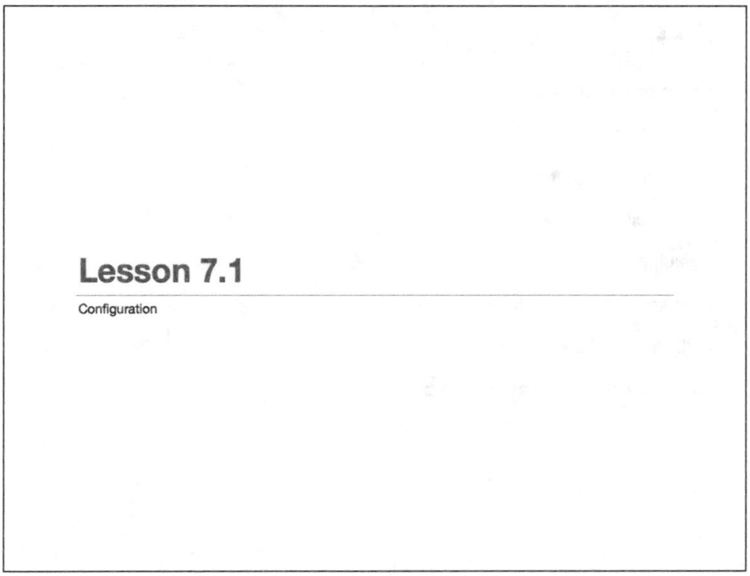


This lesson deals with the basics of web service terminology, including site-specific configuration options and Apple-specific options for all sites on a server.

## Web Service

- Web basics
- Web server modules
- Enabling websites
- Website options
- Web server logging
- Additional site creation
- Aliases and Redirects
- Web services

Web services can encompass many features with a variety of configuration options.

## Website Basics

Based on Apache version 2.

Default computer site location.

- /Library/WebServer/Documents/
- Default file is index.html.

Default port is 80.

User and group www are used by Apache

- Defines default access to sites

All users with home folders have personal sites.

- http://server17.pretendco.com/~john
- Located in user's Sites folder

Mac OS X Server's web service is based on Apache version 2. The default directory for webpages is /Library/WebServer/Documents, and the default port is the widely used port 80.

## Web Server Modules

Modules are enabled or disabled for all sites, not per site.

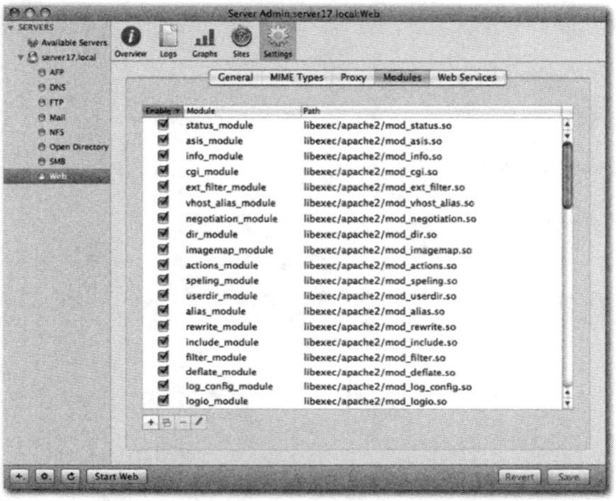


It is a good idea to review the modules that Apple enables by default. Then, if you need to quickly return to the default settings to troubleshoot issues with your site, you'll know exactly what Apple has enabled and disabled.

## Apple-Specific Modules

mod_spotlight_apple

- Permits searching a website.
  - http://server17.pretendco.com/.spotlight

mod_bonjour

- Allows edits to how websites will register with Bonjour service

mod_hfs_apple

- Requires visitors to enter correct case for site links.

There are a variety of Apple-specific modules. The Spotlight module permits searching your website pages. The Bonjour module can be used where the administrator would like to control how the sites appear via Bonjour on the local subnet. The HFS module forces case-sensitivity on URLs for sites. Remember that modules are enabled or disabled for all sites, that is, and are not site-specific.

## Apple-Specific Authentication Modules

mod_auth_apple

- Allows for restriction of users to sites or subdirectories of sites by requiring authentication

mod_digest_apple (Mac OS X Server v10.4 Open Directory Master)

- Does not send passwords in clear text

mod_auth_digest_apple (Mac OS X Server v10.5 Open Directory Master)

- Does not send passwords in clear text

mod_spnego

- Leverages Kerberos and Open Directory for authentication

Four Apple modules center around authentication. These modules should be used in conjunction with realms, which you'll learn about in the following lesson.

## Enabling Websites

Default website is based on initial IP of computer

Domain name may not be listed and does not restrict access by name

To start a website:

- Select the Enable checkbox.
- Click Start Web button.

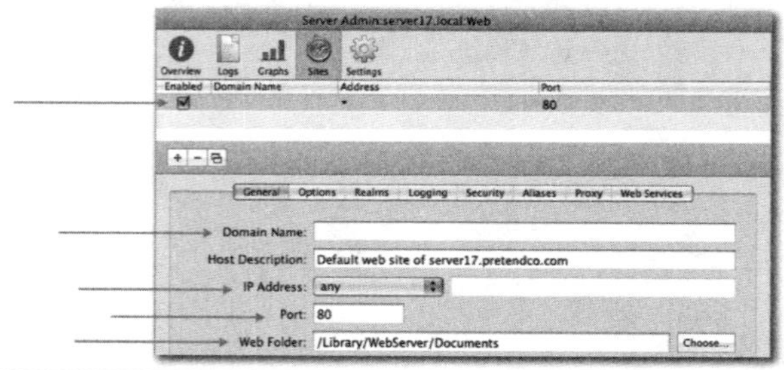


Starting a website is as simple as clicking the Start Web button, however additional configuration is generally desired. The main components of the site are the domain name, IP address, and port number.

## Website Options

Folder Listing

- Allows sites to show all files
- Can be insecure—allows viewing of files not directly linked

WebDAV

- Distributed authoring and versioning
- Folder and file access similar to AFP, SMB, FTP

Spotlight Searching

- Permits websites to be searched using Spotlight

Permission to execute various scripting languages

- CGI Execution and Server Side Includes (SSI)

Site-specific options allow for Spotlight searching, file sharing and restricting access, use of scripting languages, and listing the contents of your site in a browser window.

## Web Server Logging

Apache has the ability to log several criteria.

- Access Log
- Error Log
  - Attempts to access pages that don't exist
  - Attempts to access restricted pages

Log files for heavy traffic sites require frequent rotation to stay manageable.

The main log files for sites are the access.log and error.log. Apache has the capability to be very verbose when filling log files, and frequent rotation ensures they don't grow to an unmanageable size.

## Apache Log Formatting

Format named "Other" in Server Admin

- %h %l %u %t "%r" %>s %b
  - -h
    - Visiting computer
  - -l
    - Remote logname
  - -u
    - Remote user
  - -t
    - Time
  - -r
    - First line requested (placed in quotes)
  - -s
    - Status of the request
  - -b
    - Number of bytes transferred

Apache can log several parameters and uses a type of shorthand to describe each parameter it logs. Using Server Admin, the Other logging parameters are shown on this slide.

## Web Server Logs

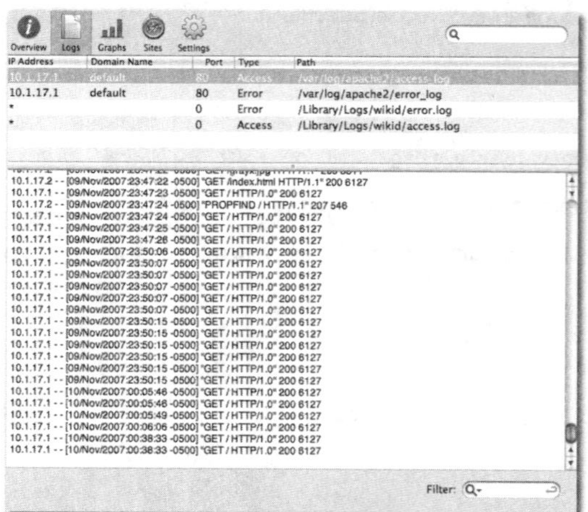


Log files should be searched using the Filter field at the bottom of Server Admin.

## Additional Website Criteria

Additional websites can be created using different criteria.

- IP address
- Domain name
- Port number

More than one website can be created and used on Mac OS X Server. Each website must be defined by one of three unique identifiers; domain name, IP address, or port number. You can choose to have many web sites point to one IP address. This is a common scenario. As long as the domain names are different, they can point to different folders, and visitors will not know that a single computer is hosting multiple sites.

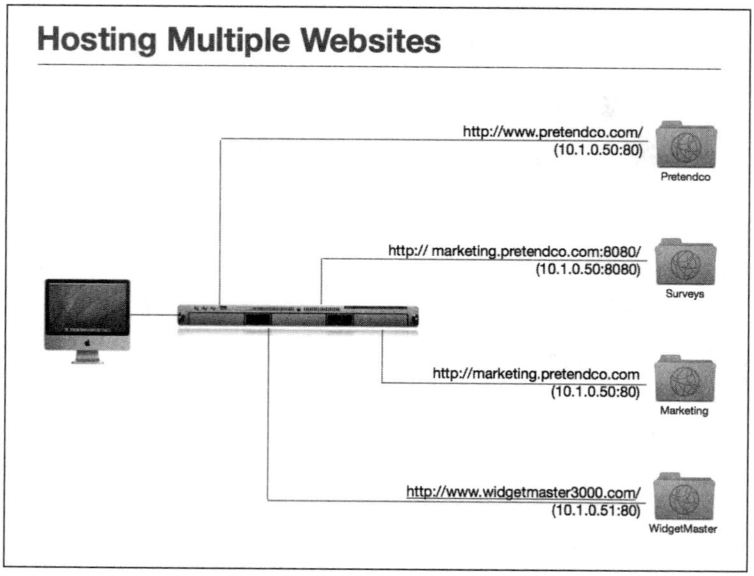


You can host multiple sites with two network interfaces. It is also possible to have more than one IP address on a single interface, and have Apache know about the second IP and direct visitors accordingly.

## Aliases and Redirects

Aliases permit more than one name for a site or folder.

- http://server17.pretendco.com also answers to http://www.pretendco.com
- Often known as virtual hosting

Redirects point visitors to another location.

- http://server17.pretendco.com/mybackpages actually goes to http://server17.pretendco.com/myotherpages
- Most commonly used to redirect users to older pages while newer ones are being updated

Aliases allow more than one name for a site. Redirects point links to a secondary site or different location than what is listed. The asterisk in the Aliases tab acts as a wildcard so any virtual hosts will be taken to your default website. To disable this feature, remove the asterisk.

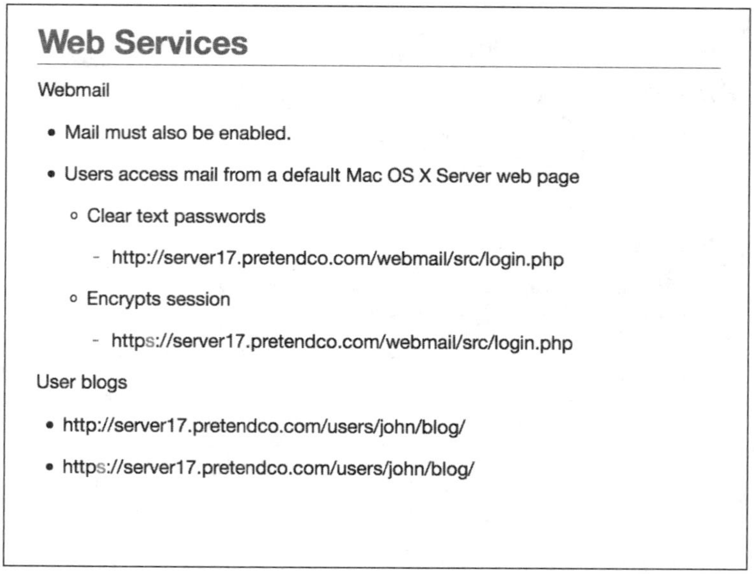


Additional web services can be turned on with Mac OS X Server's Web Services. These services include webmail and blogging, and encryption via SSL.

Myriad configuration options are available when setting up a website, and Mac OS X Server makes it easy to handle several of these options with Server Admin.

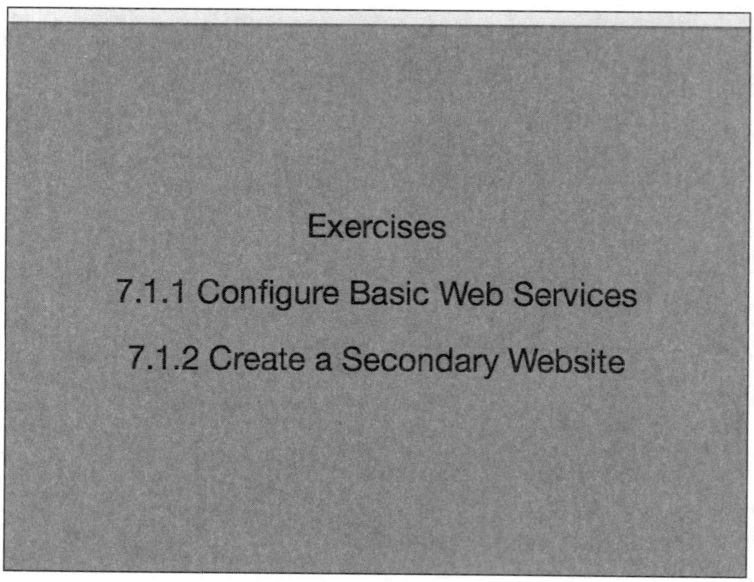

## Exercise 7.1.1

# Configure Basic Web Services

### Objective

Set up the Web Services and allow users to view and search webpages with the Spotlight plug-in. Learn which modules are enabled by default and which are enabled when functionality is added to your site.

### Summary

The web is probably the most talked about and used technology on the market. Everything from food and drugs to computers and textiles are bought and sold every day using a web browser and web servers. Our focus is an introduction to setting up two websites. The specific details of these will be used in the next chapters as we talk about collaborative services.

1. From the Server menu in Server Admin, choose Add Service.
2. Select the Web checkbox to add it to your list of services.
3. Click Save.
4. Select Web from the list under your server.
5. Click the Start button to start the Web Service.
6. Open Safari, and enter `http://10.1.n.1` in the address.

   Notice that with absolutely no configuration, you have a website running.

7. Now enter: `http://servern.pretendco.com` (where *n* is your student number).

   Notice you can also get to your website via its fully qualified domain name.

8 Attempt to click the buttons in the upper right: groups, users, and webmail.

They are not yet available. You'll make them available in this and the following chapter.

9 Back in Server Admin, in the Web service, click the Settings icon in the toolbar, and click the General tab to view the default settings for the web service.

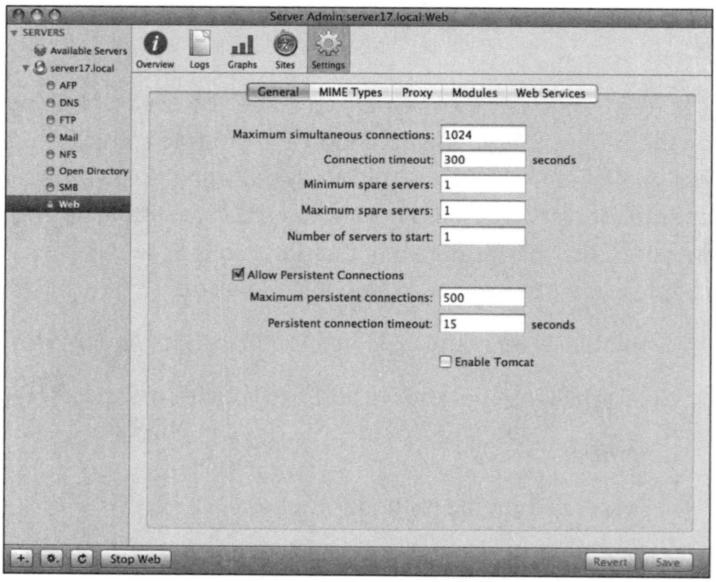


10 Click the Modules tab, and click the Enabled column to sort by modules that are enabled and disabled. Notice that the apple_spotlight_module, the php5_module, the dav_fs_module, and the dav_module are not enabled.

11 Take screen shots of the enabled and disabled modules using Command-Shift-4.

You'll probably need to take three or four screen shots as you scroll through the list.

12 Give the screen shot files names: Default Module State 1, Default Module State 2, and so on.

You'll use these screen shots for comparisons later on in this exercise.

13 Click on the Sites icon in the toolbar, and click the asterisk to select your default website.

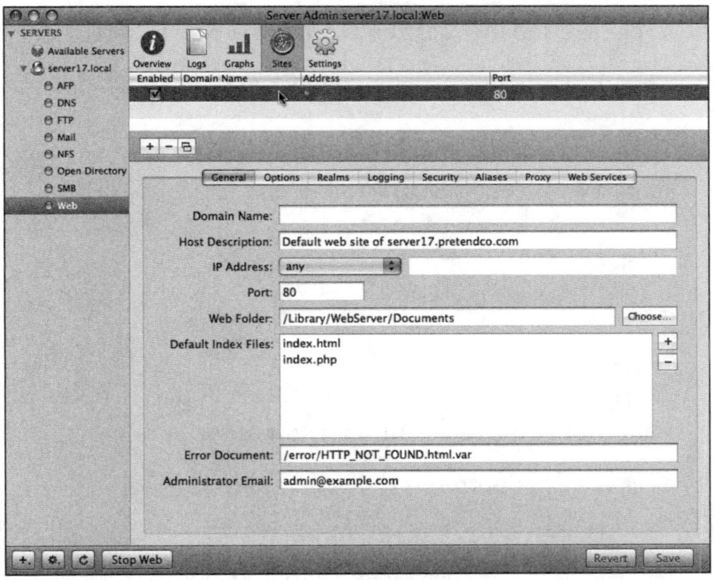


14 Notice the default settings; Domain Name (blank), IP address (any), and Port (80). These define the site.

15 Enter `servern.pretendco.com` in the Domain Name field (where *n* is your student number).

16 Choose your IP address from the IP Address pop-up menu.

17 Click the Options tab, and select the Spotlight Searching and WebDAV checkboxes.

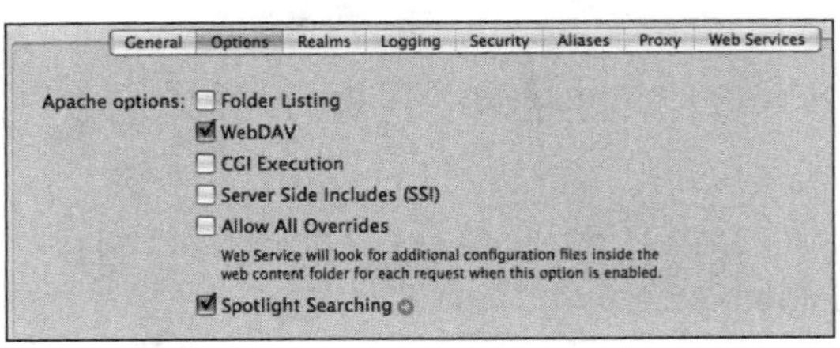

18 Click the Web Services tab, and select the Webmail and Blog checkboxes.

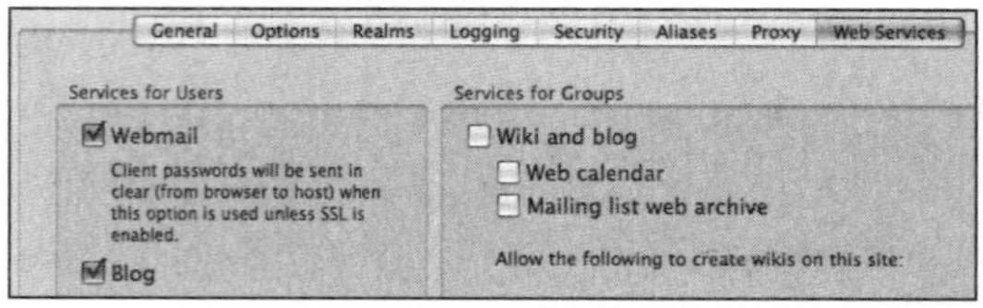


19 Click Save and then stop and restart the Web service.

20 Click the Settings icon in the toolbar, and click the Modules tab.

**Question 1** *What modules have been activated as a result of you turning on Webmail, Blog, WebDAV, and Spotlight searching?*

21 Click back in Safari, and click the Refresh button to refresh the page. Notice the users button is now active.

22 Click the users button. It shows no available users.

23 Click the Create Your Weblog button.

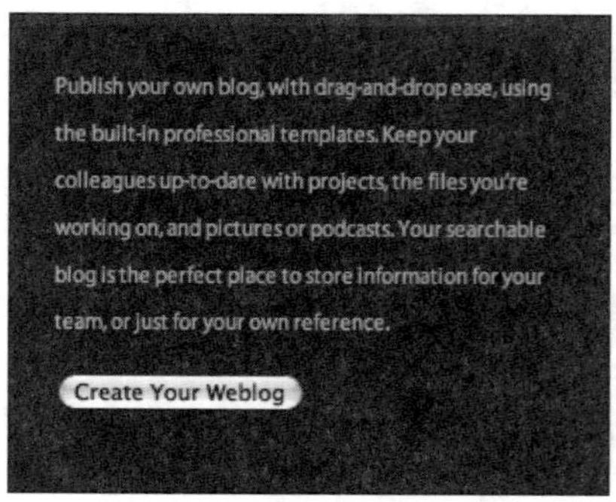


24 In the username field that appears, enter Simon's short name (simon, all lowercase). At the bottom of the window, click the Log In link.

25 Enter `simon`, the password `abcd1234`, and log in. You can now start making blog entries.

26 Click the Add (+) button, enter the title `Time`, click Create, and enter the following text: `Ever notice how the word "time" is used?`

27 Click the Save button on the right to save your changes. You've created a blog entry for others to see.

28 At the bottom of the page, click the Log Out link to log out as simon.

29 Remove all the text except http://server*n*.pretendco.com in the web address, and press Return.

30 Click the users button again, and you'll see a link for Simon Wheatgerm's blog.

31 Click the Back button, add `.spotlight` to the end of the address in the address bar, and press Return. (http://server*n*.pretendco.com/.spotlight)

32 Enter the word `server` in the field, and click Search.

You should have approximately seven returned hits. Spotlight searched inside /Library/WebServer/Documents in all the pages for the word *server* and returned those pages that contained that word.

33 In Server Admin, click the Logs icon in the toolbar and click the default site, if not already selected.

This is your default site's access log. The error log is beneath it. Below that are additional logs for the Wiki, which will be discussed in the next chapter.

34 Enter the word GET in the Filter field at the bottom of the window, and press Return to filter the access log so you can see all the log lines that have the word GET in them.

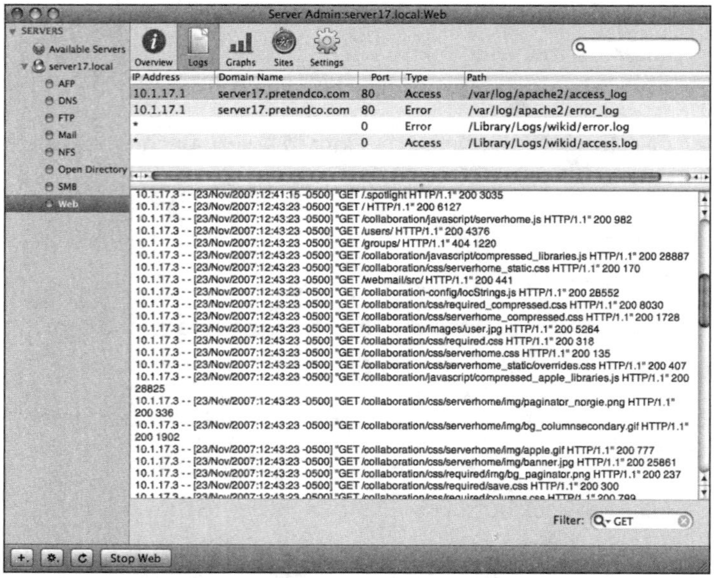

35 Click the Sites icon, and then click your default site. Click the Logging tab under your site.

36 Notice the Location of the log files and the Format string.

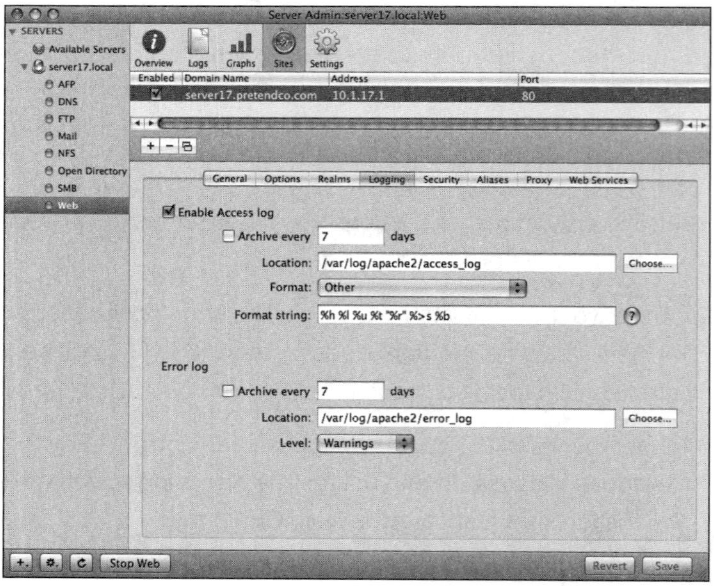

> **Note** If you were connected to the Internet, clicking the Question Mark (?) icon would take you to http://httpd.apache.org/docs/1.3/mod/mod_log_config.html, which is the older Apache log format page (version 1.3). You'll want http://httpd.apache.org/docs/2.0/en/logs.html, which is the log explanation page for Apache 2.0.

**37** Open the Terminal application and type

```
ab -n 10000 -c 50 http://servern.pretendco.com/
```

(where *n* is your student number), and press Return. Be sure to include the trailing forward slash.

You've just sent a large request to your web service. `ab` is an Apache benchmarking tool that tells your Mac OS X computer to ask for 10000 (the `-n` parameter) requests run concurrently by 50 (the `-c` parameter) pretend users on the website http://servern.pretendco.com/.

**38** Make sure Terminal is your frontmost application, and wait for the prompt to appear (`client17:~ cadmin$`).

**39** Press the Up Arrow on your keyboard to re-enter the command, and press Return.

**40** Do this several times after the prompt appears, so you know the last process was completed. You may see a timeout error occur.

**41** Quit the Terminal application.

**42** In Server Admin, click the Graphs icon in the toolbar to see the number of requests spike.

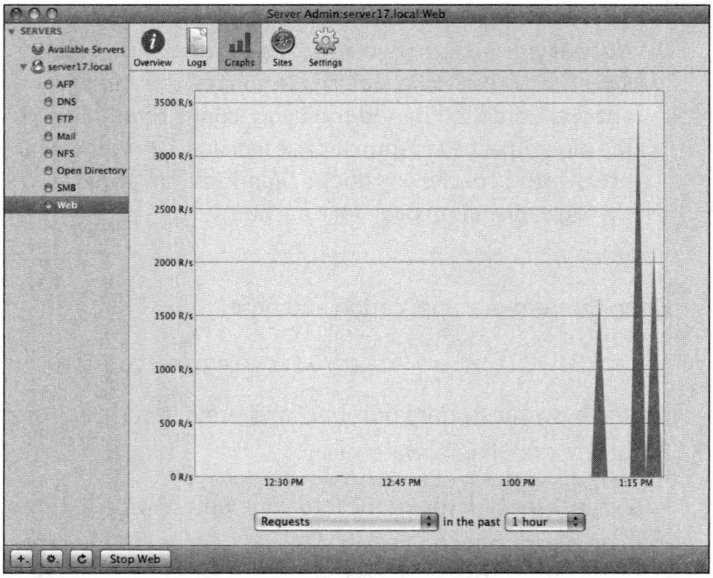


43 Select Throughput from the pop-up menu at the bottom of the window to view the throughput.

These graphs, coupled with the access log, help you keep track of website usage so you can better determine server load and network bandwidth needs.

> **Note** If you are running a web service on your Mac OS X Server, you should also watch the CPU load as it relates to web service requests. You can see your Mac OS X Server's CPU load by clicking the server name in the list in Server Admin, clicking the Graphs icon in the toolbar, and choosing CPU Usage (total) from the pop-up menu at the bottom of the window.

44 Click back on the Sites icon in the toolbar, and select your default website.

45 Click the Aliases tab, and view the default aliases and redirects.

The asterisk in the aliases tab acts as a wildcard, so any virtual hosts will be taken to your default website. If you wanted to disable this feature, you could remove the asterisk, but leave it there for this exercise.

**46** Back in Safari, enter

`http://servern.pretendco.com/allusers/`

to get an error page.

**47** Click back on the General tab of your website. Note the Error Document and path at the bottom of the window.

You may want to customize the error document for your websites. It is important to know where it is located.

**48** Quit Server Admin.

## Exercise 7.1.2

# Create a Secondary Website

## Objective

Create another website so users can access both sites.

## Summary

Often, servers running Web Services host more than one site. You'll set up an alternate site and configure that site accordingly.

1 Use Screen Sharing to connect to your server, and copy the folder PretendCoWebSite from /Users/Shared/StudentMaterials/CH07/ to /Library/WebServer.

2 While still controlling your server's screen, open System Preferences on your Mac OS X Server, and click the Network tab.

3 Ensure Ethernet is selected on the left, and choose Duplicate Service from the Action menu at the bottom of the window.

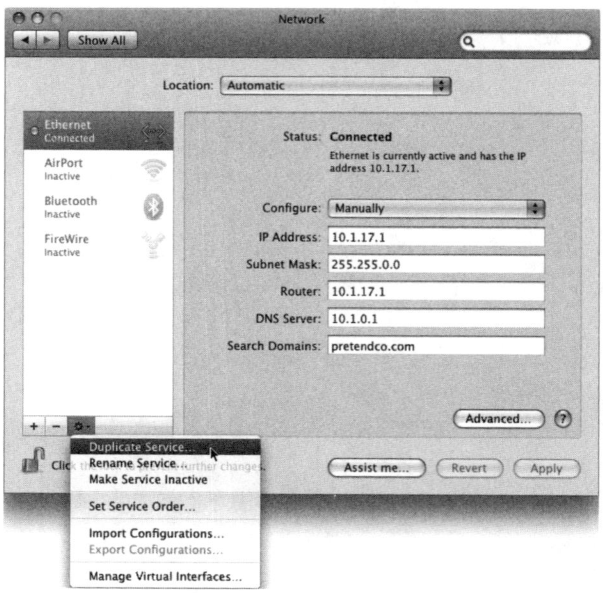

4 In the dialog that appears, leave the name unchanged and click the Duplicate button.

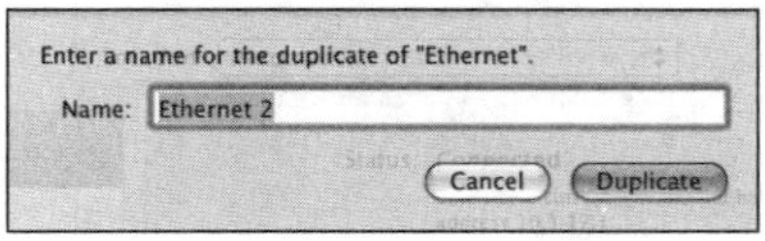


5 Change the last octet of the IP address from `1` to `5`, click the Apply button, and close System Preferences.

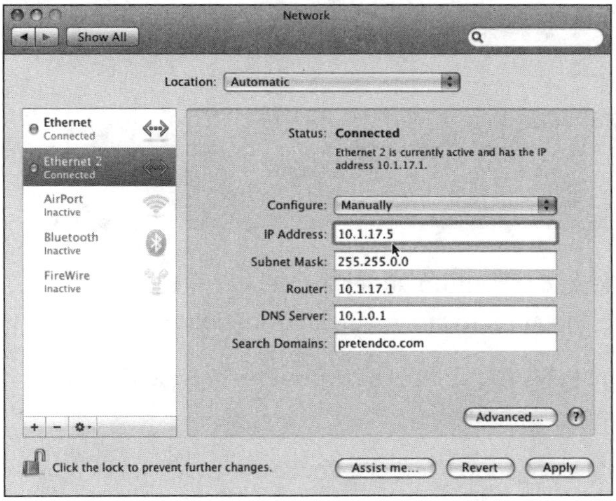


6 Disconnect from screen sharing your server.

7 You've just created a virtual interface for your server. It will now respond to both 10.1.*n*.1 and 10.1.*n*.5.

**Question 2** *What can you use to test to see if both IP addresses are responding?*

---

8 Click Server Admin in the Dock, ensure the Web Service is selected, the Sites icon is chosen in the toolbar, and the General tab is selected for the default site.

9 Stop the web service.

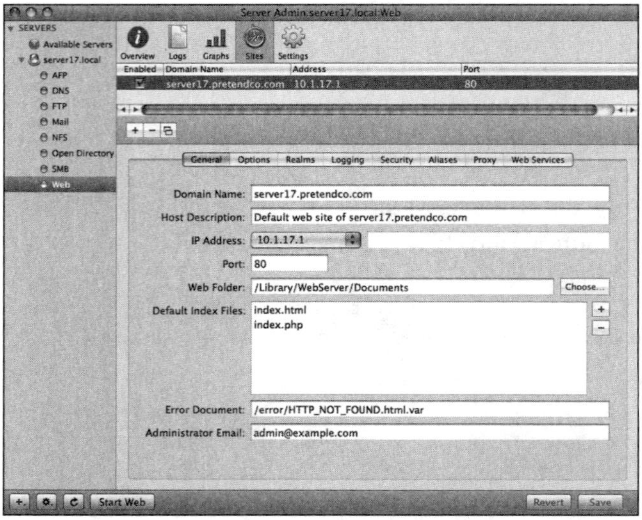

10 Click the Add (+) button under the default site to add a new website and enter the following information:

- Domain Name: `worksiten.pretendco.com` (where *n* is your student number)
- Host Description: Work Site for Server *n*
- IP Address: `10.1.n.5` (from the pop-up menu)
- Port: `80`
- Web Folder: `/Library/WebServer/PretendCoWebSite`
- Default Index Files: Leave defaults.
- Error Document: Leave defaults.
- Administrator Email: Leave default.

11 Ensure the Enabled checkbox is selected in the sites list at the top of the window.

12 Click Save.

13 Start the web service, and leave this window open in Server Admin.

14 In Safari, enter `http://servern.pretendco.com` to see your initial website.

15 In Safari, enter `http://10.1.n.5` to see your new site.

16 In Safari, enter `http://worksiten.pretendco.com` to see your new site again.

***Question 3*** *How can you see your new site with the fully qualified domain name even though you have not edited DNS?*

17 Ask the instructor to show you your machine records on the main DNS server.

18 In Server Admin, disable the worksite*n*.pretendco.com site and save changes.

19 Use Screen Sharing to connect to your server and log in as ladmin.

20 Make the Ethernet 2 interface inactive, apply the change, and log out as ladmin and quit Screen Sharing.

# 7.2 Sharing

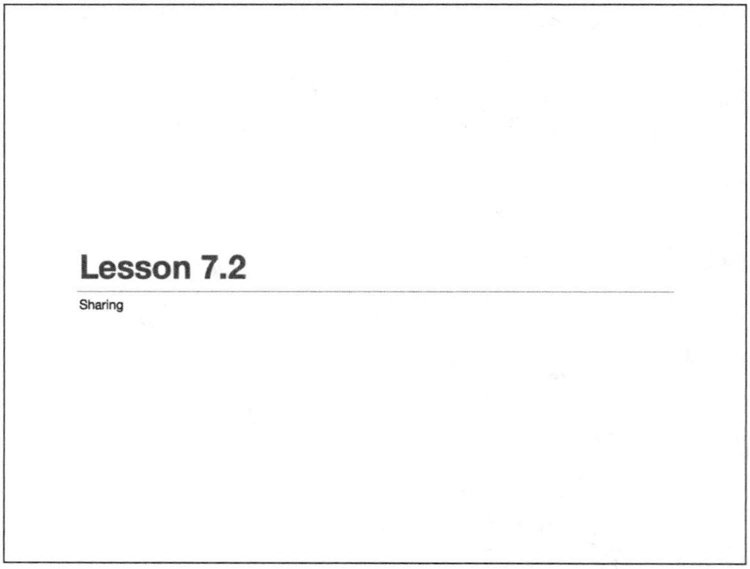

## Realms and WebDAV

WebDAV Fundamentals

Defining realms

Client Connections via WebDAV

Protocol Comparison

When talking about sharing web content, your must first consider that you are sharing your files with anyone who has access to your website. Now consider that there are likely portions of the the site that may benefit from being restricted to certain users or groups. Also consider that just as you can use AFP, SMB, FTP, or NFS to share files, so can you use HTTP. This lesson deals with how to share and restrict access to files via the http protocol.

Sharing files using the http protocol is similar to sharing them using any other protocol. However with WebDAV, you have the ability to restrict access to portions of a site so only certain users or groups have access.

## WebDAV Fundamentals

WebDAV is an open standard that allows share points to be accessed via the http protocol.

- Similar to AFP or SMB

WebDAV can be enabled on a per-site basis.

Applications benefit from WebDAV.

- Adobe Illustrator
- Adobe Dreamweaver
- iCal

WebDAV often uses Realms to dictate access.

WebDAV stands for Web Distributed Authoring and Versioning. It allows users to mount share points using HTTP, like AFP or SMB. WebDAV is useful when other protocols are blocked by a firewall, because it runs through port 80 (and 443 for HTTPS), which most firewalls leave open for web access.

## Defining and Managing Realms

Realms are directories that are given names.

- Authentication methods
  - Basic
  - Digest
  - Kerberos

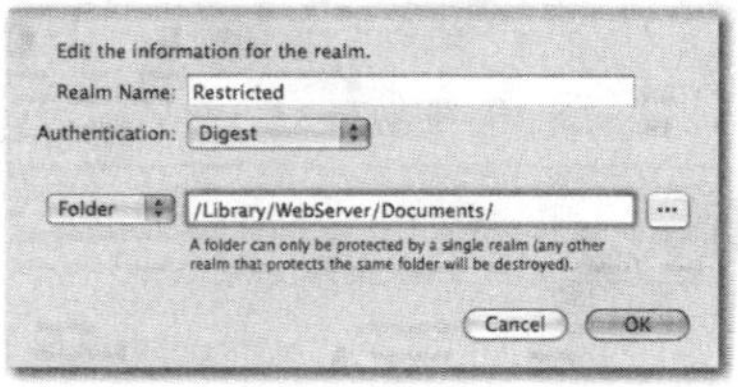


A realm is nothing more than a name given to a folder (or another site). When you define a realm, you are restricting or allowing users and groups access to that folder. Generally, that folder is also part of a website, so users are prompted with a dialog when attempting to view portions of the restricted site. Authentication can take place in one of three ways; Basic, Digest, and Kerberos.

## Realm Access

User and group access can be restricted to a realm.

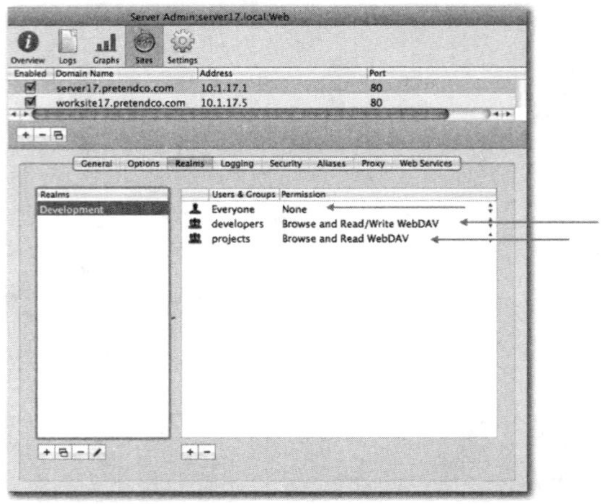


This slide shows the interface for adding users and groups to a realm and setting the level of access each user or group can have.

## Client WebDAV/Realm Experience

Clients connect to WebDAV via Connect to Server or web browser.

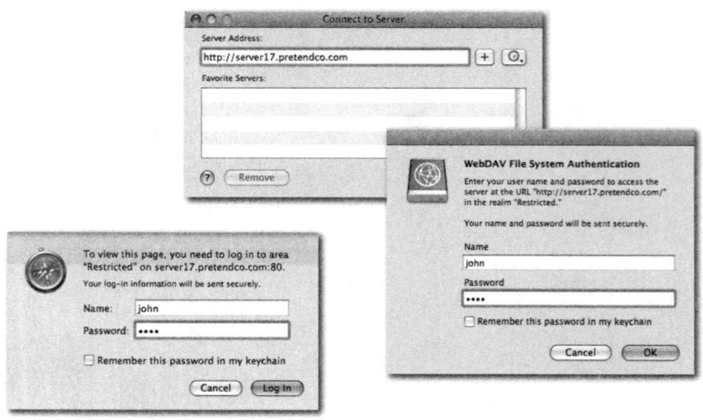


Attempting to access a restricted realm, whether via a web browser or the Finder, results in an authentication dialog, prompting the user to authenticate to gain access to that realm.

## File Sharing Protocol Comparison

| | AFP | SMB | FTP | NFS | HTTP |
|---|---|---|---|---|---|
| **Native Platform** | Mac OS | Windows | Multi-platform | *NIX | Multi-platform |
| **Security** | Encrypted - Standard or Kerberos | Encrypted - NTLMv2 or Kerberos | Clear text or Kerberos | Clear text, encrypted, or Kerberos | Clear text, encrypted, or Kerberos |
| **Browsable** | Bonjour | NetBIOS | Bonjour | Bonjour | No |
| **Example URL** | afp://server17.pretendco.com/SharePoint | smb://server17.pretendco.com/SharePoint | ftp://server17.pretendco.com/ | nfs://server17.pretendco.comSharePoint | http://server17.pretendco.comSharePoint |

You saw a version of this matrix in Chapter 5, "File Services." The capabilities of using HTTP versus the other four file sharing protocols has been added.

Exercise

7.2.1 Use Realms to Restrict Access

## Exercise 7.2.1
# Use Realms to Restrict Access

## Objective

Restrict users or groups to certain areas of your website using WebDAV realms.

## Summary

You'll choose a folder in your default website to which access will be restricted. Then you'll attempt to gain access to the restricted folder via a web browser and the Finder.

1 In Safari, enter `http://servern.pretendco.com/manual-1.3`.

  You're looking at the Apache manual folder inside your /Library/WebServer/Documents folder. You'll protect this area of your website with a realm.

2 In Server Admin, ensure the Web service is selected, and select your server*n*.pretendco.com website from the Sites list.

3 Click the Options tab, to ensure you have WebDAV selected, and if not, select it now, and save the change.

4 Click the Realms tab.

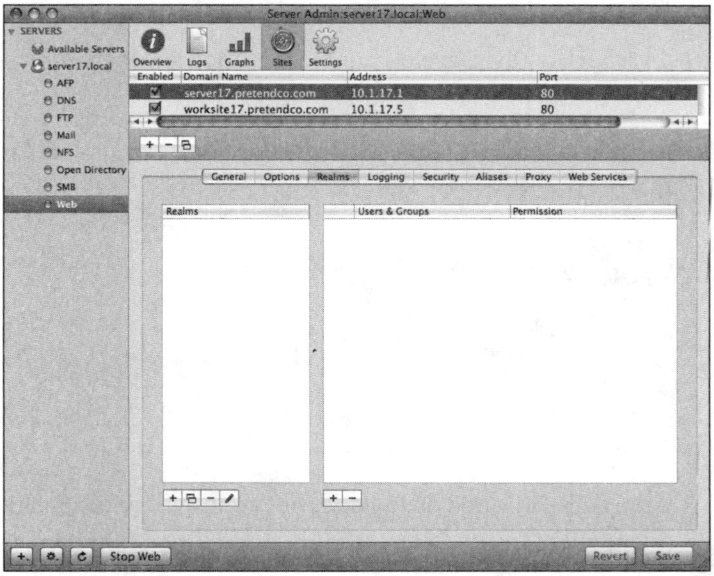


5 Click the Add (+) button under the Realms section of the window to add a realm.

You'll be using a folder inside the /Library/WebServer/Documents folder for your realm called `manual-1.3` to represent a fictional restricted area of your website.

6 Edit the realm information as follows:

- Realm Name: `Development`
- Authentication: `Digest`
- Folder: `/Library/WebServer/Documents/manual-1.3` (Rather than type the path to the folder, you can click the ellipses button and navigate to this folder to select it.)

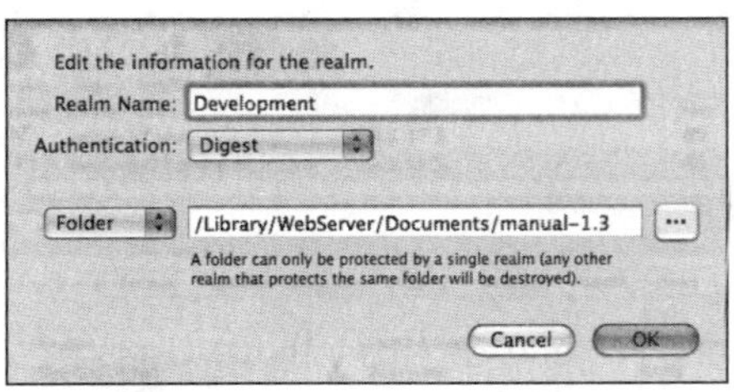

7 Click OK, and click Save.

You've now created the realm.

8 Click back on the Development realm, and view the permissions of Everyone on the right.

9 In Safari, reload the page, and view the authentication dialog that appears.

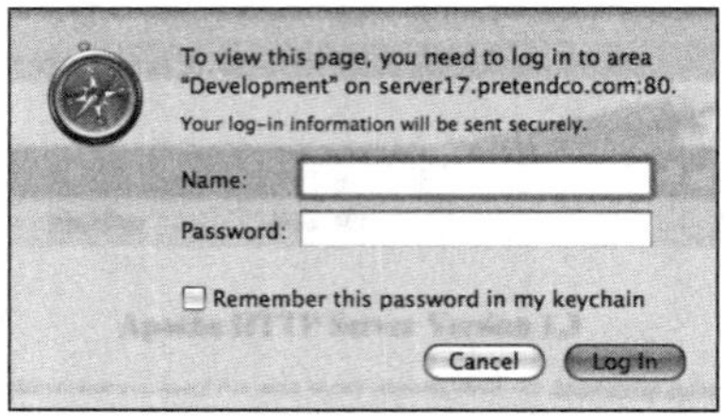


If the authentication dialog does not appear, from the Safari menu select Empty Cache, then try to load the URL again.

No one can log in at this point because you have not given anyone permissions yet.

10 Do not close the dialog.

11 In Server Admin, select the Development realm, and click the Add (+) button under the Users & Groups section to open the Users and Groups window. Click on the Groups button.

12 Drag the Developers and Projects groups into the Users & Groups window in Server Admin.

13 Select the Developers group, and set the permissions to Browse and Read/Write WebDAV.

14 Select the Projects group, and set the permissions to Browse and Read WebDAV.

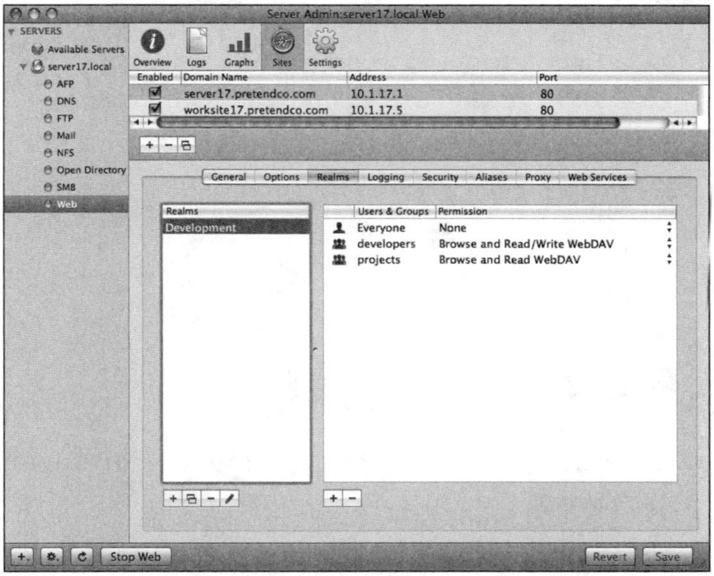


15 Click Save.

16 In the Safari log-in dialog that you left open, enter `sshores` (password: `changeme`) to log in as a member of the Projects group. Do not save the information to your Keychain. Click the Log In button.

***Question 4*** *Was Sandy able to load and browse the pages?*

17 Quit Safari and relaunch it.

18 Under history, access the same URL again.

19 Authenticate as Elizabeth (short name: `etown` and password: `changeme`).

You can load and browse the page because Elizabeth is a member of the Developers group.

20 Quit Safari.

21 In the Finder, choose Go > Connect to Server and enter `http://servern.pretendco.com/manual-1.3` in the Server Address field.

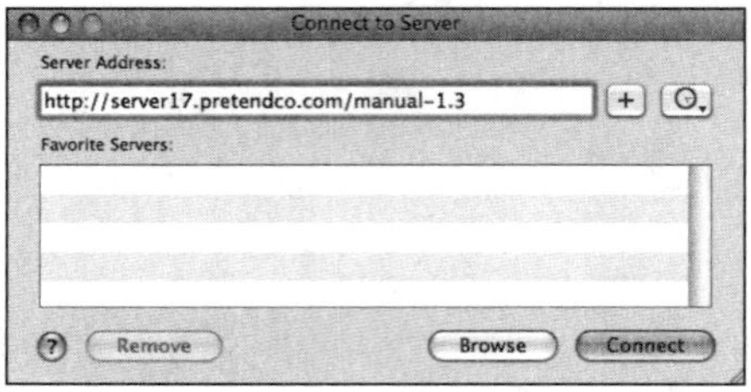


22 Authenticate as Elizabeth (short name: `etown` and password: `changeme`).

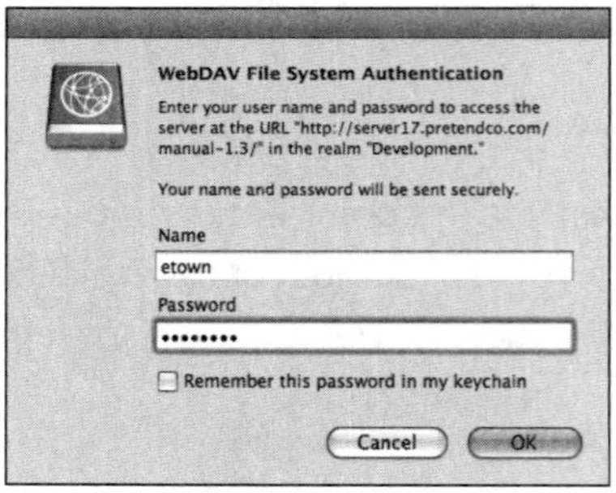


23 Drag the Dictionary.zip file from the /Users/Shared folder into the Finder window that appears, which is actually the manual-1.3 folder on your server, mounted on your Desktop.

**Question 5** *Were you able to copy the file up to your server as Elizabeth? Why or why not?*

24 Close any windows, and unmount the share point from your Desktop.

25 In the Finder, choose Go > Connect to Server again, and enter `http://server`*`n`*`.pretendco.com/manual-1.3` in the Server Address field.

26 Authenticate as Sandy (short name: `sshores` and password: `changeme`).

27 Copy the Chess.zip file from the /Users/Shared folder to the share point window.

**Question 6** *Were you able to copy the file up to your server as Sandy? Why or why not?*

29 In Server Admin, double-click the Development realm to edit the realm.

30 Change the Authentication method from Digest to Kerberos, click OK, and save the changes.

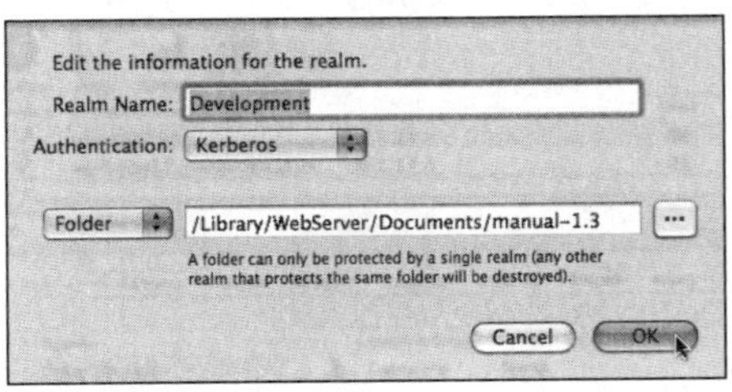


31 Log out as cadmin, and log in as Simon (short name: `simon`, and password: `abcd1234`).

32 While logged in as Simon, open Mail and send a message to developers@server*n*.pretendco.com. Check your mail to ensure you got a copy of the message.

33 Quit Mail.

**34** In the Finder, choose Go > Connect to Server and enter `http://servern.pretendco.com/manual-1.3` in the Server Address field.

**35** Again, in the Finder, choose Go > Connect to Server, enter `smb://servern.pretendco.com`, and mount the project lion folder.

**Question 7** *Other than when logging in, did Simon have to provide a password for any of the functions asked of him?*

---

**36** Open /System/Library/CoreServices/Kerberos and view all of Simon's tickets.

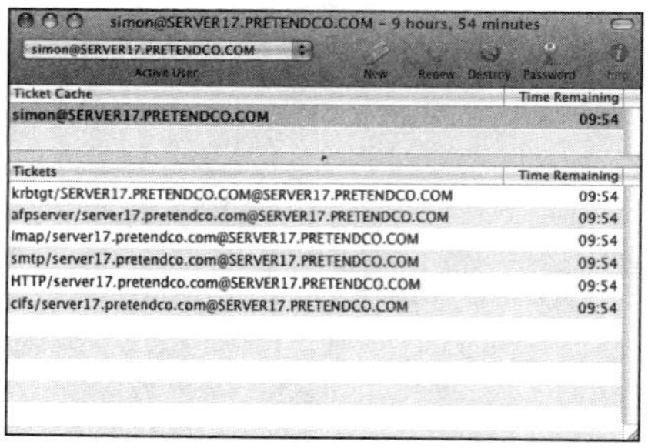


**Question 8** *What is the idea behind using Kerberos tickets to provide authentication?*

---

**Question 9** *What is the function of each ticket?*

---

---

---

---

**37** Log out as simon, and log in as cadmin.

# Security

7.3

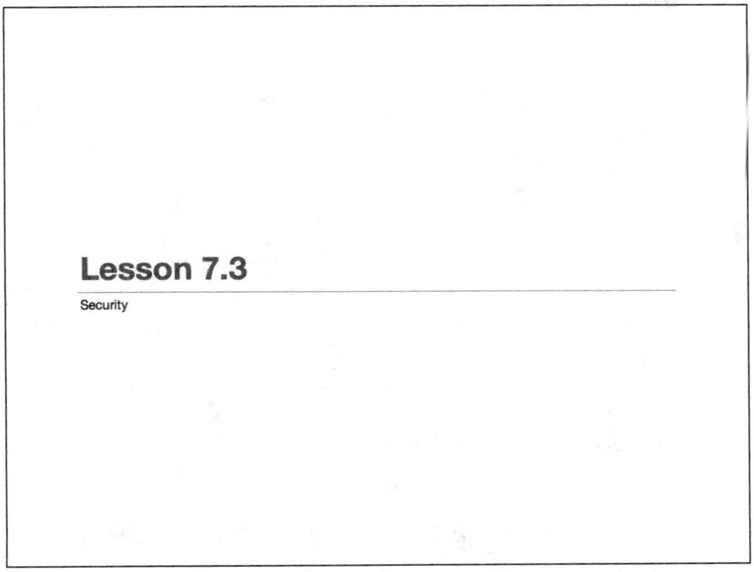


Websites are used to conduct business every minute of every day. To ensure transactions are secure, website administrators use certificates to encrypt traffic between their servers and client browsers. They also keep any languages used to create scripts—like PHP, Python, and Perl—updated to their latest versions.

## Web Security Issues

Encrypting web traffic

Web folder permissions

Potential Script vulnerabilities

Three main issues for administrators of servers hosting web services are:

- Encrypting traffic between the server and the client browser.
- Ensuring permissions are correct on folders that are part of a website.
- Securing scripting languages by keeping them updated.

## Encrypting Web Traffic

By default, all web traffic is unencrypted.

- Can be insecure
- Reasons for encryption
    - Restricted web pages
    - Internal documents
    - Monetary transfers

The first method to ensure security of your website should be to encrypt all traffic between the server running your web service and the browsers that visitors use to access your site.

## Enabling Web Encryption

Ensure fully qualified domain name has been properly entered on the General tab for the website:

1. Default to server17.pretendco.com

On the Security tab of website:

2. Turn on SSL (Secure Sockets Layer).
3. Change website port from 80 to 443.
4. Choose certificate.
    - Save changes
5. Apache requires a restart

To enable encryption (SSL), administrators first obtain a certificate from a certificate authority on the Internet or create one themselves. Second, the certificate is enabled for the site. The certificate must bear the fully qualified domain name of the site to function. Finally, if the certificate was created by the administrator, a copy of the certificate must be placed on every computer that will need to securely access the website.

## Website Encryption

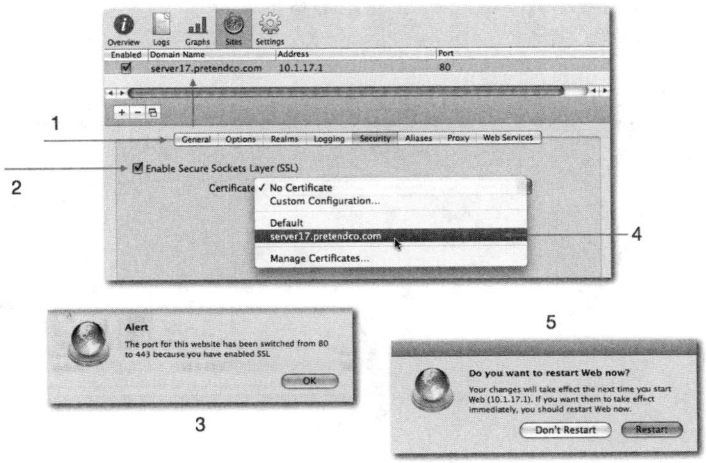


This slide shows a step-by-step process of enabling website encryption.

## Web Folder Permissions

Don't:

- Allow read-write access to web folders by all.
- Allow read-only access to restricted realms.

Review permissions model prior to taking website live.

- Ensure access to folders is tested and verified.
- Server Admin - File Sharing

Permissions on folders used in your website should be verified before going live. Most web folders should be read-only and access to areas in your website should be controlled with realms.

## Potential Script Vulnerabilities

Allowing all scripting languages can be insecure.

- Enable modules on only those being used by the website.
- Enable CGI execution only when being used by the website.
- Update scripting languages when warranted.
  - PHP
  - Perl
  - Ruby
  - Python
- Test scripts thoroughly.

When leveraging scripting languages, always ensure you have the latest security patches to reduce the possibility of an attack on your web service or worse, your server.

Exercise

7.3.1 Secure a Website Using SSL

## Exercise 7.3.1

# Secure a Website Using SSL

## Objective

Enable secure sockets layer (SSL) for your website, which will also allow you to check your webmail securely.

## Summary

Secure websites are commonplace on the Internet. You'll be using the Default certificate that was generated when Mac OS X Server was first configured. Your Mac OS X computer already has a copy of this certificate.

1 Open Server Admin, and select the web service from the list.

2 Click the Sites icon in the toolbar, and select server*n*.pretendco.com.

3 Click the Security tab, and select the Enable Secure Sockets Layer (SSL) checkbox.

4 Click OK to dismiss the dialog alerting you the port has switched from 80 to 443.

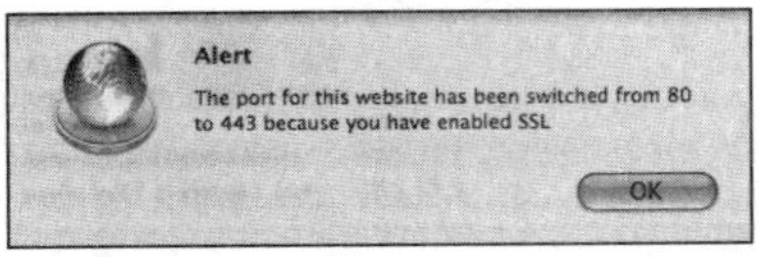

5 Ensure the Default certificate is selected, and save the changes.

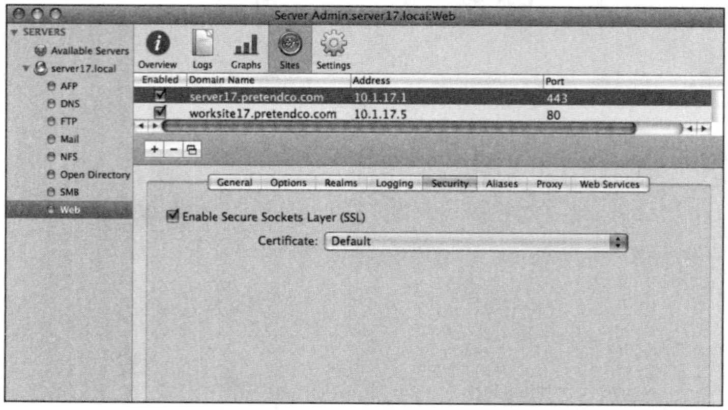


6 When prompted, restart the web service.

7 Launch Safari and enter `https://servern.pretendco.com` in the address.

Note the *s* after http, which indicates this is a secure connection.

8 Click the Webmail button in the upper right of the main Mac OS X Server webpage. A login page appears.

You've now enabled SSL on the web service, which means you can securely check and send mail via webmail. However, webmail does not understand encrypted authentication, so you must change the authentication method to clear text. Because you are using SSL, the name and password is sent over an encrypted connection.

9 In Server Admin, select Mail in the services list.

10 Click the Settings icon in the toolbar, select the Advanced tab, and then the Security tab.

11 Select the Clear checkbox for IMAP authentication. For both SMTP SSL and IMAP and POP SSL, change from Require to Use.

12 Save the changes.

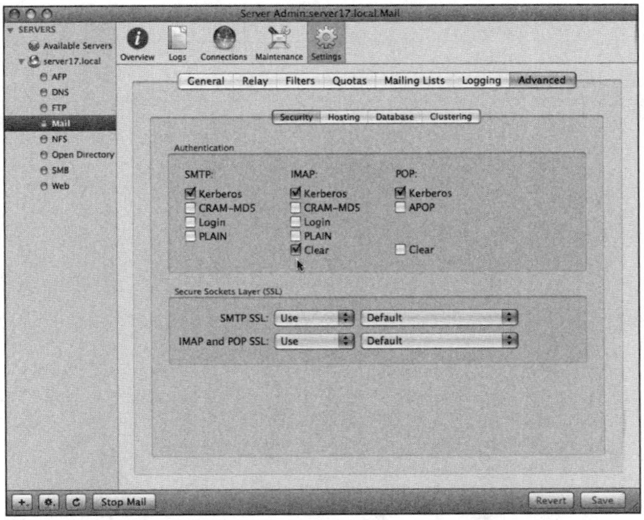


13 In Safari, log in as `simon` (password: `abcd1234`).

If you get an error logging in as Simon, try again after a few moments.

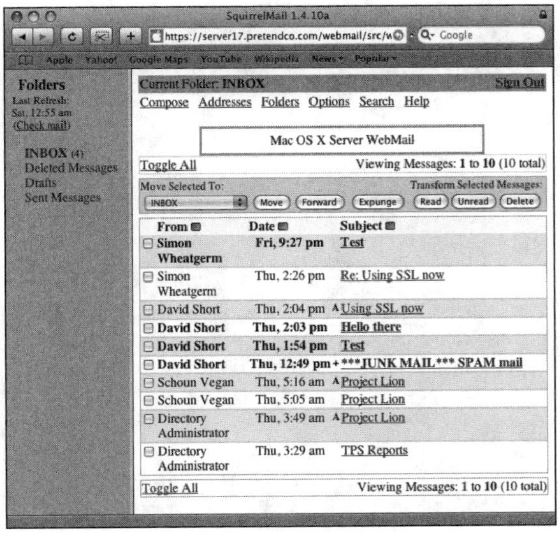

14 View Simon's mail, and reply to a mail message to ensure you can send mail.

15 After sending the mail, click "Sign Out" in webmail, and quit Safari.

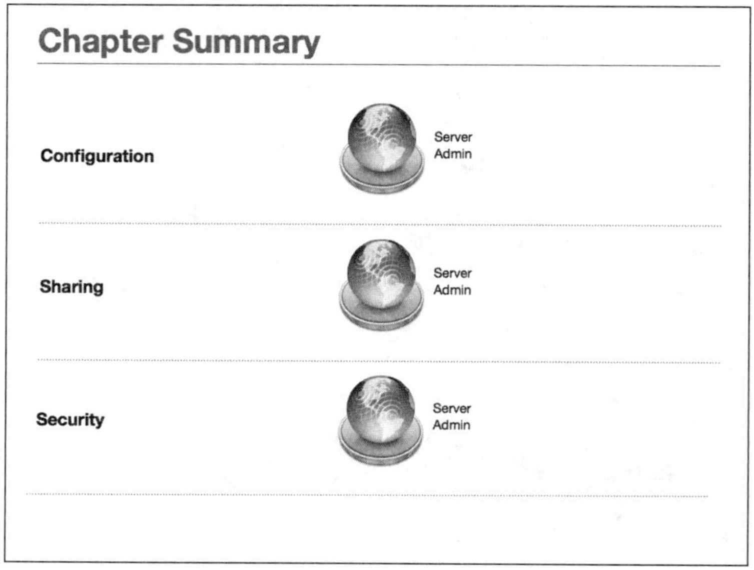

# 8

# Collaboration Services

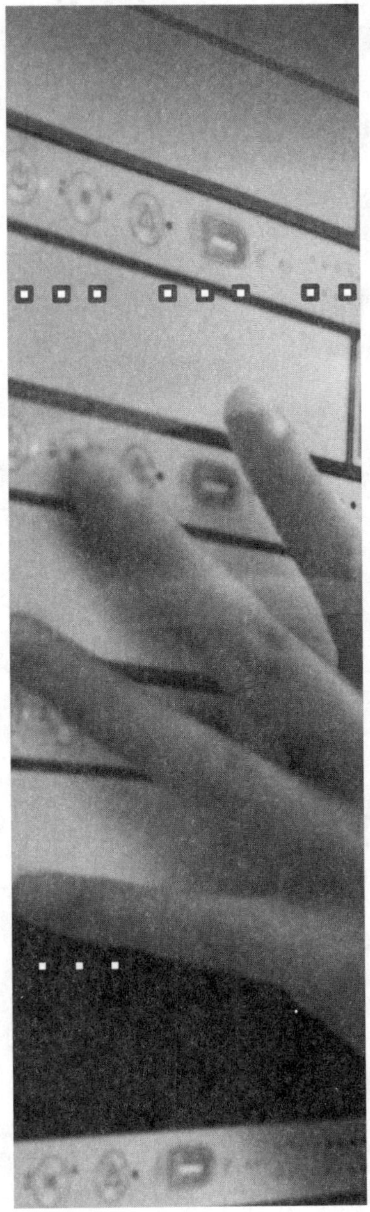


## 8.1 Wiki Services

**Exercise 8.1.1** Configure and Enable Wiki and Blog Services for Groups

**Exercise 8.1.2** Modify a User Blog

**Exercise 8.1.3** Tag and Search Blog Entries

**Exercise 8.1.4** Create and Edit a Group Wiki

**Exercise 8.1.5** Set Blog and Wiki Access Controls

## 8.2 Calendaring Services

**Exercise 8.2.1** Configure and Use iCal Service

**Exercise 8.2.2** Create Resource and Location Records Using Directory

**Exercise 8.2.3** Configure iCal Accounts

**Exercise 8.2.4** Create and Respond to Events

**Exercise 8.2.5** Edit Web Group Calendars (optional)

## 8.3 Messaging Services

**Exercise 8.3.1** Configure the iChat Service and Application

**Exercise 8.3.2** Add Jabber Buddies and Communicate

**Exercise 8.3.3** View Chat Logs

# 8.1 Wiki Services

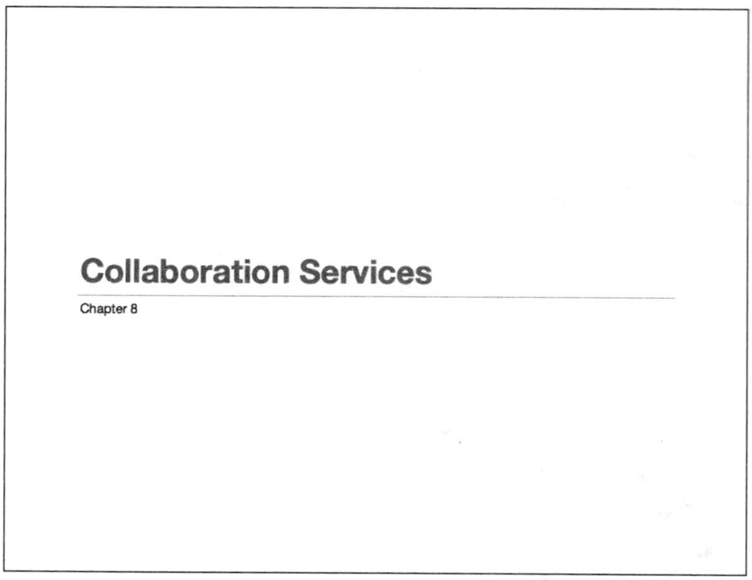

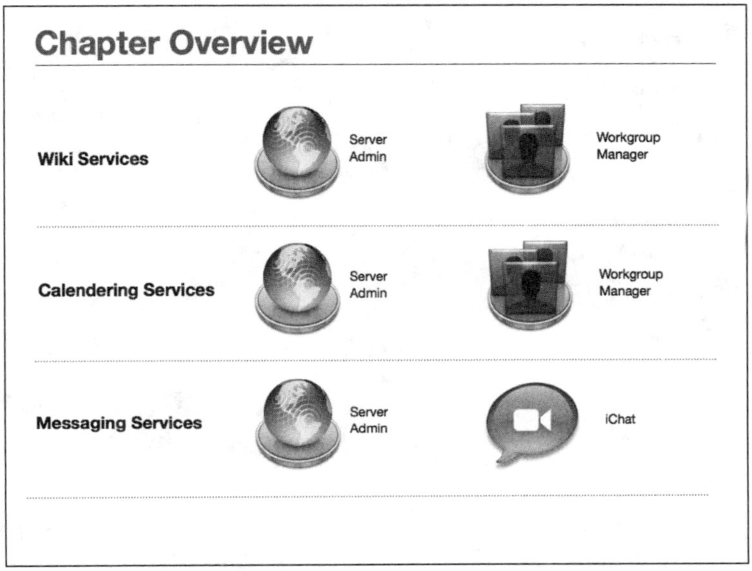


In Mac OS X Server, collaboration services involve three things, Wiki and weblog service, calendaring service, and handling messaging.

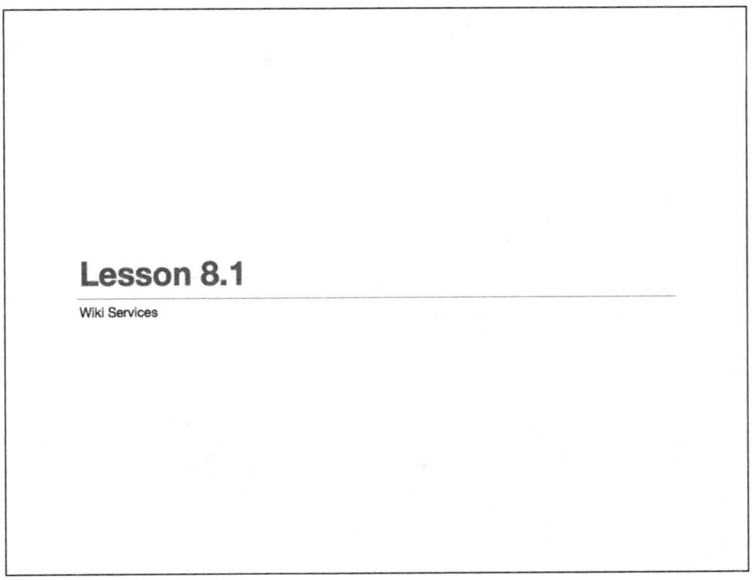


This lesson deals with the basics of Wiki and weblog services, how to set them up, configure them, and restrict access to them.

## Providing Wiki Services

- Wiki basics
- Wiki benefits
- Using Weblogs
- Enabling Wikis and Weblogs
- Restricting access to Wikis
- Wiki creation
- Modifying Wikis

A Wiki is a collaborative, web-based tool that allows users and groups to post information for the logical progression of an idea, project, theme, or any other focal point of discussion.

## Wiki Basics

- Web-based collaboration.
- Groups communicate via website and links.
- All communications are logged and captured.
- Secured by group-only access if necessary.
- Examples:
  - wikipedia.org
    - Online searchable repository of constantly updated data segregated and cross linked

Wikis are central to the idea of all users in a group being able to post, edit, review, and discuss material without interference from other groups or departments in an organization. This process can benefit a group whose Wiki is hosting a secret project or sensitive information. Mac OS X Server Wikis also keep a detailed history of a group's Wiki, for retrieval of historical information.

Each Wiki and blog hosted on your server is associated with one of your server's websites. Keep this in mind when configuring website settings for security and access controls. For example, if your server has a public site and an internal site that is only accessible from your network, you may decide to only enable Wiki and blog services on the internal site.

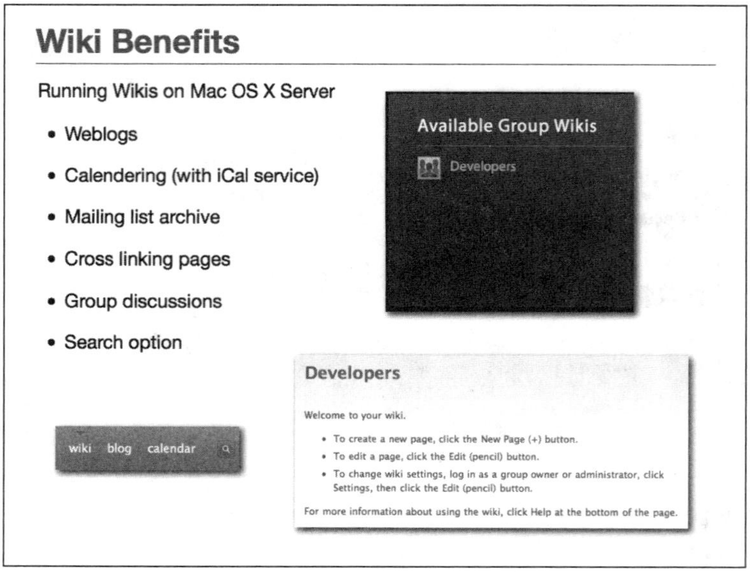


Groups associated with a Wiki can post images and files, link pages together, and format pages. They can use a group weblog and have access to a group calendar, if the iCal service is enabled.

## Weblogs and User Blogs

Weblogs are group blogs accessible by group members.

- Can be restricted or expanded
- Blog entries can contain
  - Media files
  - File attachments
- Blogs are searchable.
- Can contain comments

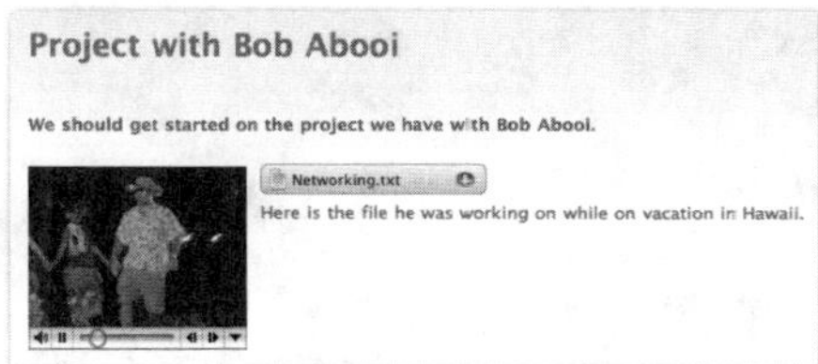


Weblogs for groups are similar to blogs for users, except the group weblogs can be restricted to just the group. Users can post images, media files, and downloadable files to their weblogs.

## Enabling Wikis and Weblogs

Web service must be enabled.

- Must have at least one site.
- Users should be a member of a group.
- Enable wiki and blog via Server Admin.
  - Web service must be running
- Group access can be restricted via Server Admin.
  - If left blank, access is granted to all users.
- Enable per group using Workgroup Manager.
  - Group records

To configure Wikis and weblogs, the web service must be running. If group mailing lists are going to be used, the Mail service must be running. Wikis and weblogs are site specific.

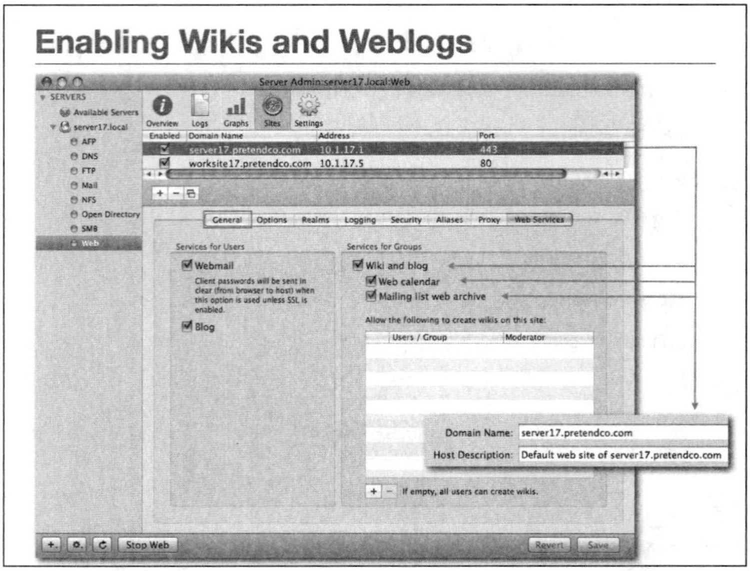


You use Server Admin to enable Wikis, weblogs, and mailing lists. Select the website on which you want Wikis enabled, and click the Web Services tab under the site. There are two Web Service tabs, one for the entire web service which you will discuss later, and this one, which is under each site.

## Enabling Wikis and Weblogs—Group Setup

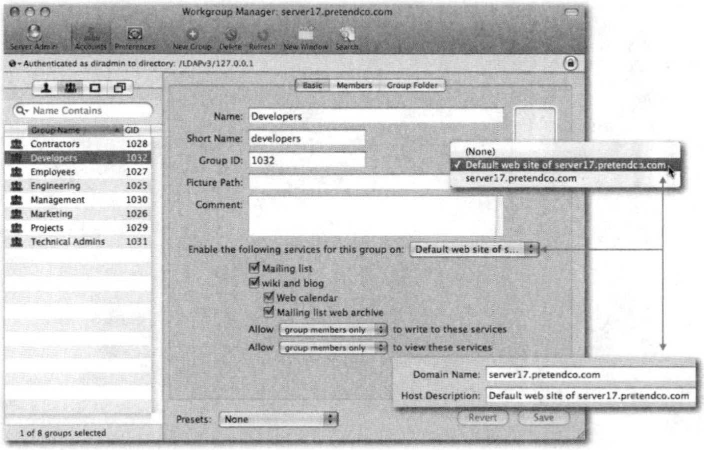


Once Wikis are enabled for a site, you use Workgroup Manager to associate the site with a group. A group can be associated only with a single Wiki. Users can be members of more than one group and, therefore, have access to more than one Wiki.

## Enabling Wikis and Weblogs—Group Access

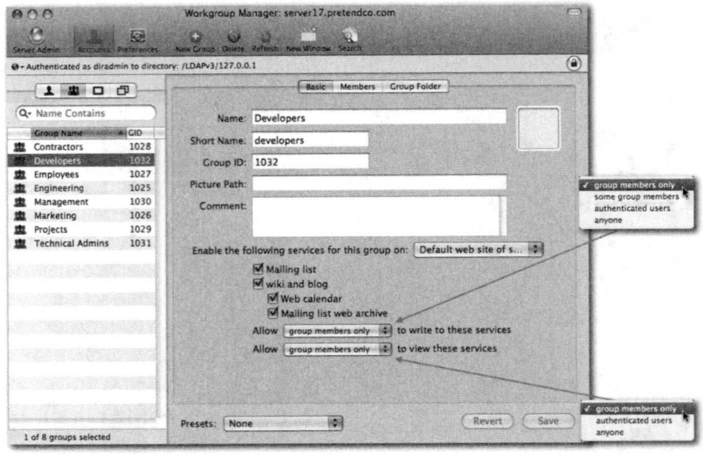


You can decide who can view the Wiki and who can write to the Wiki. In some cases, you may want the entire Wiki restricted, for example on a secret project. Conversely, a Wiki can be open to all users, as in a company-wide employee suggestion Wiki.

## Editing Group Management

Use Directory application

- /Applications/Utilities/Directory
- Don't confuse with Directory Utility

Manage

- Users
- Groups
  - Ownership
- Locations
- Resources

After group permissions are set with Workgroup Manager, group ownership can be handled with the Directory application. This is not the same application as Directory Utility. You'll learn more about the Directory application later in this chapter.

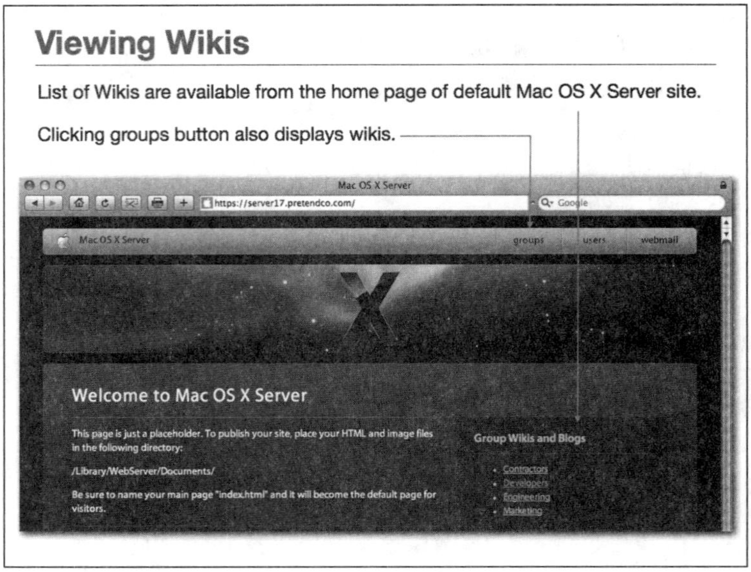


Some Wikis are accessible via the default index.html page on Mac OS X Server's default website. From the home page, you can access the Wikis in two ways, from the groups button on the top or the listed Wikis on the right.

## Wiki Entries

Authenticated users are allowed to create Wiki entries.

Posts can be read by all users in the group.

Users can also edit posts.

All changes are kept and are viewable by all members of the group.

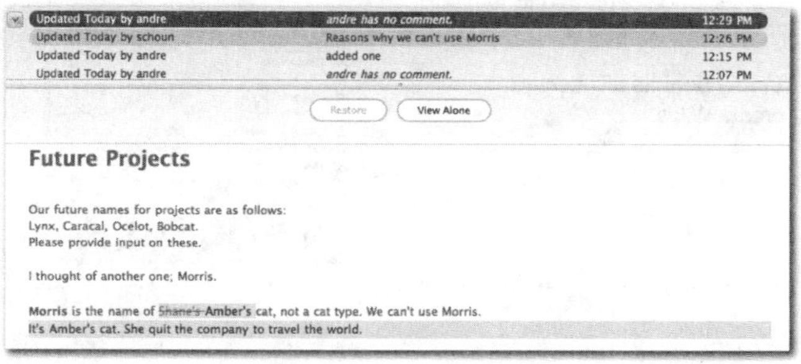


The collaborative nature of Wikis allows members of a group to edit entries. Note that when entries are removed, they are not necessarily deleted because all changes are tracked. Administrators of each group are permitted to manage the entry and all posts, including deleting comments and posts.

## Restricting Access to Wikis

Wiki creation can be restricted.

- Use the Web service in Server Admin to set restrictions for:
  - Groups
  - Users
    - Can be permitted to function as a moderator.
- Empty permits all users to create Wikis.

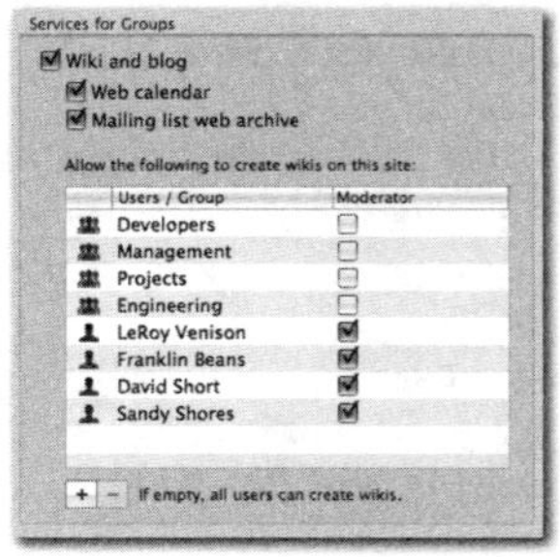


In Workgroup Manager, you give access to read or write to the group Wiki. In Server Admin, you give access to create new Wikis, and to dictate who can moderate discussions on the group Wikis.

## Wiki Modification

Wiki templates can be changed using Web Services in Server Admin.

- 20 different template styles

Data store location can be changed to other volumes.

- RAID, Xsan

Attachment size can be restricted.

- Default is 50 MB.

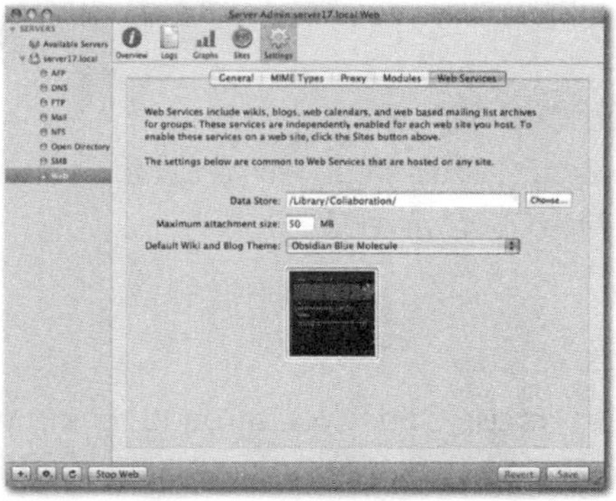

Wikis are one way Mac OS X Server provides for group collaboration and interaction. Administrators can choose among several Wiki templates and control the size of file attachments. As the popularity of Wikis grows, consider placing the Wiki database on a redundant system to ensure uninterrupted service.

### Exercises

8.1.1 Configure and Enable Wiki and Blog Services for Groups

8.1.2 Modify a User Blog

8.1.3 Tagging and Search Blog Entries

8.1.4 Create and Edit a Group Wiki

8.1.5 Set Blog and Wiki Access Controls

## Exercise 8.1.1

# Configure and Enable Wiki and Blog Services for Groups

## Objective

Configure and enable Wiki and blog services for websites hosted by Mac OS X Server.

## Summary

This exercise guides you through the configuration and use of the Wiki and blog services, for both users and groups. In order to use Wiki and blog services, the server must be configured as Open Directory Master. A group's blog and Wiki pages are shared by all members of the group, and by default are only visible and editable by members of the group. Enabling a group's Wiki and blog services is handled with Workgroup Manager. The Wiki and blog services also allow the group owner (or any admin user) to have access to additional administrative settings. You'll use the Directory application to configure group ownership for some of the groups on your server.

1. Ensure you are logged in as cadmin, and open Server Admin and Workgroup Manager.
2. In Server Admin, select Web from the list of services for your server.
3. Click the Sites icon in the toolbar, disable worksite*n*.pretendco.com, and then select server*n*.pretendco.com (where *n* is your student number).
4. Click the Web Services tab.

5 Select the "Wiki and blog," "Web calendar," and "Mailing list web archive" checkboxes under Services for Groups.

Remember that you already turned on Webmail and blogs for users in previous chapters, which is why those options under Services for Users are already selected.

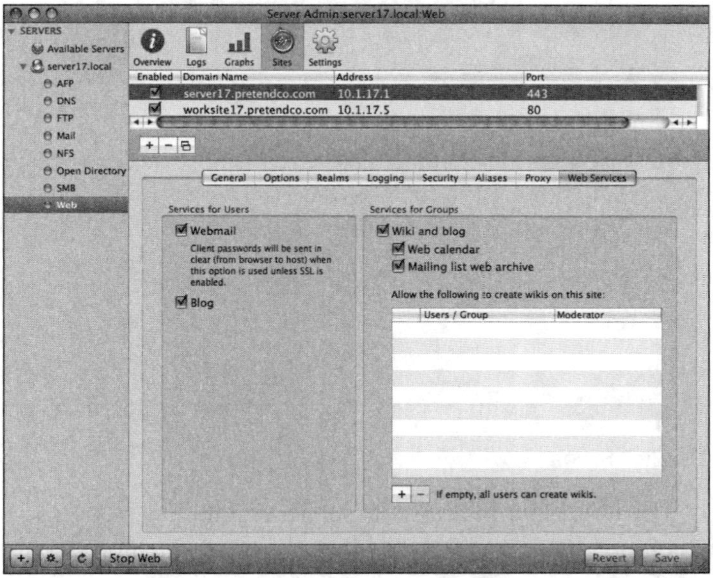


6 Click Save.

7 Using Workgroup Manager, verify you are working in /LDAPv3/127.0.0.1 (the shared data store).

8 Click the Groups button to view the list of group records.

9 Select the Developers group, and click the Basic tab.

The sites that have been enabled for Wiki and blog services for groups will be listed in the "Enable the following services for this group on" pop-up menu. This pop up is how you associate a group's Wiki and blog services with a specific website hosted on your server.

10 Choose your server's default website ("Default website of server*n*.pretendco.com") from the "Enable the following services for this group on" pop-up menu.

11 Select the "Wiki and blog," "Web calendar," and "Mailing list web archive" checkboxes.

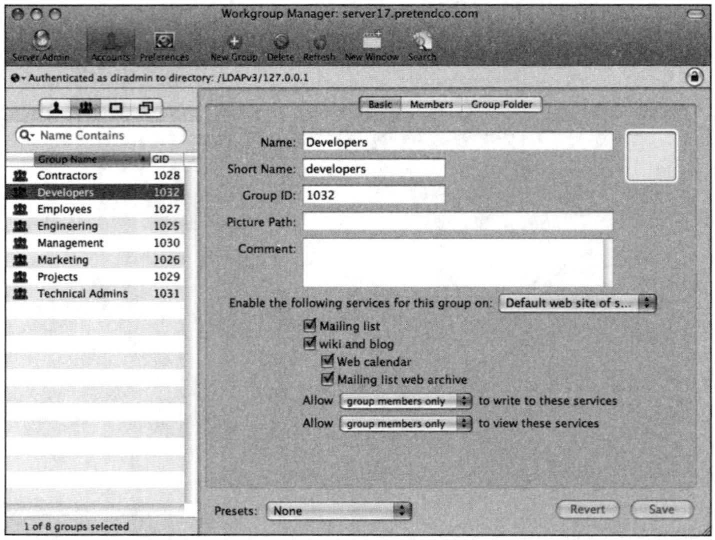


12 Click Save.

The Wiki, blog, and calendar services for the Developers group will be viewable and editable only by members of the Developers group. Now, you'll enable some collaboration services for the Engineering group, using slightly more permissive access controls.

13 Select the Engineering group.

14 Configure the Engineering group to use Wiki, blog, and calendar services on the default website. It is not necessary to enable the Mailing list.

15 Configure Engineering so that any authenticated users can view the group's enabled services, regardless of group membership.

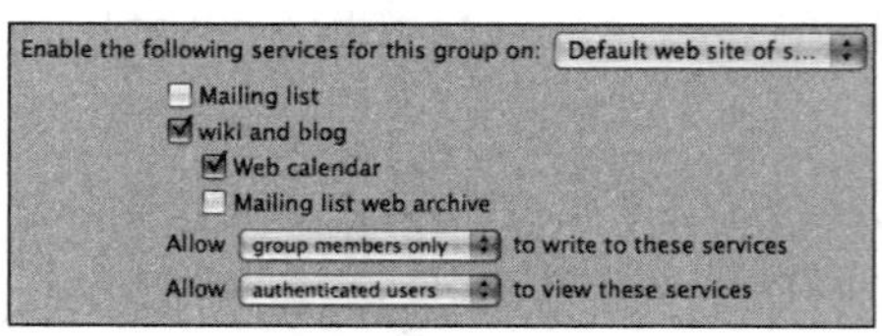

16 Click Save.

17 Configure Wiki, blog, and calendar settings for the Marketing group using the following settings:

- Allow: `some group members` to write to these services
- Allow: `anyone` to view these services

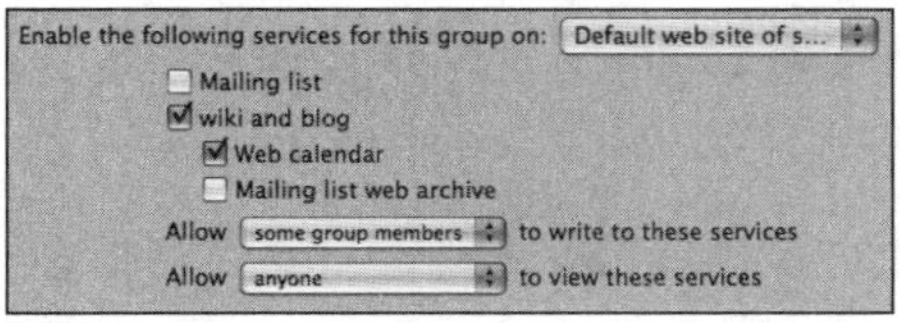


***Question 1*** *Why would you want everyone to view a Wiki and blog?*

18 Click Save.

## Set Group Ownership

Additional administrative controls for the blog and Wiki services are available to admin users and users who are a group owner. Admin users have admin access to all groups, whereas group owners only have admin access to the groups they own. You'll use the Directory application to configure group ownership. The Directory application requires that the computer running it has access to the server's Open Directory domain. Because your Mac OS X computer is bound to your server, no additional configuration is needed before using Directory.

1 Open the Directory application, located in /Applications/Utilities/.

2 Under the Directory menu, choose Preferences. Change Authentication to Password, and close the window to return to the main Directory window.

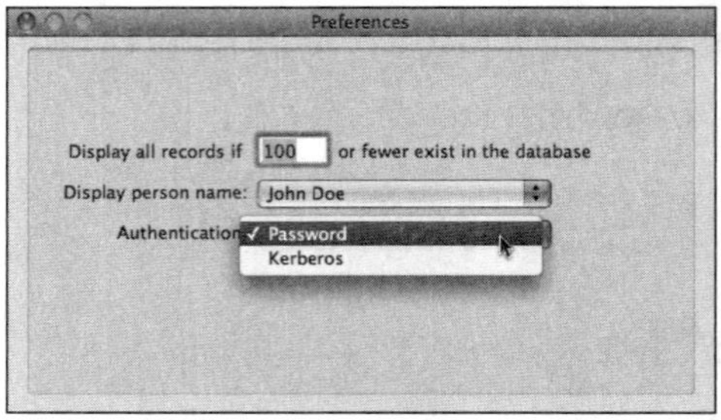


You won't need Kerberos tickets as the Directory Administrator to make changes.

3 Quit and reopen Directory.

4 Select the Developers group, and then click the Ownership tab.

5 Click the Edit button at the bottom right of the window. Authenticate as diradmin (password: diradmin).

You are authenticating so you can make a change to your shared LDAP directory. Think of the Directory application as a mini Workgroup Manager. Directory requires authentication just as Workgroup Manager does.

6 Select the name that exists in the owner field and type `Andre` in the field.

Note that Directory autocompletes the rest of the name.

7 Click Save to set Andre LeLimb as the owner of the Developers group.

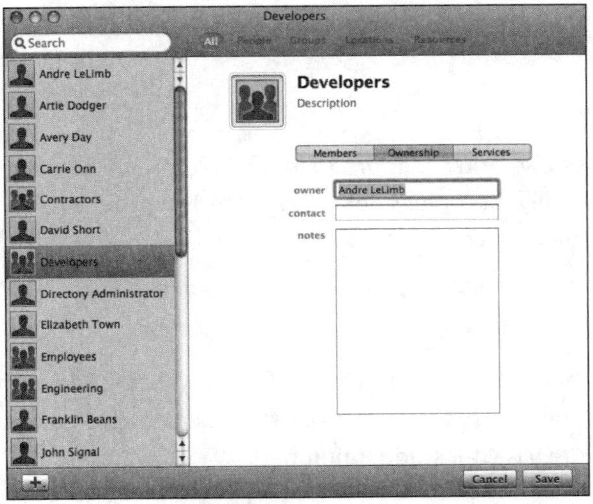


8 Configure LeRoy Venison as the owner of the Marketing group, and save the changes.

9 Configure Red Floyd as the owner of the Engineering group, and save the changes.

10 Quit the Directory application.

Exercise 8.1.2

# Modify a User Blog

## Objective

Learn how to create and edit blog and pages.

## Summary

In the last exercise, you configured Wiki and blog services for three groups on your server's default website. Now you're ready to create and edit blog content for users.

## Utilize a User Blog

1 Open Safari, and view your server's default website. Remember we are using SSL, so the address is https://server*n*.pretendco.com (where *n* is your student number).

2 To access the user blogs, click the users button at the top of the web page.

Notice that Simon created a user blog earlier in this course.

3 Click Simon's user blog.

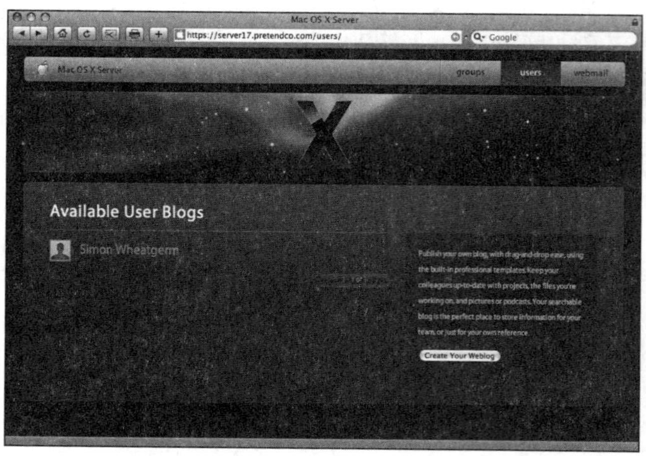

4 Click on Simon's blog entry, and view his blog.

5 Click on the "Add a new comment" link, and add a comment to Simon's blog.

You must log in to add comments.

6 Enter `carrie` (password: `changeme`).

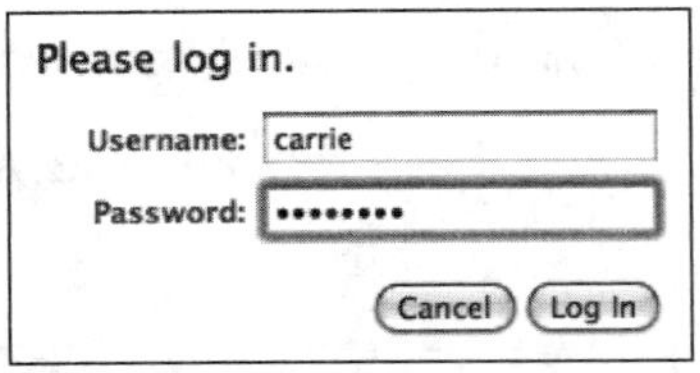


7 Click Log In.

8 Enter your comments in Simon's blog, and click the Save Comment button.

Carrie is not a member of any group. She simply has an account on the Mac OS X Server's shared LDAP database. Because of this, she can add comments to user blogs. Group blogs can be more restrictive.

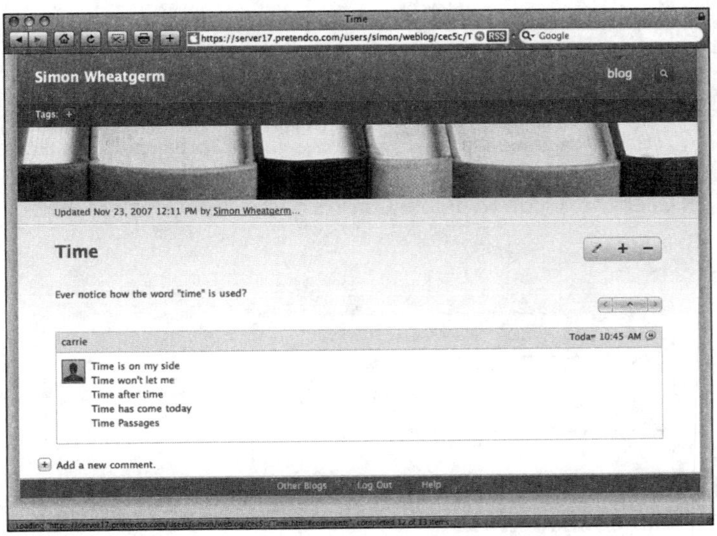

9 Log out as Carrie by clicking the Log Out link at the bottom of the page.

Once a blog comment has been created, it can be deleted by the blog owner.

10 Click the Log In link at the bottom of the page to log in as simon (password: abcd1234).

11 If necessary, click the "1 comment" link to view Carrie's comments.

12 Move your mouse near Carrie's name above her comments, and notice your cursor changes.

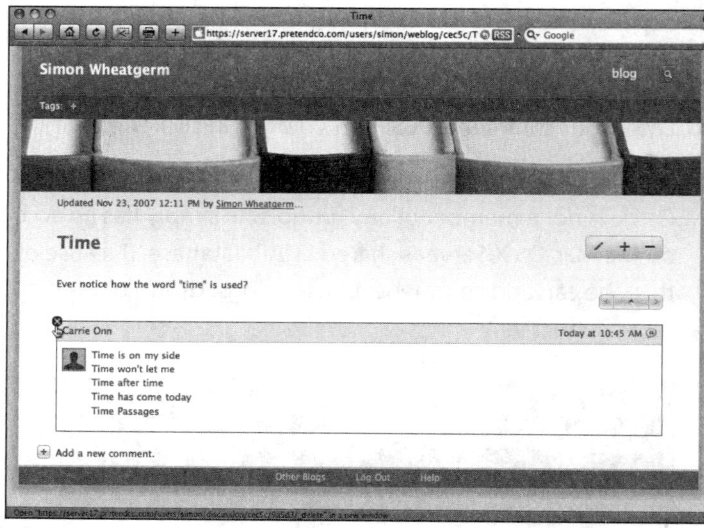


13 Click the X icon to delete Carrie's comments. An alert dialog appears.

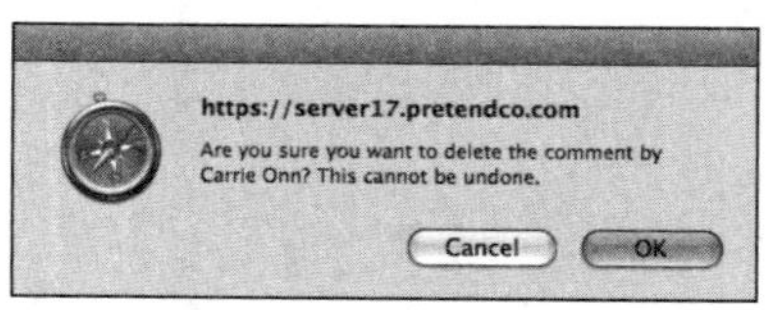


14 Click the Cancel button because you do not want to delete Carrie's comments.

## Exercise 8.1.3

# Tag and Search Blog Entries

## Objective

Experiment with adding tags to blog entries, and use tags and content searches to locate blog posts.

## Summary

Both Wiki pages and blog entries support tagging and searching. Tags can be used to create relationships among a group's Wiki and blog resources and are especially useful when browsing or searching. Each group has its own list of tags, as do each of the individual user blogs. There is no limit to the number of tags a blog or Wiki page can have.

1 Because you are logged in as Simon, click the Add (+) button on the right to create a new blog entry called Features.

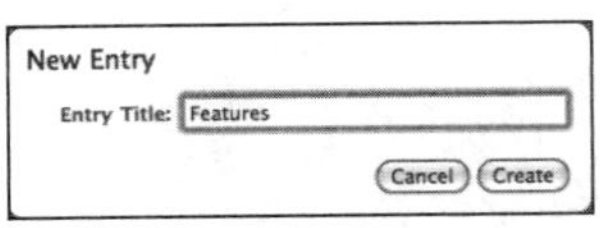


2 Enter some text in the blog entry, and save it.

3 Add a tag to the blog post by clicking the plus button in the upper left corner and entering the word `lion` in the Tags field, and then press Return.

4 Add two more tags: `cool` and `requests`.

If the tag does not exist, it will be created. Typing the partial name of an existing tag will perform a live search, so you can select the tag from a list of matches. This helps prevert typos when assigning existing tags to Wiki or blog pages.

To assign multiple tags at once, enter them as a comma-separated list.

To remove a tag from a page, hover the cursor over the tag name and drag it away from the tag list. If you are editing a blog, the tags appear with an X to delete them instead of dragging them away from the tag list.

5 Create another blog entry called Schedule. Assign some of the tags you used for the previous entry, like `requests`, but also create new tags, `meetings` and `employees`. Save the entry when finished.

6 Click the blog button at the top right to view the list of all blog posts.

Filtering controls are available that allow you to filter the displayed blog posts by tag or by date.

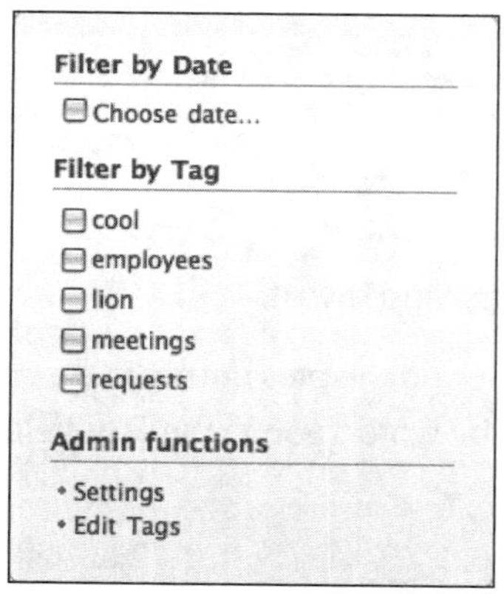


7 Experiment with filtering controls to show only posts that match certain tags.

You can also search blog pages using a full content search. Click the search icon at the top right of the page next to the blog link to access the Search menu.

8 Click the Search icon in the top right of the page to reveal the search menu.

The search menu has two dynamic components. First is the list of recent tags, which updates as new tags are used. Second is the list of recent search terms, which is revealed by clicking the triangle on the left side of the search field.

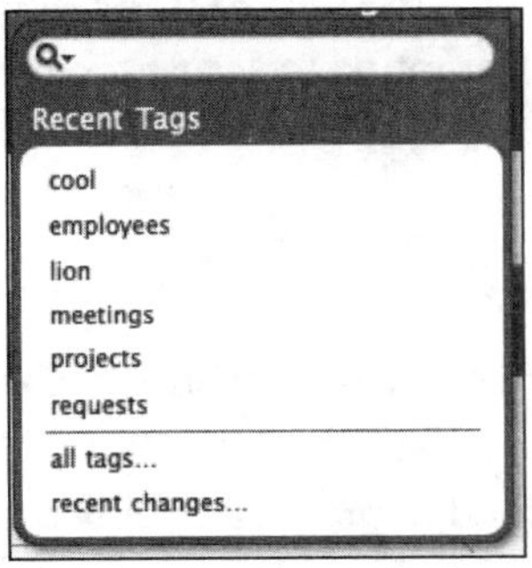


9 In the search field, type a word that appears in one of your blog entries, and then press Return to perform a content search.

10 Experiment with the special search pages that show recent changes and the list of all tags by selecting them from the search menu.

11 Log Out as Simon, and return to your default home page for Mac OS X Server (https://server*n*.pretendco.com).

12 Ensure you are logged in as cadmin and that Server Admin and Workgroup Manager are open.

## Exercise 8.1.4

# Create and Edit a Group Wiki

## Objective

Create a group Wiki page and test the access controls by logging in with different user accounts and by attempting to access the Wiki without authenticating.

## Summary

A group Wiki is a shared collection of webpages that are editable by some or all members of a group. By default, any member of a group may create or edit Wiki pages for that group, and only group members are allowed to access any of the group Wiki pages. These settings are configured in Workgroup Manager.

1. Using Safari, view your server's default website.
2. Notice the Group Wikis and Blogs available on the right. Do not click them yet.

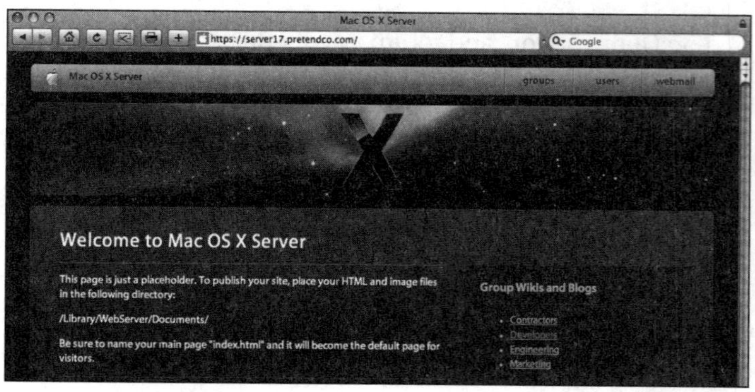


3. Click the groups button instead to display the list of groups for which Wiki and blog resources have been turned on, and click the Developers group.

4 Log in as andre (password: abcd1234), who is a member of the Developers group.

5 Click the Add button (the plus), and add a page called `Future Projects`, and add some text with the words, `Lynx`, `Caracal`, `Ocelot`, and `Bobcat`. Click Save.

Unlike blog entries, each revision of a Wiki page is stored on the server. This allows users to view the page as it existed at any point in time. It also allows group members or administrators to restore the page to any previous version. When editing Wiki pages, you can use the Comment field to store a summary of the change.

6 Click the Edit button (the pencil), make some edits to the page, enter a brief comment in the upper right each time, and click Save.

7 Repeat step 6 a few times, and add more comments and text to the post, saving each time.

8 To view the revision history of this page, click the arrow icon above the page title.

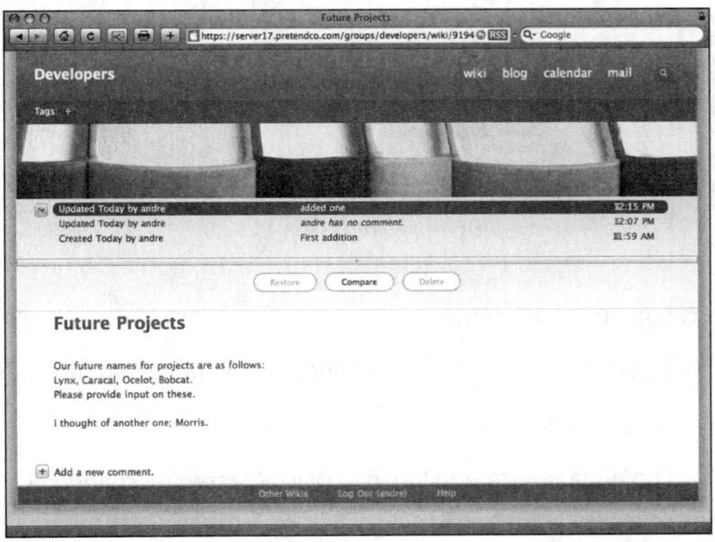


To view a previous revision of the page, select the version you want to view from the list.

9 To visually compare a page with its previous version, click the Compare button.

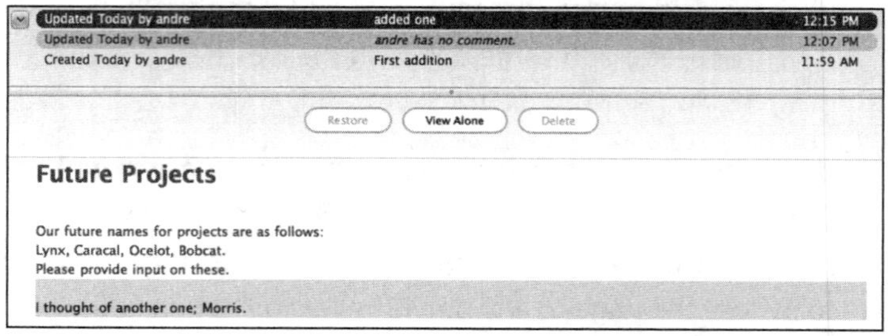


To restore the page to any previous version, select the desired version, and click Restore.

10 Log out as andre, and log in as schoun (password: changeme).

11 Click the Edit button, add some text to the post, apply bold formatting to some text, add a comment, and save the changes.

12 Compare the posts again as you did in steps 8 and 9.

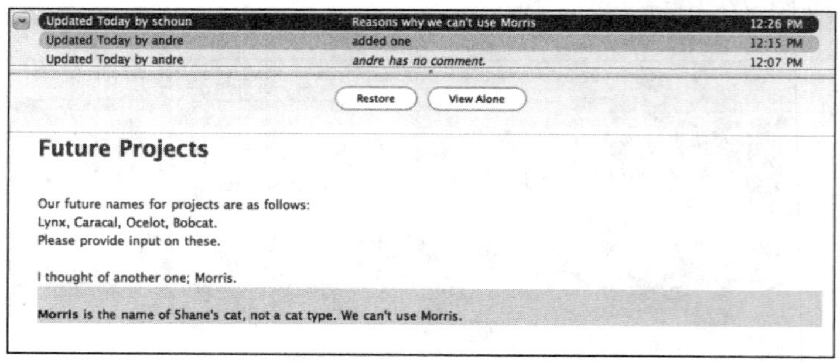


13 Log out as schoun.

14 Log in as andre, and change a word in the post. Add more text.

15 Save the changes.

16 Log out as andre, and log in as david (password: changeme).

17 Compare the changes again as you did in steps 8 and 9.

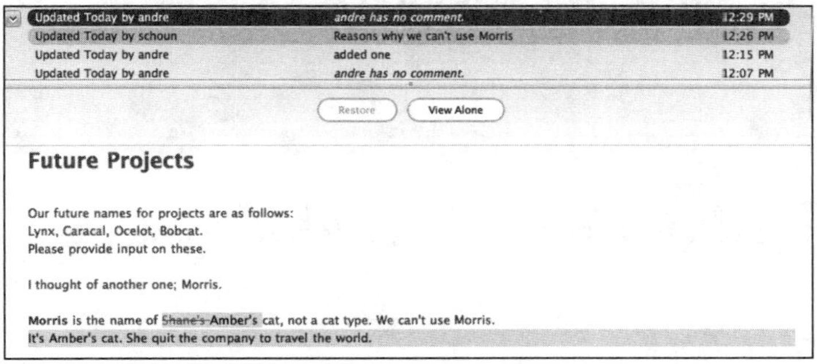


18 Log out as david, and return to your default home page for Mac OS X Server (https://server*n*.pretendco.com).

Notice that all changes are kept, even deletions. Wikis provide a detailed history of posts and allow all users in the group to make edits. Perhaps this is not as secure as you want.

## Exercise 8.1.5

# Set Blog and Wiki Access Control

## Objective

Control Wikis group access, so only certain users have access.

## Summary

In this exercise, you'll use Safari to test the access control settings you configured for the group blog and Wiki pages. Three groups were configured for blog and Wiki services: Developers, Engineering, and Marketing. Developers group resources can only be viewed and edited by members of that group. Engineering group resources are viewable by any authenticated users on the server, but only editable by group members. Marketing group resources are viewable by any user on the server, but only editable by specific group members.

1 Under the Safari menu, choose Empty Cache, and click the Empty button.

2 Wait about 15 seconds, and quit Safari.

3 Relaunch Safari, and enter your server's default website address again.

   In some cases, cached values may not permit the variety of changes attempted during this course. Clearing the cache should correct this.

4 Select the Developers group in the list on the right to view the Developers group's page.

   You're prompted to authenticate. First, try a user that is not in the group to show that membership is required.

5 Attempt to log in as franklin (password: changeme).

   This should fail because franklin is not a member of the Developers group.

6 Attempt to log in as diradmin.

This succeeds. Although diradmin is not in the Developers group, the diradmin account has access to all Wiki and blog content because it is an administrator account.

7 Click Log Out (diradmin) at the bottom of the page to log out of the diradmin account.

8 Attempt to log in as andre (password: abcd1234).

This should succeed because andre is in the Developers group. Andre is also configured as the owner of the Developers group.

9 Click Settings under the Admin functions heading on the right.

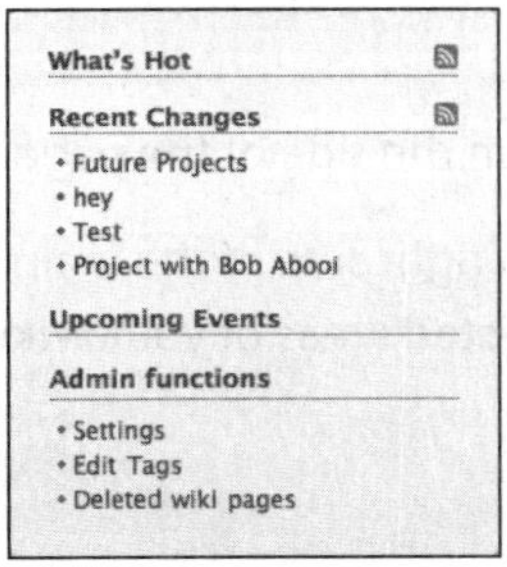


This page allows you to modify the Wiki and blog settings.

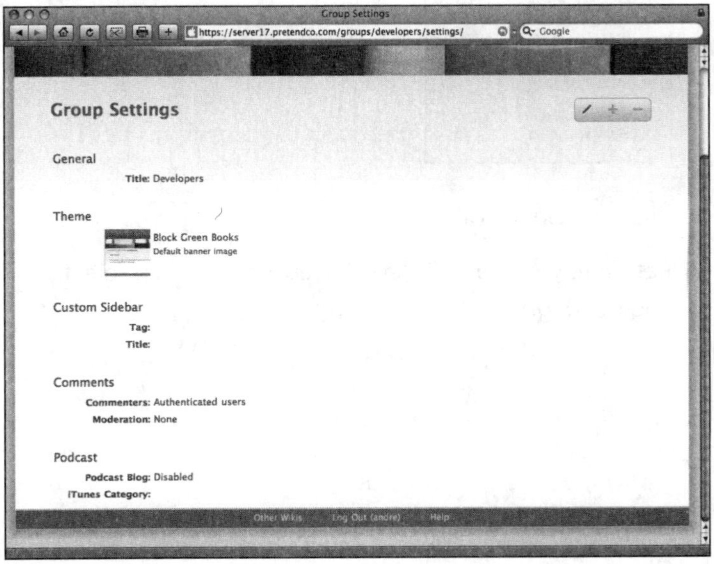

10 Click the Edit (pencil) button, and create a custom sidebar named Project Name Requests for one of the comments you created earlier; select "All comments" from the Moderation pop-up menu.

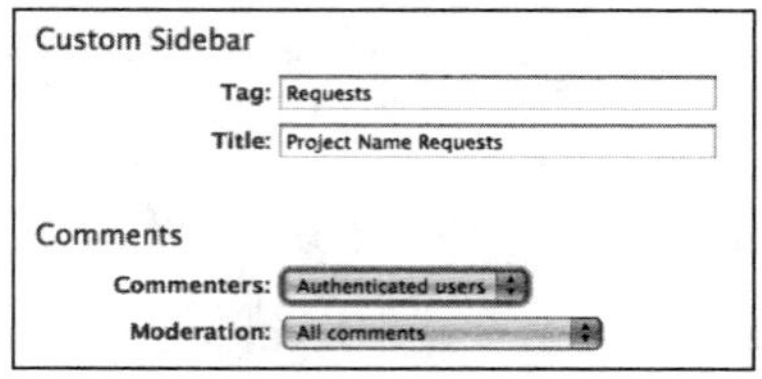


11 Click Save.

12 Click the Wiki button at the top of the page to return to the main Developer Wiki page.

13 Click the Project Name Requests link on the side of the page.

The custom sidebar will appear on the right side of the main Wiki page, allowing you to search selected areas of your Wiki.

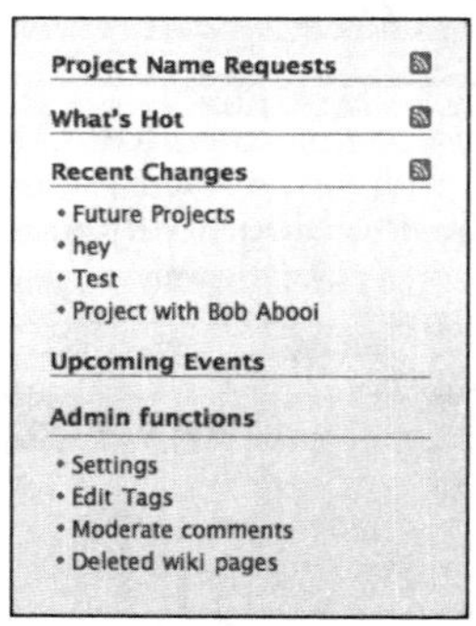


14 Click Log Out (andre).

15 Return to your server's default website, and then select Engineering.

16 Log in as john, who is a member of Engineering (but also Marketing), and create a new page in the Engineering Wiki called Twiddles.

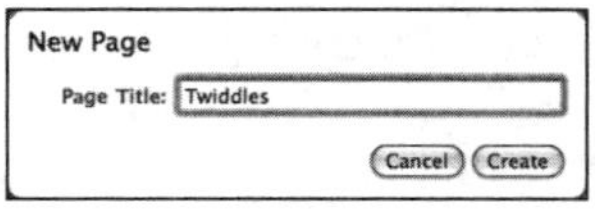


17 Enter some text, and then click Save.

The edit is posted without any moderation as long as it comes from an authenticated user; this is the default setting.

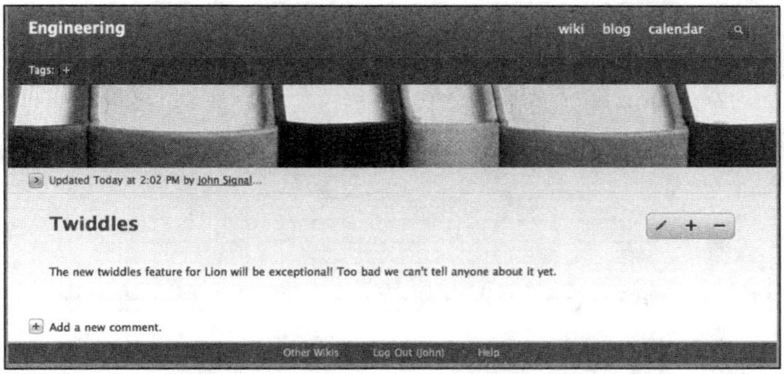


18 Click Log Out (john).

Now, experiment with the earlier configured group mail for the Developers group.

19 Return to your website's default home page (https://server*n*.pretendco.com).

20 Select the Developers group on the right.

21 Log in as Elizabeth (short name: etown and password: changeme).

22 Click the mail button at the top right of the page.

The mail page displays. Any future mail is sent by a member of the developers group to the developers@server*n*.pretendco.com address will display here.

23 Click Log Out (etown).

24 Return to your website's default home page (https://server*n*.pretendco.com).

25 Click the webmail button in the upper-right corner of the page.

26 Log in as Elizabeth using her short name.

27 Click the Compose link and create a mail message addressed to developers@server*n*.pretendco.com (where *n* is your student number). Enter a subject and some text in the body of the message.

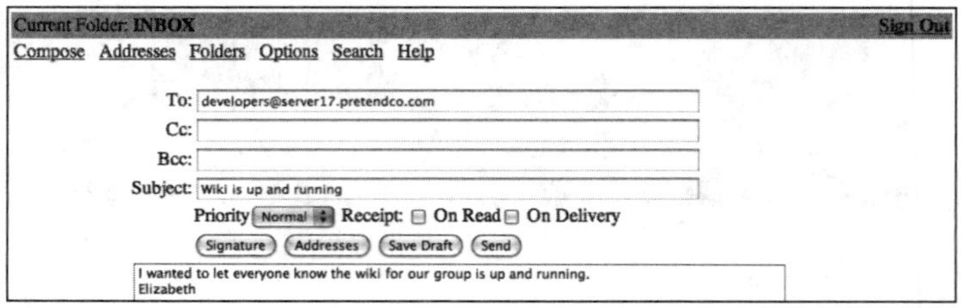


28 Click the Send button to send the mail, and then click the Sign Out link.

29 Return to your website's default home page (https://server*n*.pretendco.com).

30 Select the Developers group on the right.

31 Log in as simon (password: abcd1234).

32 Click the mail button at the top right of the page.

33 Click the new mail link sent by Elizabeth to view the mail message.

34 Log out as simon, empty Safari's cache again, and quit Safari.

***Question 2*** *Is information typed in a Wiki insecure?*

# Calendaring Services 8.2

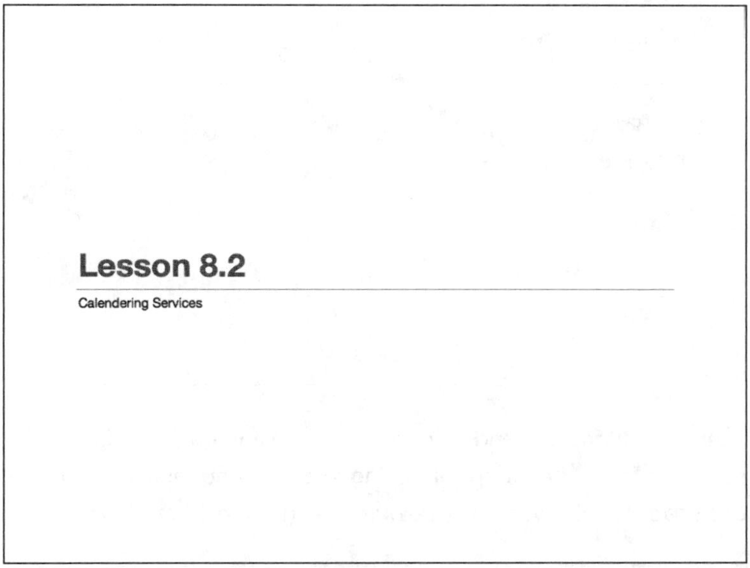


Calendaring services allow users to schedule events that can include locations and resources. Users who schedule events can invite other users and delegate access so colleagues can read or read and write to the events. Coupled with network home folders and/or the use of a Kerberos infrastructure, the ease of use and open standards behind the scenes makes managing and using the calendaring service relatively straightforward.

## Providing Calendaring Services

- Calendaring service basics
- Shared calendar benefits
- Enabling iCal service
- Restricting iCal service
- Securing iCal service
- Configuring iCal
- Delegated Users

Users benefit from calendaring services as an addition to collaborative services such as the group wiki. Using a calendaring service allows users to schedule events, use resources, and invite users to events.

## Calendaring Service Basics

iCal is built on several open source initiatives.

- CalDAV - looks for busy/free data
    - Extension of WebDAV - access control
- HTTP/HTTPS - means of accessing information
- iTIP - ability to initiate and respond to events
- iCalendar - event descriptions

Events are file based (*.ics files).

- File-system ACLs dictate read/write access.

Clients include iCal 3.x, Wiki web calendar, and third-party applications.

The iCal service is built on open source standards and communicates over the HTTP protocol. All events are *.ics files that have file-system access controls.

## Shared Calendar Benefits

- Open Directory Support
- Delegation
- File Attachment
- Multiple Calendars
- Event Invitations
- Access Control
- Locations
- Resource Allocation

Running the iCal service has several advantages: Among those are Open Directory support, the ability to delegate access to your calendar, file attachments, resource allocation, and more.

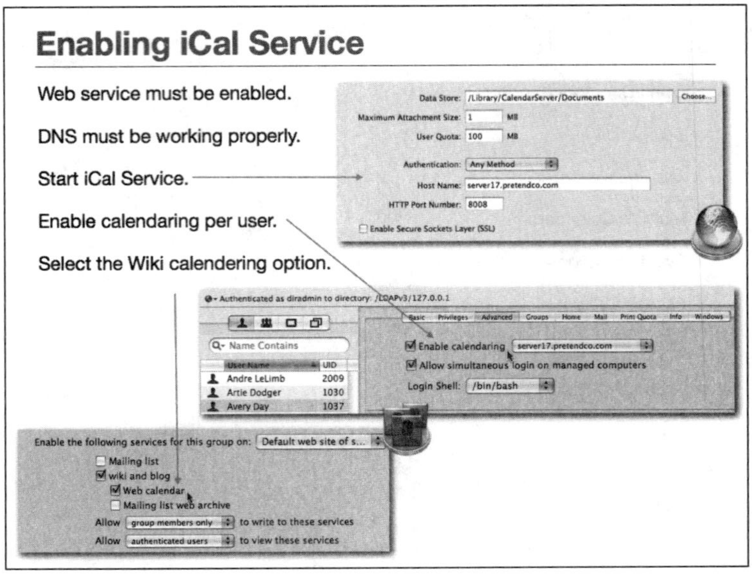


Turning on the iCal service amounts to running the web service, ensuring DNS is functioning properly, and enabling the iCal service. Once enabled, you permit users to use the service using Workgroup Manager. A ServicesLocator attribute is added per user. Resources and locations are created using the Directory application.

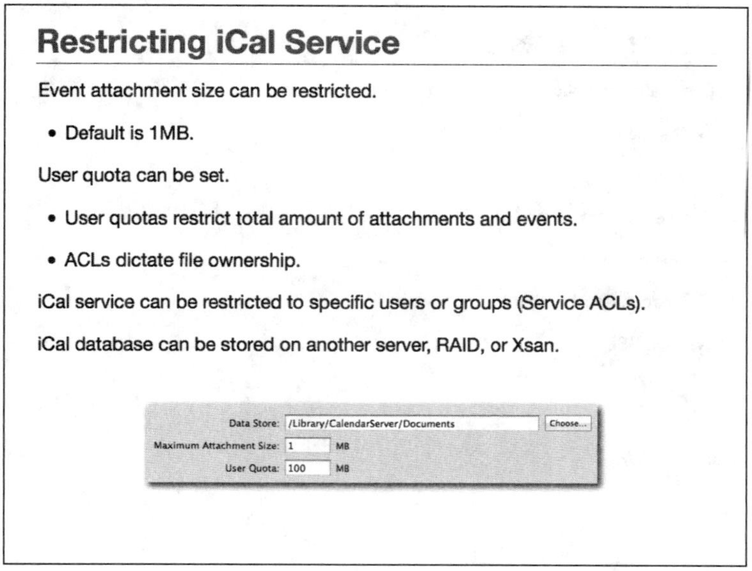


By default, the iCal Server stores all calendaring data in /Library/CalendarServer/Documents. A limit is imposed on the size of individual file attachments that may be included with calendaring events, and there is a per-user quota for all calendaring data. If file attachments are used often, these limits may need to be raised from the default values. These limits are configured in the iCal Service Settings pane. For large deployments, it may also be advisable to configure iCal Server to store calendaring data on a faster or larger storage volume.

## Securing iCal Service

Client authentication

- Standard
- Kerberos

Secure Sockets Layer (SSL)

- Use certificate
- Changes port to 8443

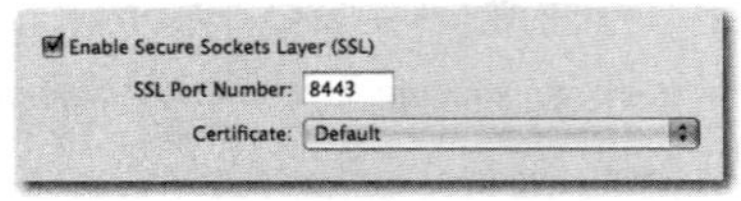


Website SSL

- https

The iCal service can be secured by using Kerberos to authenticate users and force connections over SSL. When secured, a certificate must be used for the encryption.

## Configuring iCal

Choose calendar name.

Add user.

- Authenticate with password or Kerberos.

Leave account URL blank.

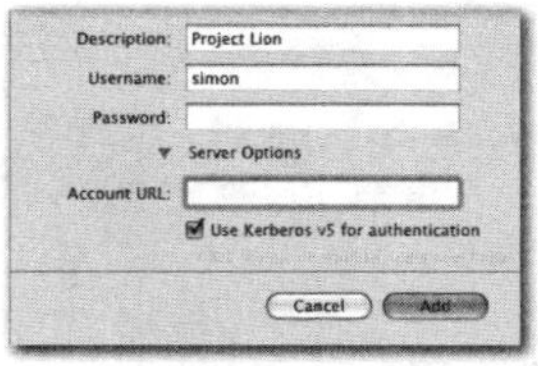


Once added:

- Automatically creates URL
  - https://server17.pretendco.com:8443/principals/__uids__/5FE6C5CA-B079-46A0-A7BB-ECD66F1B8DBC/
  - Long string of digits is user's universally unique ID (UUID)
    - NOT the UNIX ID

After the iCal service is enabled, users must configure their iCal accounts. If Kerberos is being used and network home directories are used, all users have to do is choose Kerberos as the authentication method and give their calendar a description. Their short name is already entered into iCal for them.

## Delegated Users

Users can delegate others to read or write to a shared calendar.

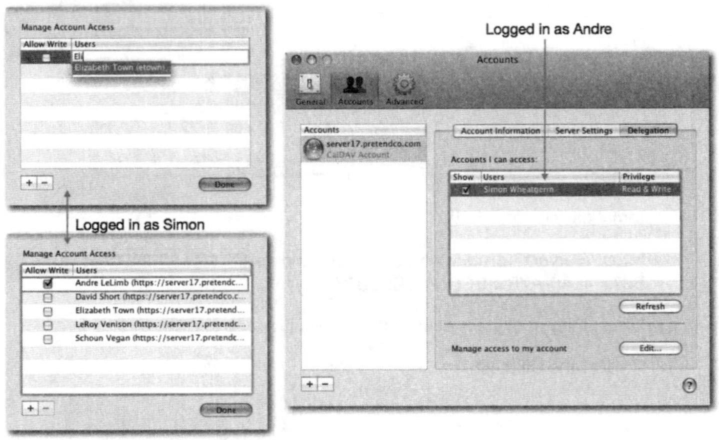


Once a user has created her account, she can delegate access to other users. Access is read only by default. With delegation, users can let someone else schedule and edit events for them.

## Creating iCal Resources

Resources can be

- Locations
- Items

Directory application is used to create resources.

Open Directory administrator can create resources and delegate access.

Resources can be reservable and invitations can be auto-accepted.

The Directory application is used to create locations and resources. The Directory administrator is, by default, permitted total access to create locations and resources.

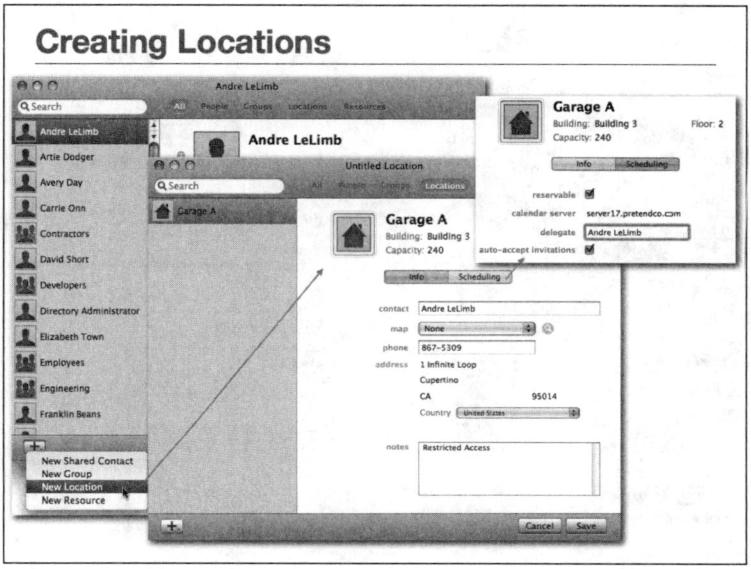


Locations are places where meetings can be held, and users can specify locations when they schedule events. Locations can be auto-accepted or can have a delegate, a user who examines the request and accepts or denies it based on whether the location is available for that date and time.

## Creating Resources

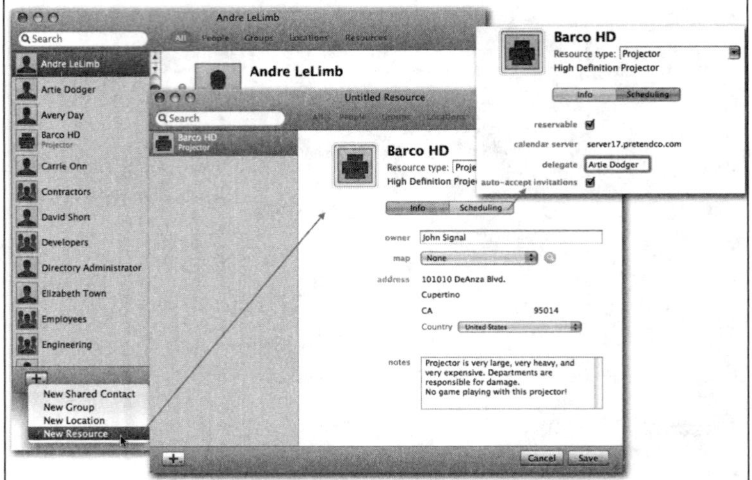


Resources, like locations, can be set to auto-accept or have a delegate answer on their behalf. Resources are treated as users and are added as users when creating events.

## Creating an iCal Event

Select calendar.

- Double-click date.
- Enter data.
- Add resources.
- Invite others.

Once the iCal service is enabled, users have created their iCal accounts, and locations and resources have been created, events can be scheduled.

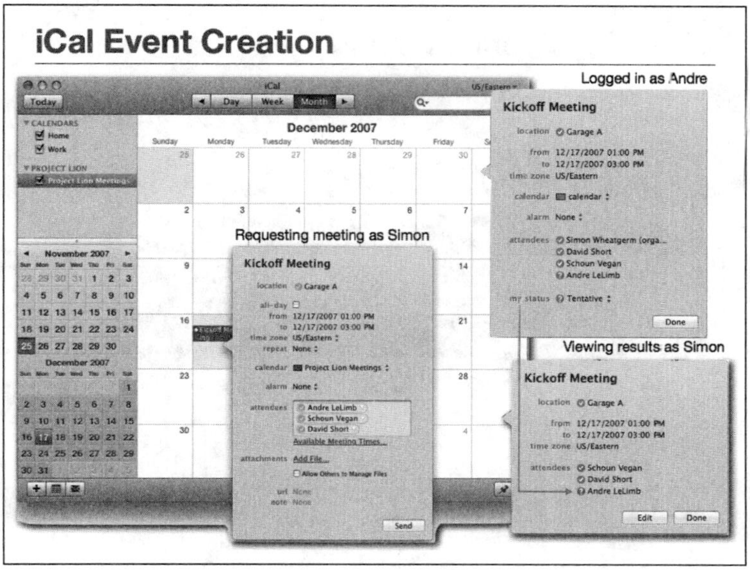


When an event is scheduled, all users invited receive an invitation. This invitation can be accepted, refused, or a "maybe" can be sent, indicating the user may not be able to respond when they get the invitation. Invitations that show up as a maybe are indicated by a question mark.

## Checking Event Conflicts

Schedulers can check for time conflicts.

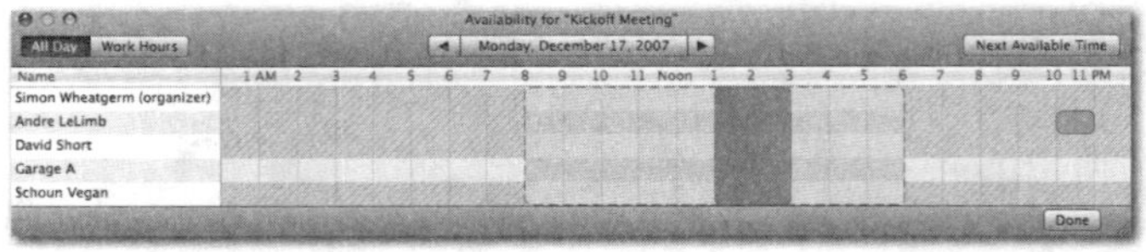


One option a scheduler has is to look for conflicts in events. This can be done only by the scheduler and is done when editing the event under the "available meeting times" link.

Exercises

8.2.1 Configure and use iCal Service

8.2.2 Create Resource and Location Records Using Directory

8.2.3 Configure iCal Accounts

8.2.4 Create and Respond to Events

8.2.5 Edit Web Group Calendars (Optional)

## Exercise 8.2.1
# Configure and Use iCal Service

## Objective

Learn how to configure and enable calendaring services for users and groups, configure iCal to access shared calendars, and use Directory to create available resources.

## Summary

Calendaring service involves three primary elements: a CalDAV service, provided in Mac OS X Server by iCal Server; a CalDAV-compatible client such as iCal; and all the directory data that represents the users, conference rooms, and other available resources used in the calendaring deployment. You'll use your server's Open Directory shared directory for this exercise.

Server Admin is used to configure and enable the iCal Service, and Workgroup Manager is used to enable calendaring service for user and group accounts. iCal will be used in these exercises as the calendaring client, although iCal Server works with a variety of third-party clients that support the CalDAV standard. The most important schedulable resources in most calendaring deployments are the users, however there may be a variety of others, such as laptop computers or projectors. The Directory application can be used to create and edit the other resource types.

1. On your Mac OS X computer, login as cadmin.
2. From the Server menu in Server Admin, choose Add Service.
3. Select the iCal checkbox next to add the service to your list of services.
4. Click Save.
5. Select iCal from the list under your server, and click the Settings icon in the toolbar.

6 Select "Enable Secure Sockets Layer (SSL), and choose the Default certificate.

7 Change the authentication to Kerberos

8 Click Save, and then click the Start iCal button to start the service.

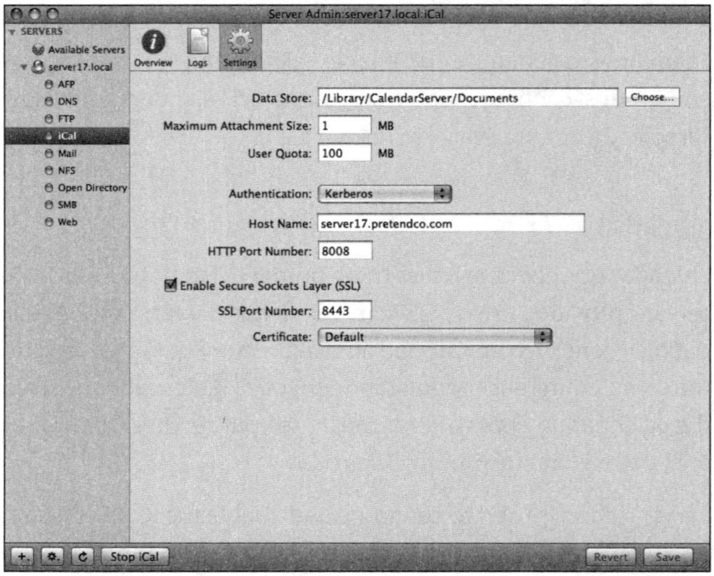


You'll use Workgroup Manager to enable calendaring for the users in your shared directory, which creates a ServicesLocator attribute in each user record.

9 Using Workgroup Manager, view the list of user accounts in your server's shared directory.

10 Select all the accounts in the shared directory, and then click the Advanced tab.

11 Select "Enable calendaring," and choose your server from the pop-up menu.

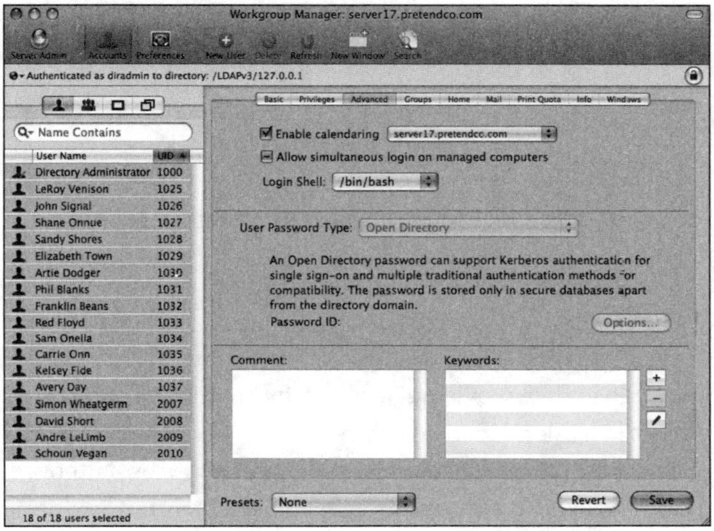


12 Click Save.

To demonstrate calendaring behavior for users who do not have calendaring support enabled, disable calendaring support for Kelsey Fide.

13 Select Kelsey Fide, deselect "Enable calendaring," and then click Save.

## Exercise 8.2.2

# Create Resource and Location Records Using Directory

### Objective

Create location and resource records to use later.

### Summary

Resource records in Mac OS X Server were designed to be generic and open ended, providing flexibility for creating all sorts of entities in a calendaring deployment. Although there is a preset list of resource types (such as projectors or automobiles), authorized users are able to create resource records that may not conform to any known resource type. Such resource records are first-class entities in the calendaring service, and fully support features such as reservation and delegation.

Location records are more specific than resource records, and are used to track locations that may be used in calendar events—most commonly conference rooms. Locations may have additional attributes such as capacity, phone number, and an associated map. Like resource records, locations can be reserved and delegated.

1. Open the Directory application, located in /Applications/Utilities.
2. Click the Add (+) button in the bottom left of the window, and choose New Location.

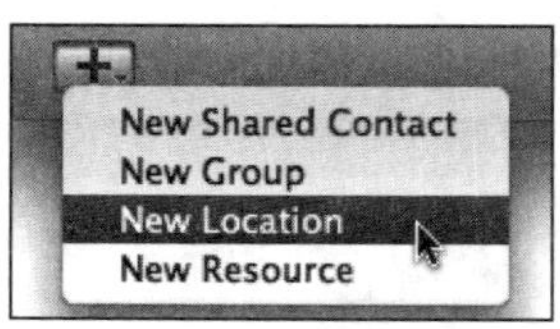

3 If prompted, authenticate as `diradmin`.

4 Add the following information to the new location record:

- Name: `Garage A` (To edit the name, click Untitled Location)
- Building: `Building 3`
- Floor: `2`
- Capacity: `240`
- Contact: `Andre LeLimb`
- Phone, address, and notes (Any values you choose)

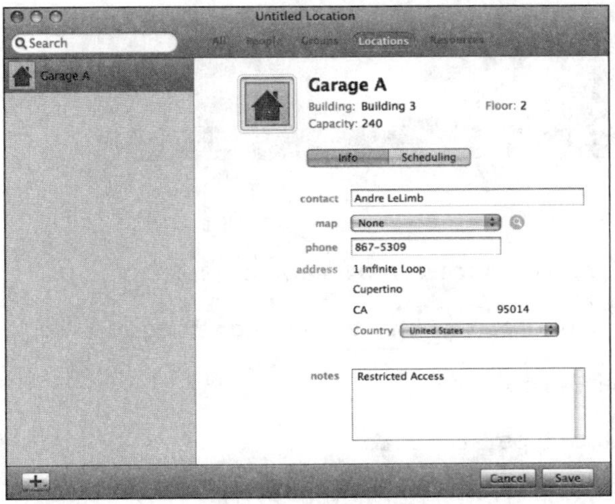


5 Click the Scheduling tab.

6 Select the "reservable" and "auto-accept invitations" checkboxes.

7 Enter `Andre LeLimb` in the “delegate” field.

Directory will autocomplete the name using a directory search.

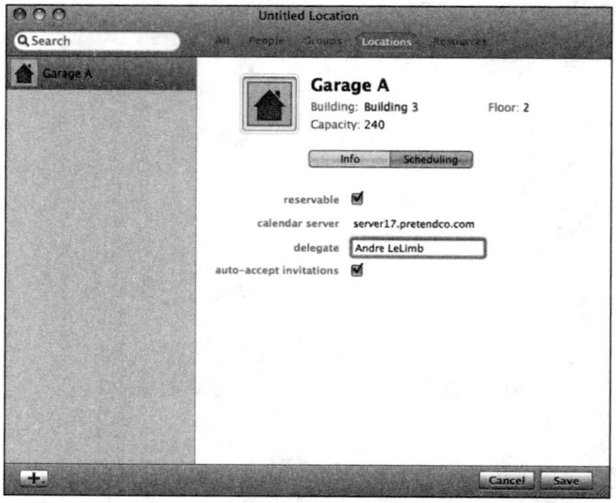


8 Click Save.

Next, create a resource record for a video projector.

9 Create a new resource with the following settings:

- Name: `Barco HD`
- Resource Type: `Projector`
- Description: `High Definition Projector`
- Owner: `John Signal`
- Address and notes (Any values you choose)
- Reservable: Selected
- Delegate: `Artie Dodger`
- Auto-accept invitations: Selected

10 Save the changes, reset the Directory authentication to Kerberos under the Directory Preferences, quit the Directory application, and log out as cadmin.

Exercise 8.2.3

# Configure iCal Accounts

## Objective

Configure iCal to access iCal service for several users.

## Summary

The iCal application will automatically connect to the Mac OS X Server's Open Directory structure because your Mac OS X computer is bound to it. This simplifies the process of configuring users for iCal.

1 Log in as simon (password: abcd1234).

2 Open iCal, located in /Applications/.

Notice you have two default calendars, home and work.

3 Choose Preferences from the iCal menu.

4 Click Accounts.

5 Click the Add (+) button to add a new CalDAV account.

6 Enter `Simon Wheatgerm` in the description, and notice that the short name already appears in the dialog.

7 Click the disclosure triangle and select the "Use Kerberos v5 for authentication" checkbox.

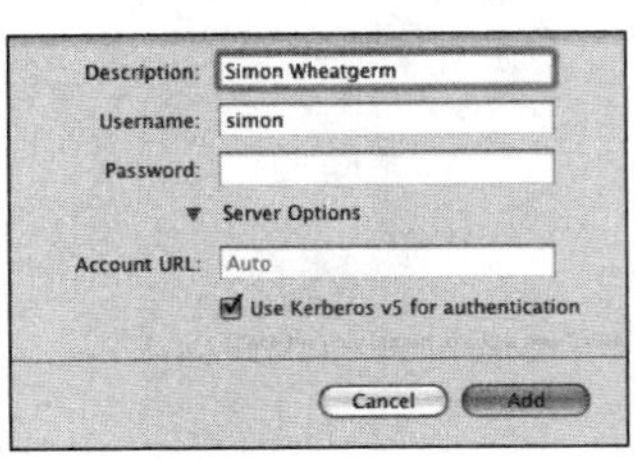


8 Click Add, and your iCal account is created automatically.

9 Click the Server Settings tab, and view the full Account URL path.

10 Notice that Simon's Universally Unique ID is located at the end of the path.

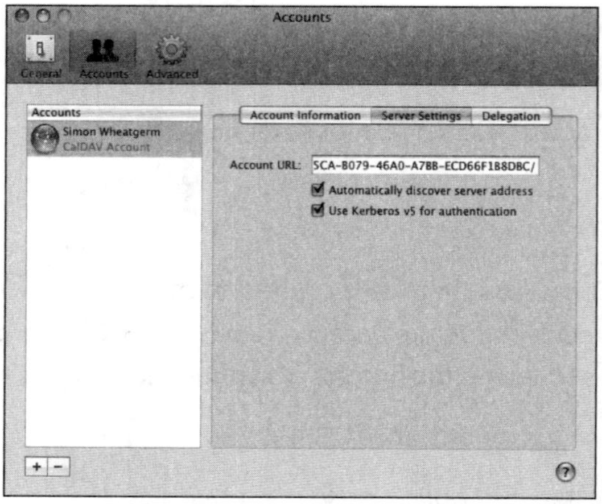


Now that the user accounts are configured, you need to configure the delegates. You'll want all members of the Developers group to have read access, and you'll want LeRoy, who is in charge of the project, to have read and write access.

11 Click the Delegation tab, and then click the Edit button at the bottom of the dialog.

12 Add the following users:

- Schoun
- David
- Andre
- Elizabeth
- LeRoy

Notice the names autocomplete.

13 Select the Allow Write checkbox for LeRoy, and click the Done button.

14 Click back on the Edit button, and you'll now see the full path for the new users. If this Mac OS X Server running the iCal service was joined with another directory server, it would search more directories for the additional names.

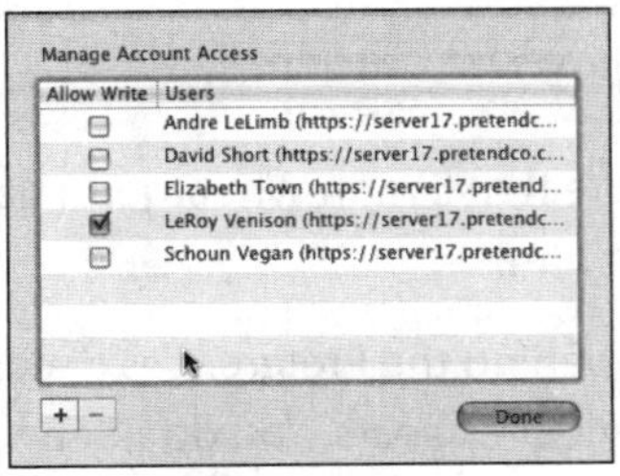


15 Close the Preferences window, and quit iCal.

16 Launch iCal again, and rename the new calendar to Project Lion Meetings.

17 Log out as Simon, and log in as Schoun (password: changeme).

18 Launch iCal, open the Preferences dialog, and click the Add (+) button.

19 Enter `Schoun Vegan` as the Description, select Kerberos authentication, and click Done.

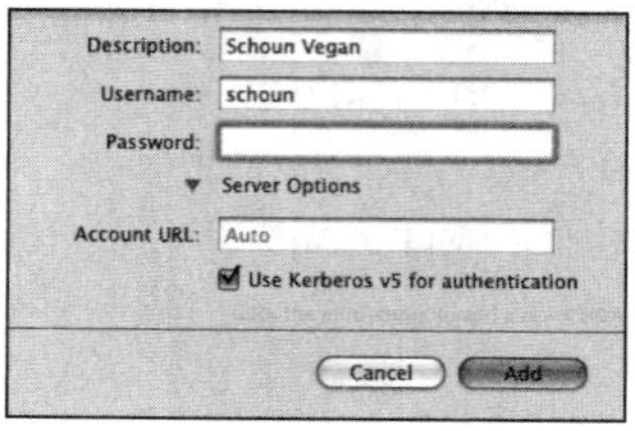


20 Click the Delegation tab, and note that Simon Wheatgerm has allowed you to be a delegate for him.

21 Select the Show checkbox, and behind the Preferences dialog in the iCal window, Simon's calendar appears. You do not need to see it now, so deselect Show.

22 Close the Preferences dialog, and rename your calendar to Schoun.

23 Log out as Schoun, and log in as andre (password: abcd1234).

24 Configure Andre's account the same as Schoun's except use Andre's name.

25 When you get to Andre's Delegation tab, note that Andre has read and write access for Garage A. Select the Show checkbox to display that calendar.

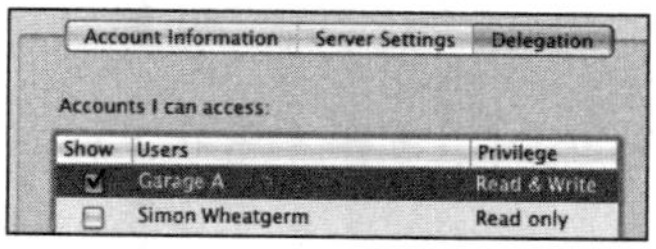


26 Rename Andre's calendar to Andre. Leave the Garage A calendar alone for now.

27 Repeat the process as LeRoy and as David.

28 Log out as David, and log in as kelsey (password: changeme).

29 Launch iCal, and attempt to create an account.

***Question 3*** *Why can't Kelsey create an account?*

______________________________________________

______________________________________________

30 Log out as Kelsey, and log in as Elizabeth (short name: etown, password: changeme).

31 Attempt to open iCal, and create an account.

***Question 4*** *Can you create an iCal account for Elizabeth? She is in the Developers group.*

______________________________________________

______________________________________________

32 Log out as Elizabeth, and log in as Simon.

## Exercise 8.2.4

# Create and Respond to Events

### Objective

Create new calendar events, invite attendees, reserve a conference room, and schedule the use of a resource.

### Summary

iCal allows you to create and work with any number of different calendars. By default, all calendar events are coalesced into a single view, and color coding is used to visually associate events with calendars. To disable the display of a calendar's events, select the checkbox by the calendar's name.

Although you can view multiple calendars at once, events are created in a single calendar. When an event is created, it is stored in whichever calendar is selected at the time.

Attendees receive notifications of events to which they are invited and have the option of accepting, denying, or deciding later. When an attendee accepts or denies an invitation, the creator of the event receives a notification of what the attendee chose.

1 Log in as simon, and open iCal.

2 Select the Project Lion Meetings calendar by clicking it in the calendar list.

3 Double-click on tomorrow to schedule a new event called Kickoff Meeting.

4 Double-click the event icon to edit the event. Configure this event as follows:

- Name: `Kickoff Meeting`
- Location: `Garage A` (notice how it auto-fills the entry)
- From: `10AM`
- To: `11AM`
- Click Add Attendees and enter: `LeRoy, David, Schoun, Andre, Barco` (You can separate them with a comma as you type.)

Do not click out of this window yet.

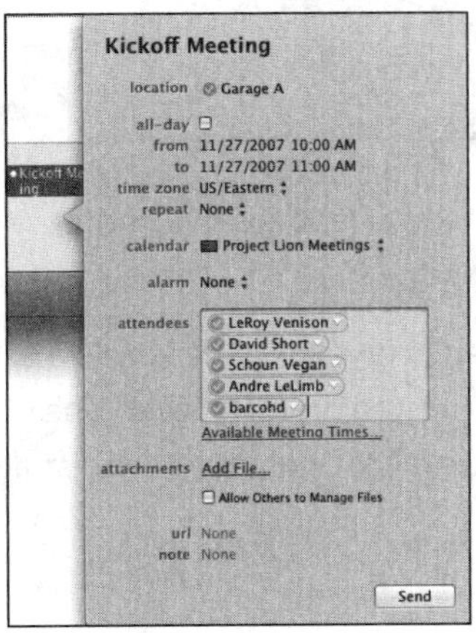


You want to send this meeting to all employees of the company, but you haven't yet added certain users to the employees group.

5 Open Workgroup Manager, and authenticate as ladmin (password: apple)

6 Select the LDAPv3/127.0.0.1 (shared) domain, and authenticate as diradmin (password: diradmin).

7 Add Avery, Carrie, Kelsey, and Sam to the Employees group.

8 Add the Projects, Contractors, and Engineering groups to the Employees group.

9 Save the changes, and quit Workgroup Manager.

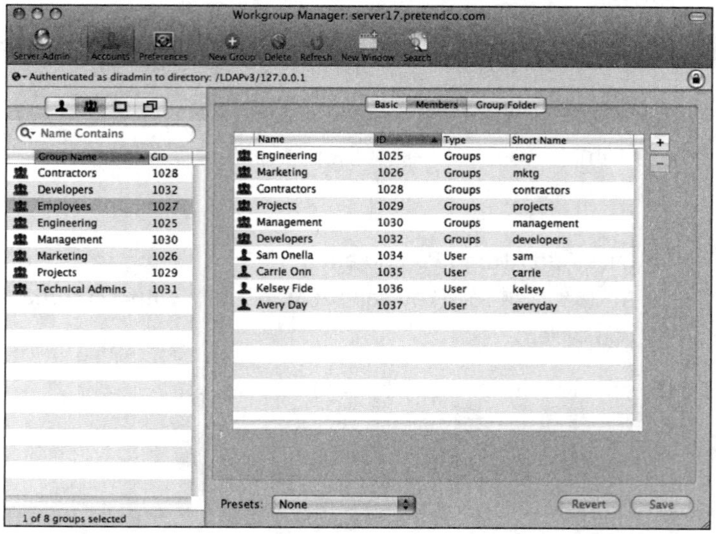

10 Back in the event dialog, click in the attendees field, enter `employees`, and press the Tab key.

Notice that because you've added everyone to the employees group—either individually or by nested groups—everyone in the company is shown in the list, except Directory Administrator, whom you did not add.

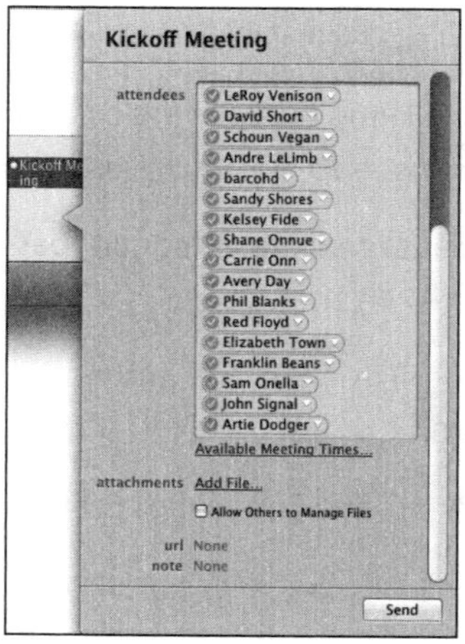

11 Click Send, quit and reopen iCal, double-click on the event, and click the Edit button.

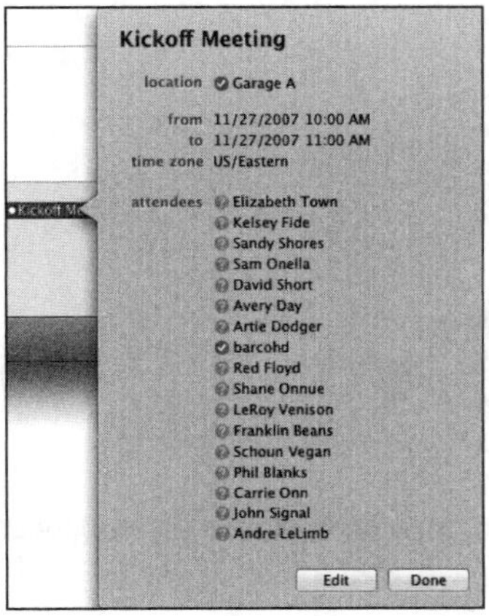


Note that all attendees other than the room and the Barco HD projector have question marks next to their name. The question mark indicates they need to respond.

iCal checks automatically for new notifications at a configurable interval, but you can also force iCal to contact iCal Server to receive any pending updates.

12 Choose Refresh All from the Calendar menu.

Now imagine that you just received a phone call that members of the engineering group will be unable to attend so you need to remove them from the event.

13 Use Workgroup Manager to locate the members of the Engineering group.

As you scroll over their names in the event dialog, an arrow appears to the right of their name.

14 Click the arrow next to the name of a person in the Engineering group, and choose Remove Attendee.

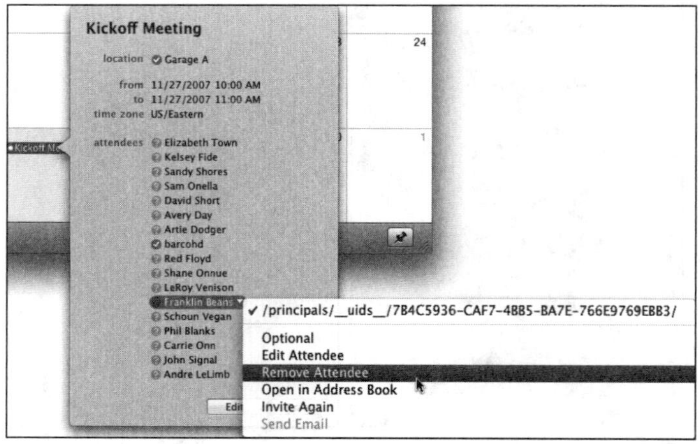


15 Remove all other members of the Engineering group, and click Update.

16 Log out as Simon, and log in as David. Launch iCal, and double-click the event.

17 Because you can see both Simon's Project calendar and your own, you see the event twice. Accept the invitation in your calendar, and log out.

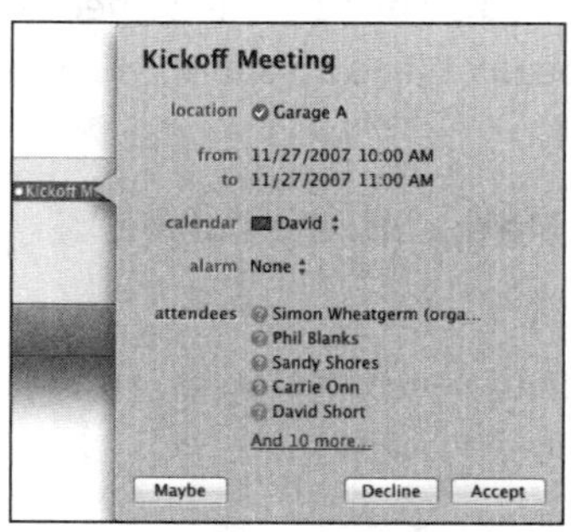


18 Log in as Andre, and launch iCal.

You have two events for the same day. One for you and one for Garage A, for whom you are the delegate.

19 Double-click the one associated with you and click Maybe, because you may be on vacation that day.

20 Double-click the event again, and you'll see you are listed as tentative. Click the Tentative pop-up menu to view your options.

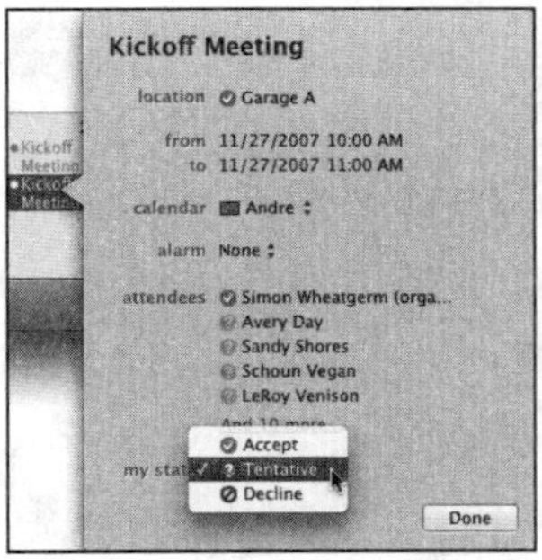

21 Choose Tentative, and click Done.

22 Double-click the Garage A event.

Because Garage A was set to auto-accept, it has accepted. As the delegate, you could override it, but you will not do so in this case.

23 Click Done, log out as Andre, and log in as Schoun.

24 Open iCal, and decline the invitation in your calendar, because you will be out of town that day.

25 Log out as Schoun, and log in as simon (password: abcd1234).

26 Open iCal, double-click your event to view it, then close that window and double-click it again and click the Edit button.

Notice the list of users have icons indicating their status with respect to the event adjacent to their names.

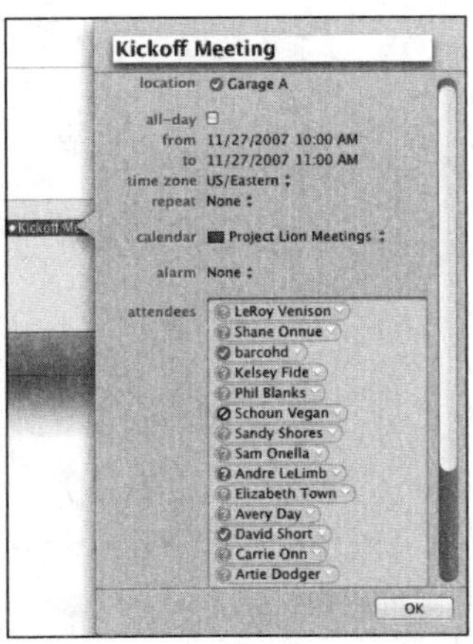

27 Click the All Day button, scroll down, and click available meeting times.

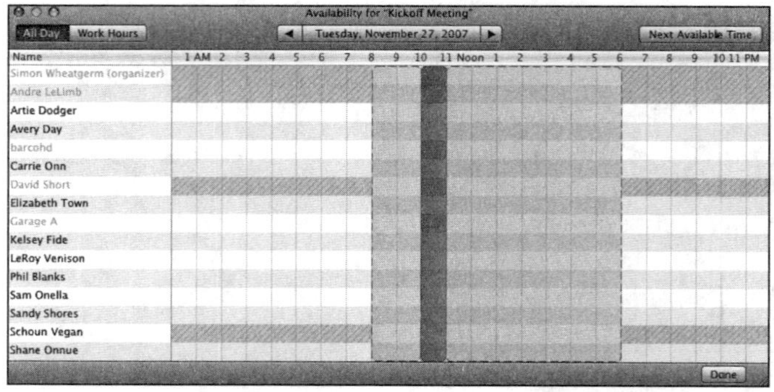


You can see if anyone who has not already responded has a conflict.

Conflicting times are indicated by dark grey. Available times are indicated by light red. The currently selected event is indicated by dark red. You can drag the event icon in the availability viewer to select a suitable time, or you can let iCal pick the next available meeting time.

28 Close the Availability window.

29 Click the Mail icon at the bottom left of iCal's main window to show any Notifications.

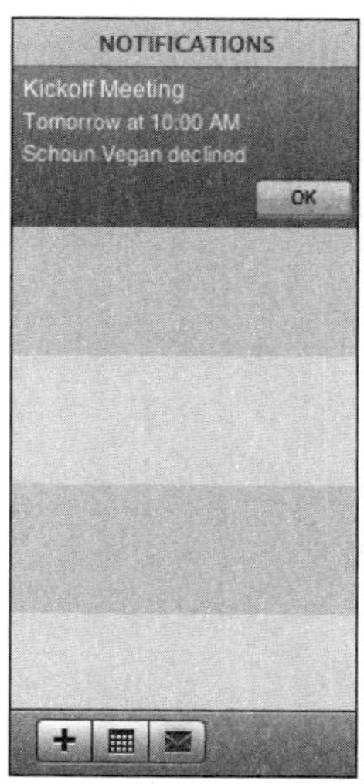

30 Click OK to dismiss the notification, and quit iCal.

31 Open the Mail application, and send a message to developers@server*n*.pretendco.com telling them the iCal service is up and running.

32 Check your mail to ensure you received a copy.

33 Mount smb://server*n*.local, and select the project lion share point.

34 Mount nfs://server*n*.pretendco.com/Shared Items/Templates

35 Mount https://server*n*.pretendco.com /manual-1.3.

36 Open Directory inside the /Applications/Utilities folder and attempt to edit the Barco Projector by clicking the edit button and dismiss the dialog when you are unable to edit the information.

37 Open /System/Library/CoreServices/Kerberos to view all your tickets.

## Exercise 8.2.5

# Edit Web Group Calendars (optional)

## Objective

Use Safari to create events on a group calendar, and subscribe to the group calendar with iCal.

## Summary

iCal Server also provides hosting for group calendars. Group calendars in Mac OS X Server are edited and viewed using a web browser, and are tightly integrated with the Wiki and blog group services. It is also possible to subscribe to a read-only version of a group calendar using iCal.

1 Use Server Admin to change the iCal service authentication method to Digest and save the change.

2 If not already logged in, log in as simon (password: abcd1234).

3 Use Safari to open your server's default web site.

4 Select Developers to visit the Developers group page.

5 Log in as andre.

   Even though you are logged in to the Finder as simon, you can log in to the group site as another person.

6 Click calendar.

7 As you did in iCal, click and drag in the calendar to create an event.

8 Configure the event with any date and time.

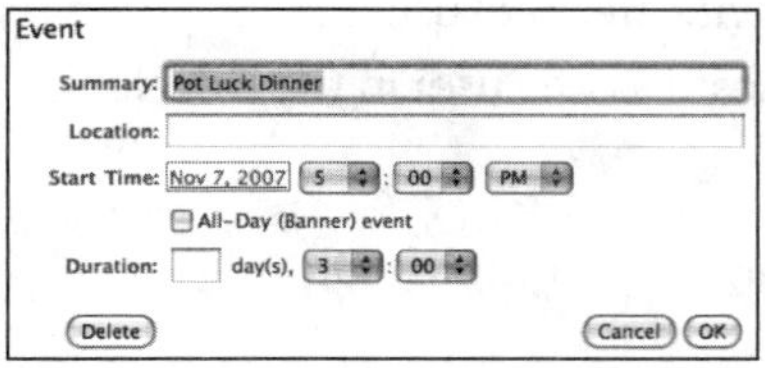


9 Click OK.

The event appears on the group calendar.

10 Click wiki to return to the main group page.

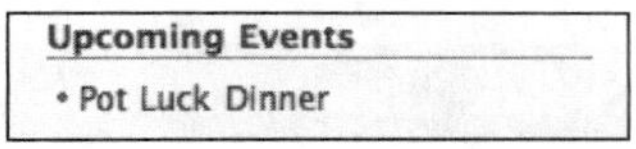


Note that the new event now appears in the list of upcoming events.

Next, you'll subscribe to this calendar to view a read-only version in iCal.

11 In iCal as Simon, choose Subscribe from the Calendar menu.

12 Enter the URL for the Developer group calendar on your server, `https://servern.pretendco.com:8443/calendars/groups/developers/calendar/` in the Calendar URL field.

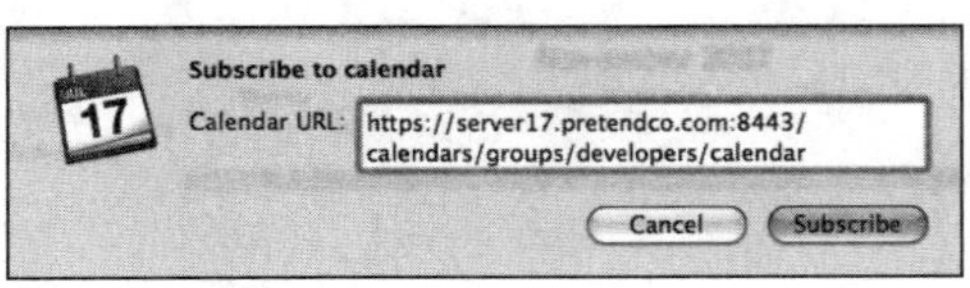

13 Click Subscribe.

You are prompted to authenticate. Because this is a group calendar, you can authenticate as any user in the Developer group, such as Simon.

14 Enter Simon's name and password and click OK.

You are now prompted to configure settings for this calendar subscription.

15 Click OK.

The event now appears in iCal.

16 Use Server Admin to reset the iCal service authentication method to Kerberos.

17 Log out.

# Messaging Services 8.3

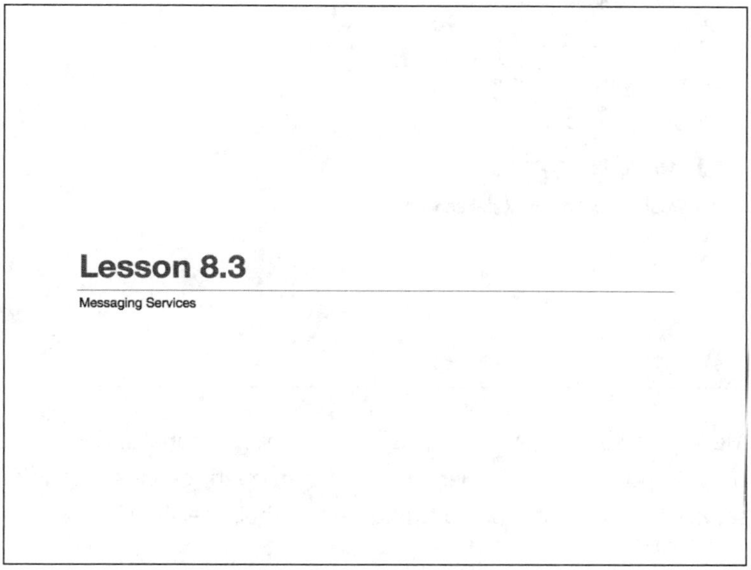


Messaging services can permit employees to chat, send files, and share their screens with one another in a secure environment. The iChat service is based on the open-source Jabber2 project, and provides chat services using XMPP, extensible message passing protocol. It features the ability to federate, or connect, your iChat Server with other XMPP compatible chat servers, enabling users of different chat servers to chat and exchange files with each other. It also supports the use of SSL certificates for encrypting client-to-server and server-to-server communications.

## Providing Messaging Services

- Messaging service basics
- Messaging service benefits
- Enabling iChat service
- Securing iChat service
- Using iChat federation
- Configuring iChat
- Logging iChat transcripts
- Troubleshooting the iChat service

Messaging services are widely used in for both personal and business purposes. Mac OS X Server provides an open source messaging service for administrators to configure and their users to use.

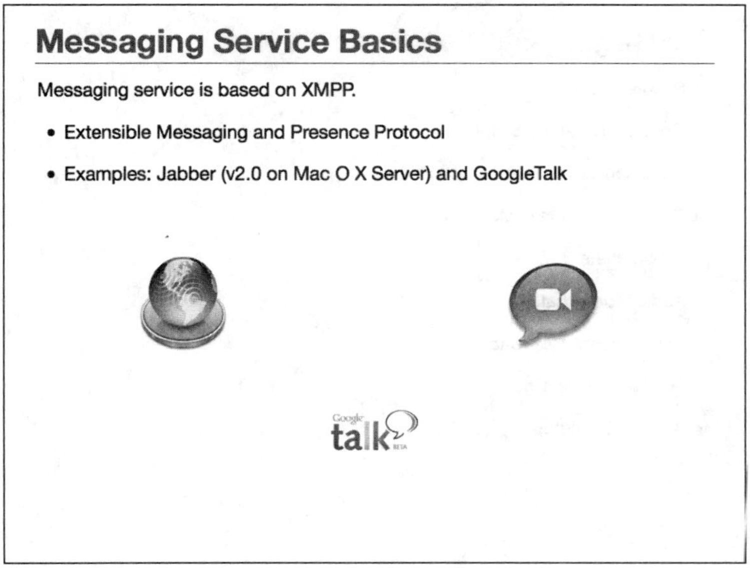


The messaging service Mac OS X Server deploys is the open source Extensible Messaging and Presence Protocol (XMPP). Mac OS X Server runs version 2.x of this software (called Jabber in some cases). Because this is open source, other companies have developed chat software around XMPP, for example Google, with GoogleTalk.

## Messaging Service Benefits

- Secure chats
- Control of chat transcripts
- iChat service to iChat service linking
- Person to person chats
- Group chats
- Audio/Video chatting
- Screen control via iChat
- File transfer via iChat
- Auto-buddy setup

There are several benefits to running a messaging service. First, it allows all communications to be kept in-house on servers protected by a firewall or virtual private connection. Secondly, even in-house, all chats can be encrypted. Third, chat transcripts can be saved on the server. These are only few of the benefits that come from implementing an in-house messaging service within your organization.

## Enabling iChat Service

DNS must be working properly.

Server Admin is used to:

- Enable the service
- Insure host name is correct.
    - Additional host names can be used
- Start the iChat Service.

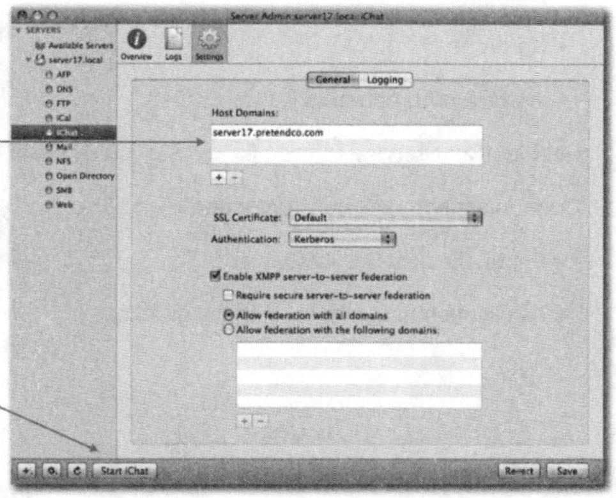


Mac OS X Server's messaging service is called iChat, but this service works with other instant message applications in addition to the iChat application. Enabling the iChat service is as easy as ensuring DNS is set up properly, ensuring a host name is set, and starting the service.

## Securing iChat Service

Authentication methods include:

- Standard
- Kerberos
- Any Method (Attempts Kerberos first)

Restrict iChat service to specific users or groups (Service ACLs).

Communication between server and clients is unencrypted.

- Enable Secure Sockets Layer (SSL).
- All clients must have copy of the certificate.

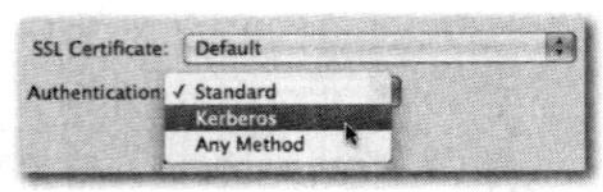


Prior to allowing users to use the chat service, administrators may want to modify the authentication scheme and use Kerberos if it has been implemented. Administrators can also increase security by using Secure Sockets Layer (SSL) to encrypt communications between the user of the chat service and the chat server. As with other services, access controls can be placed on the iChat service to restrict who can actually use the service.

## iChat Federation

Federation allows additional iChat services on other servers to communicate between one another.

- Supports chats and file transfers between servers
- S2S part of Jabber (Server To Server)

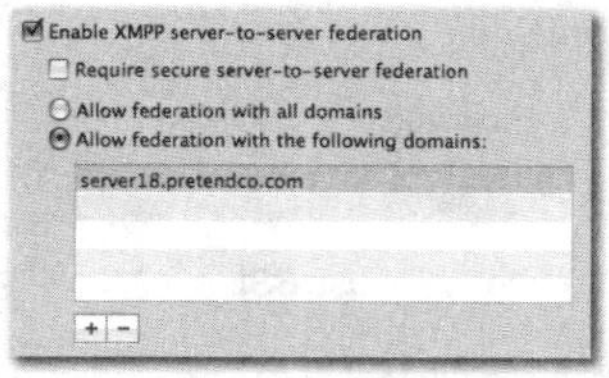


Any XMPP compatible messaging service can be in federation.

- iChat service
- GoogleTalk

While chat between client and server are encrypted, chat between servers is not set up automatically.

- All servers must have identical certificate structure to encrypt data between servers in federation.

In large scale deployments, it is feasible that there be more than one iChat service running on more than one server. The XMPP package allows for server to server connections called federation. In this way, users from one iChat service can communicate with users on another XMPP v2.x messaging service. It doesn't have to be another Mac OS X Server.

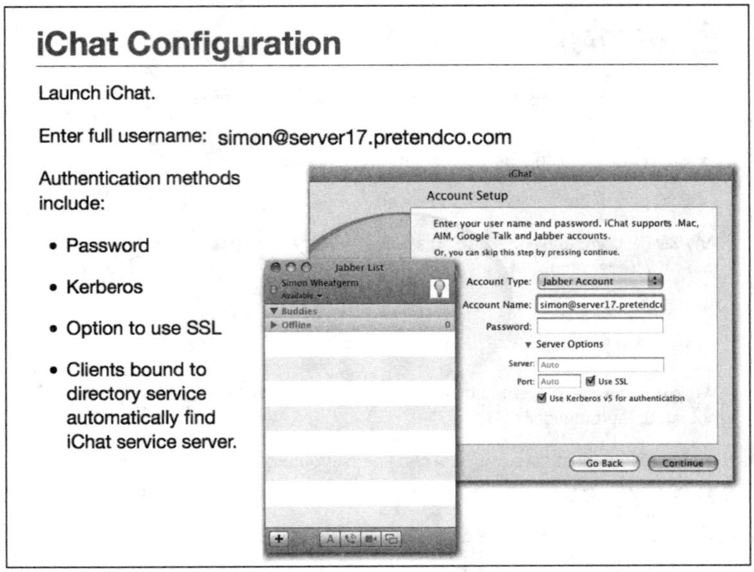


Once the iChat service is configured, the iChat application is used on Mac OS X to connect to the iChat service running on your Mac OS X Server. The iChat application supports all of the following account types: .Mac, AIM, GoogleTalk, and of course Jabber (iChat service). Because Bonjour is built into all Mac OS X computers, users can chat with each other on a local network without any server present. This method of course provides no method for centralized security, encryption, or management, which is why a centralized iChat service makes good sense.

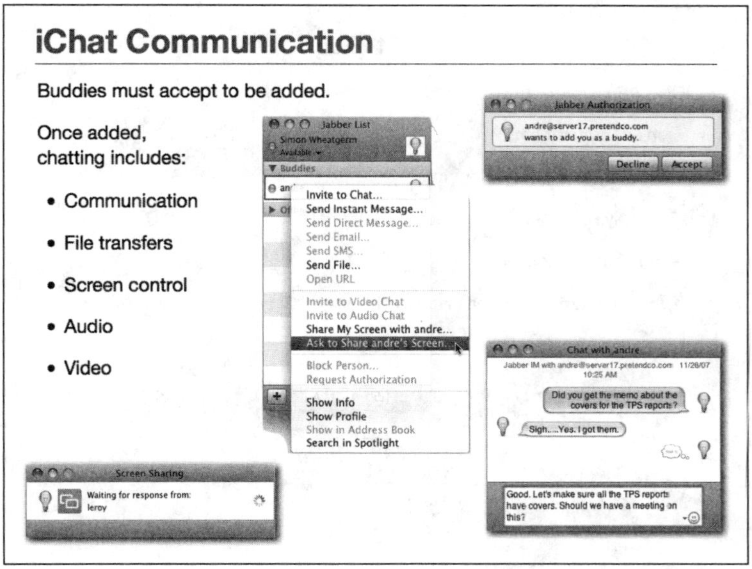


When iChat has been configured, users have several methods of communication, among them, standard peer-to-peer chat, group chats, screen control and screen sharing, audio chat, and file transfers.

## Logging iChat Transcripts

All iChat transcripts can be logged.

- Even encrypted chats
    - Unencrypted prior to logging

Log files only readable by root user.

- Default path for log files:
    - /private/var/jabberd/message_archives

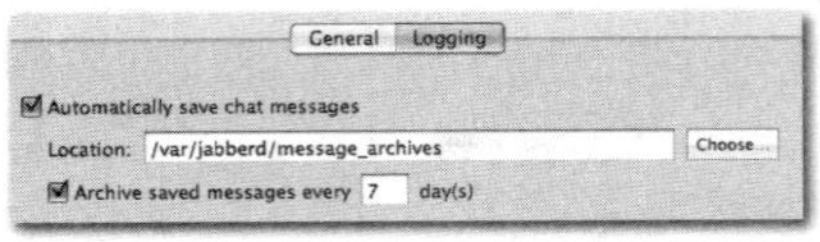


Administrators can log all iChat service transcripts to a directory. Understanding the legal ramifications of message logs, it may be worthwhile to place these transcripts on a RAID or Xsan system. Even if communications are encrypted, the text is decrypted prior to being stored in the logs. Also, in a federation environment, server-to-server communication is not encrypted but can be by using the same certificate on all servers within the federation.

## Troubleshooting iChat Service

If iChat service is not functioning properly, follow the path of networki

- DNS setup
- Firewall issues
- Authentication issues
- Certificate (SSL) issues
- Check Bonjour
- Check from server
- Check iChat entries in system.log via iChat service log pop-up

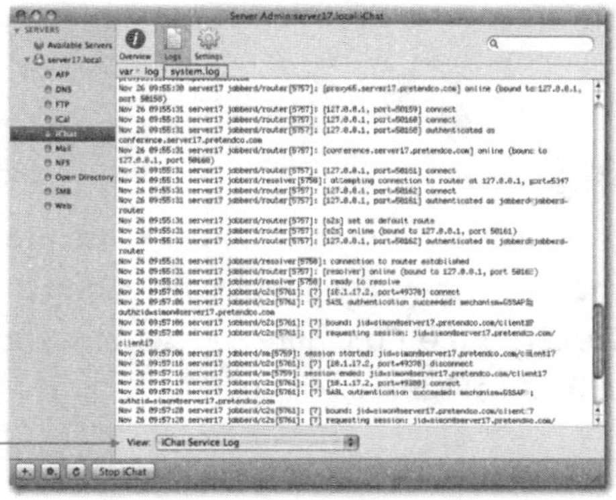


When users cannot connect or use the iChat service, consult the system.log file for any iChat service errors. Server Admin pulls out any iChat service related log entries and displays them in the Log entries under the iChat service.

Exercises

8.3.1 Configure the iChat Service and Application

8.3.2 Add Jabber Buddies and Communicate

8.3.3 View Chat Logs

## Exercise 8.3.1

# Configure the iChat Service and Application

### Objective

Learn how to configure, start, and use the iChat service. Set up encrypted chat sessions by configuring the iChat service to use an SSL certificate. Configure and perform encrypted federation with other iChat service servers.

### Summary

In this exercise, you'll configure the iChat service to allow server-to-server federation and restrict federation to the pretendco.com domain. You'll also use a self-signed SSL certificate to encrypt all chat messages that are sent over the network. For this exercise, iChat will be configured and used as the chat client so you can log in to the iChat service and send messages. The iChat service has the ability to log all chat messages to a selected folder on the server, so you'll also enable and browse the chat logs. Finally, you'll experiment with federation by chatting with other students in the classroom.

### Configure and Start iChat Server

In this section, you'll configure iChat Server to use SSL for encryption, enable federation, restrict federation to the pretendco.com domain, and save chat logs to a folder.

1 Log in as cadmin, and open the Server Admin application.

2 From the Server menu in Server Admin, choose Add Service.

3 Select the iChat checkbox to add it to your list of services.

4 Click Save.

5 Select iChat from the list under your server, and click the Settings icon in the toolbar.

6 Click the General tab to view your iChat service's general settings.

7 Choose the Default certificate for the SSL Certificate pop-up menu.

8 Ensure Authentication is set to Any Method.

   This is the first time you have not used strictly Kerberos for authentication. This is because you'll have more than one account active in iChat. Only one user's Kerberos credentials can be active at a time, so this causes problems when trying to use two different Kerberos accounts at once.

9 Select Enable XMPP server-to-server federation.

   It is possible to keep your server from federating with unknown servers by using the federation domain list. Next, you'll configure iChat Server to restrict federation.

10 Select the "Allow federation with the following domains" radio button, click the Add button, and add pretendco.com.

   This list may contain both host names and domain names. If a host name is listed, federation is allowed with that host. If a domain is listed, any hosts in that domain or any subdomains are allowed federation with your server. In the current configuration, your server will be allowed to federate with all the other servers in the classroom, because they are all in the pretendco.com domain.

   The General settings should now appear as shown in the following figure.

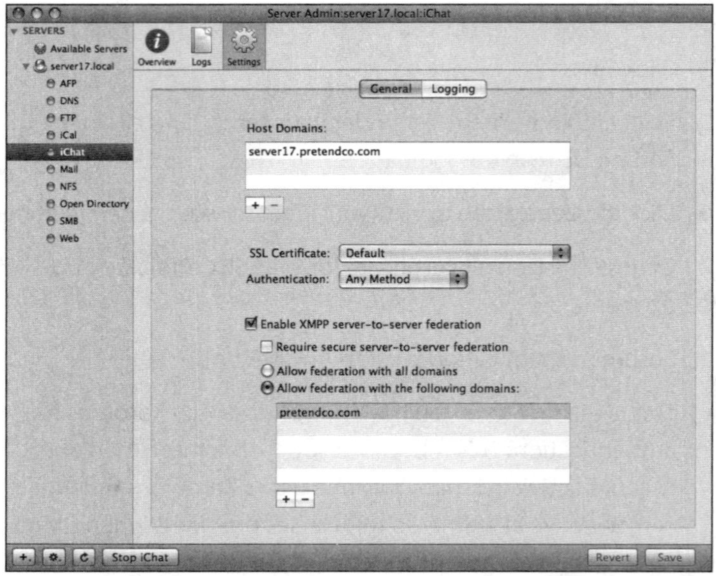


12 Click the Logging tab.

13 Select the checkbox to enable logging of all chat messages.

By default, chat message logs are archived every 7 days. Log archiving saves server disk space by compressing plain text chat messages into a binary format, which can be decompressed for viewing at any time.

14 In the Location field, enter `/Users/Shared`

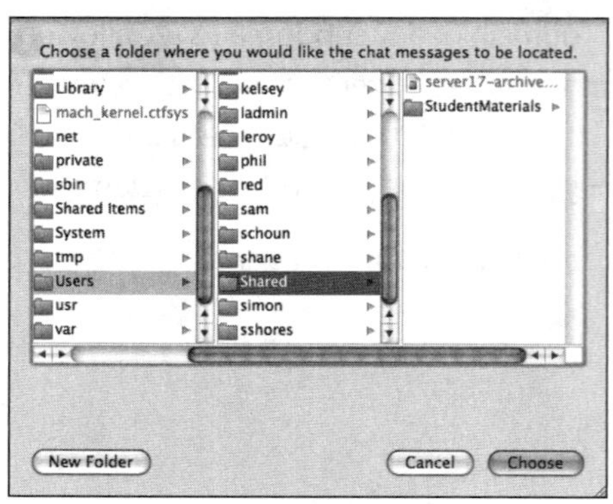


The default location for the chat logs is /var/jabberd/message_archives. This directory is difficult to access using Finder due to file permissions, so you'll store chat logs in a different location. Normally, chat logs should be stored in a secure location that only administrator accounts can access. For this exercise, you'll store the logs in /Users/Shared for the sake of simplicity. For added security, the log file itself is created with permissions that only allow read access to the jabber service account.

15 Click Save.

16 Click the Start iChat button to start the iChat service.

17 Quit Server Admin, log out as cadmin, and log in as simon (password: abcd1234).

18 Open iChat, located in /Applications/.

The first time iChat opens, a setup assistant displays.

19 At the Welcome screen, click Continue.

20 At the Account Setup screen, choose Jabber Account from the Account Type pop-up menu.

21 Enter `simon@servern.pretendco.com` as the name with no password.

22 Click the disclosure triangle, and select both "Use SSL" and "Use Kerberos v5 for authentication."

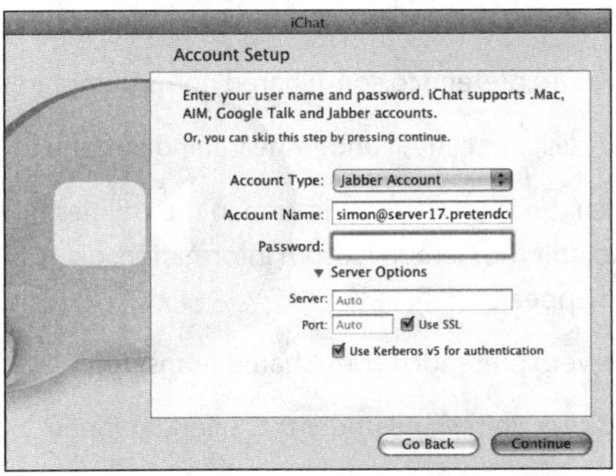


23 Click Continue to accept the account configuration.

24 At the Conclusion screen, click Done.

25 In Simon's empty Buddy List window, select View as Handle from the name pop-up menu.

Selecting View as Handle will help keep you from confusing users later in this exercise.

26 Open the Mail application and send a message to the developers group letting them know the iChat service is up and runnning.

27 Check your mail to ensure you received a copy.

28 Quit Mail.

29 Mount smb://server*n*.pretendco.com, and select the project lion share point.

30 Mount https://server*n*.pretendco.com/manual-1.3

31 Mount nfs://server*n*.pretendco.com/Shared Items/Templates

32 Open iCal, and click Refresh All under the Calendar menu.

33 Quit iCal, launch the Directory application in the Utilities folder, and attempt to edit the Garage A room information, dismissing the dialog that appears.

34 Mount nfs://server*n*.pretendco.com/Shared Items/Templates

35 Open iCal, and click Refresh All under the Calendar menu.

36 Quit iCal.

37 Open /System/Library/CoreServices/Kerberos to view your tickets.

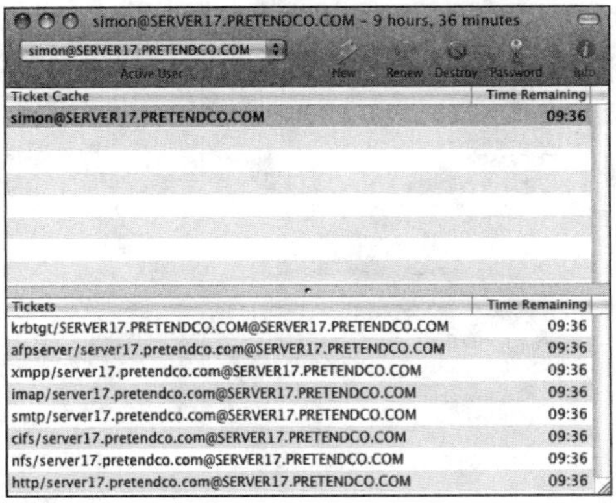


You can mount volumes, check and send mail, schedule events with iCal, and log into the iChat service, all without entering a password.

38 From the iChat menu, choose Preferences.

39 Click Accounts.

40 Click the plus button to begin configuring a new account.

41 Enter the following information:

- Account Type: `Jabber Account`
- Account Name: `andre@server`*`n`*`.pretendco.com`
- Password: `abcd1234`
- Server Options: Select Use SSL. Do *not* select "Use Kerberos v5 for authentication."

We cannot use Kerberos because iChat will not switch tickets on the fly. Therefore, even though you are logged in as simon, you effectively have two separate iChat accounts. You'll add two more accounts.

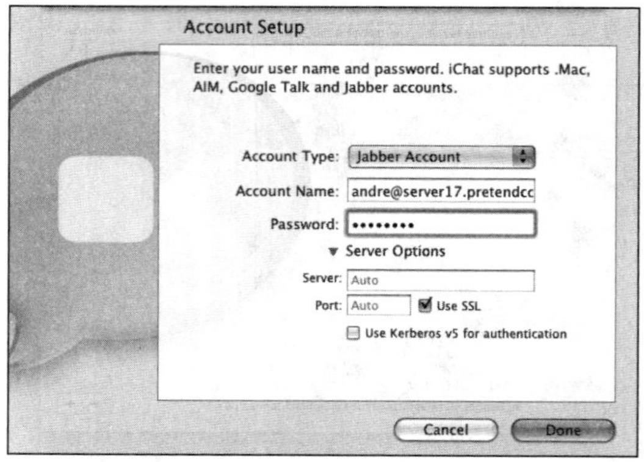


42 Click Done.

43 Configure Andre's Buddy List window to show his handle, like Simon's.

44 Repeat steps 36–38 for Schoun and David (passwords: changeme), remembering to select Use SSL.

45 Close the Accounts preferences window.

You should now have four different accounts, and you may want to arrange them in a similar way to help keep track of all four accounts.

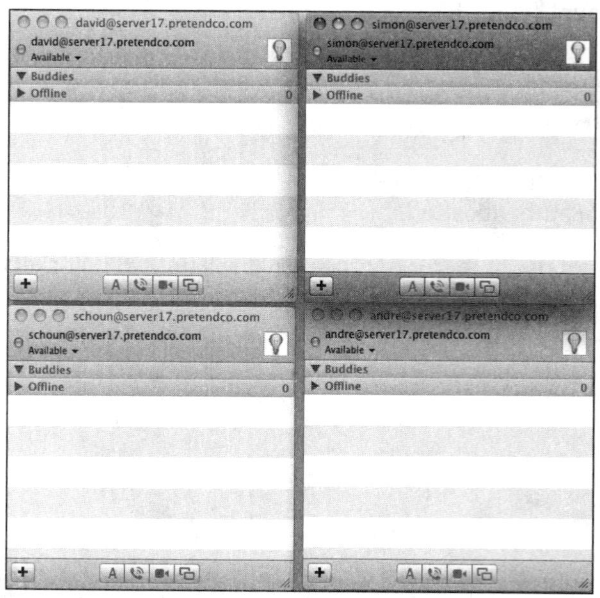

Exercise 8.3.2

# Add Jabber Buddies and Communicate

## Objective

Now that iChat is configured and connected, you will chat between the accounts to learn how to add Jabber buddies. This activity also creates some chat transcripts for later viewing.

## Summary

To send messages to another user, you must first add that user to your Buddy List. Adding a user as a buddy initiates an approval process, where the user you want to add is given the opportunity to allow or deny the buddy request. If the other user is not online, the buddy approval is presented to the user the next time they log in. You'll add buddies by sending them a message.

1 Select Simon's buddy list. Under the File menu, choose New Chat, and enter `andre@servern.pretendco.com` in the To field.

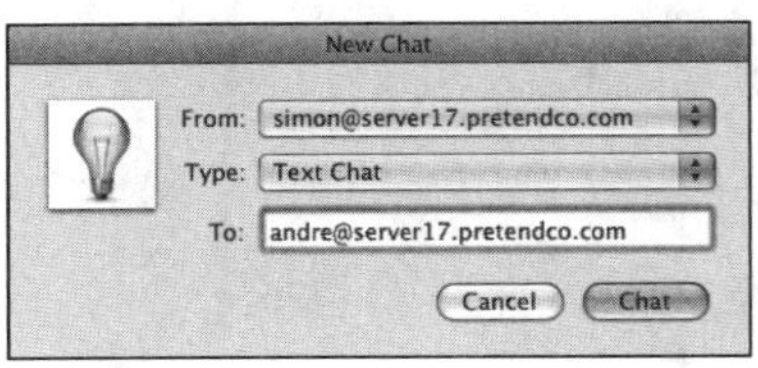


2 Click the Chat button, type some text and press Return.

3 Andre must now accept your chat by clicking in the window that appears, clicking the Display button, and then clicking the Accept button. (The Accept button appears after you click the Display button.)

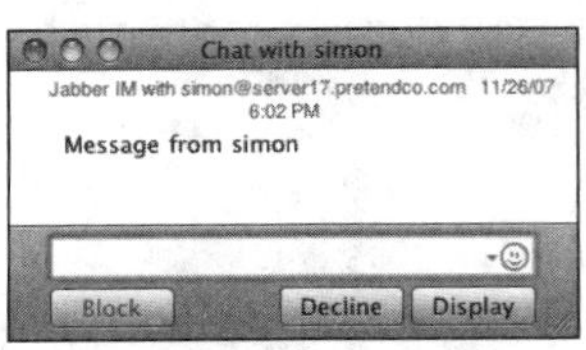

4 Click back in the window where Simon initiated the chat, and choose Add Buddy <andre@server*n*.pretendco.com> from the Buddies menu in the menu bar.

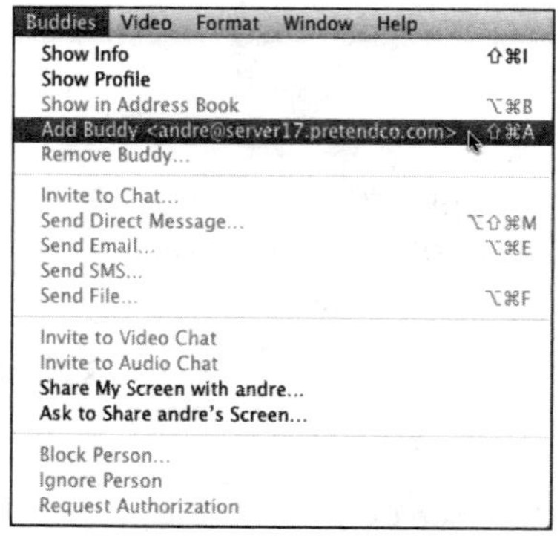


5 In the dialog that appears, click the disclosure triangle to show a small version of your Address book.

6 Click the blue Directories icon on the left.

7 In the Search field, start typing Andre's name and watch it appear in the list.

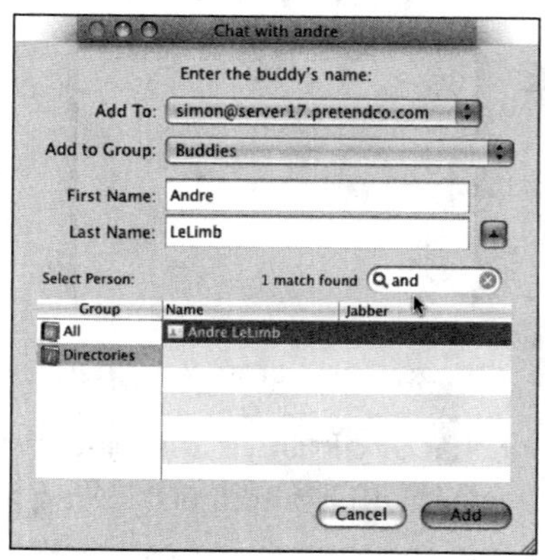


Because you are bound to your server, the Address book automatically searches the shared LDAP domain for users that may match what you are looking for.

8 Click Add.

A buddy authorization request is sent to Andre's account. Because you are also logged in as Andre, the Jabber Authorization window appears immediately.

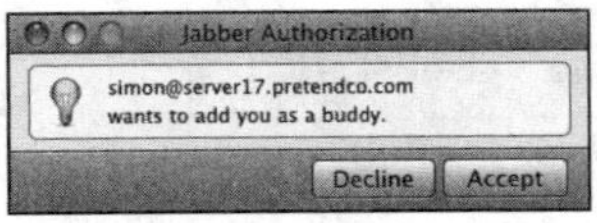


9 Click the Jabber Authorization window, then click Accept.

Adding a Jabber buddy also adds you to the other person's buddy list. Your two iChat buddy lists should now each have an entry for the other account.

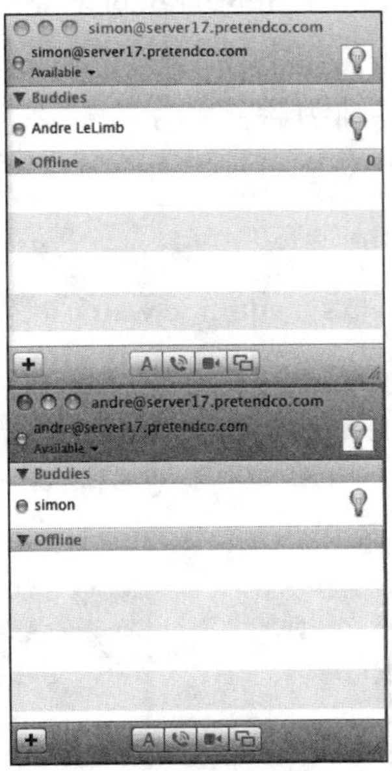

10 Take a few moments to send messages between the two accounts.

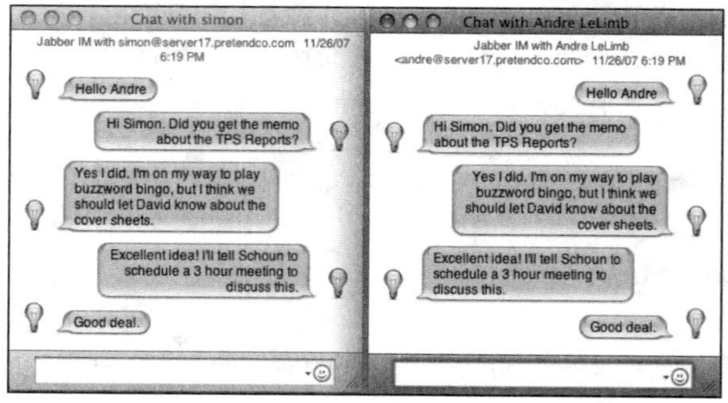


11 Close the two chat windows, and click back on Simon's buddy list.

12 Click the Add (+) button at the bottom of the window to add another buddy.

13 In the dialog that appears, click the disclosure triangle to show a small version of your Address book.

14 Click the blue Directories icon on the left.

15 In the Search field, start typing David's name, and watch it appear in the list.

16 Enter `david@servern.pretendco.com` in the Account Name field.

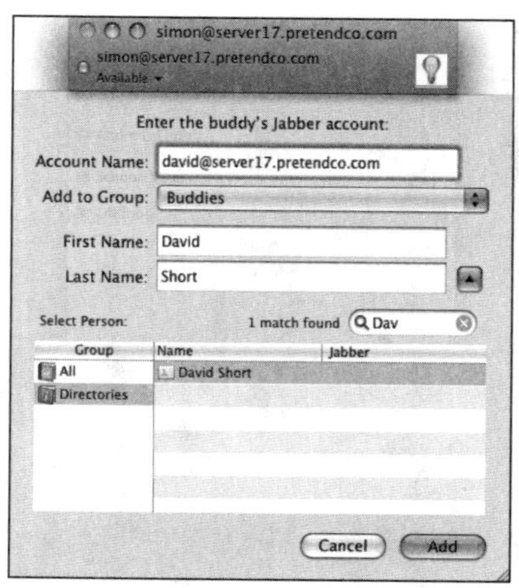


17 Click Add.

18 Accept the invitation.

19 Repeat the process to add schoun@server*n*.pretendco.com to Simon's Buddy List, accepting the invitation.

20 Repeat the process, adding all three people to the other three users' Buddy Lists by starting to type their names in the Account Name field. Notice when you do this, the names autofill, making the process much easier.

21 When you are finished, the Buddy List should appear as shown in the following figure.

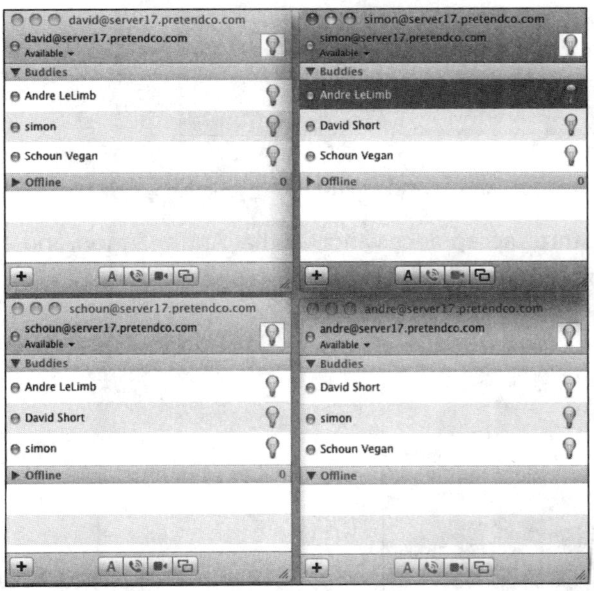


22 Select Schoun's Buddy List, and from the File menu, choose Go to Chat Room.

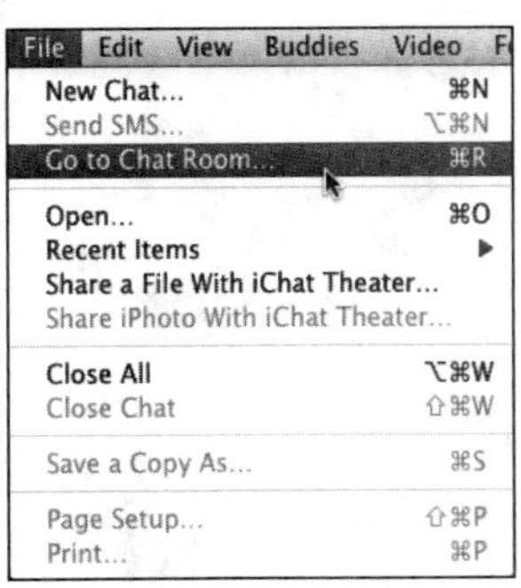

23 In the window that appears, select schoun@server*n*.pretendco.com from the list, enter Project Lion as the Chat Room name, and click the Go button.

24 In the window that appears, drag Andre from your Buddy List to the empty window to add Andre to this group chat.

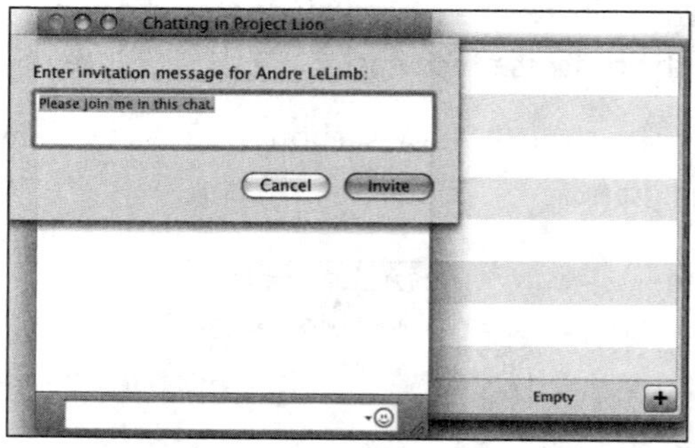


25 Repeat this for Simon and David.

26 View all three acceptance windows that Andre, Simon, and David must agree, to, and accept each one of them.

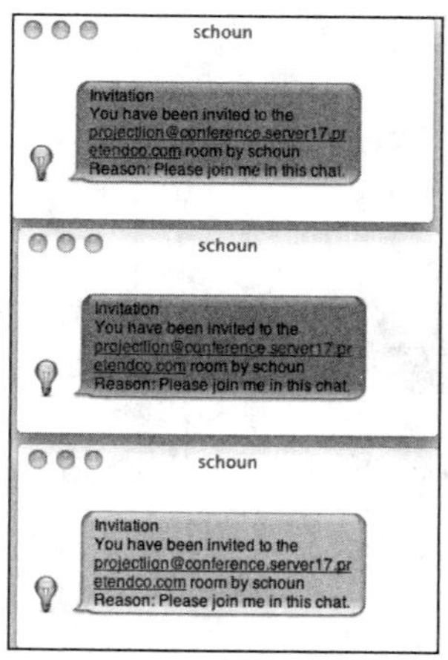

27 Back in the group chat window started by Schoun, enter some text as each participant, viewing the chat window.

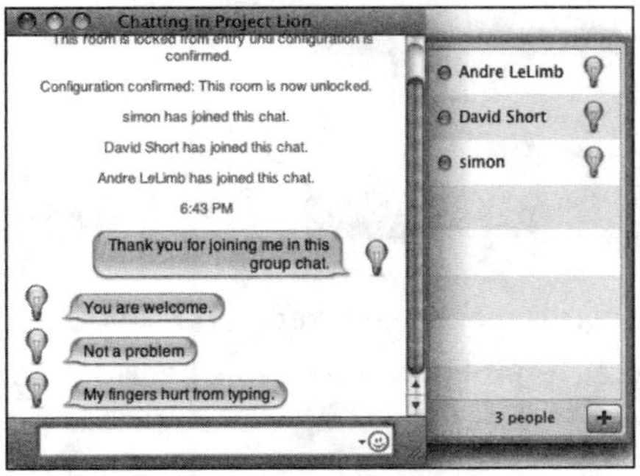


Because all users have the same icon and text color, it is difficult to tell who is who. This would not be the situation if each person had a separate account.

28 Close the group chat window, and close Schoun, Simon, and David's Buddy Lists.

29 Select Andre's Buddy List, and from the File menu, choose New Chat.

30 Start a text chat with diradmin@mainserver.pretendco.com.

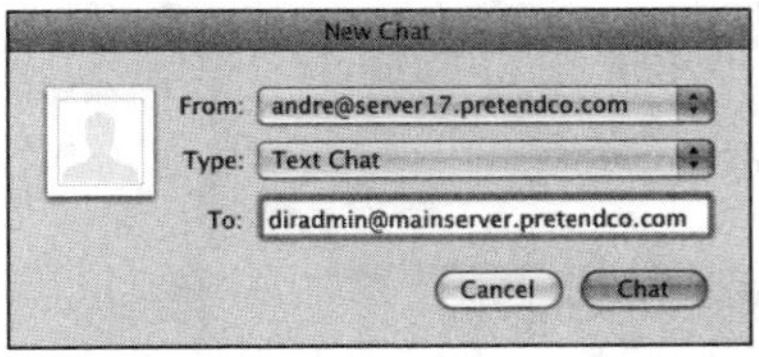


31 Add diradmin@mainserver.pretendco.com to your Buddy List:

- First Name: `Mac OS X`
- Last Name: `Instructor`

32 Wait for the instructor to accept your invitation.

You have an iChat service federation happening between your server and the instructor's server.

33 When asked to allow your screen to be shared by the instructor, click Accept.

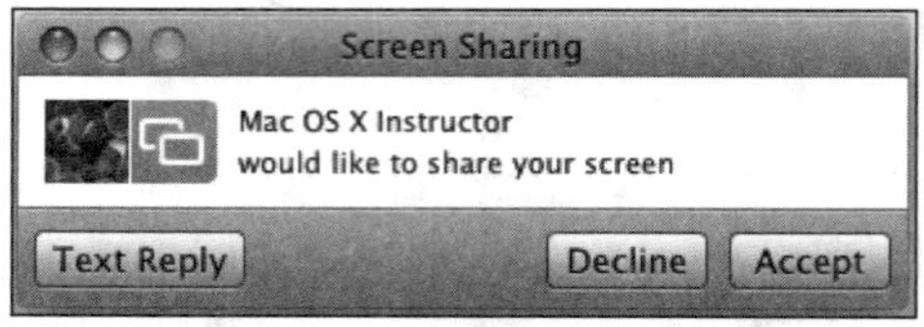


Your instructor is now controlling your screen and, if you have a microphone and speakers enabled, you can talk back and forth with your instructor.

34 Click the red double-screen icon in the menu bar, and choose End Screen Sharing.

35 Open TextEdit, create a file named Student*n*, (where n is your student number), and save it to your Desktop.

36 Select the Mac OS X Instructor in your Buddy List, and drag the Student*n* file on your Desktop over the instructor's name, to transfer the file to the instructor.

37 Click Send in the dialog that appears.

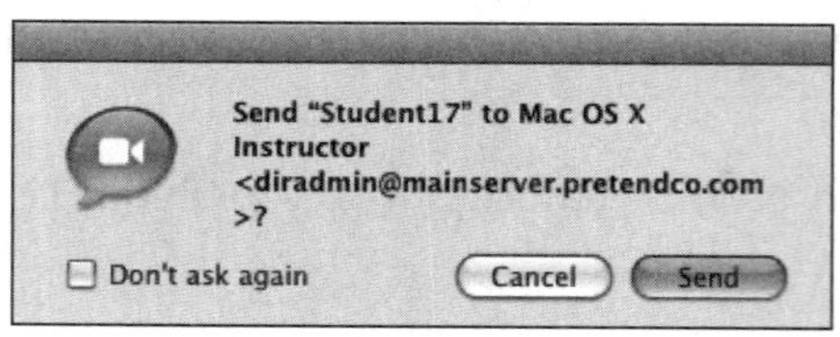


You can do peer-to-peer file sharing with iChat and the iChat service.

38 Quit iChat.

Exercise 8.3.3

# View Chat Logs

## Objective

Use Console to view the iChat logs.

## Summary

Add a share point, mount the share point, copy over a file, and look at the contents of that file. The iChat user logs are an important tool in the management of Mac OS X Server and chat services. Because you configured the iChat service to log all chat messages, the previous conversations are now stored on the server. To open the log file, you'll need to change the permissions on it to grant read access.

1 While still logged in as simon, launch Server Admin, and connect to your server as ladmin (password: apple).

2 Select your server in the list on the left, and click the File Sharing icon in the toolbar.

3 Click the Volumes and Browse buttons, and navigate to and select /Users/Shared.

4 Share this folder.

5 Select the jabberd_user_messages.log inside the Shared folder and set the permissions on the file as follows:

   - Owner: _jabber Permissions: Read & Write
   - Group: developers Permissions: Read & Write
   - Others: Permissions Read & Write

   In this case, you want to see the contents of the file, so you are giving wide access to everyone. Normally you would not want to give such free access to this particular file.

6 Save the changes, and quit Server Admin.

7 Mount the server's Shared folder on your Desktop, and double-click the jabberd_user_messages.log file to open it with Console.

8 Use the String Matching search field to look for anything you typed while chatting.

The Jabber log is a consolidation of all chat messages sent through the iChat service. Each line contains the full Jabber ID of both the sender and the receiver. Also note the "client*n*" portion of each Jabber ID. This information is the Location attribute, which is configurable in iChat Account preferences, under Server Settings. Because Jabber allows multiple, simultaneous logins with the same account, Location can be used to uniquely identify different chat sessions that are using the same account. By default, iChat sets Location based on the host name of the computer that is running iChat, but it can be manually set to any other value.

9 Quit any open applications.

10 Log out as simon, and log in as cadmin.

**Question 5** *Using the message log, how can you identify a message that begins a new conversation?*

***Question 6*** *There are log entries that contain no message body. Why are these log entries present? (Hint: Leave the log open in Console while you chat).*

## Chapter Summary

| | | |
|---|---|---|
| **Wiki Services** | Server Admin | Workgroup Manager |
| **Calendering Services** | Server Admin | Workgroup Manager |
| **Messaging Services** | Server Admin | iChat |

Apple
Certified

# 9

# Deployment Solutions

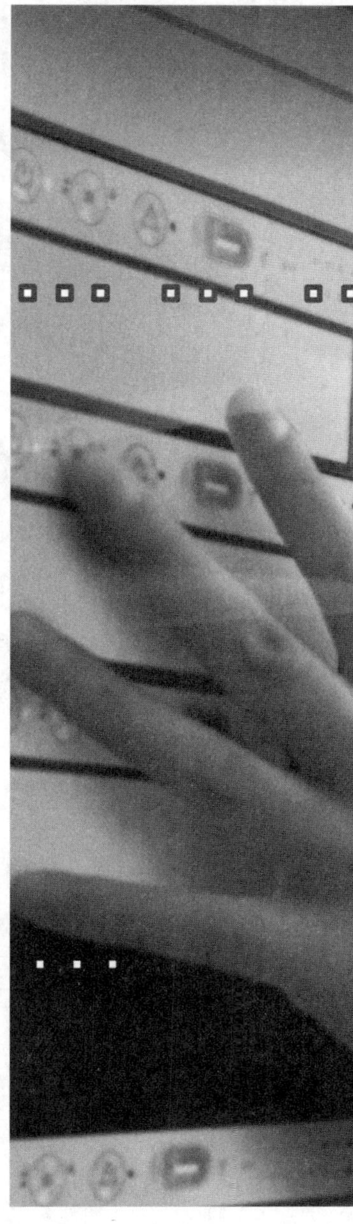


## 9.1 Configuration

**Exercise 9.1.1** Configure NetBoot Services

## 9.2 Imaging

**Exercise 9.2.1** Create a NetBoot Image

## 9.3 Deployment

**Exercise 9.3.1** NetBoot a Mac OS X Computer

# 9.1 Configuration

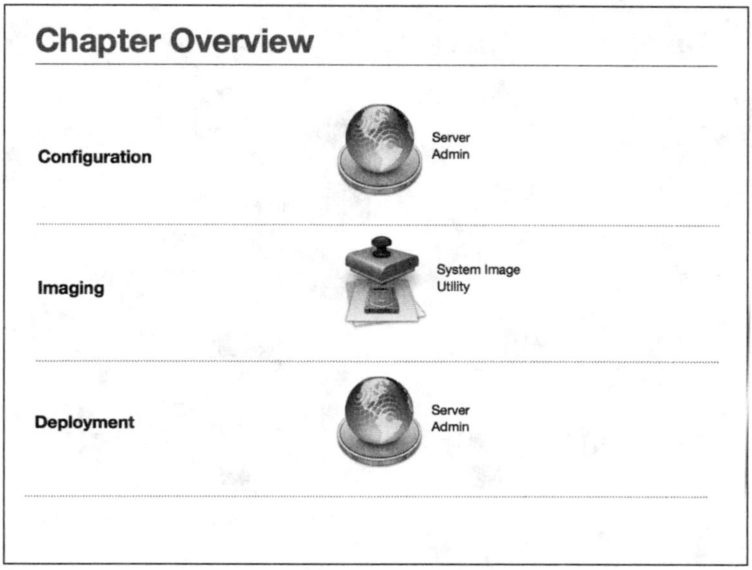


Imaging and deployment go hand in hand when managing more than a handful of computers. Although it is not platform specific like deployment, image management is a crucial part of system maintenance and management.

**Lesson 9.1**

Configuration

In this lesson you'll learn why it is advantageous to use NetBoot, how to initially implement it, and the criteria involved in making it work.

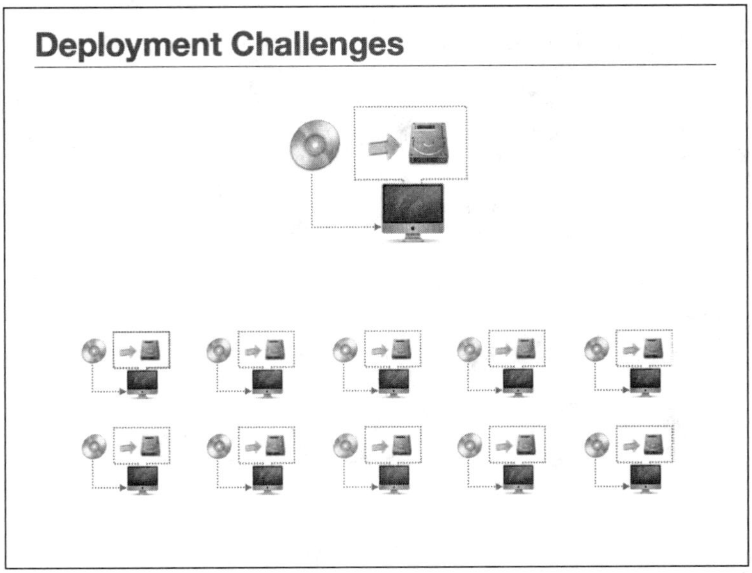


Managing one Macintosh is different than managing 100 or 1000. Installing the operating system, managing updates, and troubleshooting are all challenges faced by administrators of large networks.

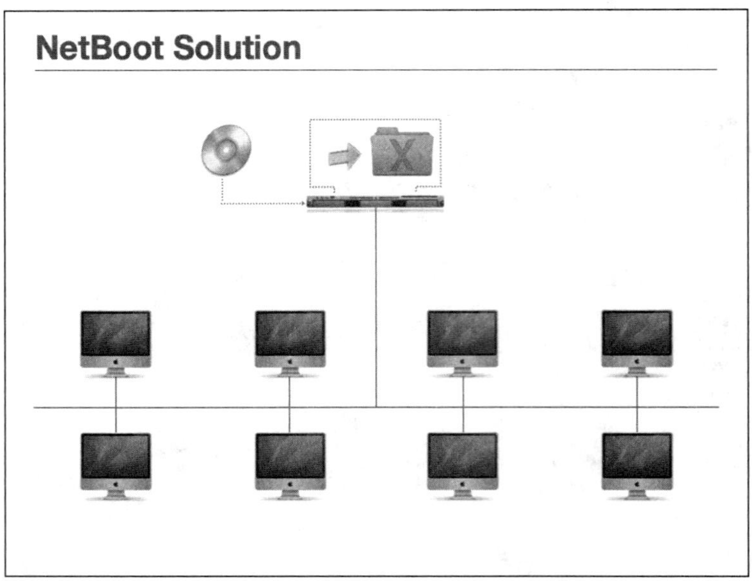


NetBoot solves the problem of individual deployment on many computers by allowing one image to boot several Apple computers.

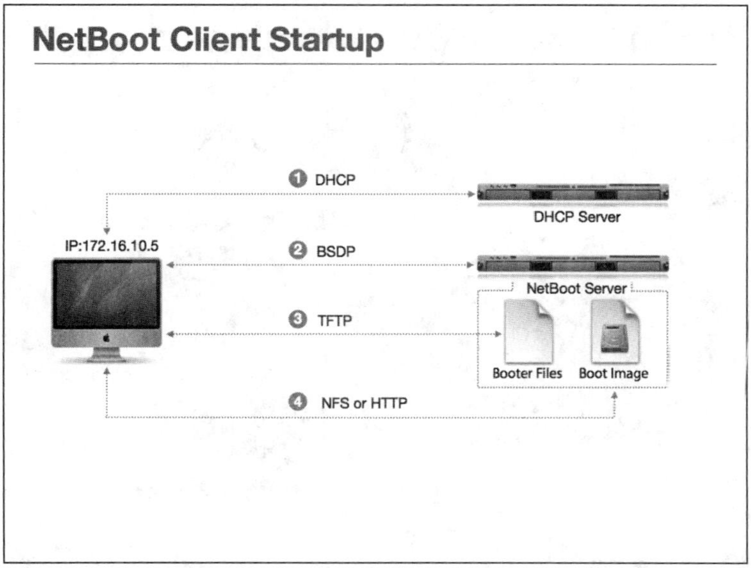


NetBoot clients start up and look for a DHCP server, obtain an address, locate the NetBoot server, and then boot off of a small boot file, transferred to the Apple computer via Trivial FTP (TFTP). The NetBoot image is then implemented over NFS or HTTP, whichever is chosen.

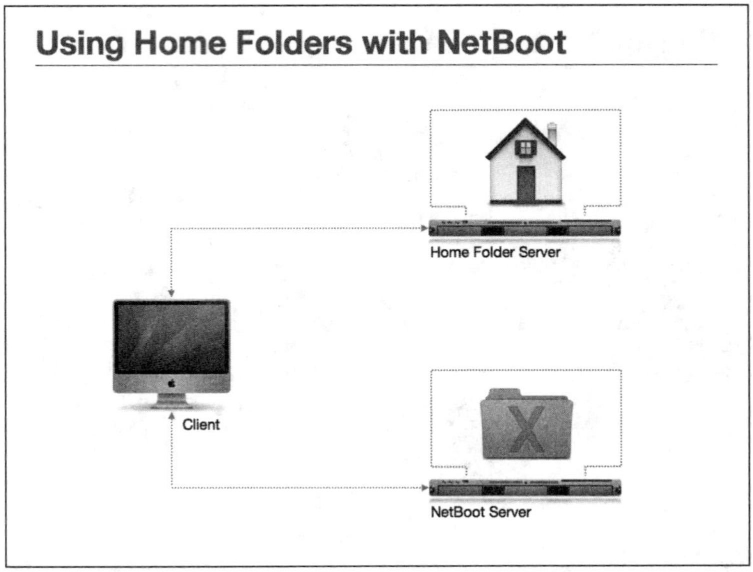


A possible scenario is to have user home folders on one Mac OS X Server and have another Mac OS X Server be the NetBoot server. It is essentially transparent to the user that they are using a network home folder and a NetBoot image.

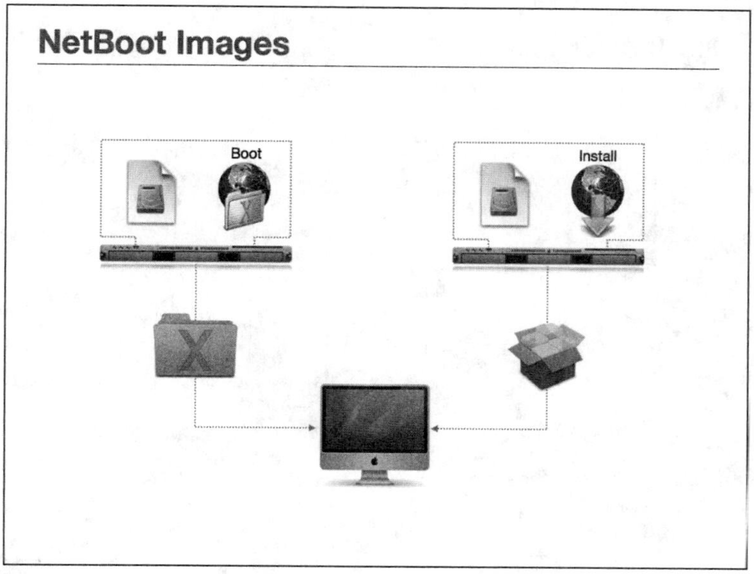


NetBoot boots the computer and provides a full Mac OS X environment. NetInstall, on the other hand, boots the computer into a limited Mac OS X environment which runs the installer, and is designed for installing packages, or an entire operating system, or both.

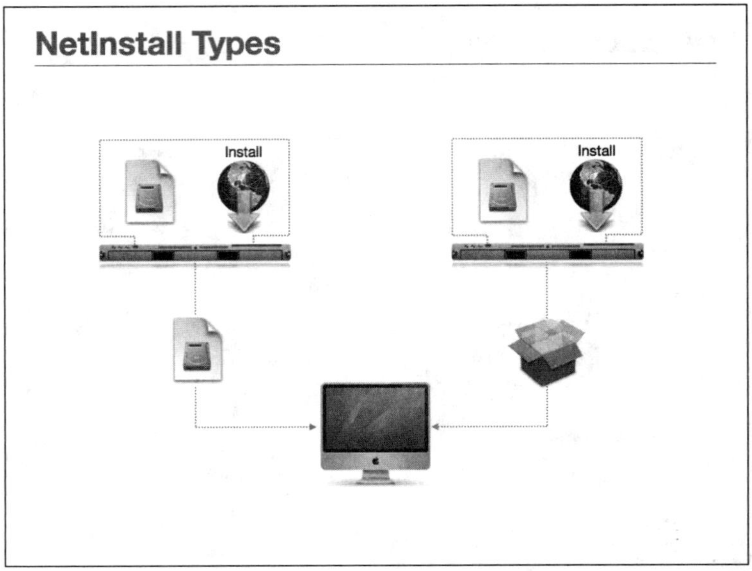


When using NetInstall, an administrator can install an entire operating system, or they can install packages that deliver files or applications. A third option is to have a package delivered that does not install a payload, but only runs some scripts, perhaps for maintenance purposes.

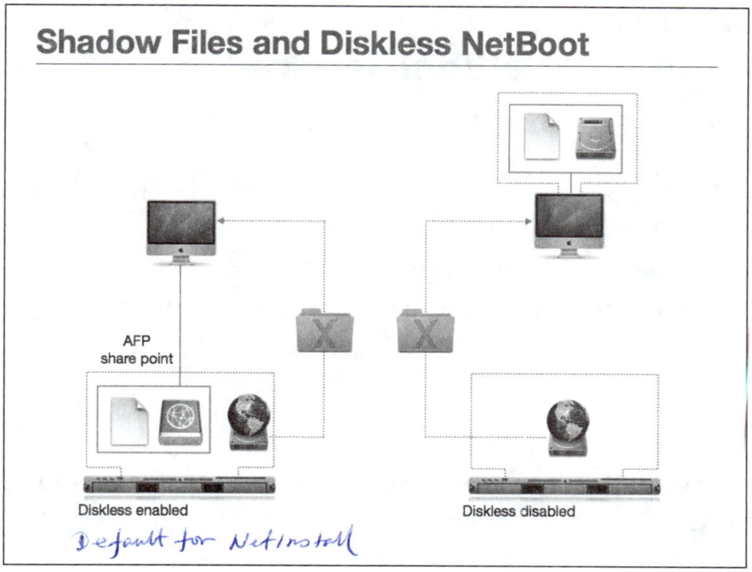


Users running an Apple computer off a NetBoot image are probably running applications and those applications need temporary space to hold files in progress. A good example of this is Safari and its cache files. Choosing diskless permits those temporary files to be stored on the server, as if the Apple computer had no hard drive at all. Not running diskless stores the temporary, or shadow files, on the local volume.

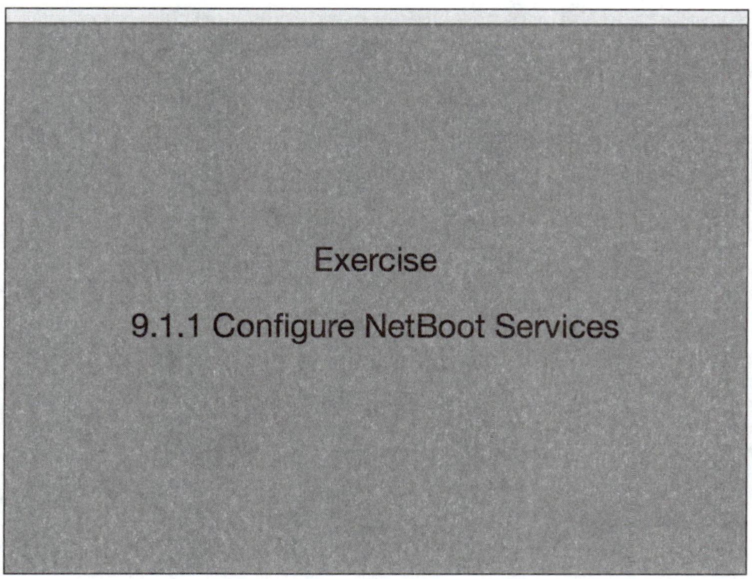

## Exercise 9.1.1

# Configure NetBoot Services

## Objective

Choose where to host the images and check your Mac OS X computer's permissions. Use that image as your Master to create a NetBoot image.

## Summary

Understanding why administrators need NetBoot is sometimes obvious. Saving time, saving resources, and reducing troubleshooting are all good reasons to institute a NetBoot server in your organization. Before you can create images and push them out to computers, you must choose the volumes on which you want these images to reside and then enable the NetBoot service. This process creates a standard folder structure on any volumes used to host images.

1. Ensure you are logged in as cadmin on your Mac OS X computer.
2. Using Server Admin, from the Server menu select Add Service.
3. Select the NetBoot and DHCP checkboxes, and click Save.
4. Select the newly added NetBoot service under your server's entry.
5. Click the Settings icon in the toolbar.
6. Click the General tab, and select the Ethernet checkbox to turn on NetBoot for your server's Ethernet port.

7 Select the Images and Client Data checkboxes for the startup volume of your server.

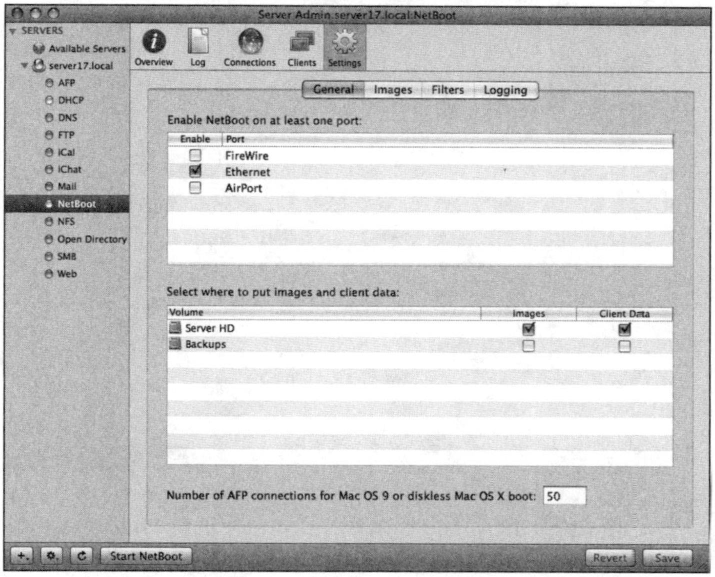


8 Click the Save button.

You don't need to start NetBoot services at this time.

9 Select the DHCP service from the list, click the Subnets icon in the toolbar, select the default configuration in the list, and delete it by clicking the Minus (-)button.

10 Click Save.

11 Click the Add (+) button to create a new DHCP configuration, and enable it.

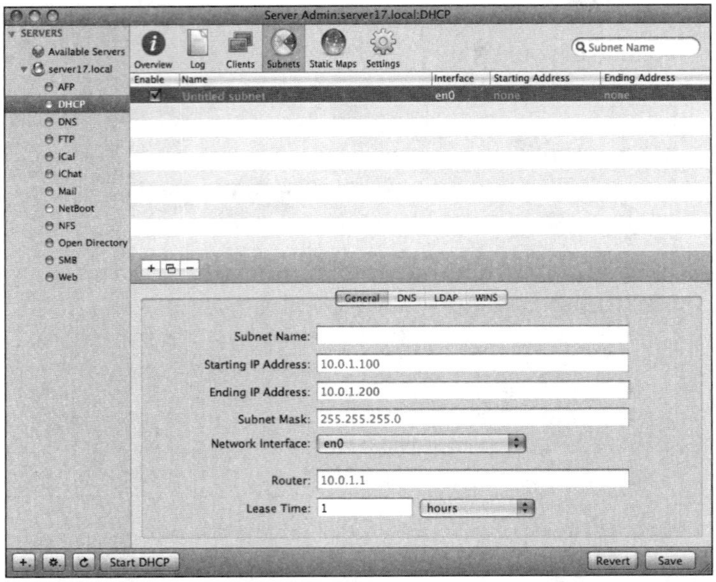


12 Ensure the General tab is selected, and edit the information as follows:

- Subnet Name: `Student`*n*`-LAN` (where *n* is your student number).
- Starting IP address: `10.1.`*n*`.2`
- Ending IP address: `10.1.`*n*`.2`
- Subnet Mask: `255.255.0.0`
- Network Interface: `en0`
- Router: `10.1.0.1`
- Lease Time: `2 days`

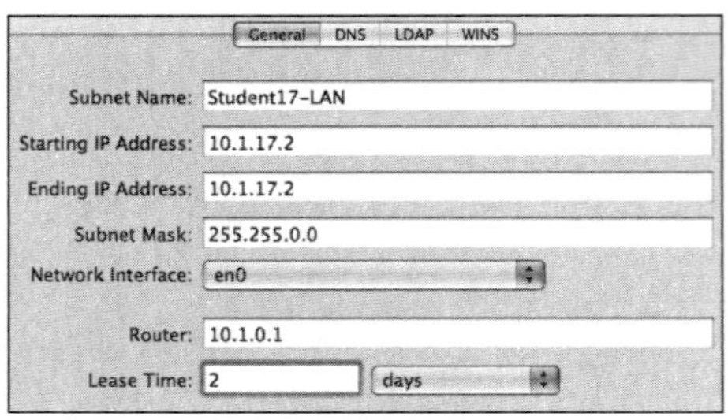

> **Warning!** You are going to be giving out the same address you statically have now. This is not a problem, because you cannot have both a static address and be accepting an address from a DHCP server at the same time at this point in the class.

13 Select the DNS tab, and edit the information as follows:DNS Servers: `10.1.0.1`

- Default Search Domain: `pretendco.com`

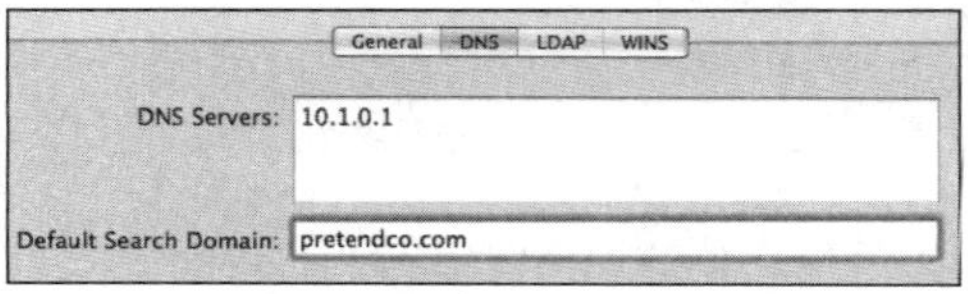


14 Select the LDAP tab, and edit the information as follows:

- Server Name: `server`*`n`*`.pretendco.com` (where *n* is your student number)
- Search Base: `dc=server`*`n`*`,dc=pretendco,dc=com` (where *n* is your student number)

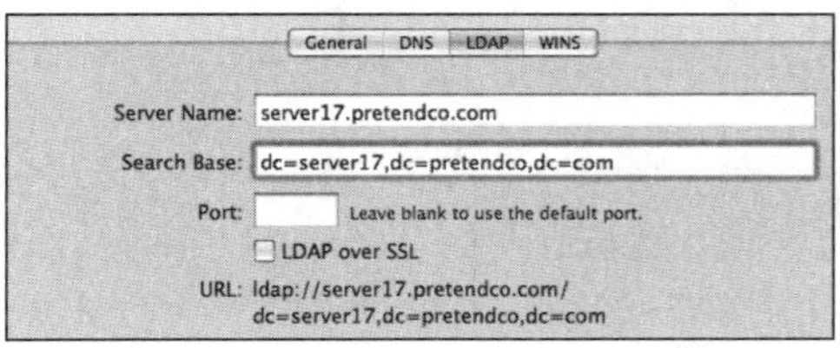


15 Click Save.

16 You've just told your DHCP server to send all this information to whatever computer receives an address from your DHCP server. Now, you must ensure your Mac OS X computer is the only computer to get an address from your DHCP server.

17 Click the Static Maps icon in the toolbar, and click the Add Computer button at the bottom of the window.

18 Leave this window open, open Network Utility inside /Applications/Utilities/, and ensure the Info tab is selected and en0 is chosen from the Network Interface pop-up menu.

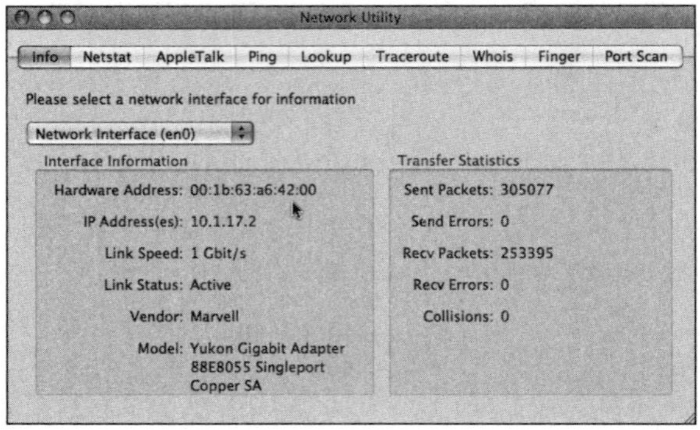


19 Carefully copy the 12-digit Hardware Address you see.

You can drag your cursor across the address and then press Command-C to copy it to your clipboard.

20 Enter `clientn` in the Computer Name field of the Static Map dialog.

21 Double-click in the MAC Address field, paste in the Hardware Address that you copied from Network Utility, enter 10.1.*n*.2 in the IP address field, and click OK.

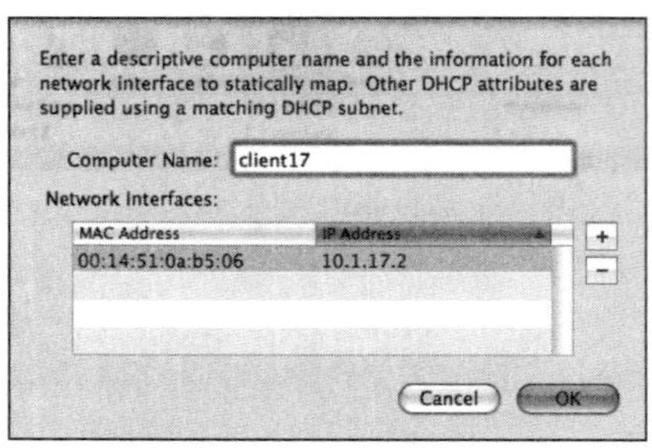


22 Save the changes, and start the DCHP service.

This ensures you are only going to give an address to your Mac OS X computer and not to other students' computers.

23 Under the Apple menu, choose Automatic from your Location menu.

This changes your network settings back to DHCP.

24 Wait about 30 seconds, and open the Terminal application. Enter

```
ipconfig getpacket en0
```

and press Return.

If you get no result, press the Up Arrow key on your keyboard, and press Return again to re-enter the command.

25 If the information returned does not look like it came from your server, notify the instructor before continuing.

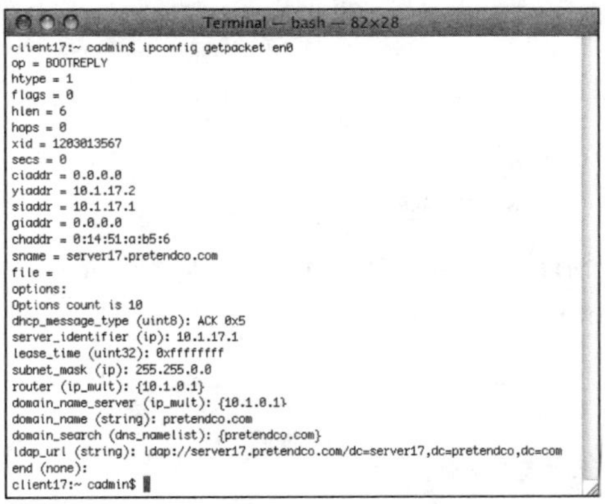


26 Quit Network Utility, Terminal, and Server Admin.

## Prepare the Client Model Machine

Your Mac OS X computer, which is already bound to your Mac OS X Server running as an Open Directory Master, will be used as the source 'model' for your NetBoot image creation. However you need to make a few adjustments, since you have been running with a static IP address so far during this course.

1 Open your Directory Utility located in /Applications/Utilities. Authentication as cadmin using the lock in the lower-left corner.

2 Click the Show Advanced Settings button to view the toolbar if necessary.

3 Click the Directory Servers icon in the toolbar.

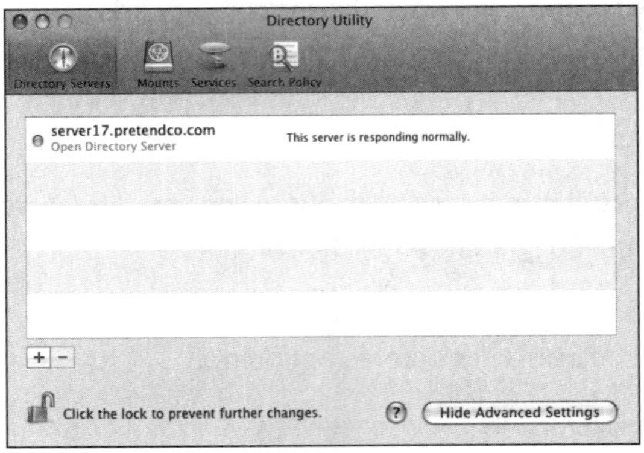


4 Select the server from the list, and click the Minus (–)button to delete the server from the list. Authenticate as diradmin (password: diradmin) if necessary.

5 Click the Services icon in the toolbar, and double-click the LDAPv3 letters to bring up the editing dialog.

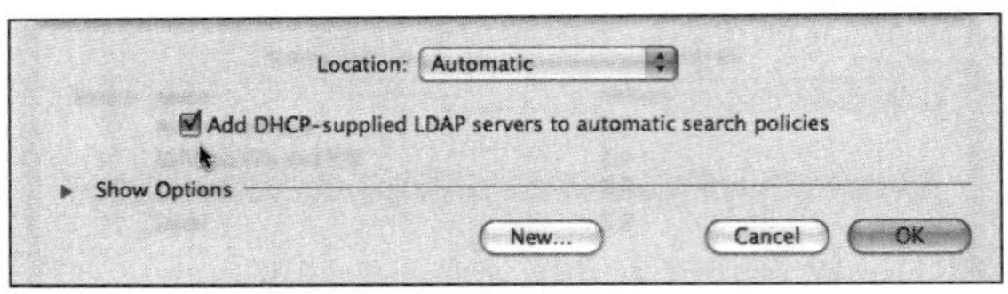


6 Ensure the Location is Automatic.

7 If not already selected, select "Add DHCP-supplied LDAP servers to automatic search policies," and click OK.

8 Click the Search Policy icon in the toolbar, and select the Authentication tab.

9 Choose Automatic from the Search pop-up menu.

10 Click the Contacts tab, and choose Automatic from the Search pop-up menu.

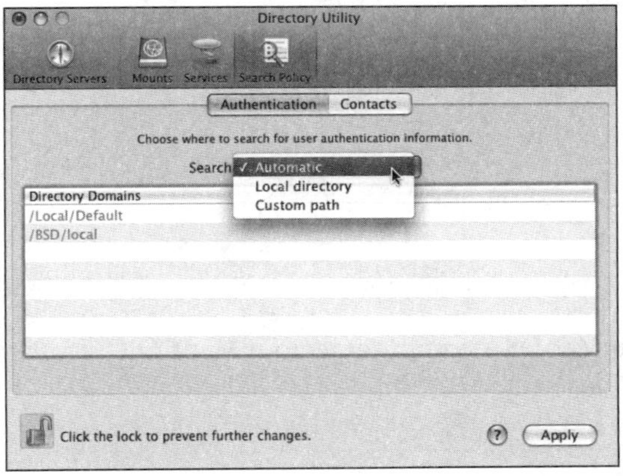


11 Click Apply, and quit Directory Utility.

You've told Directory Utility to look for directory information when you receive a DHCP address from your server.

12 Open /Applications/Utilities/Disk Utility, and run Repair Disk Permissions on your Mac OS X computer's volume.

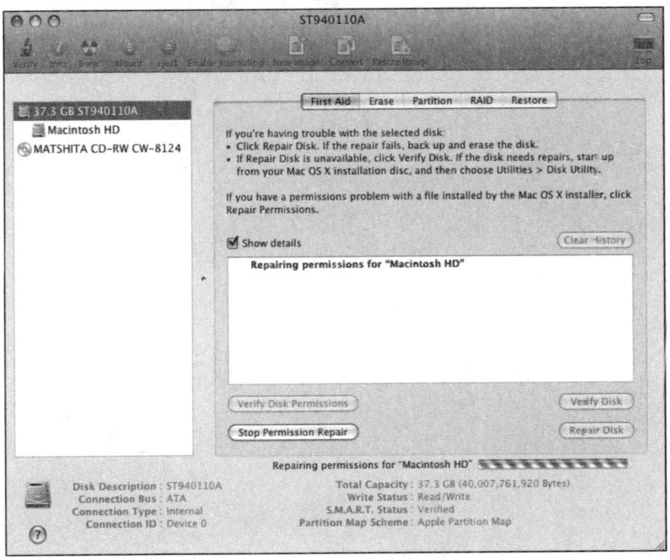

13 Open System Preferences, and from the Startup Disk preference pane, click the Target Disk Mode button. Click the Restart button in the dialog that appears (authenticate as cadmin if necessary).

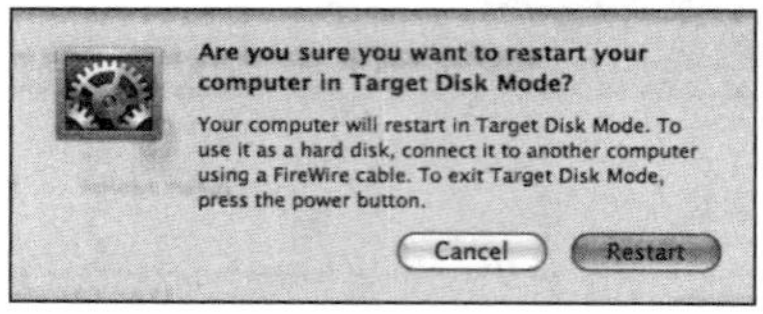


Your Mac OS X computer will now restart in target disk mode.

14 Connect your Mac OS X computer to your Mac OS X Server with a FireWire cable.

> **Note** FireWire cables are available from your instructor.

Your Mac OS X computer is now ready to be imaged.

15 Log in to your Mac OS X Server as ladmin, and click Cancel at the Time Machine dialog box.

You do not want to use your Mac OS X computer's hard drive as a Time Machine repository.

# Imaging

# 9.2

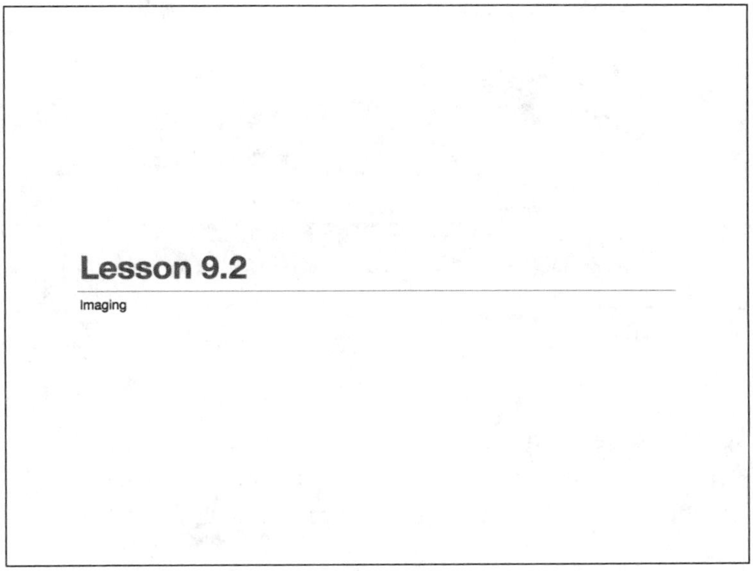


In this lesson, you'll learn how to create images and save them for later use.

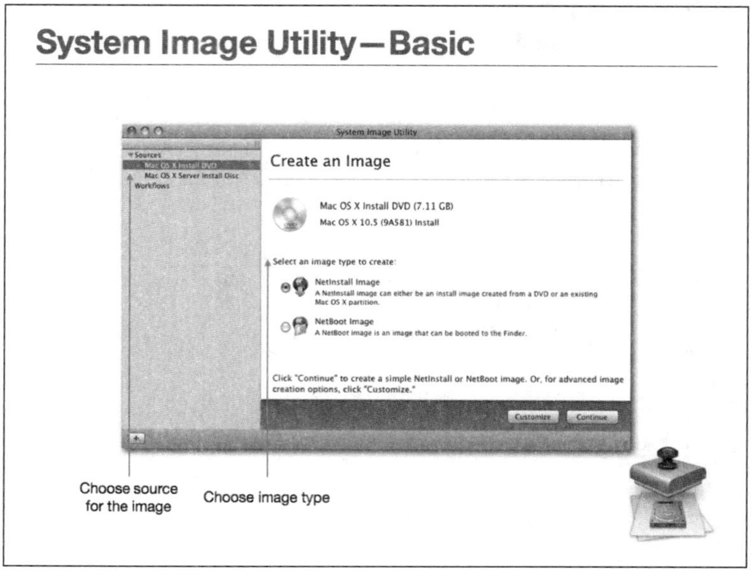


System Image Utility is the tool used to create both NetBoot and NetInstall images. When first launched, it attempts to locate a volume, disk, or DVD from which an image will be created.

## System Image Utility—Basic

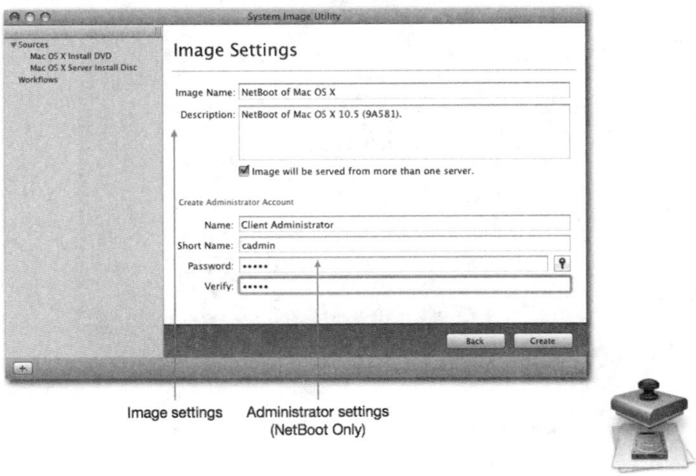


Customizing a NetBoot image permits creation of an administrator account, allowing you to choose the name, short name, and password for the new account.

## NetBoot Image Location

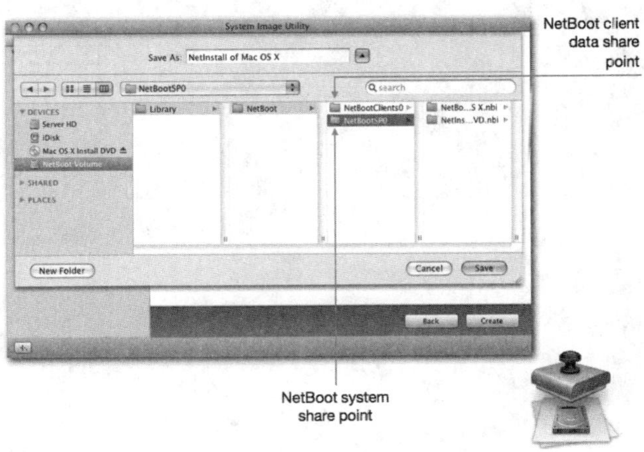


Images can be stored on any volume the NetBoot service can locate. Usually, they are stored in /Library/NetBoot/ on any volume.

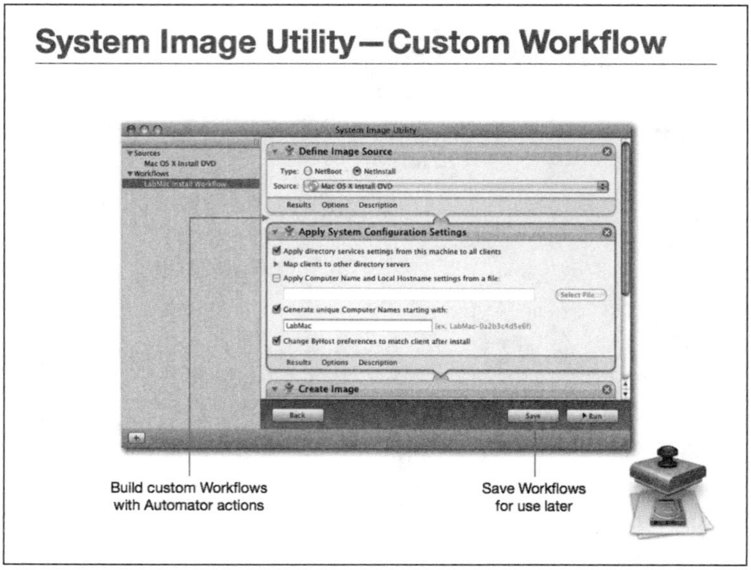


System Image Utility has a plethora of options and can be used to create a variety of customized workflows, enabling the administrator to automate the process, thus saving time, resources, and money.

Exercise

9.2.1 Create a NetBoot Image

Exercise 9.2.1

# Create a NetBoot Image

## Objective

Use System Image Utility to create an initial image, often called the Master image or Alpha image, that all other computers can use.

## Summary

You should note the amount of time it takes to create a NetBoot image so you have a good idea of how long the process might take if the image contained more software. Keeping the size of the initial image low and allowing users to locate software on NFS-mounted volumes or creating additional install packages is an efficient way of keeping NetBoot images relatively small.

## Create a NetBoot-Ready Disk Image with System Image Utility

System Image Utility is the primary tool for creating images to be delivered by NetBoot services.

1 On your Mac OS X Server, open System Image Utility (in /Applications/Server or from the Dock).

   The first time System Image Utility runs, you have the option of viewing What's New (4 pages).

   For now, close the What's New window.

By default, a new NetBoot image will be created from the hard drive connected in target disk mode.

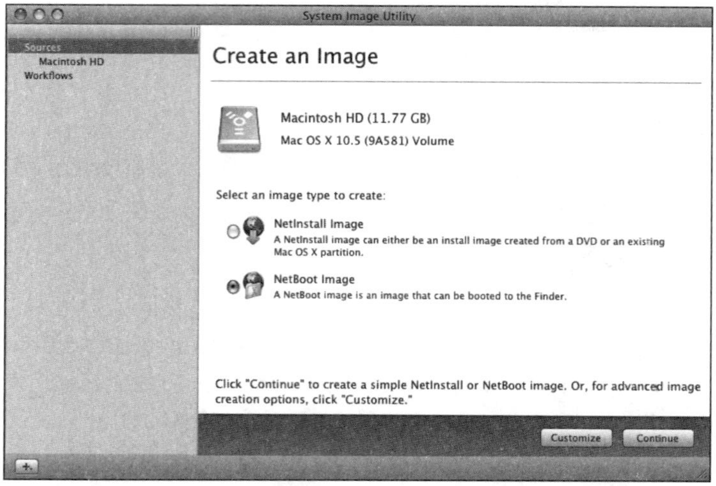


2 Click Continue.

3 Enter the following values (where *n* is your student number):

- Image Name: `MasterNB`*n*
- Description: `NetBoot of Mac OS X 10.5 - client` *n*.

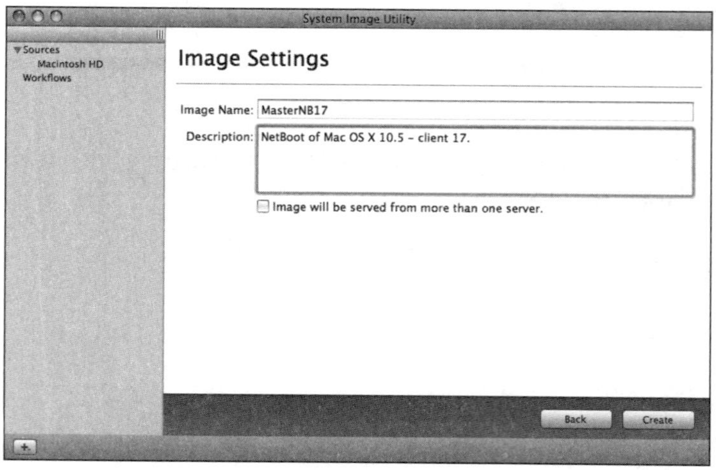

4 Click the Create button.

5 Click the Agree button when prompted to agree to Apple's licensing terms governing the use of System Image Utility.

6 In the Save As dialog, select /Library/NetBoot/NetBootSP0/ as the location for saving this image.

7 Click Save.

8 Authenticate when prompted.

Image creation will proceed through four stages. You'll be prompted to authenticate one last time before completion.

The process to create an image could take from 20 minutes to over an hour depending on the hardware used and size of the image being created.

9 Once the image creation process is complete, authenticate once more to finish.

10 Click Done, and quit System Image Utility.

11 Eject the Mac OS X computer's Macintosh HD from the Server, hold the Power button down on the Mac OS X computer to shut it off, and disconnect the FireWire cable.

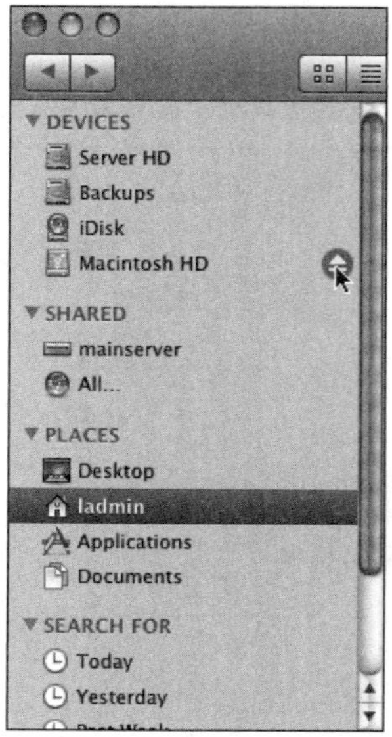


12 Do *not* start your Mac OS X computer yet.

# Deployment

# 9.3

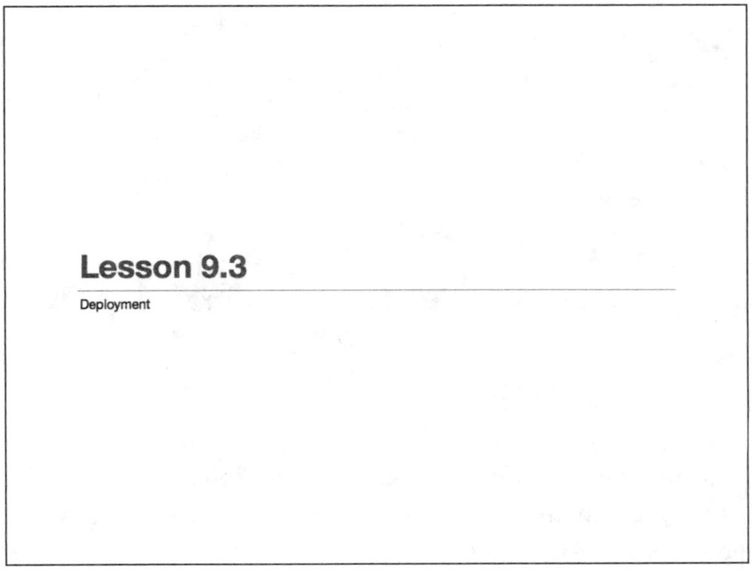


In this lesson, you'll learn how to use Mac OS X Server to deploy software to multiple Macintosh computers.

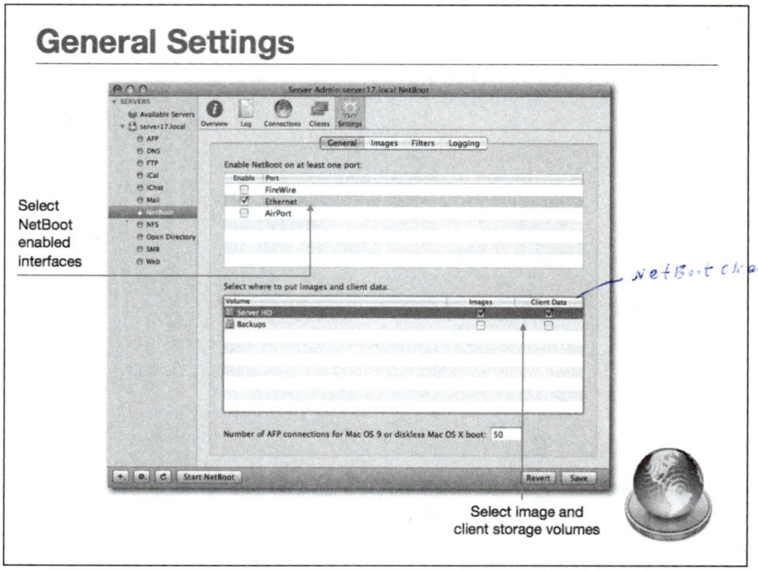


Using the General settings of NetBoot, you can choose which network interfaces you want NetBoot to use. You can also specify where you want the NetBoot service to search for client data and potentially save the NetBoot and NetInstall images.

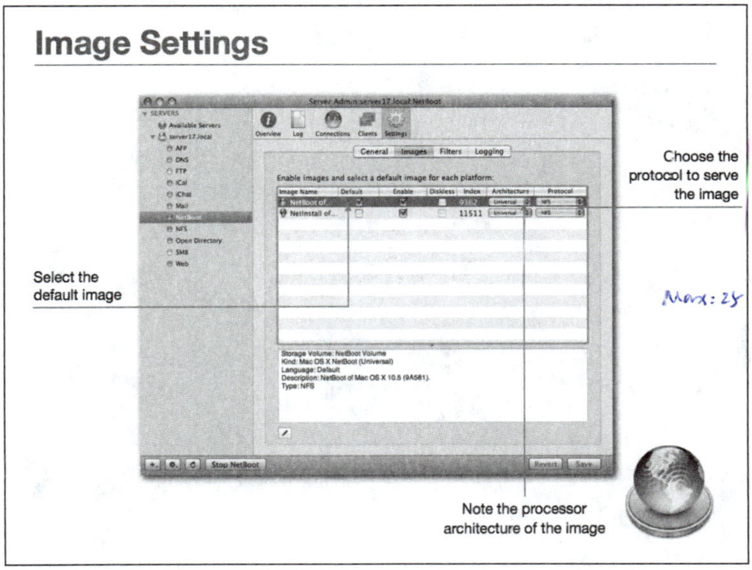


The Images tab allows the administrator to see all available NetBoot and NetInstall images. This pane allows them to enable each image and select one image as the default image for that particular architecture. Administrators also have a choice of serving up the images via NFS or HTTP.

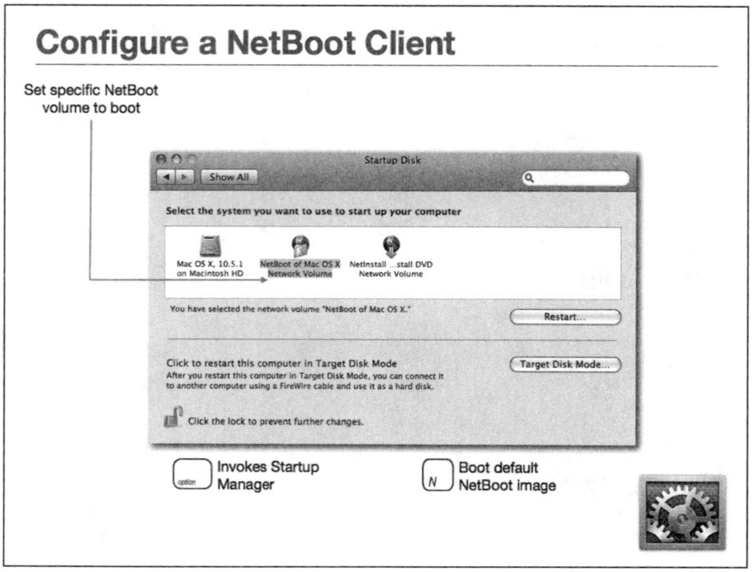


To boot an Apple computer from a NetBoot/NetInstall image, you can either hold down the Option key at boot to invoke the Startup Manager, hold down the N key to boot off the default NetBoot image for that computer's architecture, or change the Startup volume with the Startup Disk preference pane of System Preferences.

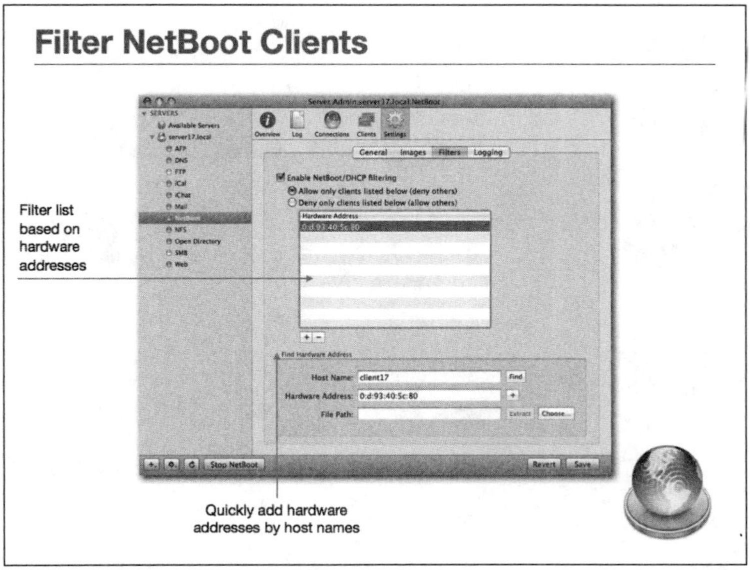


You may want to prevent other computers on your network from accidentally or intentionally using NetBoot/NetInstall. You can set filters to only allow or deny specific computers to use the NetBoot service. These filters are based on the MAC address of the computers.

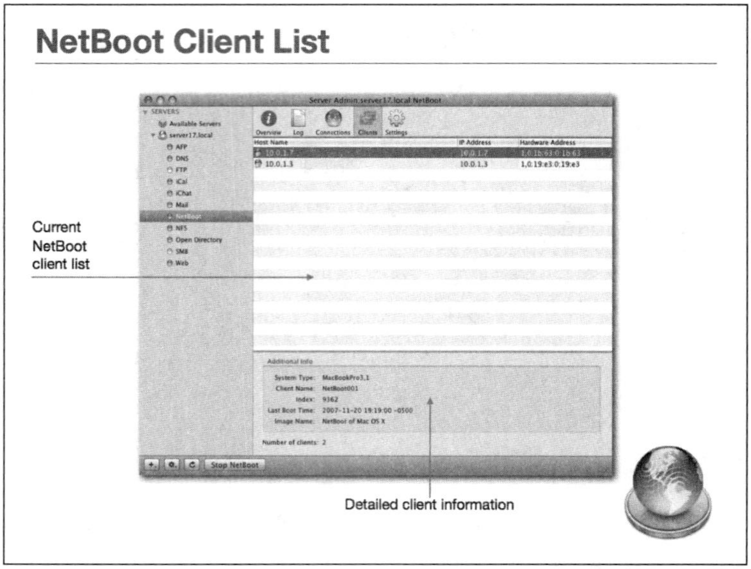


Once NetBoot is running, you can view all NetBoot/NetInstall clients by clicking the Clients icon in the toolbar of the NetBoot service in Server Admin.

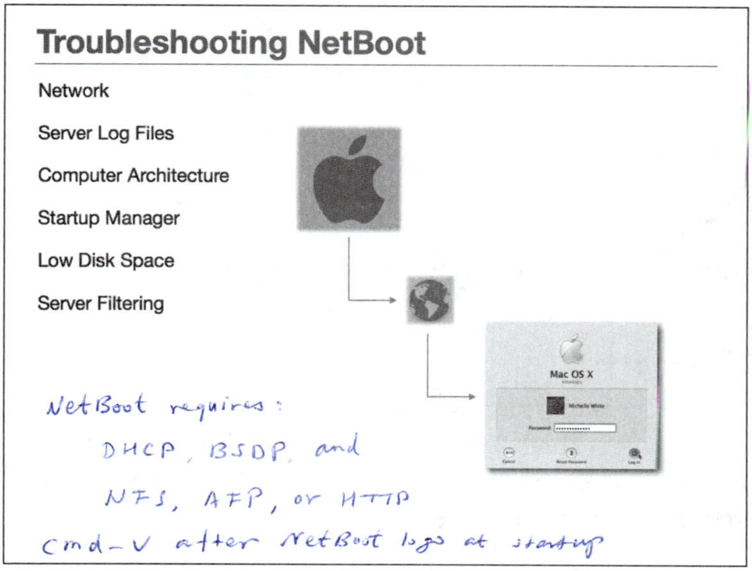


Troubleshooting NetBoot should start with the network, DHCP, firewall, and routing issues. From there, administrators can scour the log files, and ensure the computer used to create the image is of the same architecture of those who are attempting to boot from the image. Other items to check are possible misconfigured NetBoot filtering and possible low disk space on the client.

## Exercise 9.3.1
# NetBoot a Mac OS X Computer

## Objective

Boot your Mac OS X computer from the image you created.

## Summary

Once images are made, they can be deployed. In environments where there are both Intel and PowerPC Macs, there may need to be more than one image created, depending on the version of Mac OS X that is being deployed.

You could take the image you've created in this class and boot any other student's computer with it. However, you may not be able to boot older or new machines with this particular image, due to possible hardware changes or new software requirements.

## Start NetBoot Services

Now that you have configured the general NetBoot settings and created a NetBoot image, you'll enable the image and start the NetBoot service.

1. On your server, open Server Admin, and return to the NetBoot service.
2. Click the Settings icon in the toolbar, and then click the Images tab.
3. Enable MasterNB*n*, and set it as the Default image by selecting the appropriate checkboxes.

   If you wanted shadow files to be stored on the server share point (NetBootClientSP0) instead of the Mac OS X computer's local hard drive, you would also enable Diskless. For now, and for performance reasons, leave this option deselected.

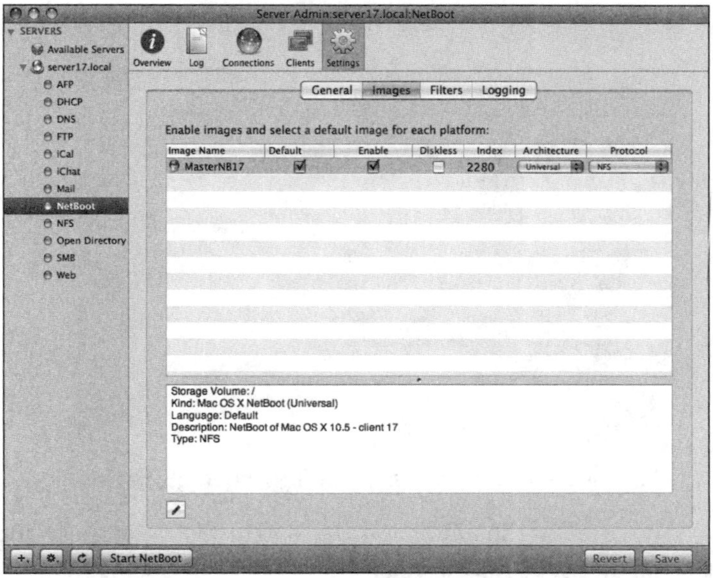


Your new NetBoot image appears in the list of available NetBoot images.

4 Click Save.

5 Click the Start NetBoot button to start the service.

## Start Up Workstations from a NetBoot Image

Once the NetBoot service is running and an image is selected, use System Preferences on your Mac OS X computer to select the served image as the startup volume.

1 Restart your Mac OS X computer, log in as cadmin, and open System Preferences.

   You could have held down the N key on the keyboard; but then you would not have been assured of getting your image, because all students are running the NetBoot service, and you have not turned on filtering.

2 Click the Startup Disk icon.

   Once open, your MasterNB*n* network volume should appear in the list of available startup volumes.

3 Click the MasterNB*n* NetBoot icon.

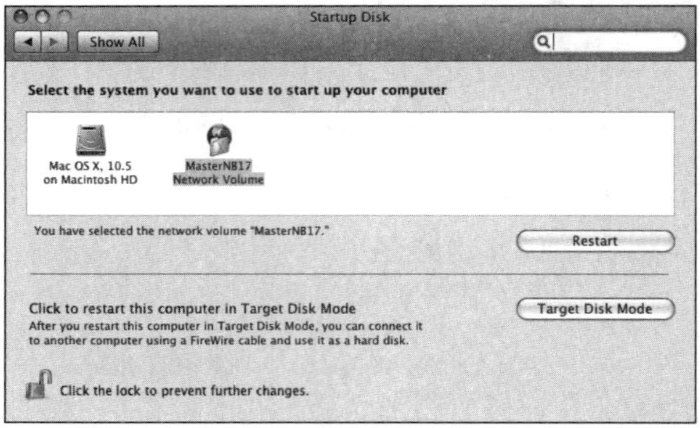


4 Click the Restart button, and confirm when prompted.

5 The computer should shut down, and restart using the NetBoot volume as the startup volume.

6 Log in to the Mac OS X computer as simon (password:abcd1234).

When successfully NetBooting, you'll see a flashing globe icon before the kernel is loaded, a spinning globe icon while the kernel is loading, and when logged in, the NetBoot network volume will appear on your desktop (Finder preferences permitting).

7 Open Mail, and send a message to the developers.

8 Send mail to instruct@mainserver.pretendco.com.

9 Check Mail to ensure it is working.

10 Mount smb://server*n*.local and mount the project lion share point.

11 Mount https://server*n*.pretendco.com/manual-1.3.

12 Open /System/Library/CoreServices/Kerberos to view all your tickets.

**Question 1** *Where is simon's home folder?*

*Question 2* *How is your Apple computer booted?*

*Question 3* *What ensures all this is working properly?*

13 Open Server Admin on your server, select the NetBoot service, and click the Clients icon in the toolbar.

Note that your client is successfully NetBooted.

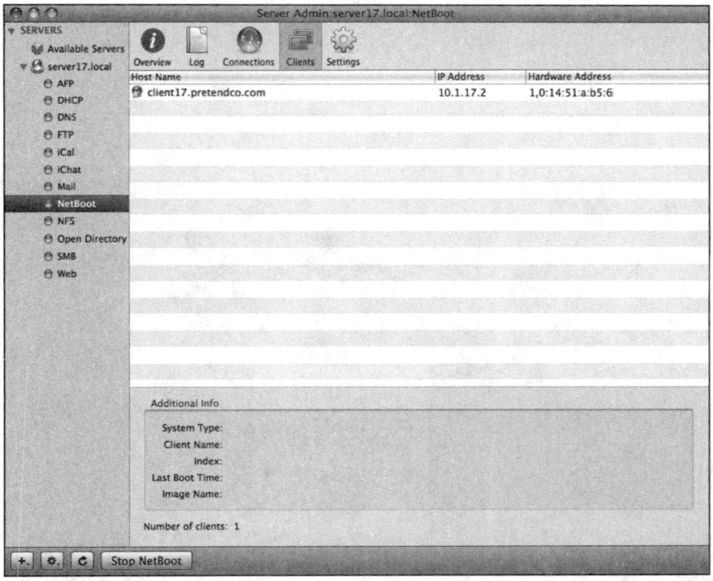


14 Use Startup System Preferences to set your Mac OS X computer to boot from its internal hard drive and then restart your computer.

15 On your Mac OS X Server, quit Server Admin and log out of your server.

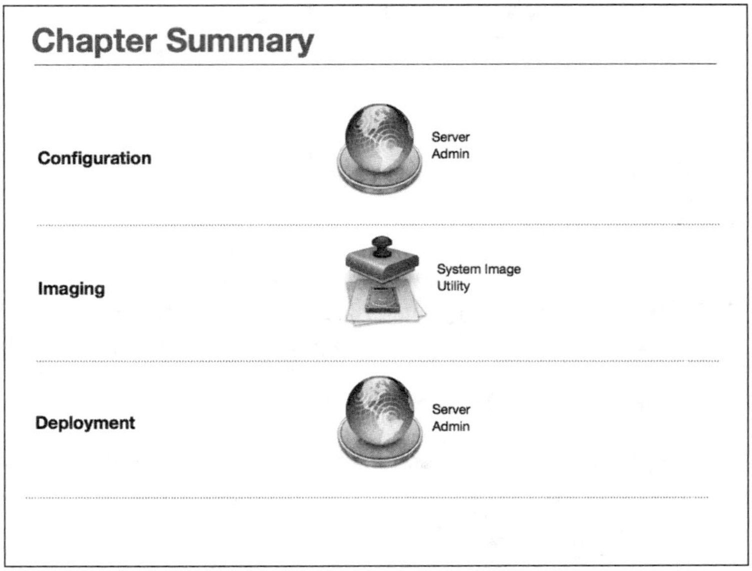
Chapter Summary
Configuration
Server Admin
Imaging
System Image Utility
Deployment
Server Admin

Apple Certified

# 10

# Managing Accounts


## 10.1 Managed Preferences

**Exercise 10.1.1** Create Group Folders

**Exercise 10.1.2** Set Managed Preferences for Users and Groups

**Exercise 10.1.3** Manage Computer Groups

## 10.2 Software Update Server

**Exercise 10.2.1** Configure and Enable Software Update Service

## 10.3 Mobile User Accounts

**Exercise 10.3.1** Configure Mobile Accounts


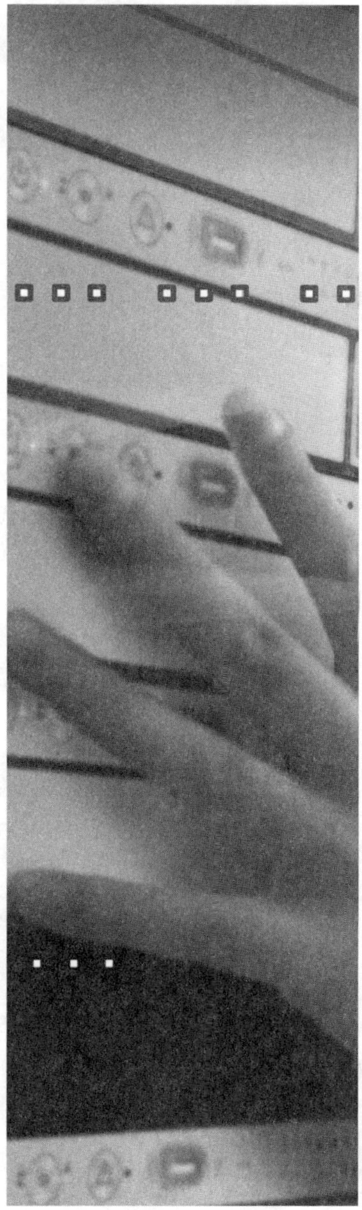

# 10.1 Managed Preferences

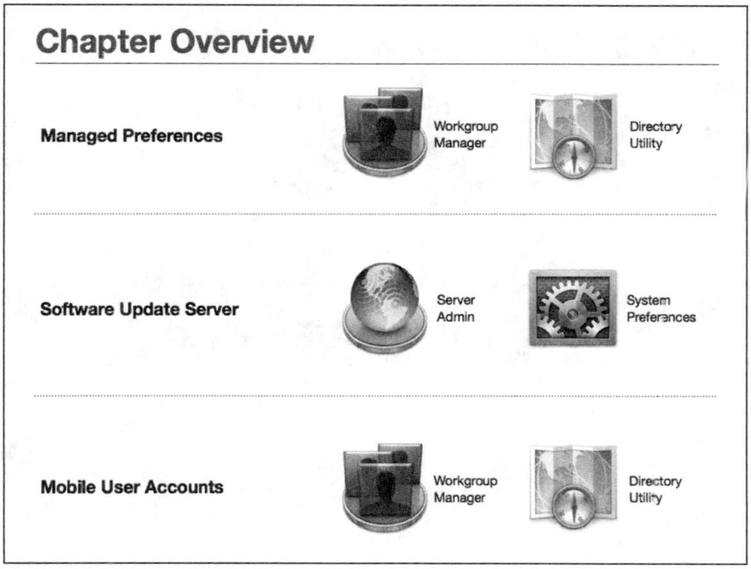


Managed Preferences can be split into three main areas: managing preferences for users, groups, and computers; managing how Apple software gets updated; and creating mobile accounts.

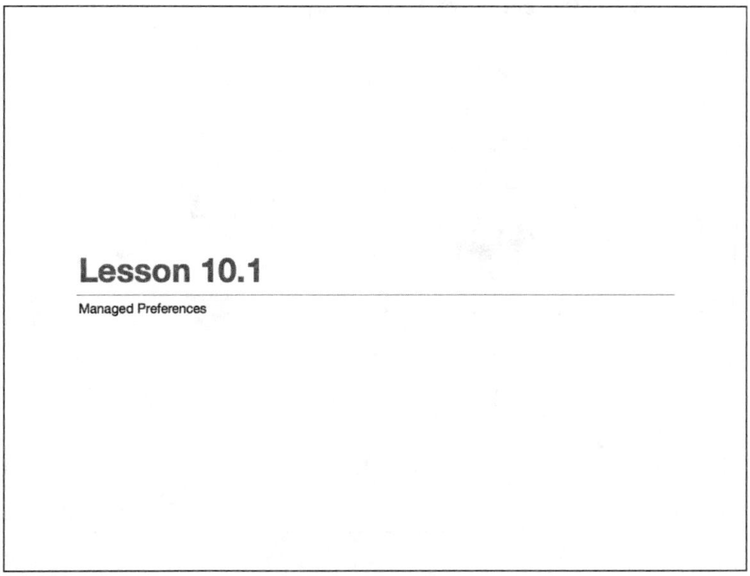


This lesson explains the four account types and how you can manage them. You'll also learn what preferences are available, hierarchy of management, and the options and types of preferences.

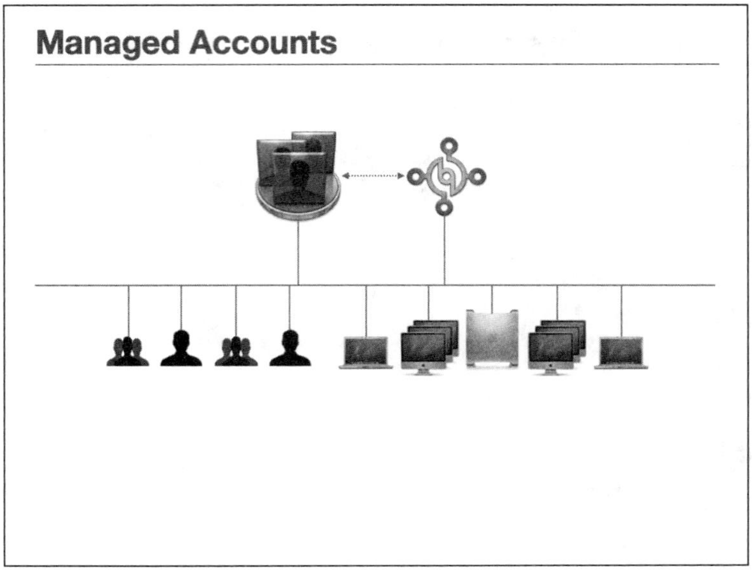


There are four types of account management in Mac OS X Server: user, group, computers, and computer groups.

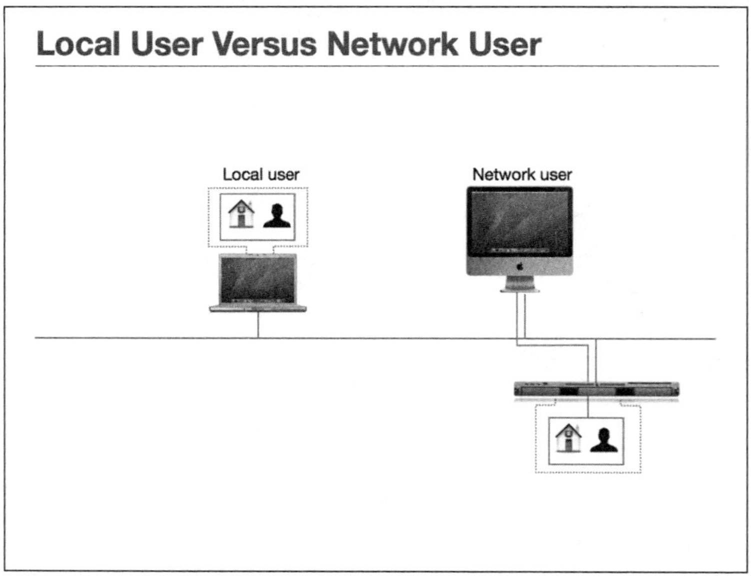


A local user is a user who has an account on a single computer. This account does not exist anywhere else on the network. A network user has an account on a server, and any computers that are properly connected to the server can be used by that network user.

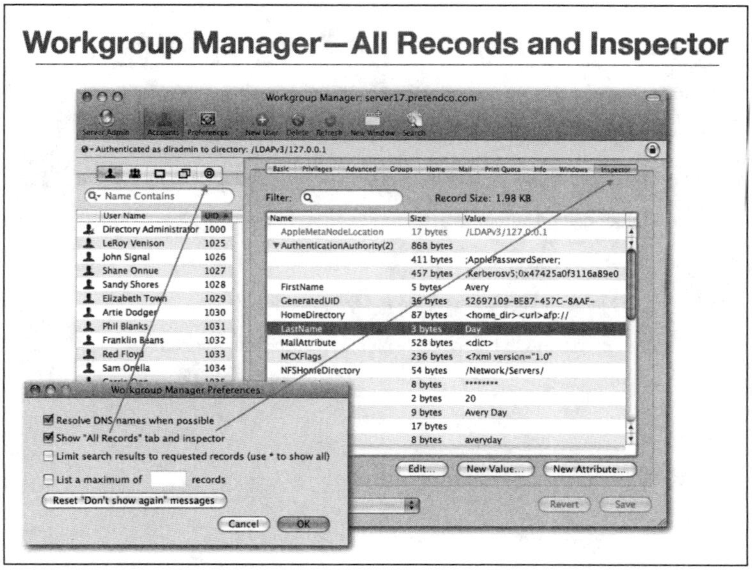


Workgroup Manager has a feature that allows you to see information about account attributes, whether they are user, group, computer, or computer group accounts.

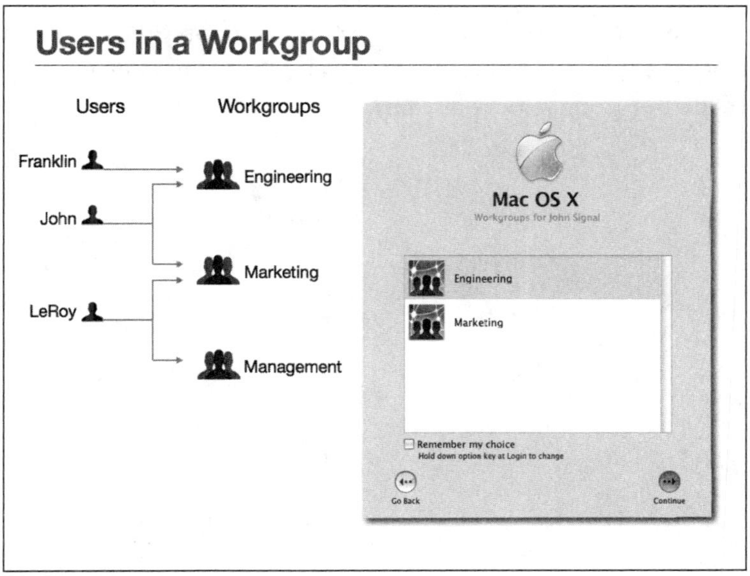


Workgroups are groups with managed preferences. Users can be members of more than one group and groups can be nested.

## Group Folders

Group folders can be located anywhere.

Mac OS X Server includes a Groups preset share point.

- Groups folder is located at root level of Mac OS X Server volume.

Groups folder can be automounted.

- Server Admin is used to set folder as automount.

Workgroup Manager is used to define the group folder owner.

Run a UNIX command to immediately create Group folder structure.

- `sudo CreateGroupFolder`

The Groups folders can exist anywhere; however, Mac OS X Server places a Groups folder at the root level of the volume on which Mac OS X Server is installed. The Groups folder, like the Users folder (and any other folder for that matter) can be automounted. If a standard Mac OS X Server group folder is needed quickly, a specific UNIX command can be run to immediately create the group folder hierarchy.

## Default Groups Folder

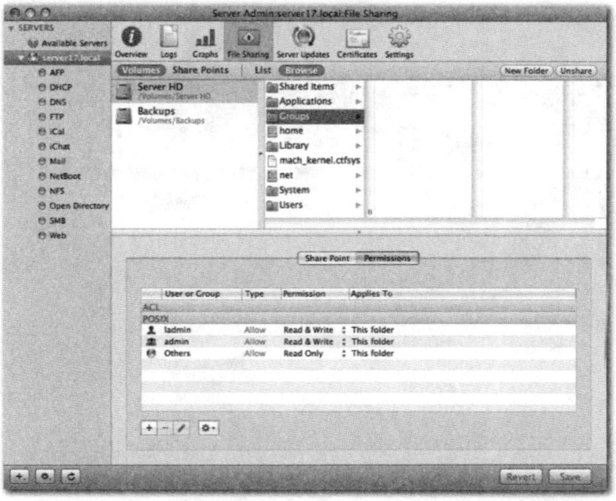


The default Groups folder is located at the root level of the volume on which Mac OS X Server is installed. You can view the default permissions for this folder using Server Admin.

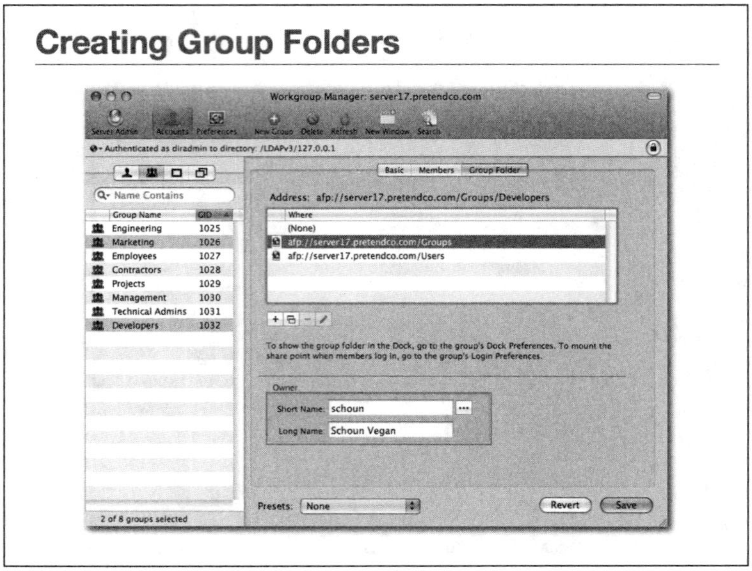


Once a folder is set to automount, it displays in a list of folders to be used for any user's home directory location and for any group's folder location. Essentially, you can select the location where the group folder is to be located. In the bottom of the window, you choose the owner of the group folder.

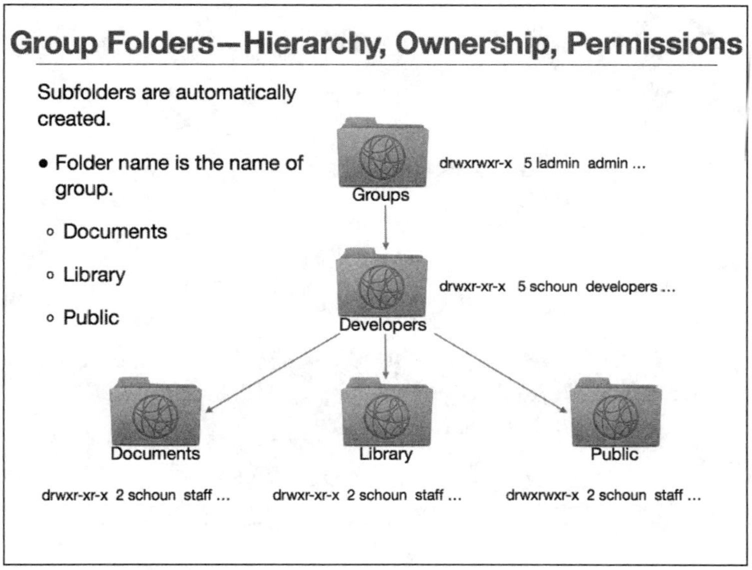


When a group has a folder created for it by Mac OS X Server, a folder hierarchy is created. This slide shows the ownership and permissions of the group folder structure.

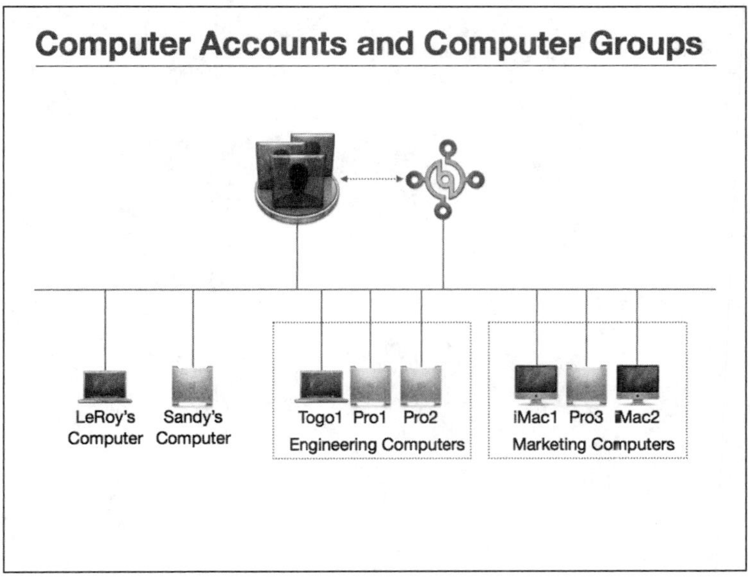

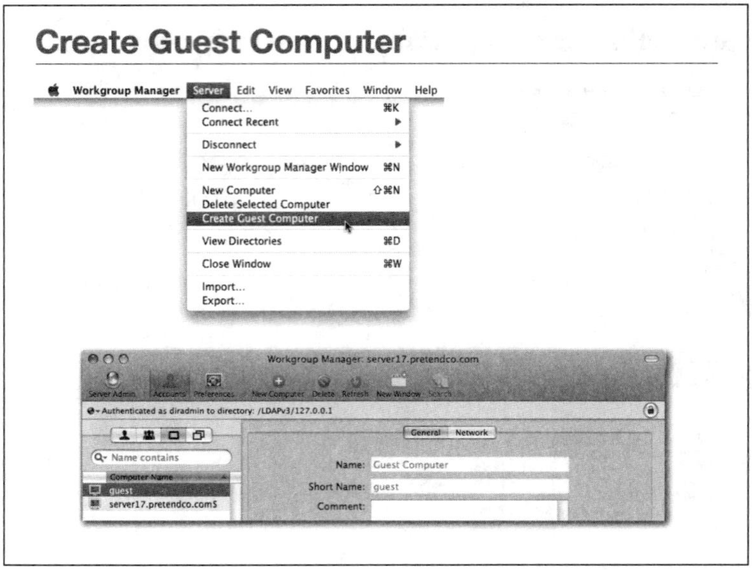


A Guest computer account is used for any Mac OS X computer that is bound to the directory but does not have any management preferences defined and is not part of any computer group.

## Create a Computer Account

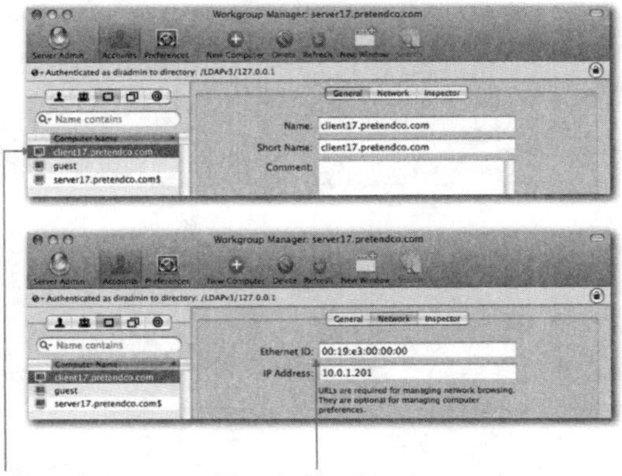


Creating a computer account is similar to creating a user or group account. The MAC address of the first built-in Ethernet interface is used to define the computer account. If authorized binding is enabled, computer accounts are created automatically.

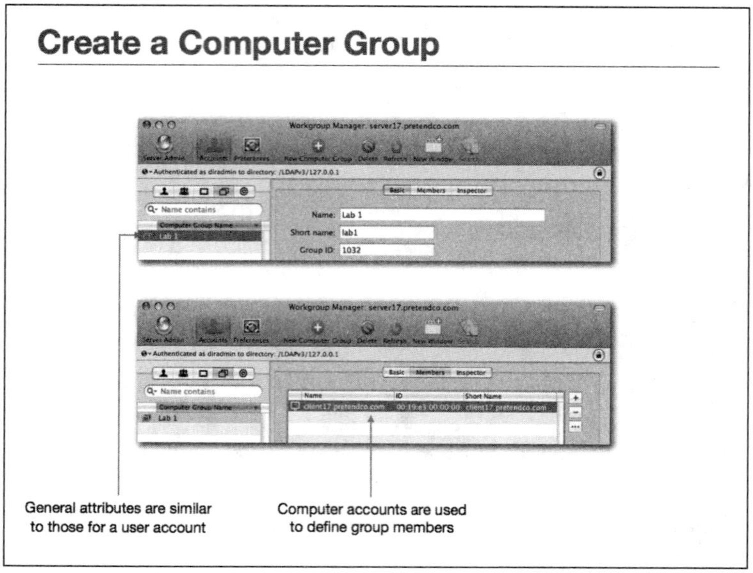


Computer groups are simply collections of computers, which are defined by their MAC addresses. Computer groups help manage settings for multiple computers, regardless of who logs in.

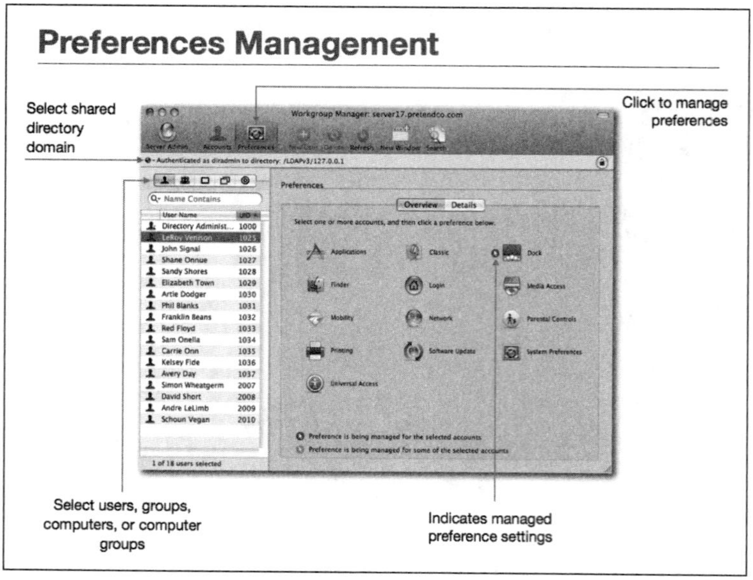


No matter the type of account, there are various preferences that can be managed for that account. The Preferences icon in Workgroup Manager is used to handle preferences management.

## When Do You Want Preferences Managed?

- Never
- Once
- Always
- Often

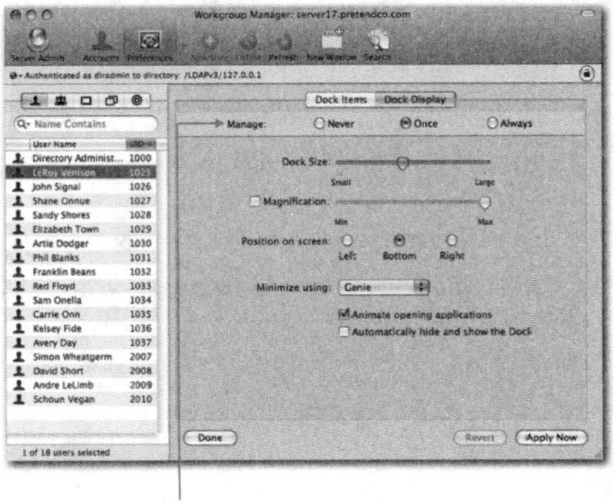


Select a management option

When managing preferences, you have the option of deciding how to manage the preferences. The options are to never manage them, always manage them, manage them once (which means after the initial management, the user manages them), or manage them often (which means the settings are managed but the user can make changes while they are logged in, but once they log out and back in, the preferences are reset to their managed state).

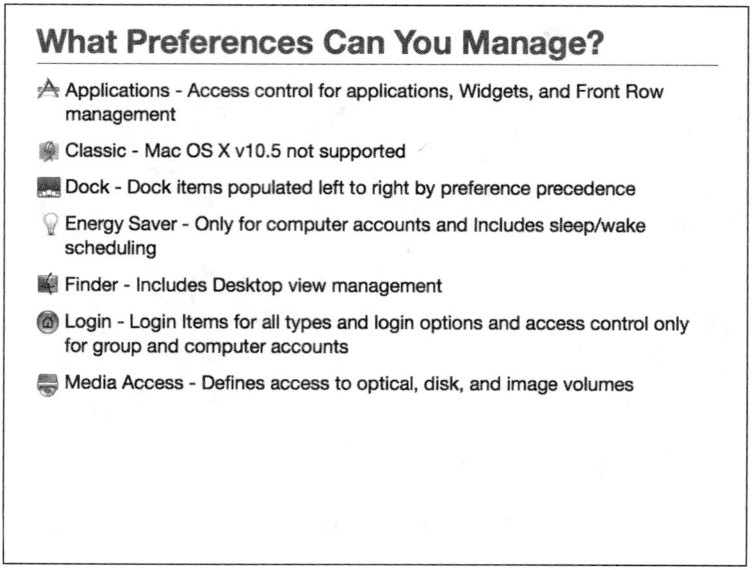


Various preferences can be managed. This is the first of two slides that show you what can be managed.

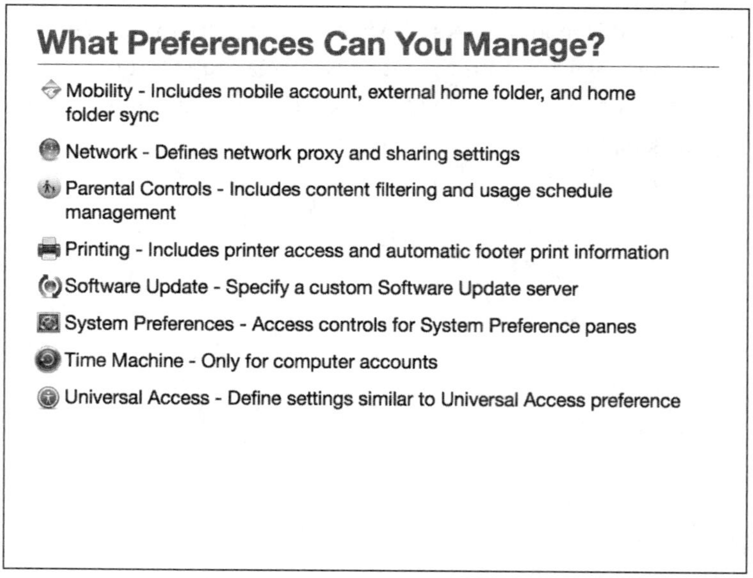

**Managed Preference Precedence—Inherit**

| | Login Items | Dock | Finder |
|---|---|---|---|
| Workgroup | Address Book | Not Managed | Not Managed |
| Computer Group | Not Managed | Right | Not Managed |
| Computer | Not Managed | Not Managed | Not Managed |
| User | Not Managed | Not Managed | ☑ Snap to grid |
| Result | Address Book | Right | ☑ Snap to grid |

When managing multiple preferences, there can be some confusion if preferences are set for a user who happens to be a member of a group and they happen to log in to a computer that is being managed. Preferences that are set for some types but not others are inherited when a user logs in.

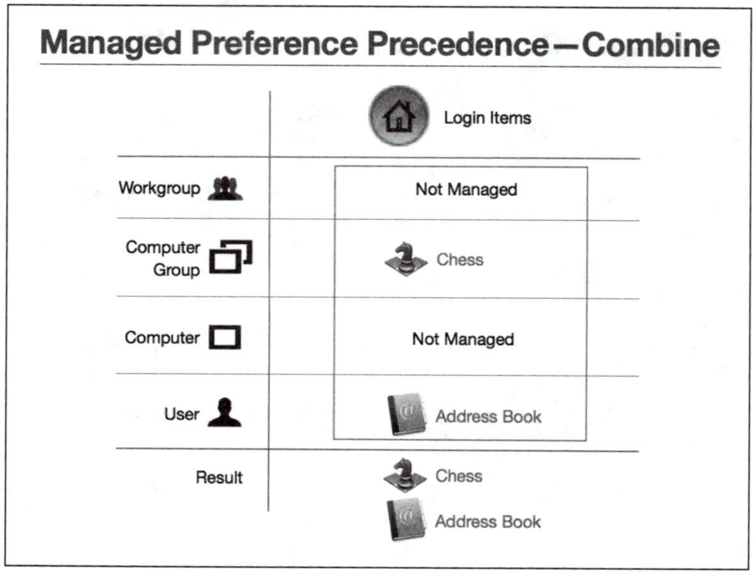


Preferences that are managed by different accounts are combined when a user logs in.

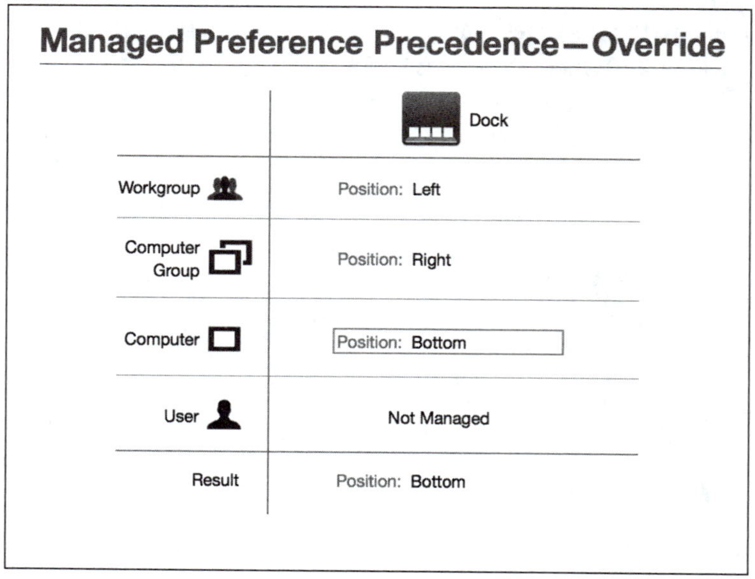


When different types of accounts have different settings for the same preference, an override situation takes place.

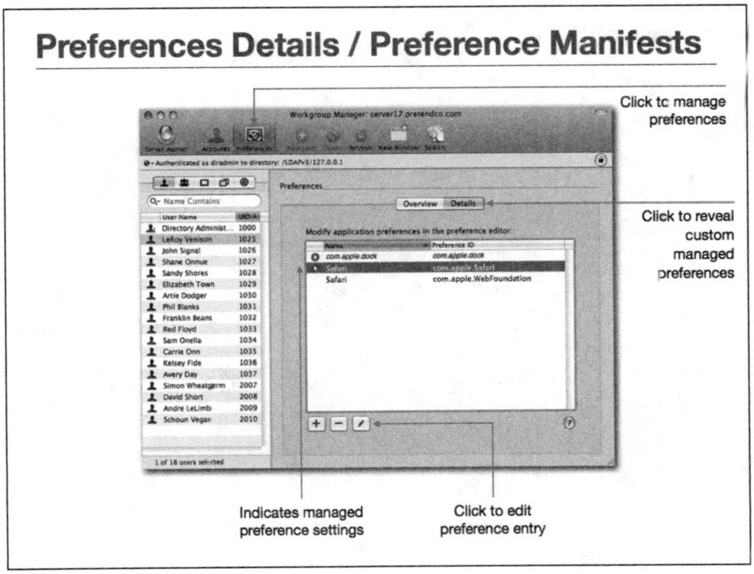


When you save managed preferences, a detailed listing of those settings is produced. It can be viewed under the Details tab in Workgroup Manager. Third-party applications that adhere to Apple's structure for saving preference files can also have their preferences managed. These are known as preference manifests.

## Editing Preference Manifests

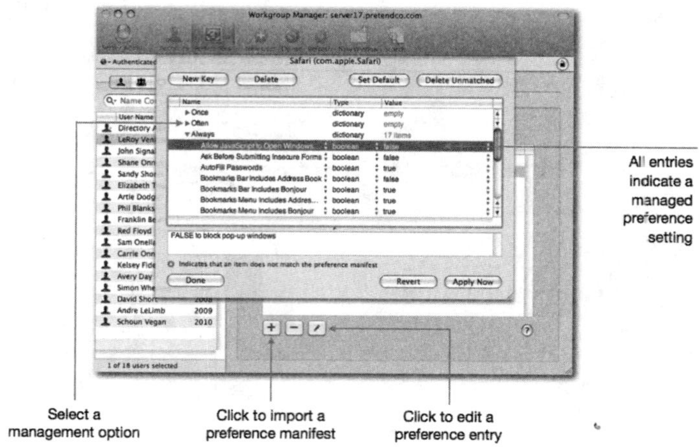


To edit preference manifests, administrators must select them from the list of managed preferences and click the edit button.

## Troubleshooting Managed Preferences

Where are your accounts managed?

- Are accounts located in a shared directory?
- Are the clients bound correctly?

At what level is the management?

- Use groups for most
- Use computer groups for static resources
- Remember precedence

View the preferences.

- Use Workgroup Manager Details functionality
- Use the Inspector

Troubleshooting managed preferences can involve the following: ensuring the computer to be managed is bound to Mac OS X Server, determining how the management is taking place, determining if there are orders of precedence to follow. Proper planning is crucial prior to setting up managed preferences.

Exercises

10.1.1 Create Group Folders

10.1.2 Set Managed Preferences for Users and Groups

10.1.3 Manage Computer Groups

## Exercise 10.1.1

# Create Group Folders

### Objective

Ensure the Groups folder can be automounted. Create a group folder for three groups.

### Summary

Group folders are often used in conjunction with collaborative services to help provide a proper work environment for members of a group in an organization.

### Restrict Access to Applications

1. Log in to your Mac OS X computer as cadmin.
2. Open Server Admin, and connect to your server as ladmin (password: apple).
3. Select your server, and click File Sharing in the toolbar.
4. Click the Share Points button, and select the Groups share point from the list.

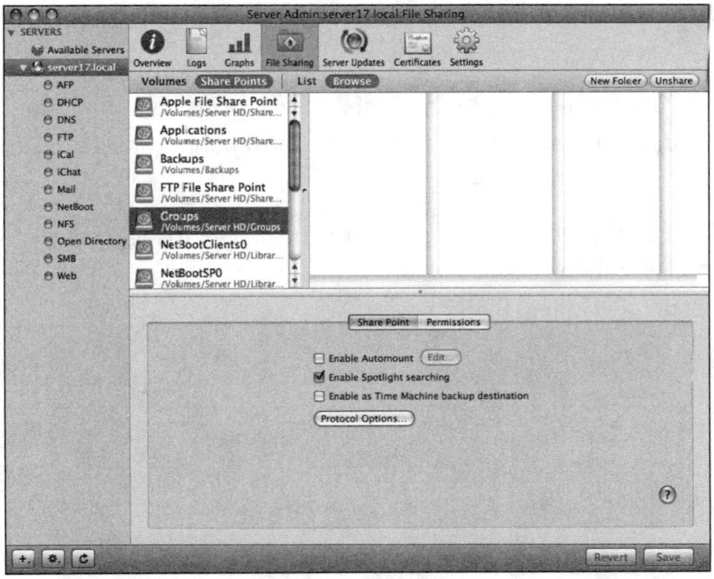


5 Click the Share Point tab, select Enable Automount, and leave all the defaults.

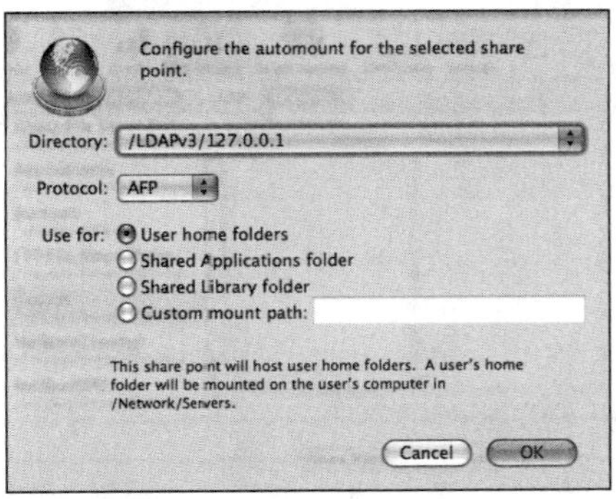


6 Click OK, enter the username `diradmin` and the password `diradmin` and click OK.

7 Click the Save button to save the automount record, and quit Server Admin.

8 Open Workgroup Manager, authenticate as ladmin, select the shared LDAP domain, and authenticate as diradmin, if necessary.

9 Click the Group accounts tab, select the Marketing group, and click the Group Folder tab.

10 Select the afp://server*n*.pretendco.com/Groups automount from the mount points list, and choose John Signal as the owner of the folder.

Use the ellipses button to open the drawer to locate the user, John.

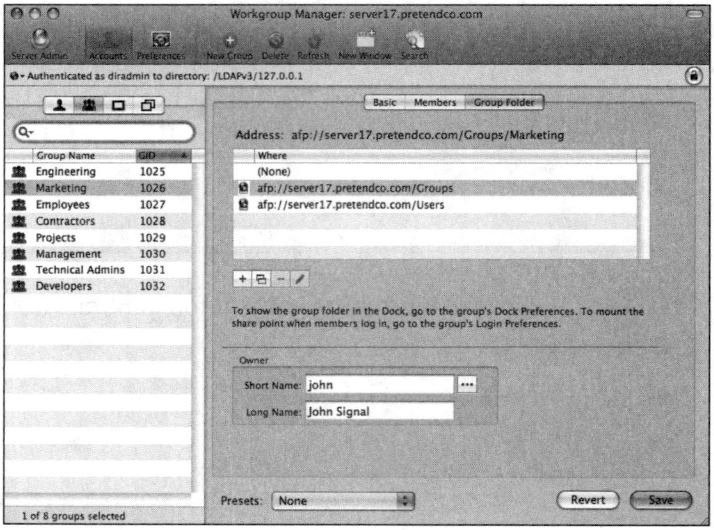


11 Click Save.

12 Select the Developers group, set the automount to the same path, and make Schoun the owner.

13 Select the Engineering group, set the automount to the same path and make Franklin the owner.

You've just set three group folders, but because Mac OS X Server will not create these immediately, you'll use a command line tool to create them.

14 Open the Terminal application located in /Applications/Utilities, type `ssh ladmin@servern.pretendco.com` and press the Return key.

15 Type `yes` if necessary when asked about keys and enter ladmin's password when prompted.

Now, you are connected to your Mac OS X Server via the SSH protocol.

16 Type `sudo CreateGroupFolder` and press the Return key.

17 Read the warning, if it appears.

18 Enter ladmin's password again.

Text appears in the Terminal window, notifying you that all your groups' folders have been created.

19 Type `exit`, and quit Terminal.

20 Use Workgroup Manager to add Simon and Schoun to the Marketing group.

You'll need these two additions to the Marketing group in a later exercise.

21 Save your changes and leave Workgroup Manager open.

## Exercise 10.1.2

# Set Managed Preferences for Users and Groups

## Objective

Use Workgroup Manager to specify various system preferences, and examine how preferences are inherited, combined, or overridden.

## Summary

Managed preferences allow administrators to strictly control what users can do with their Macs. You should plan carefully before implementing several policies.

## Restrict Access to Applications

1. Select John in the Accounts list.
2. Click the Preferences icon in the toolbar.
3. Click the Dock icon in the Preferences Overview pane, and click the Dock Display tab.

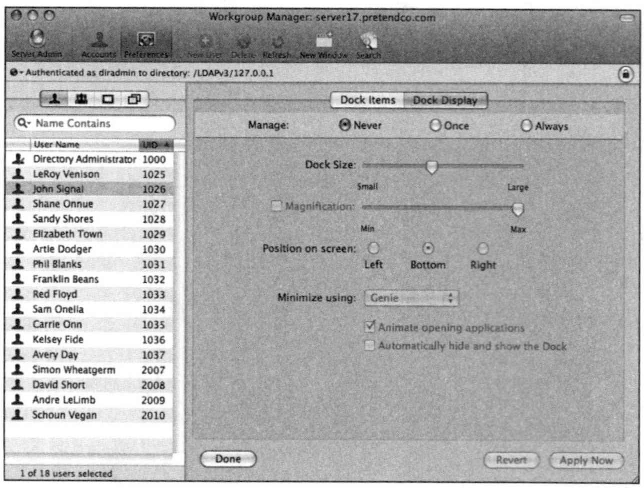

4 Select Always as the management choice.

5 Configure the Dock to appear on the Right, and choose Genie from the "Minimize using" pop-up menu.

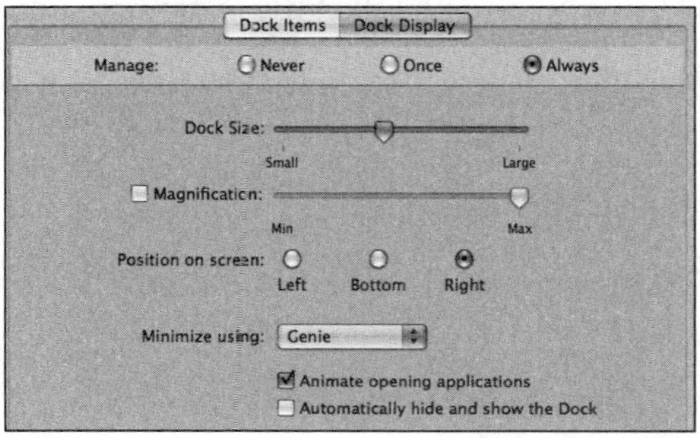


6 Click Apply Now, and then click Done.

7 Click the Finder icon, click the Commands tab, and select Always as the management choice.

8 Deselect the following:

- Go to iDisk
- Go to Folder
- Restart

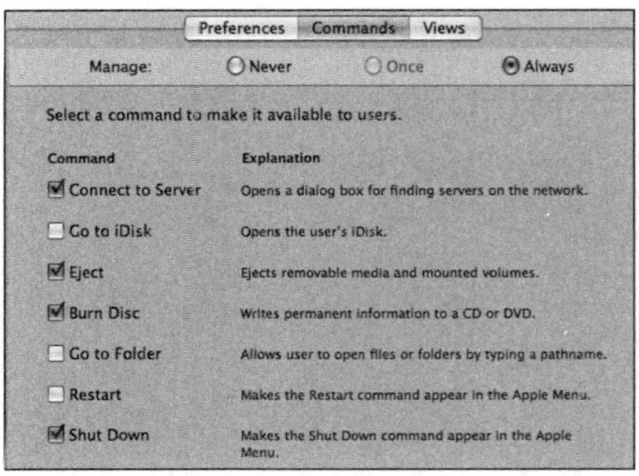


9 Click Apply Now, and then click Done.

10 Click the System Preferences icon, and select Always as the management choice.

11 Deselect .Mac and QuickTime from the Preferences pane list.

12 Click Apply Now, and then click Done.

You've just set some managed preferences for John. You'll now set managed preferences for the Marketing group.

13 Click the Groups account tab, and select the Marketing group.

14 Click the Dock icon in the Preferences Overview pane, and click the Dock Display tab.

15 Select Always as the management choice.

16 Configure the Dock to appear on the Left, and choose Scale as the minimize option.

When you log in as John later, you'll observe two conflicting preferences.

17 Click the Dock Items tab, and select Always as the management choice

18 Select Add Group Folder, click Apply Now, and click Done.

The Marketing group folder is added to the Dock.

19 Click the Login icon, and click through all the tabs.

Notice the only one active for groups is the Items tab.

20 Select Always as the management choice.

21 Click the Add (+) button, navigate to /System/Library/CoreServices, and select Kerberos.

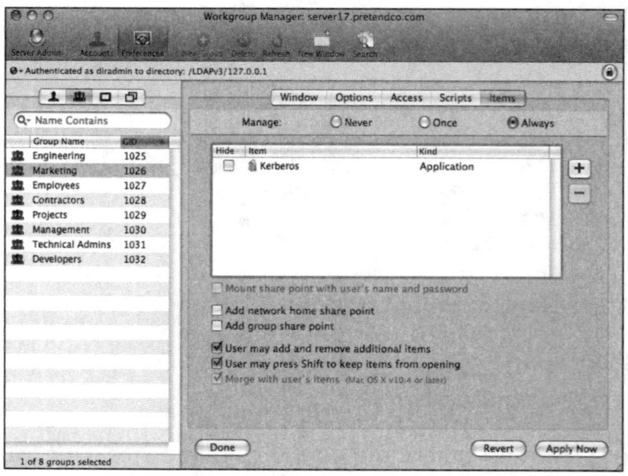

22 Click Apply Now, and then click Done.

23 Select the Engineering group, and click the Applications icon.

24 Select Always as the management choice, and click the Applications tab.

25 Click the Add (+) button, and add the following applications:

- Address Book
- iCal
- iChat
- Mail
- Safari
- System Preferences.

26 Click Apply Now.

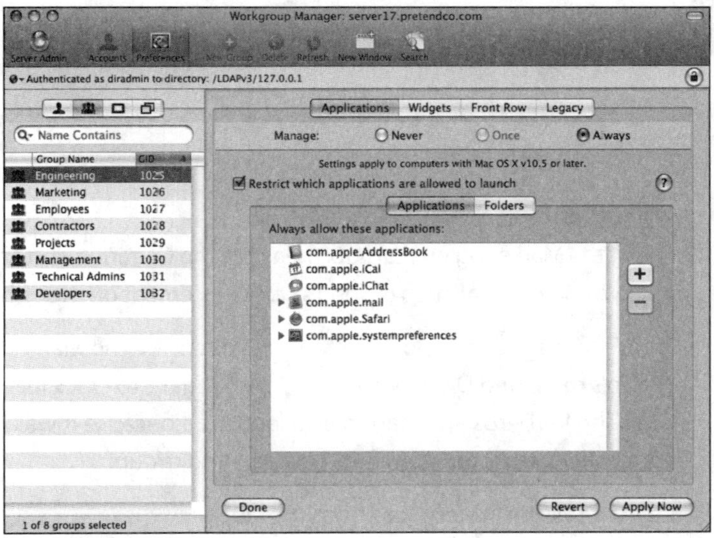


You've limited what the Engineering group can launch.

27 Quit Workgroup Manager, and log out as cadmin.

28 Log in as john (password: changeme).

Notice that because John is a member of both groups and they are both being managed in some form or another, John is presented with a screen asking him to choose which group he would prefer to associate with this session. If John were a member of a more groups, they would not appear unless they were being managed in some form or another. This is where the word Workgroups is used. John can log into either the Engineering workgroup or the Marketing workgroup.

29 Select the Marketing workgroup, then click the Continue button to log in to view the location of John's Dock placement on the right.

John's managed user Dock preferences overrode the Marketing group's managed Dock preferences with regard to Dock location. The Kerberos application also launched because it was configured as a login item for the Marketing group.

30 Launch System Preferences from the Dock.

Notice the .Mac and QuickTime preference panes are dimmed and cannot be used.

31 Hold down the shift key, and minimize System Preferences to view the Genie effect, not the Scale effect, further confirming the Dock display settings for John overrode the Marketing Dock display settings.

32 Click the question mark below the Dock line separating applications from files, folder, open windows, and the trash can.

33 The Marketing group folder appears.

You told the group folder to appear in the Dock for the Marketing group, not for John. In this case, the Dock items came from the Marketing managed preferences because John's Dock items were not being managed, showing the combine rule.

34 Click the Apple menu, and notice Restart is not showing.

35 Click the Go menu, and notice the ability to go to your iDisk and the Go to Folder items are missing.

36 Log out as John, and log back in as John, this time choosing the Engineering group.

37 Select the Go menu, and notice that Go to Folder is missing as expected.

38 Choose Applications from the Go menu.

39 Attempt to launch Image Capture, and view the error dialog.

40 Click the Apple menu, and notice Restart is missing as expected.

41 Log out as John, and log in as cadmin.

## Exercise 10.1.3

# Manage Computer Groups

### Objectives

Create a computer group, add a computer to it, and configure some preferences to see how they interact with user and group preferences.

Enable Auto Log-Out for the computer group.

### Summary

Computer groups are an excellent way to handle preferences for a lab or for users who have laptops and may roam networks. Before you can create a computer group, you must disable your DHCP server, as computer records and DHCP static mappings do not work together. You will also rebind your Mac OS X computer to your server statically.

1. Open Directory Utility, and authenticate as cadmin.
2. Click to show advanced settings, if not already shown.
3. Click the Services icon in the toolbar, and double-click the LDAPv3 letters to open the LDAP settings.
4. Deselect "Add DHCP-supplied LDAP servers to automatic search policies," and click OK, then click Apply, if necessary.
5. Click the Directory Servers icon in the toolbar, and click the Add button.
6. Enter `servern.pretendco.com` (where *n* is your student number), authenticate with cadmin's password if necessary, and click OK.
7. Click the Search Policy icon in the toolbar, and ensure Custom Path is selected for both the Authentication tab and the Contacts tab, and click Apply.

8 Quit Directory Utility.

9 Open Server Admin, authenticate if necessary, select your DHCP service from the service list, delete the static mapping for client*n*, and stop the DHCP service using the button at the bottom of the window.

10 From the Apple menu, choose Locations, and set your location to Static.

11 Go back up to the Apple menu, choose Locations, and set your location back to Automatic.

This forces your Mac OS X computer to request a new DHCP address, one it will get from the instructor server. However, your Mac OS X computer will still get its authentication information from your Mac OS X Server.

12 Open Workgroup Manager, authenticate as ladmin, select the shared LDAP domain, and authenticate as diradmin, if necessary.

13 In the left pane of the window, click the Computer Groups tab.

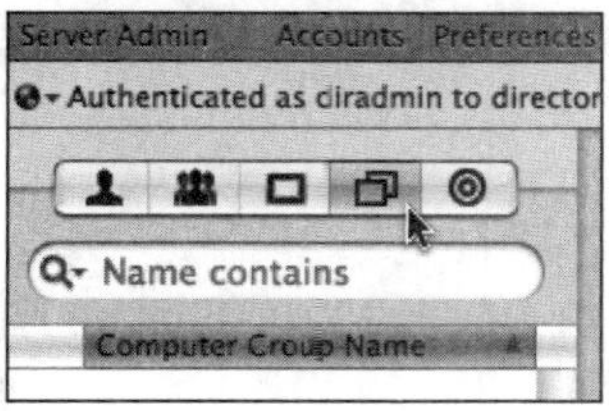


14 Click the Accounts icon in the toolbar, and then click the New Computer Group icon in the toolbar.

15 Type `Lab 1` in the Name field,

Notice the short name removes the space. When creating computer groups, you may elect to remove the space from the name so the name and short name match. Leave the space here for the example.

16 Click Save.

17 Click the Members tab.

18 Click the Ellipses (...) button.

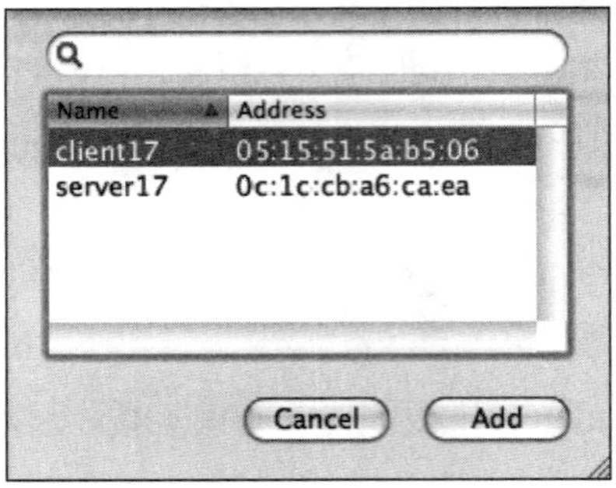


19 Select your Mac OS X computer, and click Add.

Your Mac OS X computer may be listed in the browser as a Mac number (where number is your student number written out) followed by the MAC address.

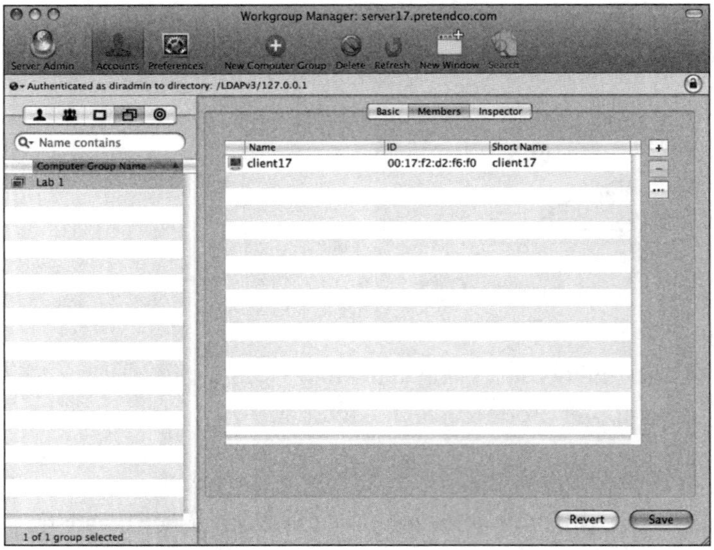


20 Click Save.

21 Click the Preferences icon in the toolbar.

22 Click the Login icon in the Preferences Overview pane.

23 Click through the tabs to view them.

24 Click the Access tab, and select the Always radio button as the management choice.

25 Click the Add (+) button.

26 Drag Marketing from the list of groups to the Access Control List area.

Only members of the Marketing group have access to the clients in the Lab 1 computer group.

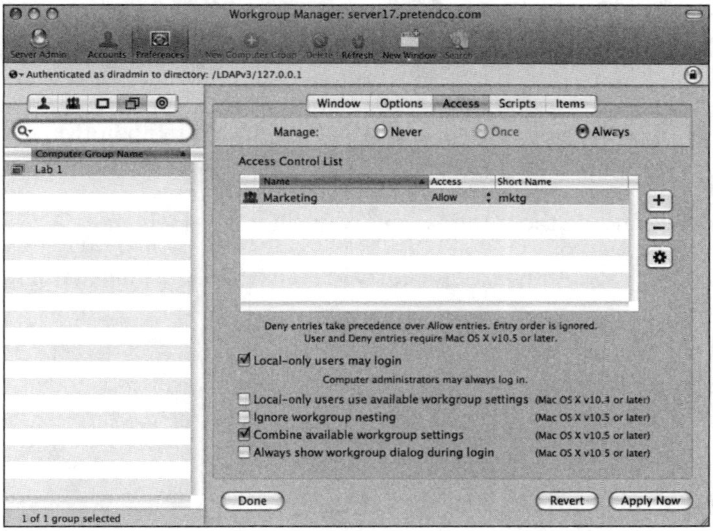


27 Click Apply Now.

28 Click the Window tab.

29 Select the Always radio button as the management choice.

30 Select Directory Status from the Heading pop-up menu.

31 In the Message box, type `Welcome to a PretendCo-owned computer. We own it, therefore if you use it, we own you. Get to work.`

32 Press the Return key to insert a line break, and in the new line type `Have a nice day.`

33 Deselect the "Show Restart button" checkbox.

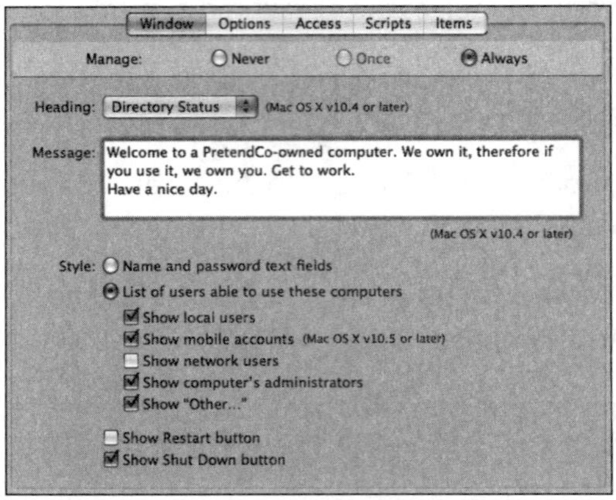


34 Click the Options tab, and select the Always radio button as the management choice.

35 Configure the settings so only two items are selected:

- Local Administrators may refresh or disable management
- Enable external accounts

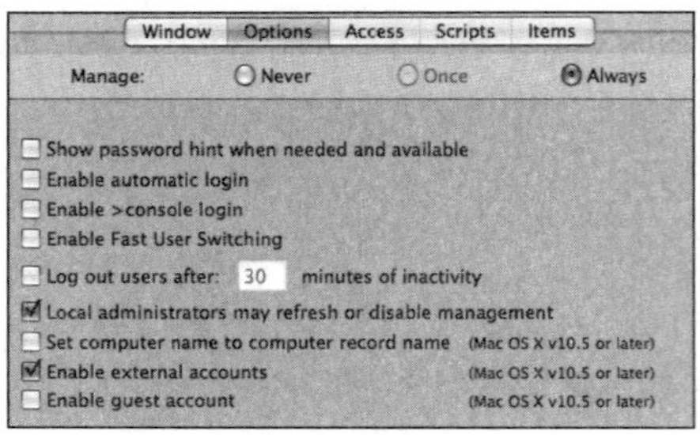


36 Click Apply Now.

37 Log out of the Mac OS X computer, and log back in as Andre.

Notice how the Login screen configuration had changed.

38 Verify that Andre can't log in.

39 Enter the username and password for cadmin, and hold the Option key down as you click the Log In button.

Notice the dialog that appears. Since you logged in as the local administrator and configured the managed preferences to refresh or disable management, you are presented with a dialog stating so.

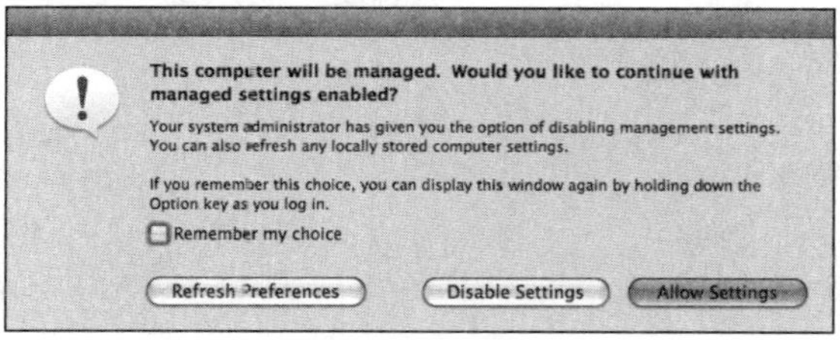


40 Click Refresh Preferences.

41 Verify that John, who is a member of the Marketing group, can log in.

42 Log out and then enter the username and password for cadmin, and hold the Option key down as you click the Log In button.

## Reset Preferences for the Lab 1 Group

Before proceeding to the next exercise, configure the Lab 1 group to allow computers to access local applications.

1 Open Workgroup Manager, authenticate as ladmin, select the shared LDAP domain, and authenticate as diradmin, if necessary.

2 Click the Accounts icon in the toolbar, select the Computer Groups button, and select the Lab 1 computer group.

3 Click the Preferences icon in the toolbar.

4 Click the Login button, and click each tab, selecting the Never option in each pane.

5 Click Apply Now, and then click Done.

6 Leave Workgroup Manager open to this window, and minimize it to your Dock.

# Software Update Server 10.2

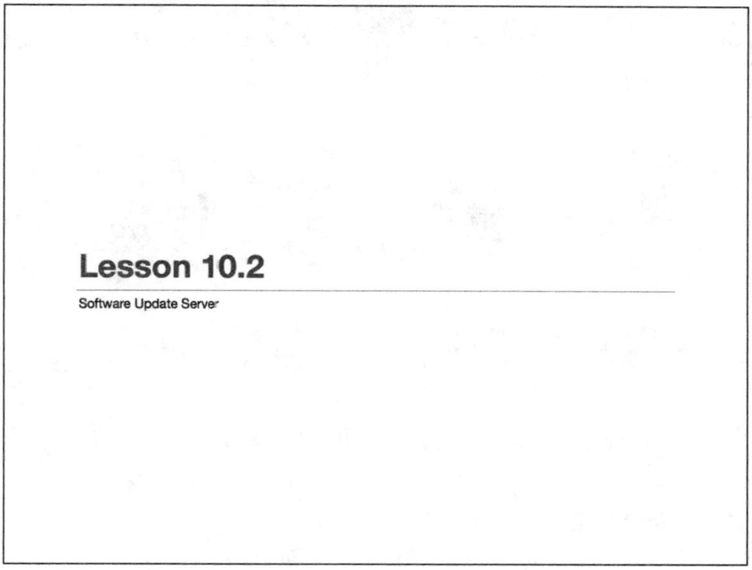


Mac OS X Server allows Mac OS X computers to connect to it and download Apple software updates. This has several benefits that you'll learn about in this lesson. The Software Update service is enabled via Server Admin, and Mac OS X computers are configured to access the service via Workgroup Manager.

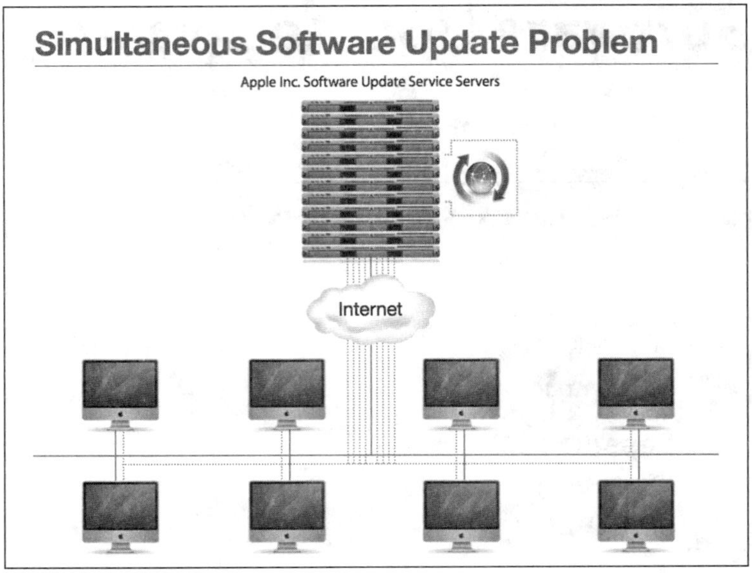


The problem with 100 computers all connecting to the Internet to download a 200 MB update at the same time is bandwidth. An organization's bandwidth limitations are tested when simultaneous downloads hoard a majority of network resources.

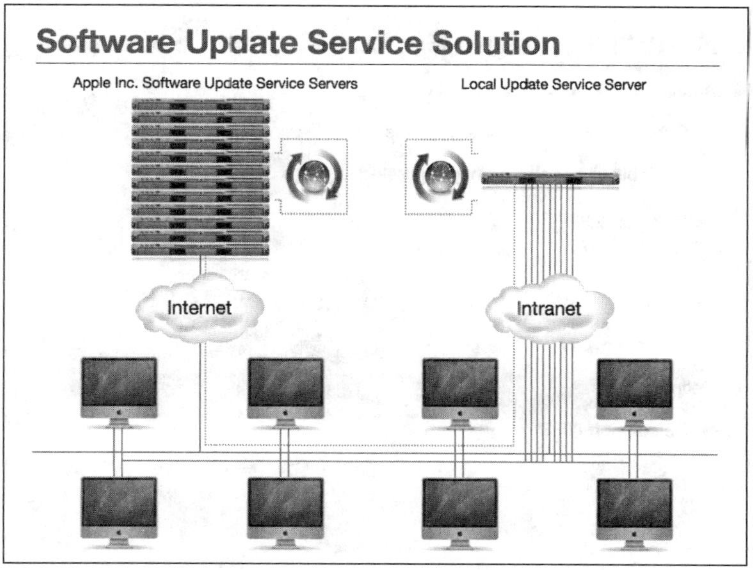


The solution to multiple, simultaneous downloads is to run a local Software Update service so Mac OS X computers can connect internally to obtain updates. Mac OS X Server offers a Software Update service that connects to Apple's software update servers and copies updates locally.

## Software Update Service General Settings

Automate actions

- Copy all new updates or all updates

Auto-enable all updates or manually select updates

Purge specific updates

- Unused
- Legacy

Restrict bandwidth

Define port

- Default port 8088

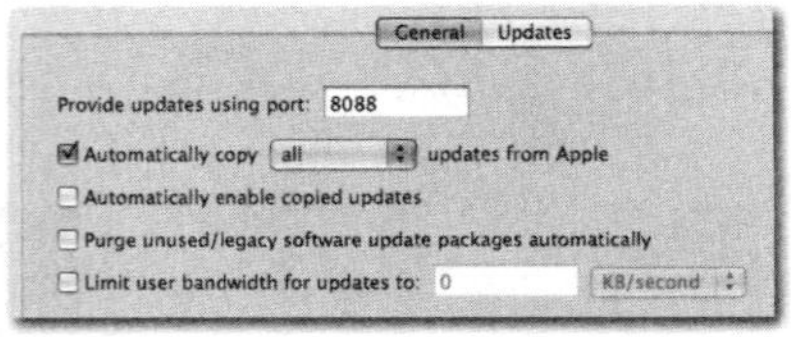


When setting up the Software Update service, administrators have a few options available, such as copying all updates, or just ones that are newer than the system hosting the Software Update service. Administrators can also automatically enable all updates, or selectively enable only certain updates, which would allow administrators to test updates before making them available to client computers.

## Software Update Service Update Settings

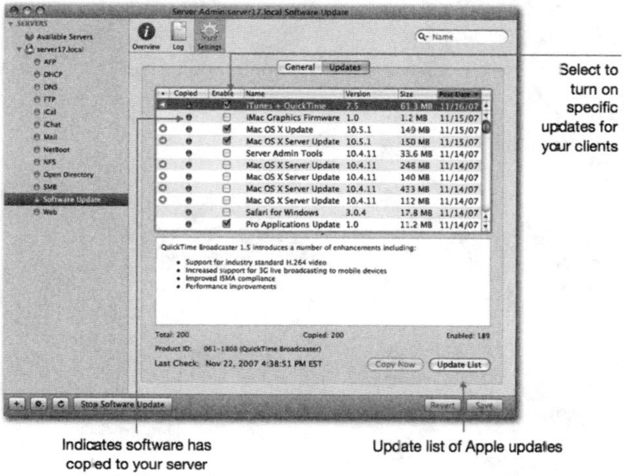


The Updates tab of the Software Update service shows all available updates and allows administrators to enable or disable updates based on need. Each update is listed with its size, version, restart requirement, and the date the update was posted.

## Software Update Managed Preference

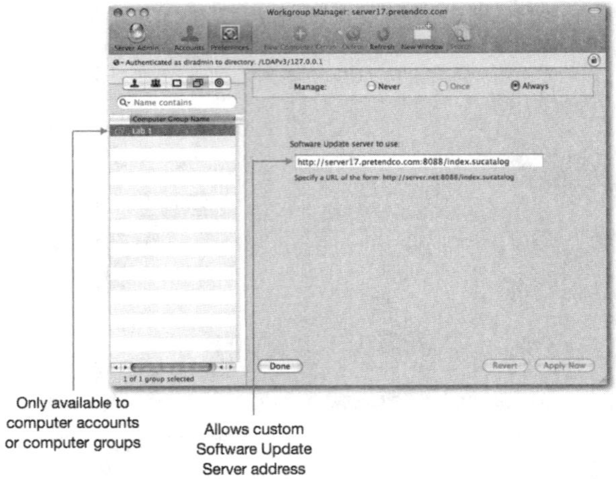


While the Software Update service is managed using Server Admin, the method of setting Mac OS X computers to specifically see the Software Update service is configured using Workgroup Manager.

Exercise

10.2.1 Configure and Enable Software Update Service

Exercise 10.2.1

# Configure and Enable Software Update Service

## Objective

Configure your server computer to run a local Software Update service.

## Summary

Running a software update service allows for more control over when Apple updates are made available to clients.

1 Launch Server Admin, and authenticate if necessary.

2 From the Server menu in Server Admin, choose Add Service.

3 Select the Software Update checkbox to add it to the your list of services.

4 Click Save.

5 Select Software Update from the list of services under your server, click the Settings icon in the toolbar, and select the General tab.

6 Leave the port number as 8088.

7 Select the "Automatically copy all updates from Apple," "Automatically enable copied updates," and "Purge unused/legacy software update packages automatically" checkboxes.

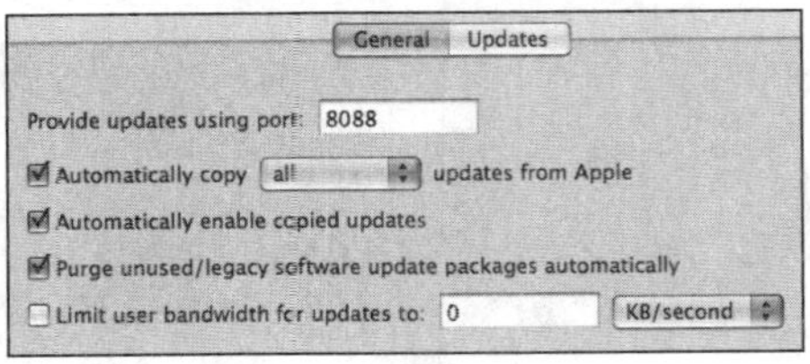

7 Click Save.

8 Ensure you are NOT connected to the Internet, and click the Start Software Update button to start the service.

> **Warning!** In classrooms with the server connected to the Internet, performing these steps will take both time and disk space. The list of updates may not appear immediately.

9 Minimize Server Admin to the Dock and select Workgroup Manager.

10 Click the Computer Groups button, and then select the Lab 1 computer group.

11 Click the Preferences button in the toolbar, and click the Software Update button in the Preferences Overview pane.

12 Select the Always radio button as the management choice.

13 Enter the URL for your server `http://servern.pretendco.com:8088/index.sucatalog` in the "Software Update server to use" field.

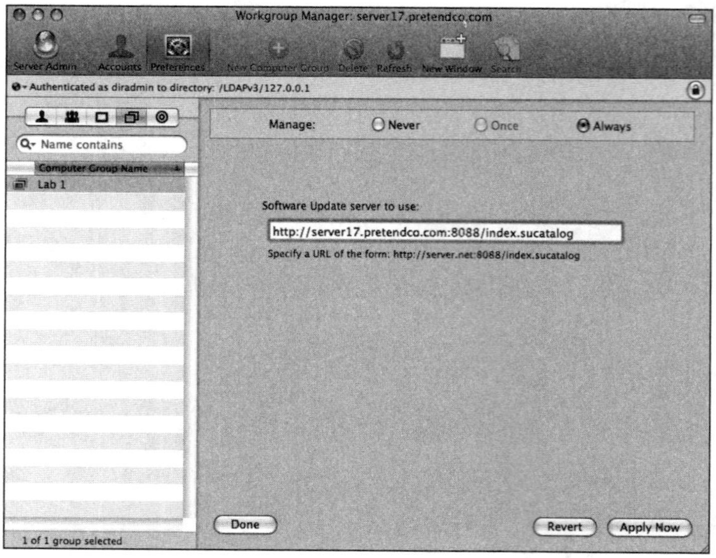

14 Click Apply Now, and then click Done.

15 Log out as cadmin, and log in as John as a member of the Marketing group.

16 Open System Preferences.

17 Click on Software Update preference, and click the Check Now button.

If your server is not able to connect to the Internet, you'll receive an error when trying to run Software Update. The error, however, still indicates that your client is contacting your local software update server.

18 Log out as John, log back in as cadmin, and launch Server Admin.

19 Using Server Admin, check the Software Update Access log of the Software Update service to see if your recent check for updates was logged.

# 10.3 Mobile User Accounts

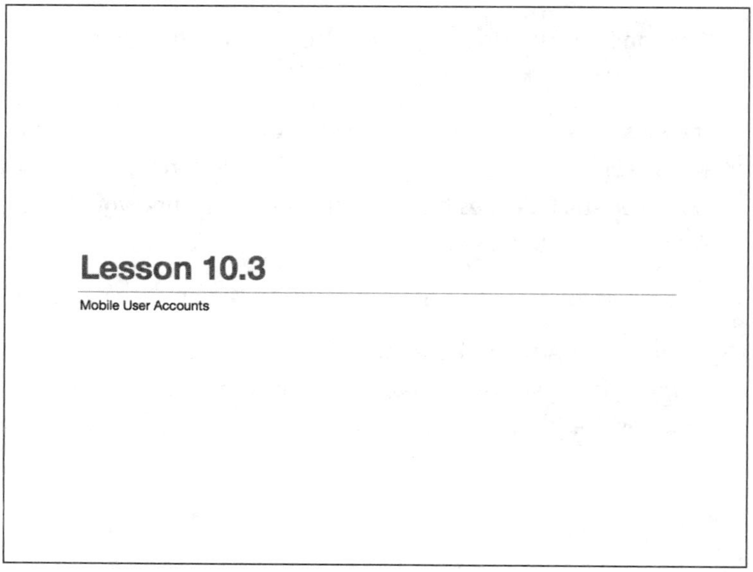


You'll examine mobile user accounts notions for when and how to configure them. You'll also explore options and policies for implementing mobile accounts including synchronization options.

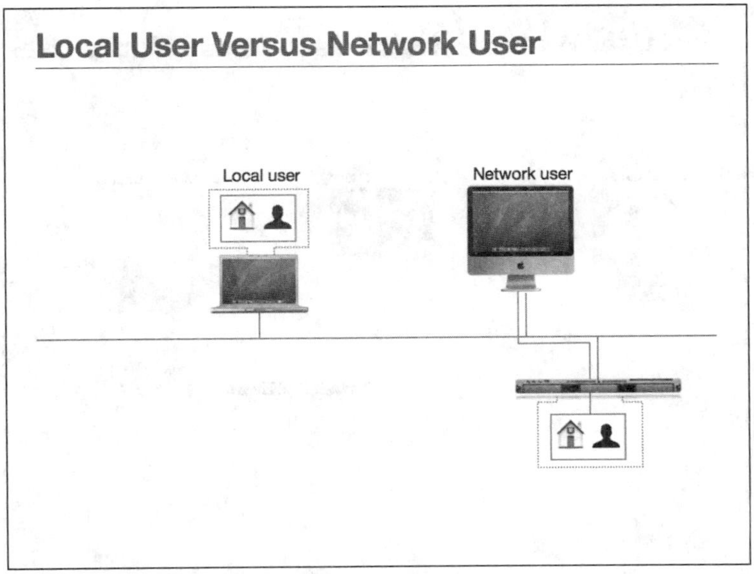


So far, you have explored two types of user accounts: local only accounts and network or shared accounts.

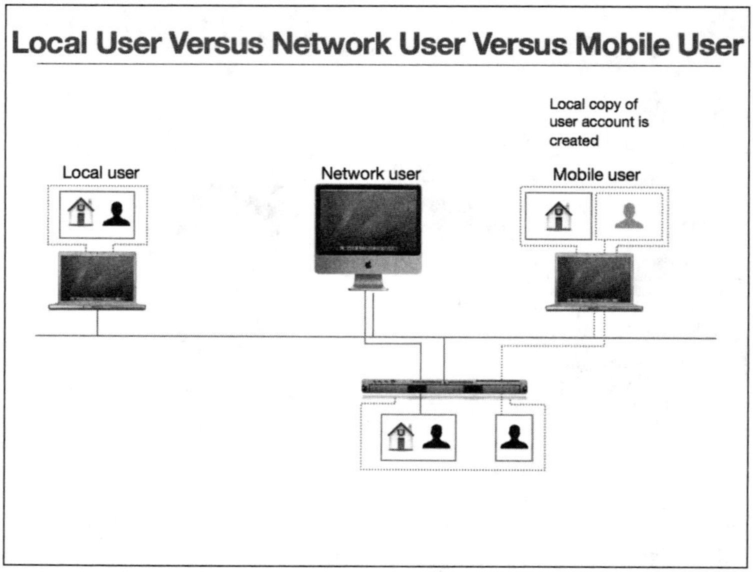


Mac OS X Server has a third type of account, a mobile account. A mobile account is a cached copy of a network account. All account attributes, including managed preferences, are synchronized but any user created data is not. This allows users to disconnect from the network and still be managed. When they connect to the network again, and log in or out any updates to their managed preferences are copied down to the mobile copy of their account.

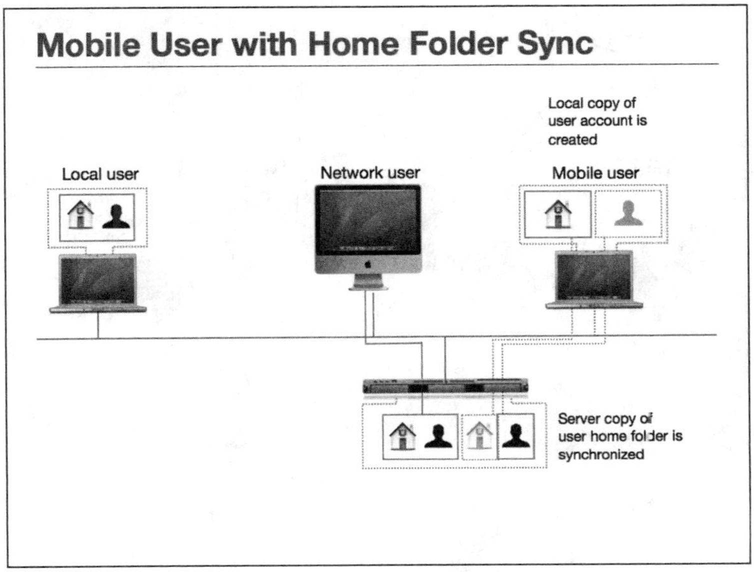


The one issue with a mobile account is that the data created by the user (folders and files) are kept locally and not synchronized with the server. Administrators do have the option of forcing synchronization of files between the local home folder on the Mac OS X computer and the network home folder on a file server. In this way, a user with a laptop can work with their files while disconnected from the server. When they return and connect to the network, any changed files (ones specified by the administrator) are synchronized back to the user's network home folder.

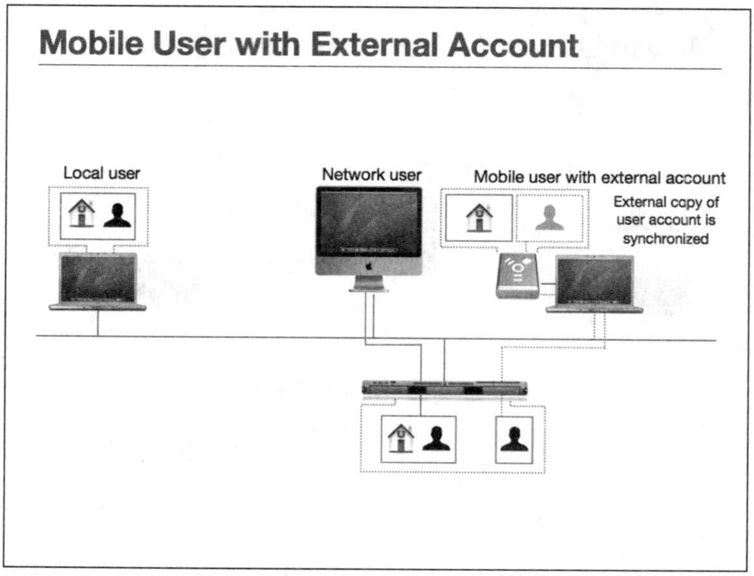


The main feature of mobile accounts allows for the user's home folder to reside in two places, on the server and the computer bound to the server. User created data is synchronized between the two. A third option is to allow the user's entire home folder to reside on a removable device, such as a FireWire or USB device.

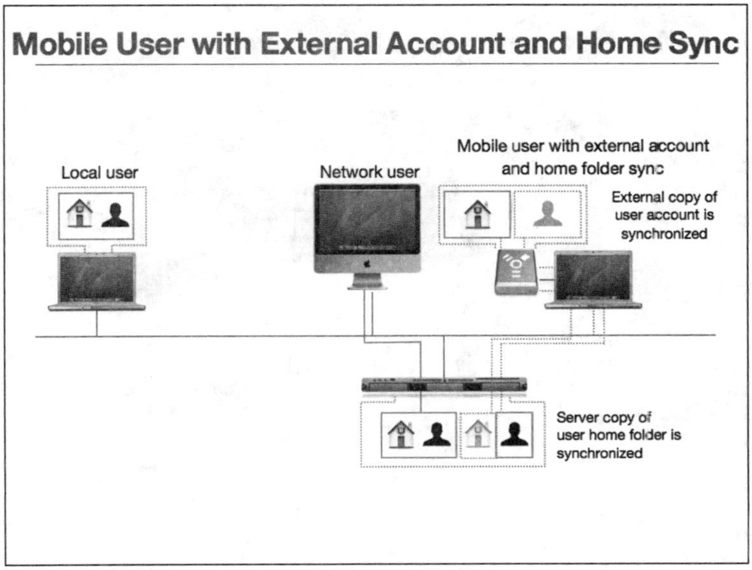


A fourth option is to take the feature of mobile synchronization and the feature of allowing a user's home folder to reside on a removable device and have them work together, allowing a user to carry their home folder on a removable device and plug into any computer bound to the server. User data selected by the administrator is then synchronized back to the server.

## Network Home Folder Review

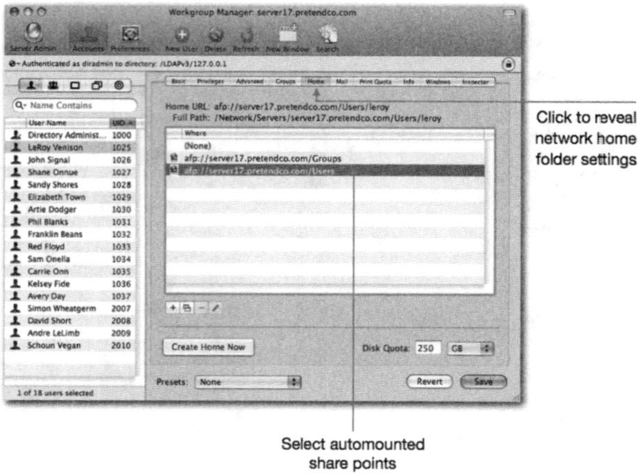


This slide is a quick review of network home folders for users. In order for network accounts to function in any of the previous scenarios, a home folder for each user must be available.

## Mobile User Account

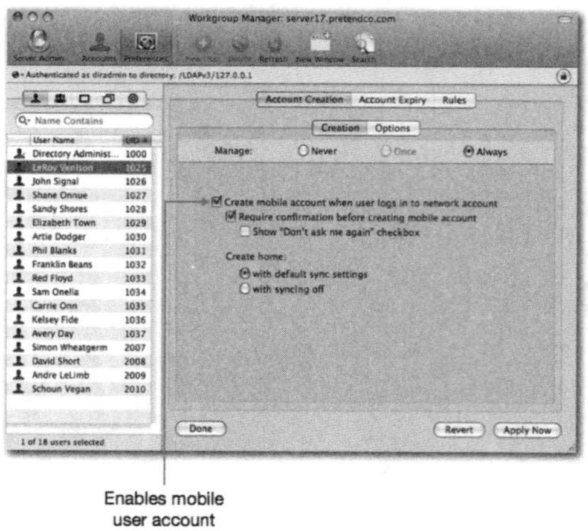


When creating a mobile user account, administrators have the option of requiring confirmation of the process and to decide whether default home folder syncing should be set.

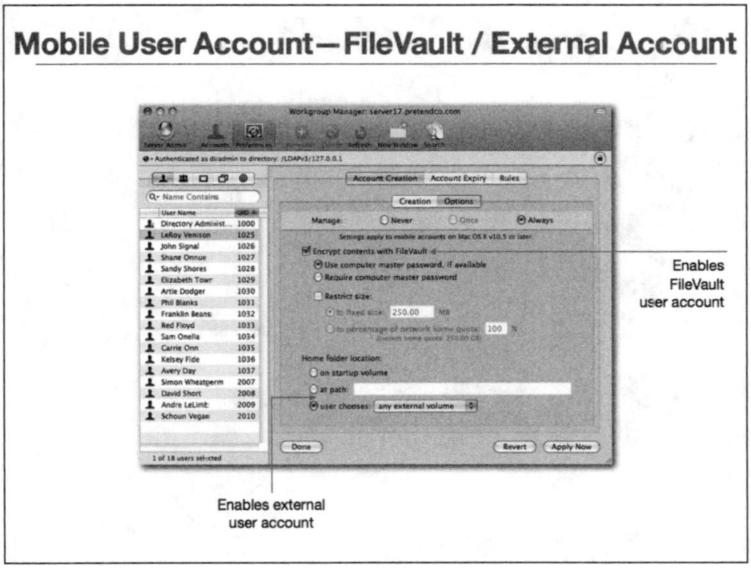


When creating a mobile account, administrators have the options of creating that account with FileVault, which is essentially an encrypted disk image of the user's home folder, and placing that home folder on a removable device or another volume.

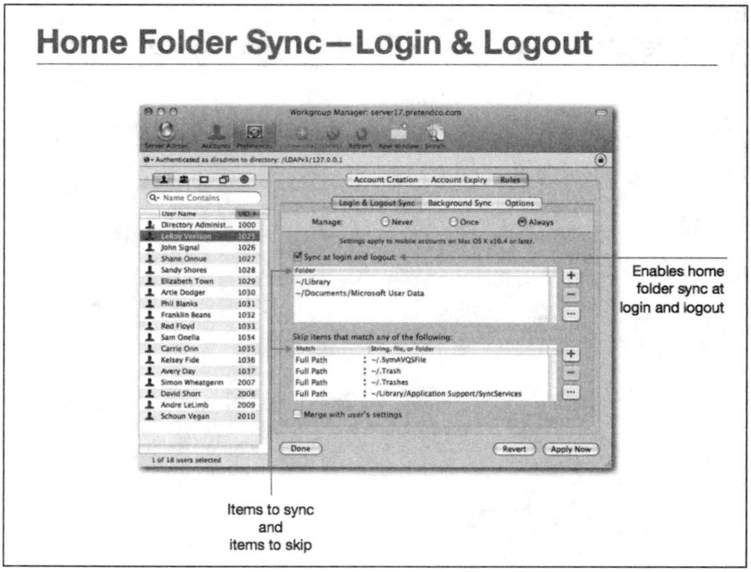


When the decision is made to synchronize the user's home folder, the administrator should decide what folders to synchronize. Mac OS X Server has suggestions for what not to synchronize. When deciding what to synchronize and what not to synchronize, administrators can use a variety of criteria to help them narrow their selections, such as wildcards and name matching. Syncing can take place at login and logout.

## Home Folder Sync—Background

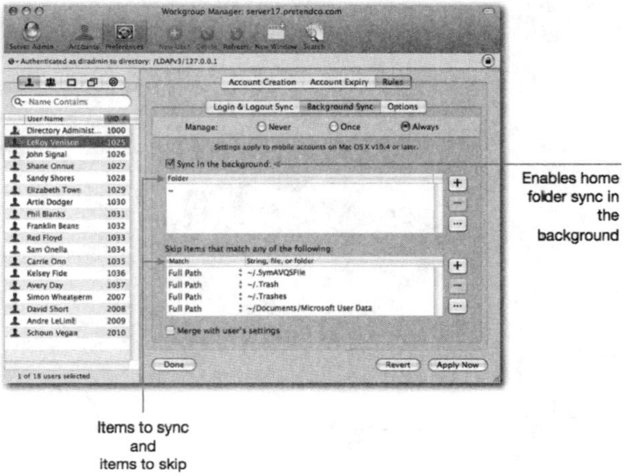


Syncing can also take place in the background, with the same options as log in and log out.

## Home Folder Sync Options

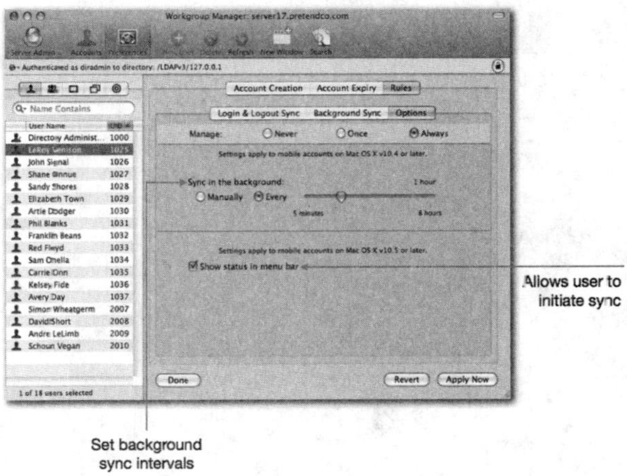


When handling background syncing, administrators have the option of deciding how often the background syncing takes place.

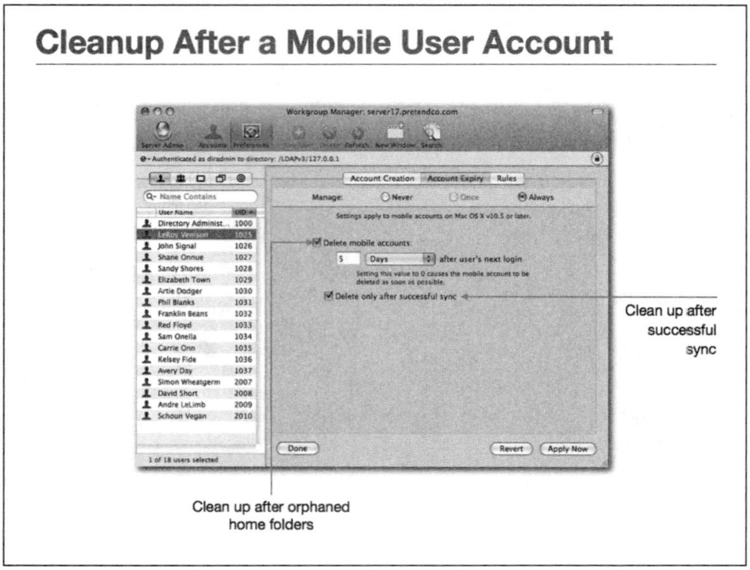


In some cases, administrators may not want the mobile accounts to be left on computers after a user has finished using it. Administrators have the option of deleting the mobile home folder.

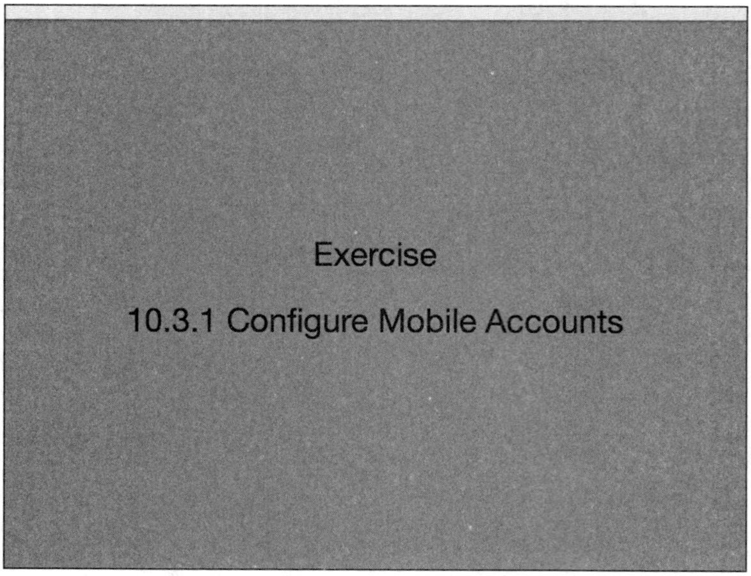

## Exercise 10.3.1
# Configure Mobile Accounts

## Objective

Configure and use a mobile home folder, manipulate synchronization settings, and verify synchronization.

## Summary

Mobile home folders and home folder synchronization are powerful tools that enhance the user experience with Mac OS X. Keep in mind that synchronization does not necessarily mean backup. If a user with a mobile account is disconnected from the network, and they delete an important file and then reconnect to the network, the server will begin the synchronization process and delete that file from their network home folder as well.

1 Open Workgroup Manager, authenticate as ladmin, select the shared LDAP domain, and authenticate as diradmin, if necessary.

2 Click the Accounts button in the toolbar, and then click the Users button.

3 Select Simon from the list of users, and verify Simon is a member of the Marketing group (you should have added him in a previous exercise). If not, update and save.

4 Click the Preferences button in the toolbar, and then click the Mobility button.

5 Select the Always radio button as the management choice.

6 Select "Create mobile account when user logs in to network account."

7 Deselect Require confirmation before creating mobile account.

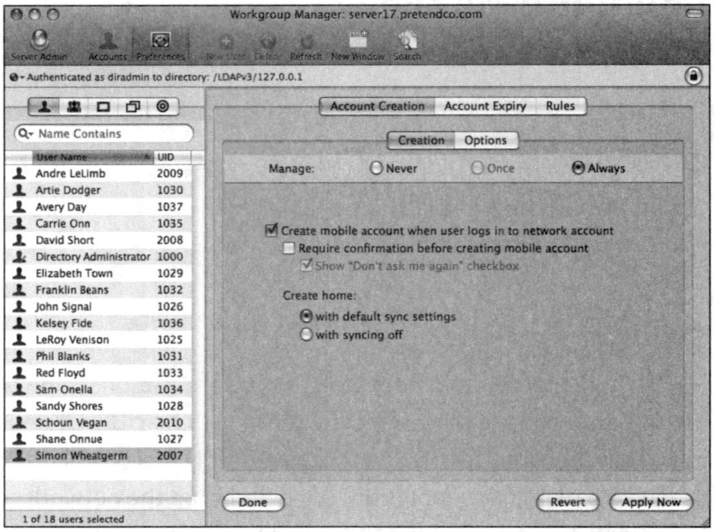

8 Click Apply Now.

9 Click the Options tab, and select the Always radio button as the management choice.

10 For "Home Folder Location" select the "user chooses" checkboxes, and select "any volume" from the pop-up menu.

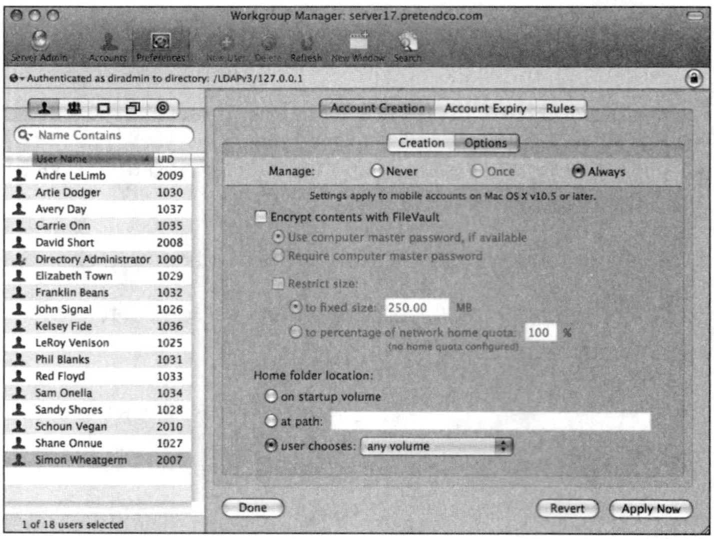

11 Click Apply Now and then click Done.

12 Log out as cadmin, and log in as simon.

13 View the Portable Home Directory dialog that appears asking you to select the home folder's volume location. Click Create Now.

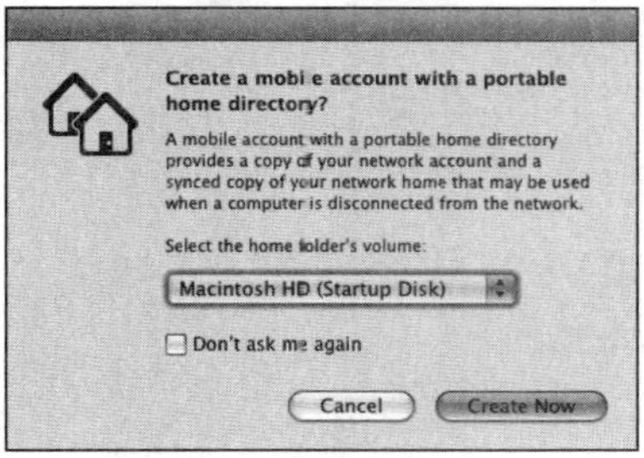


14 Click the lower question mark near the Trash Can to mount the Marketing group folder, and move the window so you can see your Kerberos application window.

You get an AFP Kerberos ticket.

15 Mount smb://server*n*.local and select the project lion share point.

16 Mount https://server*n*.pretendco.com/manual-1.3

17 Mount nfs://server*n*.pretendco.com/Shared Items/Templates.

18 Open iCal, and choose Refresh All from the Calendar menu.

19 Quit iCal.

20 Open Mail, and send an email to developers@server*n*.pretendco.com notifying that Preference Management is working.

21 Check your mail to ensure you received a copy of the message and quit Mail.

22 Launch iChat, and then quit iChat.

23 Bring the Kerberos application to the front, and view all your tickets.

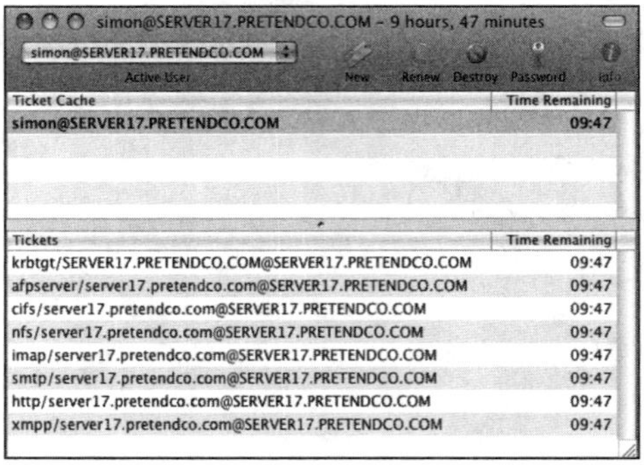


You did not have to enter a password to get access to any of the services. Other services on Mac OS X Server that use Kerberos are VPN and Xgrid. FTP can also use Kerberos, but Mac OS X does not currently support FTP uploads from Safari or the Finder, so a third party FTP utility that supports Kerberos will work.

24 Create a TextEdit file called MyNewFile, and save it to the Desktop.

25 Click the new Sync icon in Simon's menu bar, and choose Sync Home Now.

The file is synced back to Simon's home folder on the server.

26 Copy the entire StudentMaterials folder from /Users/Shared to the Desktop.

27 Log out as simon, and view the new Login Window.

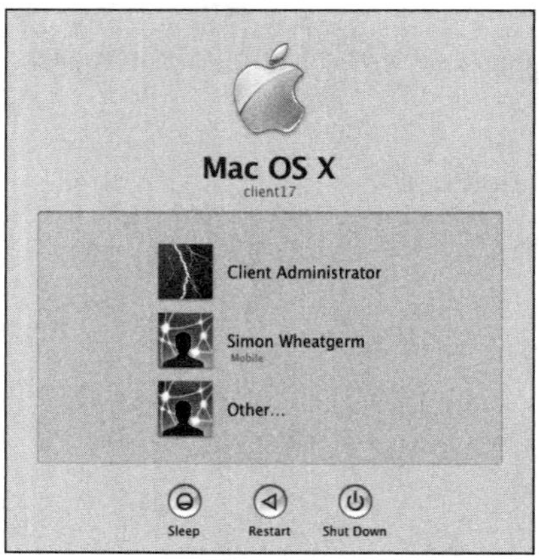

Now, you now have a new account, Simon Wheatgerm, which is a mobile account.

28 Log in as cadmin.

29 Open Workgroup Manager, authenticate as ladmin, select the shared LDAP domain, and authenticate as diradmin, if necessary.

30 Select Simon's account, click the Preferences icon in the toolbar, and select the Mobility button.

31 Click the Rules tab, and the click the Login & Logout Sync tab.

Notice that login and logout syncing is turned on by default as indicated by the grayed out checkbox in the middle of the window.

32 Select the Always radio button as the management choice.

33 Remove all items in the Sync at login and logout pane, and enter a tilde (~), indicating you want to sync Simon's entire home folder at login and logout.

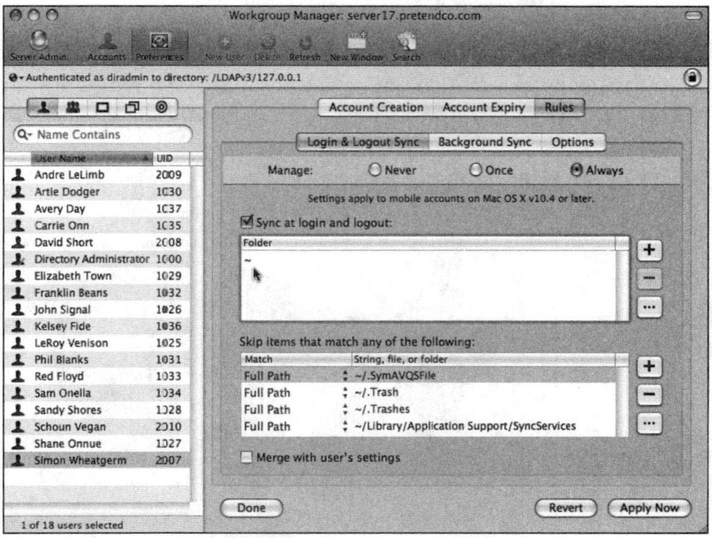


34 Click Apply Now and click Done.

35 Log out as cadmin, and log in as simon.

36 Choose Home Sync Preferences from under the Sync menu in the menu bar. The Accounts preference pane opens so you can view the sync settings.

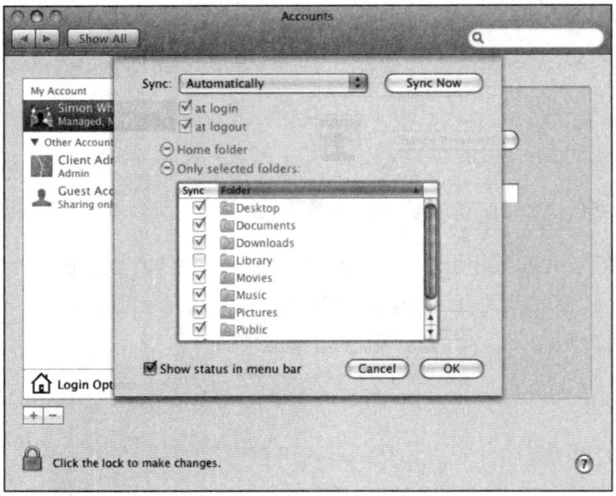


Notice that login and logout are grayed out, indicating that they are always managed. However, because background syncing is never managed, Simon has the option of syncing his information in the background. Also notice Simon does not have a choice of what is synced because that was also set in the previous steps.

37 Click Cancel, and log out as Simon.

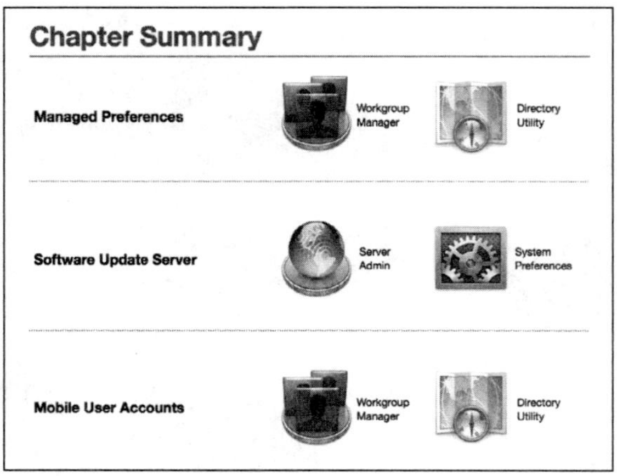

# 11

# Optional Challenges

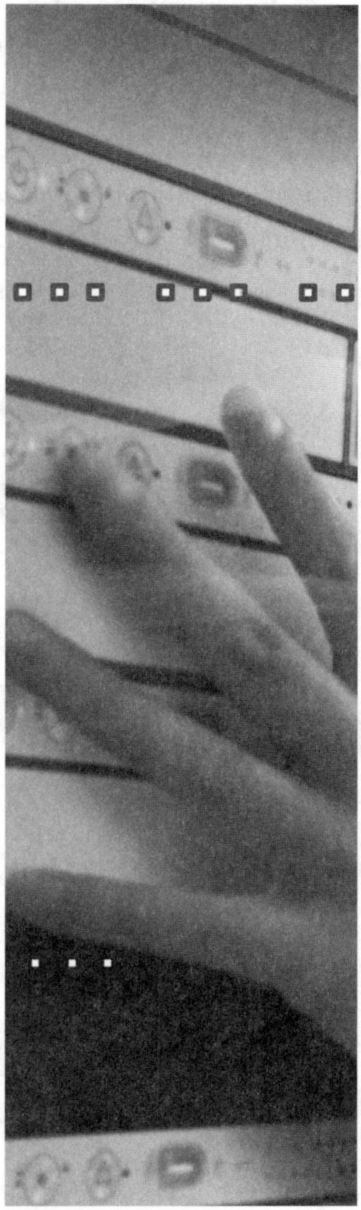

| | |
|---|---|
| **Exercise 11.1** | Take the Challenge |
| **Exercise 11.2** | Plan the Implementation |
| **Exercise 11.3** | Server 1: Configure the Directory and Collaborative Services |
| **Exercise 11.4** | Server 2: Configure the File Server |
| **Exercise 11.5** | Server 3: Configure NetBoot Services (optional) |
| **Exercise 11.6** | Test Your Solution |
| **Exercise 11.7** | Reassess the Situation |

## Prerequisites

Before attempting these exercises, you must first complete the Chapters 1 through 10 in this course.

### Exercise 11.1

# Take the Challenge

## Summary

In this challenge you'll be given an assignment. With one or two partners you'll set up from one to three servers. Each server will be configured to perform a different task. When finished, the three servers will provide a complete solution.

This exercise introduces you to the challenge while you install the software.

- Perform an installation or setup of Mac OS X Server.
- Read the assignment.

## Set Up Computers

While the software is being installed, read the assignment and start planning. You can use the documents from the next exercise for your plans.

Install Mac OS X Server from DVD (optional-You may elect to NetBoot and restore the server image)

1. Insert the Installer DVD, and reboot your server computer while holding down the C key.
2. Provide the initial information to erase the hard drive and install the server software.
3. Deselect extra languages and printer drivers. For specific information you can refer to "Setting Up Mac OS X Server."
4. Stop when the server is at the Welcome screen.

## The Assignment

You are tasked with configuring a solution for ten users. The solution must be scalable so you can add users easily in the future. The solution should be high performance, so services should be spread across multiple servers.

1 Configure an Open Directory server to handle user account information and handle the collaborative services.

   This server will be where you'll store all user information and accounts and allow users to access collaborative services.

2 Set up and configure the file server for network home folders.

3 Set the users to have home directories on the file server.

4 Configure NetBoot services on a third server.

This will allow any user to use any computer without impacting configurations. This last step requires a third person or set of equipment. You have access to one server and one client for each participant. The instructor server will act as your DNS and DHCP server for these exercises.

## Exercise 11.2
# Plan the Implementation

## Summary

You have been given your assignment. Now, you need to plan out how to implement your solution.

## Complete the Plan

With your partner(s), decide which of the servers will be configured for which service. Using the following template as a guide, plan out the account names, determine which services are required, determine the network configuration, and determine what services need to be implemented.

This solution should be accomplished in the classroom network environment.

You don't need to provide all the DNS or DHCP services to support your implementation. Each person will be completing some but not all the remaining exercises.

- The person configuring the directory and collaborative services server should complete "Server 1: Configure the Directory and Collaborative Services."
- The person configuring the file server should complete "Server 2: Configure the File Server."
- The person setting up NetBoot should complete "Server 3: Configure NetBoot Services (Optional)."

Not every team will install NetBoot. Identify the person in class, if anyone, who is installing NetBoot. You can boot your clients off their server. Coordinate your efforts with that person's team.

## Server Configuration Plan

Use the following as an aid to help you format your communication with your team.

- Networking:
  - Describe the network configuration.
  - How will the server be connected?
- Account Information:
  - Describe account data.
  - Server Admin—account name and passwords
  - User—Account names and passwords
  - Directory—account name and password
- Services List:
  - Which services to establish.
  - File Services: On which server?
  - Directory/Collaborative Services?
  - NetBoot?
  - Other?
- Who Will Do What Detail—Show who will perform which task.
- Outstanding Issues
- Action Items List

## Exercise 11.3

# Server 1: Configure the Directory and Collaborative Services

### Summary

You'll need to store user data in a centralized directory.

### Background

You only need to complete this exercise if your server will be acting as the Directory Services and collaborative services server. You'll need to coordinate with the person setting up the File Services.

### Set Up the Mac OS X Server

The main classroom server has been configured to act as a DNS server for this course.

The data you enter in the following steps corresponds to the configuration in the DNS server.

1 Administrator Account:

- Name: <enter planning data here>
- Short Name: <enter planning data here>
- Password: <enter planning data here>

2 Network Names: (replace n with your student number)

- Host Name: servern.pretendco.com
- Computer Name: server*n*
- Bonjour Name: server*n*

3 Network Interfaces:

- Port Name: `Built-in Ethernet`
- Device Name: `en0`
- Ethernet Address: blank
- Verify only TCP/IP is selected for Built-in Ethernet

4 Configure Manual Address:

- IP Address: `10.1.`*`n`*`.1`
- Subnet Mask: `255.255.0.0`
- Router: `10.1.0.1`
- DNS Servers: `10.1.0.1`
- Search Domains: `pretendco.com`

5 Configure the server to start as a Standalone Server.

This is the initial installation setting. Once installed, you can change the server to an Open Directory Master. It is good practice to always configure a server as a standalone first. There should be only one Directory Master. From the Directory Master, you'll start mail, web, Wiki, calendaring, and messaging services.

## Configuration Assignment: Set Up Users

### Configuration Files

This exercise calls for entering only ten user accounts. You should not limit yourself to thinking in terms of specific number of users. Design your directory structure with scalability and growth in mind. Also, design a schema for user configuration.

### Coordination

User accounts do not exist in isolation. In this exercise you are to coordinate the services across servers. Using the following form as a guide, take into consideration the other areas and services the user might need, even outside the scope of this exercise. Will the users need account management? Will there be shared printers and perhaps a print queue? What will the password policy be? Will the users be acting collaboratively and therefore need shared directories?

### Configuration Job Aid

- User Information: Full Name Short Name

  1 ______________________________

  2 ______________________________

  3 ______________________________

  4 ______________________________

  5 ______________________________

  6 ______________________________

  7 ______________________________

  8 ______________________________

  9 ______________________________

  10 ______________________________

- Account Information
- Password Type
- Primary Group
- Other Groups
- Home Path
- Printer
- Print Quotas
- Shared Directory Path Permissions:
  - Owner Name: RW - WO - RO - None
  - Group Name: RW - WO - RO - None
  - Everyone RW - WO - RO - None

- Shared Directory Path Permissions:
    - Owner Name: RW - WO - RO - None
    - Group Name: RW - WO - RO - None
    - Everyone RW - WO - RO - None
- Shared Directory Path Permissions:
    - Owner Name: RW - WO - RO - None
    - Group Name: RW - WO - RO - None
    - Everyone RW - WO - RO - None
- Workgroup Preference Management
- Computer Preference Management
- User Preference Management

## Exercise 11.4

# Server 2: Configure the File Server

### Summary

This exercise is part of the challenge. Configuring home folders will allow your users to save files without having an account on the local system.

### Background

You only need to complete this exercise if your server will be acting as the file server. You'll need to coordinate with the person setting up the directory server.

### Set Up the Mac OS X Server

The main classroom server has been configured to act as a DNS server for this course.

The following data corresponds to the configuration in the DNS server.

1 Administrator Account:

- Name: `<enter planning data here>`
- Short Name: `<enter planning data here>`
- Password: `<enter planning data here>`

2 Network Names: (replace n with your student number)

- Host Name: `servern.pretendco.com`
- Computer Name: `server`*`n`*
- Bonjour Name: `server`*`n`*

3 Network Interfaces:

- Port Name: `Built-in Ethernet`
- Device Name: `en0`

- Ethernet Address: blank
- Verify only TCP/IP is selected for Built-in Ethernet

4 Configure Manual Address:

- IP Address: `10.1.n.1`
- Subnet Mask: `255.255.0.0`
- Router: `10.1.0.1`
- DNS Servers: `10.1.0.1`
- Search Domains: `pretendco.com`

Configure the server to start as a Standalone Server.

## Challenge Assignment: Set Up a Home Folder Server

### Configuring the Server

The challenge is to configure the server that will house the home folders. This server will only be running as a file server. There are no network-visible users on your server. As part of this exercise you'll need to give the address of the server to the administrator of the directory server in your group. Specific user folders may not be created until the user actually logs in to the server. This process occurs automatically the first time the user connects via AFP or logs in using the home folder.

### Configuration Job Aid

Use this job aid to record the appropriate data.

- User Folder Information Server Address

  1 DNS NAME: ______________________________

  2 URL of File Server (i.e., afp//server*n*.pretendco.com)

  ______________________________

  3 Path Name to User Folder (usually Users)

  ______________________________

- Password Type
- Primary Group
- Other Groups
- Home Path
- Printer
- Print Quotas
- Shared Directory Permissions
    - Owner Name: RW - WO - RO - None
    - Group Name: RW - WO - RO - None
    - Everyone RW - WO - RO - None
- Shared Directory Path Permissions
    - Owner Name: RW - WO - RO - None
    - Group Name: RW - WO - RO - None
    - Everyone RW - WO - RO - None
- Shared Directory Path Permissions
    - Owner Name: RW - WO - RO - None
    - Group Name: RW - WO - RO - None
    - Everyone RW - WO - RO - None
- Workgroup Preference Management
- Computer Preference Management
- User Preference Management

## Exercise 11.5

# Server 3: Configure NetBoot Services (optional)

### Summary

NetBoot is a read-only instance of the operating system. This section is optional because it requires additional resources. It there are only two students working this lab, you can choose to skip this lab.

### Background

Data on configuring NetBoot was not in any specific exercises. You only need to complete this exercise if your server will be acting as the NetBoot server. You'll need to coordinate with the person setting up the directory server and the file server. It is also possible that this will be the only NetBoot server in your class. If that is the case, share the following data with all the other students.

### Set Up the Mac OS X Server

The main classroom server has been configured to act as a DNS server for this course.

The following data corresponds to the configuration in the DNS server.

1 Administrator Account:

- Name: <enter planning data here>
- Short Name: <enter planning data here>
- Password: <enter planning data here>

2 Network Names: (replace *n* with your student number)

- Host Name: server*n*.pretendco.com
- Computer Name: server*n*
- Bonjour Name: server*n*

3 Network Interfaces:

- Port Name: `Built-in Ethernet`
- Device Name: `en0`
- Ethernet Address: blank
- Verify only TCP/IP is selected for Built-in Ethernet

4 Configure Manual Address:

- IP Address: `10.1.`*`n`*`.1`
- Subnet Mask: `255.255.0.0`
- Router: `10.1.0.1`
- DNS Servers: `10.1.0.1`
- Search Domains: `pretendco.com`

5 Configure the server to start as a Standalone Server.

## Challenge Assignment: Set Up a NetBoot Server

### Setup

Unless you have configured the NetBoot server to start automatically, there is no NetBoot folder inside /Library. The NetBoot folder is where images are stored by default. We will configure NetBoot to create this folder.

1 Open Server Manager and authenticate.

2 Click the NetBoot server.

3 Click Settings.

4 Select the hard drive, usually Server HD, and enable it for Images and Data.

5 Select the Built-In Ethernet Port, and enable it.

6 Click Start NetBoot Service.

7 Quit Server Admin.

### Create and Host a NetBoot Image Bound to Your Open Directory Master

On your Mac OS X computer, use Directory Utility to bind to your group's Open Directory Master. To further prepare your Mac OS X computer to be imaged, you may want to remove the extra materials in /Users/Shared, or just start with a fresh installation of Mac OS X that is customized to install only the bare essentials of Mac OS X (be sure to define an initial administrator account before imaging).

Use System Image Utility to create a NetBoot image, and save it to /Library/NetBoot/NetBootSP0. Use filters to disallow any clients except for your group's computers.

### Start the NetBoot Server

Now that the file is copied and configured you need to enable this image to make it available to clients.

1 Open Server Admin.

2 Select the NetBoot service and click Settings.

3 Click Images.

4 Select your NetBoot image, enable it, and make it the default.

5 Click Save.

6 Click Start Service.

You can now verify a client using NetBoot, either by holding down the "N" key or selecting the image in the Startup pane of System Preferences. If you are assisting other teams by acting as their NetBoot server, you'll need to repeat these steps and create a separate image file for each Directory Master server. Remember only one image can be the default. Other teams will have to point their client to the correct images to work properly. Naming the NetBoot image copies will help the other groups make the proper selection.

## Exercise 11.6

# Test Your Solution

### Summary

You should now have your servers and clients correctly configured. It is always a good practice to test the implementation before you roll it out to customers or users.

### Test the Setup

The easiest way to test the configuration is to actually log in as one of the network users. In the planning phase, you could have set up some test user accounts.

- Can the user change preferences?
- Can the user save documents to his or her folder and other folders?
- Are these paths remembered across boots?
- Does it make any difference which client machine the user logs in to?
- Was testing part of your original plan, or was it an afterthought?

Repeat until you are satisfied the configuration is complete and properly functioning.

### The Instructor Verifies the Installation

The instructor will take some or all of the following steps to validate your installation.

1 Go to each client machine and NetBoot it manually.

2 Log in to the client as the NetBoot admin, and verify that there are no local user accounts in the boot image.

3 Reconnect as a network user with information provided by the team.

4 Change preferences for that user, and create a document saved in the user's home or Documents folder.

5 Reconnect as another network user on the same machine.

6 On another client computer, log in as the original network user.

7 Validate the preferences are consistent and documents are available.

8 View the directory binding using Directory Access on the client.

9 Connect to the server computers, and view your configuration.

10 Observe that the path to the home folders is not on the directory server.

11 View the directory bindings on each server, and verify there is only one Directory Master.

Your instructor may not perform these actual steps in the order given, but they are an excellent starting point for your validation. If you cannot perform these tasks, you may not have a valid configuration.

## Exercise 11.7
# Reassess the Situation


## Summary

Completing a solution rollout is not the end of a project. Once you have implemented a solution there will always be on-going maintenance. The scope of the project will change and so will the goals. Nothing succeeds like success. Having completed a successful implementation you can be sure that you'll be asked to make changes, improvements, and upgrades.


## Writing Reports

In this exercise you'll write a report and document what you have implemented so that others can make changes to your implementation. There are two reports to be implemented.

Write an implementation report. Using the materials from your team, create a comprehensive document detailing the networking, servers, and user lists. Use collaborative services to communicate, send mail, create a Wiki and group folder, set meeting dates. Detail what software was installed and where it was installed. What users and groups were created? What policies were implemented? What password policies were used, if any? Was there a schema for user names or IDs? Were any restrictions or management implemented? Describe a plan for updating the software and how to add resources to the product.

Another important process to accomplish when a project completes a significant milestone is an assessment. Also known as a post mortem, these assessments aid in planning for future projects. Sit down with your team members, and go over the project process. Document what went well and what did not go as expected. Document the practices that should be carried forward and the pitfalls to watch out for next time. The important part of this evaluation is to learn from the successes and mistakes. Problems happen, and the only mistake is to repeat the same difficulties when they are known and can be avoided. Your team might have implemented a novel solution to a thorny issue that all the teams experienced. Try to create a document that, if you had read it before completing the exercise, could have saved you and your team significant time and trouble.

## Escalation Job Aid

Use this document a job aid to help you format your communication to your ACSA.

- Escalation Report ACTC Name:
- Problem Description—Clearly describe the problem.
- What You've Done So Far—Describe the steps you've taken to resolve the problem.
- Results—What are the results of your actions?
- Resolved issues
- Outstanding Issues
- Recommendations—What do you recommend as next steps?

# Answer Key

## Chapter 1

***Question 1*** *What tools are installed inside the* `Server` *folder by the* `ServerAdministrationSoftware.mpkg` *metapackage?*

Server Assistant, Server Admin, Server Monitor, Server Preferences, Workgroup Manager, System Image Utility, and Xgrid Admin.

***Question 2*** *What does Remote Management permit?*

Remote Management allows additional management and control of your Mac OS X Server via the Apple Remote Desktop application. You can configure Mac OS X Server to be controlled via any Virtual Network Client (VNC) application, such as Screen Sharing, found in `/System/Library/CoreServices/`.

## Chapter 2

***Question 1*** *Why are you able to ping some fully qualified domain names but not others?*

You are running and looking at your own DNS service, and you cannot resolve names associated with the instructor's DNS service anymore.

***Question 2*** *Why are you able or not able to look up other students' fully qualified domain names?*

You can only see your own DNS service and cannot utilize other students' DNS services, so you will be unable to see their fully qualified domain names.

## Chapter 3

***Question 1*** *What are the differences between the accounts?*

The "administer the server" option is selected on Local Administrator and not on the others.

***Question 2*** *What is the password for Simon Wheatgerm? What is the password for Schoun Vegan?*

When the first record shows the word "Password" as the value, all subsequent records have the actual password for the shown user. In Simon's case, his password is wheatgerm2007. Schoun's password is vegan2010.

***Question 3*** *What other folders are set up as shared folders on Mac OS X Server?*

The Users folder, the Groups folder, and the Public folder are all shared by default.

***Question 4*** *Who can connect, and who cannot connect?*

Only LeRoy and Franklin can connect because they are the only individuals who are members of the Employees group (each is in a different subgroup). Even though ladmin is an administrator, ladmin cannot connect.

## Chapter 4

***Question 1*** *What are the names of the local directories that have the potential to hold local directory data store information?*

Aliases, config, machines, users, computers, groups, networks.

***Question 2*** *Do they match?*

They do not match.

***Question 3*** *Why or why not?*

The Kerberos realm is derived from the DNS name, which you set up in Chapter 2, "Providing DNS Service." Your DNS name is server.student*n*.pretendco.com (where *n* is your student number).

Your search base is derived from your host name, which you entered when you ran Server Assistant. This does not change even though you have your own DNS server in the Network Preferences Pane.

***Question 4*** *Do they match?*

They do match.

***Question 5** Why or why not?*

The Kerberos realm now matches the search domain.

## Chapter 5

***Question 1** Where is the Users share point located?*

The Users share point is located at /Volumes/Server HD/Users.

***Question 2** What kind of access does Red have to the Press Releases folder?*

Red has read-only access to the Press Releases folder.

***Question 3** What happens when you try to connect?*

You cannot connect to the AFP share point because the Mac OS X computer does not have the appropriate information about the Kerberos database or the shared directory.

***Question 4** Were you prompted to authenticate?*

Your AFP Kerberos ticket is still valid for this AFP server and its share points (for about 10 hrs).

***Question 5** Which subfolders does artie have access to without further authentication?*

Lion Development and Press Releases

***Question 6** Can you still copy files to both mount points even though you don't have any tickets? Why or why not?*

Yes, because you already have both share points mounted. Note that you can mount additional share points using the same protocol as any share points you already have mounted (as long as it is from the same server of course), even if you do not have tickets for that service.

***Question 7** What happens if you drag the Podcast Capture application from the Shared applications folder to your desktop?*

You get an error message because you have a 5 MB quota and the application is bigger than 5 MB.

**Question 8** *How many tickets do you have and for what services?*

You should have at least four tickets. One is a ticket granting ticket (krbtgt), and you should also have one each for AFP, CIFS, and NFS.

**Question 9** *How do you account for each ticket being in the list?*

You get the TGT by logging in at the login window. You get the AFP ticket because your home directory is automounted via AFP. You get the CIFS and NFS tickets because you manually connected to the server and requested volumes with those protocols.

**Question 10** *What file(s) do you see in the share points folder?*

A sparse bundle disk image should be created for each client that uses this share point for Time Machine backups.

## Chapter 6

**Question 1** *Did your mail server balk at all when sending mail messages to people who do not have their Mail accounts set up yet?*

No. As long as they are set to receive mail, the mail server will hold their mail in their mailbox until they choose to view it, download it, or delete it.

**Question 2** *Steve is not a user in Workgroup Manager. What happens to the mail that is addressed improperly?*

It is sent to the diradmin account.

**Question 3** *How can you send mail to the instructor?*

Because your network mask and the instructor's network mask is set to 255.255.0.0, the mail service is allowing mail to be sent to anyone in the 10.1.x.x range. The instructor's server is 10.1.0.1, and your server is 10.1.*n*.1. They both fall in that range.

**Question 4** *Can Elizabeth set up mail? Why or why not?*

No, because Elizabeth has a 5 MB disk quota and is prevented from opening the Mail application.

***Question 5*** *Why does setting up David's mail differ from that of Schoun's and the Directory Administrators?*

Kerberos was enabled on the mail service, so no passwords are required, only tickets that are granted automatically.

***Question 6*** *What is each ticket for and how did you obtain them?*

imap, smtp

***Question 7*** *Why does David have more than one IMAP connection?*

Because IMAP opens multiple connections per client.

***Question 8*** *What happened when you attempted to change the settings?*

Because Kerberos is required for IMAP, a Kerberos dialog appeared asking for cadmin's password. Because cadmin is not an account on Mac OS X Server, in either the local or shared LDAP database, you can cancel this as many times as it appears, close the preferences, save the changes, and then quit and launch Mail again.

***Question 9*** *What happens when you try to delete them and how can this be corrected?*

The mail quota can be expanded to allow the user to move his mail to the Trash to delete the messages.

***Question 10*** *What log files are being searched by both the IMAP and SMTP entries in the View pop-up menu?*

The mailaccess.log and mail.log are searched.

## Chapter 7

***Question 1*** *What modules have been activated as a result of you turning on Webmail, Blog, WebDAV, and Spotlight searching?*

apple_spotlight_module, dav_module, php5_module, dav_fs_module

**Question 2** *What can you use to test to see if both IP addresses are responding?*

The Ping tab of Network Utility.

**Question 3** *How can you see your new site with the fully qualified domain name even though you have not edited DNS?*

You are using the instructor's server for DNS, not yours, and the instructor's DNS service has three machine entries for all students: 1) server*n*.pretendco.com maps to 10.1.*n*.1, 2) client*n*.pretendco.com maps to 10.1.*n*.2, and 3) worksite*n*.pretendco.com maps to 10.1.*n*.5.

**Question 4** *Was Sandy able to load and browse the pages?*

Yes, Sandy can load and browse the page because Sandy is a member of the Projects group.

**Question 5** *Were you able to copy the file up to your server as Elizabeth? Why or why not?*

Yes, you can copy the file because Elizabeth is in the Developers group, which has browse and read/write rights for WebDAV.

**Question 6** *Were you able to copy the file up to your server as Sandy? Why or why not?*

No, you cannot copy any files to the WebDAV volume. Sandy is a member of the Projects group, which has browse and read only rights for WebDAV.

**Question 7** *Other than when logging in, did Simon have to provide a password for any of the functions asked of him?*

No, all the functions took advantage of single sign-on.

**Question 8** *What is the idea behind using Kerberos tickets to provide authentication?*

Single sign-on.

**Question 9** *What is the function of each ticket?*

krbtgt is the Ticket Granting Ticket, which was granted at login; afpserver is for the automounted home directory; imap is for checking mail; smtp is for sending mail; HTTP is for WebDAV; and cifs is for mounting the SMB volume.

## Chapter 8

***Question 1*** *Why would you want everyone to view a Wiki and blog?*

Perhaps this is an internal company website and all users are permitted to view the Wiki.

***Question 2*** *Is information typed in a Wiki insecure?*

Because you set up secure sockets layer (SSL) for your website, all communication has been encrypted.

***Question 3*** *Why can't Kelsey create an account?*

Kelsey does not have access to calendaring, so he cannot create an account. You disabled calendaring access in Workgroup Manager.

***Question 4*** *Can you create an iCal account for Elizabeth? She is in the Developers group.*

You cannot open iCal because Elizabeth has already exceeded her home folder quota.

***Question 5*** *Using the message log, how can you identify a message that begins a new conversation?*

The first message in a conversation does not log the Location attribute of the recipient. Because that user has not yet responded, iChat Server does not know what the recipient's Location is yet.

***Question 6*** *There are log entries that contain no message body. Why are these log entries present? (Hint: Leave the log open in Console while you chat).*

Whenever you begin typing in a chat window of an established conversation, iChat indicates to the other party that you are typing by displaying a thought bubble graphic next to your buddy icon in the chat window. The log entries with no message body appear whenever this indication is shown, or whenever it is hidden because the input line is cleared.

## Chapter 9

*Question 1 Where is simon's home folder?*

Simon's home folder is on the server.

*Question 2 How is your Apple computer booted?*

The computer is NetBooted from your Mac OS X Server.

*Question 3 What ensures all this is working properly?*

DNS ensures everything is working properly.

## Chapter 10

None

## Chapter 11

None